Engineering Dynamics Labs with SolidWorks Motion 2014

Huei-Huang Lee
Department of Engineering Science
National Cheng Kung University, Taiwan

SDC Publications

SDC Publications
P.O. Box 1334
Mission, KS 66222
913-262-2664
www.SDCpublications.com
Publisher: Stephen Schroff

ISBN-13: 978-1-58503-898-5
ISBN-10: 1-58503-898-9

Printed and bound in the United States of America.

Contents

Preface

A New Way of Thinking in Engineering Mechanics Curricula

Figure 1. illustrates how engineering mechanics curricula are implemented nowadays. Engineering students learn physics and mathematics in their high school years and their first college year. Based on this foundation, the students go further into studying engineering mechanics courses such as Statics, Dynamics, Mechanics of Materials, Heat Transfer, Fluid Mechanics, etc. This paradigm has been practiced for as long as any university professor can remember. I've grown up with this paradigm too. More than 30 years has passed since I graduated from my college, and even the contents of the textbooks remain essentially identical. The only "improvement" is that we have CAD and CAE courses now (as shown in the figure). So, what are the problems of this conventional paradigm of engineering mechanics curricula?

First, conventional curricula relies too much on mathematics to teach the concepts of engineering mechanics. Many students are good at engineering thinking but not good at mathematical thinking. For these students, especially in their junior years, mathematics is an inefficient tool (a nightmare, some would say). As a matter of fact, very few students enjoy mathematics as a tool of learning engineering ideas and concepts. Nowadays, CAE software has matured to a point that it can be used as a tool to learn engineering ideas, concepts, and even formulas. We'll show this through each section of this book. Often, mathematics is not the only way to show engineering concepts, or to explain formulas. Using graphics-based CAE tools is often a better way. It is possible to reduce the dependency on mathematics by a substantial extent.

Second, as shown in the figure, the CAD course is usually taught as a standalone subject in a sense that it doesn't serve as part of foundation for engineering mechanics courses. The 3D modeling techniques learned in the CAD course can be a powerful tool. For example, modern CAD software usually allows you to build a mechanism and study the motion of parts. However, our engineering mechanics textbooks haven't illuminated these advantages yet.

Third, the CAE course is usually taught in the senior or graduate years, because the CAE textbook requires some background knowledge of engineering mechanics. It is my long-term observation that the CAE course should be taught as early as junior years, for the following reasons: (a) If a student begins to learn CAE in his junior years, he will have many years to become proficient at this important engineering skill. (b) After knowing what and how CAE can help him solving problems, a student would be more knowledgeable and confident about what direction he should concentrate on when learning engineering mechanics courses. (c) As mentioned earlier, CAE can be used as a learning tool, just like mathematics, for the ensuing subjects. It'll largely facilitate the learning of engineering mechanics courses.

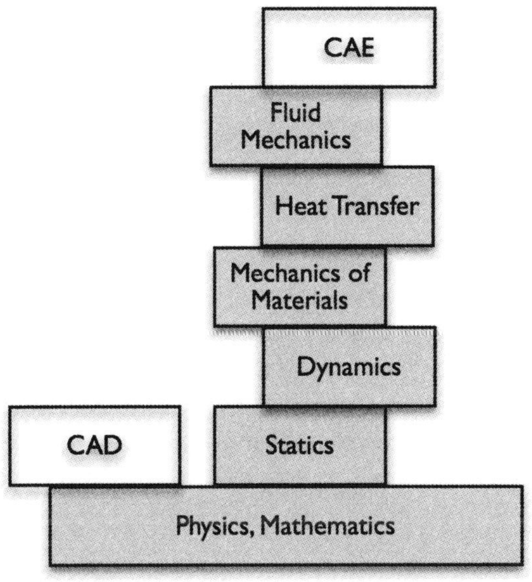

Figure 1. Conventional Paradigm of Engineering Mechanics Curricula

Figure 2. shows an idea that I'd like to propose for engineering mechanics curricula; this book is developed based on this idea. Engineering students usually learn CAD tools in their junior years. For example, among many CAD tools, **SolidWorks** has been popularized in many colleges. Naturally **SolidWorks** might serve as a "virtual laboratory" for the ensuing engineering mechanics courses, such as Statics, Dynamics, Mechanics of Materials, Heat Transfer, Fluid Mechanics, etc. The idea is simple, the benefits should be appreciated, but the implementation needs much more elaboration.

First, a series of well-designed lab exercise books are the key to the success of this idea. These software-based lab books must map their contents to contemporary textbooks.

Second, a CAE software platform must be chosen to serve as the virtual laboratory. We (Mr. Stephen Schroff of SDC Publications and I) have chosen **SolidWorks Motion** as the platform for this book, for the following reasons: (a) As mentioned, **SolidWorks** has been popularized in many colleges. Many students are familiar with this software. (b) The **Motion** is an integrated part of **SolidWorks** and a natural extension of **SolidWorks**. (c) The licensing of the **Motion** is included with a **SolidWorks** license. (d) Compared with other CAE software I've investigated, the **Motion** is very friendly for college juniors. (e) Finally, after a thorough investigation, I've concluded that **SolidWorks Motion** has capabilities to implement all of the ideas I want to cover.

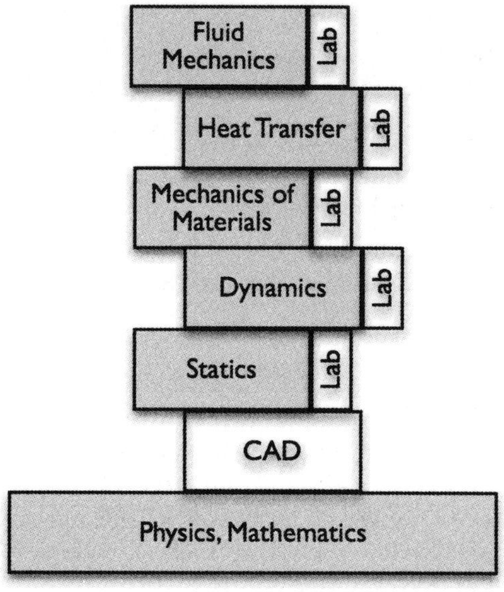

Figure 2. Proposed Paradigm of Engineering Mechanics Curricula

Use of This Book

This book is designed as a software-based lab book to complement a standard textbook in an Engineering Dynamics course, which is usually taught in junior undergraduate years.

There are 11 chapters in this book. Each chapter contain two sections. Each section is designed for a student to follow the exact steps in that section and learn a concept or topic of Engineering Dynamics. Typically, each section takes 20-40 minutes to complete the exercises.

Companion Webpage

A webpage is maintained for this book:

http://myweb.ncku.edu.tw/~hhlee/Myweb_at_NCKU/SWD2014.html

The webpage contains links to following resources: (a) videos that demonstrate the steps of each section in the book; (b) finished **SolidWorks** files of each section; and (c) a 121-page PDF tutorial, *Part and Assembly Modeling with SolidWorks 2014*. The videos, hosted by YouTube, have a maximum resolution of 1280x720 (half HD).

As for the finished **SolidWorks** files, if everything works smoothly, you may not need them at all. Every model can be built from scratch by following the steps described in the book. I provide these files just in cases you need them. For example, when you run into trouble and you don't want to redo it from the beginning, you may find these files useful. Or you may happen to have trouble following the steps in the book, you can then look up the details in the files. In fact, the main reason I provide these finished files is as follows. It is strongly suggested that, in the beginning of a section when previously saved **SolidWorks** files are needed, you use my files rather than your own files so that you are able to obtain results that have minimum deviations in numerical values from those in the book.

I provide the 121-page PDF tutorial (*Part and Assembly Modeling with SolidWorks 2014*), for those students who have no experience in **SolidWorks** and want to acquire some, to feel more comfortable working on the exercises in this book. Please note that this book (*Engineering Dynamics Labs with SolidWorks Motion 2014*) is self-contained and requires no pre-existing experience in geometric modeling with **SolidWorks**.

Companion DVD

For each hardcopy of the book, we also provide a DVD containing some of the resources in the webpage to save your time of downloading the files, including (a) the finished **SolidWorks** files of each section (b) the 121-page PDF tutorial, *Part and Assembly Modeling with SolidWorks 2014*.

Notations

Chapters and sections are numbered in a traditional way. Each section is further divided into subsections. For example, the first subsection of the second section of Chapter 3 is denoted as "3.2-1." Text boxes in a subsection are ordered with numbers, each of which is enclosed by a pair of square brackets (e.g., [4]). We refer to that text box as "3.2-1[4]." When referring to a text box from the same subsection, we drop the subsection identifier. For example, we simply write "[4]." Equations are numbered in a similar way, except that the equation number is enclosed by a pair of round brackets rather than square brackets. For example, "3.2-1(2)" refers to the 2nd equation in the subsection 3.2-1. Notations used in this book are summarized as follows (see page 6 for more details):

3.2-1	Numbers after a hyphen are subsection numbers.
[1], [2], ...	Numbers with square brackets are text box numbers.
(1), (2), ...	Numbers with round brackets are equation numbers.
SolidWorks	**SolidWorks** terms are boldfaced to facilitate the readability of text.
Round-cornered text boxes	A round-cornered text box indicates that mouse or keyboard actions are needed.
Sharp-cornered text boxes	A sharp-cornered box is used for commentary only; i.e., mouse or keyboard actions are not needed in that step.
#	A symbol # is used to indicate the last textbox of a subsection.

Huei-Huang Lee

Associate Professor
Department of Engineering Science
National Cheng Kung University, Tainan, Taiwan
e-mail: hhlee@mail.ncku.edu.tw
webpage: myweb.ncku.edu.tw/~hhlee

Chapter 1

Particle Kinematics

Rigid Body

In the real world, all solid bodies are more or less deformable. There are no such things as **rigid bodies**. However, if the deformation of a body is not our concern and if the deformation is negligible relative to the motion of the body, we can treat the body as a **rigid body**. In this book, we assume all bodies studied in this book are **rigid bodies**. In rigid body dynamics, **springs** are the only elements that are deformable.

Particle

Similarly, in the real world, there are no such things as particles, which occupy zero volume in the space. However, when a body doesn't rotate (therefore no angular velocity, angular acceleration, angular kinetic energy, or angular momentum), we can treat the body as though its entire mass concentrates at its mass center and regard it as a **particle**.

Even when a body does rotate but its angular velocity remains constant, we still can treat the body as a particle, since its rotational quantities (angular velocity, angular acceleration, angular kinetic energy, or angular momentum) remain unchanged during the motion. For example, in the study of space mechanics, we often treat a planet as a particle, even though it does rotate. Keep in mind that *a body is treated as a particle not because of it size, but because of its insignificancy of rotation*.

Chapters 1-4 provides exercises on dynamic systems involving bodies that can be treated as particles.

Kinematics

What is kinematics? To answer this question, let's first explain how a dynamics problem is solved (either by computer or hand-calculation). Like any other engineering analysis, solving a dynamics problem involves two main steps: (a) write down a set of equations and (b) solve the equations.

For rigid body dynamics, these equations can be divided into two groups: (a) Equations based on **physical principles**. For each body, some equilibrium equations (e.g., Newton's 2nd Law) or conservation equations (e.g., principle of work and energy) can be written down. (b) Equations describing the **kinematics relations** among bodies. That is, the relations among motions of bodies. The motions of a particle can be fully described by its **position**, **velocity**, and **acceleration**.

Particle kinematics is the study of the relations among **positions**, **velocities**, and **accelerations** of particles involved in a dynamics system. Examples of kinematics problems are: (a) If a particle has an acceleration of $\vec{a}(t)$, what are its velocity $\vec{v}(t)$ and position $\vec{r}(t)$? (b) If particle A is moving with a constant acceleration of $\vec{a}_A$, what are the acceleration, velocity, and position of particle B at time t?

Chapter 1 provides exercises on particle kinematics.

Section 1.1

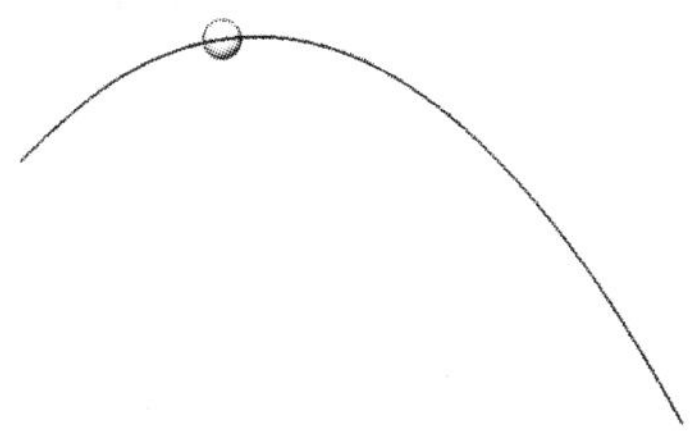

Rectangular Components: Falling Ball

1.1-1 Introduction

[1] Imagine that you throw a ball with an initial velocity [2-5]. The velocity and the position of the ball at time t = 1 sec can be calculated as follows.

In X-direction, the velocity component is constant,

$$v_X = v_0 \cos\theta = (5 \text{ m/s})(\cos 45^\circ) = 3.54 \text{ m/s} \quad (1)$$

and the position is

$$X = (v_0 \cos\theta)t = (5 \text{ m/s})(\cos 45^\circ)(1 \text{ s}) = 3.54 \text{ m} \quad (2)$$

In Y-direction, the velocity component is

$$v_Y = v_0 \sin\theta - gt = (5 \text{ m/s})(\sin 45^\circ) - (9.81 \text{ m/s}^2)(1 \text{ s}) = -6.27 \text{ m/s} \quad (3)$$

and the position is

$$Y = (v_0 \sin\theta)t - \frac{1}{2}gt^2 = (5 \text{ m/s})(\sin 45^\circ)(1 \text{ s}) - \frac{1}{2}(9.81 \text{ m/s}^2)(1 \text{ s})^2 = -1.37 \text{ m} \quad (4)$$

These values are shown in [6, 7]. In this section, we'll perform a simulation for this scenario and validate the simulation results with the values in Eqs. (1-4).

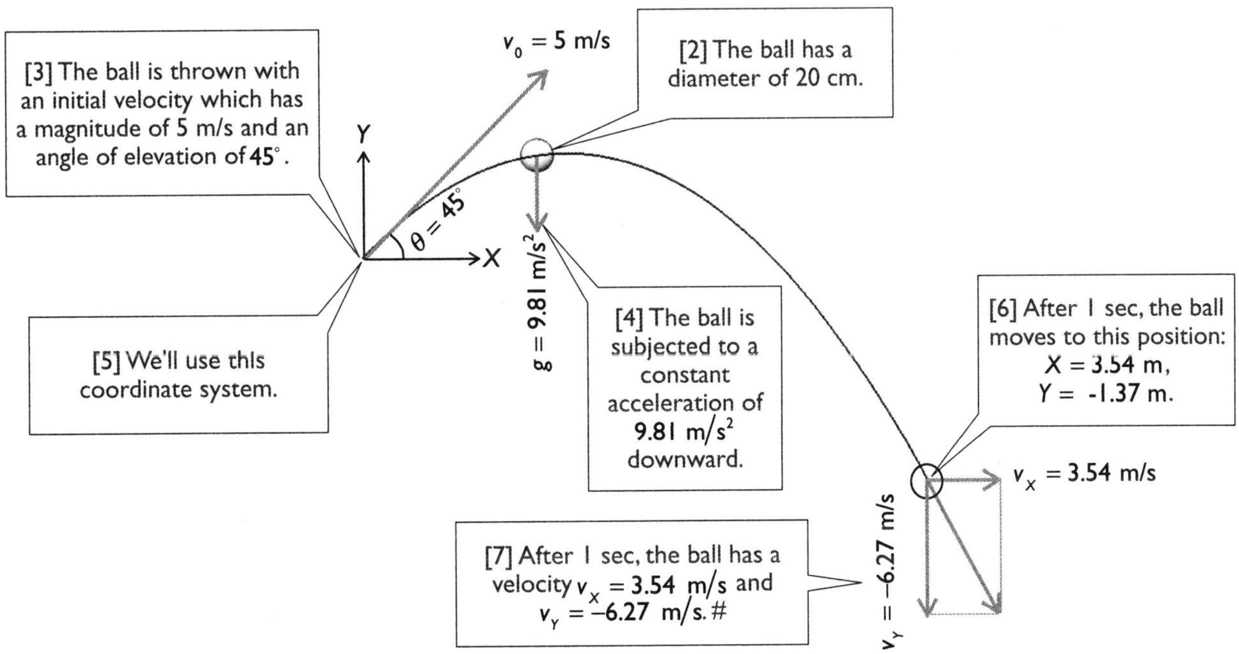

1.1-2 Launch **SolidWorks** and Create a New Part

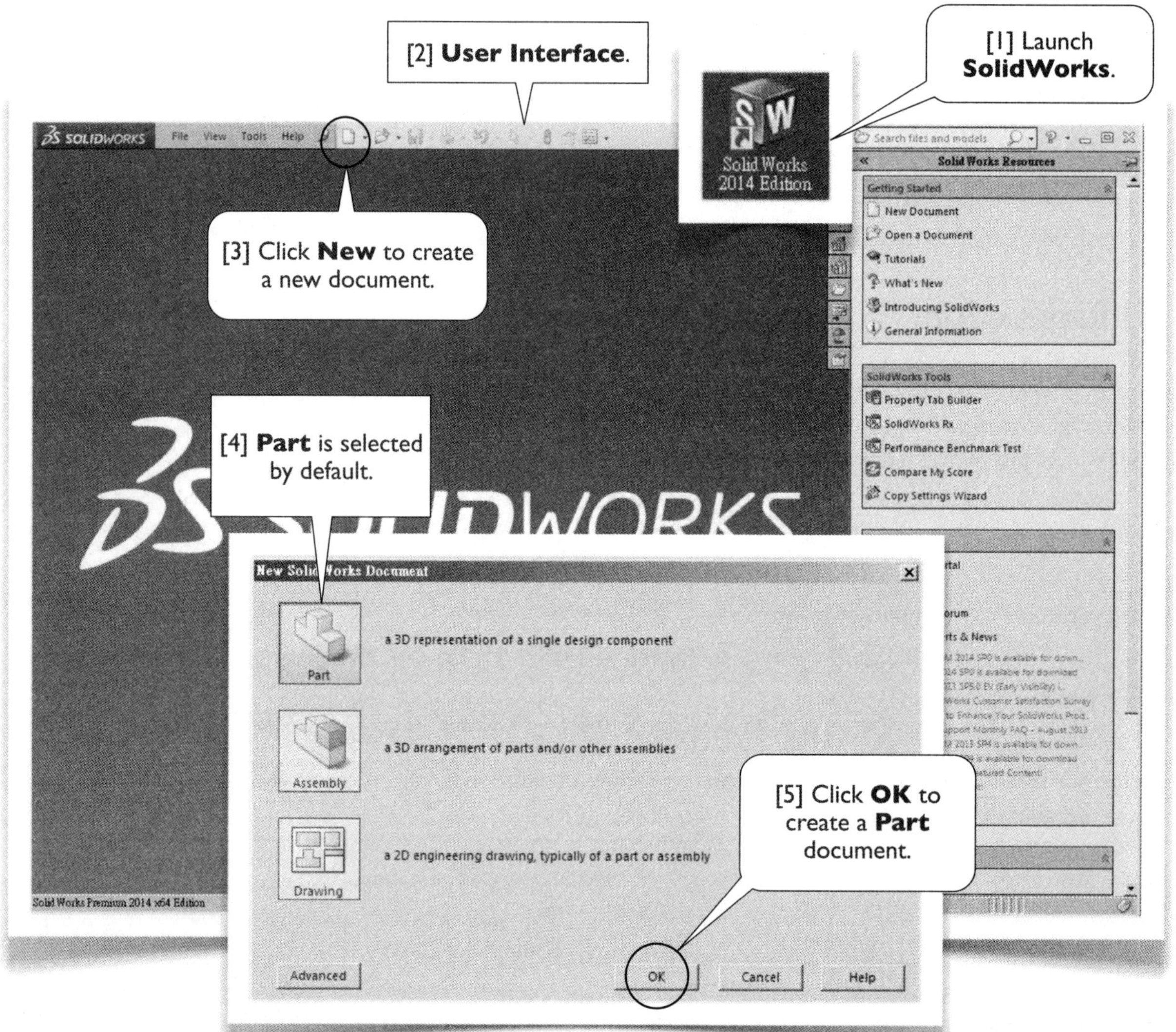

About the Text Boxes

1. Within each subsection (e.g., 1.1-2), text boxes are ordered with numbers, each of which is enclosed by a pair of square brackets (e.g., [1]). When you read the contents of a subsection, please follow the order of the text boxes.
2. The text box numbers are also used as reference numbers. In the same subsection, we simply refer to a text box by its number (e.g., [1]). From other subsections, we refer to a text box by its subsection identifier and the text box number (e.g., 1.1-2[1]).
3. A text box is either round-cornered (e.g., [1, 3, 5]) or sharp-cornered (e.g., [2, 4]). A round-cornered box indicates that **mouse or keyboard actions** are needed in that step. A sharp-cornered box is used for commentary only; i.e., mouse or keyboard actions are not needed in that step.
4. A symbol # is used to indicate the last text box of a subsection, so that you don't leave out any text boxes.

SolidWorks Terms

In this book, terms used in the **SolidWorks** are boldfaced (e.g., **Part** in [4, 5]) to facilitate the readability. #

1.1-3 Set Up Unit System

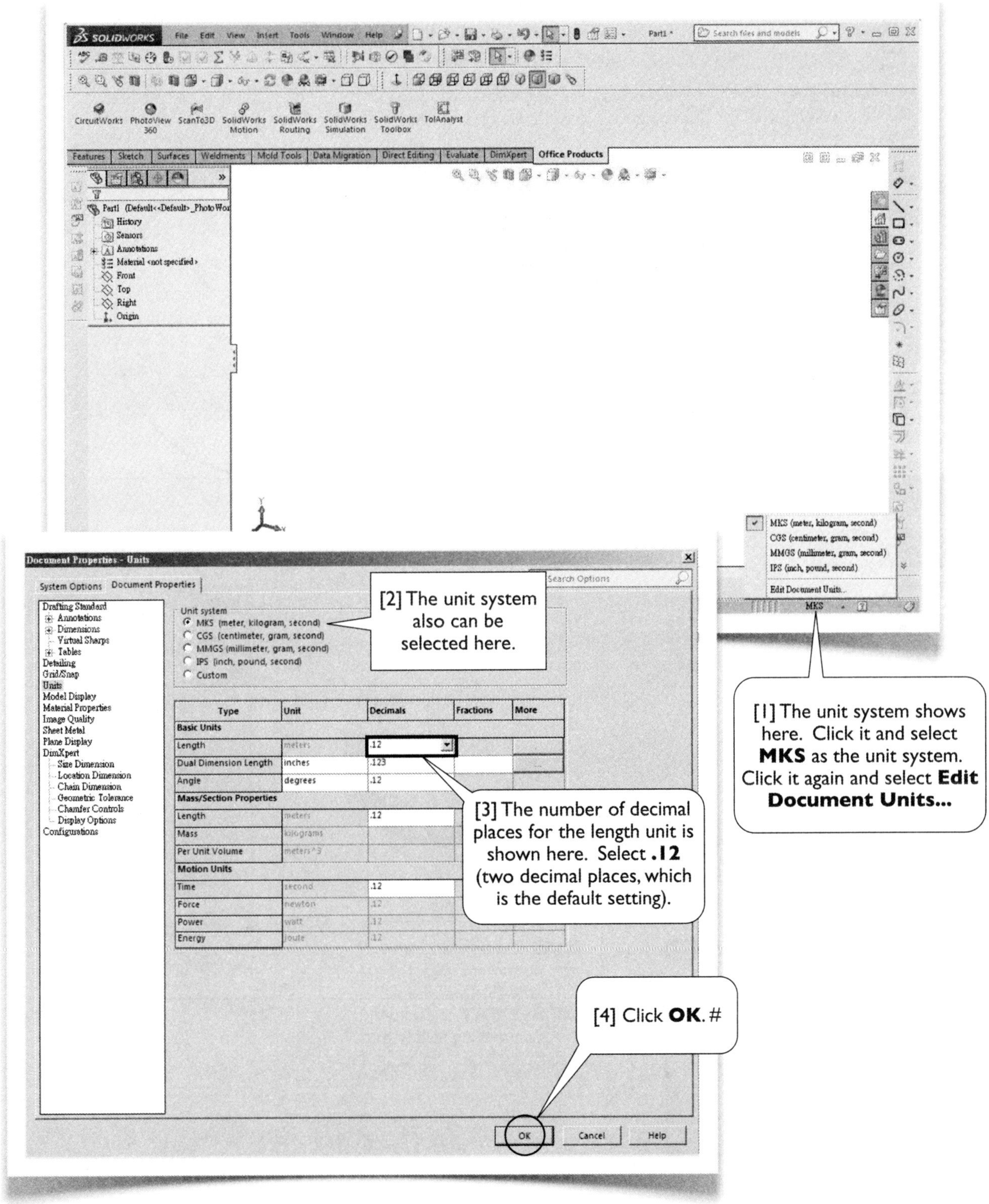

1.1-4 Create a Part: **Ball**

[1] In the **Features Tree** (on the left of the user interface), right-click **Front** plane and select **Sketch** from the **Context Menu**.

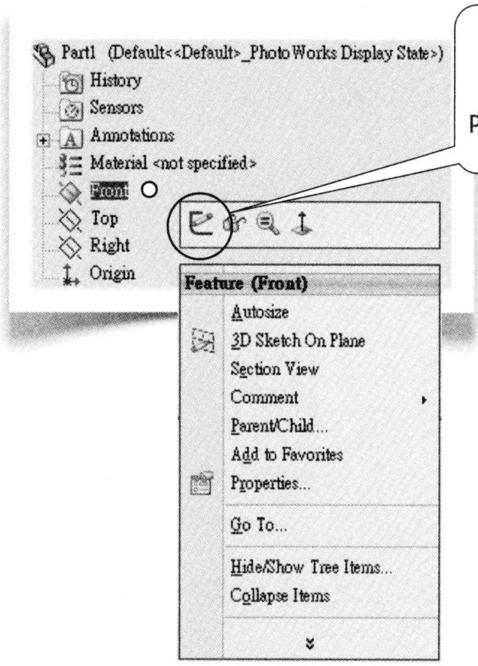

[2] Draw a sketch like this.

[4] Select this line as **Axis of Revolution**.

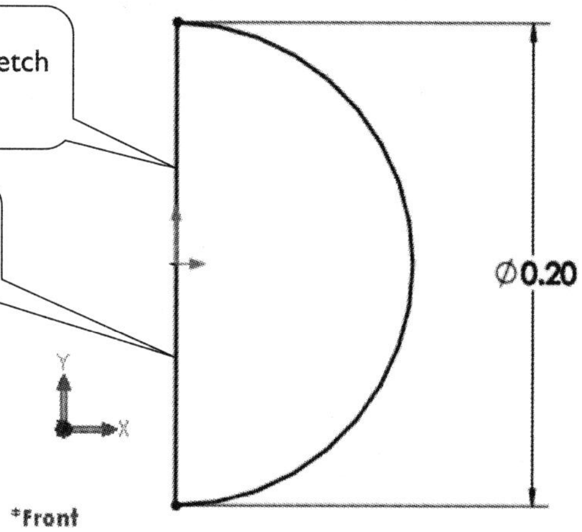

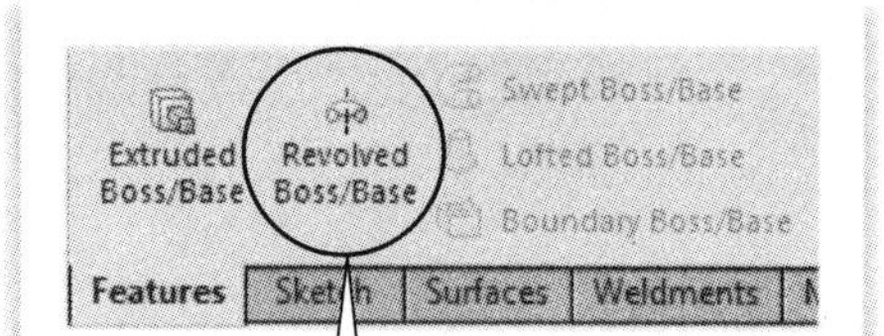

[3] In the **Features Toolbar**, click **Revolved Boss/Base**.

[5] Click **OK**.

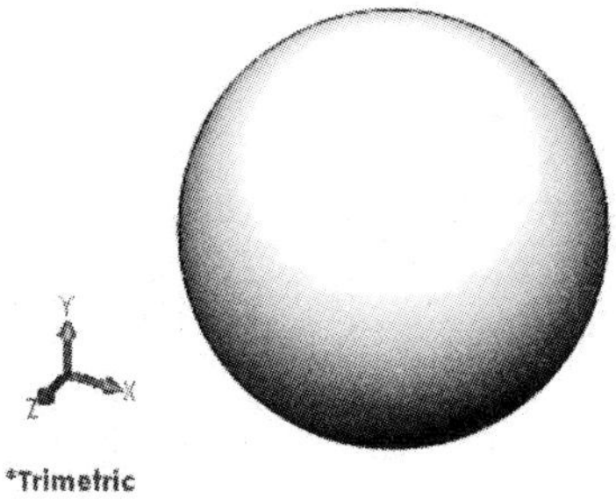

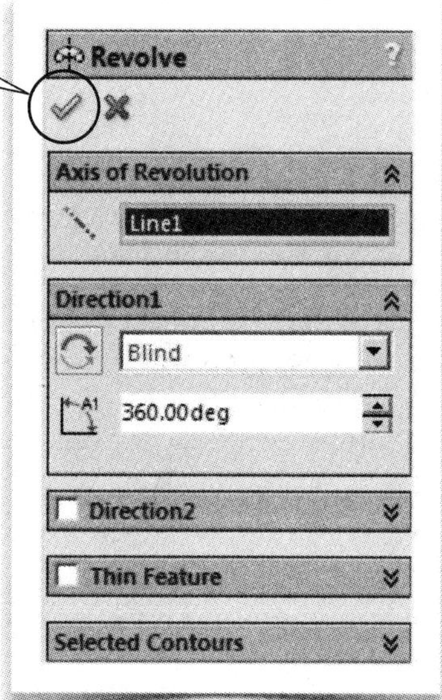

[6] This is the **Features Tree** of the **Part**. In this book, we simply call it a **Part Tree**.

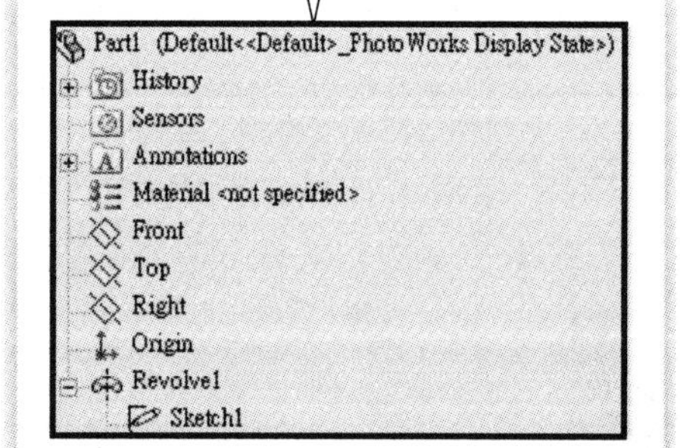

[7] Click **Save** and save the document with the name **Ball**. A file **Ball.SLDPRT** is created in your working folder. #

1.1-5 Create an Assembly: **Ball-In-Space**

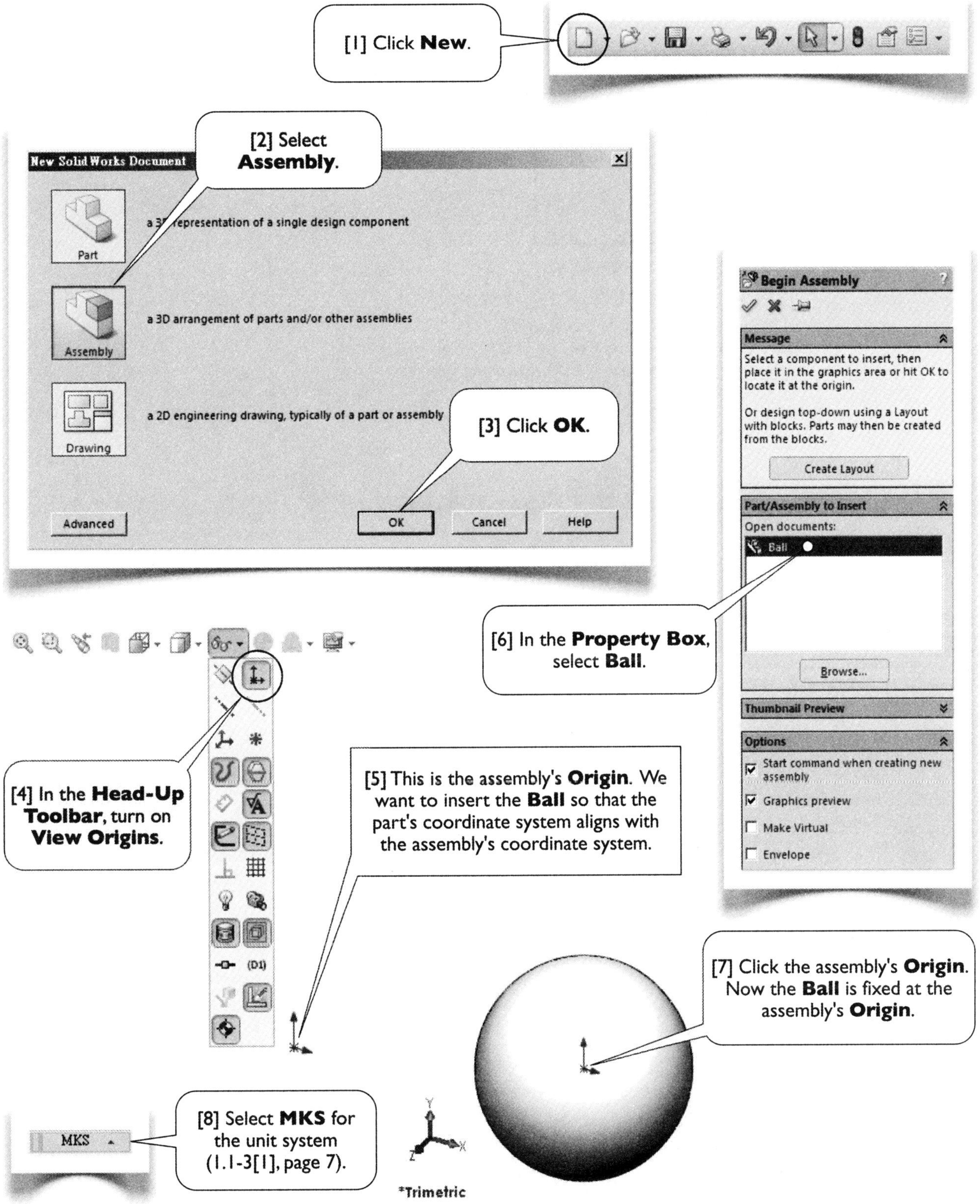

[10] This is the **Features Tree** of the **Assembly**. In this book, we simply call it the **Assembly Tree**.

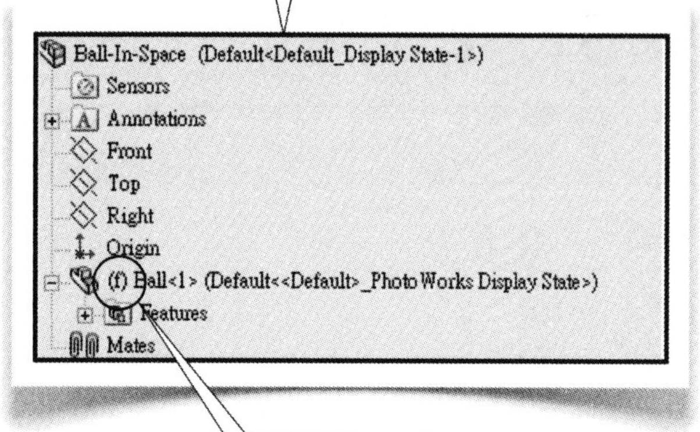

[11] In the **Assembly Tree**, an **(f)** sign before **Ball<1>** indicates that the **Ball** is fixed in the space. We'll release it before running the simulation (1.1-11[11], page 14). #

[9] Click **Save** and save the document with the name **Ball-In-Space**. A file **Ball-In-Space.SLDASM** is created in your working folder.

1.1-6 Create a **Sketch** in the **Assembly**

[1] Right-click **Front** plane and select **Sketch** from the **Context Menu**.

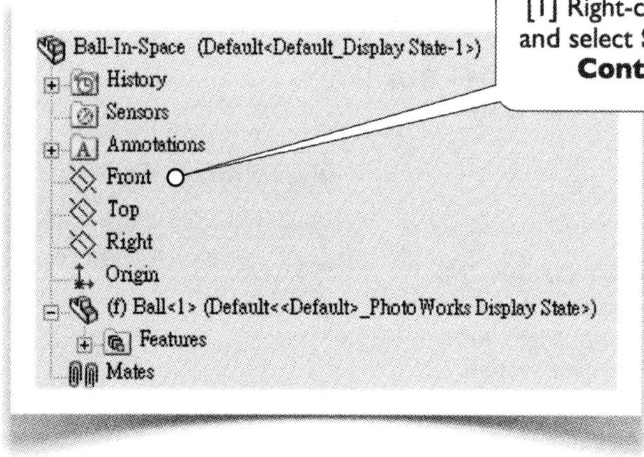

[2] In the **Standard Views Toolbar**, click **Normal To**.

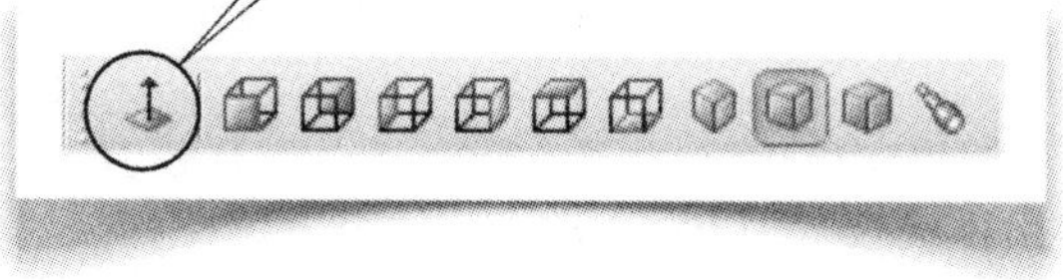

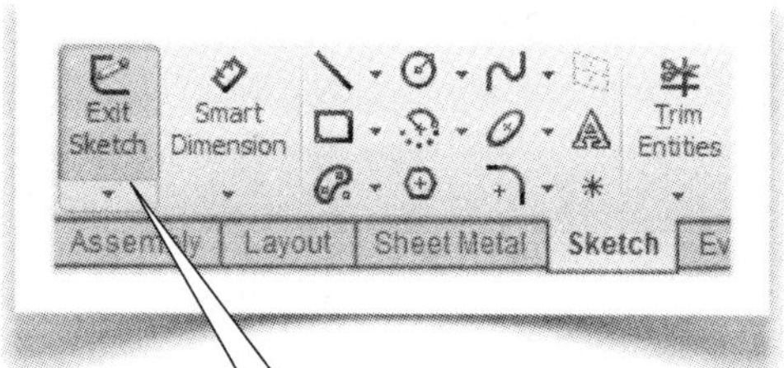

[4] Click **Exit Sketch**. #

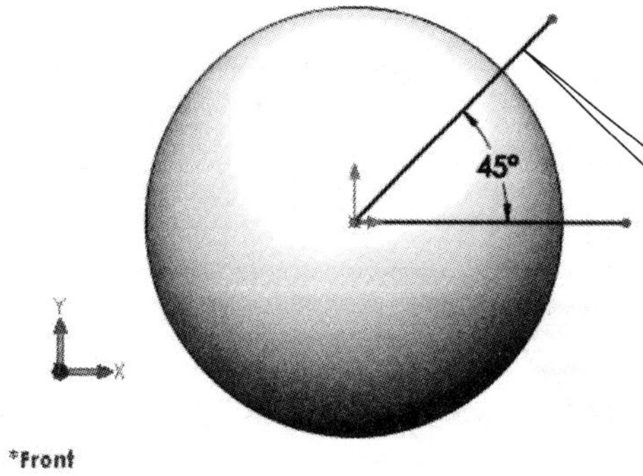

[3] Draw a sketch like this. The lengths of the lines are not relevant. We'll use this line to define the direction of the initial velocity of the **Ball**.

1.1-7 Load **SolidWorks Motion**

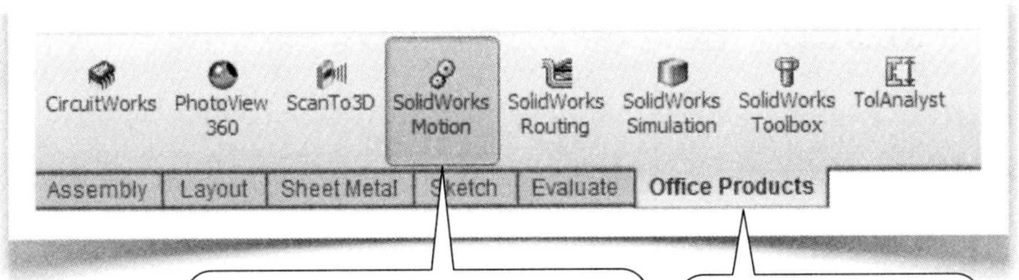

[1] Click **Office Products** tab.

[2] If this button is highlighted, that means **SolidWorks Motion** has already been loaded, you may jump to next page. Otherwise, click to load **SolidWorks Motion**.

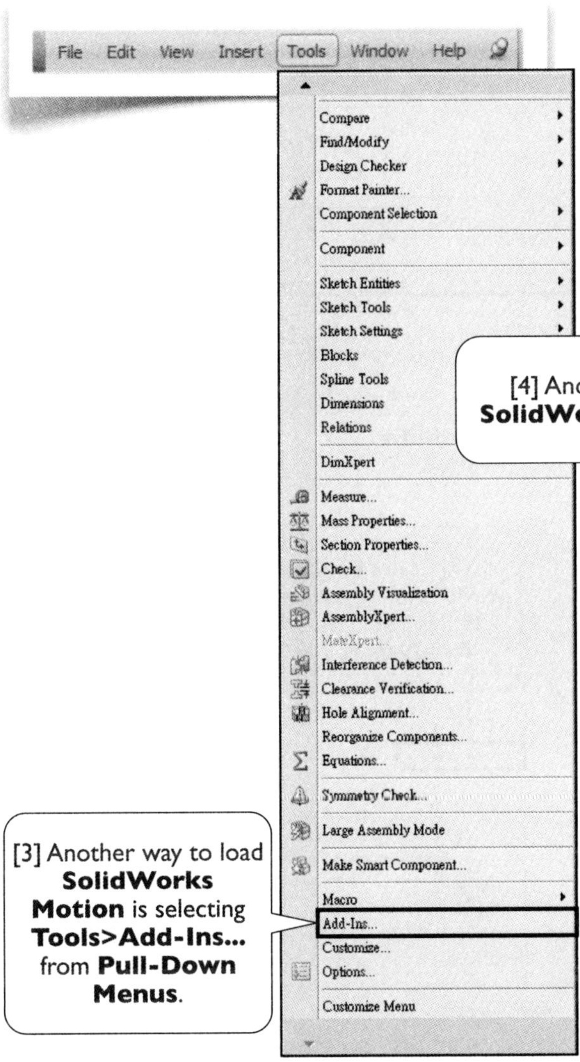

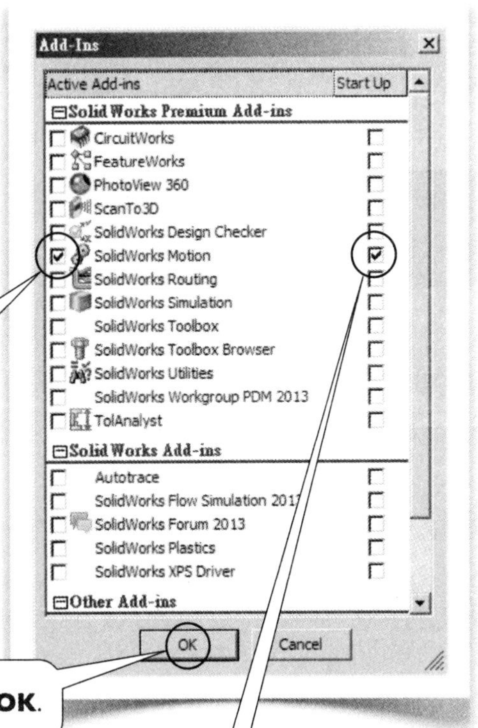

[3] Another way to load **SolidWorks Motion** is selecting **Tools>Add-Ins...** from **Pull-Down Menus**.

[4] And then select **SolidWorks Motion**.

[5] Also click here so that the **Motion** will be loaded automatically each time you start up **SolidWorks**. In this book, we assume that you set up this way so that the **Motion** is loaded automatically each time you start up **SolidWorks**. #

[6] Click **OK**.

1.1-8 Create a **Motion Study**

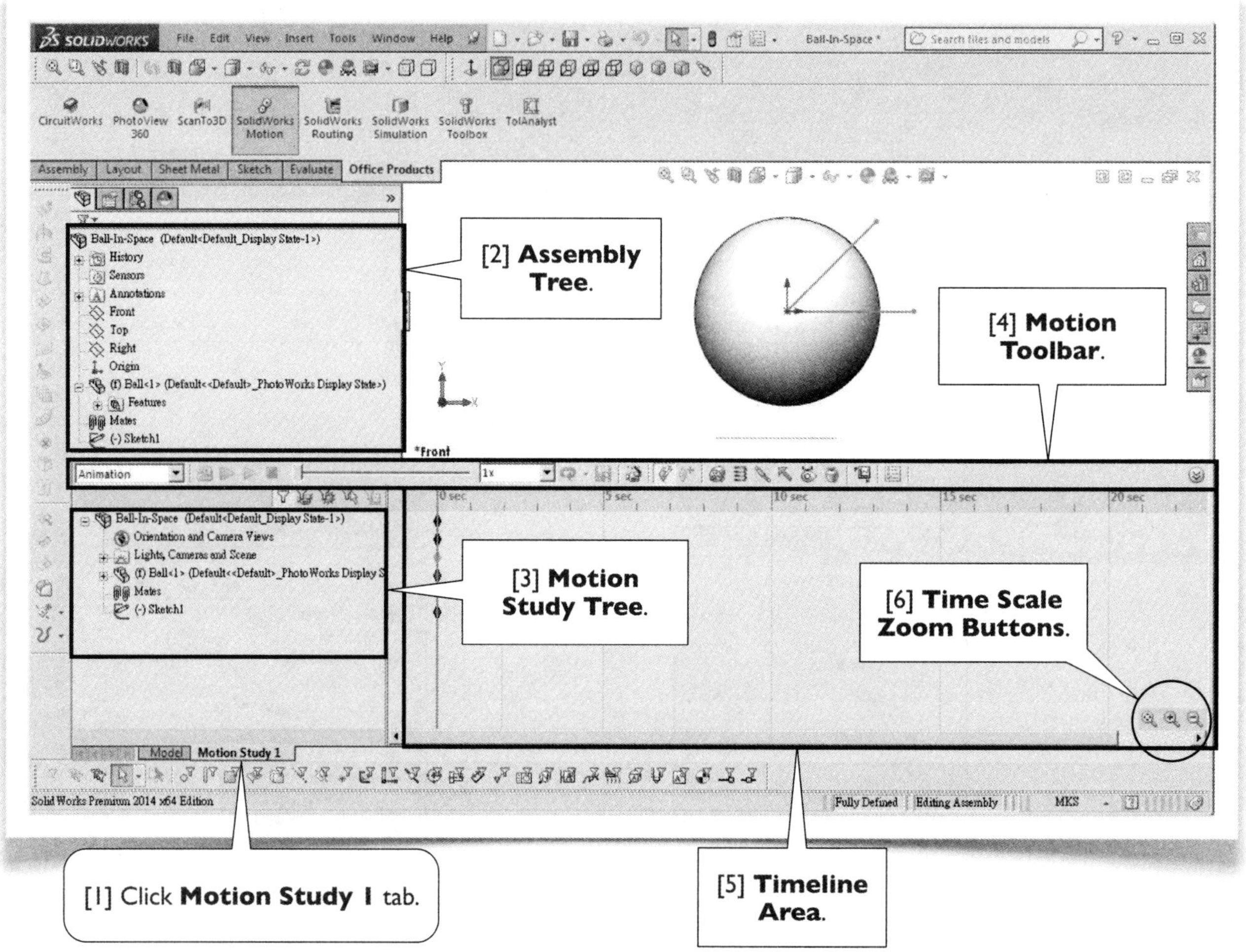

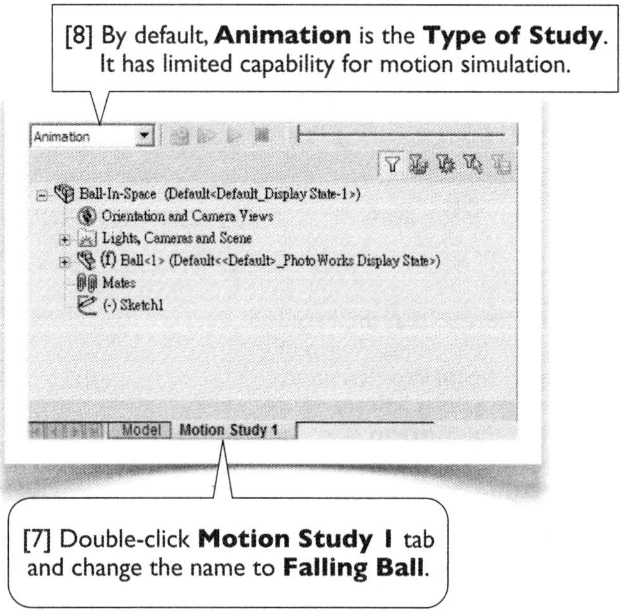

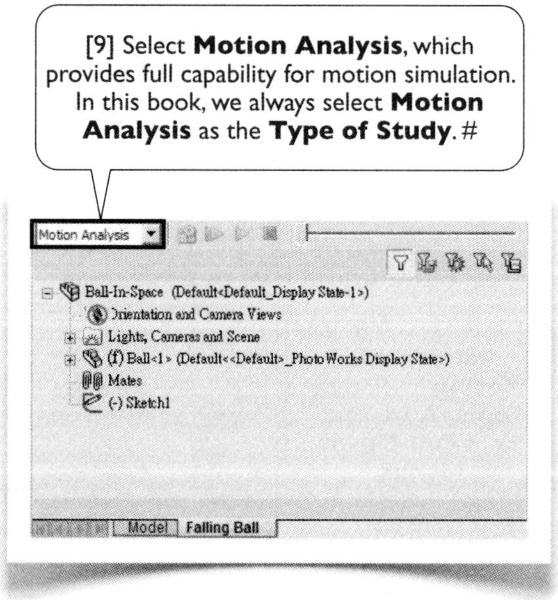

1.1-9 Set Up **Gravity**

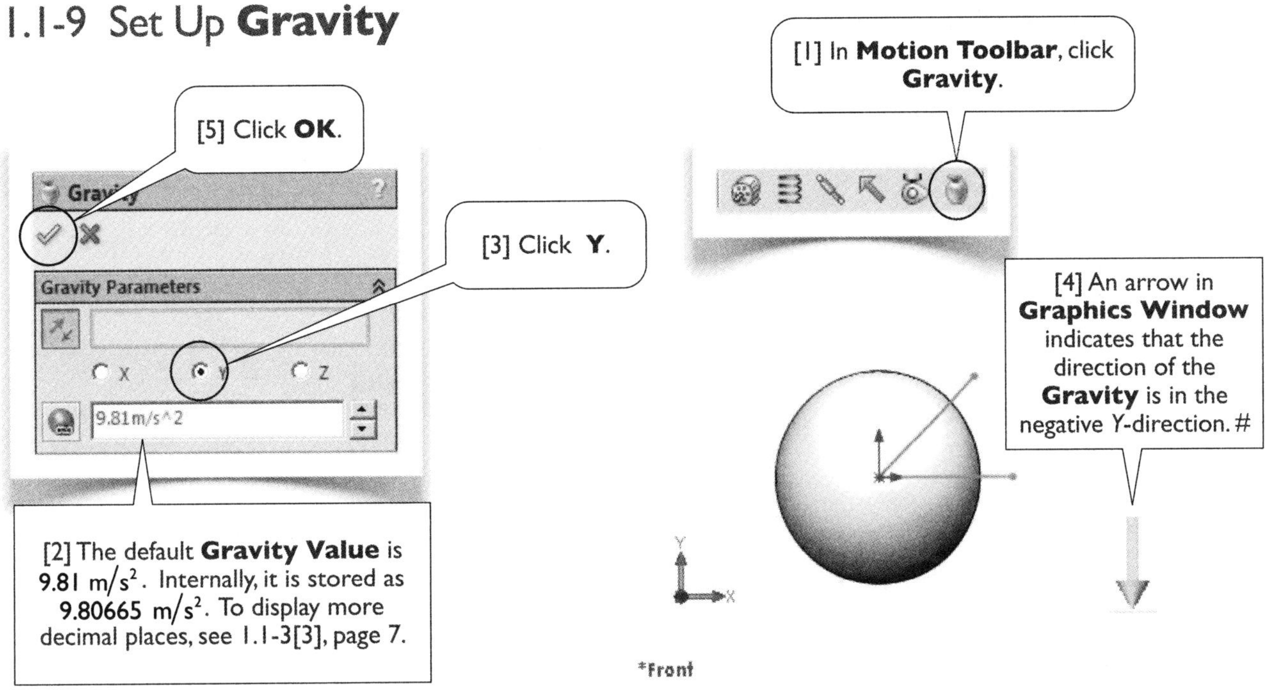

[1] In **Motion Toolbar**, click **Gravity**.

[2] The default **Gravity Value** is 9.81 m/s^2. Internally, it is stored as 9.80665 m/s^2. To display more decimal places, see 1.1-3[3], page 7.

[3] Click **Y**.

[4] An arrow in **Graphics Window** indicates that the direction of the **Gravity** is in the negative *Y*-direction. #

[5] Click **OK**.

1.1-10 Set Up **Initial Velocity** for the **Ball**

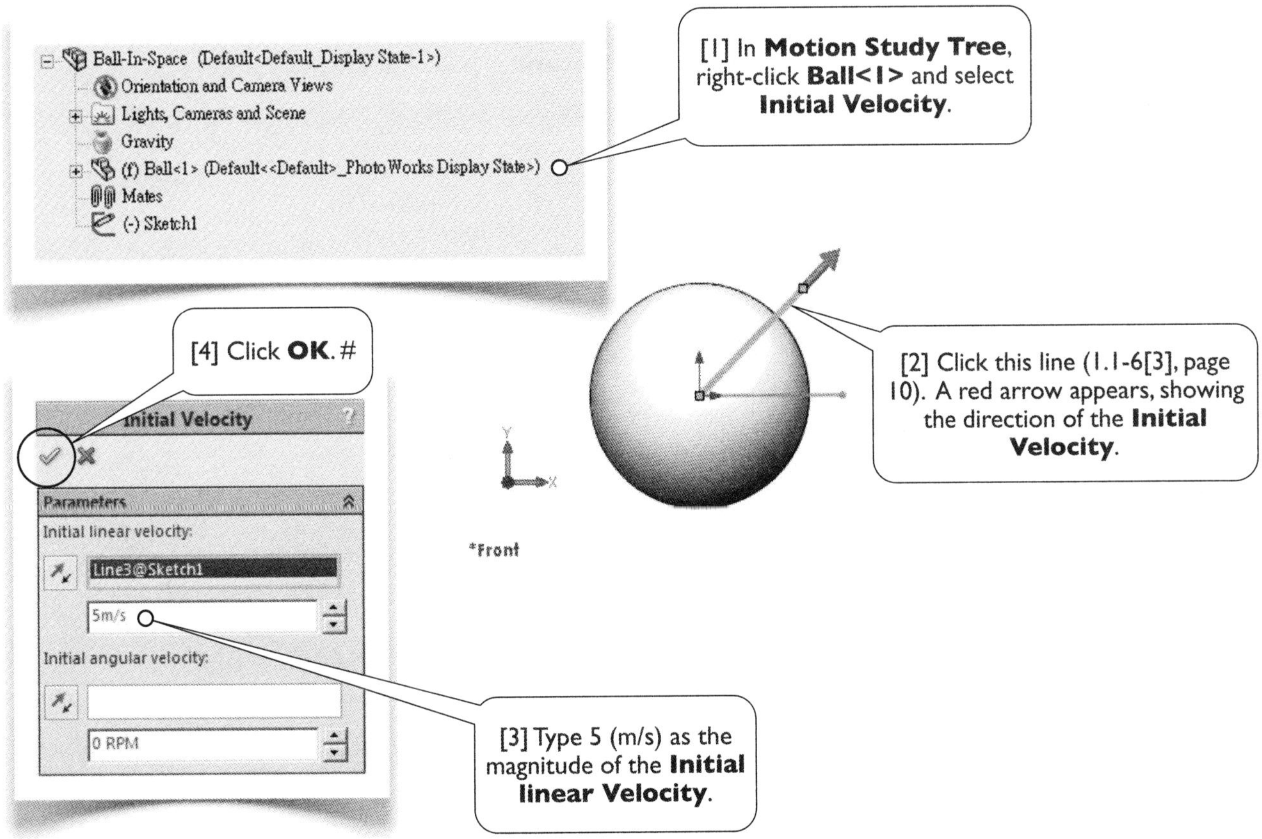

[1] In **Motion Study Tree**, right-click **Ball<1>** and select **Initial Velocity**.

[2] Click this line (1.1-6[3], page 10). A red arrow appears, showing the direction of the **Initial Velocity**.

[3] Type 5 (m/s) as the magnitude of the **Initial linear Velocity**.

[4] Click **OK**. #

1.1-11 Calculate and Animate **Results**

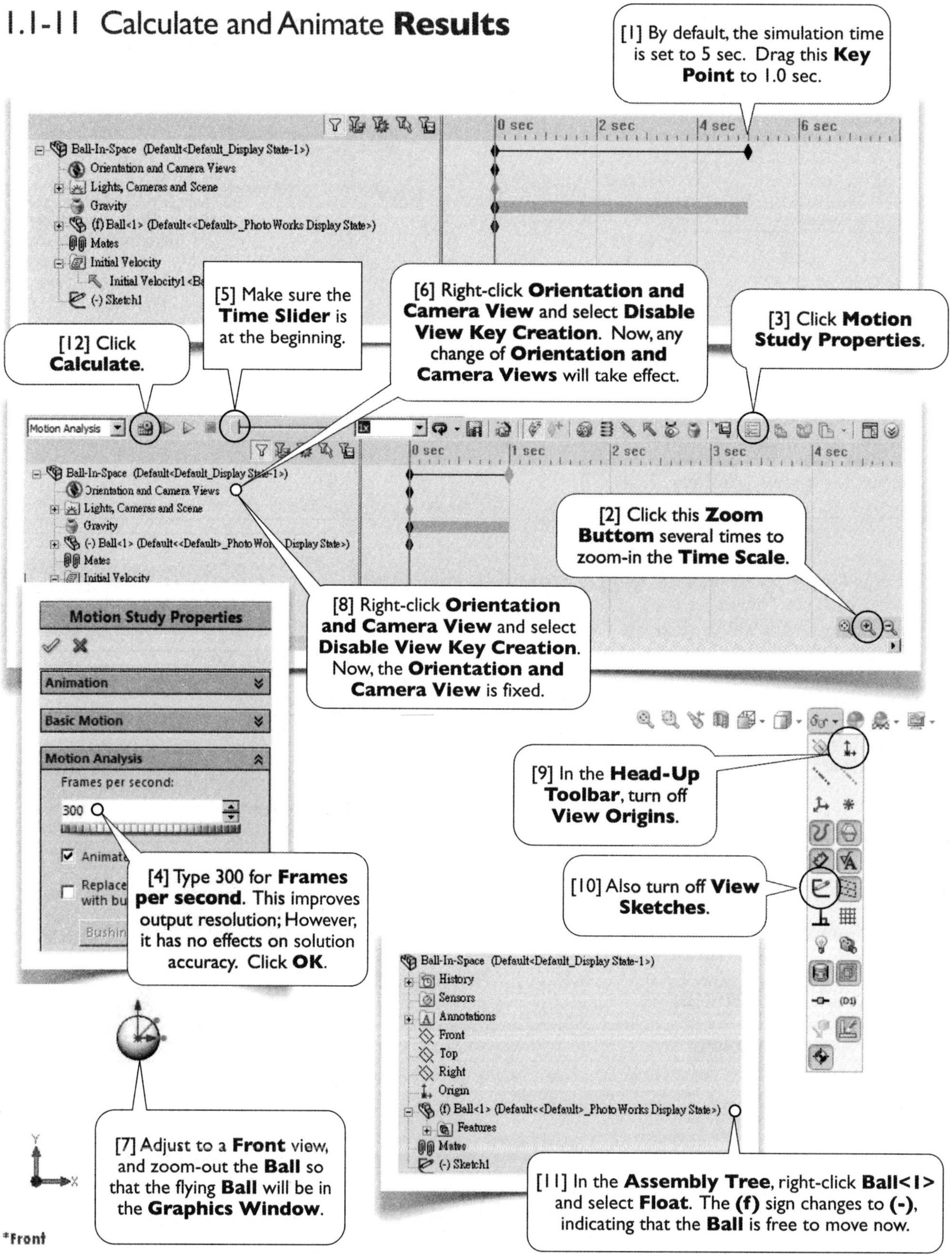

[13] A **Motion Analysis Messages** window may appear with useful information. This feature can be disabled (see 2.1-9[4], page 41). If you don't see this window, never mind and skip to [15].

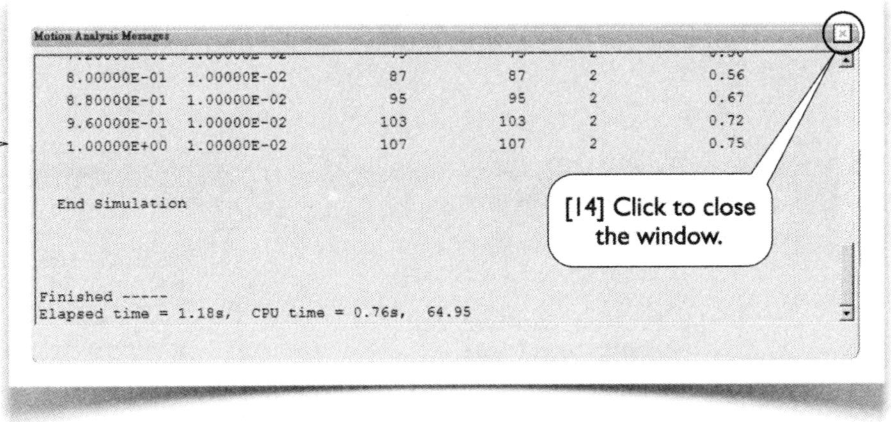

[14] Click to close the window.

[17] Click to **Stop** the animation. #

[16] Click **Play from Start**.

[15] Select **0.1x** for **Playback Speed**. We now play a slow motion.

1.1-12 Results: **Trace Path**

[1] In **Motion Toolbar**, click **Results and Plots**.

[5] Click **OK**.

[2] Select **Displacement/Velocity/Acceleration**.

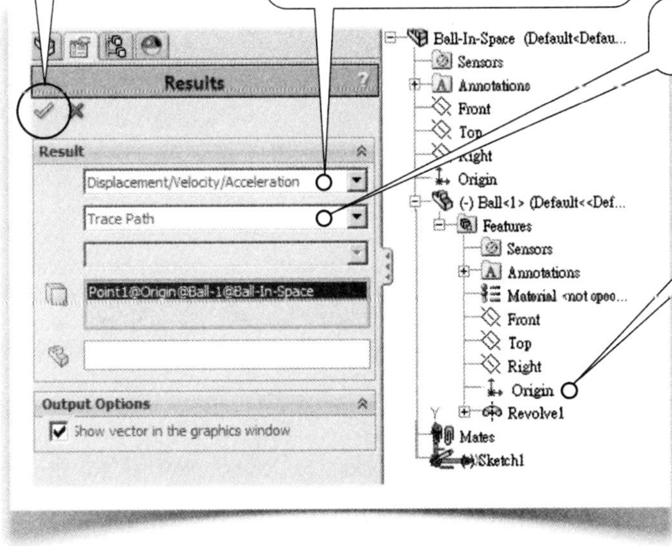

[3] Select **Trace Path**.

[4] Expand the **Assembly Tree** in the **Graphics Window** and select the **Origin** of **Ball<1>**.

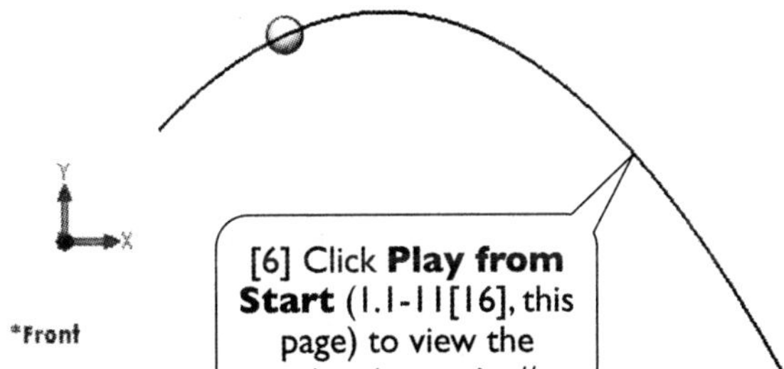

[6] Click **Play from Start** (1.1-11[16], this page) to view the animation again. #

1.1-13 Results: **Positions-X**

[1] In **Motion Toolbar**, click **Results and Plots**.

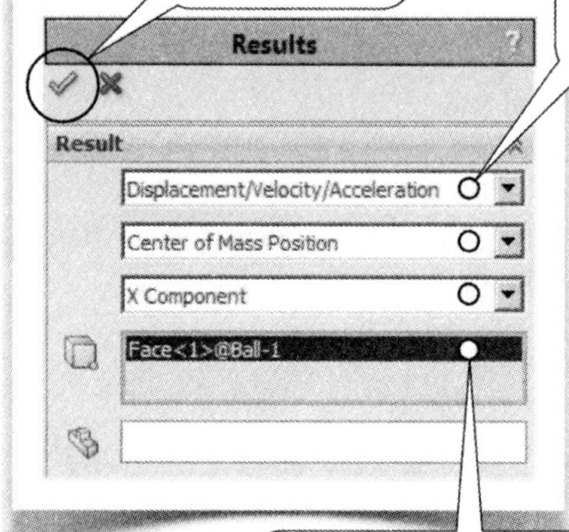

[2] Set up the **Results** like this.

[3] In the **Graphics Window**, click the **Ball**. The positions of the **Center of Mass** will be reported.

[4] Click **OK**.

[5] The scale is somehow misleading. Double-click the vertical axis.

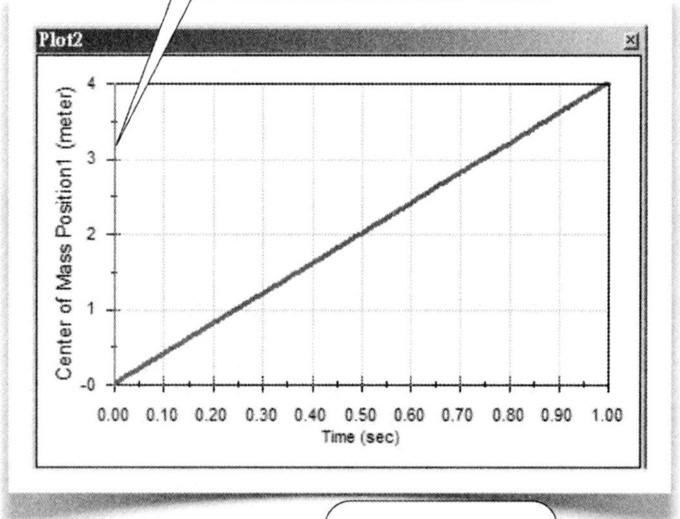

[6] Click **Scale** tab and set the scale like this. Click **OK**.

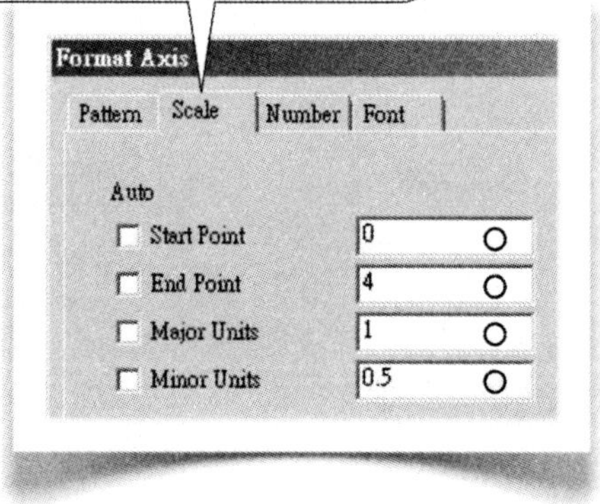

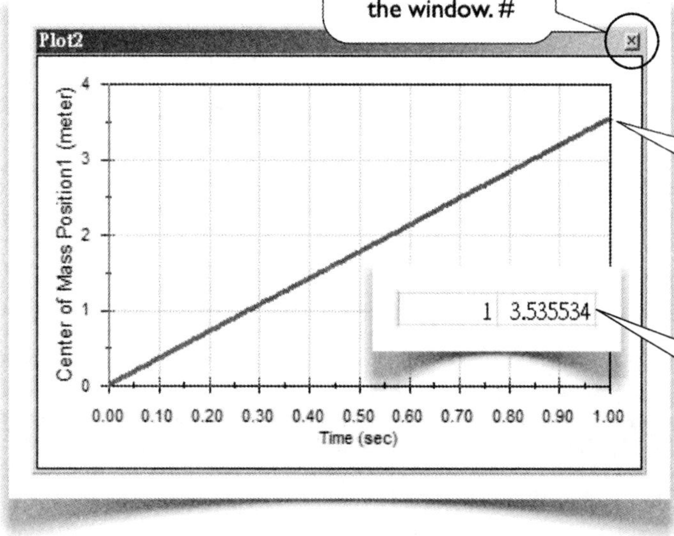

[7] Now, it looks better. Let's obtain numerical data. Right-click anywhere inside the window and select **Export CSV**. Save the file with the name **Ball-Position-X**.

[8] In your working folder, double-click to open the file **Ball-Position-X.CSV**. Look up the position at time = 1 sec, which is 3.535534 m, consistent with the value in Eq. 1.1-1(2), page 5. Close the **CSV file**.

[9] Click to close the window. #

1.1-14 Results: **Positions-Y**

[1] In **Motion Toolbar**, click **Results and Plots**.

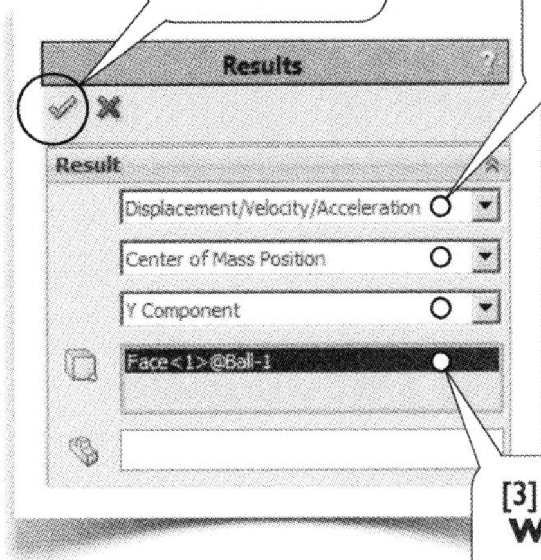

[2] Set up the **Results** like this.

[3] In the **Graphics Window**, click the **Ball**.

[4] Click **OK**.

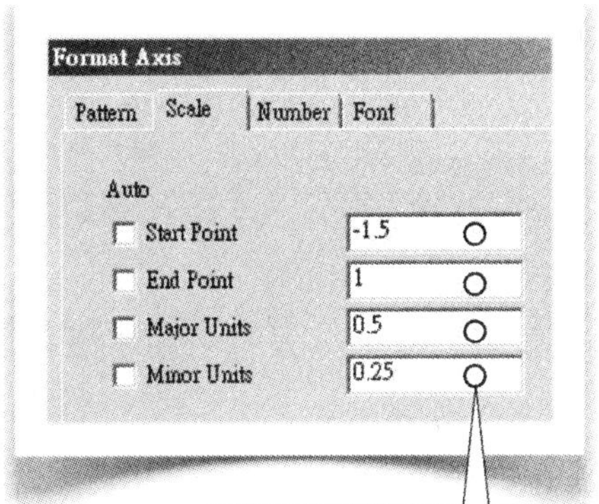

[5] Set the scale for the vertical axis like this.

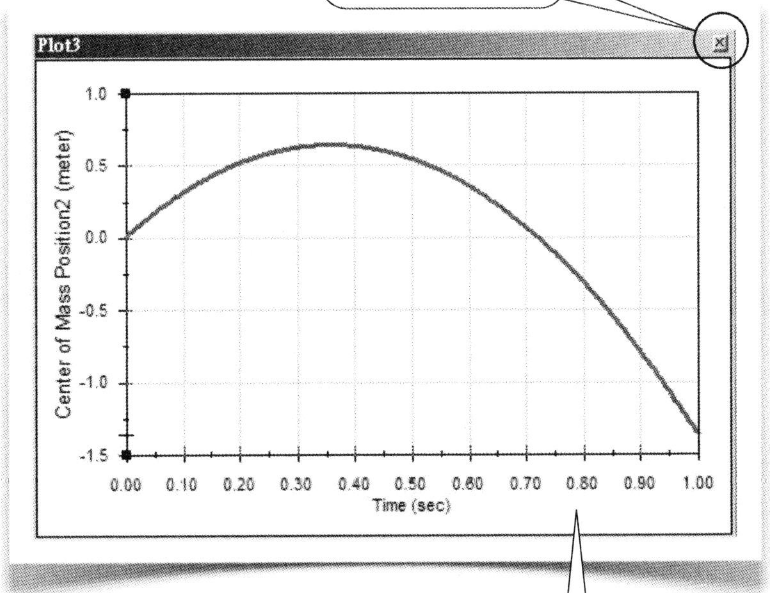

[6] Right-click anywhere inside the window and select **Export CSV**. Save the file with the name **Ball-Position-Y**.

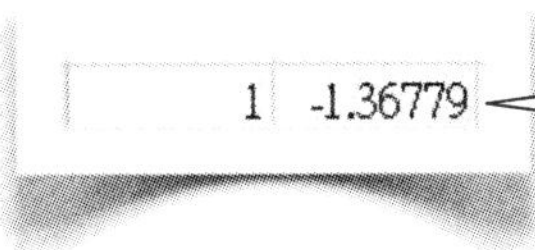

[7] In your working folder, double-click to open the file **Ball-Position-Y.CSV**. Look up the position at time = 1 sec, which is -1.36779 m, consistent with the value in Eq. 1.1-1(4), page 5. Close the **CSV** file.

[8] Click to close the window. #

1.1-15 Results: **Velocity-X**

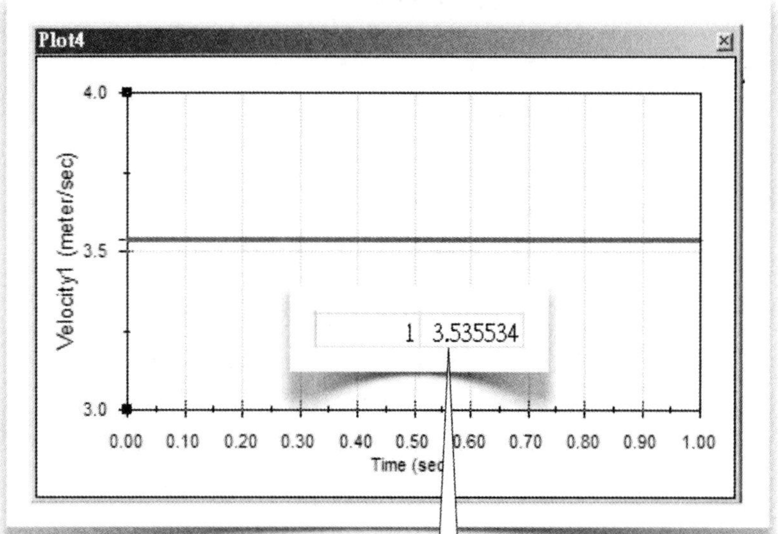

[1] Follow a similar procedure in 1.1-14 to obtain the **Ball's** velocity in *X*-direction, which is a constant (3.535534 m/s) over the time, consistent with the value in Eq. 1.1-1(1), page 5. #

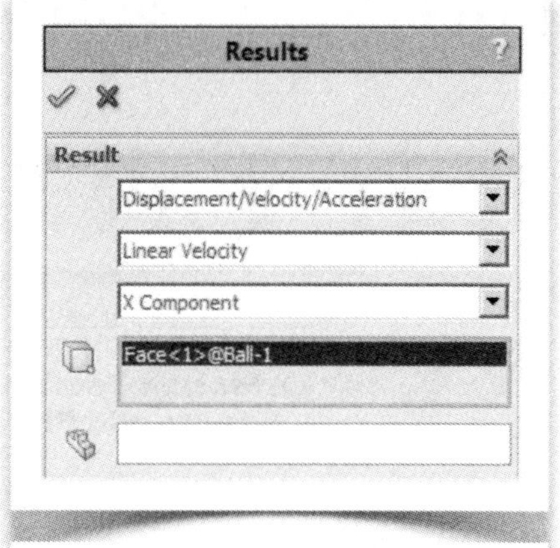

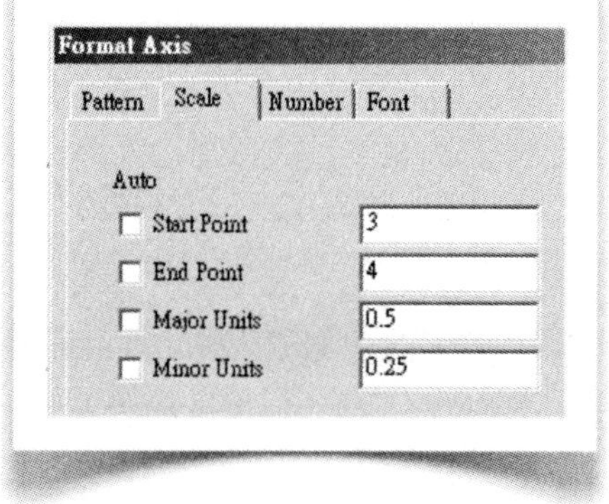

1.1-16 Results: **Velocity-Y**

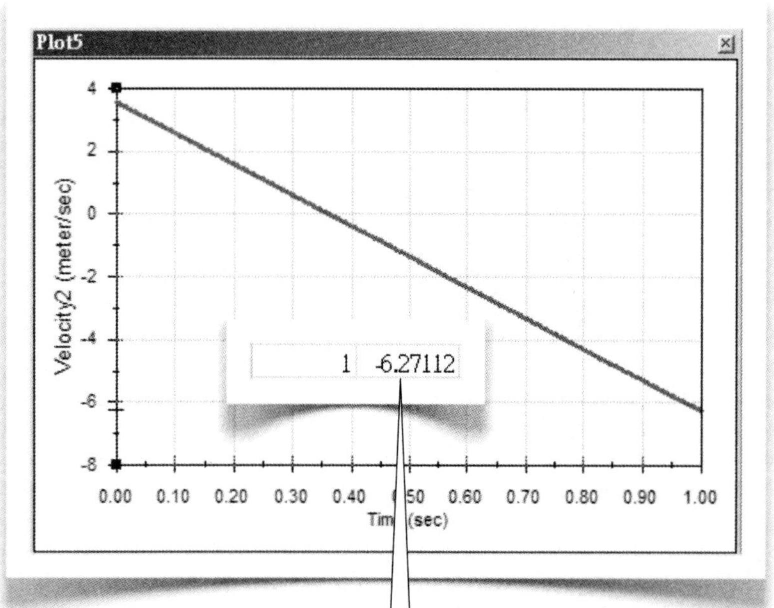

[1] Follow a similar procedure in 1.1-14 to obtain the **Ball's** velocity in *Y*-direction, which is -6.27112 m/s at time = 1 sec, consistent with the value in Eq. 1.1-1(3), page 5. #

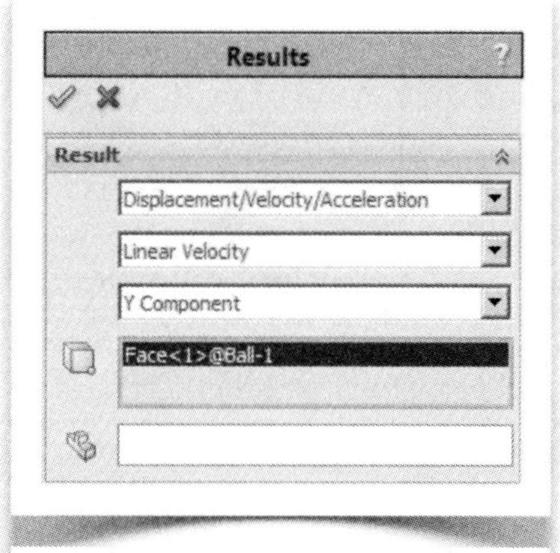

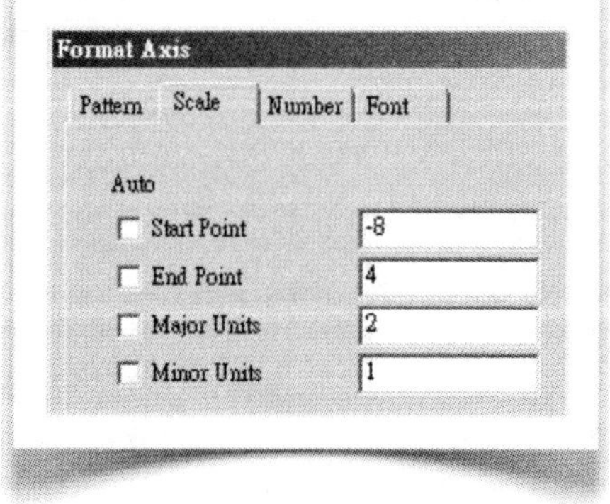

1.1-17 Do It Yourself

[1] **Motion Study Tree**.

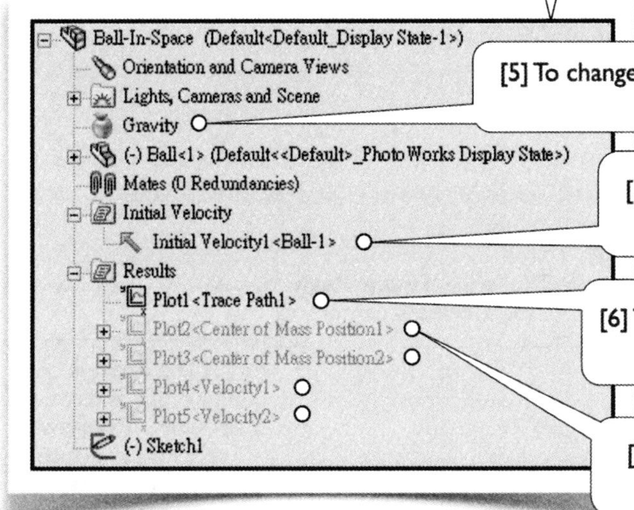

[5] To change the **Gravity**, right-click here and select **Edit Feature**.

[3] To change the magnitude of the **Initial Velocity**, right-click here and select **Edit Feature**.

[6] To hide the **Trace Path** in the **Graphics Window**, right-click here and select **Hide Plot**.

[7] To show any of the **Plot**, right-click it and select **Show Plot**.

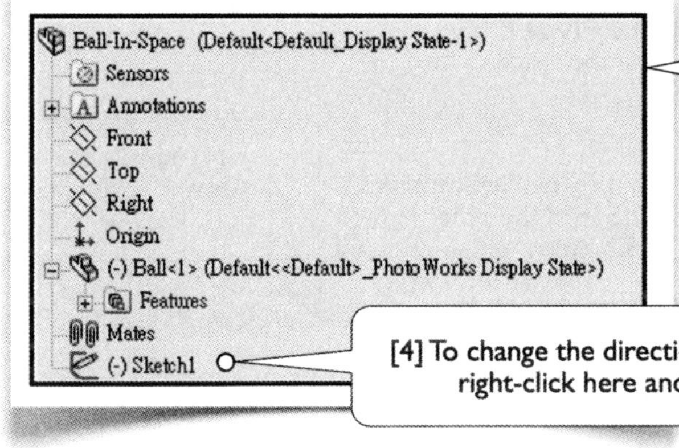

[2] **Assembly Tree**.

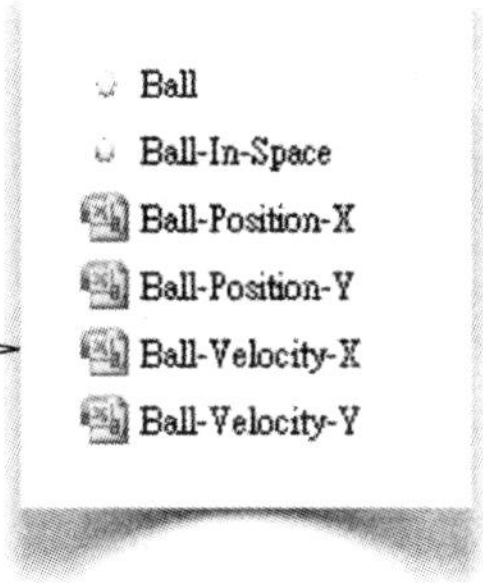

[8] Your working folder should contain these files. #

[4] To change the direction of the **Initial Velocity**, right-click here and select **Edit Sketch**.

1.1-18 Wrap Up

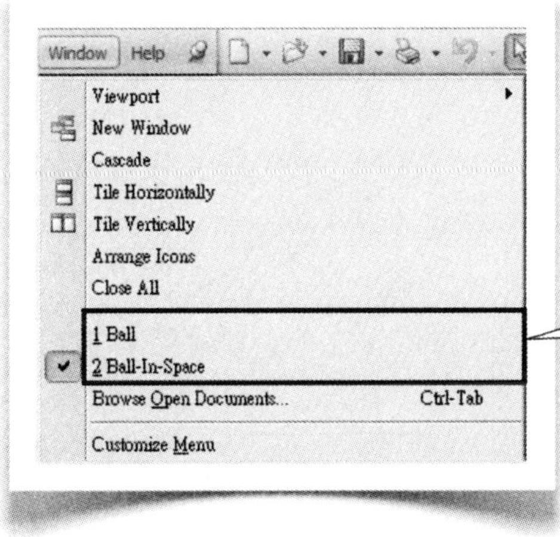

[1] From the **Pull-Down Menus**, click **Window** to see that there are two opened files.

[2] Select **Save>Save All** to save all changes in the two files. Click **Rebuild**, if a warning message window appears.

[3] From the **Pull-Down Menus**, Select **File>Exit** to quit **SolidWorks**. #

Section 1.2

Radial and Transverse Components: Sliding Collar on Rotating Arm

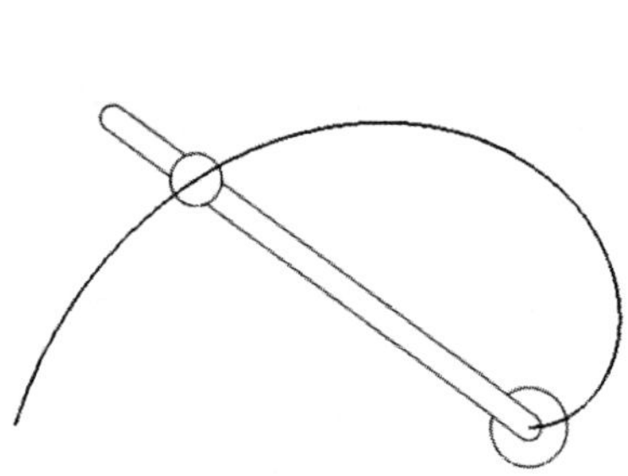

1.2-1 Introduction

[1] Consider an **Arm** rotating about a **Pivot** with an angular speed $\dot{\theta} = \pi$ rad/s [2-4]. A **Collar** initially aligned with the **Pivot** slides along the **Arm** with a constant speed $\dot{r} = 1.0$ m/s [5-6].

Let's use a polar coordinate system centered at the **Pivot** and let (r, θ) be the position of the **Collar's** center. Denote $\vec{e}_r$ the unit vector in radial direction and $\vec{e}_\theta$ the unit vector in transversal direction [7, 8]. Then the position, velocity, and acceleration of the **Collar's** center are respectively

$$\begin{aligned} \vec{r} &= r\vec{e}_r \\ \vec{v} &= \dot{r}\vec{e}_r + r\dot{\theta}\vec{e}_\theta \\ \vec{a} &= (\ddot{r} - r\dot{\theta}^2)\vec{e}_r + (r\ddot{\theta} + 2\dot{r}\dot{\theta})\vec{e}_\theta \end{aligned} \tag{1}$$

Let's calculate these values at an arbitrary time, say $t = 0.8$ s. At that time [9, 10],

$$\begin{aligned} r &= 0.8 \text{ m} & \theta &= 0.8\pi \\ \dot{r} &= 1.0 \text{ m/s} & \dot{\theta} &= \pi \text{ rad/s} \\ \ddot{r} &= 0 \text{ m/s}^2 & \ddot{\theta} &= 0 \text{ rad/s}^2 \end{aligned}$$

Then, the position is

$$\begin{aligned} \vec{r} &= r\vec{e}_r \\ &= 0.8\vec{e}_r \\ &= 0.8(\cos 144^\circ)\vec{i} + 0.8(\sin 144^\circ)\vec{j} \\ &= -0.647\vec{i} + 0.470\vec{j} \end{aligned} \tag{2}$$

where $\vec{i}$ is the unit vector in X-direction and $\vec{j}$ is the unit vector in Y-direction. The origin of the XY-coordinate system is the same as that of the polar coordinate system.

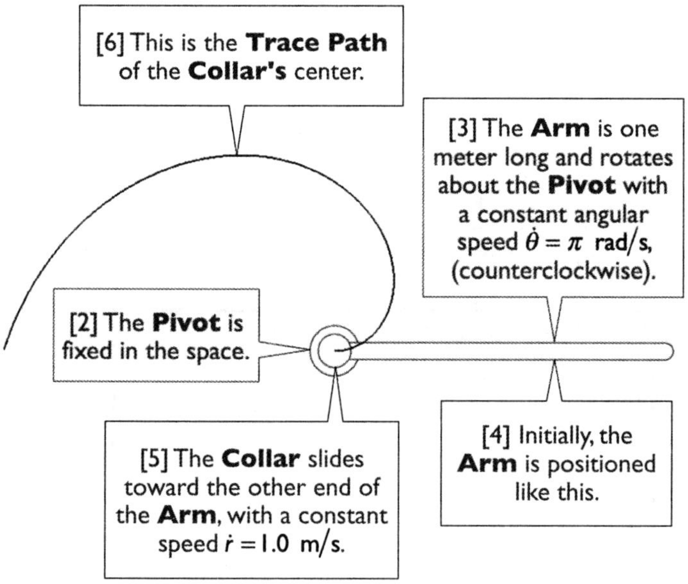

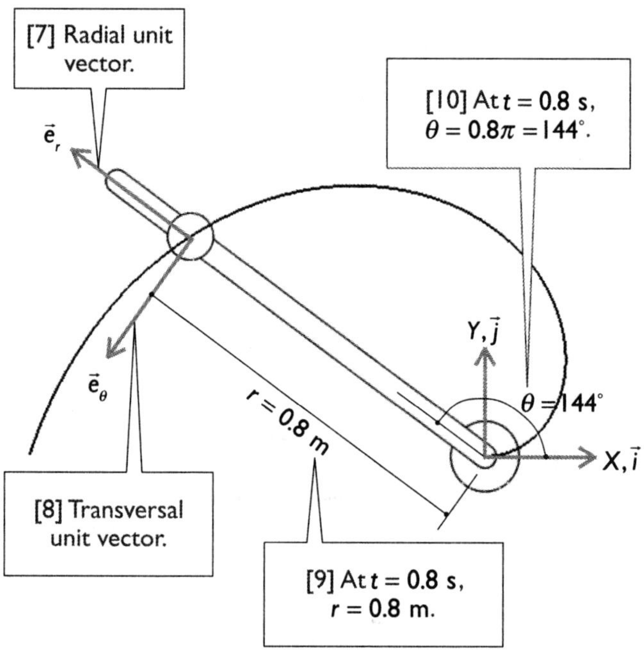

[11] The velocity is [12]

$$
\begin{aligned}
\vec{v} &= \dot{r}\vec{e}_r + r\dot{\theta}\vec{e}_\theta \\
&= 1.0\vec{e}_r + 0.8\pi\vec{e}_\theta \\
&= 1.0\vec{e}_r + 2.513\vec{e}_\theta \\
&= (\cos 144^\circ \vec{i} + \sin 144^\circ \vec{j}) \\
&\quad + (-2.513\sin 144^\circ \vec{i} + 2.513\cos 144^\circ \vec{j}) \\
&= -2.286\vec{i} - 1.445\vec{j}
\end{aligned} \tag{3}
$$

The acceleration is [13]

$$
\begin{aligned}
\vec{a} &= (\ddot{r} - r\dot{\theta}^2)\vec{e}_r + (r\ddot{\theta} + 2\dot{r}\dot{\theta})\vec{e}_\theta \\
&= \left[0 - 0.8(\pi)^2\right]\vec{e}_r \\
&\quad + \left[0.8(0) + 2(1.0)(\pi)\right]\vec{e}_\theta \\
&= -7.896\vec{e}_r + 6.283\vec{e}_\theta \\
&= (-7.896\cos 144^\circ \vec{i} - 7.896\sin 144^\circ \vec{j}) \\
&\quad + (-6.283\sin 144^\circ \vec{i} + 6.283\cos 144^\circ \vec{j}) \\
&= 2.695\vec{i} - 9.724\vec{j}
\end{aligned} \tag{4}
$$

In this section, we'll perform a simulation for this system and validate the simulation results with the values in Eqs. (2-4).

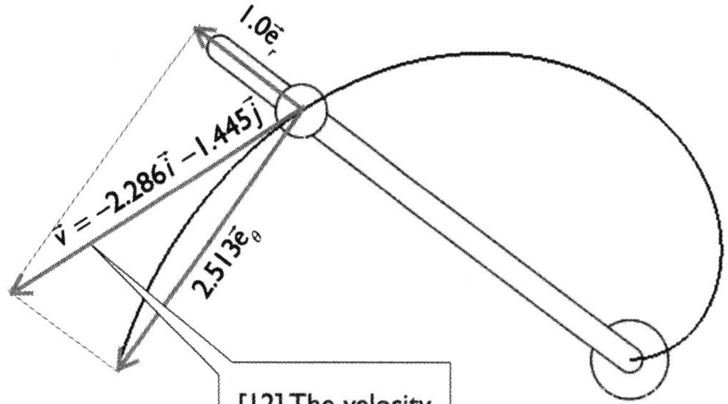

[12] The velocity at $t = 0.8$ s.

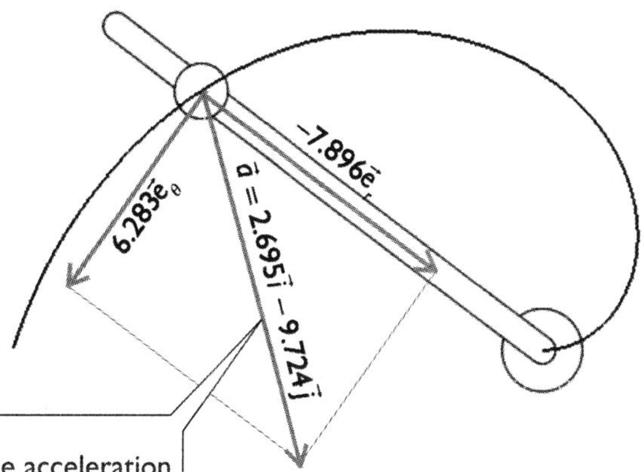

[13] The acceleration at $t = 0.8$ s. #

1.2-2 Start Up and Create a Part: **Pivot**

[1] Launch **SolidWorks** (1.1-2[1], page 6) and click **New** to create a new **Part**. Set up **MMGS** unit system with zero decimal places for the length unit (1.1-3, page 7).

[2] On the **Front** plane, draw a circle like this.

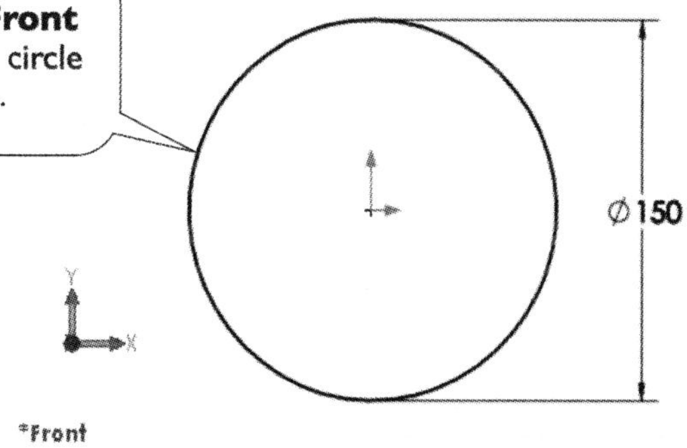

[3] In the **Features Toolbar**, click **Extruded Boss/Base**.

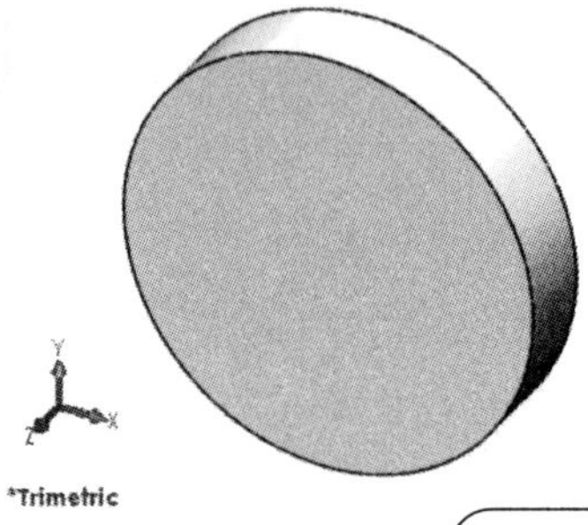

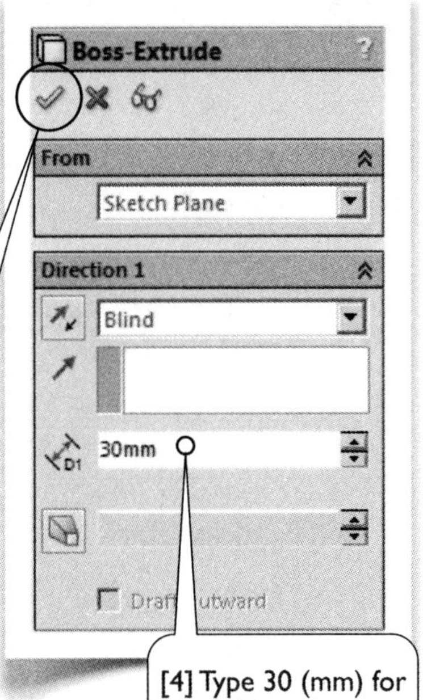

[4] Type 30 (mm) for **Depth**.

[5] Click **OK**.

[6] Save the **Part** with the name **Pivot**. #

1.2-3 Create a Part: **Arm**

[1] Click to create a new **Part**. Set up **MMGS** unit system with zero decimal places for the length unit.

[4] Save the **Part** with the name **Arm**. #

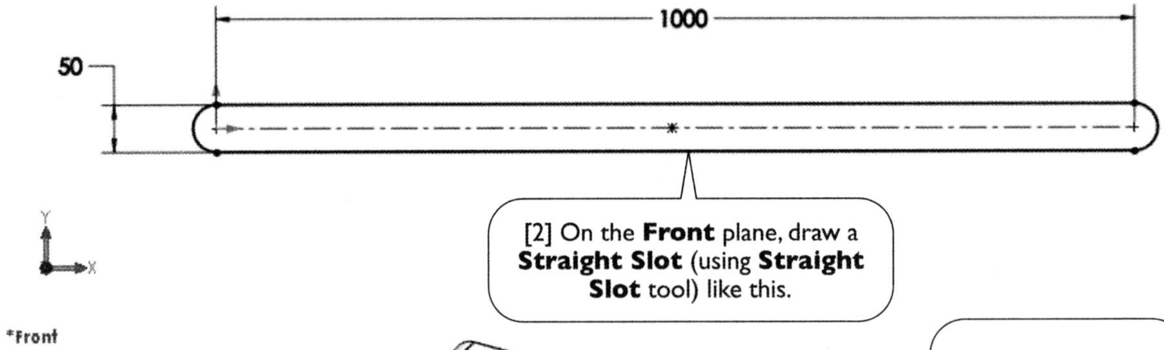

[2] On the **Front** plane, draw a **Straight Slot** (using **Straight Slot** tool) like this.

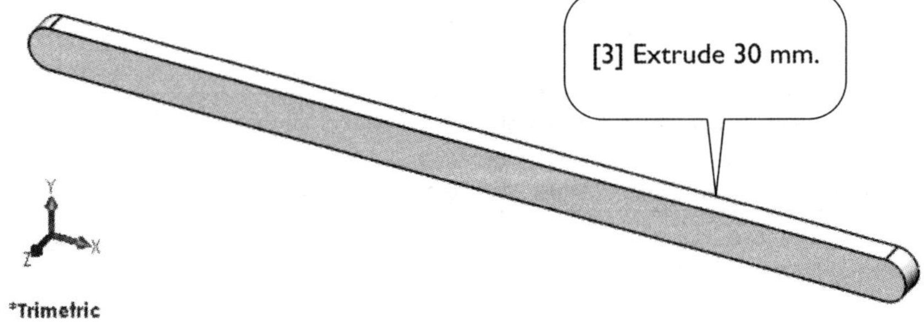

[3] Extrude 30 mm.

1.2-4 Create a Part: **Collar**

[1] Create a new **Part**. Set up **MMGS** unit system with zero decimal places for the length unit.

[2] On the **Front** plane, draw a circle like this.

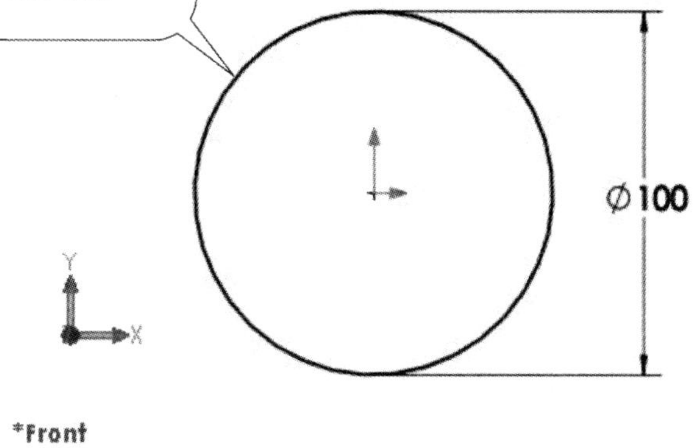

[3] Extrude 30 mm.

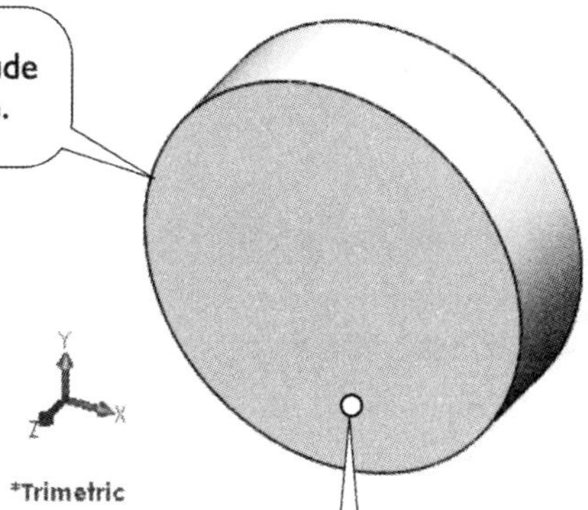

[4] Right-click this face and select **Sketch**.

[5] In the **Standard Views Toolbar**, click **Normal To** (1.1-6[2], page 10).

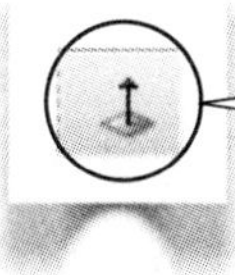

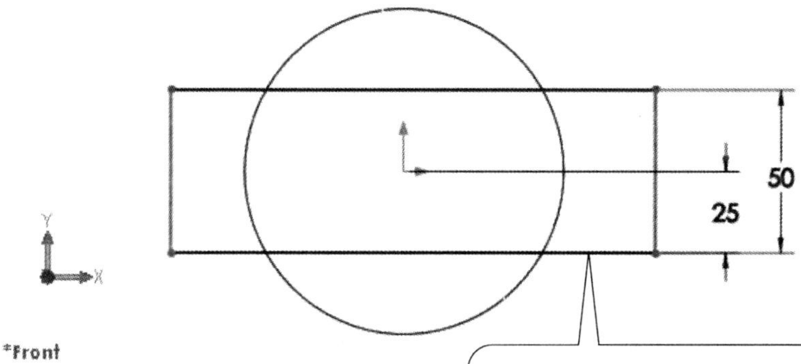

[6] Draw a rectangle like this. The width of the rectangle is not important.

[7] In **Features Toolbar**, click **Extruded Cut**.

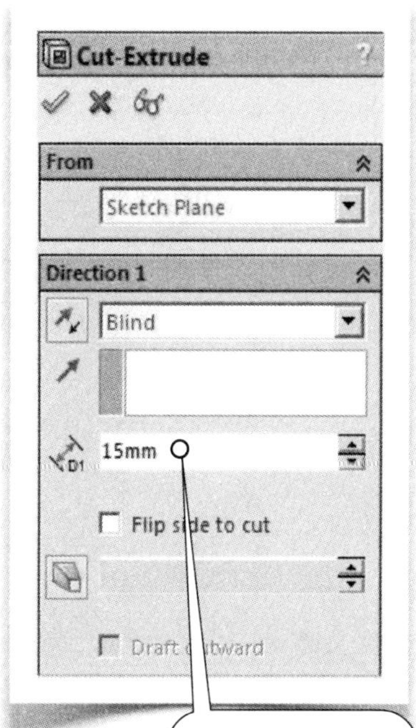

[8] Type 15 (mm). Click **OK**.

[9] Save the **Part** with the name **Collar**. #

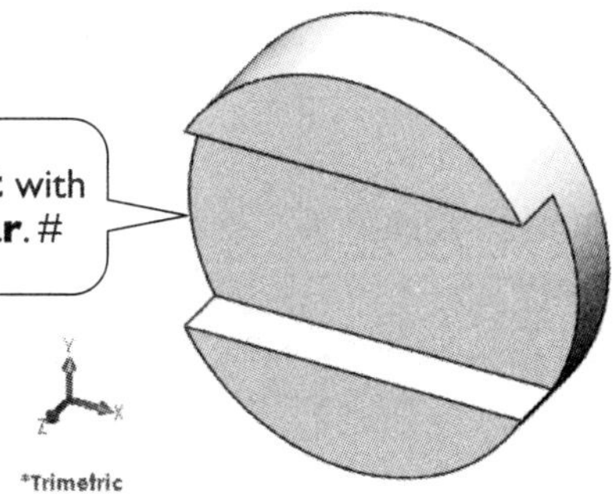

1.2-5 Create an Assembly: **Collar-On-Arm**

[1] Click **New** and create an **Assembly** (1.1-5[1-3], page 9).

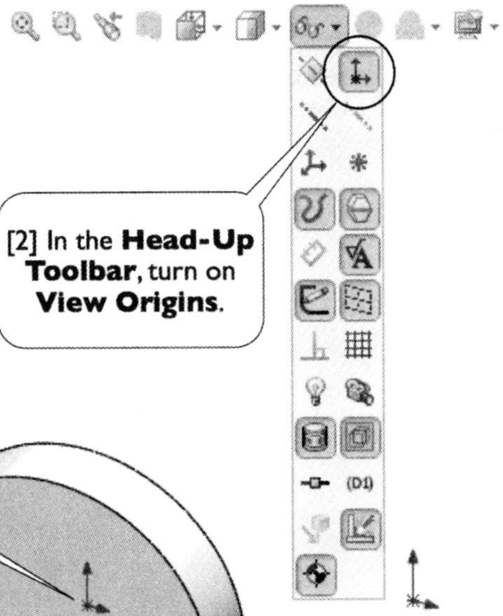

[2] In the **Head-Up Toolbar**, turn on **View Origins**.

[4] Click the **Origin**. Now the **Pivot** is fixed at the assembly's **Origin**.

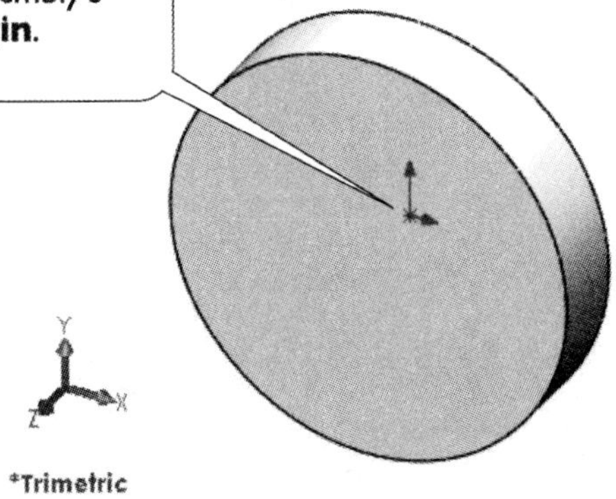

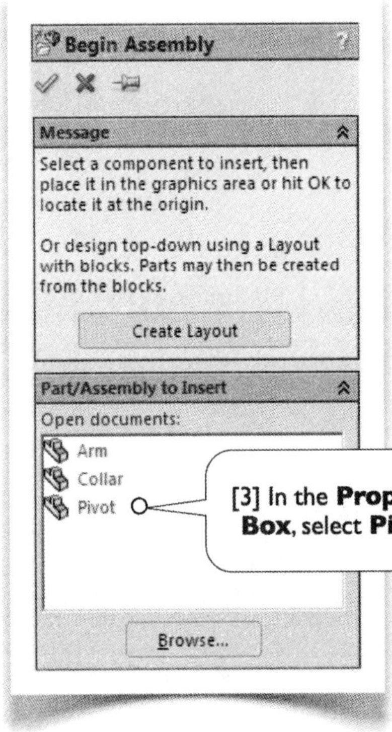

[3] In the **Property Box**, select **Pivot**.

[5] Select **MKS** for the unit system (see 1.1-3[1], page 7).

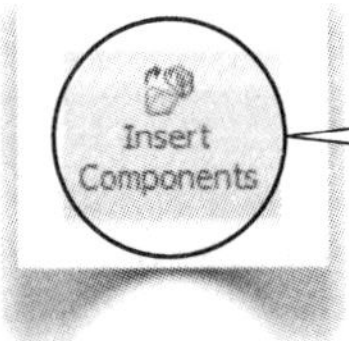

[6, 8] In the **Assembly Toolbar**, click **Insert Components**.

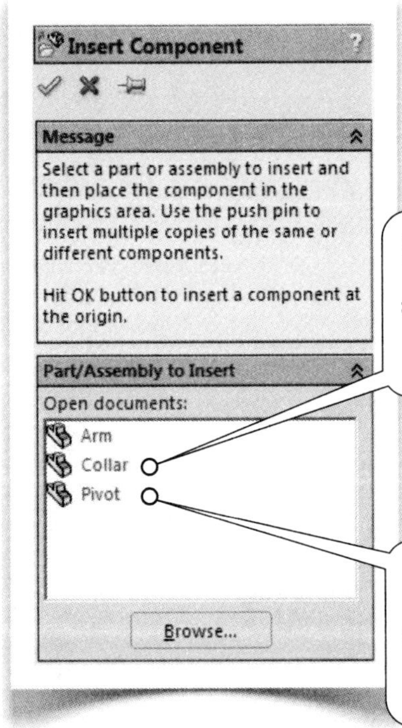

[7] In the **Property Box**, select **Arm** and click anywhere in the **Graphics Window** to temporarily park the part.

[9] In the **Property Box**, select **Collar** and click anywhere in the **Graphics Window** to temporarily park the part.

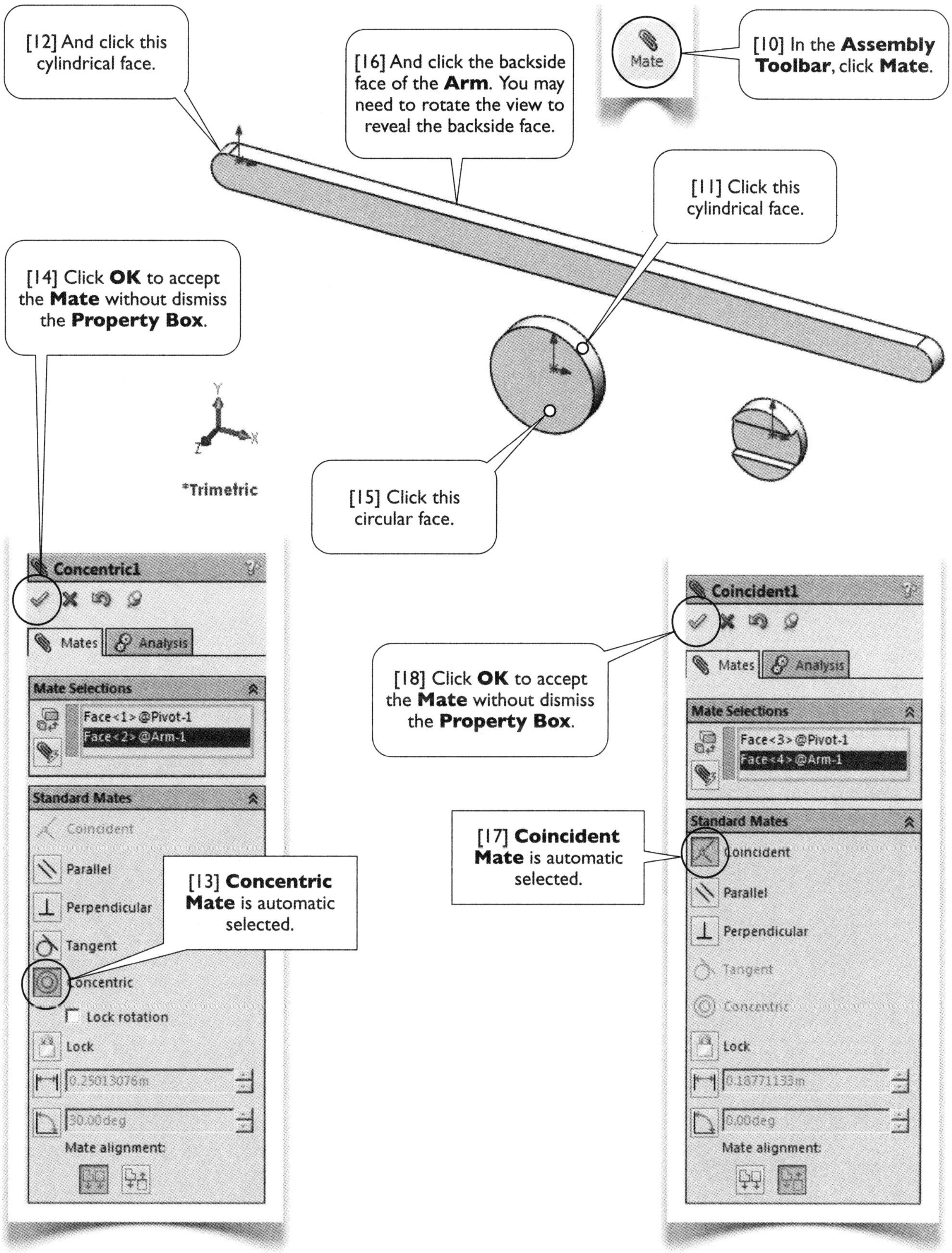
[10] In the **Assembly Toolbar**, click **Mate**.
Mate
[11] Click this cylindrical face.
[12] And click this cylindrical face.
[13] **Concentric Mate** is automatic selected.
[14] Click **OK** to accept the **Mate** without dismiss the **Property Box**.
[15] Click this circular face.
[16] And click the backside face of the **Arm**. You may need to rotate the view to reveal the backside face.
[17] **Coincident Mate** is automatic selected.
[18] Click **OK** to accept the **Mate** without dismiss the **Property Box**.
*Trimetric
Concentric1
Mates
Analysis
Mate Selections
Face<1>@Pivot-1
Face<2>@Arm-1
Standard Mates
Coincident
Parallel
Perpendicular
Tangent
Concentric
Lock rotation
Lock
0.25013076m
30.00deg
Mate alignment:
Coincident1
Mates
Analysis
Mate Selections
Face<3>@Pivot-1
Face<4>@Arm-1
Standard Mates
Coincident
Parallel
Perpendicular
Tangent
Concentric
Lock
0.18771133m
0.00deg
Mate alignment:

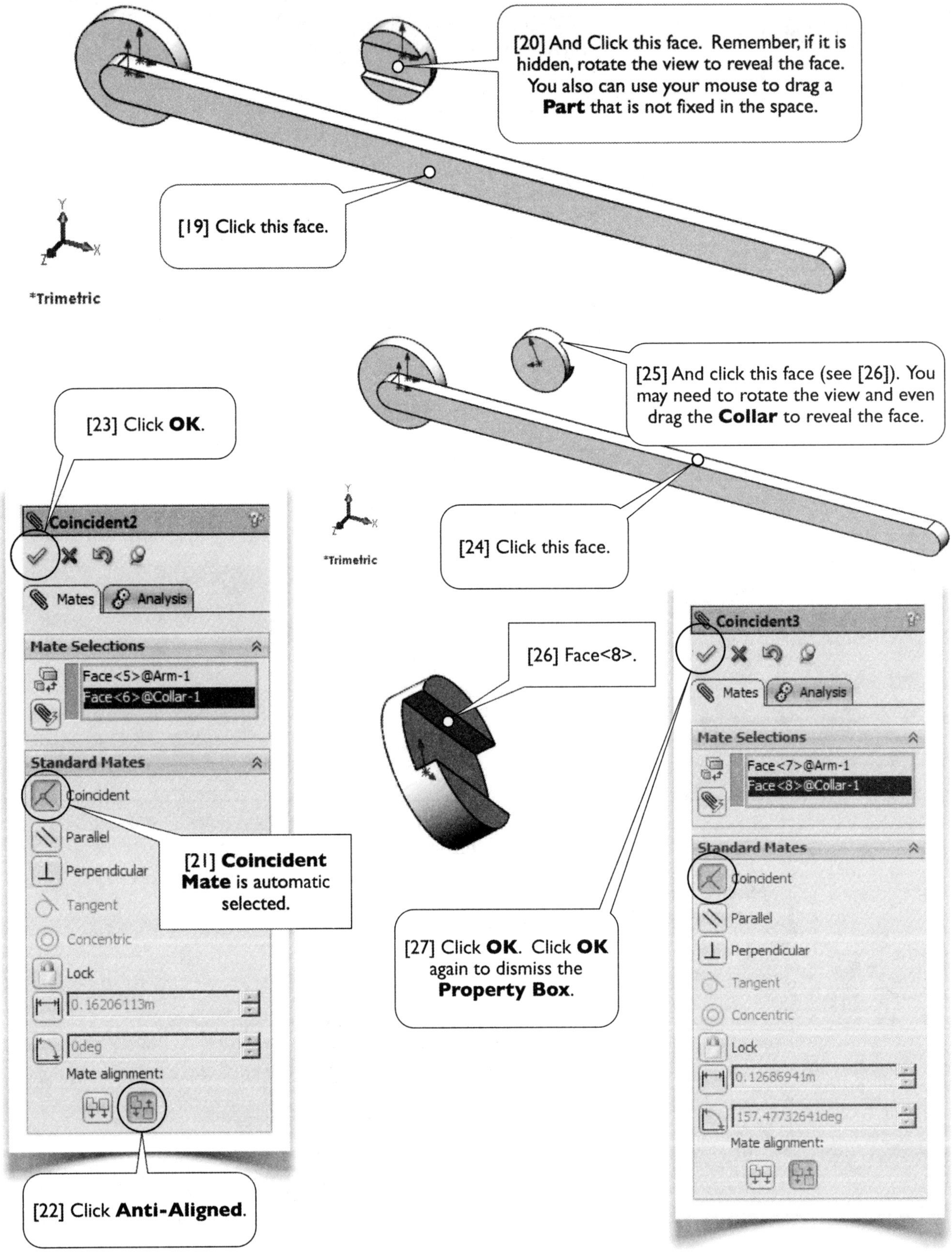
[20] And Click this face. Remember, if it is hidden, rotate the view to reveal the face. You also can use your mouse to drag a **Part** that is not fixed in the space.
[19] Click this face.
*Trimetric
[25] And click this face (see [26]). You may need to rotate the view and even drag the **Collar** to reveal the face.
[23] Click **OK**.
[24] Click this face.
*Trimetric
Coincident2
Mates
Analysis
Mate Selections
Face<5>@Arm-1
Face<6>@Collar-1
Standard Mates
Coincident
Parallel
Perpendicular
Tangent
Concentric
Lock
0.16206113m
0deg
Mate alignment:
[21] **Coincident Mate** is automatic selected.
[22] Click **Anti-Aligned**.
[26] Face<8>.
[27] Click **OK**. Click **OK** again to dismiss the **Property Box**.
Coincident3
Mates
Analysis
Mate Selections
Face<7>@Arm-1
Face<8>@Collar-1
Standard Mates
Coincident
Parallel
Perpendicular
Tangent
Concentric
Lock
0.12686941m
157.47732641deg
Mate alignment:

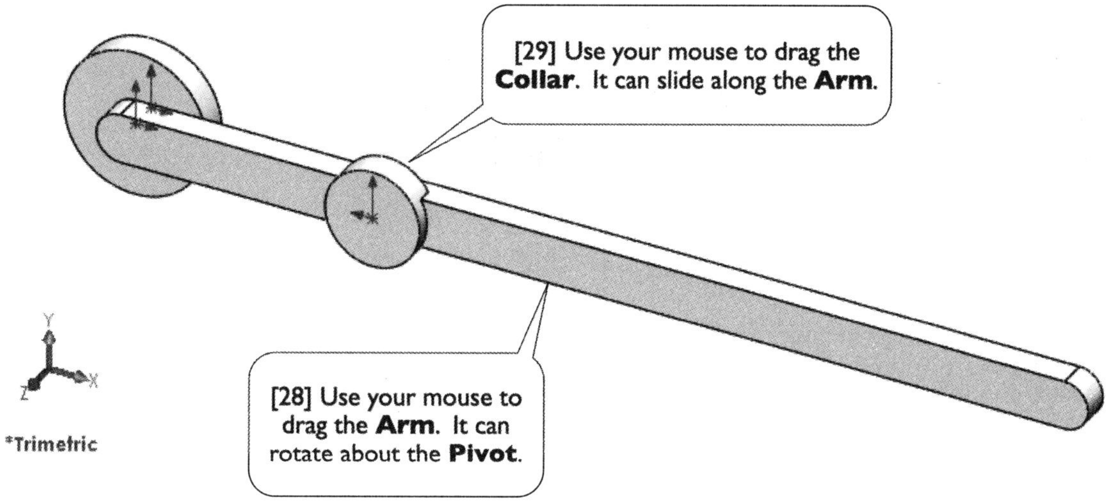
[29] Use your mouse to drag the **Collar**. It can slide along the **Arm**.
[28] Use your mouse to drag the **Arm**. It can rotate about the **Pivot**.
*Trimetric

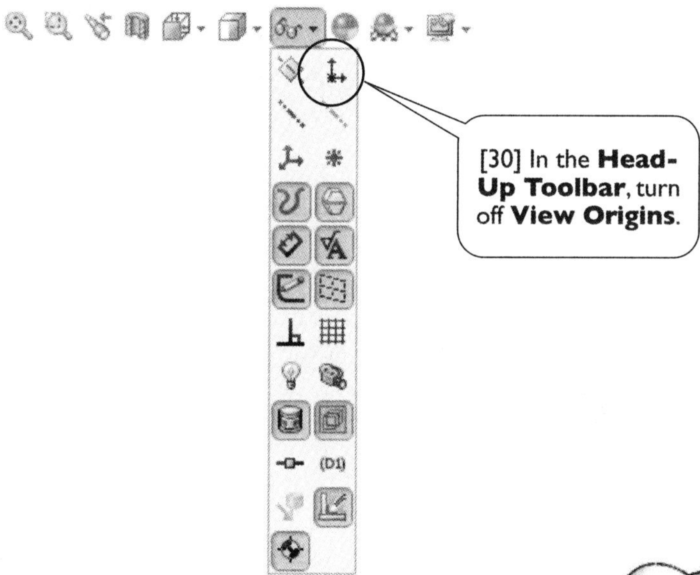
[30] In the **Head-Up Toolbar**, turn off **View Origins**.

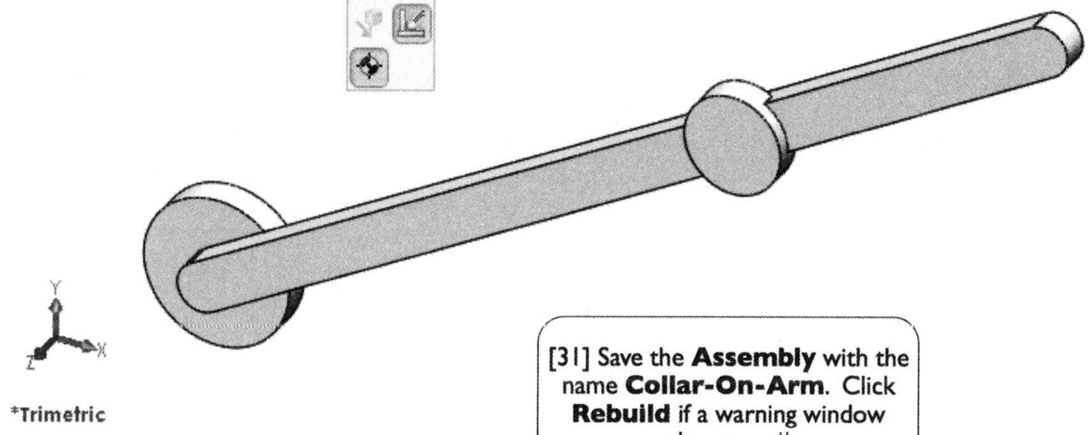
*Trimetric

[31] Save the **Assembly** with the name **Collar-On-Arm**. Click **Rebuild** if a warning window shows up. #

1.2-6 Set Up Initial Positions

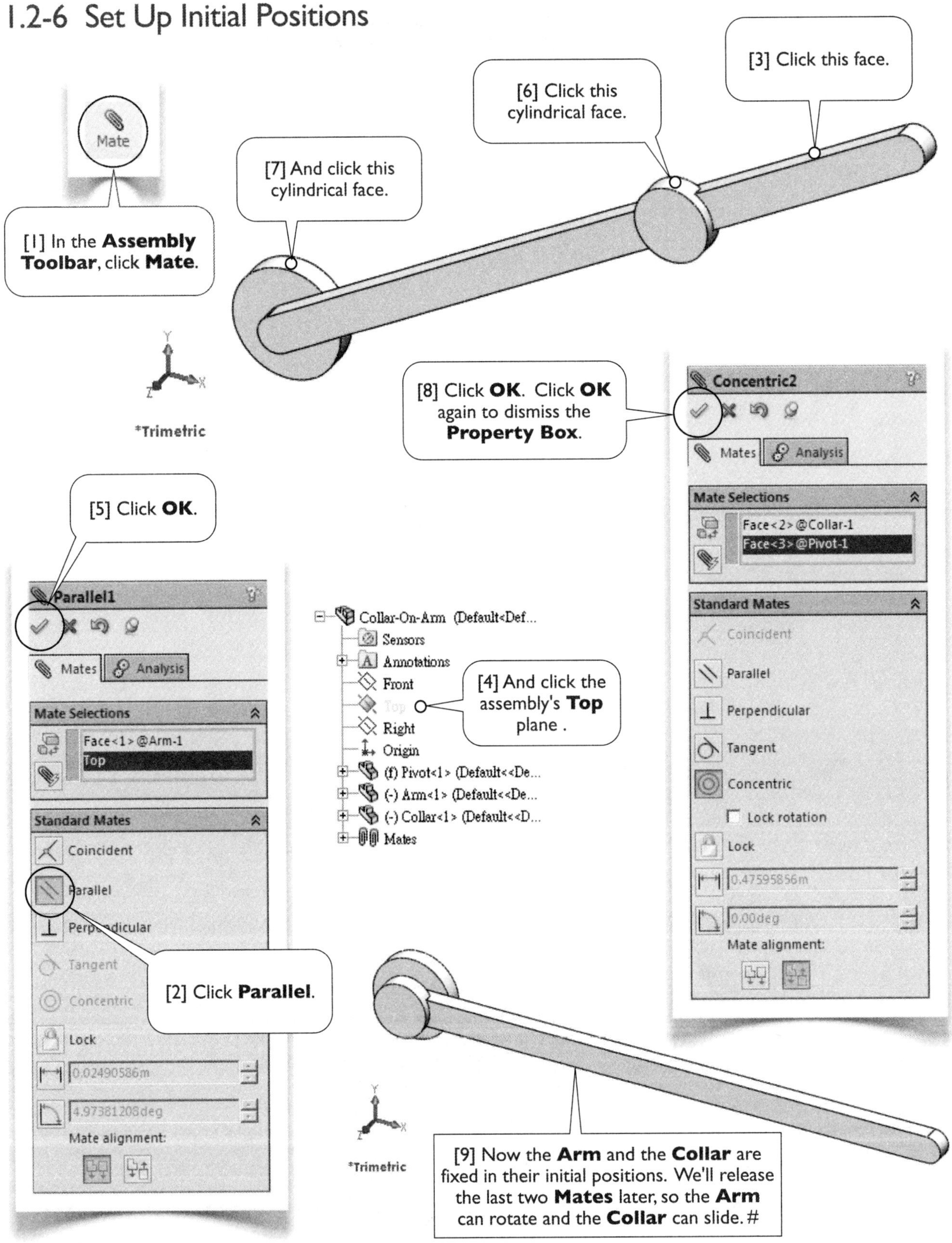

1.2-7 Create a **Motion Study**

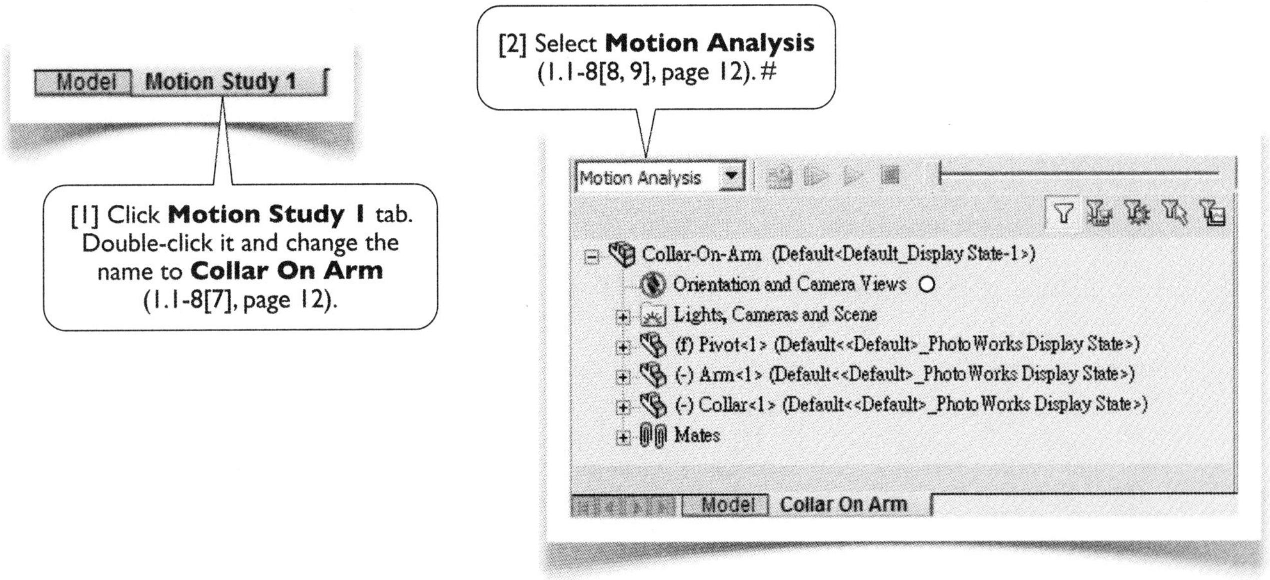

1.2-8 Set Up **Motor** at the **Arm**

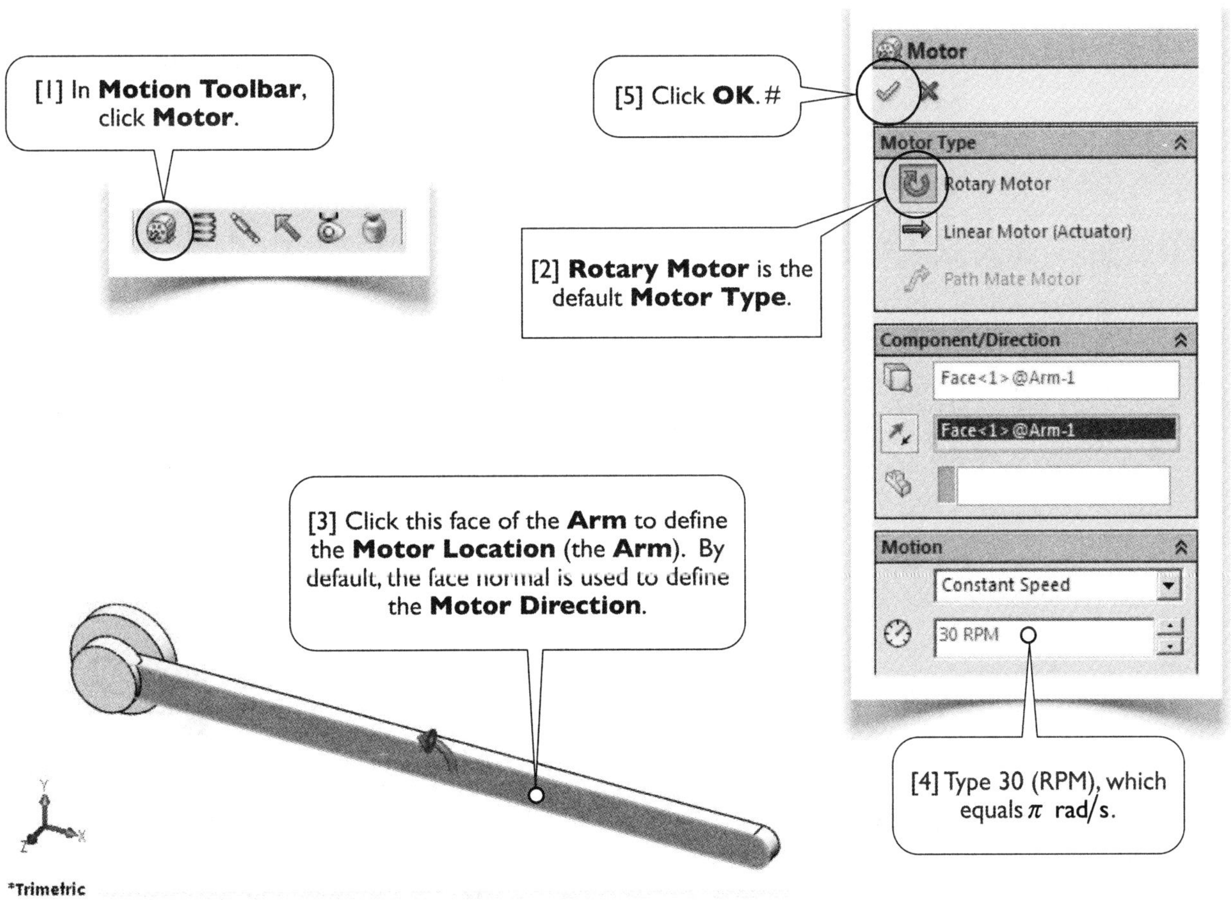

1.2-9 Set Up **Motor** at the **Collar**

[1] In **Motion Toolbar**, click **Motor**.

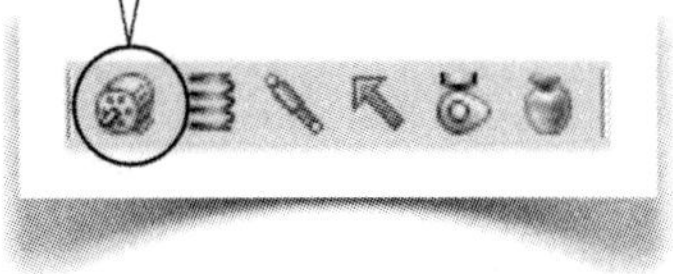

[2]Click **Linear Motor**.

[3] Click the **Collar** as **Motor Location**.

[4] Click this edge of the **Arm** as **Motor Direction**.

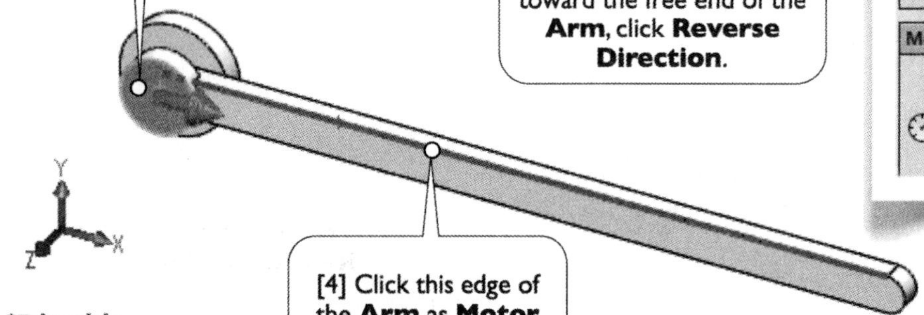

[5] If the direction is not toward the free end of the **Arm**, click **Reverse Direction**.

[6] Type 1 (m/s) for **Speed**.

[7] Click **OK**. #

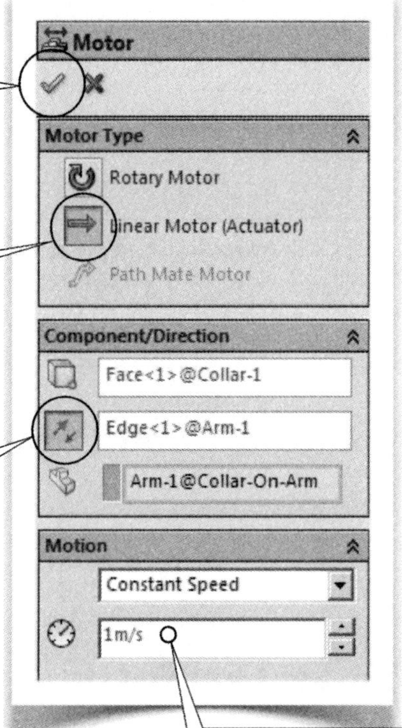

1.2-10 Calculate and Animate **Results**

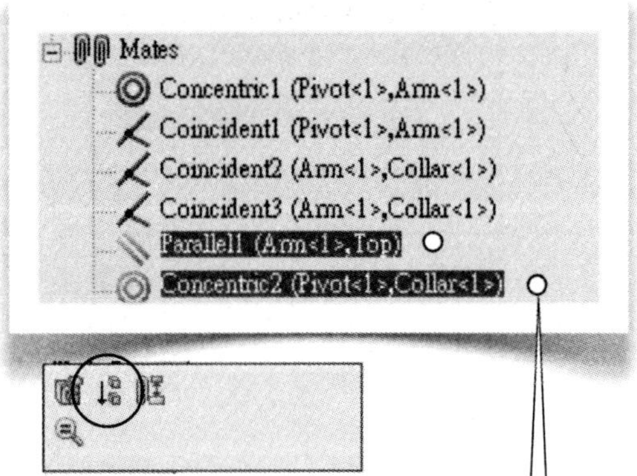

[1] In the **Assembly Tree**, under **Mates**, select the last two **Mates** (**Parallel1** and **Concentric2**) and right-click-select **Suppress**.

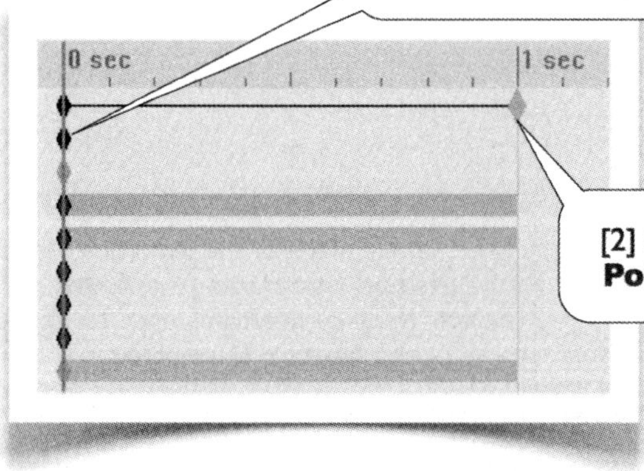

[2] Drag this **Key Point** to 1.0 sec.

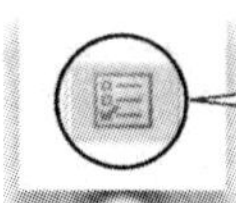

[3] In the **Motion Toolbar**, click **Motion Study Properties**, and type 300 for **Frames per second** (1.1-11[3, 4], page 14).

[4] Right-click this **Key Point** and select **View Orientation>Front**.

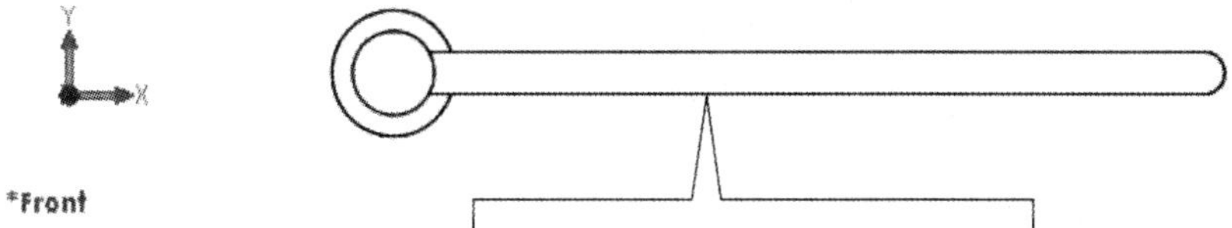

[5] For this case, a **Front** view has a better visual effect.

[6] In the **Motion Toolbar**, Click **Calculate**. If a **Motion Analysis Messages** window appears, close it (1.1-11[13, 14], page 15).

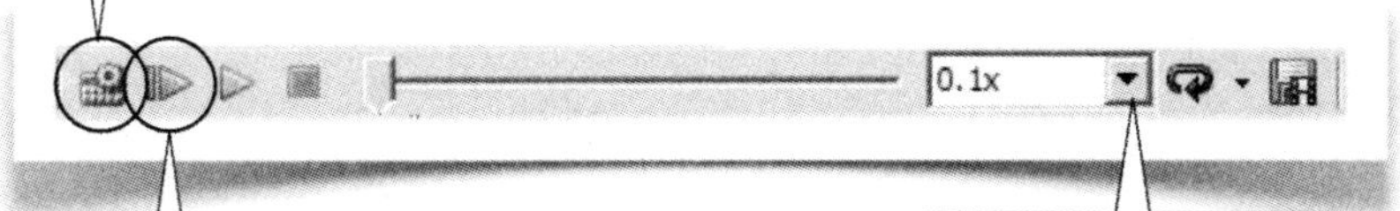

[7] Select **0.1x** for **Playback Speed**.

[8] Click **Play from Start**. #

1.2-11 Results: **Trace Path**

[1] In the **Timeline**, click at 0.8 sec.

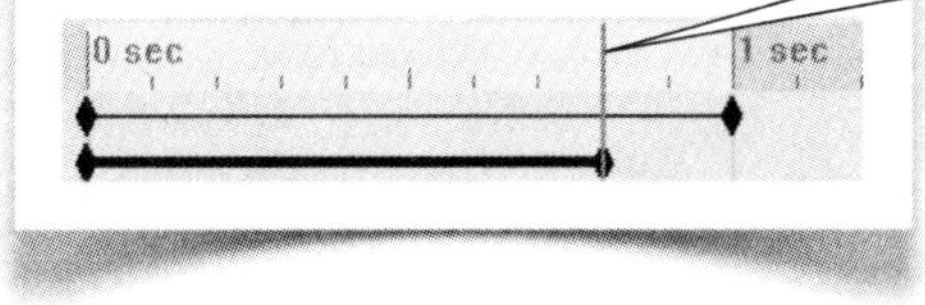

[2] In **Motion Toolbar**, click **Results and Plots**.

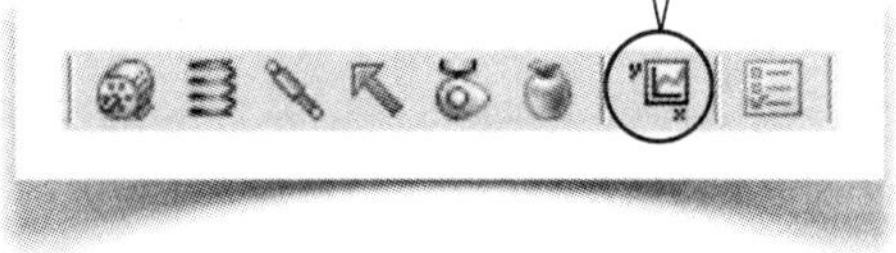

[3] Select **Trace Path**.

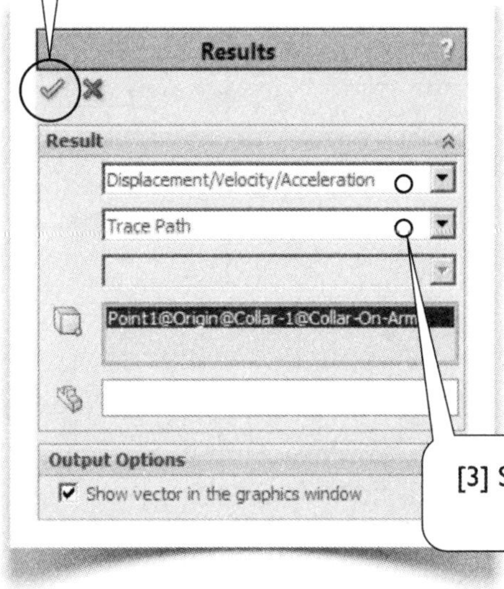

[4] From the **Assembly Tree** (in the **Graphics Window**), select the **Origin** of the **Collar<1>**.

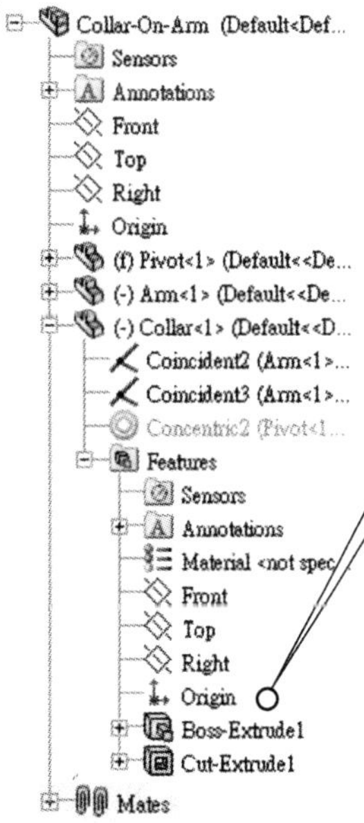

[5] Click **OK**.

[6] Click **Play from start** (1.2-10[8], this page) to view the animation again. #

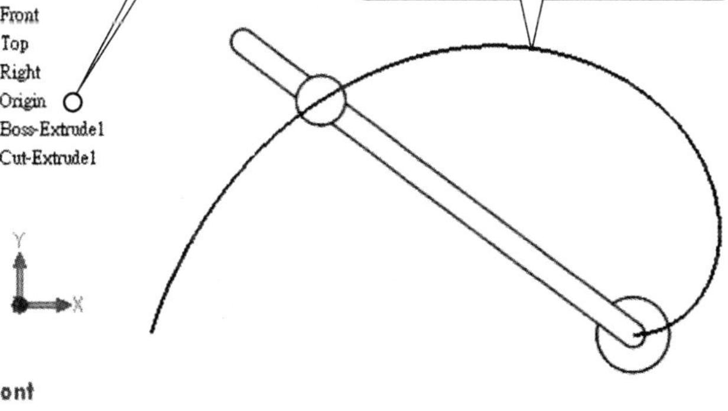

1.2-12 Results: **Acceleration**

[1] In **Motion Toolbar**, click **Results and Plots**.

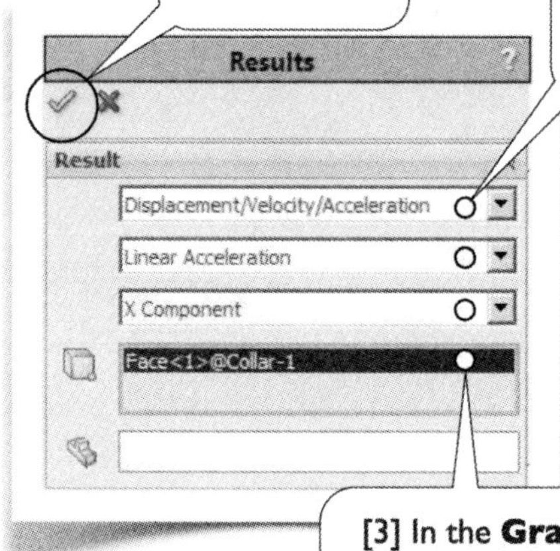

[2] Set up the **Results** like this.

[3] In the **Graphics Window**, click the **Collar**. The acceleration will be reported at the mass center of the **Collar**.

[4] Click **OK**.

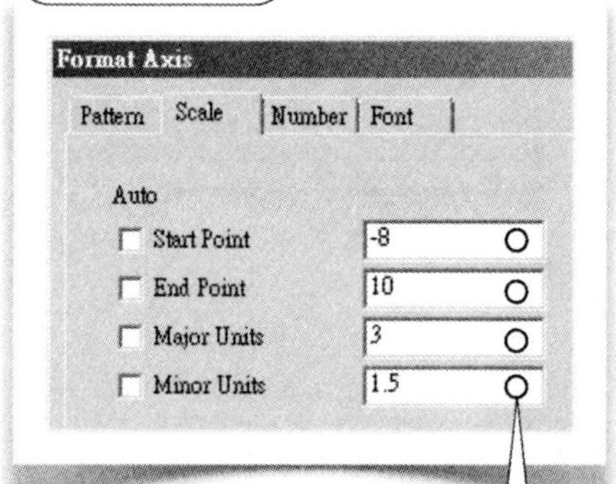

[5] Set the scale for the vertical axis like this.

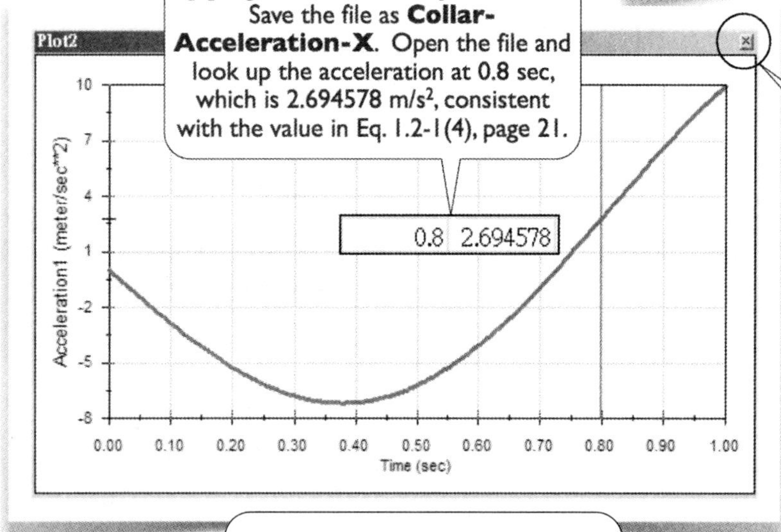

[6] Right-click-select **Export CSV**. Save the file as **Collar-Acceleration-X**. Open the file and look up the acceleration at 0.8 sec, which is 2.694578 m/s^2, consistent with the value in Eq. 1.2-1(4), page 21.

[7] Close the window.

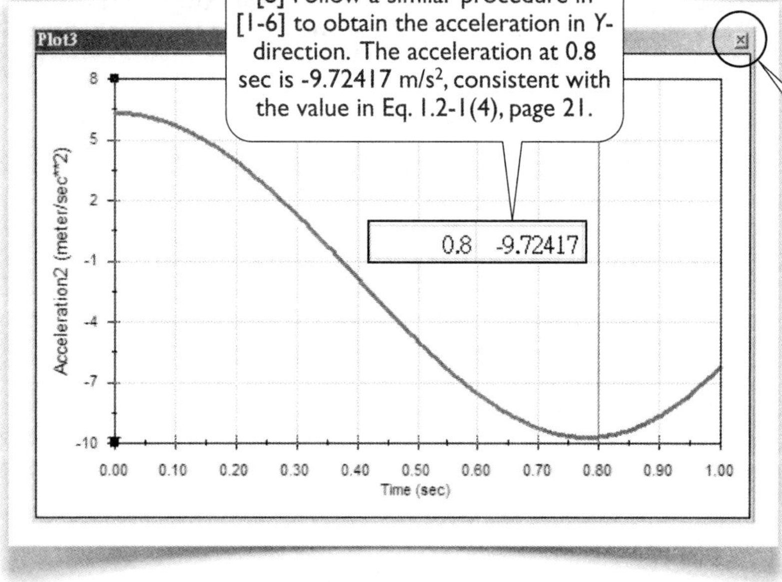

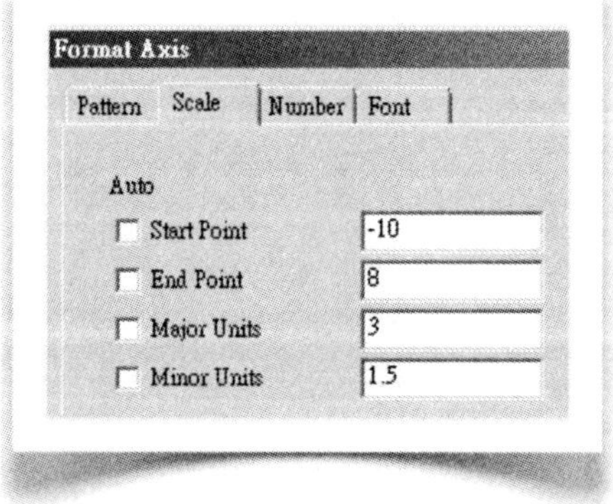

[8] Follow a similar procedure in [1-6] to obtain the acceleration in Y-direction. The acceleration at 0.8 sec is -9.72417 m/s^2, consistent with the value in Eq. 1.2-1(4), page 21.

[9] Close the window. #

1.2-13 Do It Yourself

[1] We leave you to obtain the velocities (Eq. 1.2-1(3), page 21) and the positions (Eq. 1.2-1(2), page 20). These plots are shown in [2-5].

[2] Velocity in *X*-direction.

[3] Velocity in *Y*-direction.

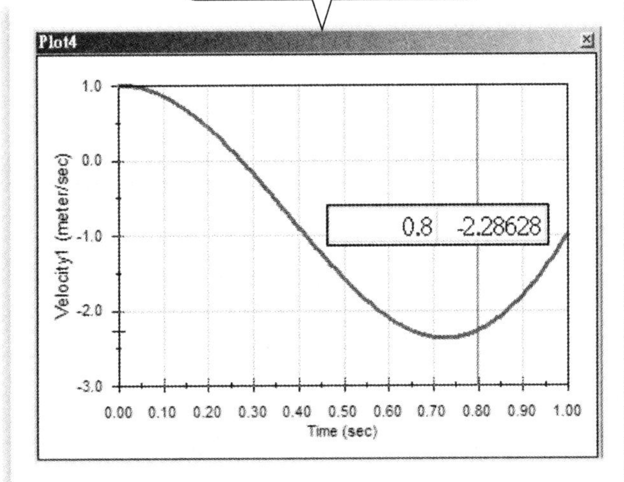

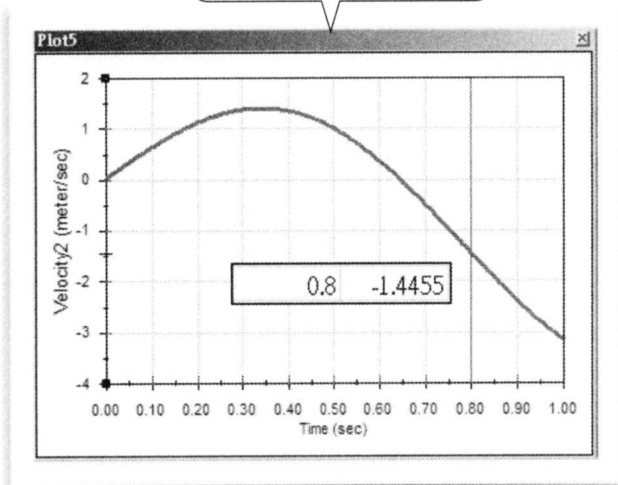

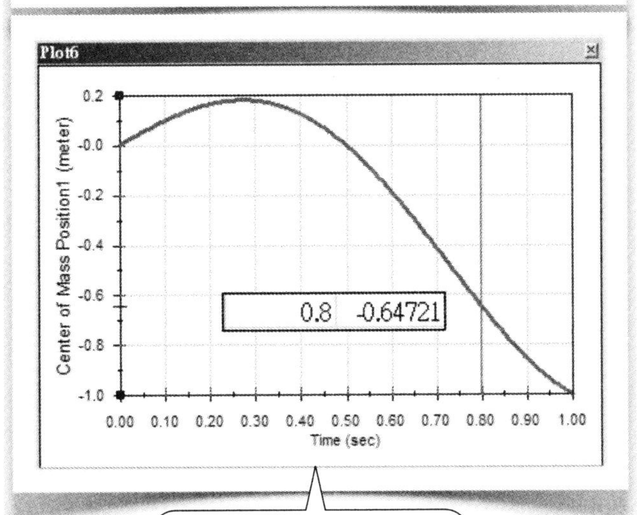

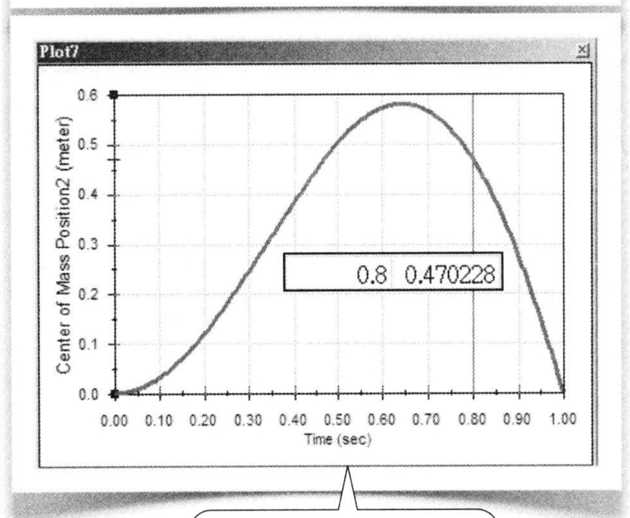

[4] Position in *X*-direction.

[5] Position in *Y*-direction.

[6] **Wrap Up**

Save all files and exit **SolidWorks** (1.1-18[1-3], page 19). #

Chapter 2

Particle Dynamics: Force and Acceleration

Newton's 2nd Law

Imagine a particle either remaining at rest or moving with constant speed in a straight line (i.e., constant velocity). If we apply a constant force $\vec{F}$ on the particle, it will gain a constant acceleration $\vec{a}$, which remains until the force is removed. Experiments show that the acceleration is proportional to the force,

$$\vec{F} \propto \vec{a} \tag{1}$$

For example, if the force is doubled, the acceleration is also doubled. Eq. (1) implies that there exists a proportional constant m, such that

$$\vec{F} = m\vec{a} \tag{2}$$

The proportional constant m is defined as the **mass** of the particle. In SI, the unit for the mass is kg, the unit for the acceleration is m/s^2, and the unit for the force is N (or, in terms of base units,kg-m/s^2).

Eq. (2) is called the *Newton's 2nd Law for a particle*. If more than one force act on the particle, the resultant force $\sum\vec{F}$ is used in place of the force $\vec{F}$. The *Newton's 2nd Law for a particle* is then stated as follows: The resultant force on a particle causes the particle to accelerate; the relation between the resultant force $\sum\vec{F}$, the acceleration $\vec{a}$, and the mass m of the particle is

$$\sum\vec{F} = m\vec{a} \tag{3}$$

In a mechanical system involving several particles, each particle must satisfy Eq. (3). This chapter will show how Eq. (3) is satisfied by each particle in motion.

Section 2.1

Newton's 2nd Law: Block and Wedge

2.1-1 Introduction

[1] Consider a 6-kg **Block** sliding down a 30° slope of a 15-kg **Wedge** due to the gravity [2-4]. Assume no friction between any two surfaces. This problem is adapted from Sample Problem 12.3, *Vector Mechanics for Engineers: Dynamics, 9th ed. in SI Units*, by F. P. Beer, E. R. Johnston, Jr., and P. J. Cornwell. The acceleration of the **Wedge** calculated by the textbook is

$$a_X^{Wedge} = 1.544 \text{ m/s}^2 \text{ (rightward)} \quad (1)$$

We'll perform a simulation for this system and validate the simulation results with the value in Eq. (1). Further, we'll show how Newton's 2nd Law is satisfied for the **Block** and the **Wedge**.

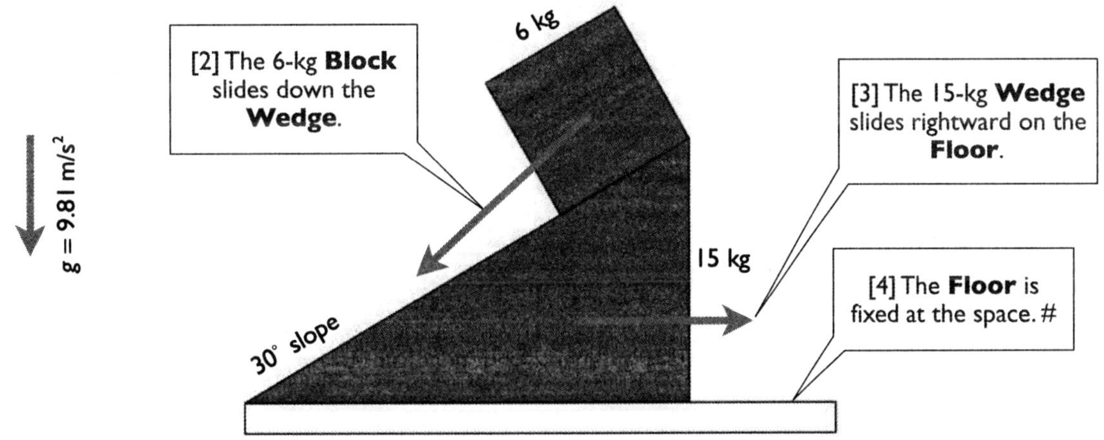

2.1-2 Start Up and Create a Part: **Block**

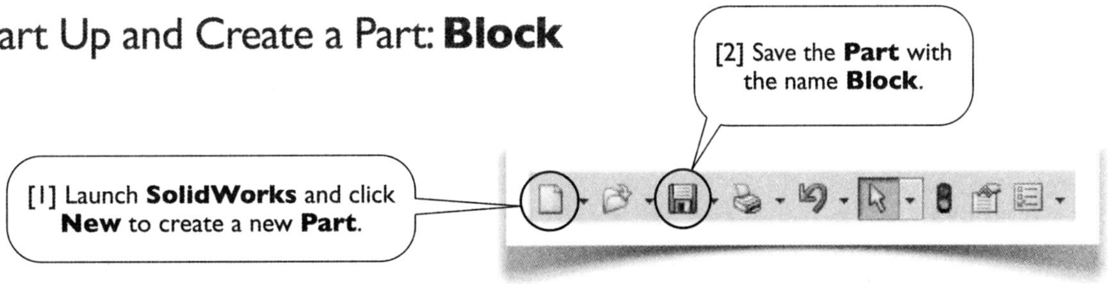

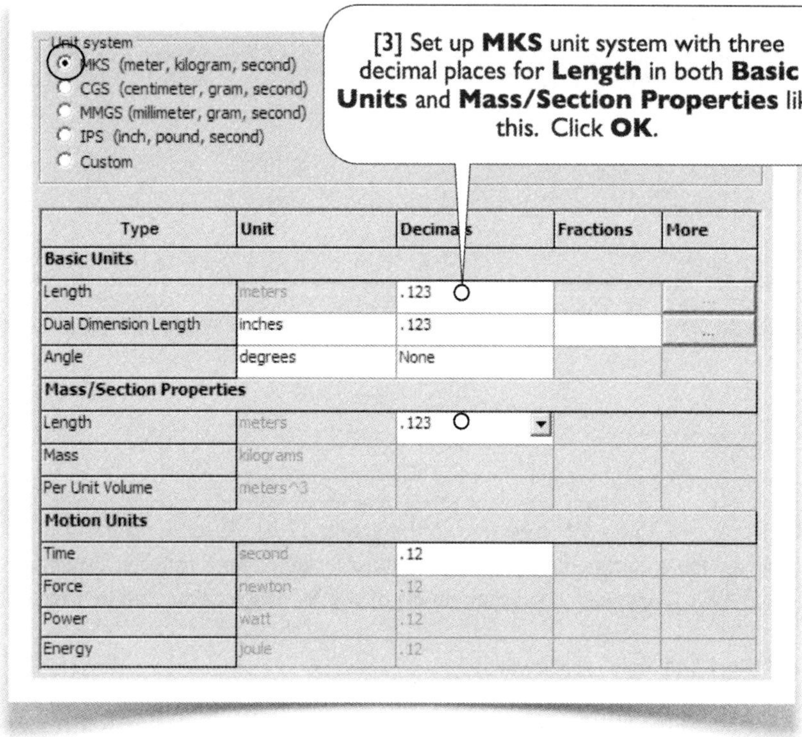

[3] Set up **MKS** unit system with three decimal places for **Length** in both **Basic Units** and **Mass/Section Properties** like this. Click **OK**.

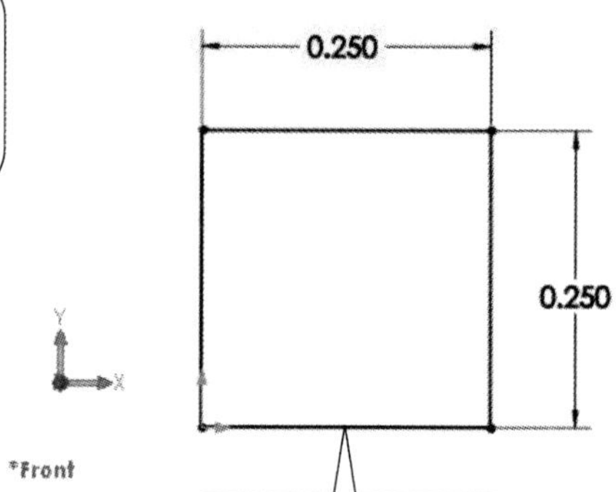

[4] On the **Front** plane, draw a rectangle like this.

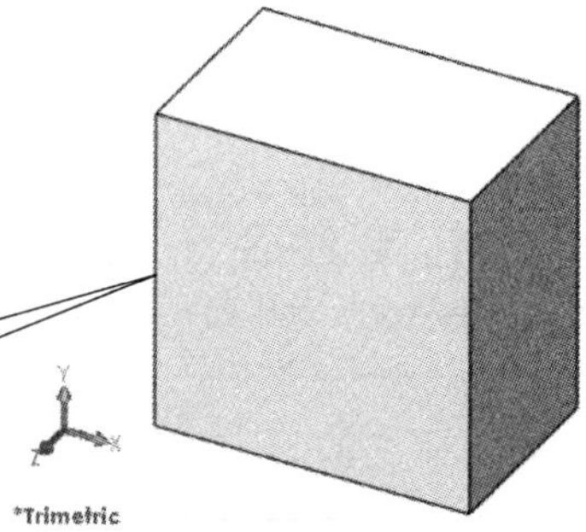

[5] Extrude 0.16 m.

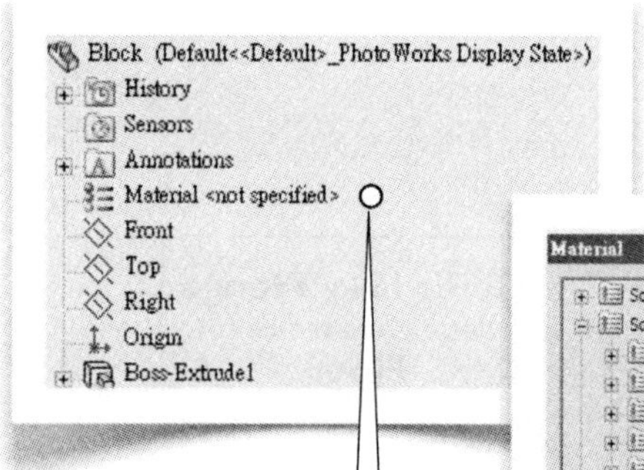

[6] In the **Part Tree**, right-click **Material** and select **Edit Material**.

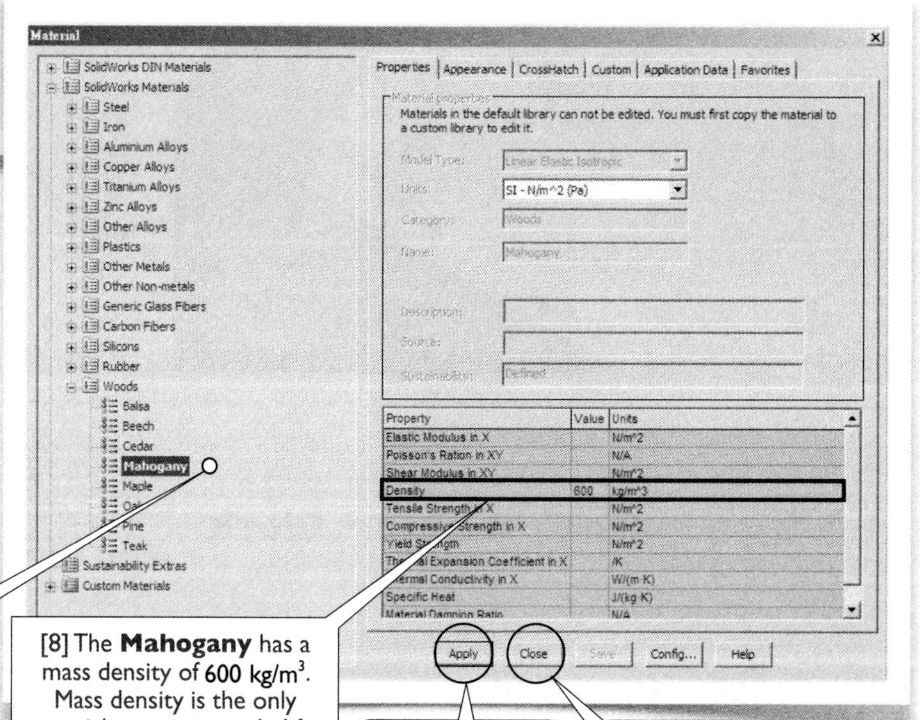

[7] Select **SolidWorks Materials>Woods>Mahogany**.

[8] The **Mahogany** has a mass density of 600 kg/m^3. Mass density is the only material property needed for a **Motion Study**.

[9] Click **Apply**.

[10] Click **Close**.

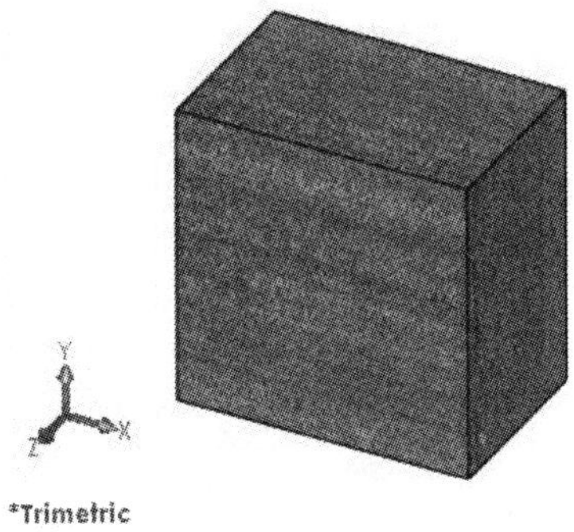

[11] From **Pull-Down Menus**, select **Tools>Mass Properties...** The **Mass Properties** command is also available in the **Evaluate Toolbar**.

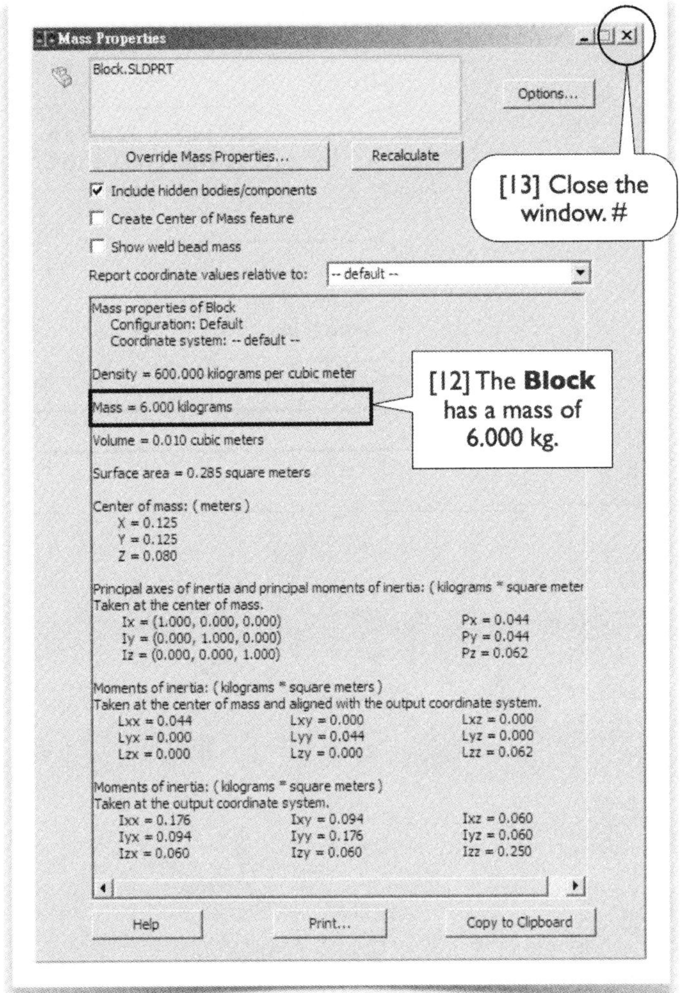

[12] The **Block** has a mass of 6.000 kg.

[13] Close the window. #

2.1-3 Create a Part: **Wedge**

[1] Click **New** to create a new **Part**.

[2] Save the **Part** with the name **Wedge**. Set up **MKS** unit system with three decimal places for **Length** in both **Basic Units** and **Mass/Section Properties** (2.1-2[3], last page).

[3] On the **Front** plane, draw a sketch like this.

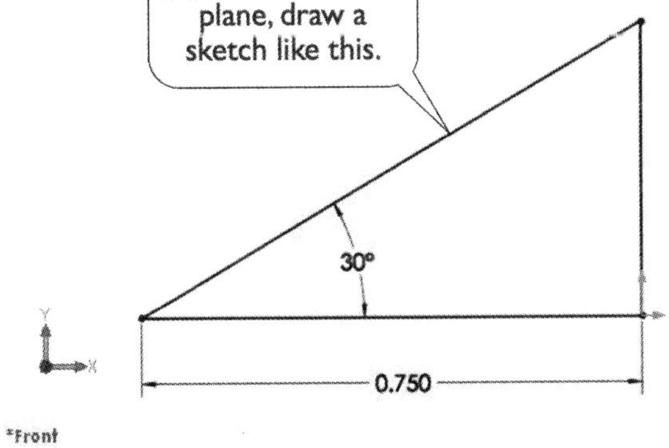

[4] Extrude 0.154 m. And apply **Mahogany** to the **Wedge** (2.1-2[6-10], last page).

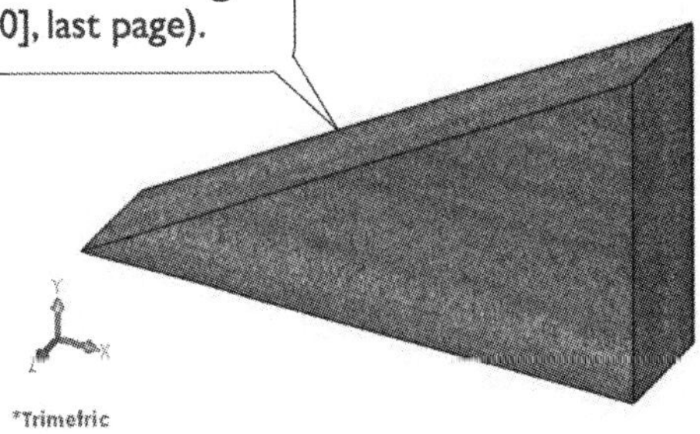

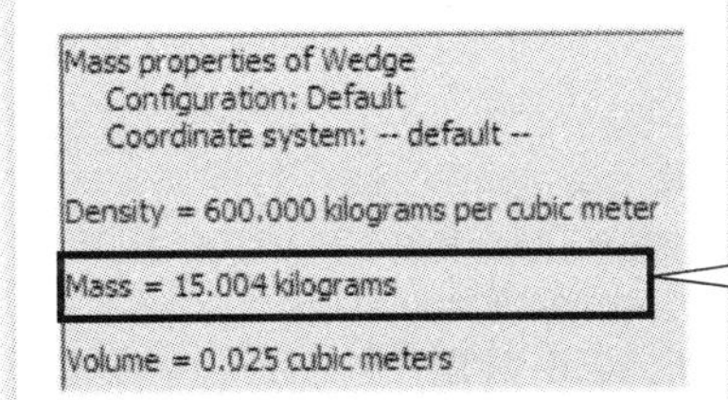

[5] Make sure the **Wedge** has a mass of 15.004 kg (2.1-2[11-13], this page). #

2.1-4 Create a Part: **Floor**

[1] Click **New** to create a new **Part**.

[2] Save the **Part** with the name **Floor**. Set up **MKS** unit system with three decimal places for **Length** in **Basic Units** (2.1-2[3], page 36).

[3] On the **Front** plane, draw a sketch like this.

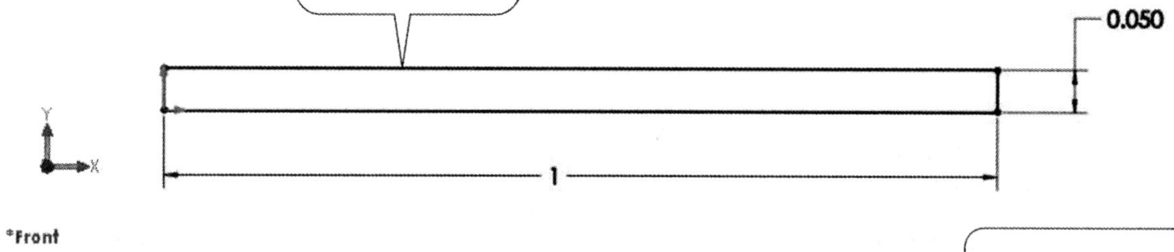

[4] Extrude 0.2 m. The mass of the floor is not relevant, since it is not a moving part. #

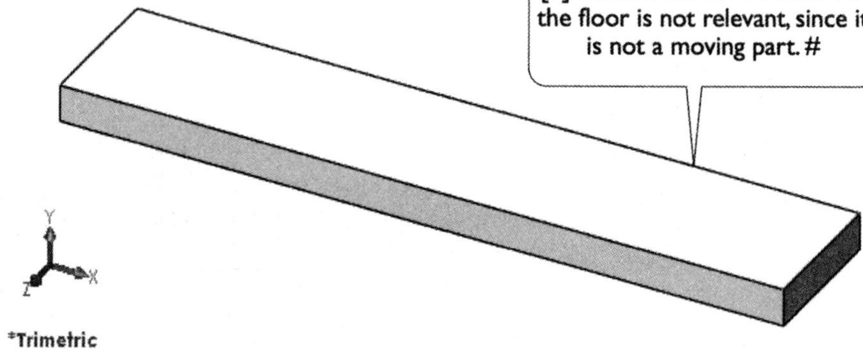

2.1-5 Create an Assembly: **Block-And-Wedge**

[1] Click **New** and create an **Assembly**.

[3] Save the **Assembly** with the name **Block-And-Wedge**. Click **Save All** if a warning window shows up. Set up **MKS** unit system with three decimal places for **Length** in **Basic Units**.

[2] Select **Floor** and click anywhere in the **Graphics Window**. The **Floor** is fixed in an arbitrary position.

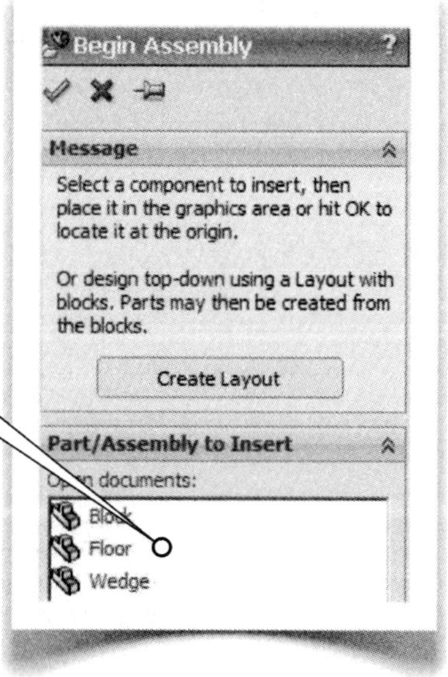

[4, 6] In the **Assembly Toolbar**, click **Insert Components**.

[8] In the **Assembly Toolbar**, click **Mate**.

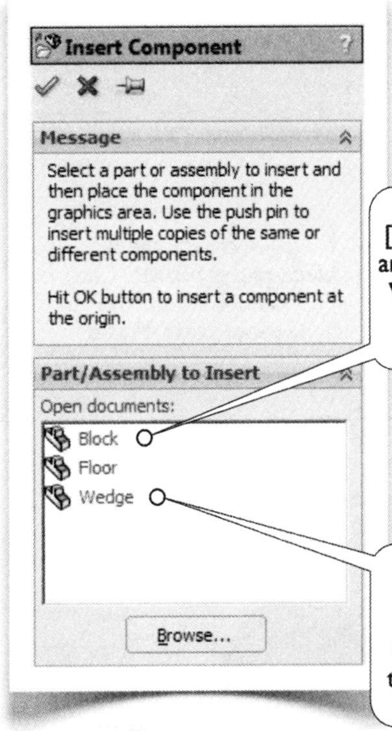

[5] Select **Block** and click anywhere in the **Graphics Window** to temporarily park the part.

[7] Select **Wedge** and click anywhere in the **Graphics Window** to temporarily park the part.

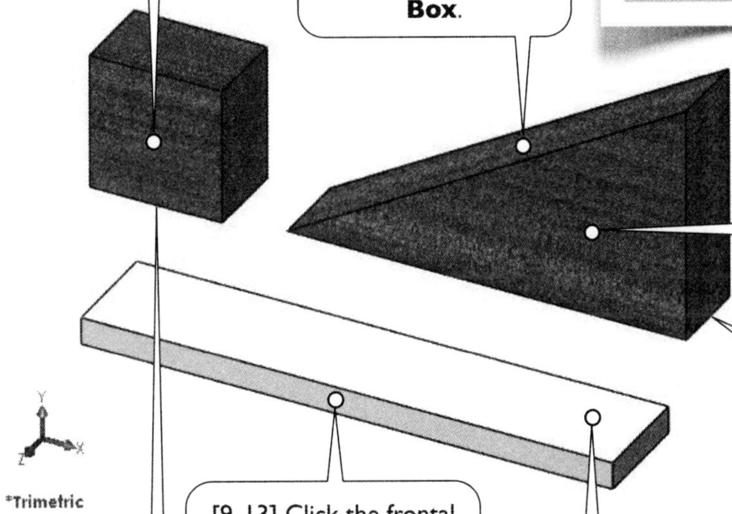

[9, 13] Click the frontal face of the **Floor**...

[10] And click the frontal face of the **Wedge**. Click **OK** to accept the **Coincident Mate**.

[11] Click the upper face of the **Floor**...

[12] And click the bottom face of the **Wedge**. Click **OK** to accept the **Coincident Mate**.

[14] And click the frontal face of the **Block**. Click **OK** to accept the **Coincident Mate**.

[15] Click the bottom face of the **Block**...

[16] And click the sloping face of the **Wedge**. Click **OK** to accept the **Coincident Mate**. Clock **OK** again to dismiss the **Property Box**.

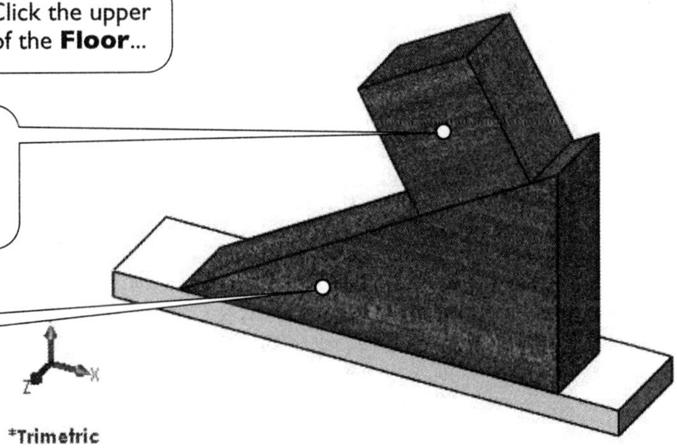

[17] Use your mouse to drag the **Wedge**. It can slide on the **Floor**.

[18] Use your mouse to drag the **Block**. It can slide on the slope of the **Wedge**. #

2.1-6 Set Up Initial Positions

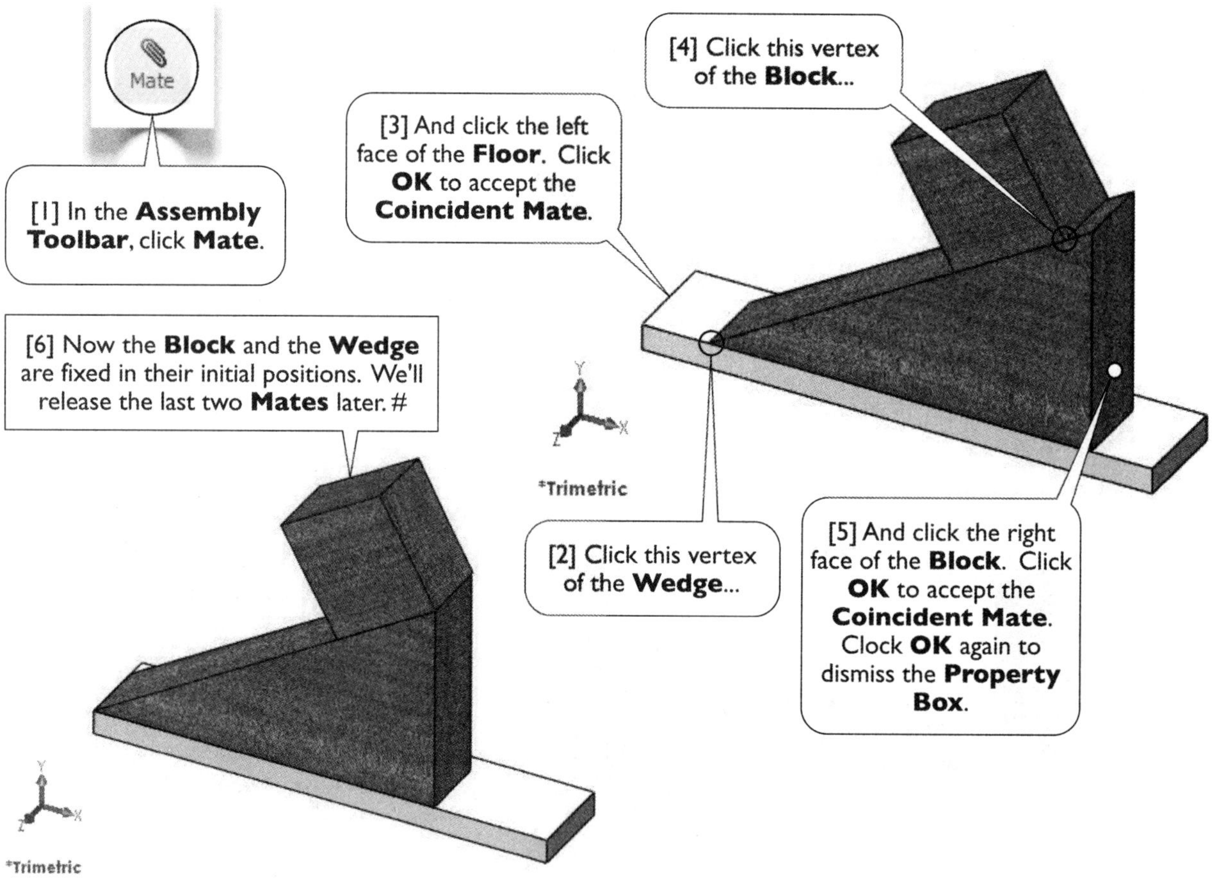

2.1-7 Create a **Motion Study**

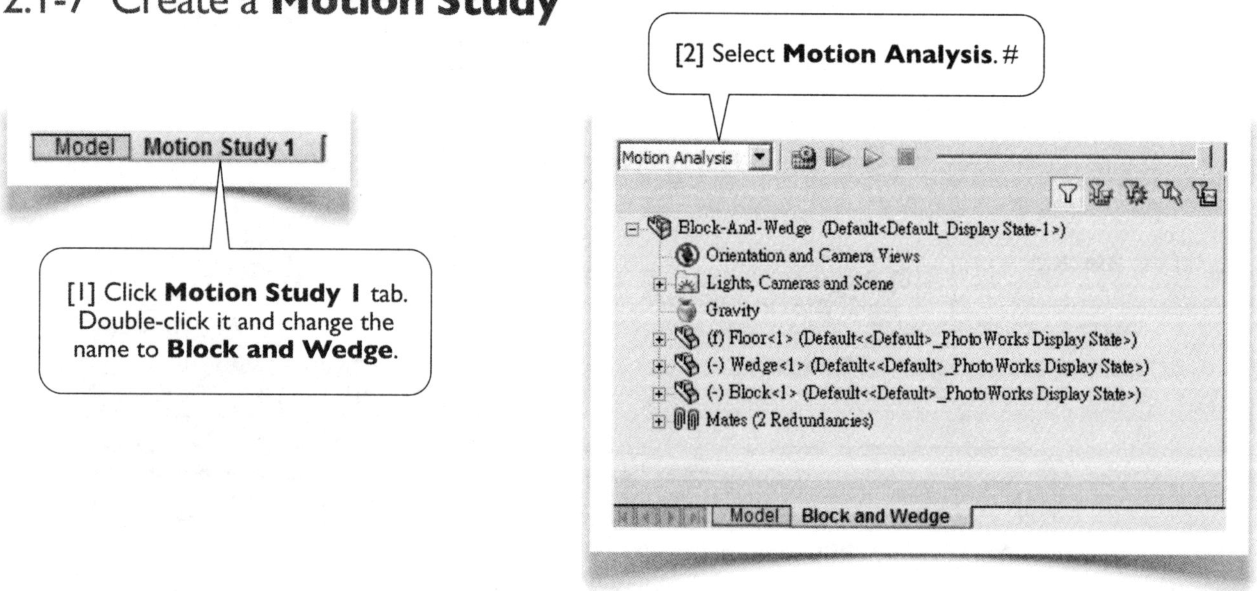

2.1-8 Set Up **Gravity**

[1] In **Motion Toolbar**, click **Gravity**.

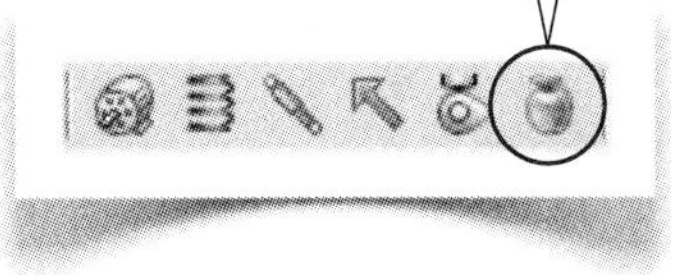

[2] The default **Gravity Value** is 9.807 m/s^2. The precise value is 9.80665 m/s^2.

[3] Click **Y**.

[4] The direction of the **Gravity**.

[5] Click **OK**. #

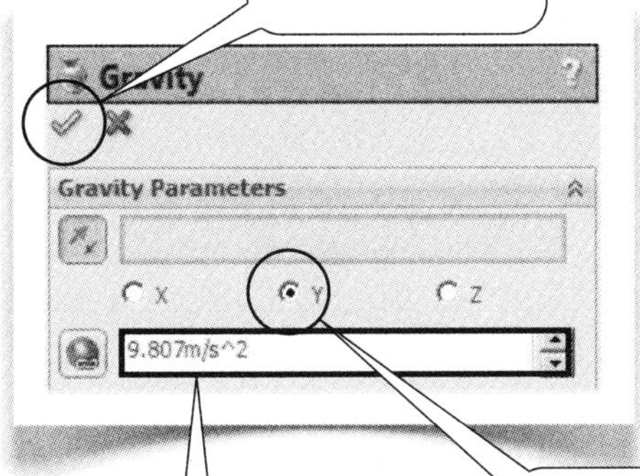

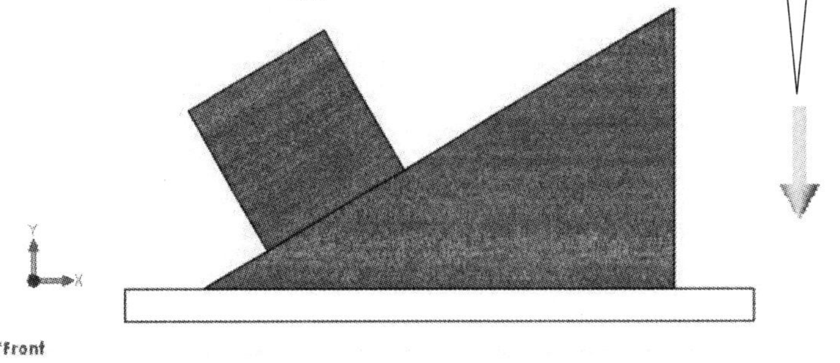

2.1-9 Calculate and Animate **Results**

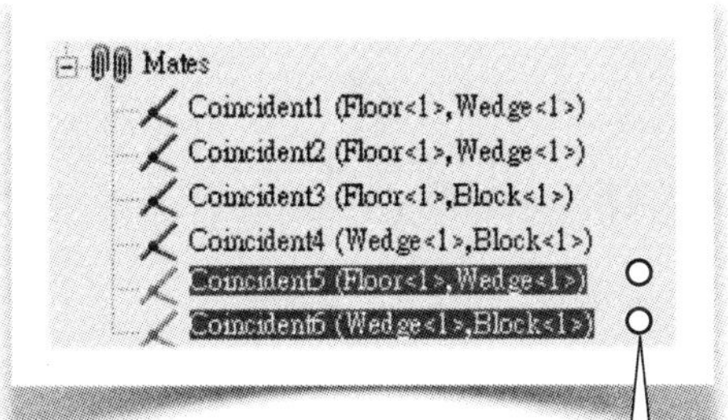

[1] In the **Assembly Tree**, under **Mates**, select the last two **Mates** (**Coincident5** and **Coincident6**) and right-click-select **Suppress**.

[2] In the **Motion Toolbar**, Click **Motion Study Properties**.

[3] Type 100 for **Frames per second**.

[4] Turn off **Show all Motion Analysis messages**. The **Motion Analysis Messages** (1.1-11[13], page 15) will not show up.

[5] Click **OK**.

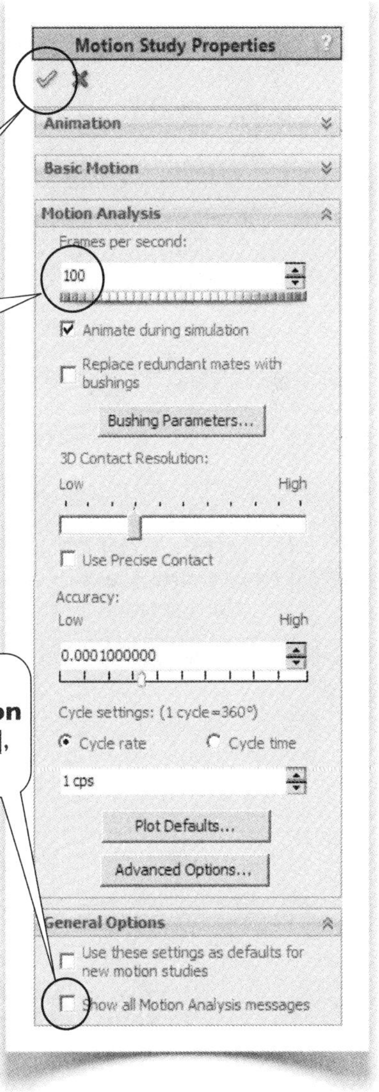

[6] Drag this **Key Point** to 0.4 seconds.

[7] Right-click this **Key Point** and select **View Orientation>Front**.

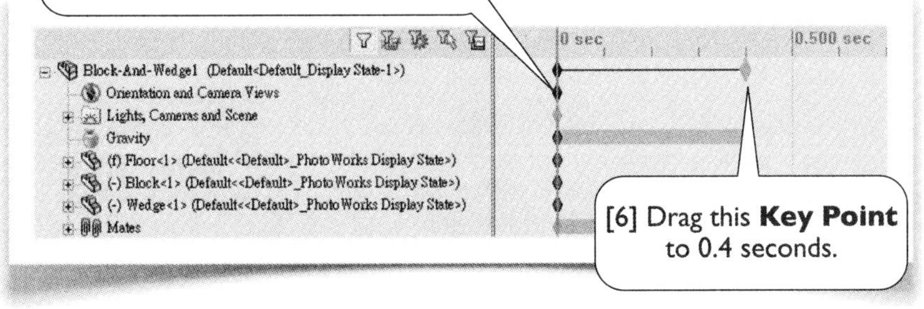

[8] In the **Motion Toolbar**, click **Calculate**. Click **No** in response to a warning message.

[9] Select **0.1x** for **Playback Speed**.

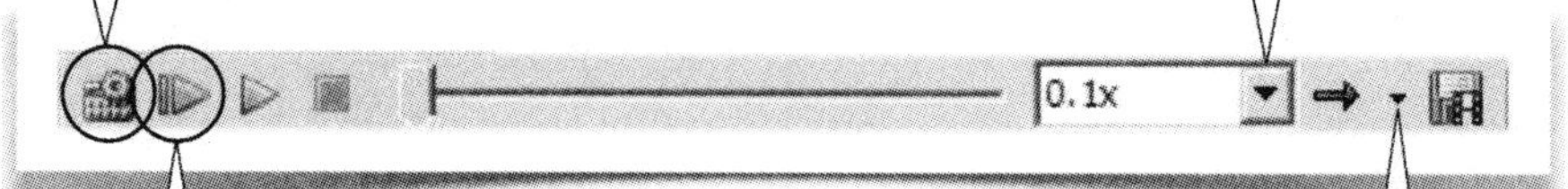

[11] Click **Play from Start**. #

[10] Select **Playback Mode: Normal**. The animation will not looped.

2.1-10 Results: **Trace Path**

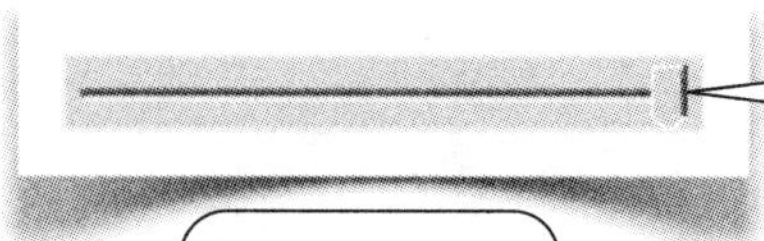

[1] Make sure the **Time Slider** is at the end.

[2, 7] In **Motion Toolbar**, click **Results and Plots**.

[6] Click **OK**.

[3] Select **Displacement/Velocity/Acceleration**. And select **Trace Path**.

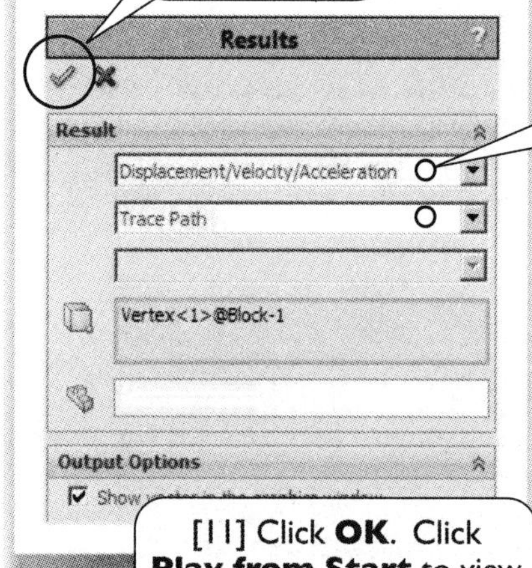

[11] Click **OK**. Click **Play from Start** to view the animation again.

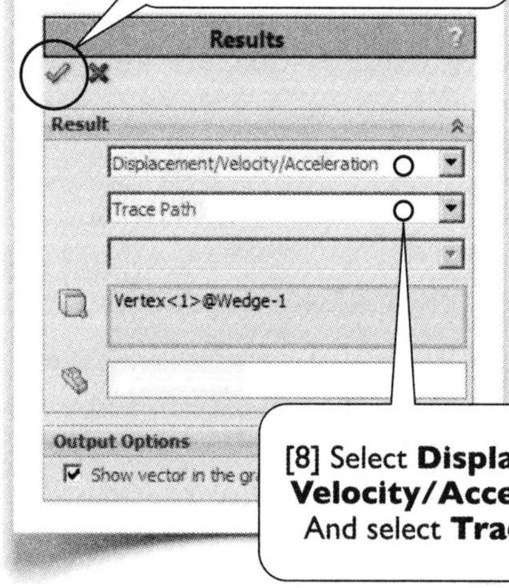

[8] Select **Displacement/Velocity/Acceleration**. And select **Trace Path**.

[5] The initial position of the vertex.

[10] The initial position of the vertex.

[4] Select this vertex of the **Block**.

[9] Select this vertex of the **Wedge**.

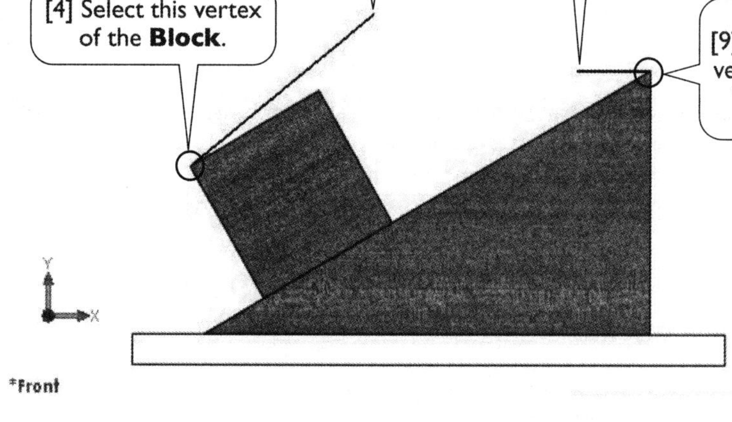

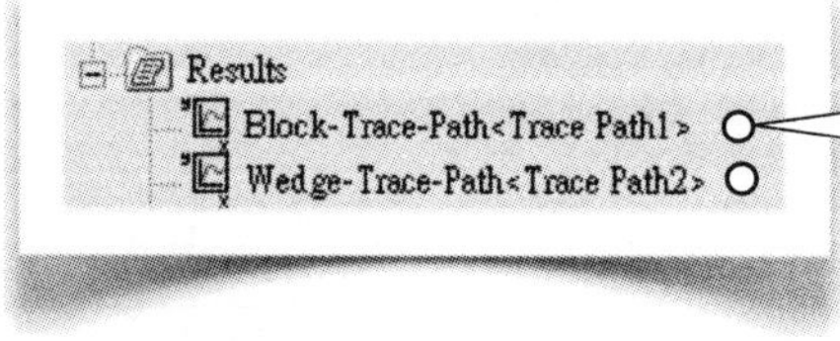

[12] In the **Motion Study Tree**, rename the **Plots** like this. #

2.1-11 Results: **Acceleration** of **Block**

[1] In **Motion Toolbar**, click **Results and Plots**.

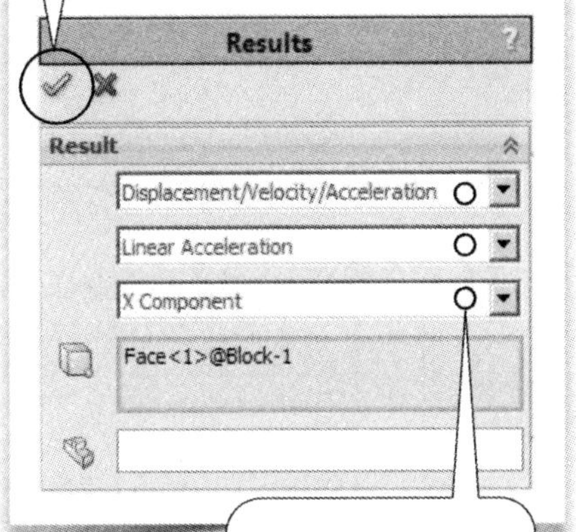

[2] Set up the **Results** like this.

[3] In the **Graphics Window**, click the **Block**. The acceleration will be reported at the mass center of the **Block**.

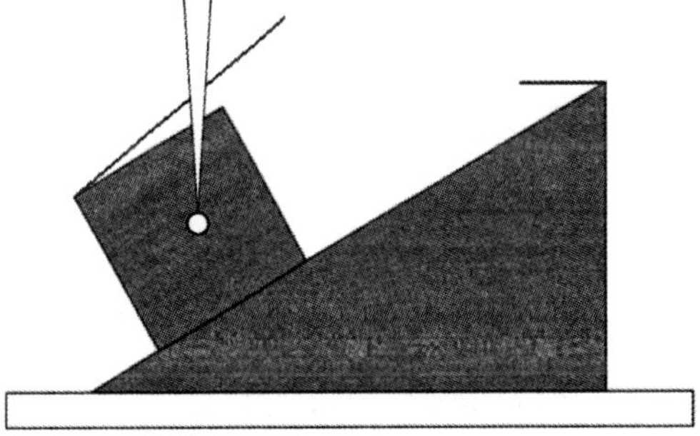

[4] Click **OK**.

[5] In the **Motion Study Tree**, rename the **Plot** like this.

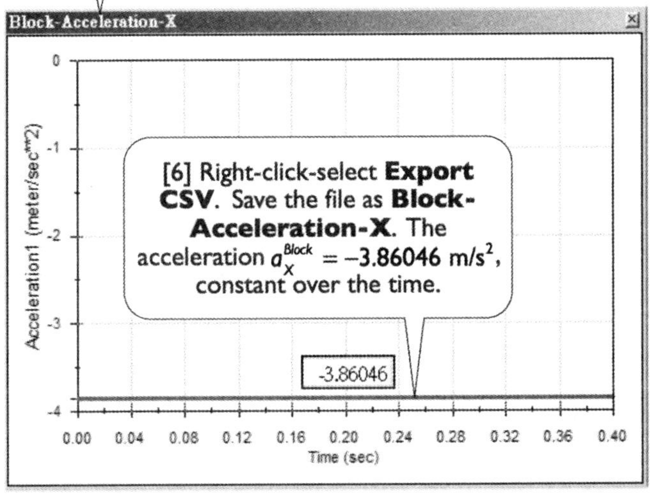

[6] Right-click-select **Export CSV**. Save the file as **Block-Acceleration-X**. The acceleration $a_X^{Block} = -3.86046$ m/s^2, constant over the time.

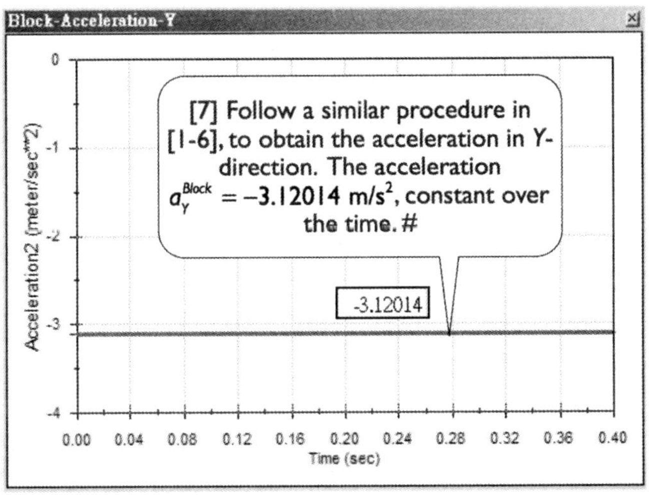

[7] Follow a similar procedure in [1-6], to obtain the acceleration in Y-direction. The acceleration $a_Y^{Block} = -3.12014$ m/s^2, constant over the time. #

2.1-12 Results: **Acceleration** of **Wedge**

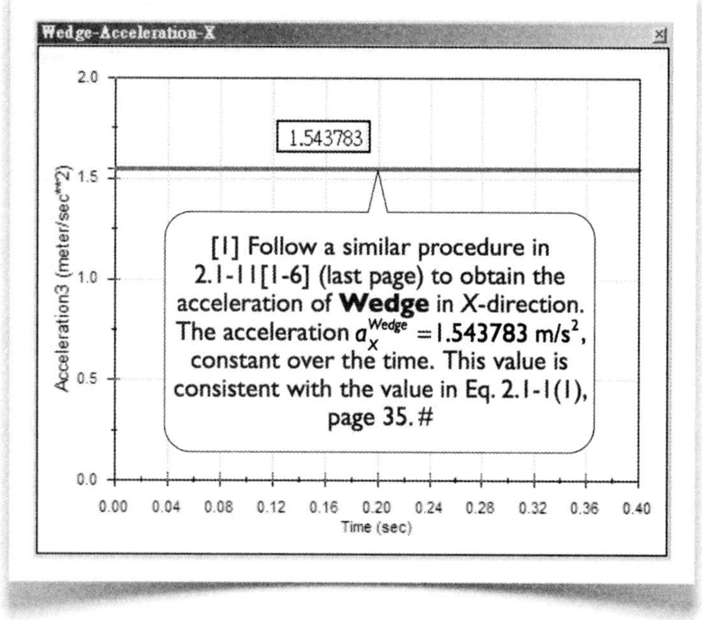

[1] Follow a similar procedure in 2.1-11[1-6] (last page) to obtain the acceleration of **Wedge** in *X*-direction. The acceleration $a_x^{Wedge} = 1.543783$ m/s^2, constant over the time. This value is consistent with the value in Eq. 2.1-1(1), page 35. #

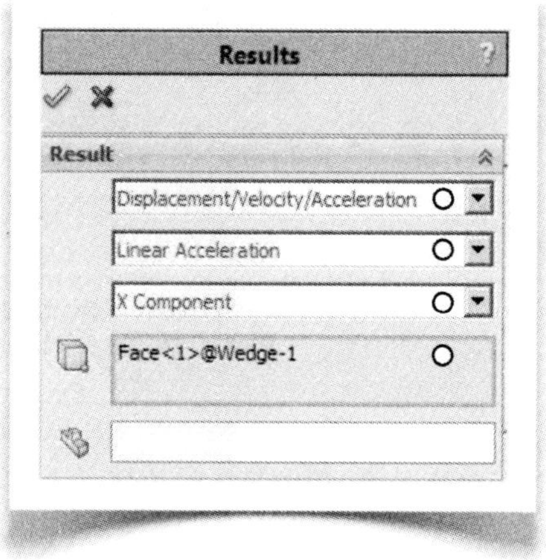

2.1-13 Results: **Reaction** between **Wedge** and **Floor**

[1] In **Motion Toolbar**, click **Results and Plots**.

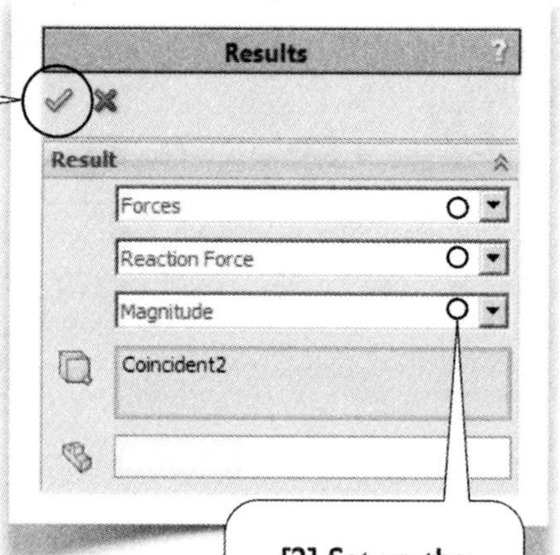

[2] Set up the **Results** like this.

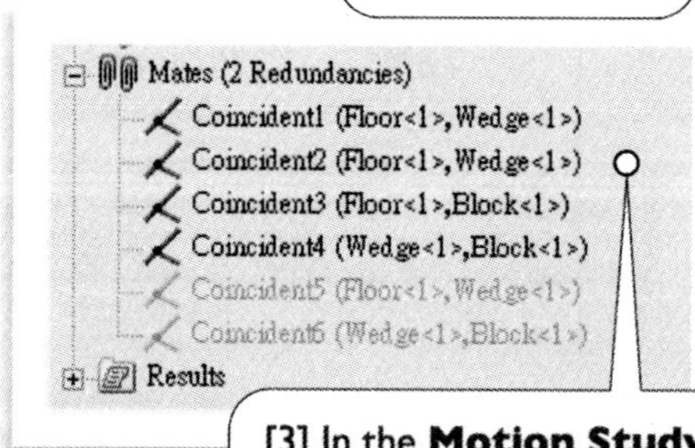

[3] In the **Motion Study Tree**, click **Coincident2**, which is the contact between **Wedge** and **Floor**.

[4] Click **OK**. Click **No** if a warning message shows up.

[5] In the **Motion Study Tree**, rename the **Plot** like this.

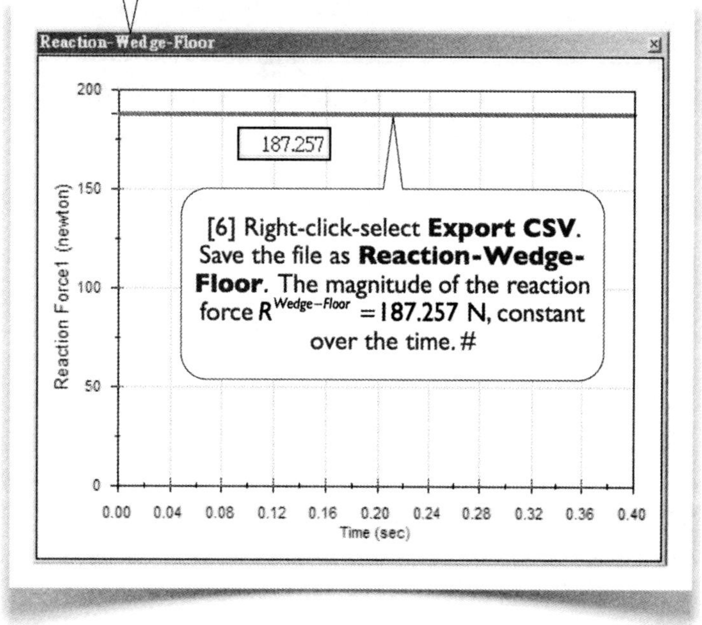

[6] Right-click-select **Export CSV**. Save the file as **Reaction-Wedge-Floor**. The magnitude of the reaction force $R^{Wedge-Floor} = 187.257$ N, constant over the time. #

2.1-14 Results: **Reaction** between **Block** and **Wedge**

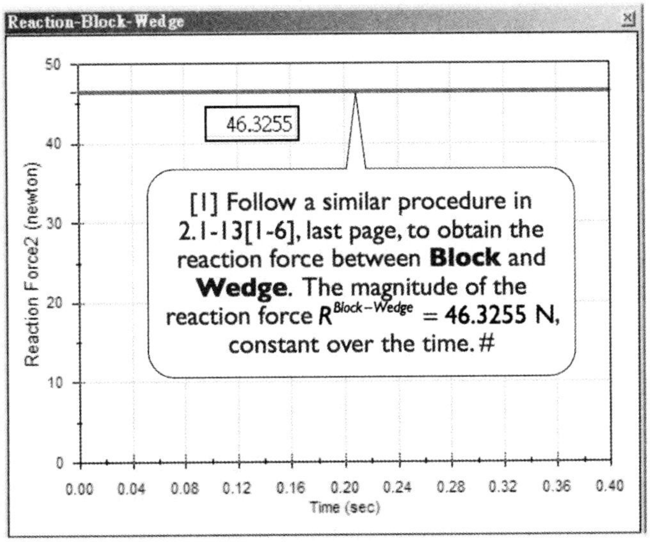

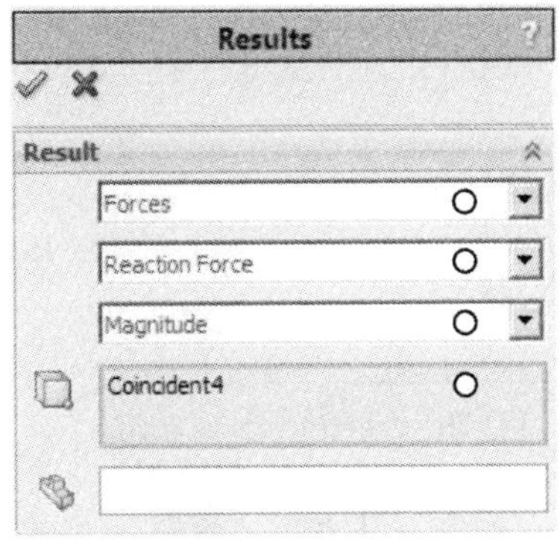

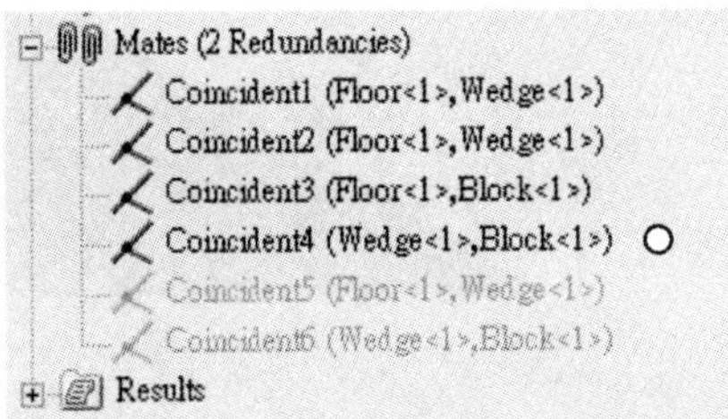

2.1-15 Newton's 2nd Law: **Block**

[1] Newton's 2nd Law states that *the resultant external forces acting on a particle is equivalent to the* ***effective force*** *acting on the particle. The effective force of a particle is simply the product of its mass and its acceleration.*

The external forces acting on the **Block** and the effective forces on the **Block** are shown in [2-5]. It's easy to confirm that these forces indeed satisfy Newton's 2nd Law; i.e., in X-direction,

$$-46.3255(\sin 30^\circ) = -6(3.86046)$$

In Y-direction,

$$-6(9.80665) + 46.3255(\cos 30^\circ) = -6(3.12014)$$

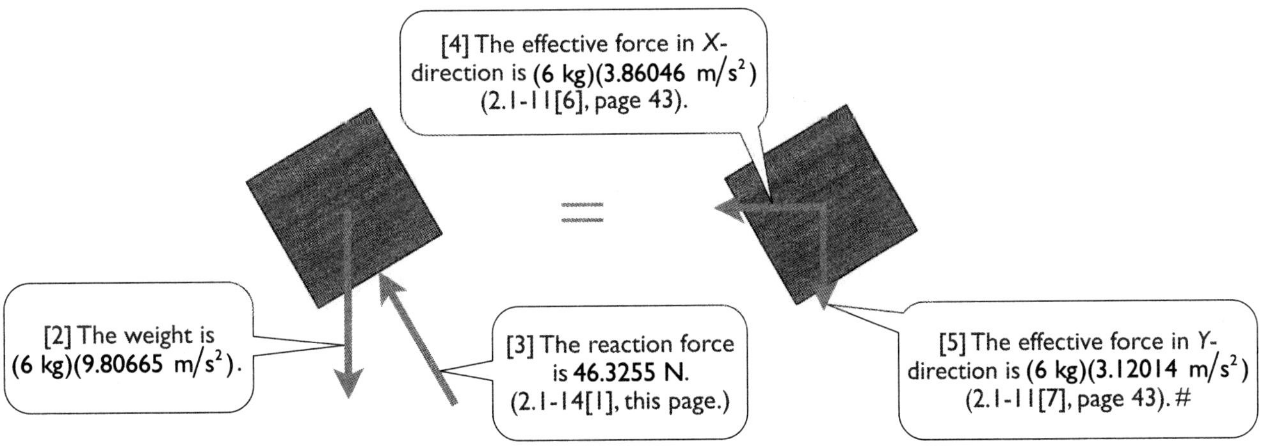

2.1-16 Newton's Second Law: **Wedge**

[1] The forces acting on the **Wedge** and the effective forces on the **Wedge** are shown in [2-5]. It's easy to confirm that these forces indeed satisfy Newton's 2nd Law; i.e., in *X*-direction,

$$46.3255(\sin 30^\circ) \approx 15.004(1.543783)$$

In *Y*-direction,

$$-15.004(9.80665) - 46.3255(\cos 30^\circ) + 187.257 \approx 0$$

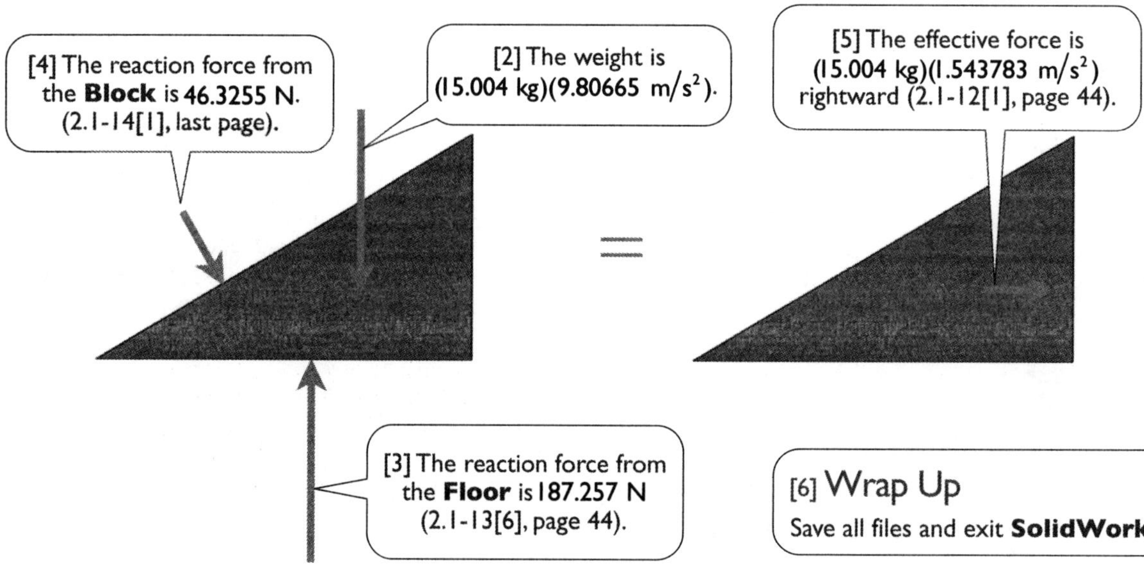

[6] Wrap Up

Save all files and exit **SolidWorks**. #

2.1-17 (Do It Yourself) Newton's 2nd Law: Sliding **Collar**

[1] The forces acting on the **Collar** and the effective forces on the **Collar** at 0.8 seconds are shown in [2-5]. The mass of the **Collar** is $m = 0.16387$ kg, which can be obtained by a similar procedure in 2.1-2[11-13], page 37. Note that, since material is not specified for the **Collar**, the mass density is assumed to be 1000 kg/m³ by default. It leaves for you to confirm that these forces indeed satisfy Newton's 2nd Law.

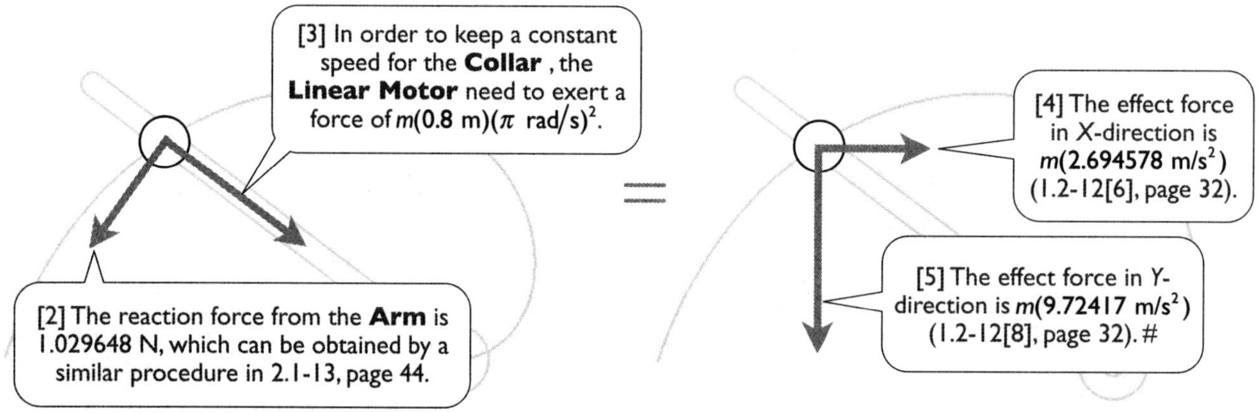

Section 2.2

Newton's 2nd Law: Billiard Balls

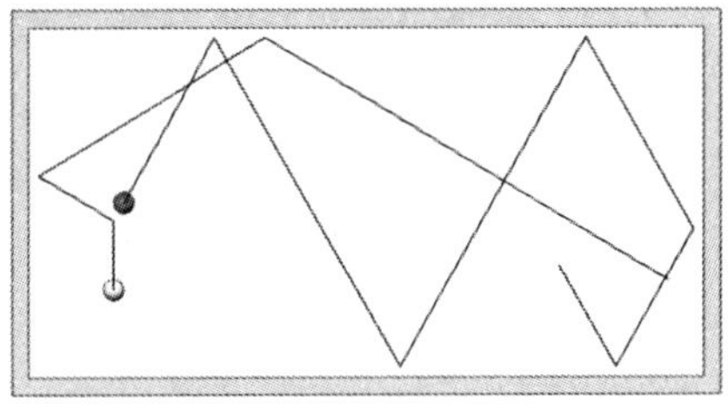

2.2-1 Introduction

[1] In this section, we'll simulate a scenario where a cue ball strikes an object ball and both balls rebound against the cushion of a billiard table [2-5]. All the impacts (between the two balls and between a ball and the cushion) are assumed to be perfectly elastic (i.e., no energy loss) and all frictions are negligible. We'll examine the dynamic behavior of the cue ball at the time when it collides with the object ball. The impact force and the acceleration will be retrieved and testified with Newton's 2nd Law.

$$\vec{F} = m\vec{a} \tag{1}$$

The velocity after the impact is also retrieved and the impacting time Δt is calculated with the simple relations

$$\vec{v}_f = \vec{v}_i + \vec{a}\Delta t \tag{2}$$

where $\vec{v}_i$ is the velocity before impact, and $\vec{v}_f$ is the velocity after impact. Eq. (2) is calculated based on the assumption that the acceleration is constant during the impacting time.

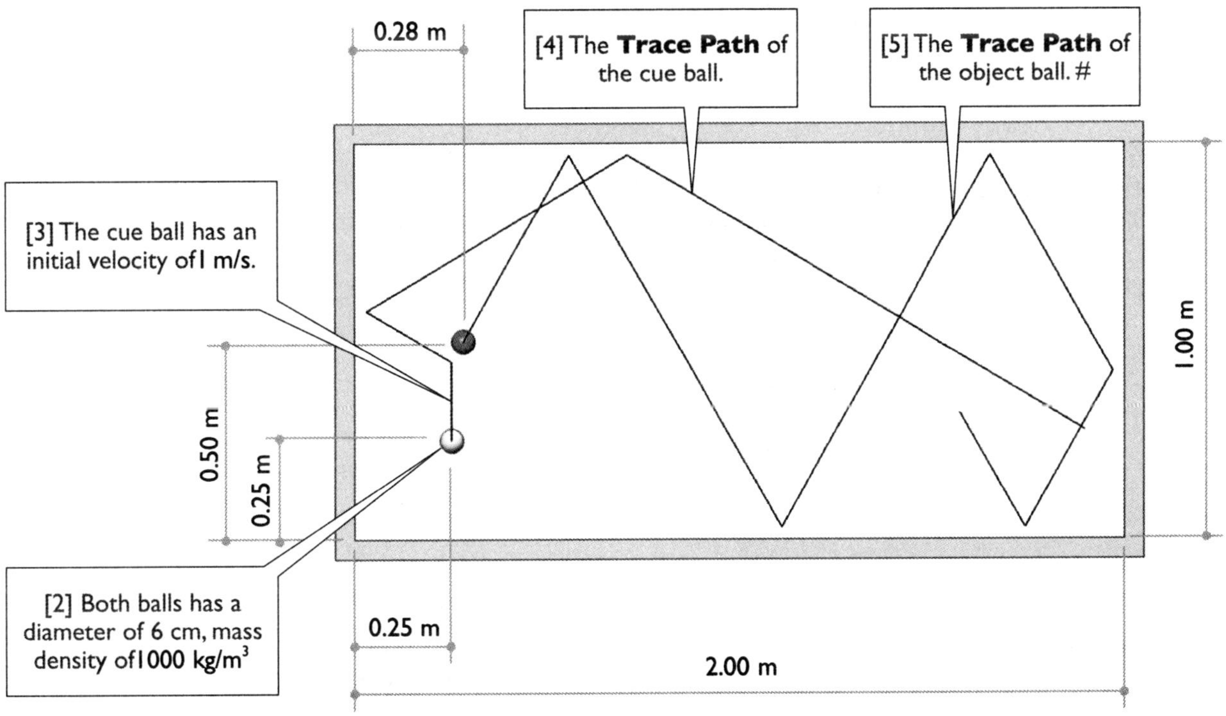

2.2-2 Start Up and Create a Part: **Ball**

[1] Launch **SolidWorks** and click **New** to create a new **Part**.

[2] Save the **Part** with the name **Ball**.

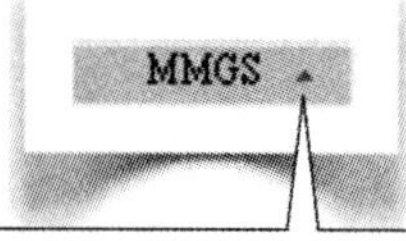

[3] Set up **MMGS** unit system with three decimal places for **Length** in both Basic Units and **Mass/Section Properties**.

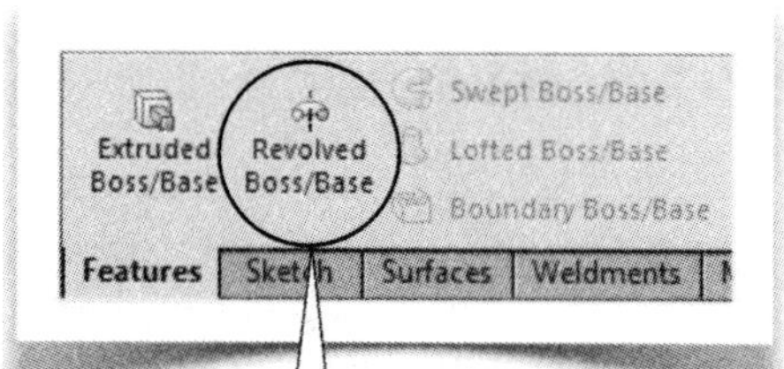

[4] On the **Front** plane, draw a sketch like this.

[5] In **Features Toolbar**, click **Revolved Boss/Base**.

[6] Select this line as **Axis of Revolution**.

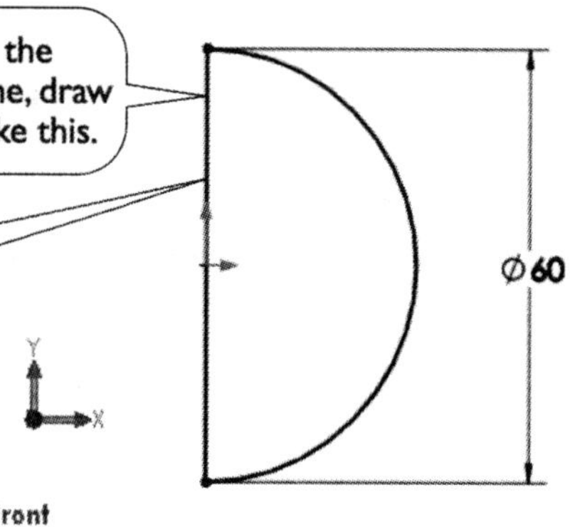

[7] Click **OK**.

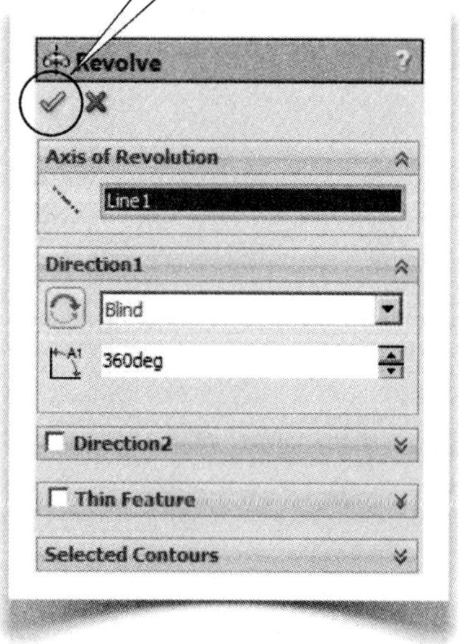

[8] In the **Evaluate Toolbar**, click **Mass Properties**. (Or, from **Pull-Down Menus**, select **Tools>Mass Properties...**)

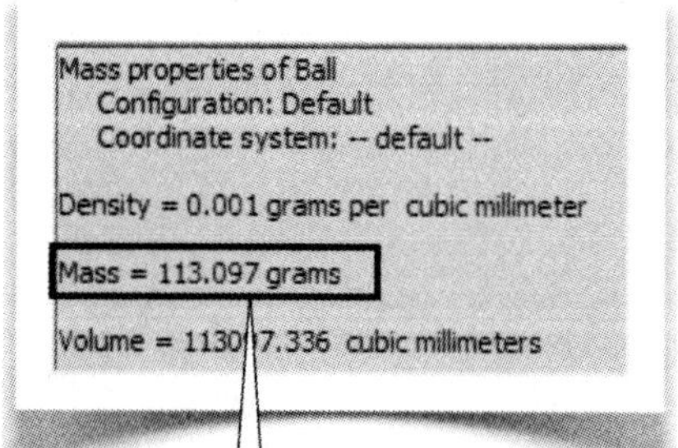

[9] The ball has a mass of 113.097 grams. Remember that, if the material is not specified, the mass density is assumed to be 1000 kg/m^3 by default (2.1-17[1], page 46). #

2.2-3 Create a Part: **Table**

[1] Click **New** to create a new **Part**.

[2] Save the **Part** with the name **Table**.

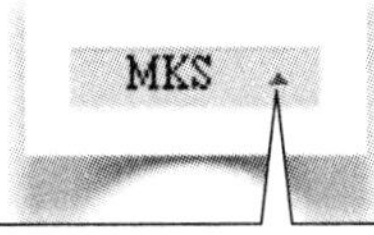

[3] Set up **MKS** unit system with three decimal places for **Length** in **Basic Units**.

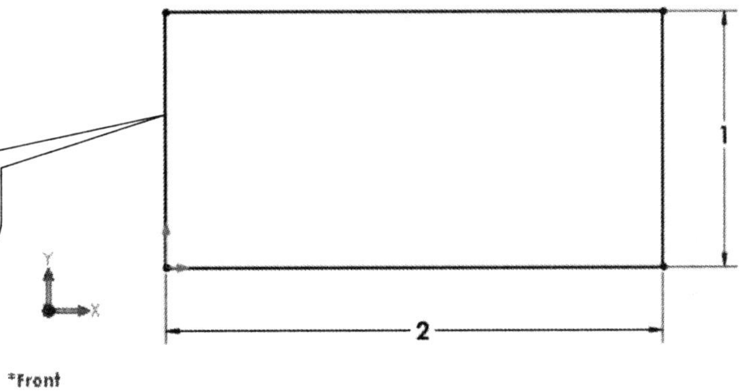

[4] On the **Front** plane, draw a rectangle like this.

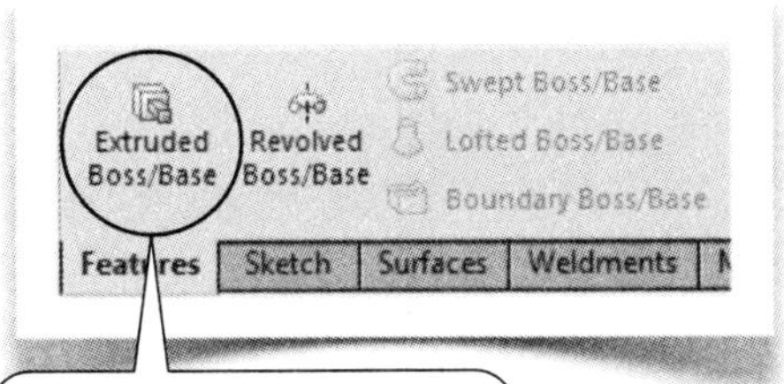

[5] In **Features Toolbar**, click **Extruded Boss/Base**.

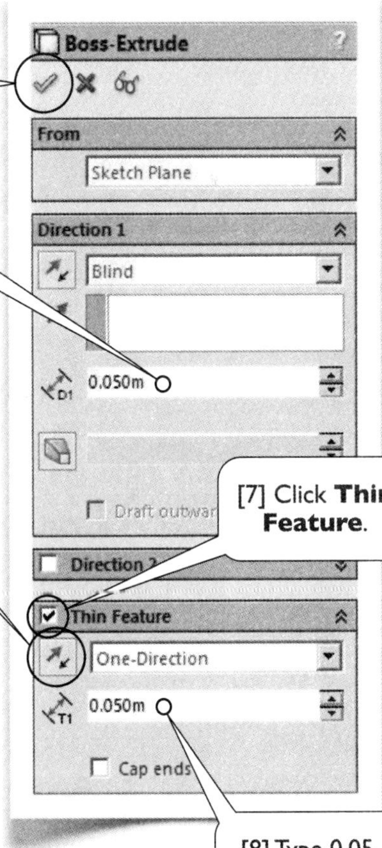

[6] Type 0.05 (m) for **Depth**.

[7] Click **Thin Feature**.

[8] Type 0.05 (m) for **Thickness**.

[9] The thickness should grow outward. If not, click **Reverse Direction**.

[10] Click **OK**. #

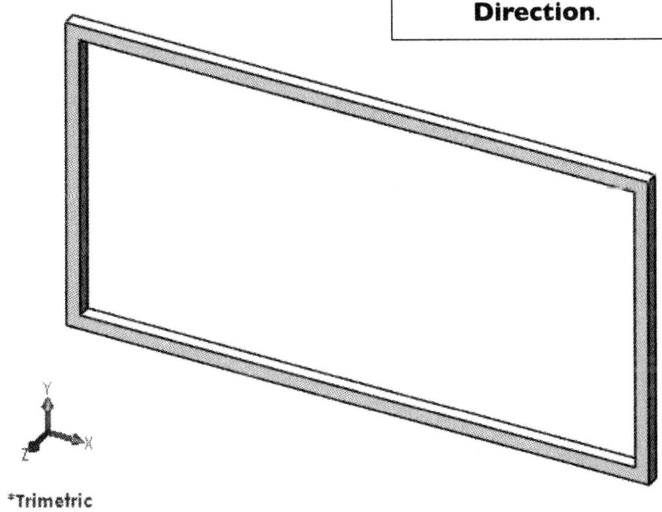

2.2-4 Create an Assembly: **Billiards**

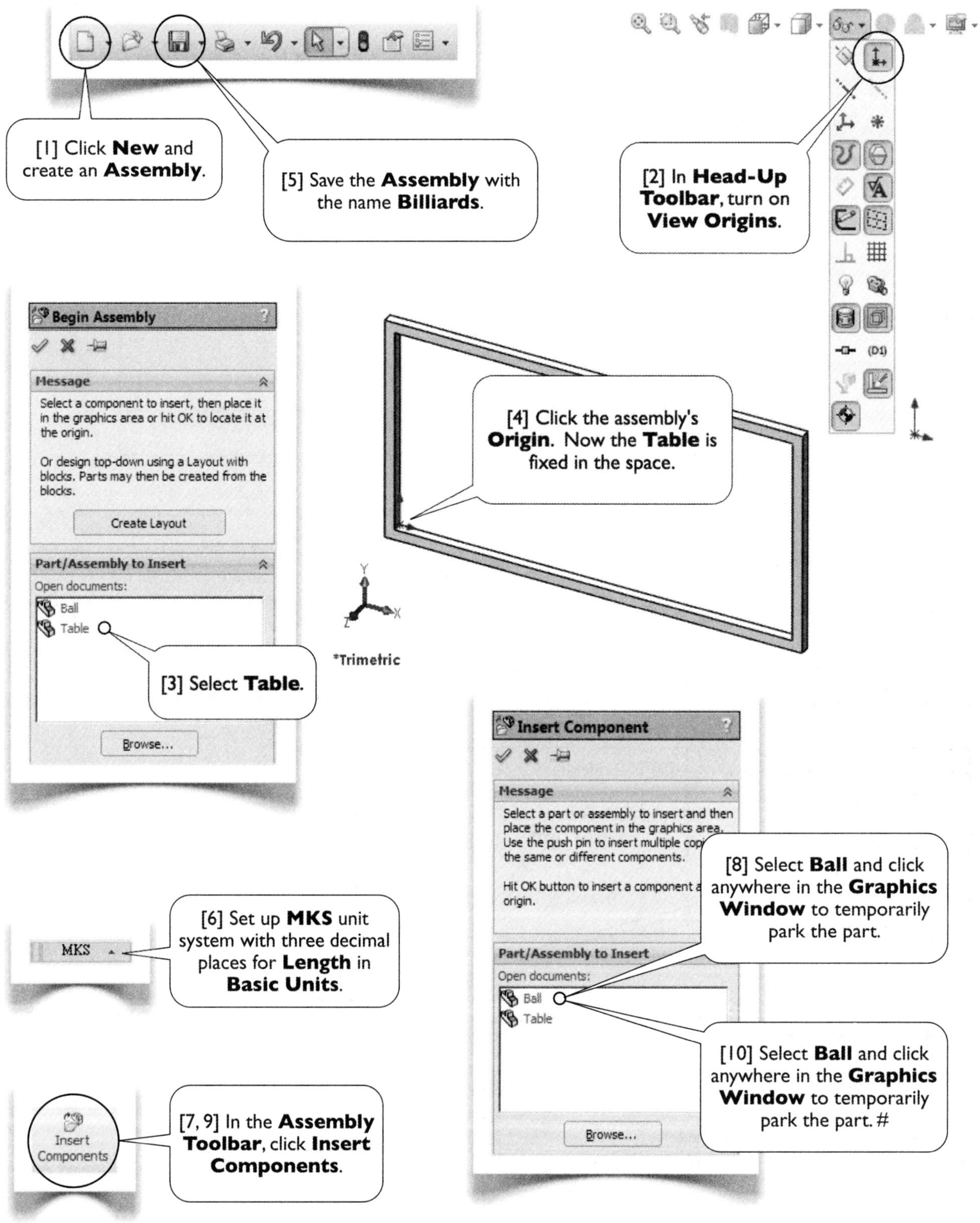

2.2-5 Set Up **Initial Positions**

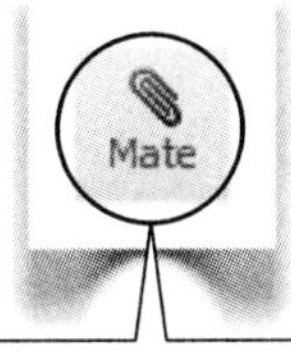

[1] In the **Assembly Toolbar**, click **Mate**.

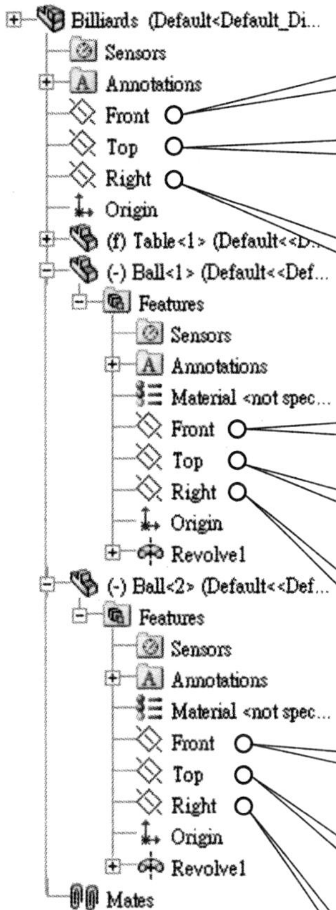

[2, 8] Click assembly's **Front** plane.

[4, 10] Click assembly's **Top** plane.

[6, 12] Click assembly's **Right** plane.

[3] Click **Front** plane of **Ball<1>**. Click **OK**.

[5] Click **Top** plane of **Ball<1>**. Type 0.25 (m) for **Distance**. Click **OK**.

[7] Click **Right** plane of **Ball<1>**. Type 0.25 (m) for **Distance**. Click **OK**.

[9] Click **Front** plane of **Ball<2>**. Click **OK**

[11] Click **Top** plane of **Ball<2>**. Type 0.5 (m) for **Distance**. Click **OK**.

[13] Click **Right** plane of **Ball<2>**. Type 0.28 (m) for **Distance**. Click **OK**. Click **OK** again to dismiss the **Property Box**.

[15] Right-click **Ball<2>** and select **Appearances>Ball-2@Billiards**. Select a red color from the palette. Click **OK**.

[16] Similarly, assign a green color to **Table**.

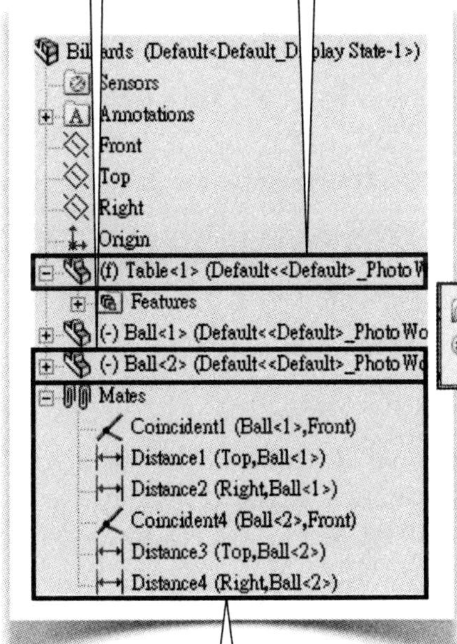

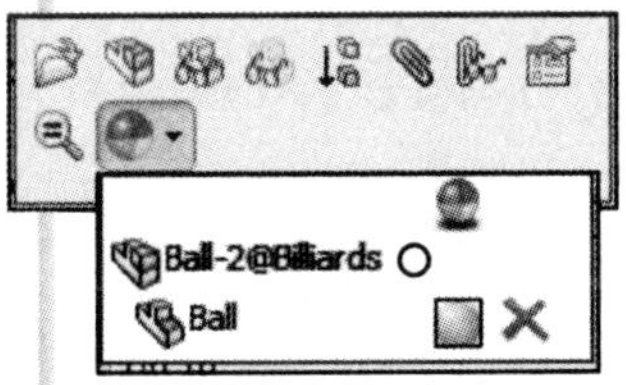

[14] We'll suppress **Distance1**, **Distance2**, **Distance3**, and **Distance4** before running the simulation (2.2-9[1], page 53).

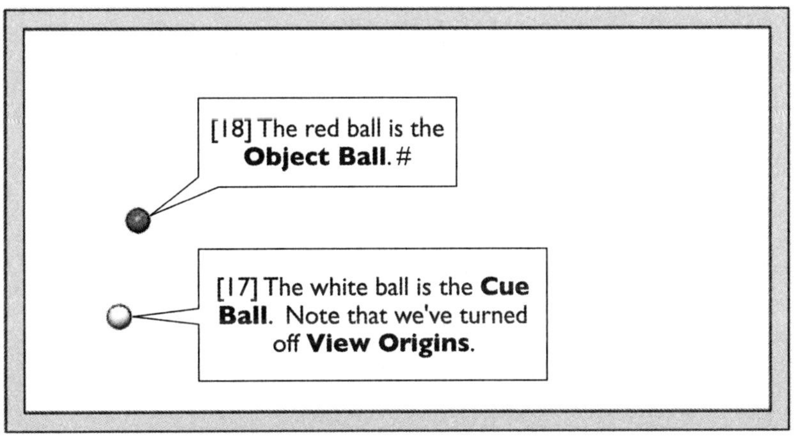

[18] The red ball is the **Object Ball**.#

[17] The white ball is the **Cue Ball**. Note that we've turned off **View Origins**.

2.2-6 Create a **Motion Study**

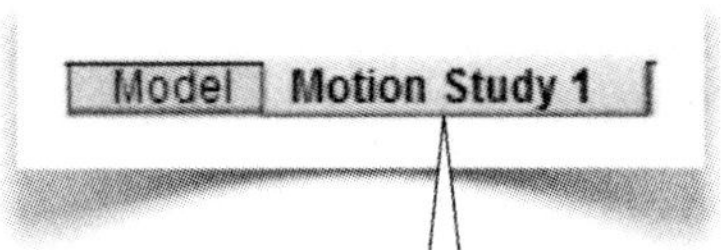

[1] Click **Motion Study 1** tab. Leave **Motion Study 1** as default name.

[2] Select **Motion Analysis**. #

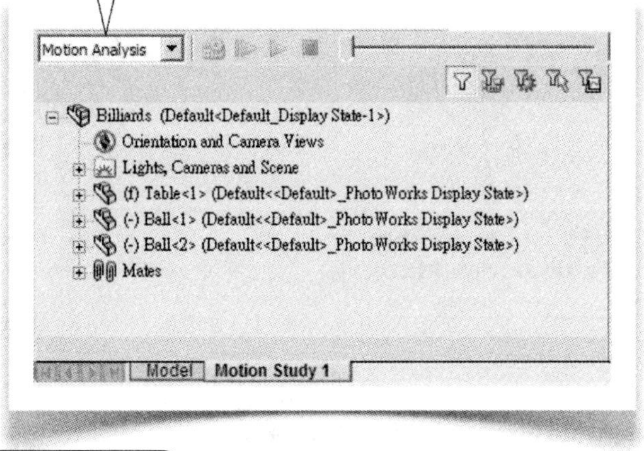

2.2-7 Set Up **Contacts**

[1] In **Motion Toolbar**, click **Contact**.

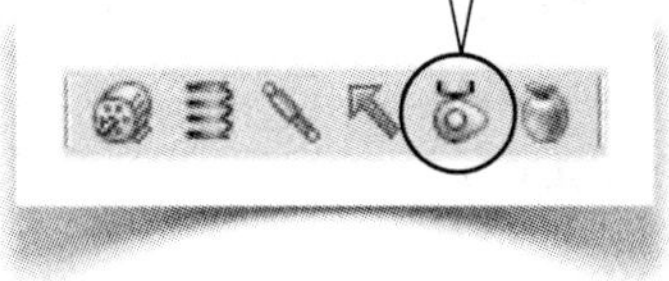

[2] In the **Graphics Window**, select the two **Balls**. This sets up a **Contact** between the two **Balls**.

[3] De-select **Material**.

[4] De-select **Friction**.

[5] Select **Restitution coefficient**.

[6] Type 1 (perfectly elastic) for **Coefficient**.

[7] Click **OK**.

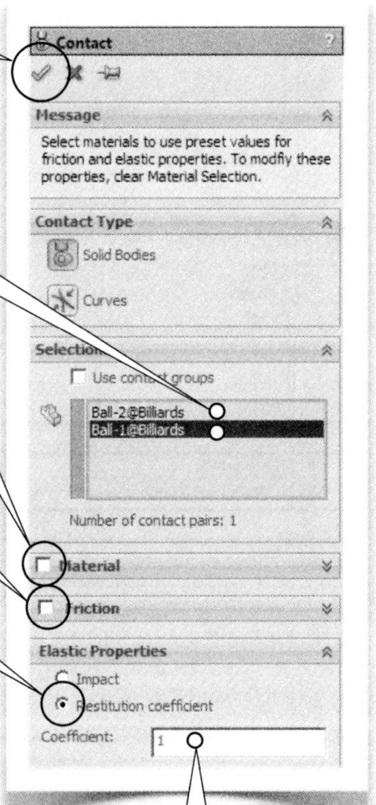

[8] Follow a similar procedure in steps [1-7] to set up a **Contact** (perfectly elastic and no friction) between **Object Ball** and **Table**.

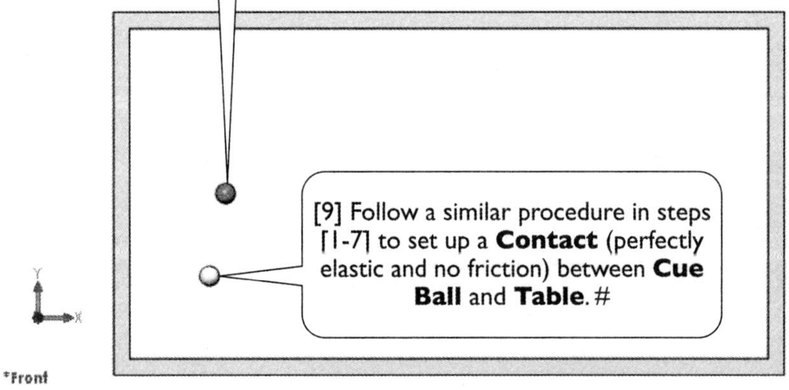

[9] Follow a similar procedure in steps [1-7] to set up a **Contact** (perfectly elastic and no friction) between **Cue Ball** and **Table**. #

2.2-8 Set Up **Initial Velocity** for the Cue Ball

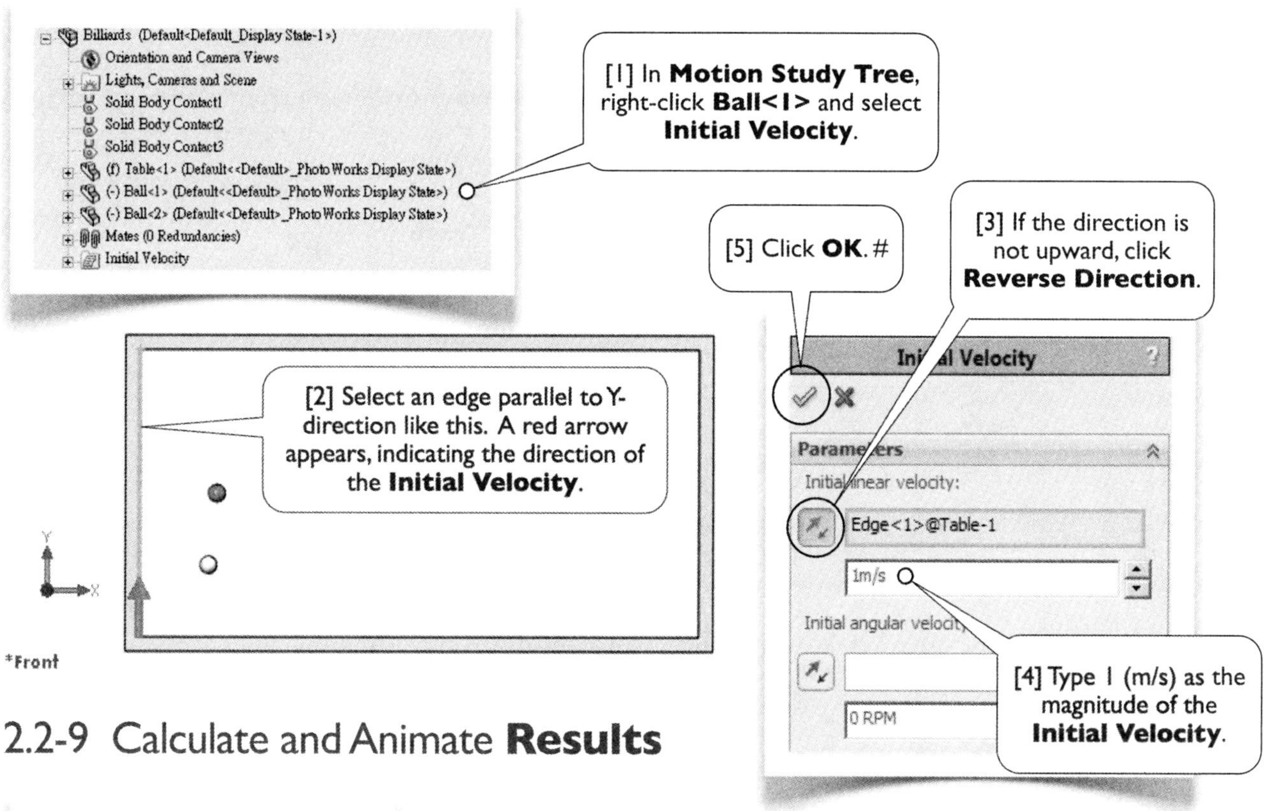

2.2-9 Calculate and Animate **Results**

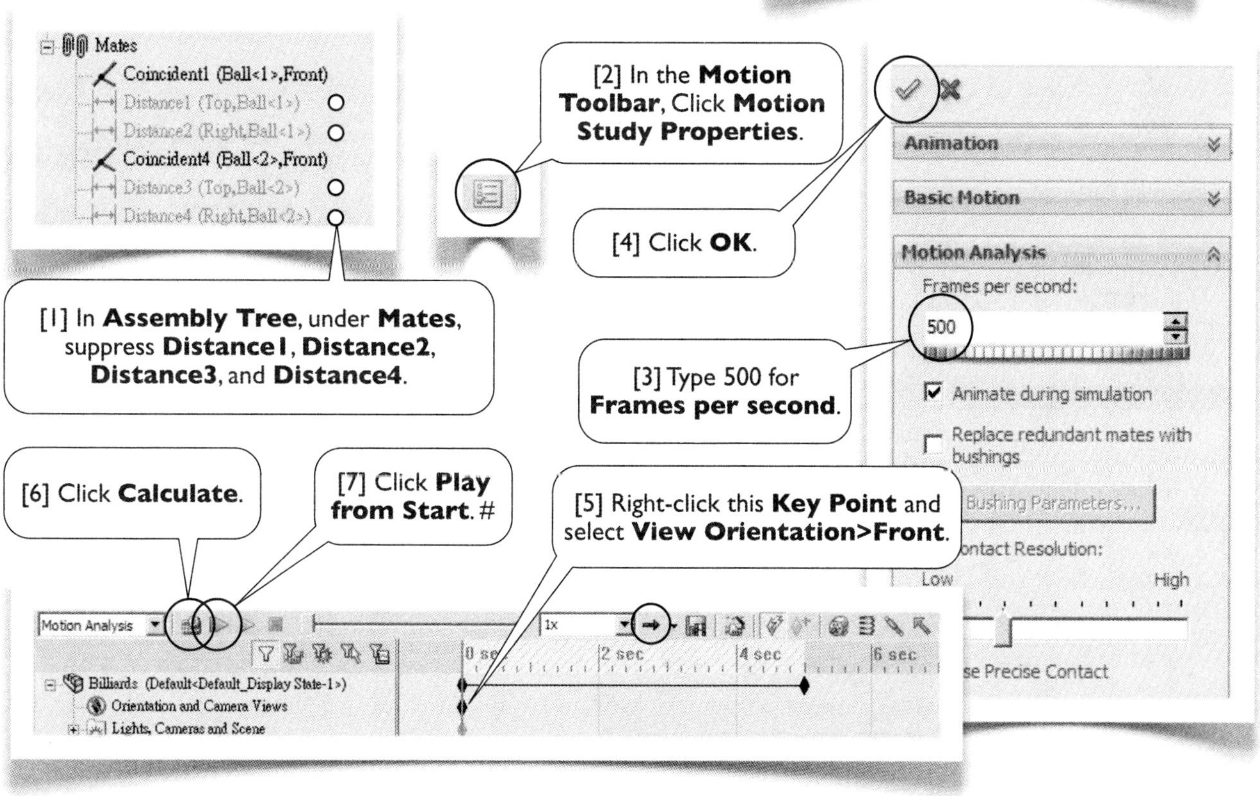

2.2-10 Results: **Trace Path**

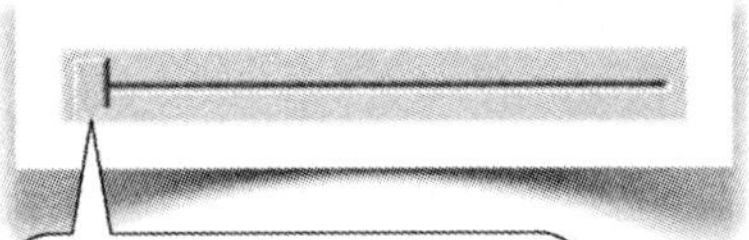

[1] Drag the **Time Slider** to the beginning.

[2] Create a **Trace Path** for **Cue Ball**.

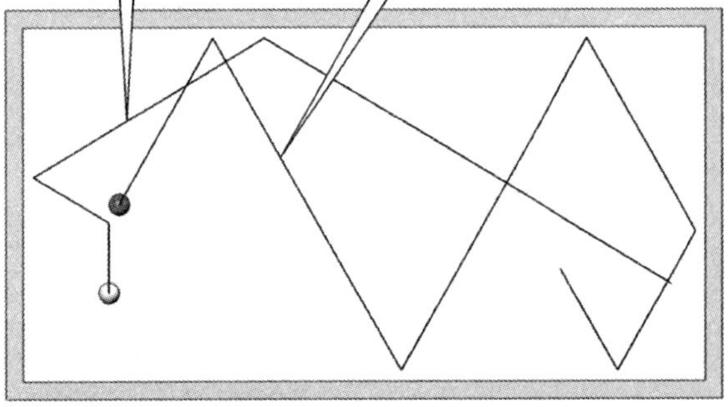

[3] The **Origin** may be selected either from the **Assembly Tree**, or from the **Graphics Window** (you need to turn on **View Origins**).

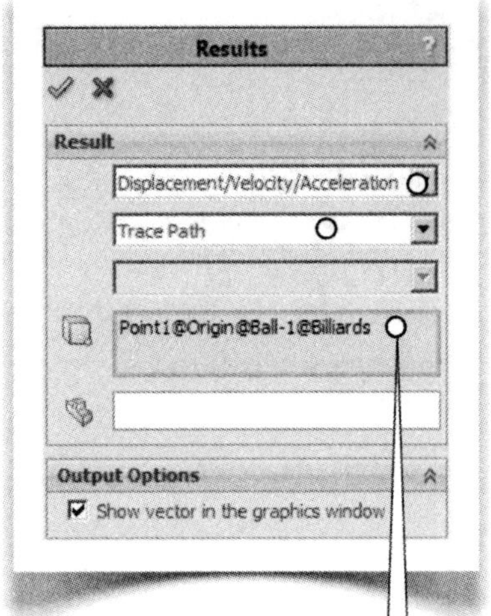

[4] Create a **Trace Path** for **Object Ball**.

[5] Rename the **Trace Paths** like this.

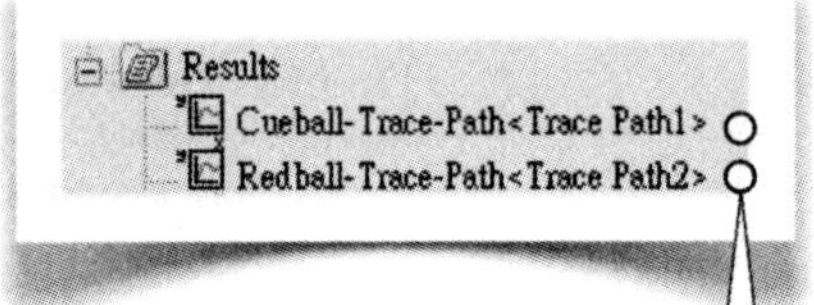

[6] Click **Play from Start**. #

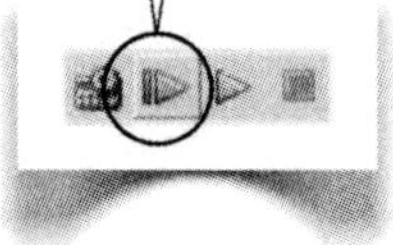

2.2-11 Results: **Contact Force**

[1] In **Motion Toolbar**, click **Results and Plots**.

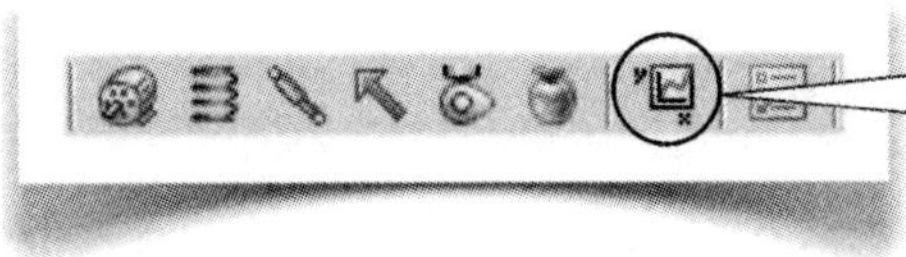

[2] In the **Graphics Window**, click **Object Balls** and **Cue Ball**.

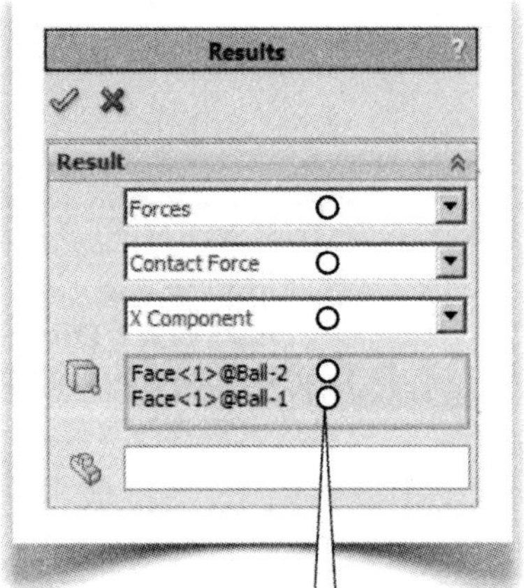

[3] Rename the plot like this.

[4] At 0.198493 sec, the cue ball collides with the object ball and the impact force in *X*-direction is 354.6498 N. (The numerical data are taken from the exported **CSV** file.)

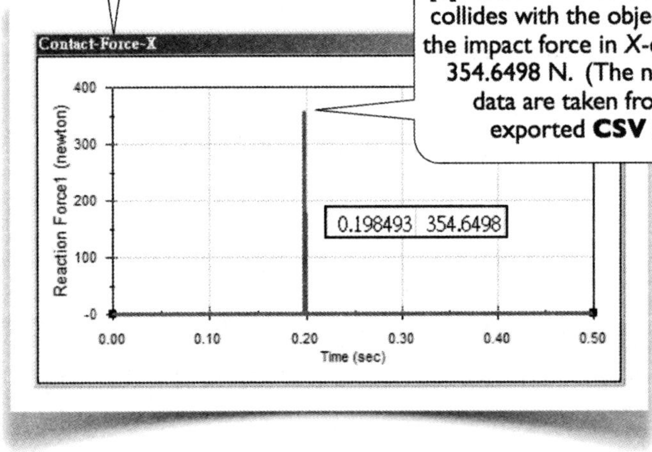

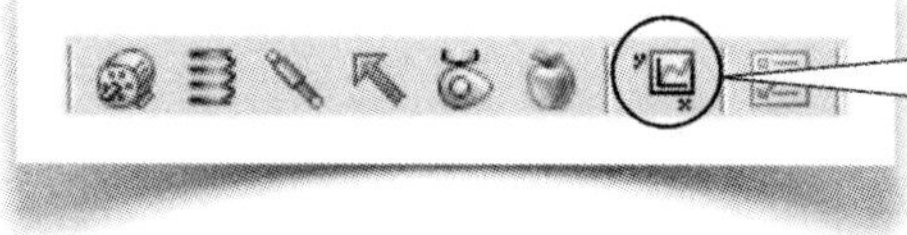

[5] In **Motion Toolbar**, click **Results and Plots**.

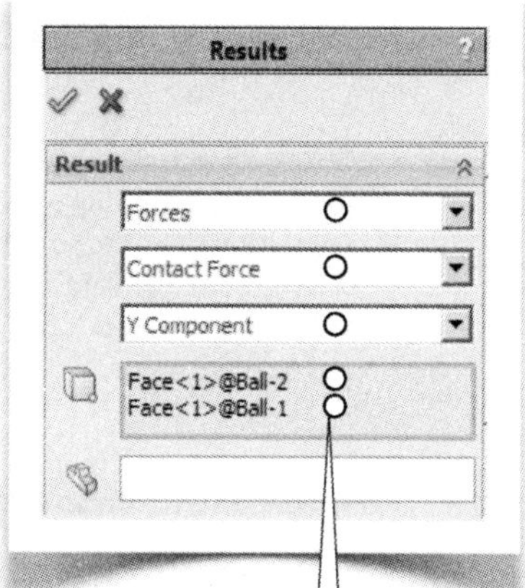

[6] In the **Graphics Window**, click the two **Balls**.

[7] Rename the plot like this.

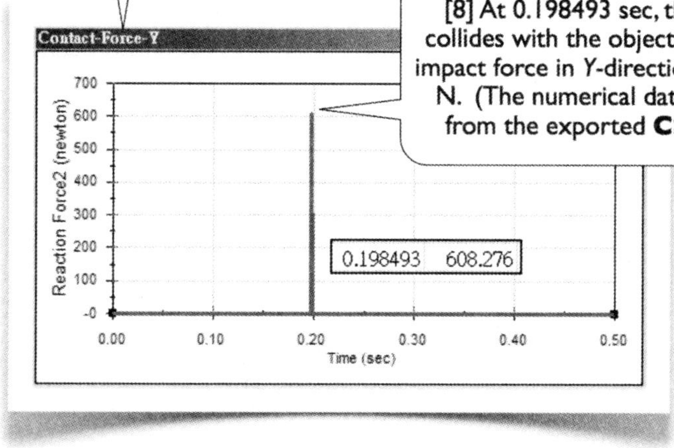

[8] At 0.198493 sec, the cue ball collides with the object ball and the impact force in *Y*-direction is 608.276 N. (The numerical data are taken from the exported **CSV** file.) #

2.2-12 Results: **Acceleration** of **Cue Ball**

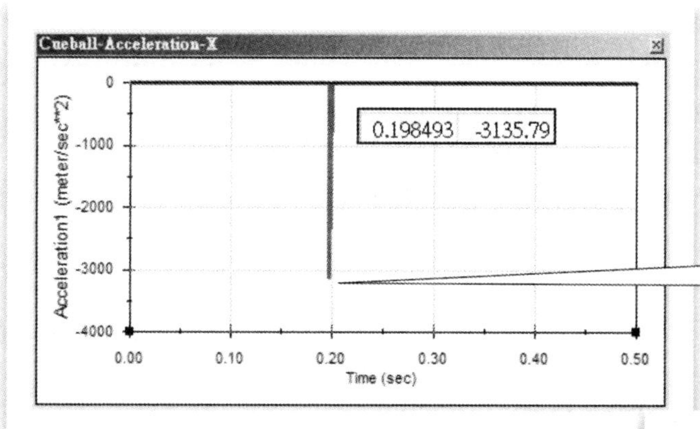

[1] At 0.198493 sec, the cue ball's acceleration in *X*-direction is **–3135.79 m/s^2**. (The numerical data are taken from the exported **CSV** file.)

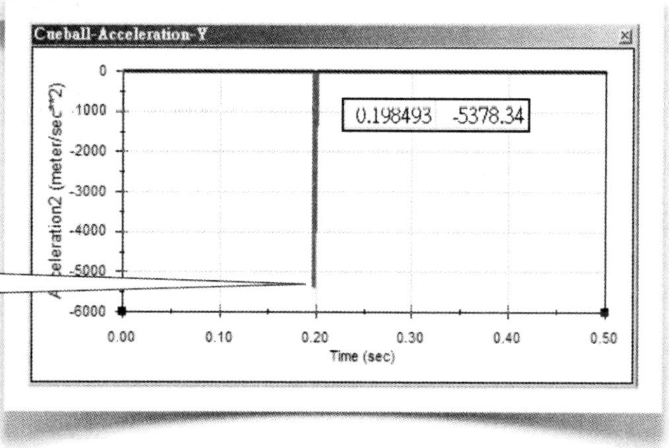

[2] At 0.198493 sec, the cue ball's acceleration in *Y*-direction is **–5378.34 m/s^2**. (The numerical data are taken from the exported **CSV** file.) #

2.2-13 Results: **Velocity** of **Cue Ball**

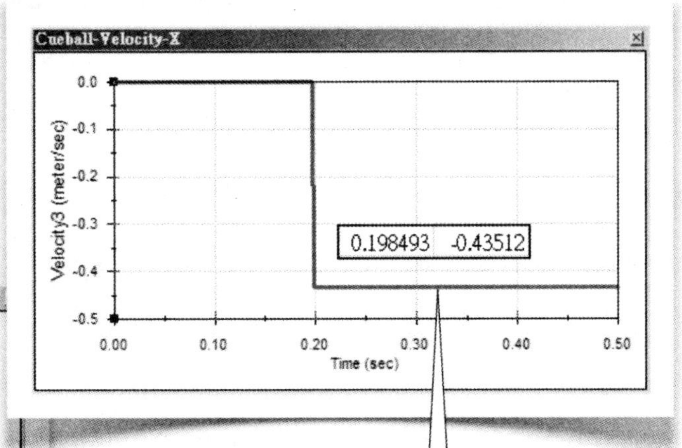

[1] After the impact, the cue ball's velocity in *X*-direction is **–0.43512 m/s.** (The numerical data are taken from the exported **CSV** file.)

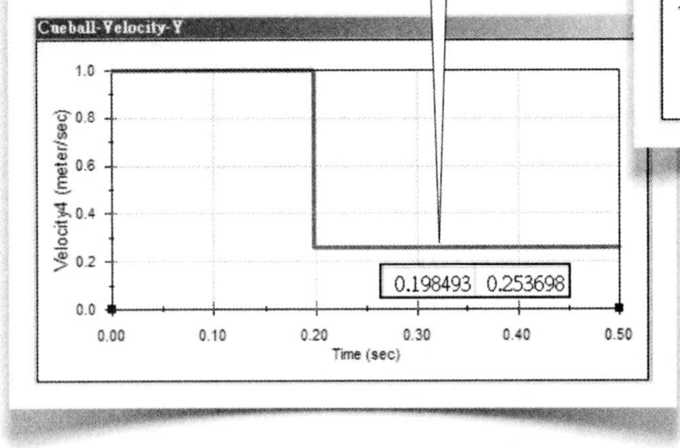

[2] After the impact, the cue ball's velocity in *Y*-direction is **0.253698 m/s.** (The numerical data are taken from the exported **CSV** file.) #

2.2-14 Newton's 2nd Law: **Cue Ball**

[1] The forces acting on the **Cue Ball** and the effective forces on the **Cue Ball** are shown in [2-5]. It's easy to confirm that these forces indeed satisfy Newton's 2nd Law, Eq. 2.2-1(1). page 47; i.e., in *X*-direction,

$$-354.6498 \text{ N} \approx (0.113097 \text{ kg})(-3135.79 \text{ m/s}^2)$$

In *Y*-direction,

$$-608.276 \text{ N} \approx (0.113097 \text{ kg})(-5378.34 \text{ m/s}^2)$$

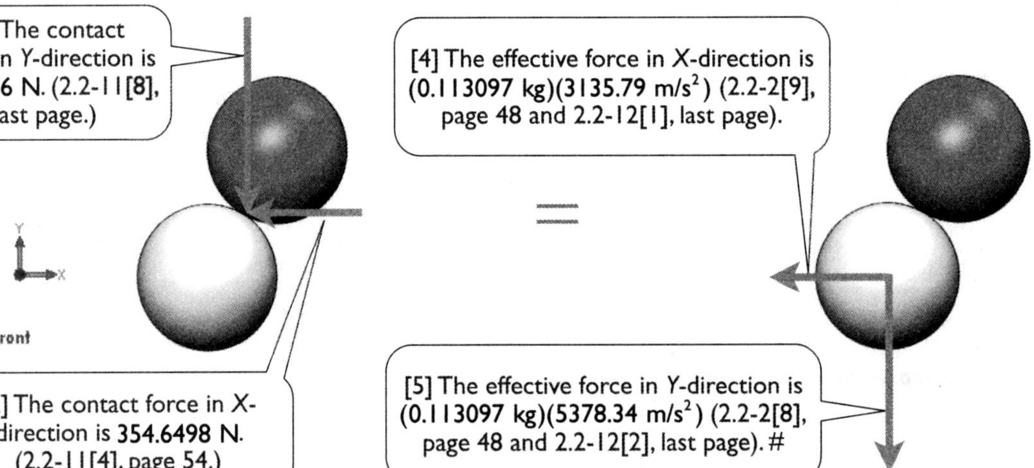

[3] The contact force in *Y*-direction is **608.276 N.** (2.2-11[8], last page.)

[2] The contact force in *X*-direction is **354.6498 N.** (2.2-11[4], page 54.)

[4] The effective force in *X*-direction is **(0.113097 kg)(3135.79 m/s²)** (2.2-2[9], page 48 and 2.2-12[1], last page).

[5] The effective force in *Y*-direction is **(0.113097 kg)(5378.34 m/s²)** (2.2-2[8], page 48 and 2.2-12[2], last page). #

2.2-15 Impacting Time Δt

[1] The acceleration of the cue ball during the impact is (2.2-12[1, 2], page 55)

$$\vec{a} = -3135.79\,\vec{i} - 5378.34\,\vec{j} \text{ (m/s}^2\text{)}$$

the velocity before impact is

$$\vec{v}_i = 1.0\,\vec{j} \text{ (m/s)}$$

the velocity after impact is (2.2-13[1, 2], last page)

$$\vec{v}_f = -0.43512\,\vec{i} + 0.253698\,\vec{j} \text{ (m/s)}$$

By Eq. 2.2-1(2) (page 47), the impacting time Δt is

$$\Delta t = \frac{-0.43512}{-3135.79} \approx \frac{0.253698 - 1.0}{-5378.34} \approx 0.00013876 \text{ (sec)} \qquad (1)$$

Note that Eq. (1) is calculated based on the assumption that the reaction forces (2.2-11[4, 8], pages 54, 55) and the accelerations (2.2-12[1, 2], page 55) are constant during the impacting time.

[2] Wrap Up

Save all files and exit **SolidWorks**. #

Chapter 3
Particle Dynamics: Work and Energy

Kinetic Energy

Energy is the ability to do **work**. Imagine that you throw a particle of mass m right upward with an initial speed v. You've transferred some energy to the particle. How much is the energy? To answer this question, let's calculate how much **work** this energy can do. The particle moves upward until a height h,

$$h = \frac{v^2}{2g}$$

the work done is

$$W = mgh = mg\frac{v^2}{2g} = \frac{mv^2}{2}$$

We conclude that *a moving particle with a speed of v possesses an energy of* $mv^2/2$. This energy is defined as the **kinetic energy** T of the particle,

$$T = \frac{mv^2}{2} \tag{1}$$

Principle of Work and Energy

Consider a particle of mass m acted upon by a force $\vec{F}$ and moving along a path. Applying Eq. 2(2) (page 34), in the tangential direction, we write

$$F_t = ma_t = m\frac{dv}{dt} = m\frac{dv}{ds}\frac{ds}{dt} = mv\frac{dv}{ds}$$

or

$$F_t ds = mvdv \tag{2}$$

where v is the speed of the particle and s is the accumulative length along the path. Integrating both sides of Eq. (2) for any duration from t_1 to t_2, where the accumulative lengths are s_1 and s_2 and the speeds of the particle are v_1 and v_2, we write

$$\int_{s_1}^{s_2} F_t\, ds = \int_{v_1}^{v_2} mv\, dv = \frac{mv_2^2}{2} - \frac{mv_1^2}{2} = T_2 - T_1 \tag{3}$$

where T_1 and T_2 are the kinetic energy possessed by the particle at t_1 and t_2 respectively. The left hand side $\int_{s_1}^{s_2} F_t\, ds$ is the **work done** $U_{1\to2}$ by the force during t_1 and t_2. We may rewrite Eq. (3) in the form

$$T_1 + U_{1\to2} = T_2 \tag{4}$$

Eq. (4) is called the **principle of work and energy**.

Work done by **conservative forces** (e.g., gravitational force or spring force, by which the work done is independent of path) can be expressed in terms of **potential energy** V. Incorporating potential energy into Eq. (4), we may write the **principle of work and energy** in a more useful form:

$$T_1 + V_1 + U_{1\to2} = T_2 + V_2 \tag{5}$$

This chapter will show how Eq. (5) is satisfied in a particle system.

Section 3.1

Principle of Work and Energy: Oscillating Block

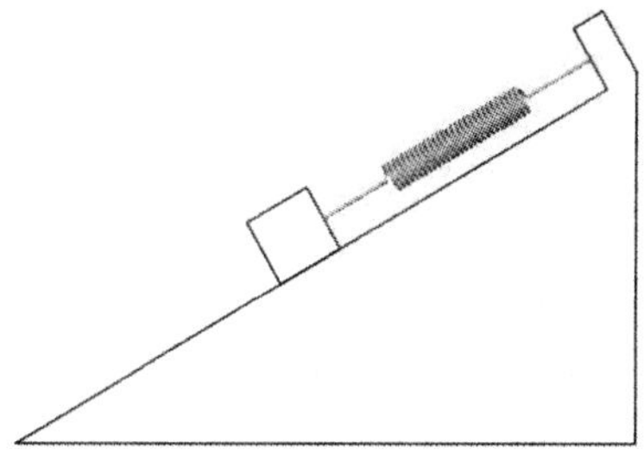

3.1-1 Introduction

[1] Consider a **Block** [2] connected to the **Ground** [3] with a **Spring** [4], sliding along a 30° slope. The **Block** is initially positioned such that the **Spring** has an initial elongation of 30 cm [5]. The **Dynamic Friction Coefficient** between the **Block** and the **Ground** is 0.3 [6].

Using this example, we'll illustrate the **principle of work and energy**, which states

$$T_0 + V_0 + U_{0\to t} = T_t + V_t \tag{1}$$

where T_0 and V_0 are respectively the initial kinetic energy and potential energy of the system, and T_t and V_t are respectively the kinetic energy and potential energy of the system at time t, and $U_{0\to t}$ is the work done by non-conservative force (work done by conservative forces always can be expressed as potential energies). In this case $T_0 = 0$ and $V_0 = (100\ \text{N/m})(0.3\ \text{m})^2/2 = 4.5\ \text{J}$ (the initial position is taken as the baseline of the gravitational potential energy); therefore, Eq. (1) can be rewritten as

$$T_t + V_t - U_{0\to t} = 4.5\ \text{J} \tag{2}$$

In other words, the **principle of work and energy** can be restated as follows: *at any time, the sum of kinetic energy and potential energy, minus the work done by non-conservative forces (in this case, the friction forces), remains a constant.* The statement can be viewed as a form of **conservation of energy**.

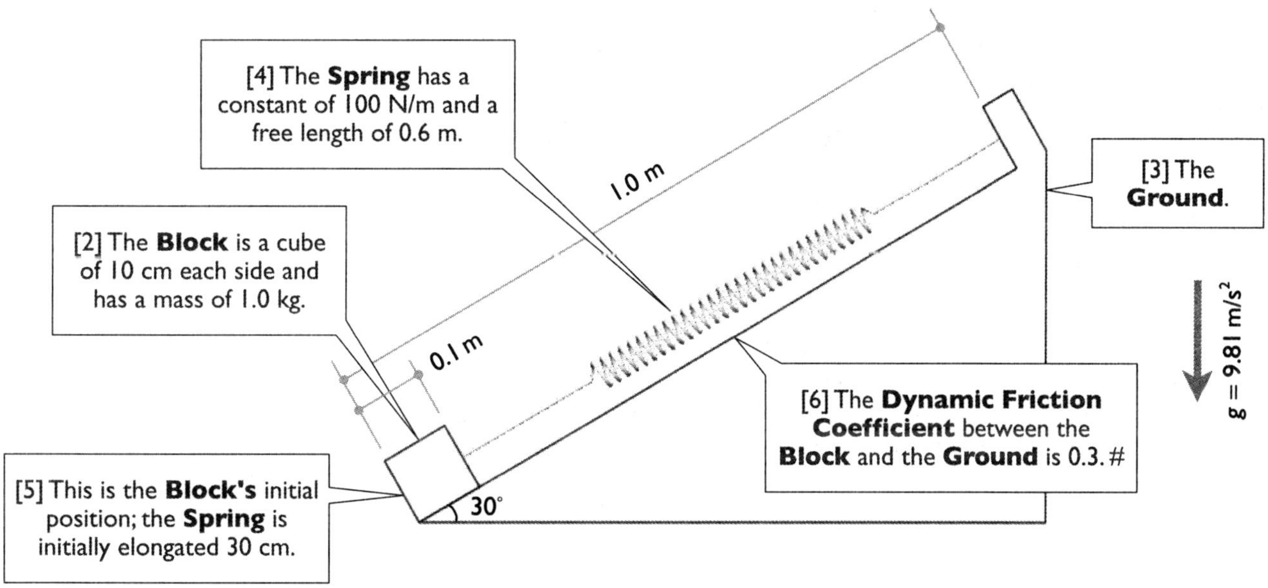

3.1-2 Start Up and Create a Part: **Block**

[1] Launch **SolidWorks** and click **New** to create a new **Part**.

[2] Save the **Part** with the name **Block**.

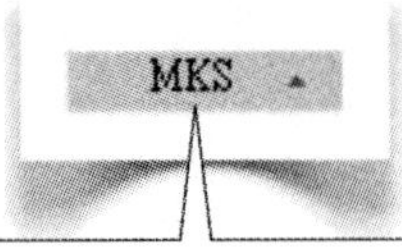

[3] Set up **MKS** unit system with three decimal places for **Length**.

[4] On the **Front** plane, draw a sketch like this.

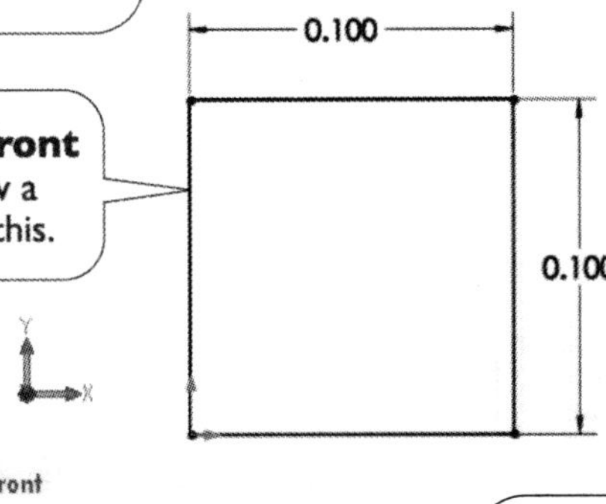

[5] Extrude 0.1 m.

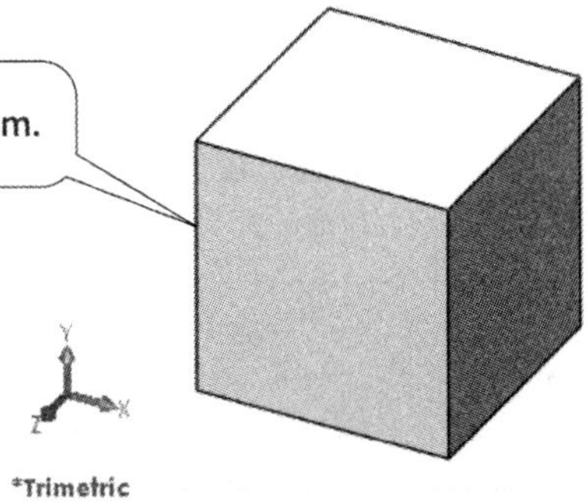

[6] In the **Evaluate Toolbar**, click **Mass Properties** (2.2-2[8], page 48) and make sure the mass of the **Block** is 1.000 kg. #

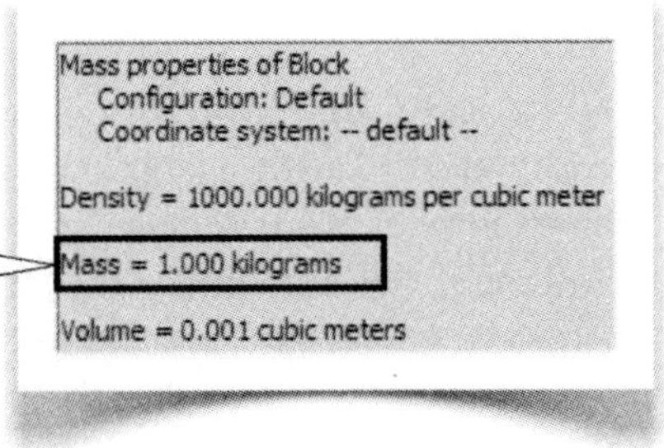
Mass properties of Block
Configuration: Default
Coordinate system: -- default --

Density = 1000.000 kilograms per cubic meter

Mass = 1.000 kilograms

Volume = 0.001 cubic meters

3.1-3 Create a Part: **Ground**

[1] Click **New** to create a new **Part**.

[2] Save the **Part** with the name **Ground**.

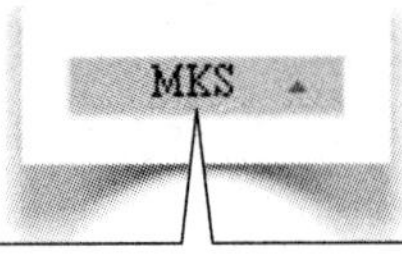

[3] Set up **MKS** unit system with three decimal places for **Length**.

[4] On the **Front** plane, draw a sketch like this.

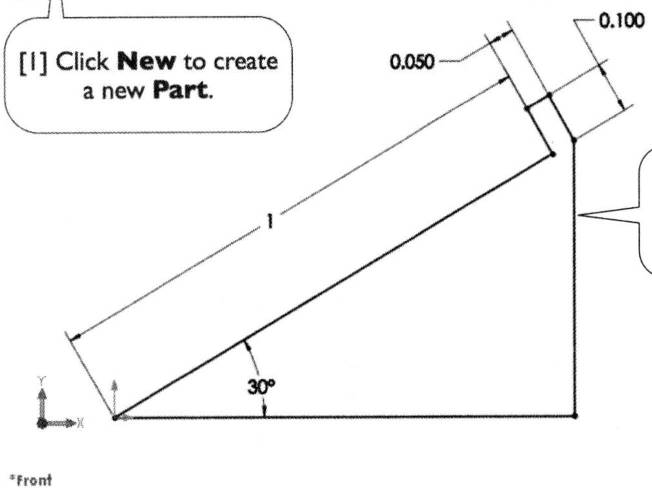

[5] Extrude 0.1 m. #

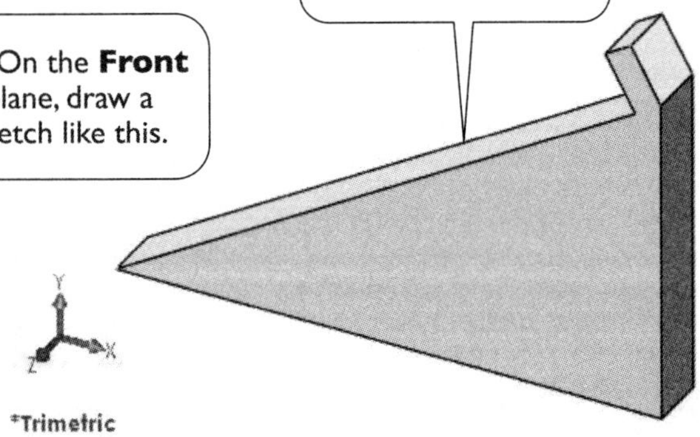

3.1-4 Create an Assembly: **Oscillating-Block**

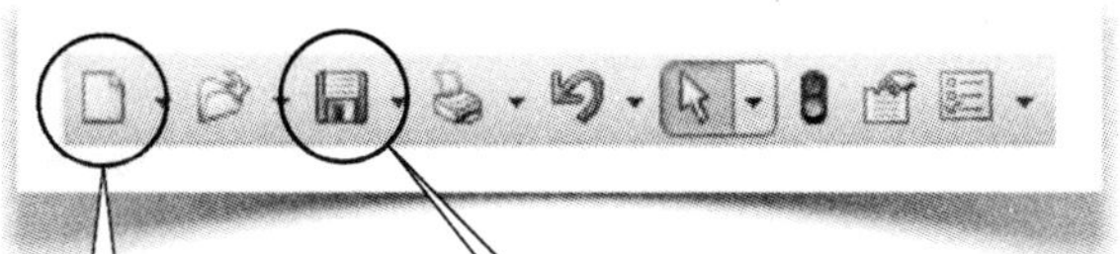

[1] Click **New** and create an **Assembly**.

[5] Save the **Assembly** with the name **Oscillating-Block**.

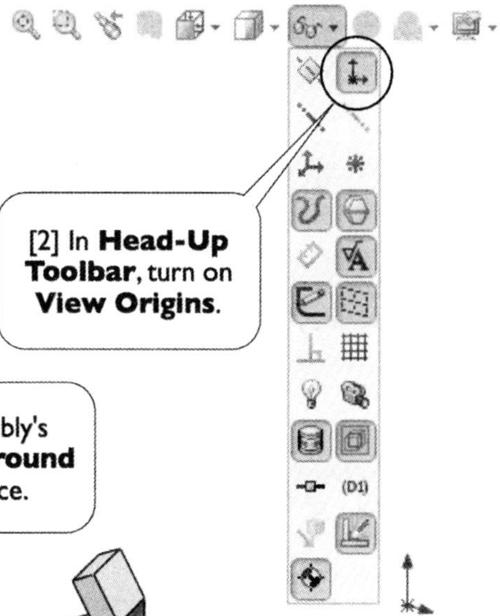

[2] In **Head-Up Toolbar**, turn on **View Origins**.

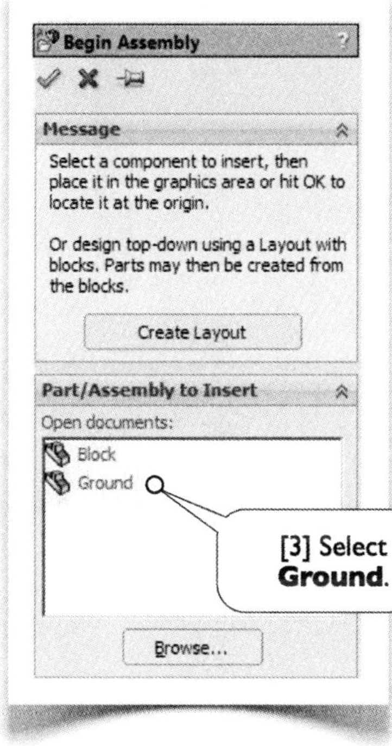

[3] Select **Ground**.

[4] Click the assembly's **Origin**. Now the **Ground** is fixed in the space.

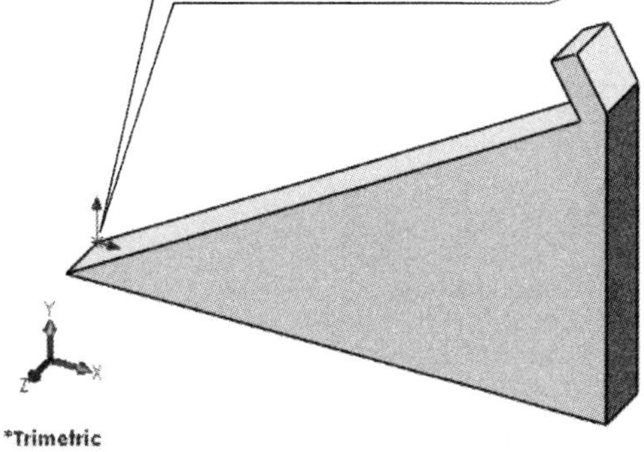

[6] Set up **MKS** unit system with three decimal places for **Length**.

[7] In the **Assembly Toolbar**, click **Insert Components**.

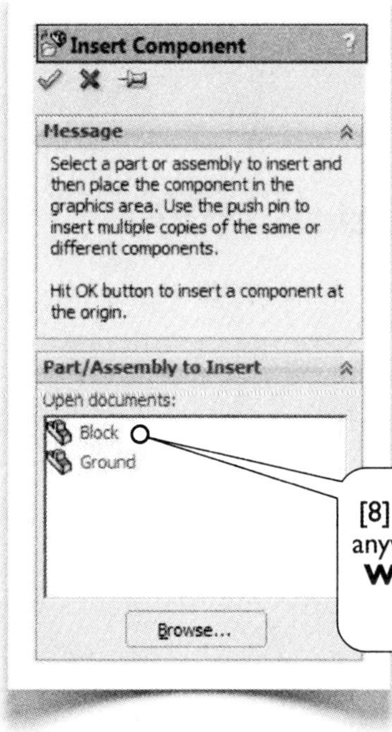

[8] Select **Block** and click anywhere in the **Graphics Window** to temporarily park the part.

[9] In **Assembly Toolbar**, click **Mate**.

[11] And click the frontal face of **Block**. Click **OK**.

[12] Click the sloping face of **Ground**.

[15] And click this vertex of **Block**. Click **OK**. Click **OK** again to dismiss the **Property Box**. Turn off **View Origin**.

[13] And click the bottom face of **Block**. You may need to rotate the view. Click **OK**.

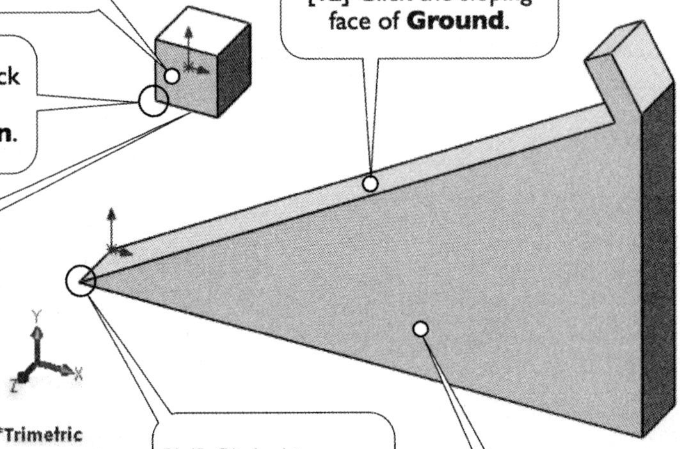

[14] Click this vertex of **Ground**.

[10] Click the frontal face of **Ground**.

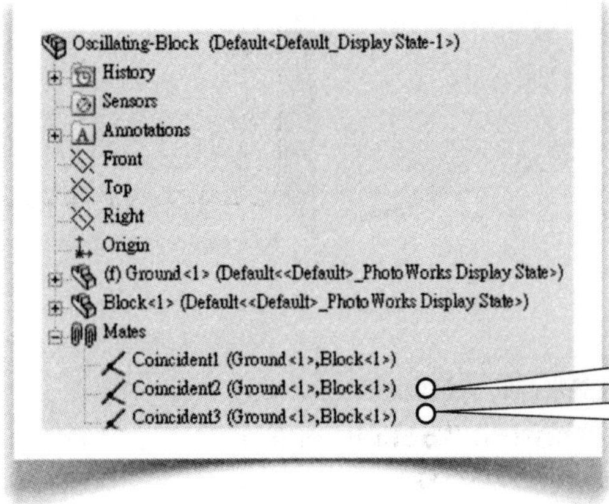

[16] We'll set up **Friction** for **Coincident2** in 3.1-8, page 64.

[17] We'll suppress **Coincident3** before running the simulation (3.1-9[1], page 65). #

3.1-5 Create a **Motion Study**

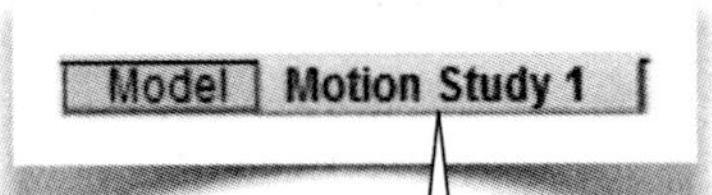

[1] Click **Motion Study 1** tab.

[2] Select **Motion Analysis**. #

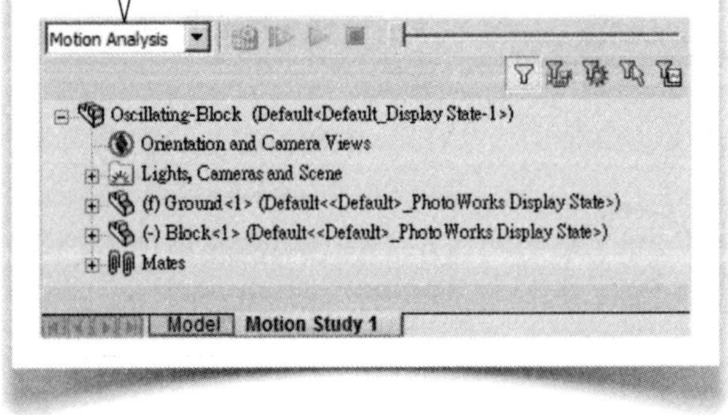

3.1-6 Set Up **Spring**

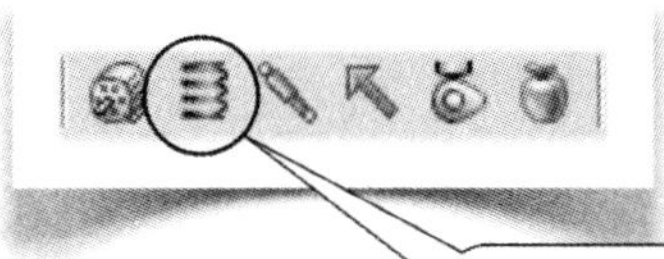

[1] In **Motion Toolbar**, click **Spring**.

[2] Click this face of **Block**.

[3] Click this face of **Ground**. You may need to rotate the view.

[4] Type 100 (N/m) for **Spring Constant**.

[5] Type 0.6 (m) for **Free Length**.

[6] Set up **Display** like this. These parameters have no effects on mechanical behavior.

[7] Click **OK**. #

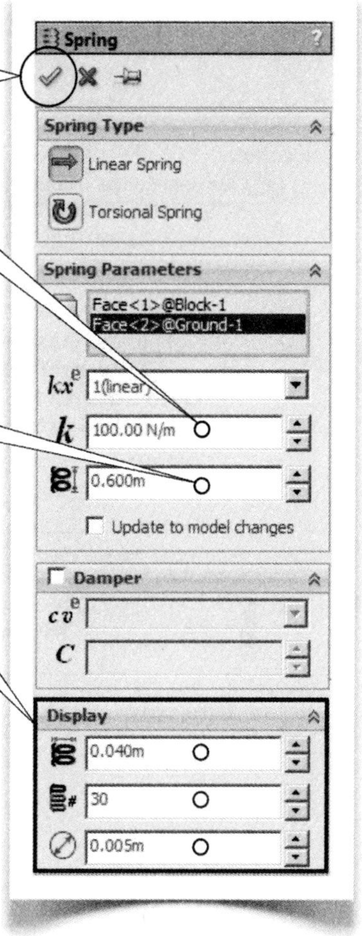

3.1-7 Set Up **Gravity**

[1] In **Motion Toolbar**, click **Gravity**.

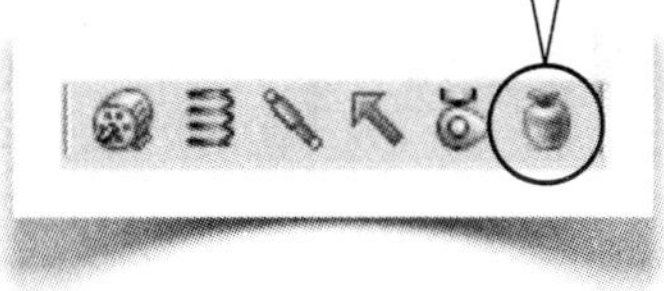

[4] Click **OK**. #

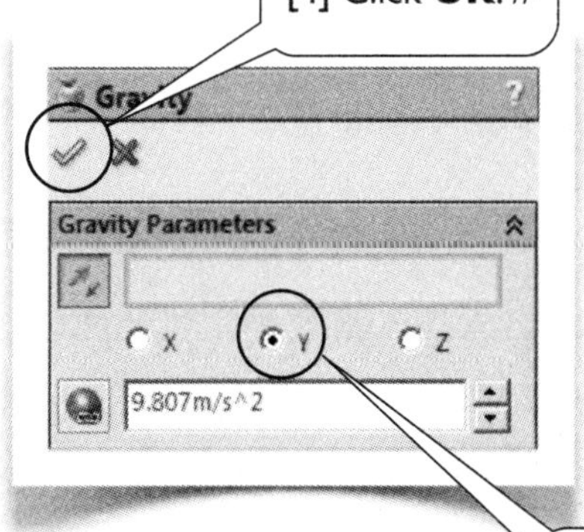

[2] Click **Y**.

[3] The direction of the **Gravity**.

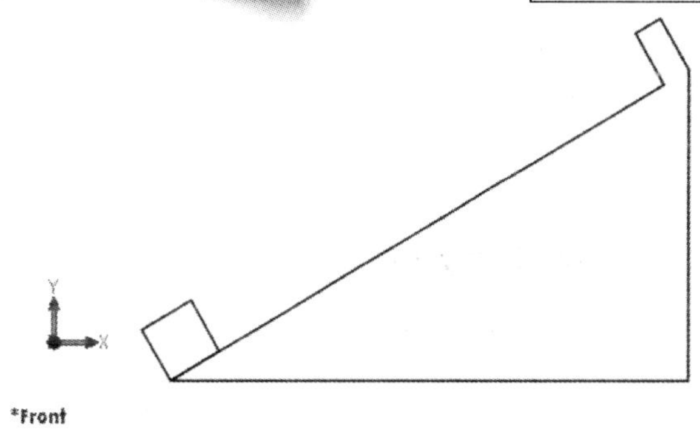

3.1-8 Set Up **Friction**

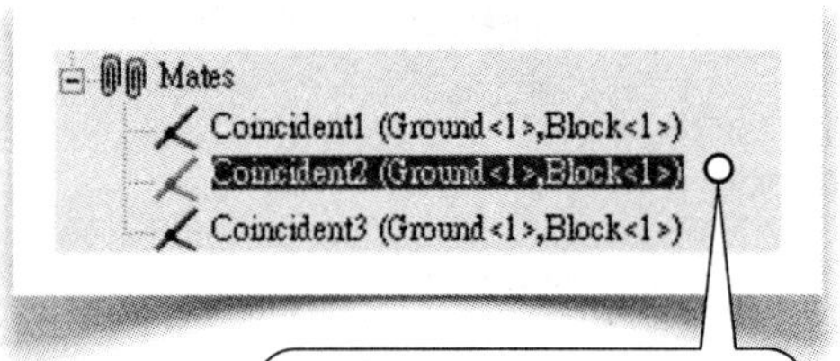

[1] In the **Assembly Tree**, right-click **Coincident2** and select **Edit Feature**.

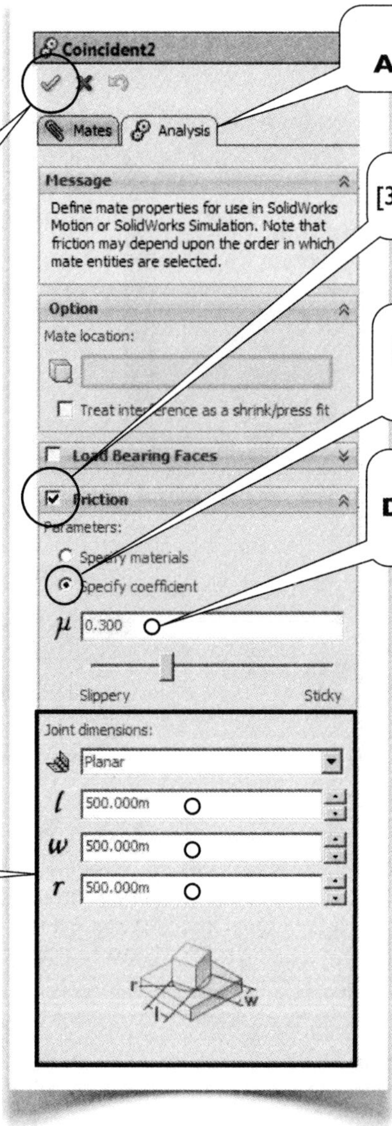

[2] Click **Analysis** tab.

[3] Click **Friction**.

[4] Click **Specify coefficient**.

[5] Type 0.3 for **Dynamic Friction Coefficient**.

[6] **SolidWorks Motion** uses a friction model for **Mates** that includes **Joint dimensions** effects. To disable the **Joint dimensions** effects, simply input large dimensions. Here, we type 500 (m) for all the three dimensions.

[7] Click **OK**. Click **OK** again to dismiss the **Property Box**. #

3.1-9 Calculate and Animate **Results**

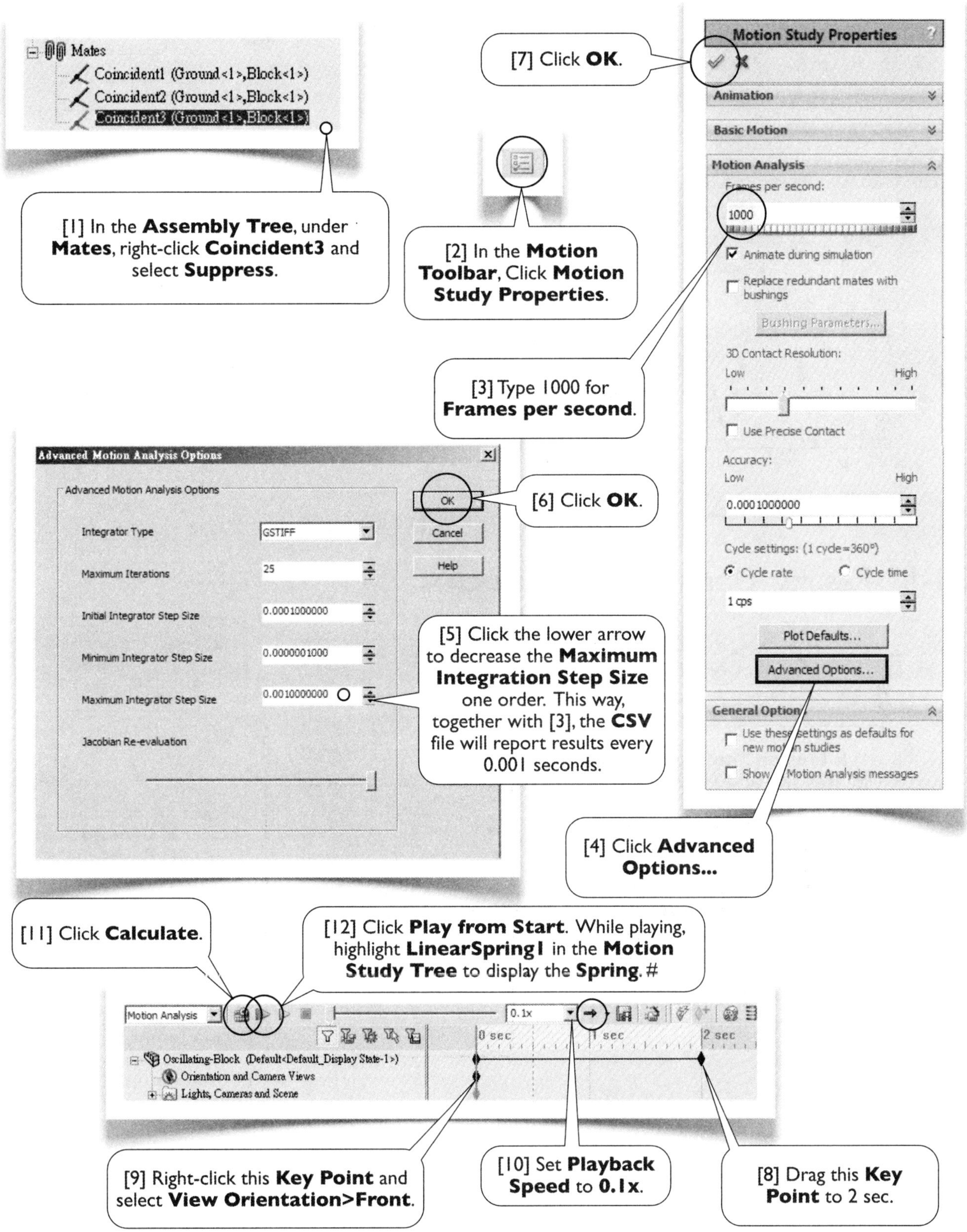

3.1-10 Results: Velocity of **Block**

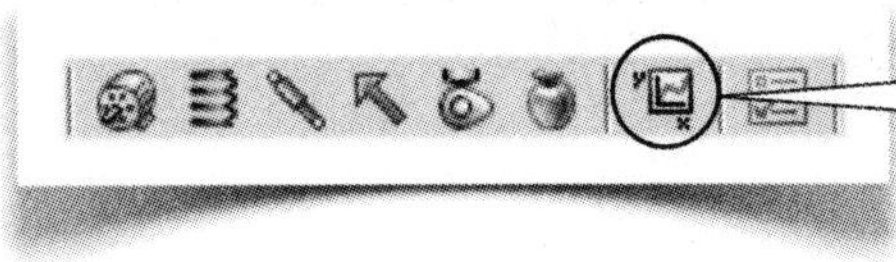

[1] In **Motion Toolbar**, click **Results and Plots**.

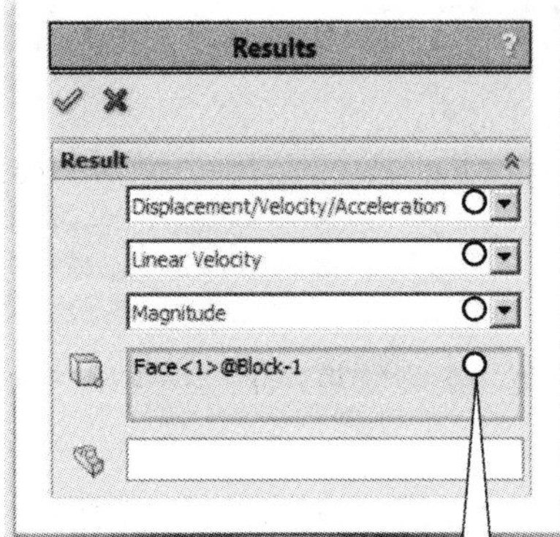

[2] Click the **Block**.

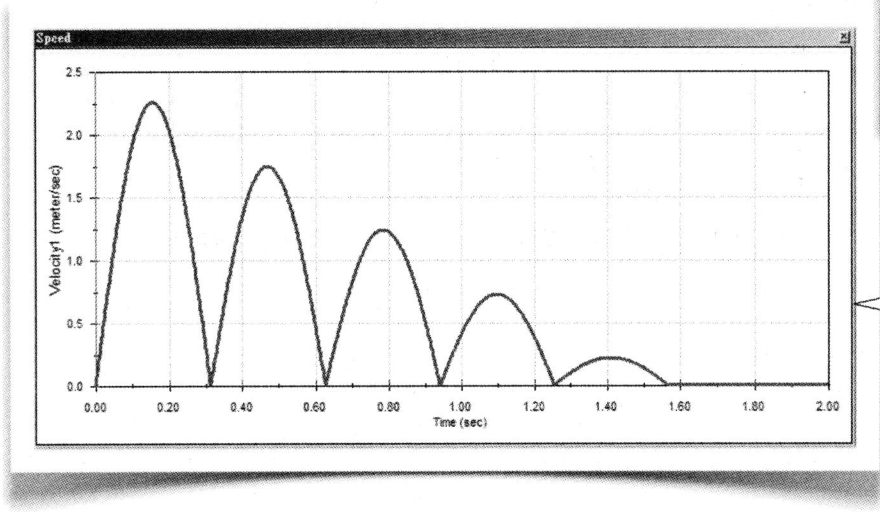

[3] Rename the plot as **Speed**. Export the file as **Speed.CSV**. #

3.1-11 Results: Displacement of **Block**

[1] In **Motion Toolbar**, click **Results and Plots**.

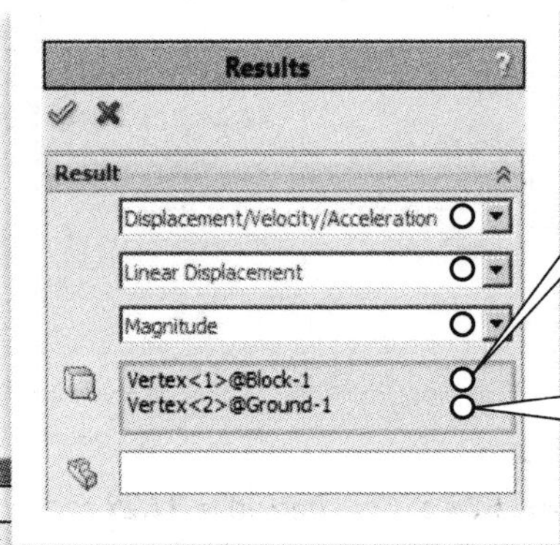

[2] Select the front-lower-left corner of **Block** (see 3.1-4[15], page 62).

[3] Select the front-lower-left corner of **Ground** (see 3.1-4[14], page 62).

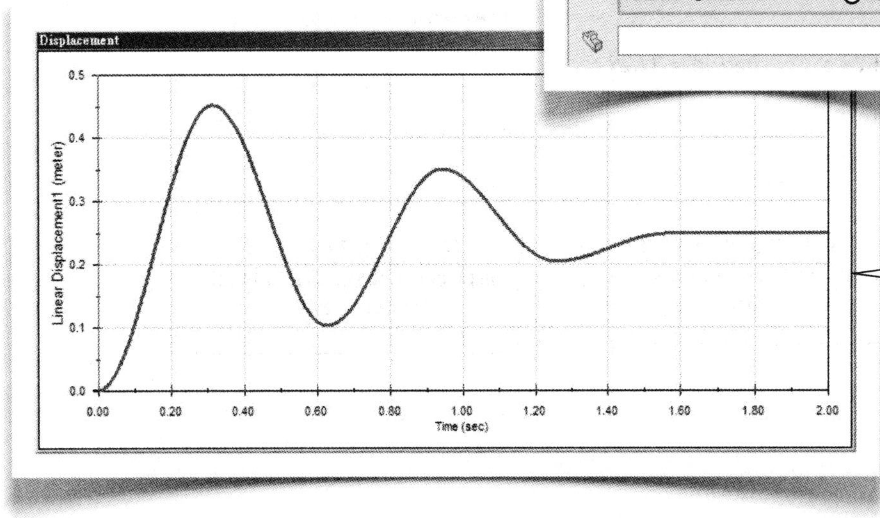

[4] Rename the plot as **Displacement**. Export the file as **Displacement.CSV**. #

3.1-12 Results: Period of the Oscillation

[1] The angular frequency of an **undamped free vibration** can be calculated

$$\omega = \sqrt{\frac{k}{m}} = \sqrt{\frac{100 \text{ N/m}}{1 \text{ kg}}} = 10 \text{ rad/s}$$

In terms of Hertz (cycle/s), the frequency is

$$f = \frac{\omega}{2\pi} = \frac{10 \text{ rad/s}}{2\pi \text{ rad}} = 1.59155 \text{ cycle/s (Hz)}$$

The period is then

$$p = \frac{1}{f} = \frac{1}{1.592 \text{ cycle/s}} = 0.62832 \text{ s/cycle} \qquad (1)$$

The period in our case [2-4] is close to the value calculated in Eq. (1), although our case is a **damped free vibration** case (due to the friction).

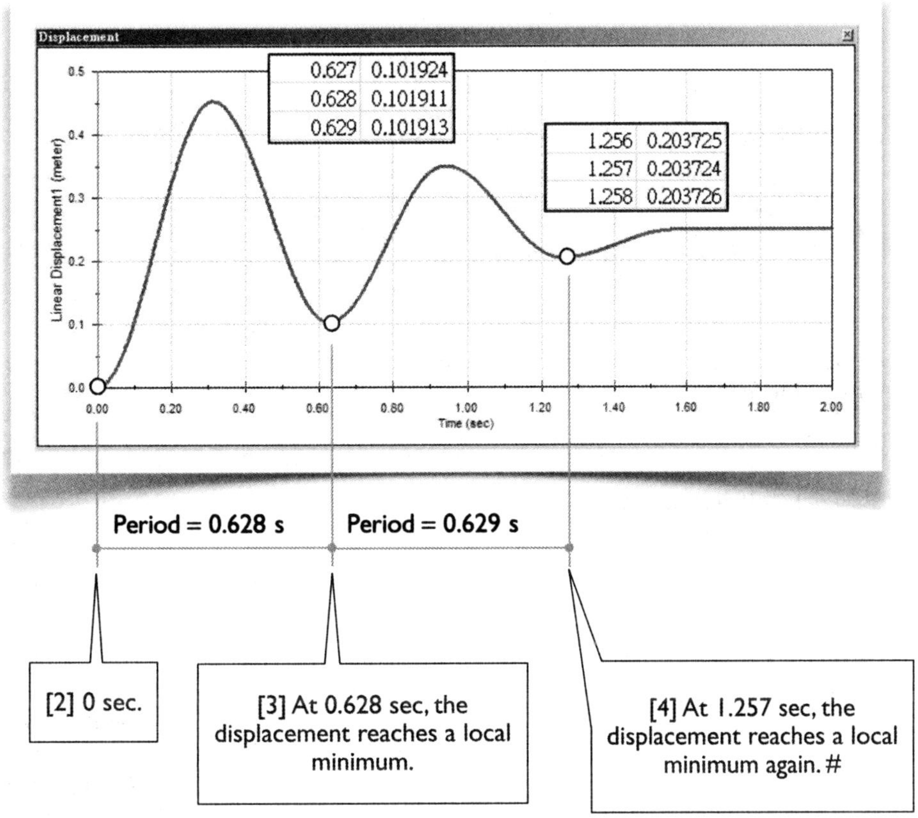

3.1-13 Conservation of Energy

[1] Here, we illustrate Eq. 3.1-1(2) (page 59) at some selected time points [2-12], when the speed of the **Block** either reaches a maximum or approaches zero. These time points are obtained by looking up **Speed.CSV**. The results [13-20] shows that the total energy (including the dissipated energy due to friction) is conserved at these time point. In fact, the total energy is conserved at any time, not just these selected time points. We select these points simply because the calculation of travel distance is easier.

[3] 0.157 sec. [5] 0.471 sec. [7] 0.785 sec. [9] 1.099 sec.

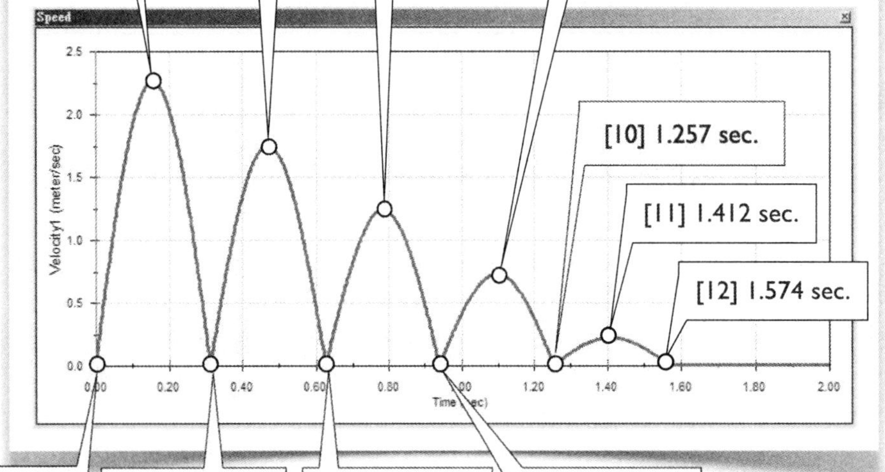

[10] 1.257 sec.

[11] 1.412 sec.

[12] 1.574 sec.

[2] 0 sec. [4] 0.314 sec. [6] 0.628 sec. [8] 0.943 sec.

[18] $V_g = mgD(\sin 30^\circ) = (1)(9.80655)D(\sin 30^\circ)$.

[13] The speed is copied from **Speed.CSV**.

[15] This is the accumulative travel distance. For example, at $t = 0.471$ s, $0.450969 + |0.276684 - 0.450969| = 0.625254$.

[19] $V_e = k(0.3 - D)^2/2$
$= (100)(0.3 - D)^2/2$.

Time t (s)	Speed v (m/s)	Displacement D (m)	Travel Distance S (m)	Work Done by Friction $U_{0\to t}$ (J)	Kinetic Energy T (J)	Gravitational Potential Energy V_g (J)	Elastic Potential Energy V_e (J)	Total Energy (J)
0	0	0	0	0	0	0	4.500000	4.500
0.157	2.254733	0.225364	0.225364	-0.574193	2.541910	1.105035	0.278523	4.500
0.314	0.003991	0.450969	0.450969	-1.148998	0.000008	2.211248	1.139585	4.500
0.471	1.745399	0.276684	0.625254	-1.593049	1.523209	1.356672	0.027181	4.500
0.628	0.004531	0.101911	0.800028	-2.038344	0.000010	0.499701	1.961968	4.500
0.785	1.235857	0.225249	0.923365	-2.352590	0.763671	1.104467	0.279388	4.500
0.943	0.004576	0.349091	1.047208	-2.668121	0.000010	1.711708	0.120498	4.500
1.099	0.726886	0.276546	1.119753	-2.852955	0.264182	1.355996	0.027504	4.501
1.257	0.001163	0.203724	1.192576	-3.038495	0.000001	0.998923	0.463457	4.501
1.412	0.219225	0.225678	1.214530	-3.094431	0.024030	1.106572	0.276189	4.501
1.574	0.000127	0.247574	1.236426	-3.150219	0.000000	1.213936	0.137424	4.502

[14] The displacement is copied from **Displacement.CSV**.

[16] $U_{0\to t} = (\mu mg\cos 30^\circ)S$
$= 0.3(1)(9.80665)(\cos 30^\circ)S$.

[17] $T = mv^2/2$
$= (1)v^2/2$.

[20] Total energy $= T + V_g + V_e - U_{0\to t}$. #

3.1-14 Principle of Minimum Potential Energy

[1] The 2nd, 3rd, and 4th columns of this table are copied from 3.1-13[14, 18, 19], last page.

[2] Total potential energy $V = V_g + V_e$.

Time t (s)	Displacement D (m)	Gravitational Potential Energy V_g (J)	Elastic Potential Energy V_e (J)	Total Potential Energy $V_g + V_e$ (J)
0	0	0	4.500000	4.5000
0.157	0.225364	1.105035	0.278523	1.3836
0.314	0.450969	2.211248	1.139585	3.3508
0.471	0.276684	1.356672	0.027181	1.3839
0.628	0.101911	0.499701	1.961968	2.4617
0.785	0.225249	1.104467	0.279388	1.3839
0.943	0.349091	1.711708	0.120498	1.8322
1.099	0.276546	1.355996	0.027504	1.3835
1.257	0.203724	0.998923	0.463457	1.4624
1.412	0.225678	1.106572	0.276189	1.3828
1.574	0.247574	1.213936	0.137424	1.3514

[6] Any infinitesimal change of displacement will not change the total potential energy; therefore doing zero work.

[3] This is a plot of the **Total Potential Energy** versus the **Displacement** *D*.

[4] The system (**Block** and **Spring**) stabilizes at a displacement where the **Total Potential Energy** is at its minimum.

[5] The **principle of minimum potential energy** states that, *among all possible configurations, a structural system stabilizes at a configuration in which the total potential energy is at its minimum*. The **Principle of virtual work** is actually another way of saying the principle of minimum potential energy: *when a structural system is in a stable configuration (i.e., the total potential energy is at its minimum), any infinitesimal changes of the configuration will not change the total potential energy; therefore doing zero work* [6].

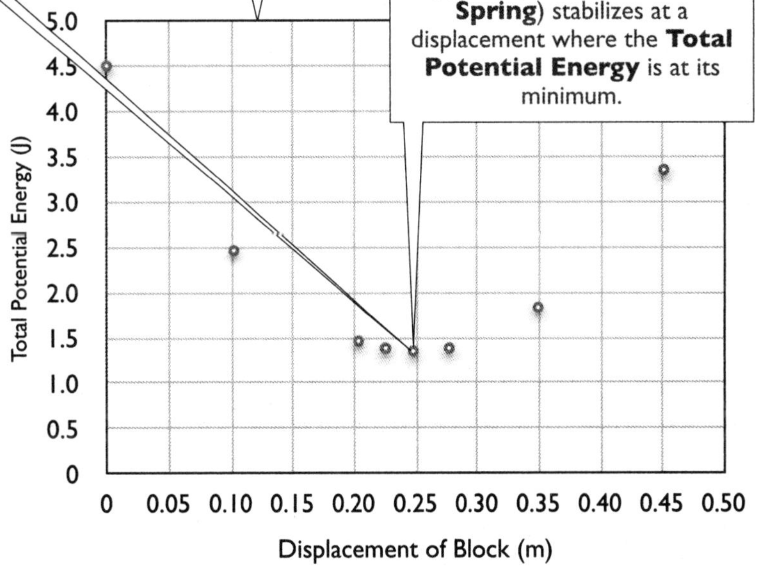

[7] Wrap Up

Save all files and exit **SolidWorks**. #

3.1-15 (Do It Yourself) Conservation of Energy: Block and Wedge

Revisit the **Block and Wedge** (Section 2.1) and investigate the energy at some arbitrarily selected time points. Verify the **conservation of energy**

$$T_0 + V_0 = T_t + V_t \tag{1}$$

where T_0 and V_0 are respectively the initial (t = 0) kinetic energy and potential energy of the system, and T_t and V_t are respectively the kinetic energy and potential energy of the system at time t. The table below demonstrates a possible results.

Time (s)	Block Kinetic Energy T_1 (J)	Wedge Kinetic Energy T_2 (J)	Block Y-Displacement (m)	Block Potential Energy V (J)	Total Energy $T_1 + T_2 + V$ (J)
0	0	0	0	0	0
0.1	0.739152	0.178791	-0.015601	-0.917946	-0.000003
0.2	2.956610	0.715165	-0.062403	-3.671777	-0.000003
0.3	6.652371	1.609122	-0.140406	-8.261496	-0.000003
0.4	11.826438	2.860661	-0.249611	-14.687101	-0.000003

Section 3.2

Principle of Minimum Potential Energy: Sliding Collar on Rod

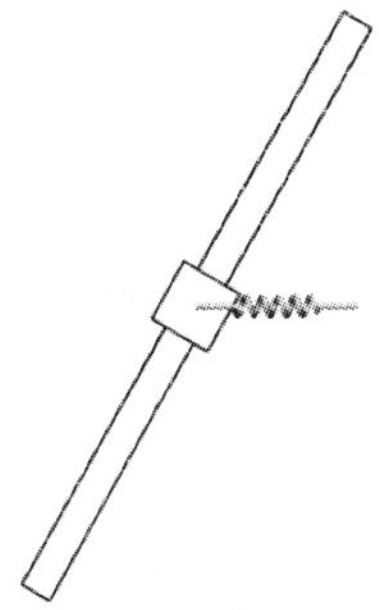

3.2-1 Introduction

[1] The **principle of minimum potential energy** (3.1-14, page 69) plays an important role in Engineering Mechanics. Many of modern finite element analysis programs are formulated based on this principle. The **principle of virtual work** is actually a variant version of the principle of minimum potential energy. It is so important that this section will use another example to reinforce the appreciation of the principle.

Consider a 6-kg **Collar** sliding along a **Rod** which is fixed in the space and forms **60°** with horizon [2]. A **Spring** is connected to the collar at one end and to a fixed point in the space at the other end [3]. The spring has a constant of 400 N/m and a free (unstretched) length of 0.5 m. The **Collar** is released at a position where the **Spring** is horizontal and unstretched [4]. The **Dynamic Friction Coefficient** between the **Collar** and the **Rod** is 0.05. We'll show that the **Collar** will oscillate up-and-down and eventually stabilize at a position where the total potential energy (the sum of gravitational potential energy and elastic potential energy) is at its minimum [5].

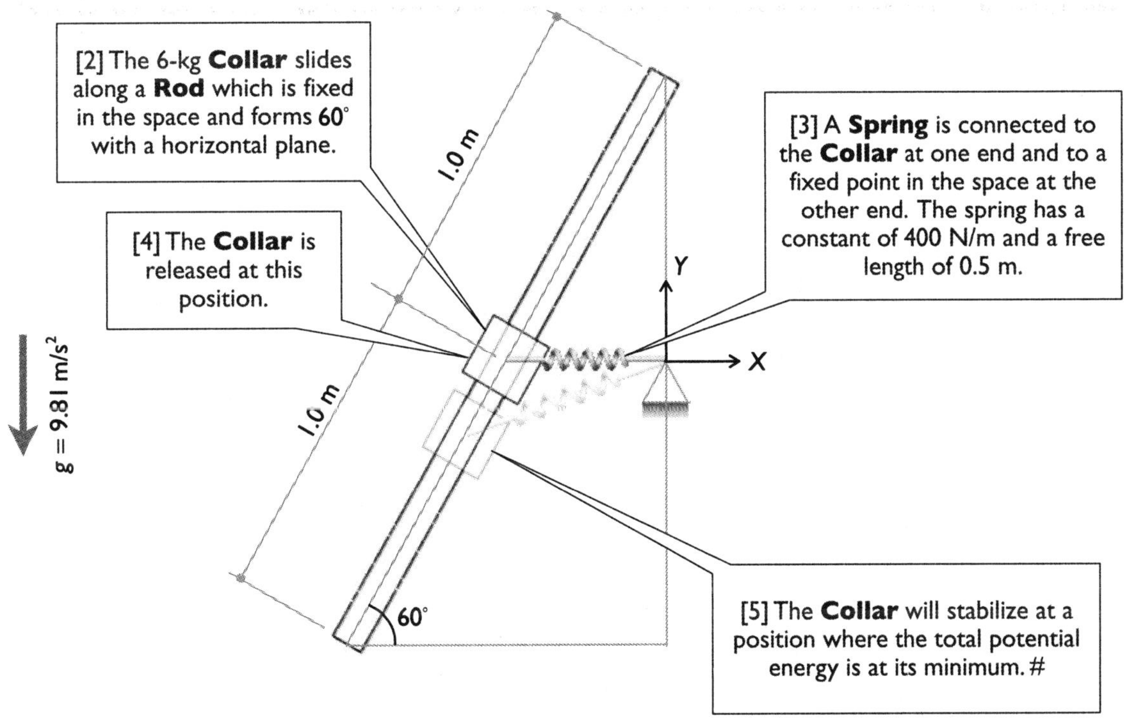

3.2-2 Start Up and Create a Part: **Rod**

[1] Launch **SolidWorks** and click **New** to create a new **Part**.

[2] Save the **Part** with the name **Rod**.

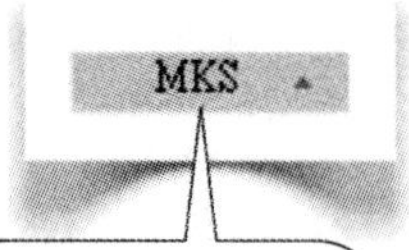

[3] Set up **MKS** unit system with three decimal places.

[4] On the **Front** plane, draw a rectangle (using **Center Rectangle** tool) like this.

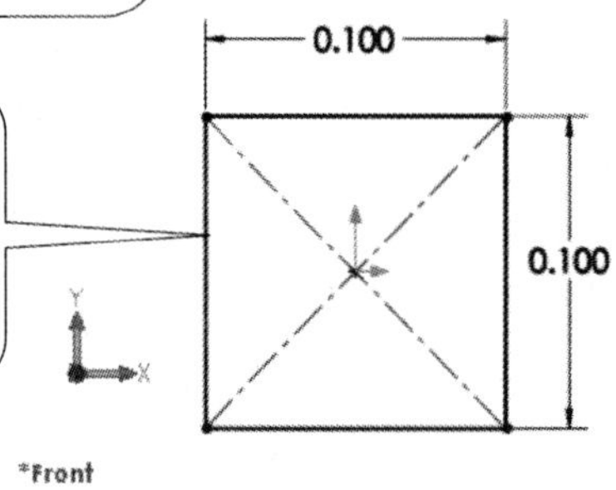

[5] Extrude 2 m. #

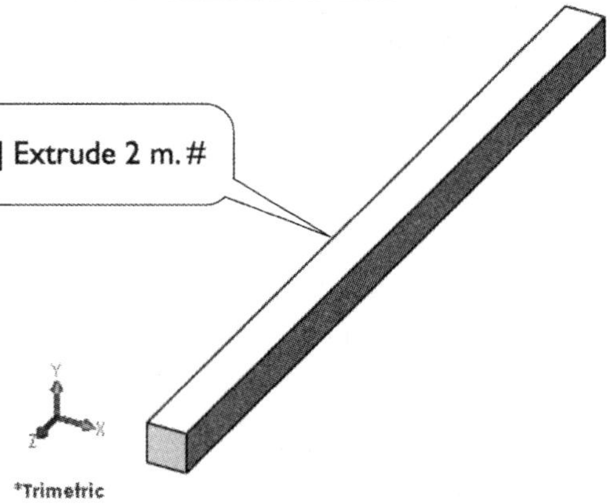

3.2-3 Create a Part: **Collar**

[1] Click **New** to create a new **Part**.

[2] Save the **Part** with the name **Collar**.

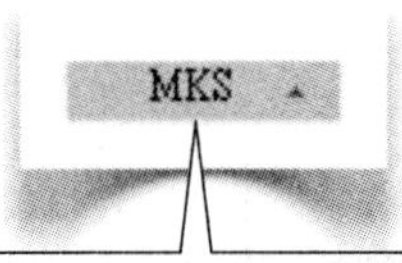

[3] Set up **MKS** unit system with three decimal places.

[4] On the **Front** plane, draw two rectangles (using **Center Rectangle** tool) like this.

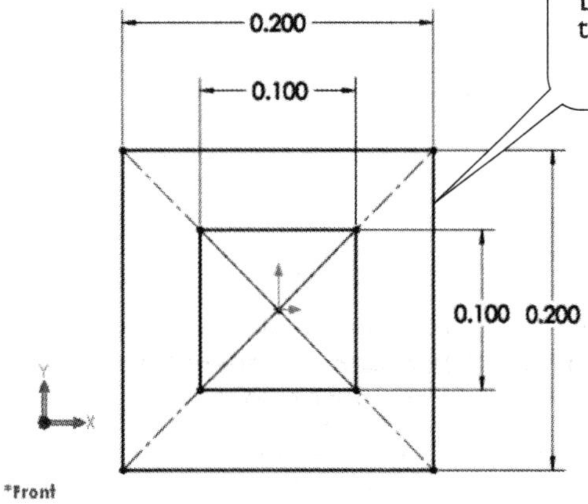

[5] Extrude 0.2 m, using **Mid Plane** option (5.1-2[5], page 101).

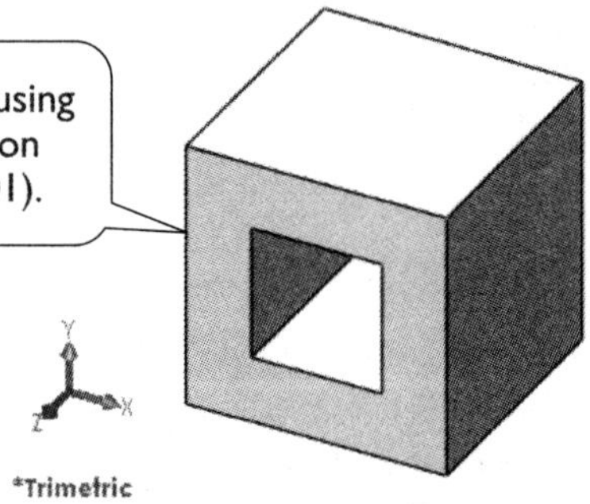

[6] In the **Evaluate Toolbar**, click **Mass Properties** and make sure the mass of the **Collar** is 6.000 kg. #

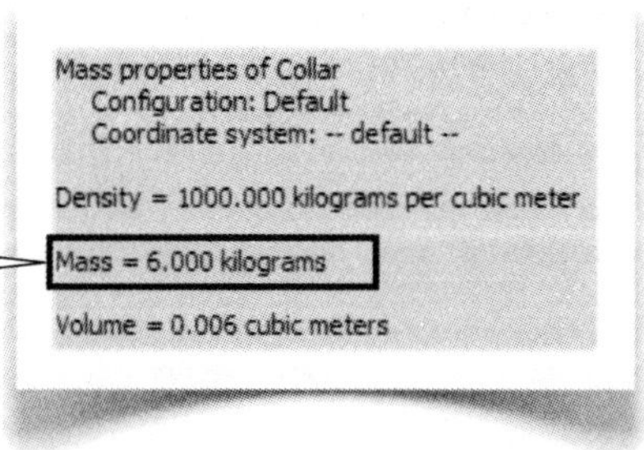
Mass properties of Collar
Configuration: Default
Coordinate system: -- default --

Density = 1000.000 kilograms per cubic meter

Mass = 6.000 kilograms

Volume = 0.006 cubic meters

3.2-4 Create an Assembly: **Collar-On-Rod**

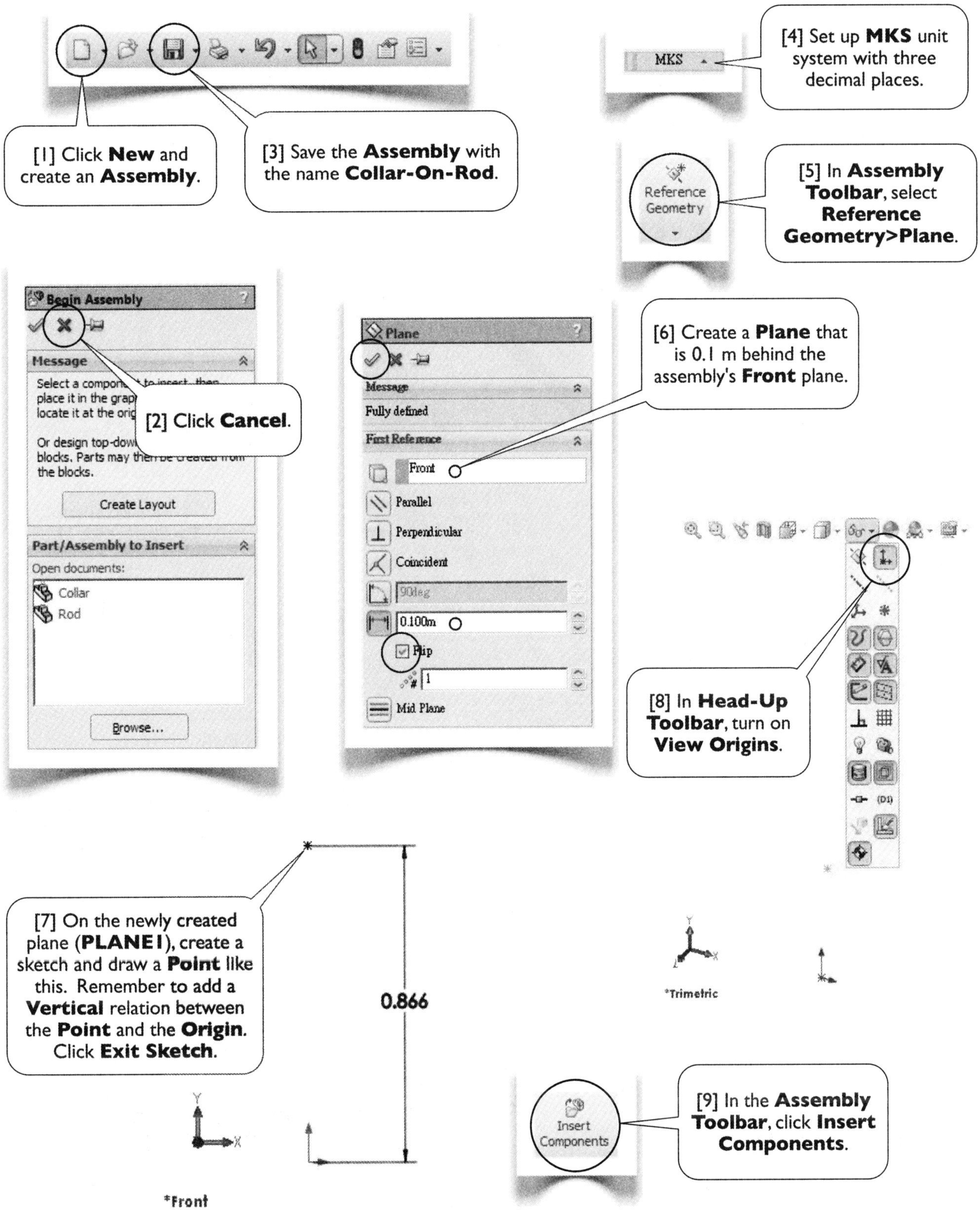

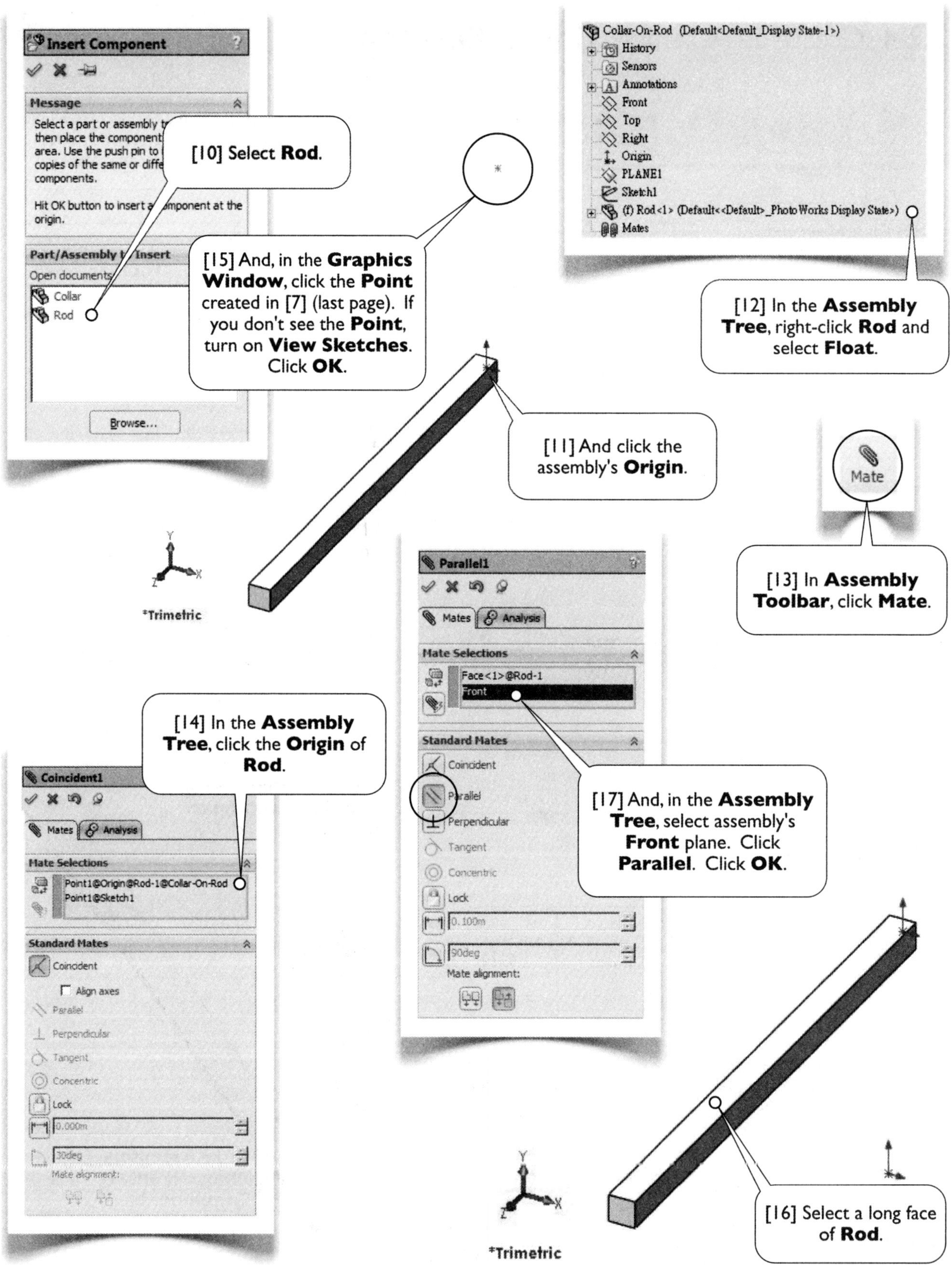
Insert Component
Message
Select a part or assembly
Hit OK button to insert a component at the origin.
Part/Assembly to Insert
Open documents
Collar
Rod
Browse...
[10] Select **Rod**.
[11] And click the assembly's **Origin**.
*Trimetric
Collar-On-Rod (Default<Default_Display State-1>)
History
Sensors
Annotations
Front
Top
Right
Origin
PLANE1
Sketch1
(f) Rod<1> (Default<<Default>_PhotoWorks Display State>)
Mates
[12] In the **Assembly Tree**, right-click **Rod** and select **Float**.
Mate
[13] In **Assembly Toolbar**, click **Mate**.
[14] In the **Assembly Tree**, click the **Origin** of **Rod**.
Coincident1
Mates
Analysis
Mate Selections
Point1@Origin@Rod-1@Collar-On-Rod
Point1@Sketch1
Standard Mates
Coincident
Align axes
Parallel
Perpendicular
Tangent
Concentric
Lock
0.000m
30deg
Mate alignment:
[15] And, in the **Graphics Window**, click the **Point** created in [7] (last page). If you don't see the **Point**, turn on **View Sketches**. Click **OK**.
Parallel1
Mates
Analysis
Mate Selections
Face<1>@Rod-1
Front
Standard Mates
Coincident
Parallel
Perpendicular
Tangent
Concentric
Lock
0.100m
90deg
Mate alignment:
[16] Select a long face of **Rod**.
[17] And, in the **Assembly Tree**, select assembly's **Front** plane. Click **Parallel**. Click **OK**.
*Trimetric

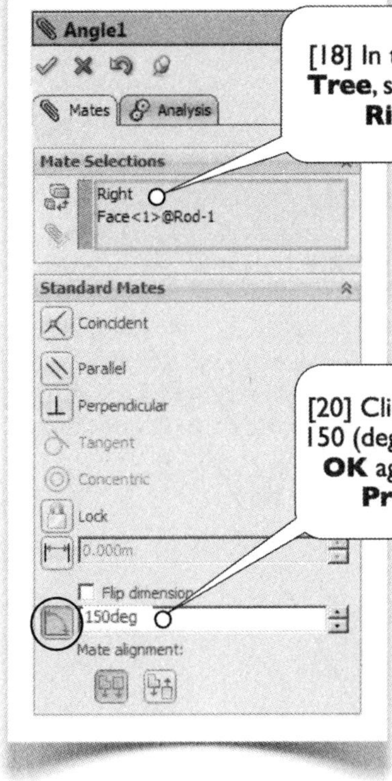

[18] In the **Assembly Tree**, select assembly's **Right** plane.

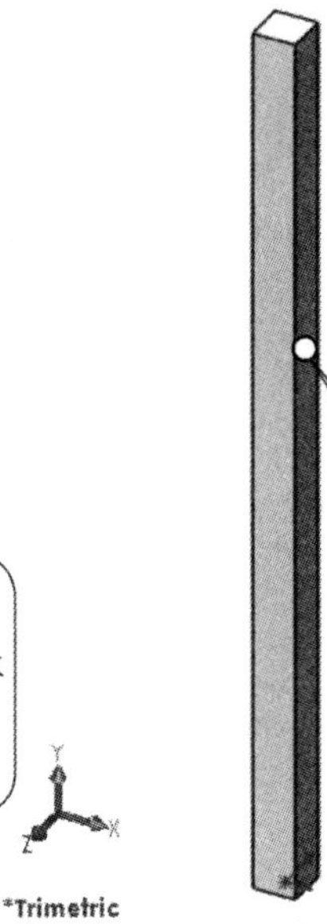

[19] Select this long face of **Rod**.

[20] Click **Angle** and type 150 (deg). Click **OK**. Click **OK** again to dismiss the **Property Box**.

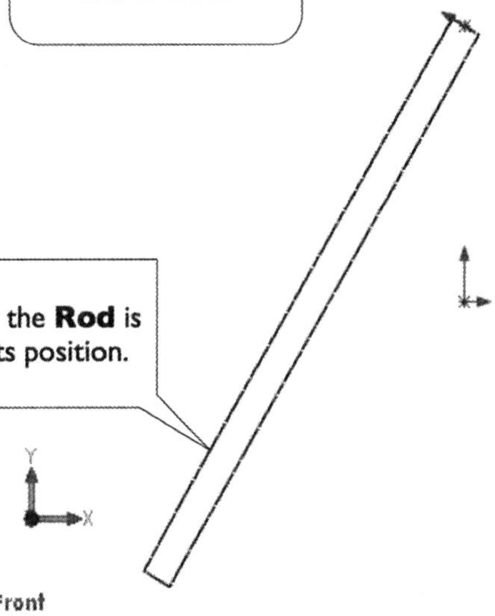

[21] Now the **Rod** is fixed in its position.

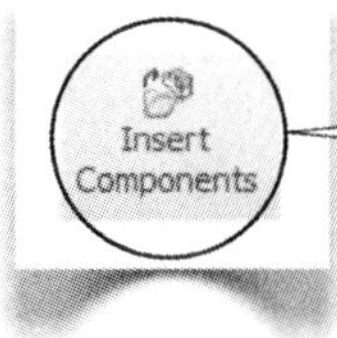

[22] In the **Assembly Toolbar**, click **Insert Components**.

[23] Select **Collar** and click anywhere in the **Graphics Window** to temporarily park the part.

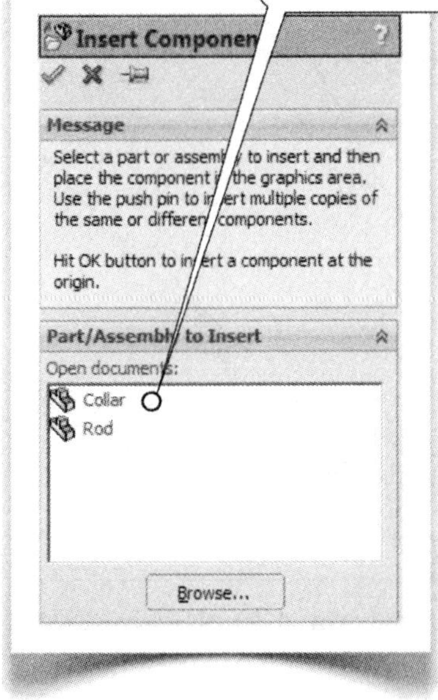

[24] In **Assembly Toolbar**, click **Mate**.

[25] Click the inner-upper face of the **Collar**. You may need to rotate the view.

[26] And click the upper long face of the **Rod**. You may need to rotate the view. Click **OK**.

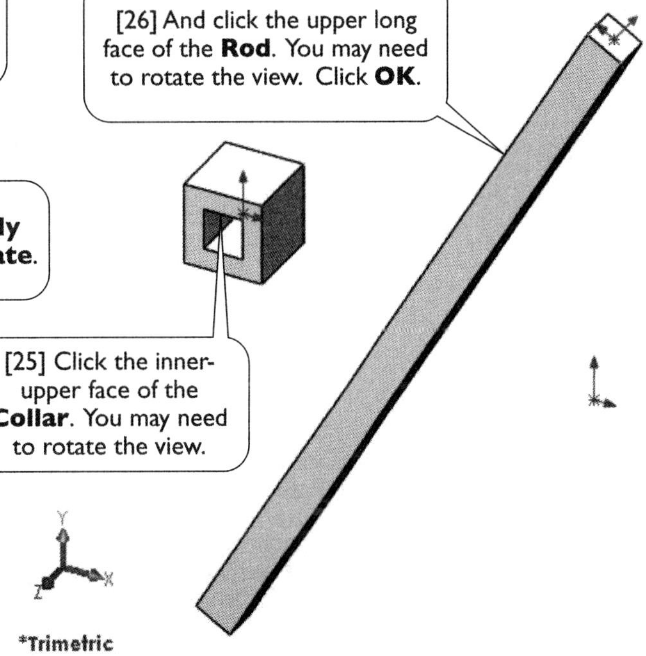

[27] Drag the **Collar** to a more convenient position and click this face of the **Collar**. You may need to rotate the view.

[28] And click this face of the **Rod**. Click **OK**.

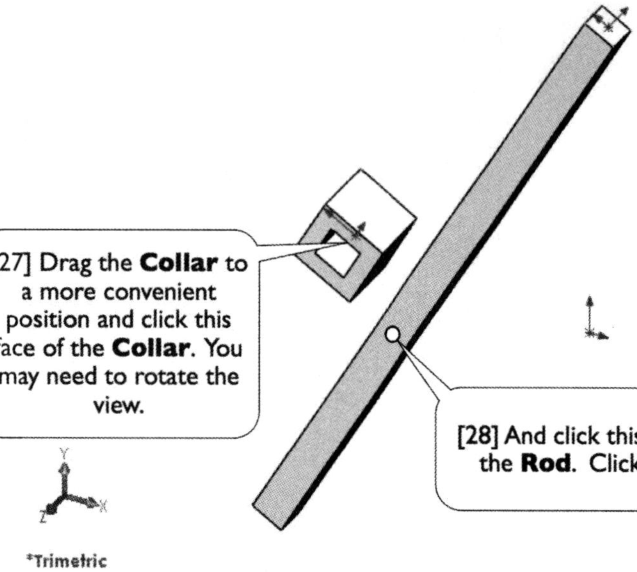

[29] Click the **Origin** of the **Collar**.

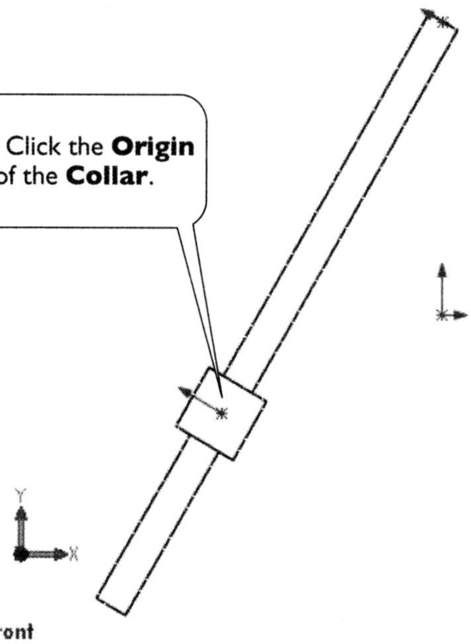

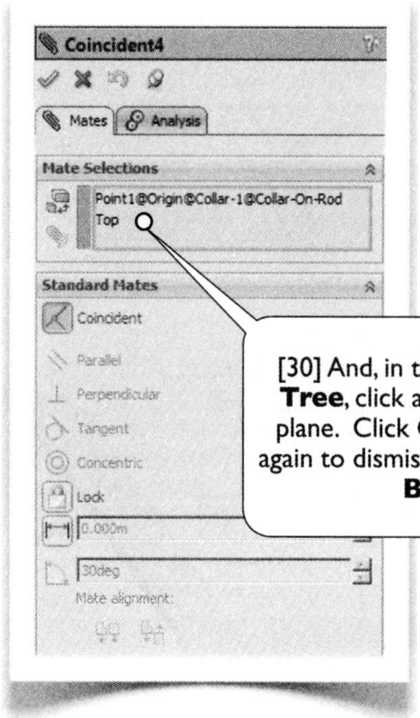

[30] And, in the **Assembly Tree**, click assembly's **Top** plane. Click **OK**. Click **OK** again to dismiss the **Property Box**.

[31] Now the **Collar** is in its initial position.

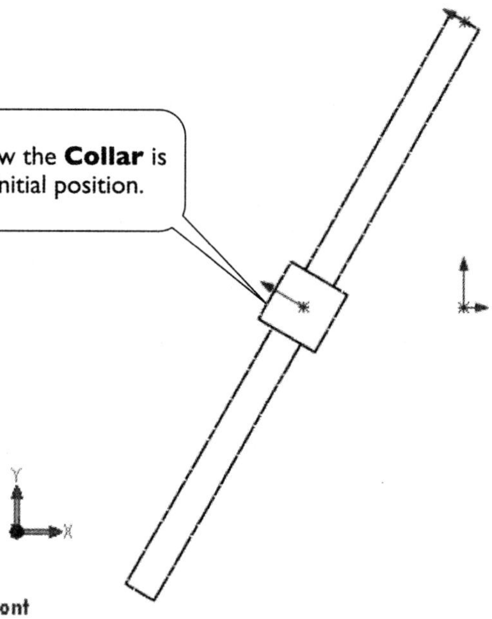

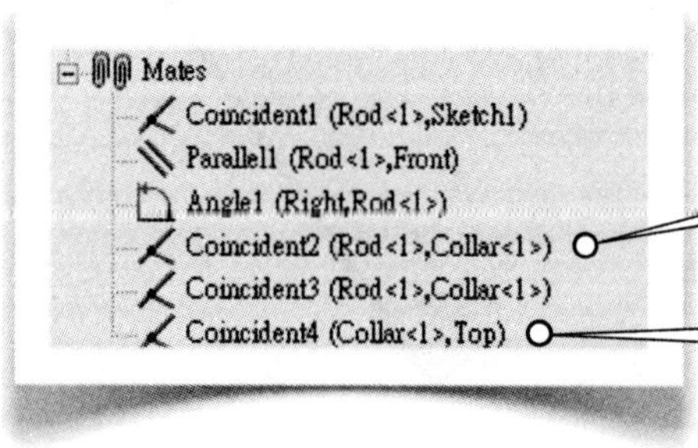

[32] We'll specify **Friction** for this **Mate**, which is created in [25, 26], last page.

[33] We'll suppress this **Mate**, which is created in [29, 30], before running the simulation. #

3.2-5 Create a **Motion Study**

3.2-6 Set Up **Spring**

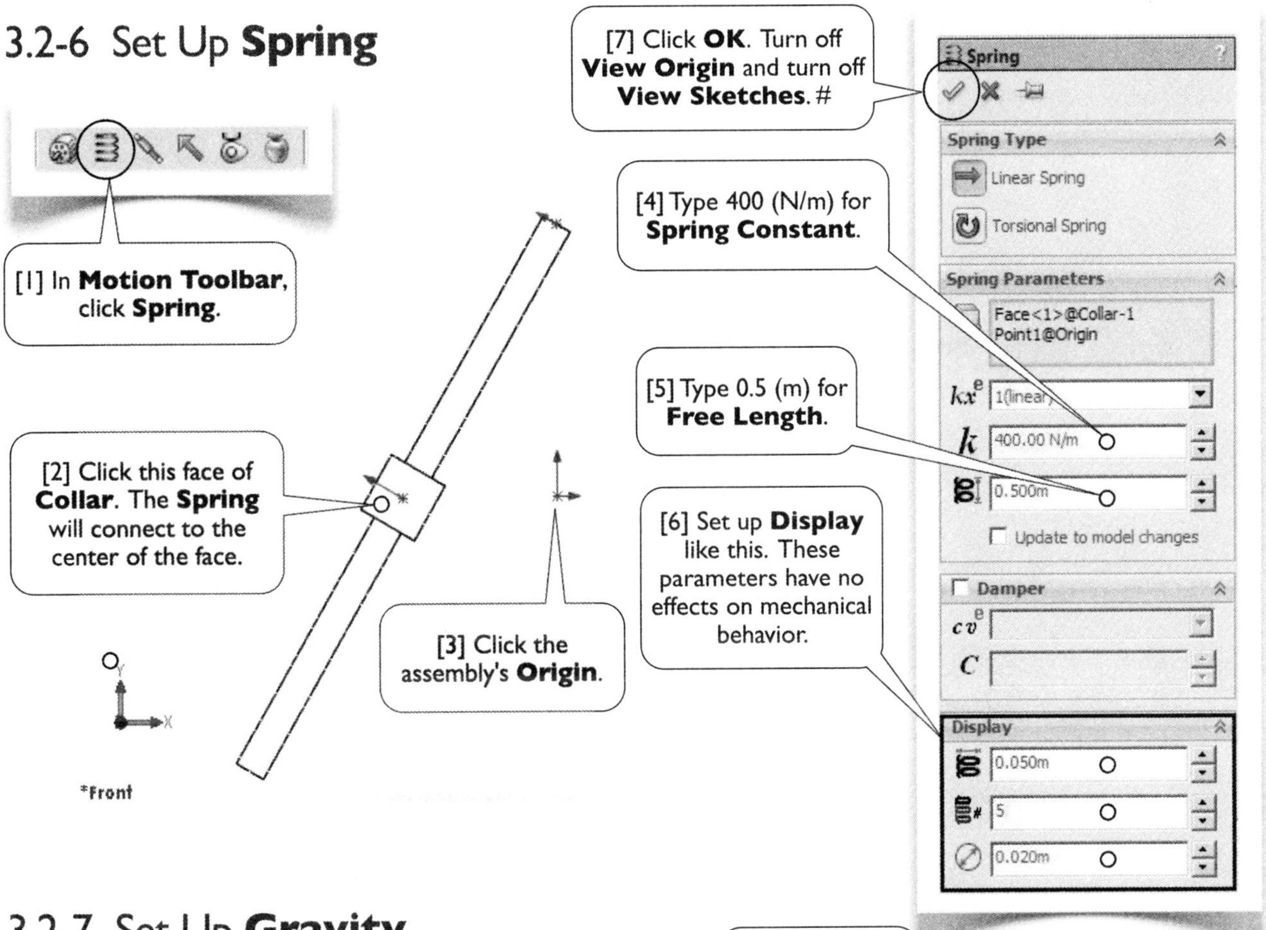

3.2-7 Set Up **Gravity**

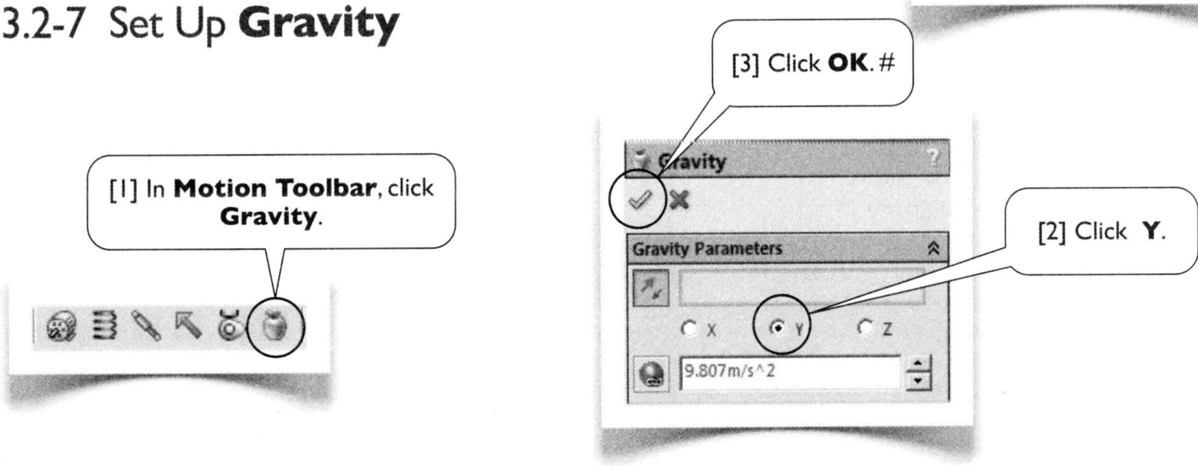

3.2-8 Set Up **Friction**

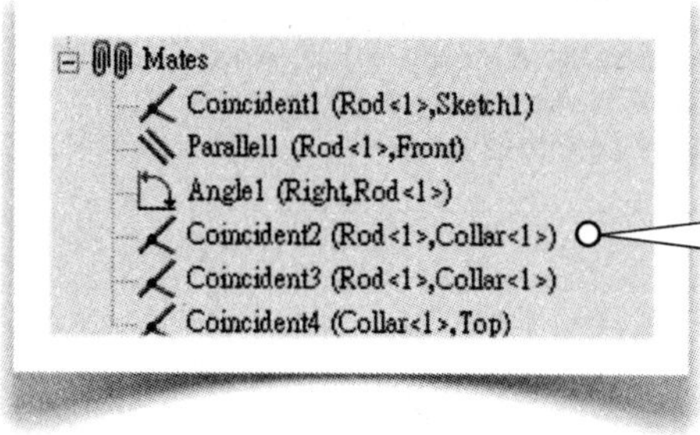

[1] In **Assembly Tree**, under **Mates**, right-click **Coincident2** and select **Edit Feature**.

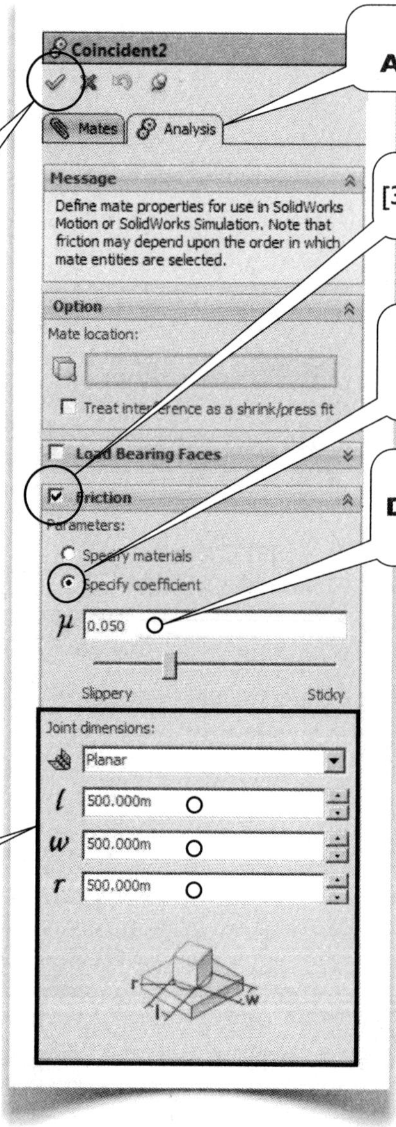

[2] Click **Analysis** tab.

[3] Click **Friction**.

[4] Click **Specify coefficient**.

[5] Type 0.05 for **Dynamic Friction Coefficient**.

[6] Type 500 (m) for all the three dimensions. This is to disable the **Joint dimensions** effects (3.1-8[6], page 64).

[7] Click **OK**. Click **OK** again to dismiss the **Property Box**. #

3.2-9 Calculate and Animate **Results**

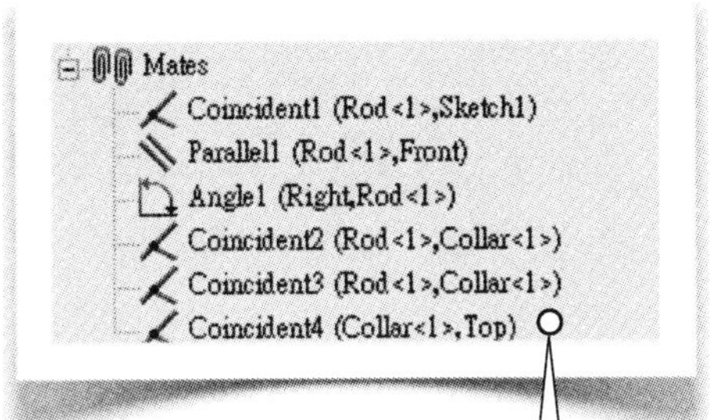

[1] In the **Assembly Tree**, under **Mates**, select **Coincident4** and right-click-select **Suppress**.

[2] In the **Motion Toolbar**, Click **Motion Study Properties**.

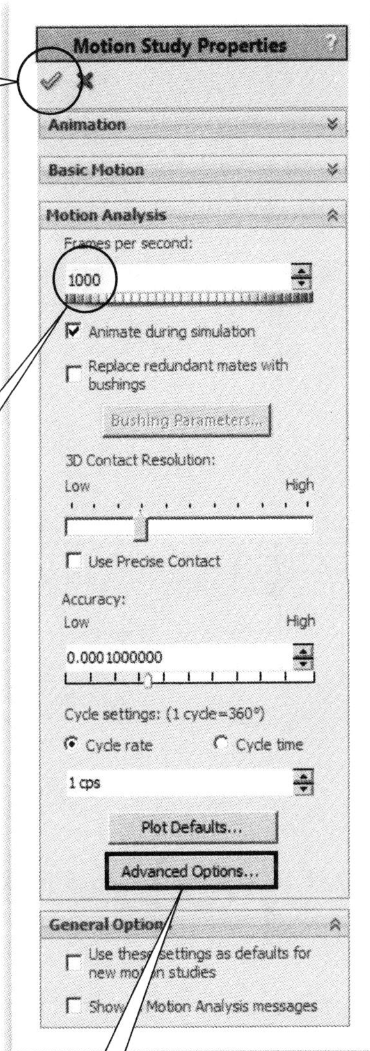

[3] Type 1000 for **Frames per second**.

[4] Click **Advanced Options...**

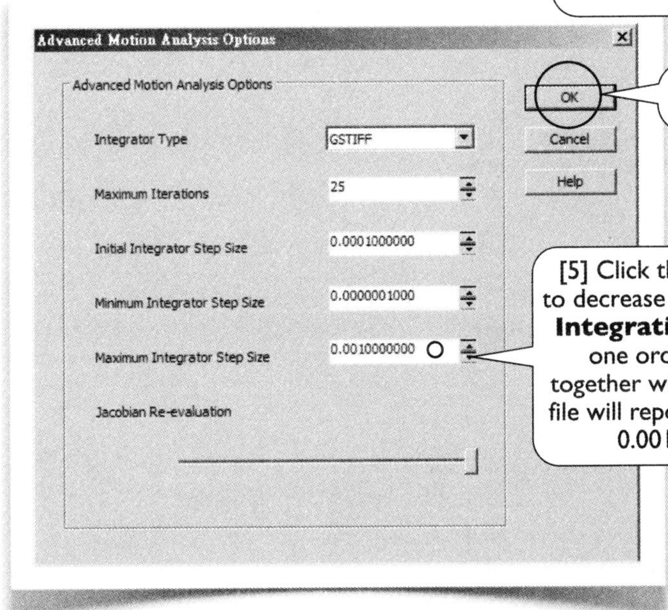

[5] Click the lower arrow to decrease the **Maximum Integration Step Size** one order. This way, together with [3], the **CSV** file will report results every 0.001 seconds.

[6] Click **OK**.

[7] Click **OK**.

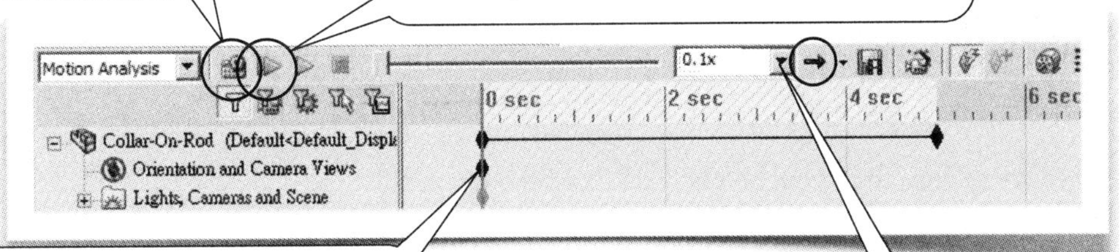

[8] Right-click this **Key Point** and select **View Orientation>Front**.

[9] Set **Playback Speed** to **0.1x**.

[10] Click **Calculate**.

[11] Click **Play from Start**. While playing, highlight **LinearSpring1** in the **Motion Study Tree** to display the **Spring**. #

3.2-10 Results: Collar Elevation

[1] In **Motion Toolbar**, click **Results and Plots**.

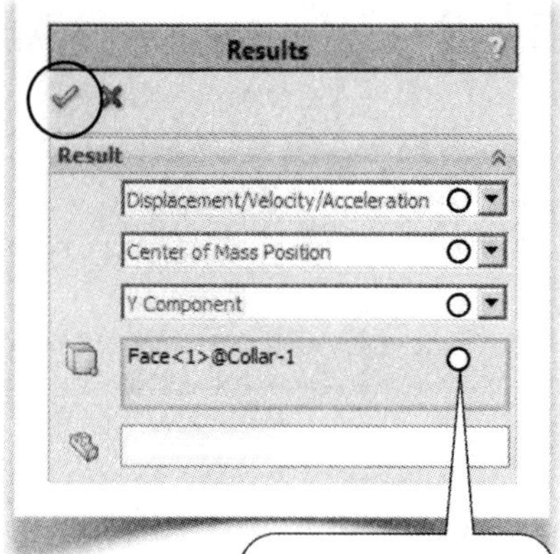

[2] Click the **Collar**.

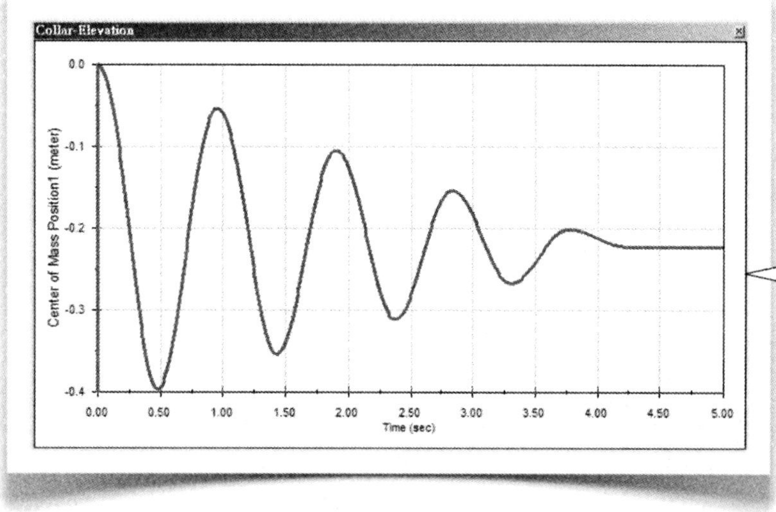

[3] Rename the plot as **Collar-Elevation**. Export the file as **Collar-Elevation.CSV**. #

3.2-11 Principle of Minimum Potential Energy

[1] Knowing the elevation y (a negative value), the gravitational potential relative to the initial position is calculate by

$$V_g = mgy = (6\ \text{kg})(9.80655\ \text{m/s}^2)y \qquad (1)$$

The elastic potential energy is calculate by (see [2])

$$V_s = k(\Delta L)^2/2$$

$$= (400\ \text{N/m})\left[\sqrt{y^2 + (|y|\tan 30^\circ + 0.5\ \text{m})^2} - 0.5\ \text{m}\right]^2 \Big/ 2 \qquad (2)$$

The total potential energy is

$$V_{Total} = V_g + V_e \qquad (3)$$

These potential energies are calculated at time points 0, 0.2, 0.4 seconds, etc., and tabulated in [3]. Note that these time points are arbitrarily chosen.

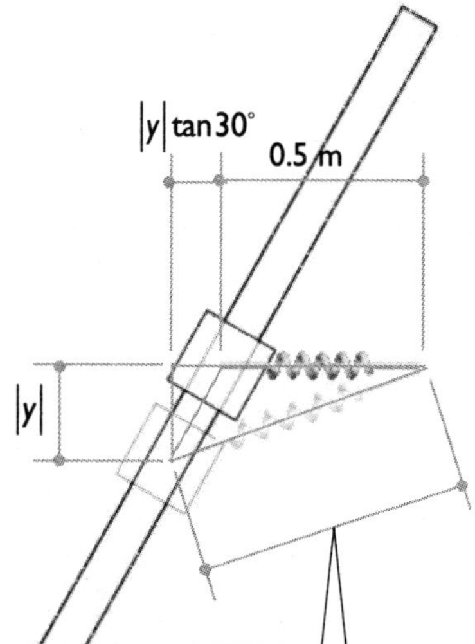

[2] Elongated spring length.

[3] The time points are arbitrarily chosen.

Time t (s)	Collar Elevation y (m)	Gravitational Potential Energy Eq. (1) V_g (J)	Spring Potential Energy Eq. (2) V_e (J)	Total Potential Energy $V_g + V_e$ (J)
0	0	0	0	0
0.2	-0.13240	-7.7903	1.6726	-6.1177
0.4	-0.36591	-21.5302	17.9835	-3.5467
0.6	-0.34336	-20.2034	15.4678	-4.7356
0.8	-0.13311	-7.8321	1.6931	-6.1390
1.0	-0.05883	-3.4614	0.2767	-3.1847
1.2	-0.19976	-11.7538	4.3185	-7.4353
1.4	-0.35090	-20.6471	16.2846	-4.3625
1.6	-0.28237	-16.6145	9.7371	-6.8774
1.8	-0.13318	-7.8362	1.6952	-6.1411
2.0	-0.12398	-7.2950	1.4406	-5.8544
2.2	-0.24604	-14.4772	7.0375	-7.4397
2.4	-0.31061	-18.2764	12.1994	-6.0770
2.6	-0.23575	-13.8717	6.3649	-7.5068
2.8	-0.15755	-9.2705	2.4912	-6.7793
3.0	-0.18276	-10.7537	3.5111	-7.2425
3.2	-0.25286	-14.8782	7.5050	-7.3732
3.4	-0.26126	-15.3726	8.1059	-7.2667
3.6	-0.22154	-13.0355	5.5009	-7.5347
3.8	-0.20192	-11.8809	4.4282	-7.4527
4.0	-0.21199	-12.4734	4.9614	-7.5119
4.2	-0.22230	-13.0798	5.5448	-7.5350
4.4	-0.22261	-13.0986	5.5635	-7.5351
4.6	-0.22263	-13.0993	5.5641	-7.5351
4.8	-0.22264	-13.1000	5.5648	-7.5351
5.0	-0.22265	-13.1006	5.5655	-7.5352

[5] The system (**Collar** and **Spring**) stabilizes at a configuration that the **Total Potential Energy** is at its minimum.

[7] Any infinitesimal change of configuration will not change the total potential energy, thus doing zero work.

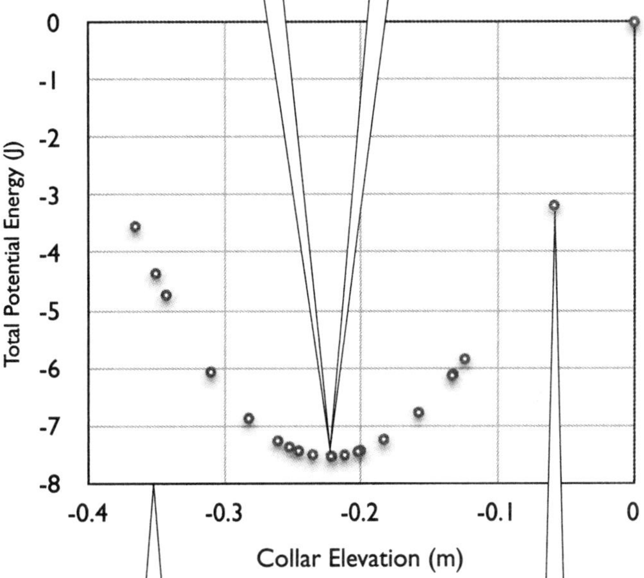

[4] This is a plot of **Total Potential Energy** versus **Collar Elevation** y.

[6] Other configurations are not stable, because the total potential energy is not at a minimum.

[8] Summary

The **principle of minimum potential energy** states that, *among all possible configurations, a structural system will stabilize at a configuration in which the total potential energy is at its minimum.*

The **Principle of virtual work** states that, *when a structural system is in a stable configuration (i.e., the total potential energy is at its minimum), any infinitesimal changes of the configuration will not change the total potential energy, therefore doing zero work.*

[9] Wrap Up

Save all files and exit **SolidWorks**. #

Chapter 4

Particle Dynamics: Impulse and Momentum

Linear Momentum of a Particle

Consider a particle of mass m moving in the space with a velocity of $\vec{v}$. The **linear momentum** of the particle is defined by $m\vec{v}$. In SI, which has a unit of **kg-m/s**, or equivalently **N-s**.

Principle of Impulse and Momentum

For a particle of mass m acted upon by a force $\vec{F}$, Eq. 2(2) (page 34) can be rewritten in the form

$$\vec{F} = m\frac{d\vec{v}}{dt}$$

Multiplying both sides by dt and integrating from time t_1 to t_2, we write

$$\int_{t_1}^{t_2} \vec{F}\,dt = \int_{\vec{v}_1}^{\vec{v}_2} m\,d\vec{v} = m\vec{v}_2 - m\vec{v}_1 \qquad (1)$$

The left hand side $\int_{t_1}^{t_2} \vec{F}\,dt$ is defined as the **linear impulse** $\overrightarrow{Imp_{1\to2}}$ of the force $\vec{F}$ during the time interval from t_1 to t_2. The **linear impulse** has the same unit as the **linear momentum**. When several forces act on a particle, the impulse of each force must be added up. Eq. (1) can be written in the form

$$m\vec{v}_1 + \sum \overrightarrow{Imp_{1\to2}} = m\vec{v}_2 \qquad (2)$$

Eq. (2) is known as the **principle of impulse and momentum** for a particle. This chapter will show how Eq. (2) is satisfied in a particle system.

Section 4.1

Principle of Impulse and Momentum: Block and Wedge

4.1-1 Introduction

[1] In this section, we'll revisit the **Block and Wedge** example, introduced in Section 2.1. Using this example, we'll illustrate the **principle of impulse and Momentum**, which states

$$\left(\sum m\vec{v}\right)_0 + \sum \int_0^t \vec{F}\, dt = \left(\sum m\vec{v}\right)_t \qquad (1)$$

where $\left(\sum m\vec{v}\right)_0$ is the initial linear momentum of the system, $\left(\sum m\vec{v}\right)_t$ is the linear momentum of the system at time t, and $\sum \int_0^t \vec{F}\, dt$ is the linear impulse by external forces during the time from 0 to t.

4.1-2 Start Up and Open the File **Block-And-Wedge.SLDASM**

[1] Launch **SolidWorks** and open the file **Block-And-Wedge.SLDASM**, which is saved in Section 2.1.

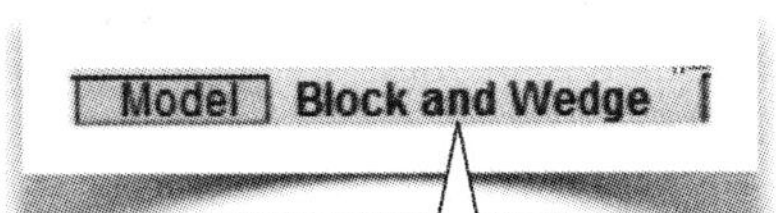

[2] Click **Block and Wedge** tab.#

4.1-3 Results: **Velocities**

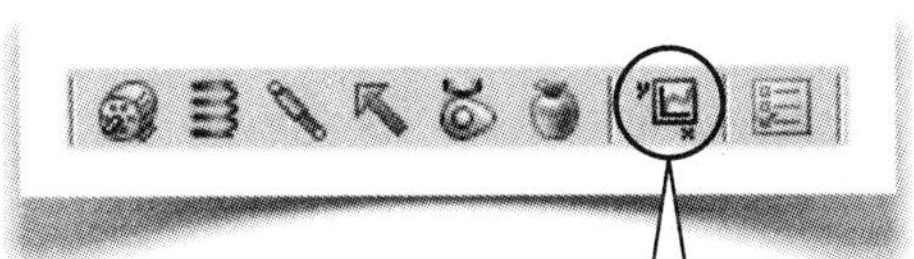

[1] In **Motion Toolbar**, click **Results and Plots**.

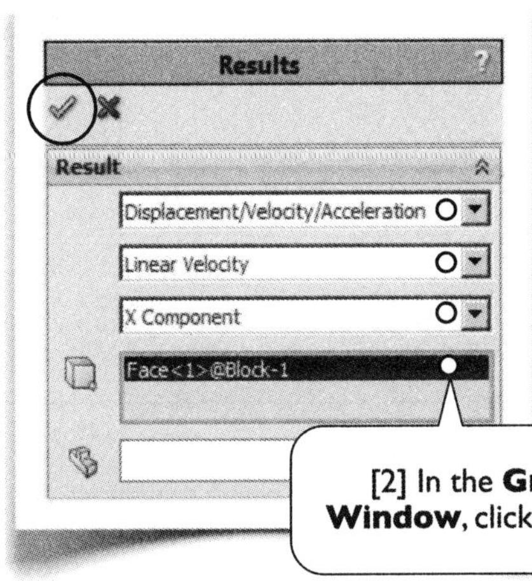

[2] In the **Graphics Window**, click the **Block**.

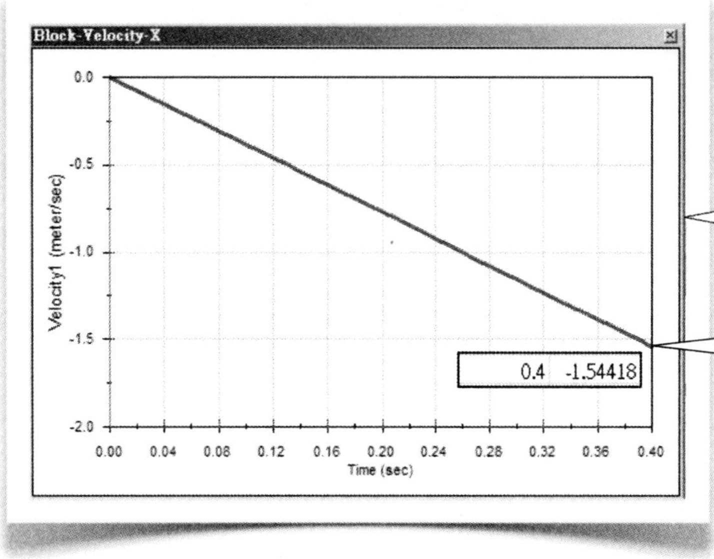

[3] This is the velocity of the **Block** in *X*-direction. Rename the plot as **Block-Velocity-X**. Export the file as **Block-Velocity-X.CSV**.

[4] It changes linearly. At 0.4 seconds, the velocity in *X*-direction is -1.54418 m/s (see the **CSV** file).

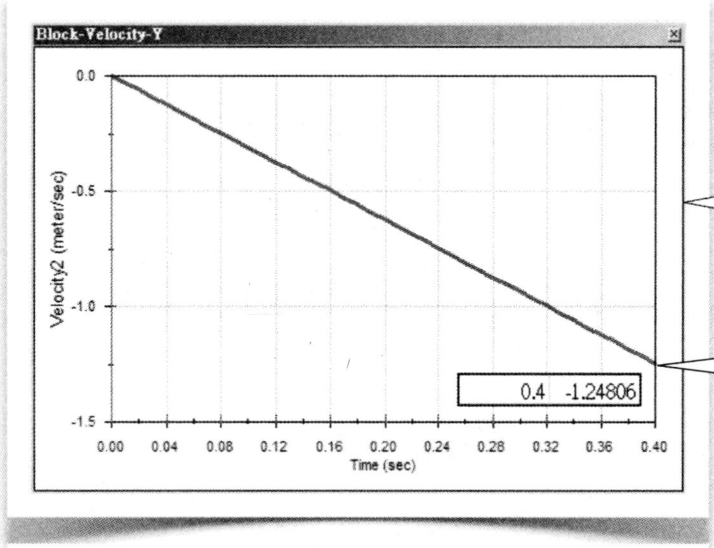

[5] Follow a similar procedure to obtain the velocity of the **Block** in *Y*-direction. Rename the plot as **Block-Velocity-Y**. Export the file as **Block-Velocity-Y.CSV**.

[6] It changes linearly. At 0.4 seconds, the velocity in *Y*-direction is -1.24806 m/s (see the **CSV** file).

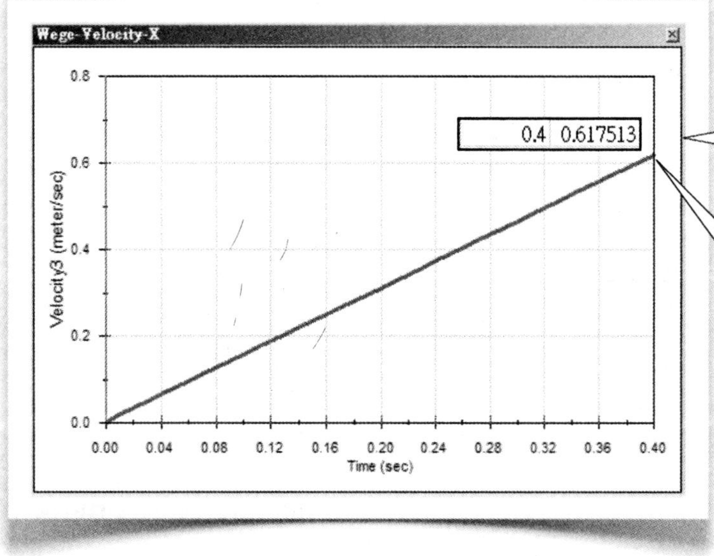

[7] Follow a similar procedure to obtain the velocity of the **Wedge** in *X*-direction. Rename the plot as **Wedge-Velocity-X**. Export the file as **Wedge-Velocity-X.CSV**.

[8] It changes linearly. At 0.4 seconds, the velocity in *X*-direction is +0.617513 m/s (see the **CSV** file). #

4.1-4 Principle of Impulse and Momentum: Entire System

[1] This is a graphical interpretation of Eq. 4.1-1(1) (page 83) for the entire system.

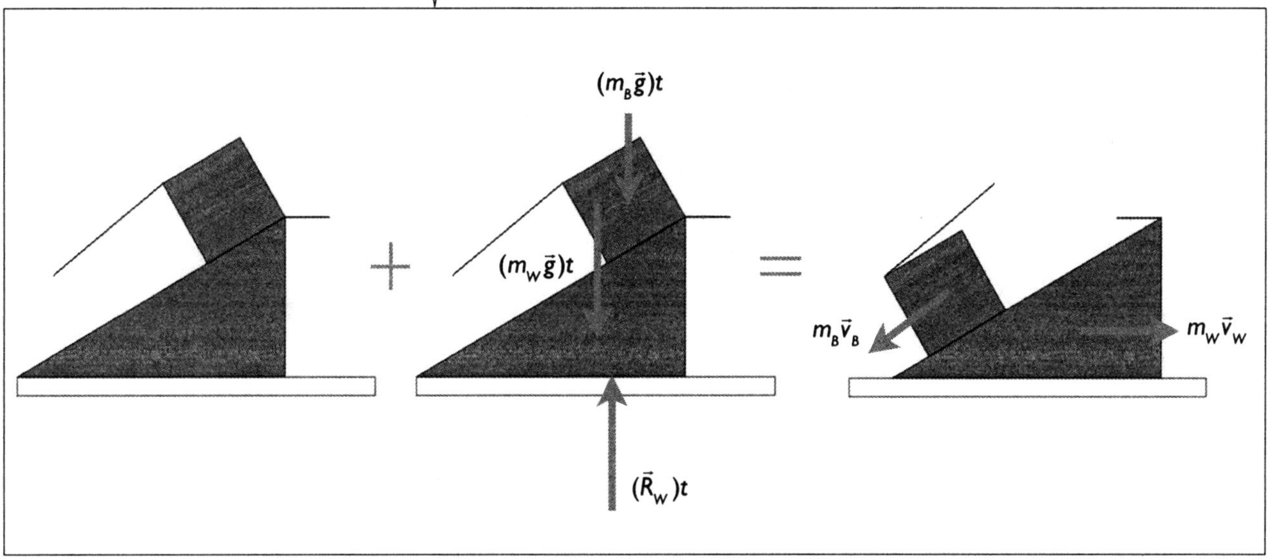

[2] We want to confirm Eq. 4.1-1(1) for the entire system, at $t = 0.4$; i.e.,

$$0 + (m_B\vec{g})t + (m_W\vec{g})t + (\vec{R}_W)t = m_B\vec{v}_B + m_W\vec{v}_W \quad (1)$$

where

$t = 0.4$ sec	
$m_B = 6$ kg	(2.1-2[12], page 37)
$m_W = 15.004$ kg	(2.1-3[5], page 37)
$\vec{g} = -9.80665\,\vec{j}$ m/s^2)	(2.1-8[2], page 41)
$\vec{R}_W = 187.257\,\vec{j}$ (N)	(2.1-13[6], page 44)
$\vec{v}_B = -1.54418\,\vec{i} - 1.24806\,\vec{j}$ (m/s)	(4.1-3[4, 6], last page)
$\vec{v}_W = 0.617513\,\vec{i}$ (m/s)	(4.1-3[8], last page)

It leaves for you to substitute these values into both sides of Eq. (1) and conclude that Eq. 4.1-1(1) holds for the entire system. #

4.1-5 Principle of Impulse and Momentum: **Block**

[1] This is a graphical interpretation of Eq. 4.1-1(1) (page 83) for the **Block**.

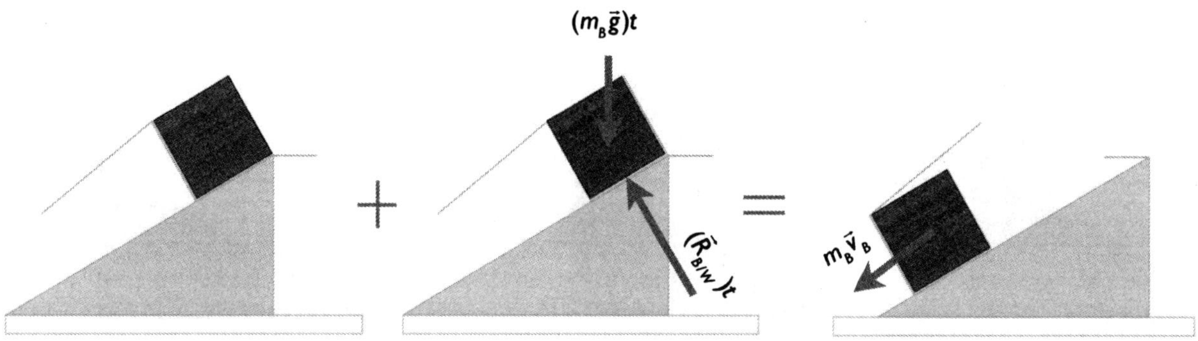

[2] We want to confirm Eq. 4.1-1(1) for the **Block**, at $t = 0.4$; i.e.,

$$(m_B\vec{g})t + (\vec{R}_{B/W})t = m_B\vec{v}_B \qquad (1)$$

where

$t = 0.4$ sec
$m_B = 6$ kg (2.1-2[12], page 37)
$\vec{g} = -9.80665\,\vec{j}$ (m/s^2) (2.1-8[2], page 41)
$\vec{R}_{B/W} = -46.3255\sin 30^\circ\,\vec{i} + 46.3255\cos 30^\circ\,\vec{j}$ (N) (2.1-14[1], page 45)
$\vec{v}_B = -1.54418\,\vec{i} - 1.24806\,\vec{j}$ (m/s) (4.1-3[4, 6], page 84)

It leaves for you to substitute these values into both sides of Eq. (1) and conclude that Eq. 4.1-1(1) holds for the **Block**.
#

4.1-6 Principle of Impulse and Momentum: **Wedge**

[1] This is a graphical interpretation of Eq. 4.1-1(1) (page 83) for the **Wedge**.

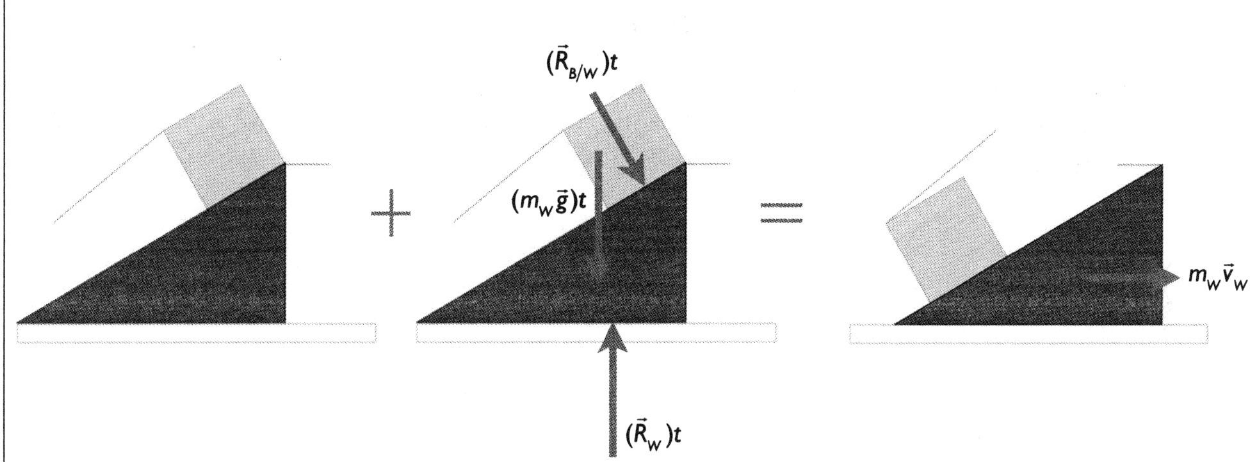

[2] We want to confirm Eq. 4.1-1(1) for the **Wedge**, at $t = 0.4$; i.e.,

$$0 + (m_W\vec{g})t + (\vec{R}_{W/B})t + (\vec{R}_W)t = m_W\vec{v}_W \tag{1}$$

where

$t = 0.4$ sec
$m_W = 15.004$ kg (2.1-3[5], page 37)
$\vec{g} = -9.80665\,\vec{j}$ (m/s^2) (2.1-8[2], page 41)
$\vec{R}_{W/B} = 46.3255\sin 30^\circ\,\vec{i} - 46.3255\cos 30^\circ\,\vec{j}$ (N) (2.1-14[1], page 45)
$\vec{R}_W = 187.257\,\vec{j}$ (N) (2.1-13[6], page 44)
$\vec{v}_W = 0.617513\,\vec{i}$ (m/s) (4.1-3[8], page 84)

It leaves for you to substitute these values into both sides of Eq. (1) and conclude that Eq. 4.1-1(1) holds for the **Wedge**.

[3] Wrap Up

Save all files and exit **SolidWorks**. #

4.1-7 (Do It Yourself)
Principle of Impulse and Momentum: **Billiard Balls**

Revisit the **Billiard Balls** example (Section 2.2) and verify Eq. 4.1-1(1) (page 83) for the entire system (cue ball and object ball), for the cue ball, an for the object ball.

Note that, for the entire system, because there are no external forces involved, Eq. 4.1-1(1) reduces to

$$\left(\sum m\vec{v}\right)_0 = \left(\sum m\vec{v}\right)_t \qquad (1)$$

Eq. (1) is called the **principle of conservation of momentum**.

Section 4.2

Conservation of Momentum: Impact of Two Balls

4.2-1 Introduction

[1] As mentioned in 4.1-7 (last page), when there are no external forces involved in a system, the **principle of impulse and momentum** (Eq. 4.1-1(1), page 83) reduces to the **principle of conservation of momentum** (Eq. 4.1-7(1), last page), which can be rewritten in the following form

$$\left(\sum m\bar{v}\right)_t = \text{constant} \tag{1}$$

In this section, we'll consider a system of two balls without any external forces involved, and thus Eq. (1) holds. In order to simulate the elasticity of the balls using a rigid body model, each ball is cut into two halves, which are then connected by a spring [2, 3]. Using this simple model, we may observe how the kinetic energy transfer to "internal energy," the internal oscillations of the material. To describe the degree of energy loss due to impact, a **coefficient of restitution** is often used, which can be defined as

$$e = \frac{v'_B - v'_A}{v_A - v_B} \tag{2}$$

where $(v_A - v_B)$ is the difference between the speeds of the balls before the impact, and $(v'_B - v'_A)$ is the difference between the speeds of the balls after the impact. In an impact problem, both **momentum equation** (Eq. (1)) and the **energy equation** (Eq. (2)) must be satisfied.

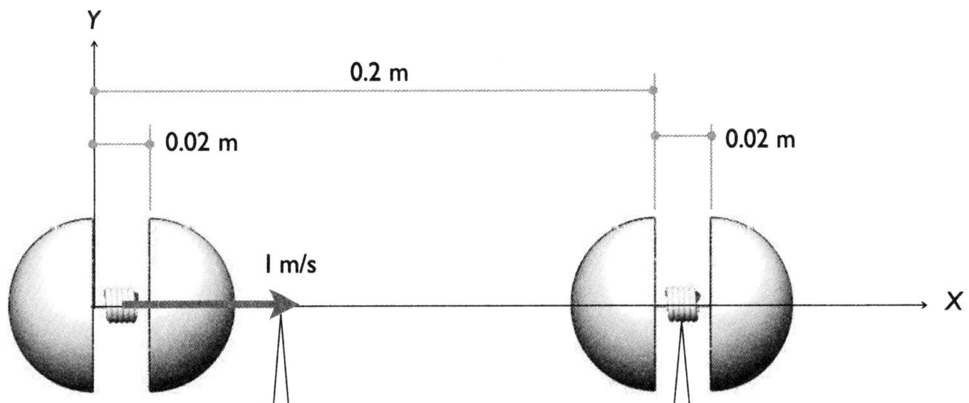

[3] The ball has an initial velocity of 1 m/s. #

[2] The spring has a constant of 100 N/m and a free length of 0.02 m.

4.2-2 Start Up and Create a Part: **Halfball**

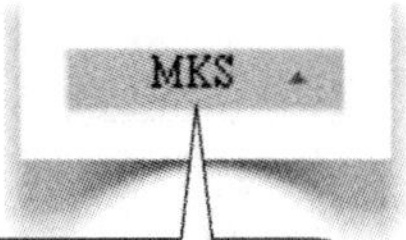

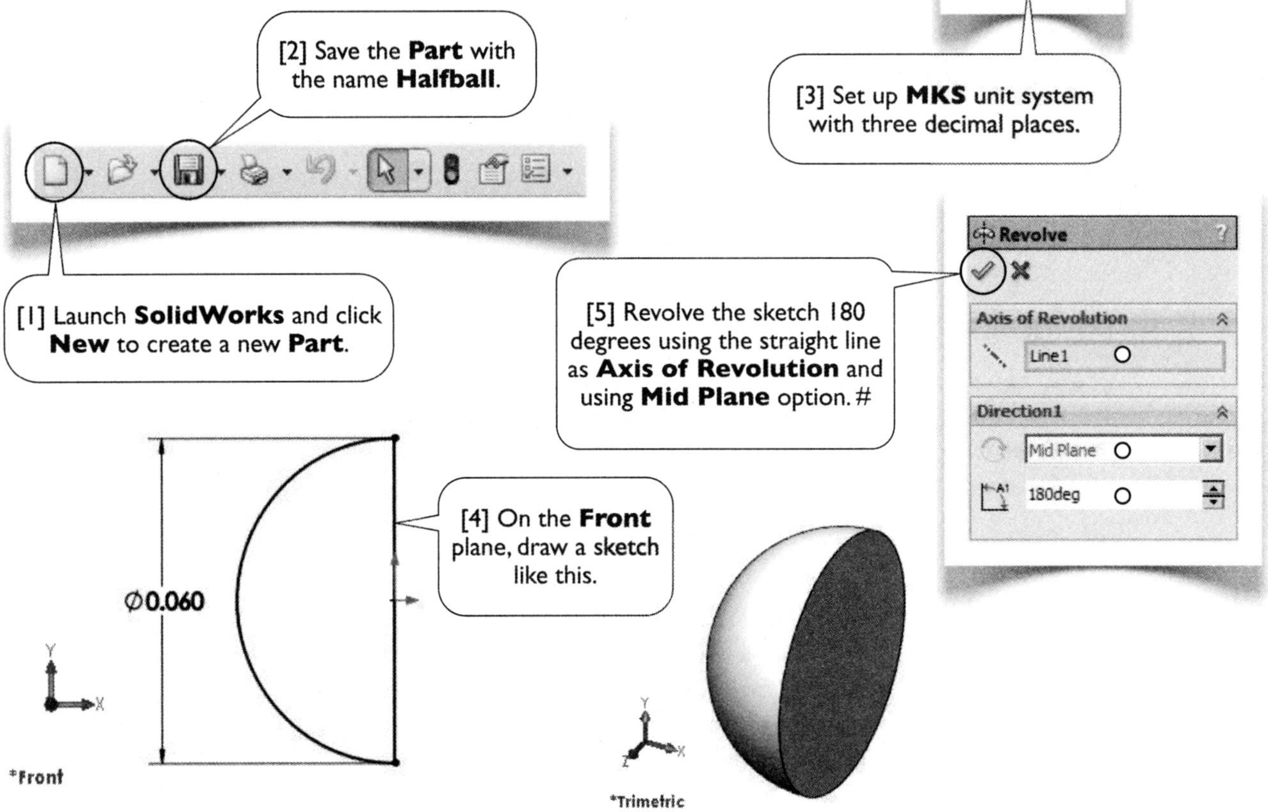

4.2-3 Create an Assembly: **Two-Elastic-Balls**

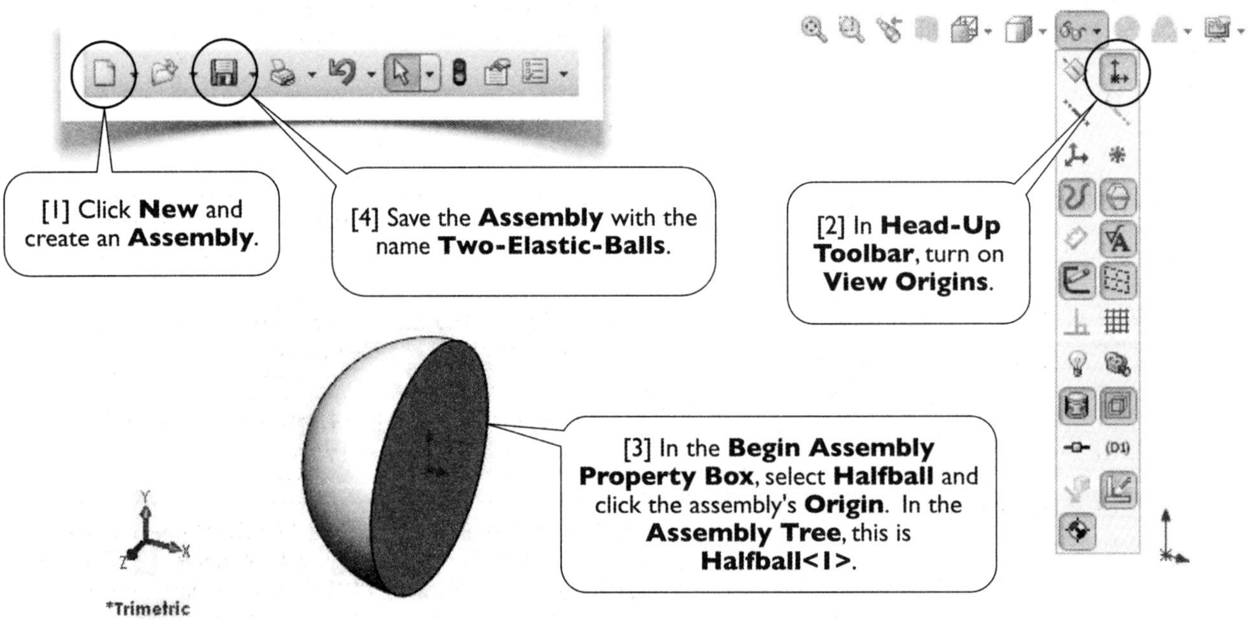

[5] Set up **MKS** unit system with three decimal places.

[6] Hold **Control** key and use your mouse to drag the first **Halfball** to this position. A **Halfball** is duplicated. In the **Assembly Tree**, this is **Halfball<2>**.

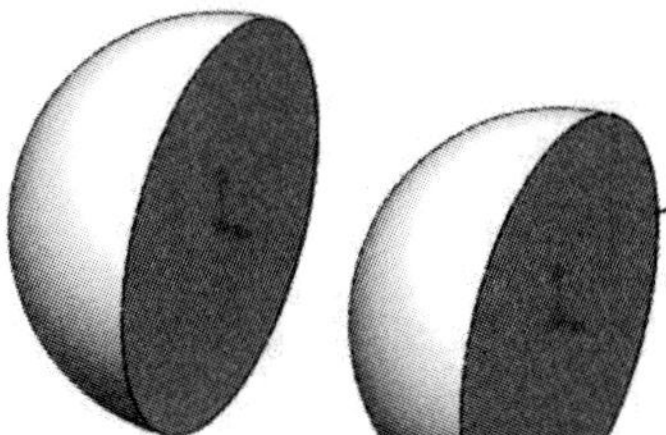

[7] Repeat [6] twice to create two more **Halfballs**. In the **Assembly Tree**, these are **Halfball<3>** and **Halfball<4>**.

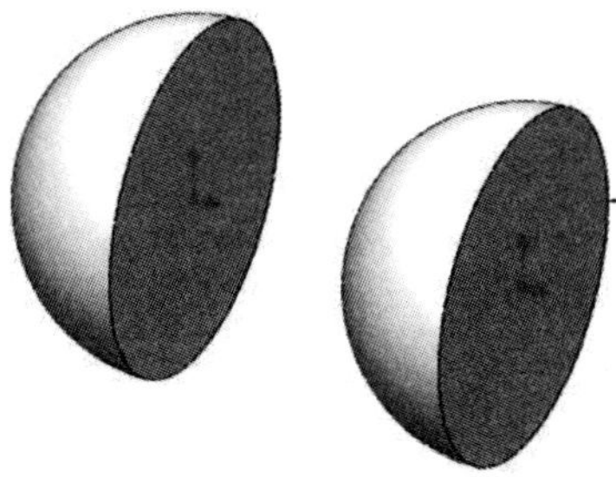

[9] In **Assembly Toolbar**, click **Mate**.

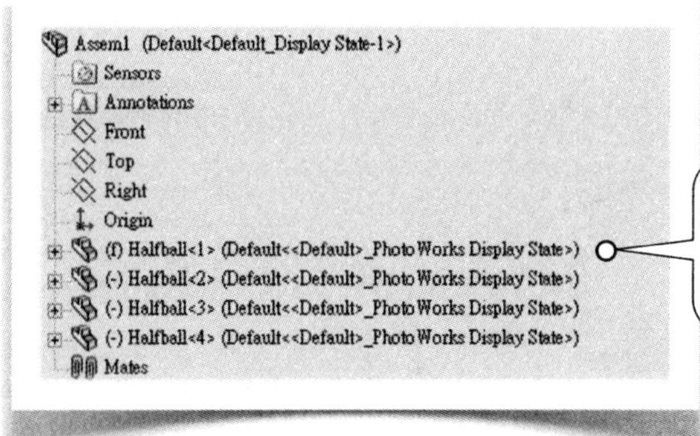

[8] Right-click **Halfball<1>** and select **Float**.

[10] We'll create these 12 **Mates** in [11-25].

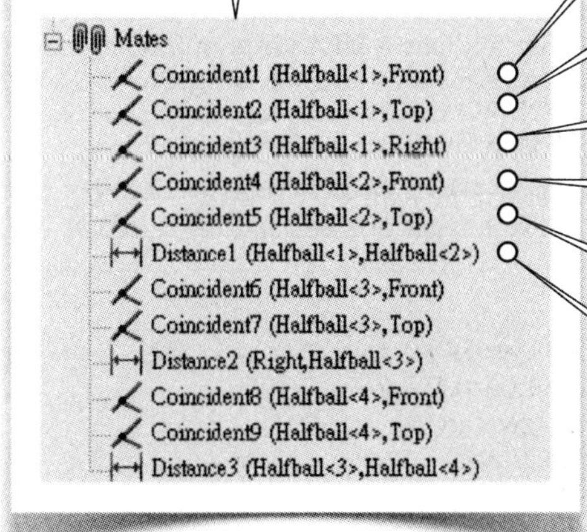

[11] The **Assembly's** and the **Halfball<1>'s Front** planes are **Coincident**.

[12] The **Assembly's** and the **Halfball<1>'s Top** planes are **Coincident**.

[13] The **Assembly's** and the **Halfball<1>'s Right** planes are **Coincident**. This **Mate** will be suppressed later.

[14] The **Assembly's** and the **Halfball<2>'s Front** planes are **Coincident**.

[15] The **Assembly's** and the **Halfball<2>'s Top** planes are **Coincident**.

[16] The **Halfball<1>'s** and the **Halfball<2>'s** circular faces are faced each other and has a **Distance** of 0.02 m (see [17, 18], next page). This **Mate** will be suppressed later.

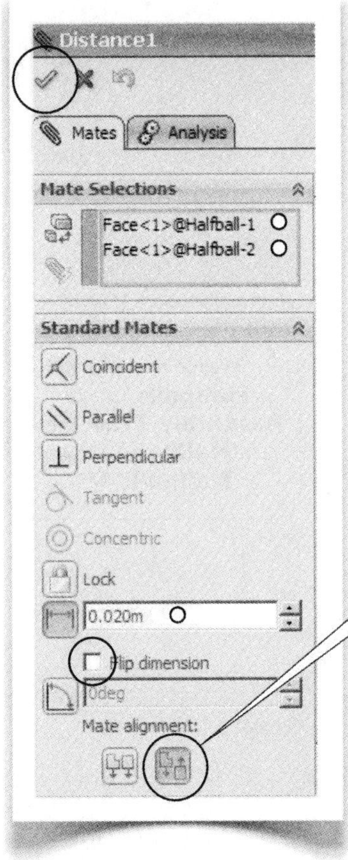

[17] The **Halfball<1>'s** and the **Halfball<2>'s** circular faces are faced each other and has a **Distance** of 0.02 m.

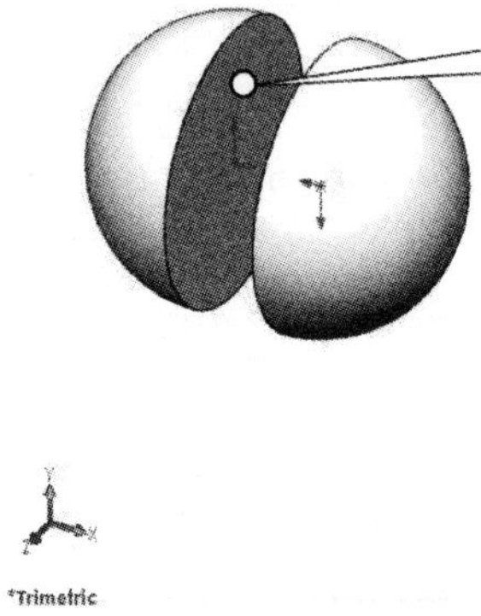

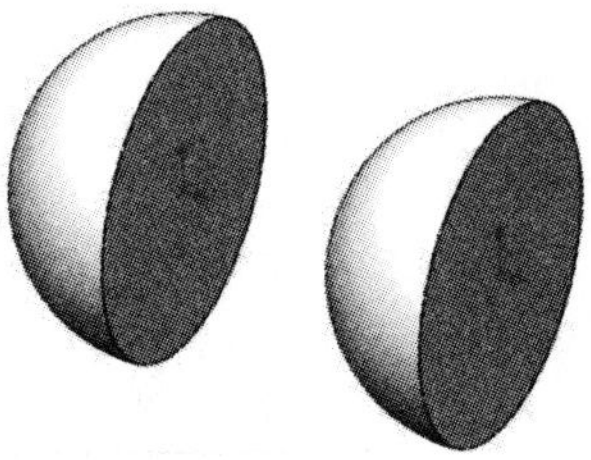

[18] Click **Anti-Aligned**. If a warning message window appears, click **OK** for the message.

[19] The **Assembly's** and the **Halfball<3>'s Front** planes are **Coincident**.

[20] The **Assembly's** and the **Halfball<3>'s Top** planes are **Coincident**.

[21] The **Assembly's** and the **Halfball<3>'s Right** planes has a **Distance** of 0.2 m. This **Mate** will be suppressed later.

[22] The **Assembly's** and the **Halfball<4>'s Front** planes are **Coincident**.

[23] The **Assembly's** and the **Halfball<4>'s Top** planes are **Coincident**.

[24] The **Halfball<3>'s** and the **Halfball<4>'s** circular faces are faced each other and has a **Distance** of 0.02 m (see [25, 18]). This **Mate** will be suppressed later.

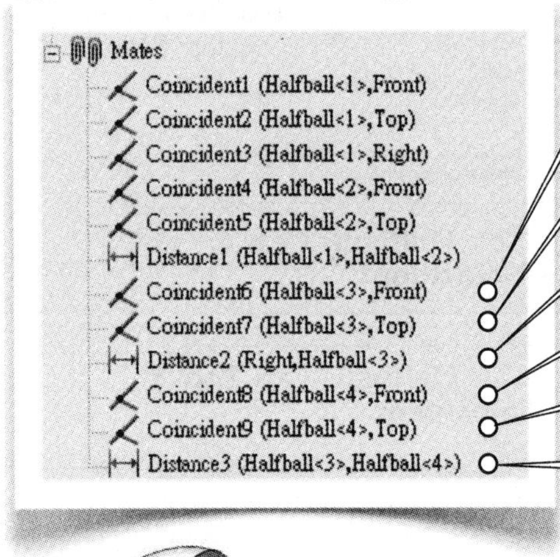

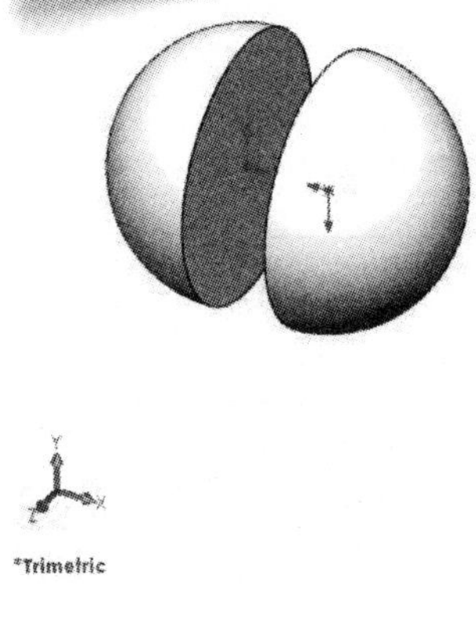

[25] The **Halfball<3>'s** and the **Halfball<4>'s** circular faces are faced each other and has a **Distance** of 0.02 m (the steps are similar to [17, 18]). #

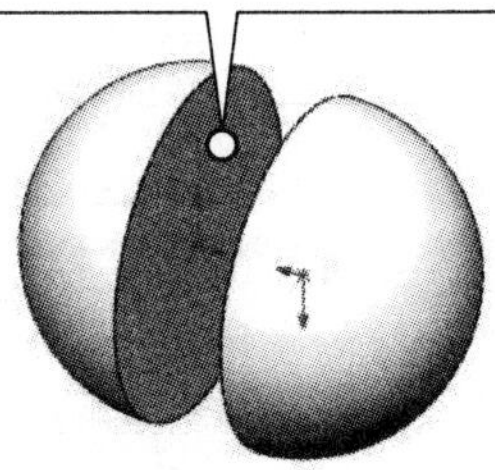

4.2-4 Create a **Motion Study**

[1] Click **Motion Study 1** tab.

[2] Select **Motion Analysis**. #

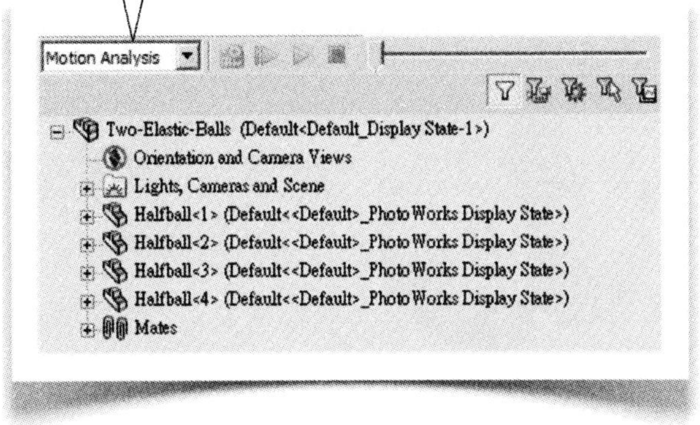

4.2-5 Set Up **Spring**

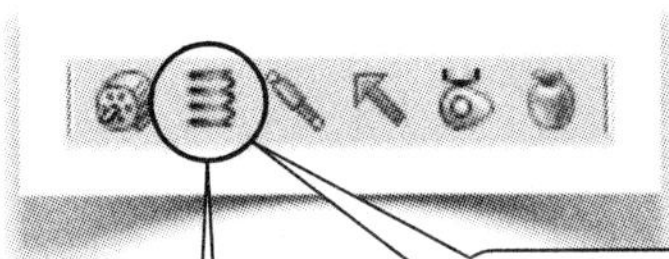

[1] In **Motion Toolbar**, click **Spring**.

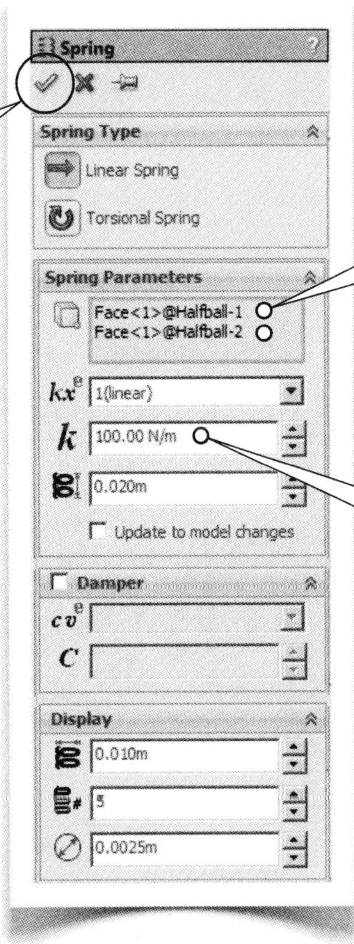

[2] Select the circular faces of **Halfball<1>** and **Halfball<2>**.

[3] Type 100 (N/m) for **Spring Constant** and leave other parameters as their default settings.

[4] Click **OK**.

[5] Click **Spring** again and set up a second **Spring** ([2-4]) between the circular faces of **Halfball<3>** and **Halfball<4>**. #

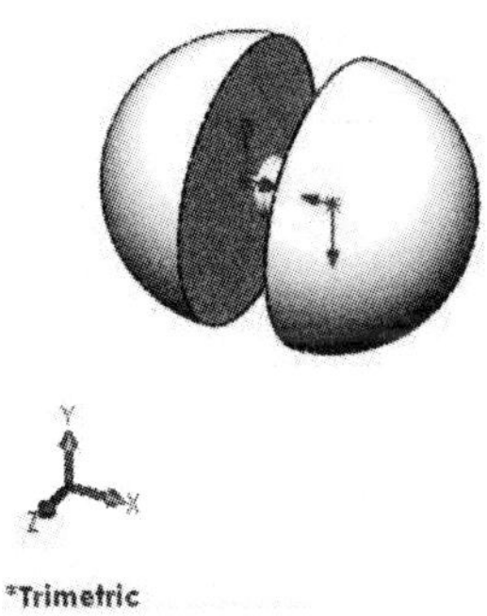

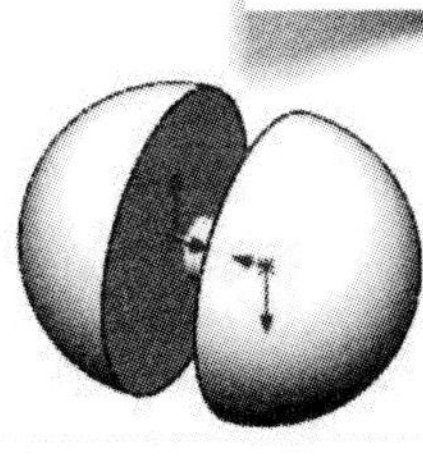

4.2-6 Set Up **Contacts**

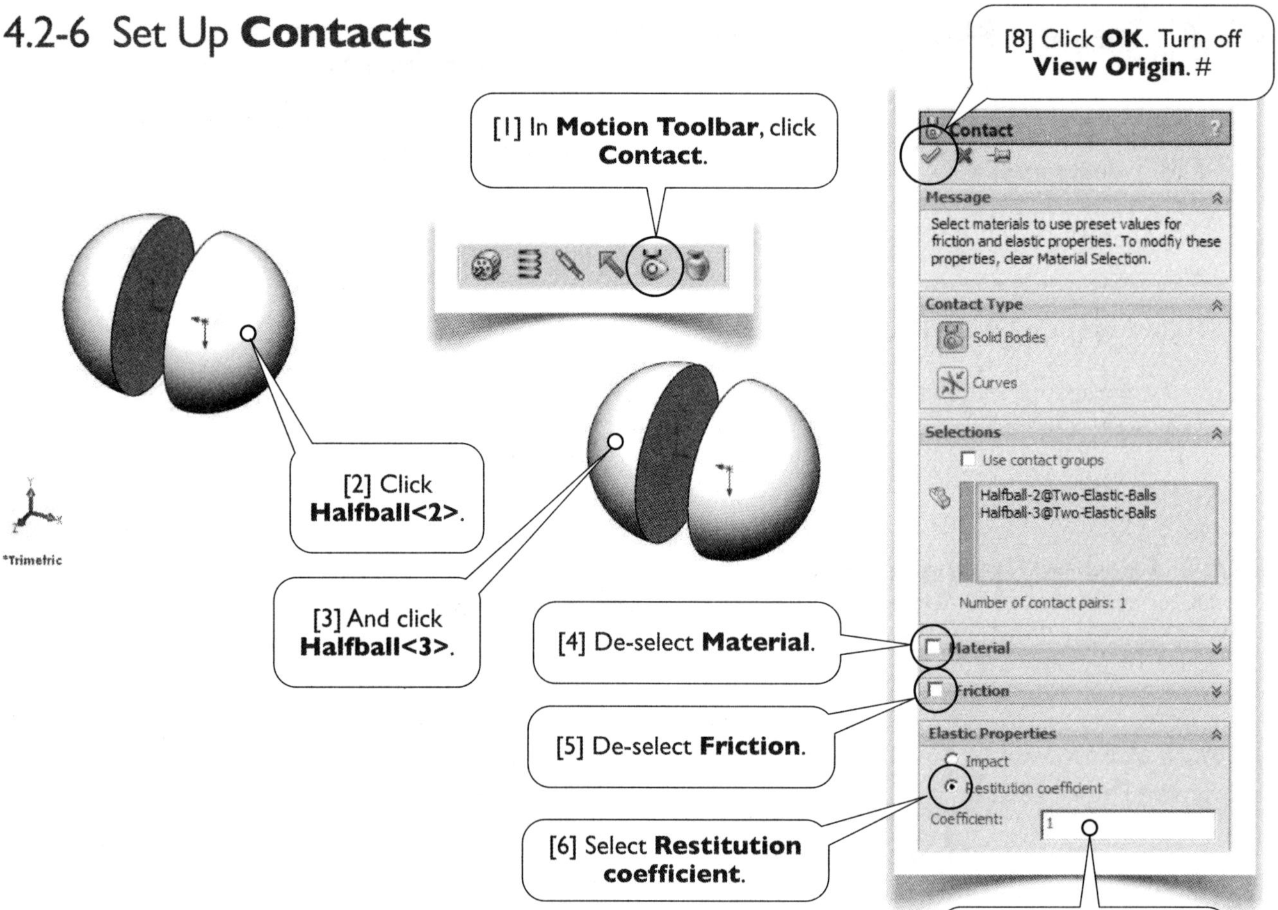

4.2-7 Set Up **Initial Velocity**

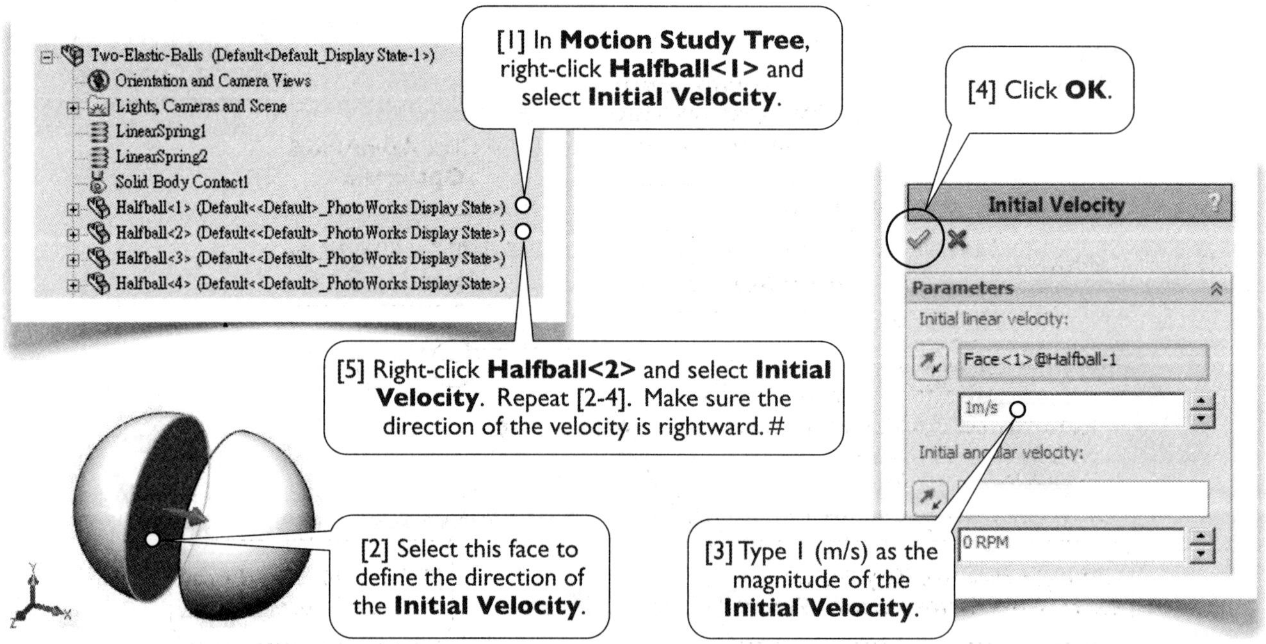

4.2-8 Calculate and Animate **Results**

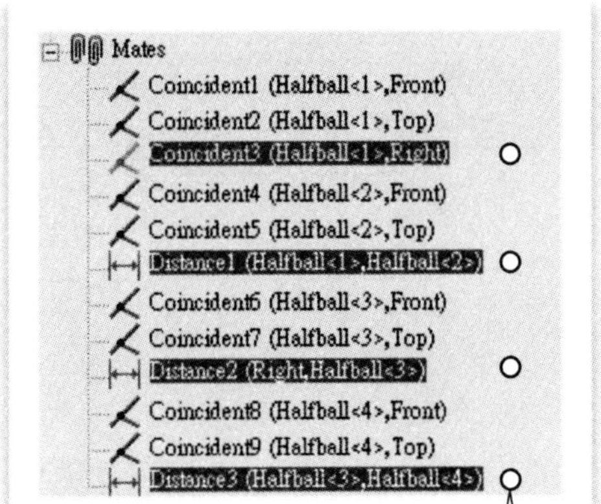

[1] In the **Assembly Tree**, under **Mates**, suppress **Coincident3**, **Distance1**, **Distance2**, and **Distance3** (see 4.2-3[13, 16, 21, 24], pages 91, 92).

[2] In the **Motion Toolbar**, Click **Motion Study Properties**.

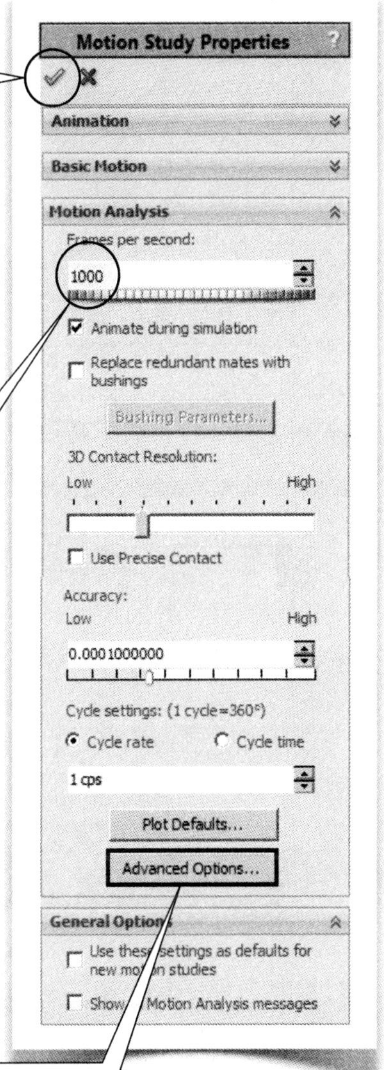

[3] Type 1000 for **Frames per second**.

[4] Click **Advanced Options...**

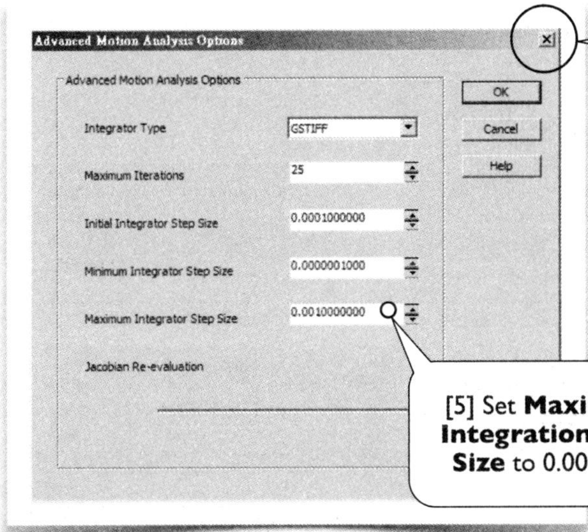

[5] Set **Maximum Integration Step Size** to 0.001 sec.

[6] Click **OK**.

[7] Click **OK**.

[8] Drag this **Key Point** to 0.5 seconds.

[9] Right-click this **Key Point** and select **View Orientation>Front**.

[10] Set **Playback Speed** to **0.1x**.

[11] Click **Calculate**.

[12] Click **Play from Start**. #

4.2-9 Results: Spring Lengths

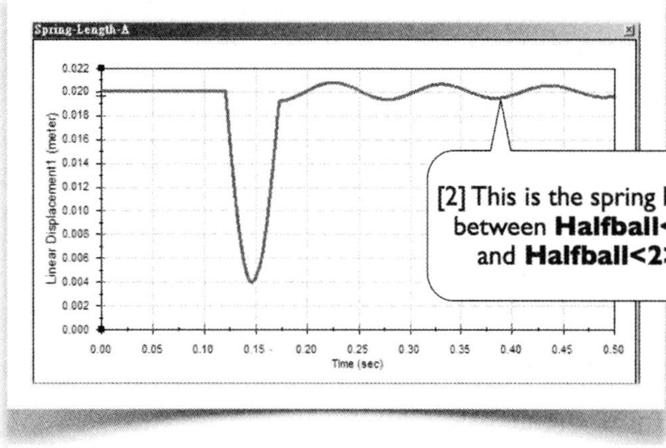

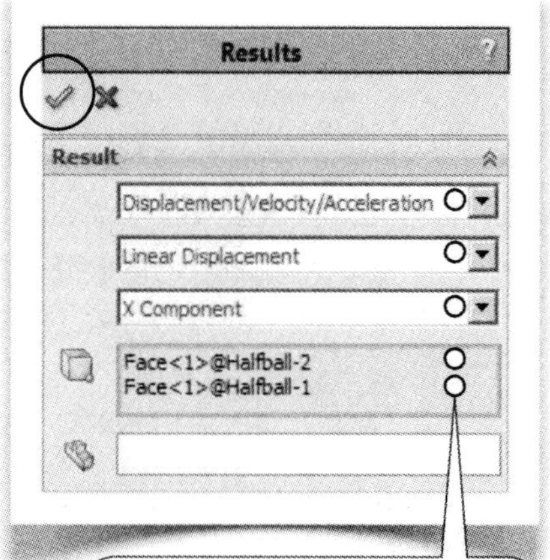

[1] Set up **Results** like this. Select the circular face of **Halfball<2>** first and then that of **Halfball<1>**. The order determines the sign of **Displacement**.

[2] This is the spring length between **Halfball<1>** and **Halfball<2>**.

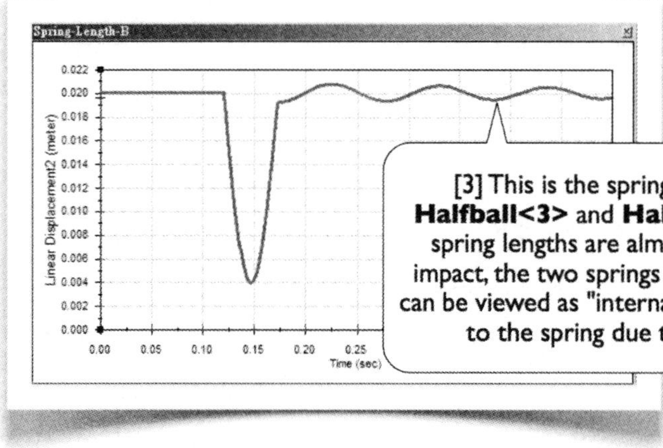

[3] This is the spring length between **Halfball<3>** and **Halfball<4>**. The two spring lengths are almost identical. After impact, the two springs oscillate; this energy can be viewed as "internal energy," transferred to the spring due to the impact. #

4.2-10 Results: Contact Forces

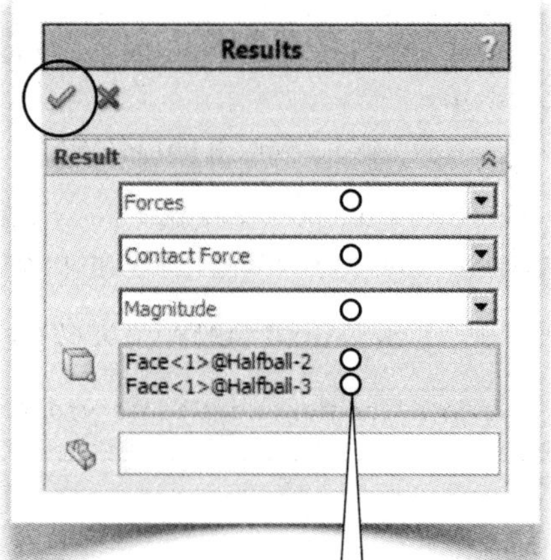

[1] Set up **Results** like this. To define the contacting components, select **Halfball<2>** and **Halfball<3>**.

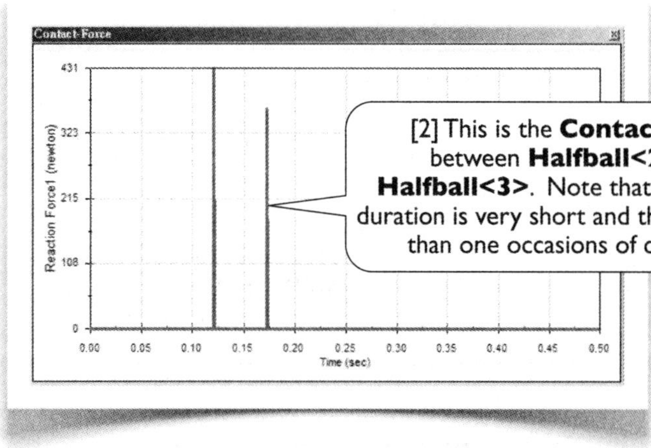

[2] This is the **Contact Force** between **Halfball<2>** and **Halfball<3>**. Note that the contact duration is very short and there are more than one occasions of contact. #

4.2-11 Coefficient of Restitution

[5] Coefficient of Restitution

After the completion of the impact, the four half balls remain oscillating; however, the mass center of each ball has a constant velocity, which can be calculated by averaging the velocities of the two halves of each ball. The velocity of the ball consisting of **Halfball<1>** and **Halfball<2>** is

$$v'_A = (0.035987 + 0.05060)/2 = 0.04329$$

The velocity of the ball consisting of **Halfball<3>** and **Halfball<4>** is

$$v'_B = (0.94940 + 0.964013)/2 = 0.95671$$

The coefficient of restitution is then

$$e = \frac{v'_B - v'_A}{v_A - 0} = \frac{0.95617 - 0.04329}{1} \approx 0.913$$

#

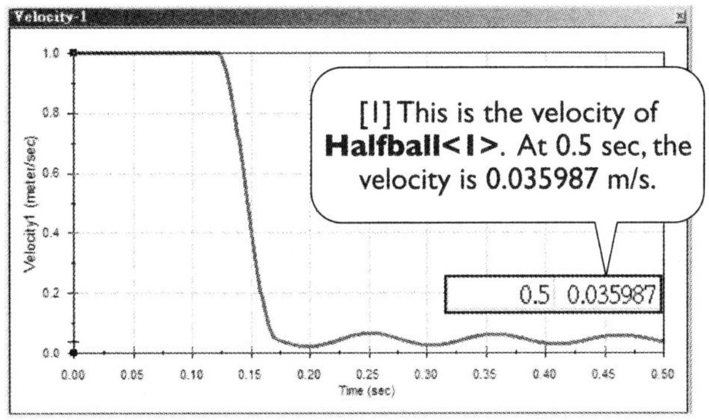

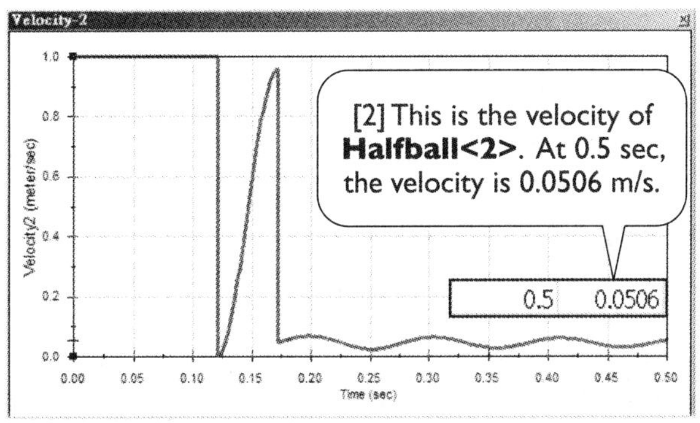

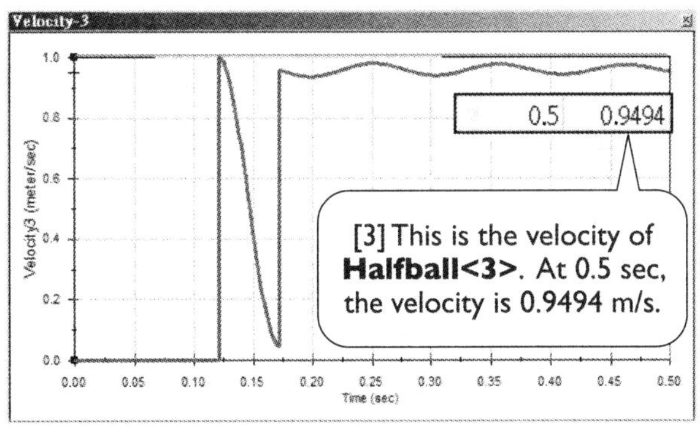

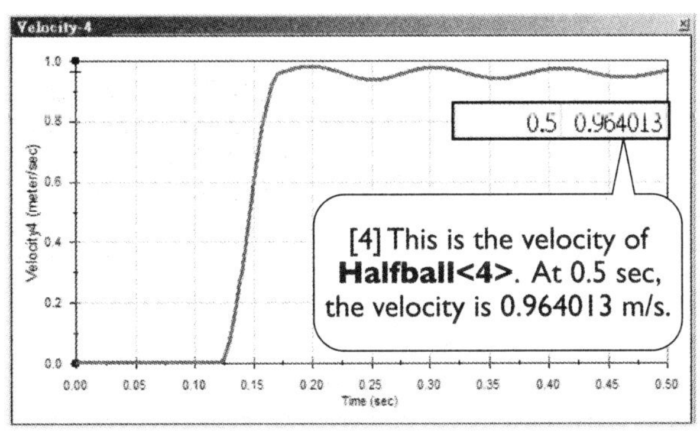

4.2-12 Conservation of Momentum

Before the impact, the linear momentum of the system is

$$mv_A = m(1.0 \text{ m/s})$$

where m is the mass of a ball. After the completion of the impact, the linear momentum of the system is

$$mv'_A + mv'_B = m(0.04329 + 0.95671) = m(1.0 \text{ m/s})$$

The linear momentum is conserved. #

4.2-13 (Do It Yourself) Change the Spring Constants

[1] Do It Yourself

Change both the spring constants and re-run the simulation. Calculate the coefficient of restitution. Observe the relation between the elasticity of the balls and the coefficient of restitution.

[2] Coefficient of Restitution for the Spring Constants of 1000 N/m

The figures at right are the resulting velocities when the spring constants change to 1000 N/m.

The velocity of the ball consisting of **Halfball<1>** and **Halfball<2>** is

$$v'_A = (0.120288 + 0.119969)/2 = 0.12013$$

The velocity of the ball consisting of **Halfball<3>** and **Halfball<4>** is

$$v'_B = (0.880031 + 0.879712)/2 = 0.87987$$

The coefficient of restitution is then

$$e = \frac{v'_B - v'_A}{v_A - 0} = \frac{0.87687 - 0.12013}{1} \approx 0.757$$

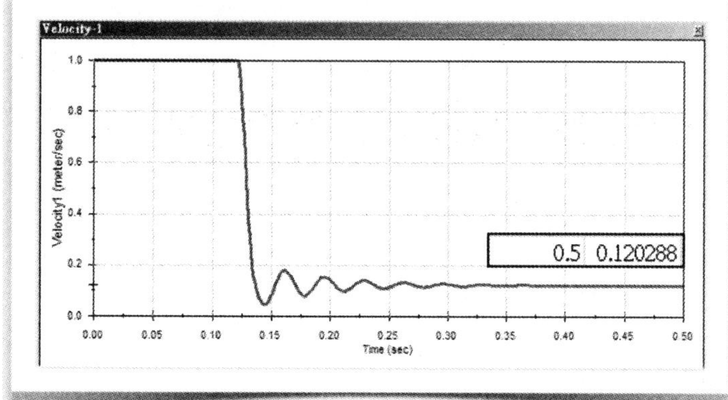

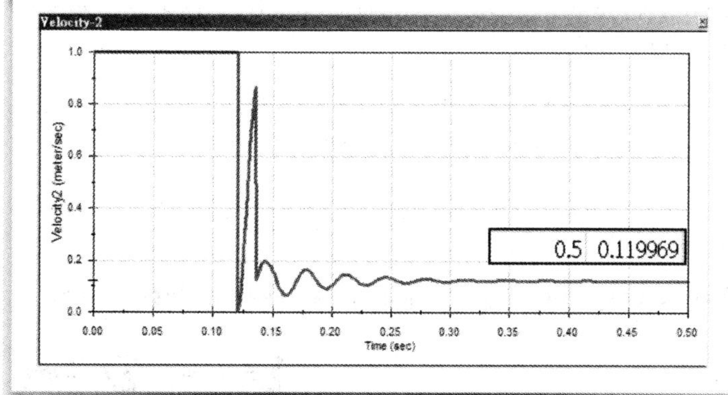

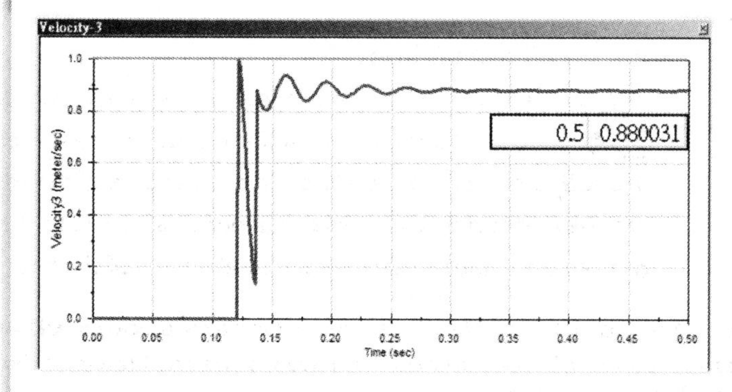

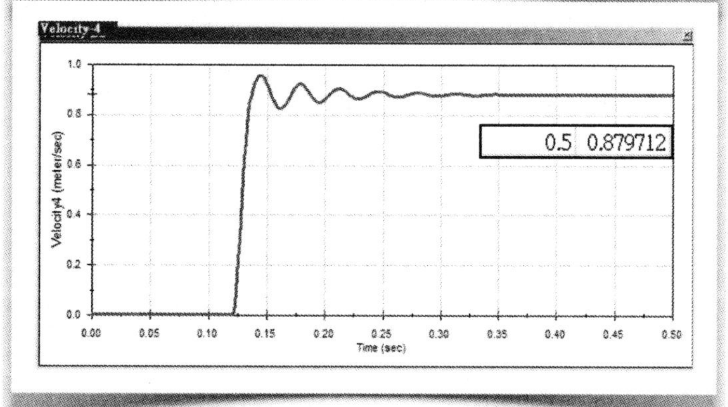

[3] Conservation of Momentum

Before the impact, the linear momentum of the system is

$$mv_A = m(1.0 \text{ m/s})$$

After the completion of the impact, the linear momentum of the system is

$$mv'_A + mv'_B = m(0.12013 + 0.87987) = m(1.0 \text{ m/s})$$

The linear momentum is conserved.

[4] Wrap Up

Save all files and exit **SolidWorks**. #

Chapter 5

Planar Rigid Body Kinematics

Plane Motion

From this chapter on, we no longer treat a body as a particle and consider each body as a rigid body. A rigid body is said to be moving in *xy*-plane if

(a) Each particle of the body moves in a plane parallel to the *xy*-plane, and
(b) The body is symmetric with respect to the *xy*-plane.

Newton's 2nd Law

When a body is moving in *xy*-plane, the following three equations hold for the body:

$$\sum F_x = m\bar{a}_x,\ \sum F_y = m\bar{a}_y,\ \sum M_G = \bar{I}\alpha \tag{1}$$

where

m is the mass of the body;
$\sum F_x$ and $\sum F_y$ are the resultant force components acting on the body;
$\sum M_G$ is the resultant moment acting on the body with respect to the mass center G;
$\bar{a}_x$ and $\bar{a}_y$ are the linear acceleration components of the **mass center** of the boy;
$\bar{I}$ is the body's moment of inertia about an axis passing through the **mass center** and normal to the *xy*-plane;
α is the magnitude of the angular acceleration of the body.

Eq. (1) is known as the Newton's 2nd Law for a rigid body in **plane motion**. How the plane motion conditions (a, b) lead to Eq. (1) will become clear after we discuss the Newton's 2nd Law for a rigid body in general 3D motion, Eqs. 10.1-1(1, 2), page 188.

Chapters 5-8 will devote to rigid bodies in **plane motion**.

Section 5.1

Crank-Link-Piston Mechanism

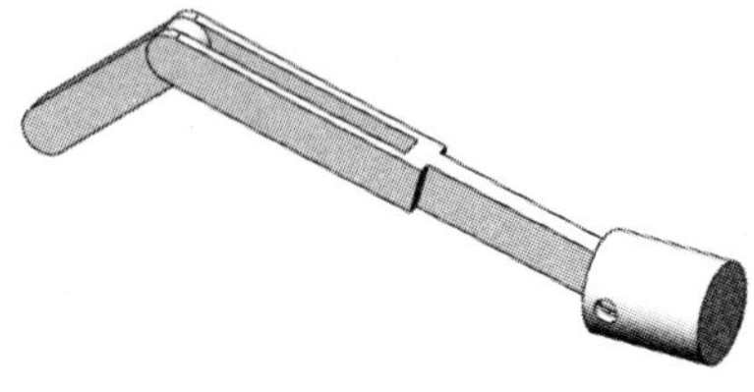

5.1-1 Introduction

[1] Consider a **Crank-Link-Piston** mechanism [2-4]. This problem is adapted from Sample Problem 15.7, *Vector Mechanics for Engineers: Dynamics, 9th ed in SI Units.*, by F. P. Beer, E. R. Johnston, Jr., and P. J. Cornwell. Some of the quantities calculated by the textbook are: when $\theta = 40^\circ$ (as shown in the figure),

The angular velocity of the **Link**	$\vec{\omega}_{BD} = 62.0\ \vec{k}$ rad/s)	(1)
The angular acceleration of the **Link**	$\vec{\alpha}_{BD} = 9940\ \vec{k}$ (rad/s^2)	(2)
The linear velocity of the **Piston**	$\vec{v}_D = 13.08\ \vec{i}$ (m/s)	(3)
The linear acceleration of the **Piston**	$\vec{a}_D = -2790\ \vec{i}$ (m/s^2)	(4)

In this section, after performing a simulation for the **Crank-Link-Piston** system, we'll validate the simulation results with the values in Eqs. (1-4) and then demonstrate two of the most fundamental kinematic equations for a rigid body:

$$\vec{v}_D = \vec{v}_B + \vec{\omega}_{BD} \times \vec{r}_{D/B} \tag{5}$$

$$\vec{a}_D = \vec{a}_B + \vec{\alpha}_{BD} \times \vec{r}_{D/B} + \vec{\omega}_{BD} \times \left(\vec{\omega}_{BD} \times \vec{r}_{D/B}\right) \tag{6}$$

Note that B and D can be any two points in a rigid body. Also note that Eqs. (5, 6) are valid for general 3D motions (not restricting to plane motions).

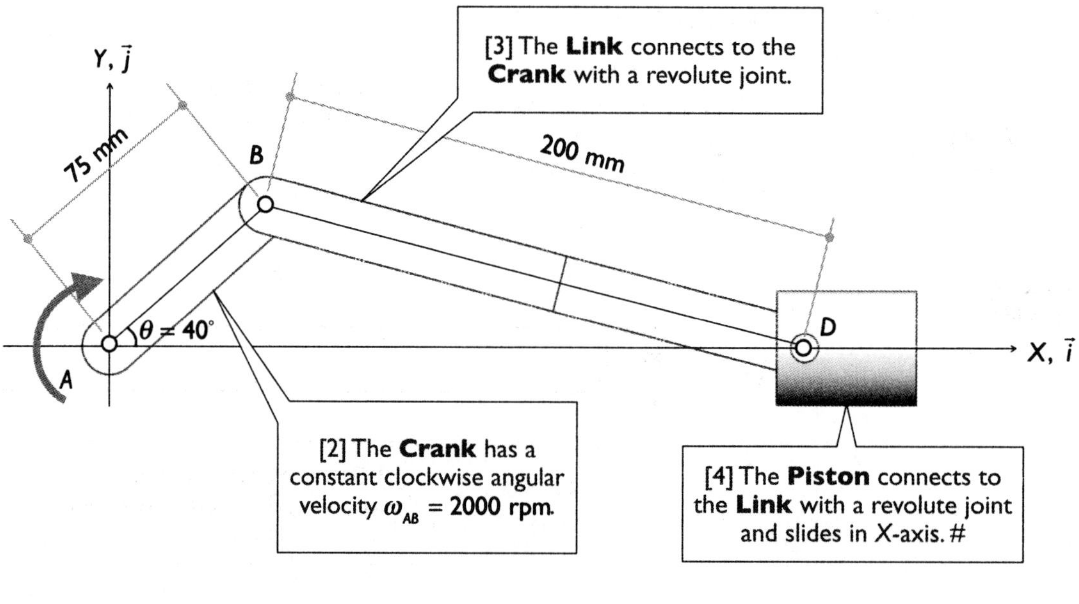

5.1-2 Start Up and Create a Part: **Crank**

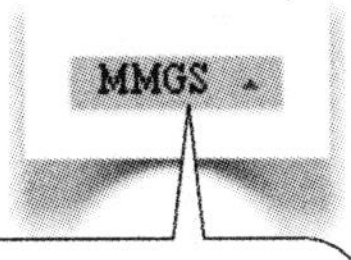

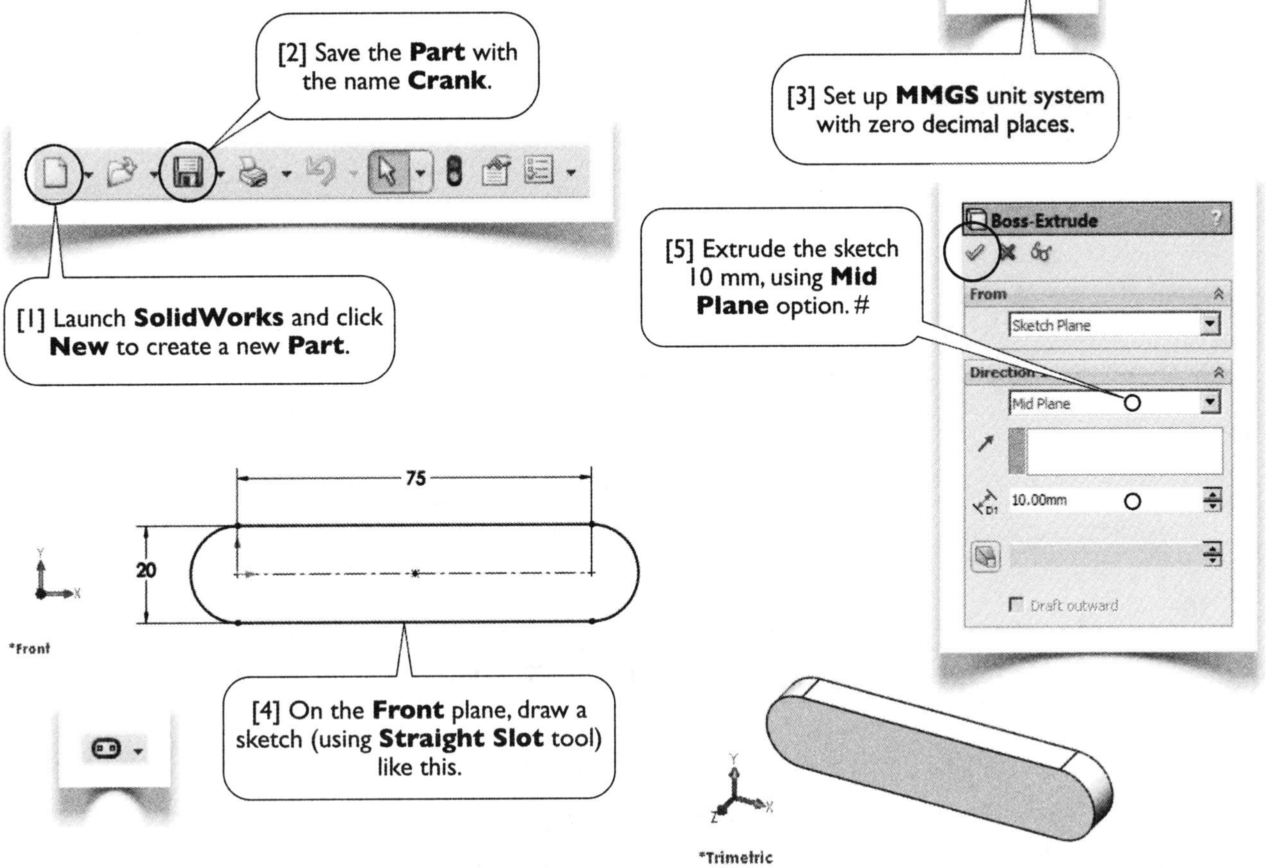

5.1-3 Create a Part: **Link**

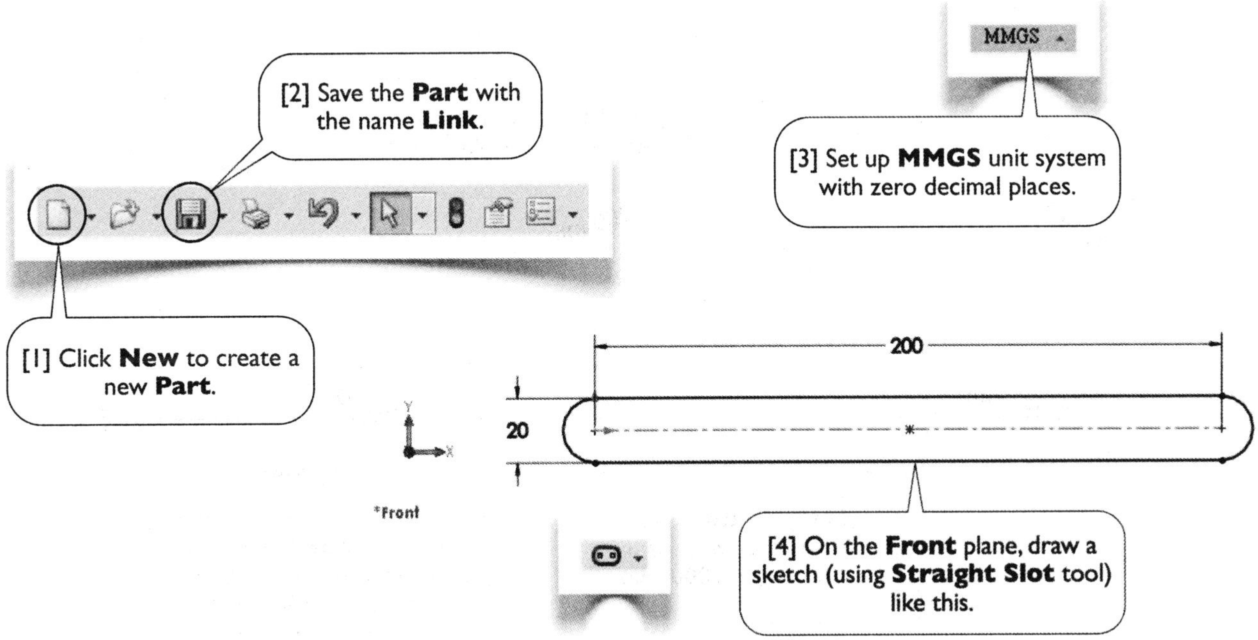

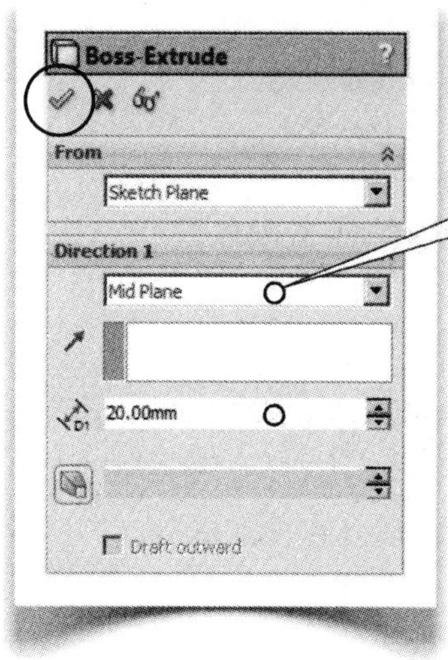

[5] Extrude the sketch 20 mm, using **Mid Plane** option.

[6] Right-click this face and select **Sketch**.

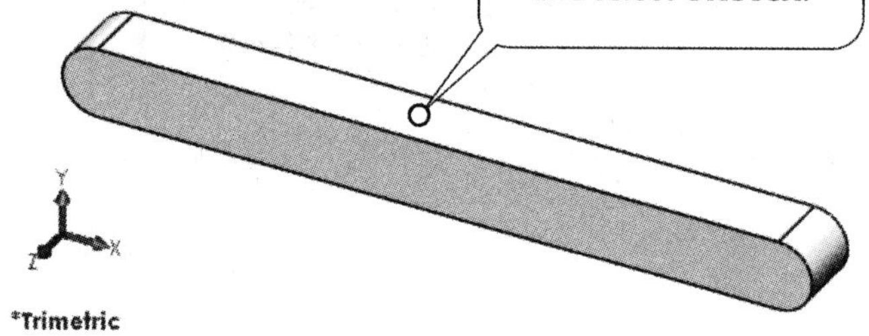

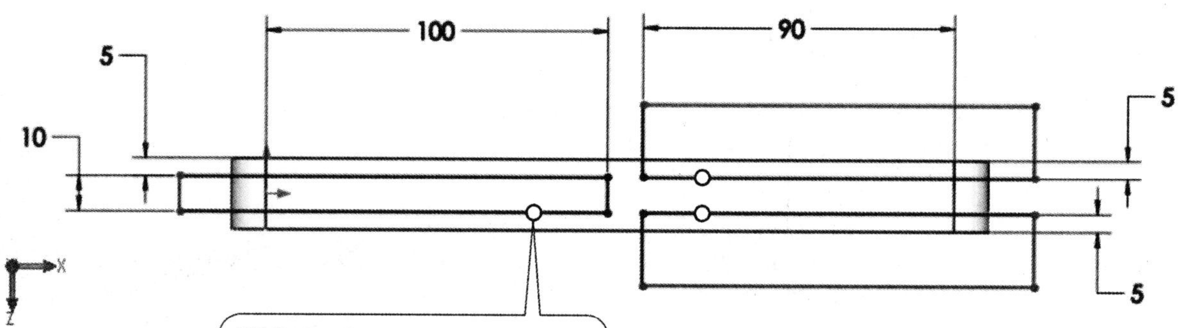

[7] Draw three rectangles like this. Note that some dimensions are not important and need not to be specified.

[8] In the **Features Toolbar**, click **Extruded Cut**.

[9] Select **Through All**. #

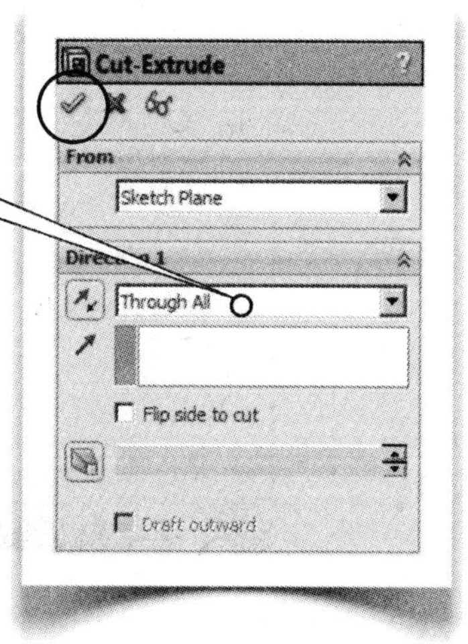

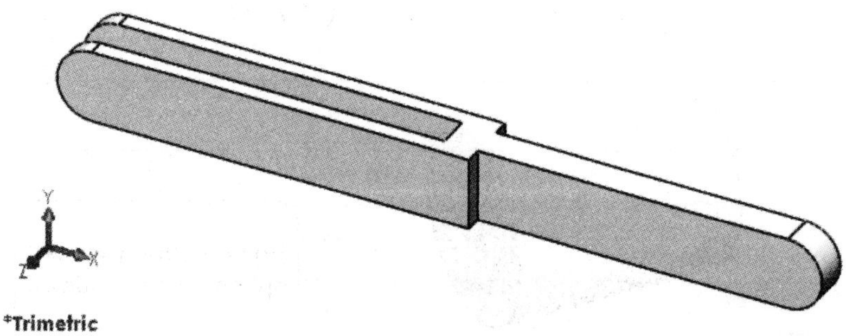

5.1-4 Create a Part: **Piston**

[1] Click **New** to create a new **Part**.

[2] Save the **Part** with the name **Piston**.

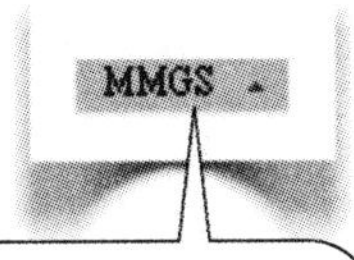

[3] Set up **MMGS** unit system with zero decimal places.

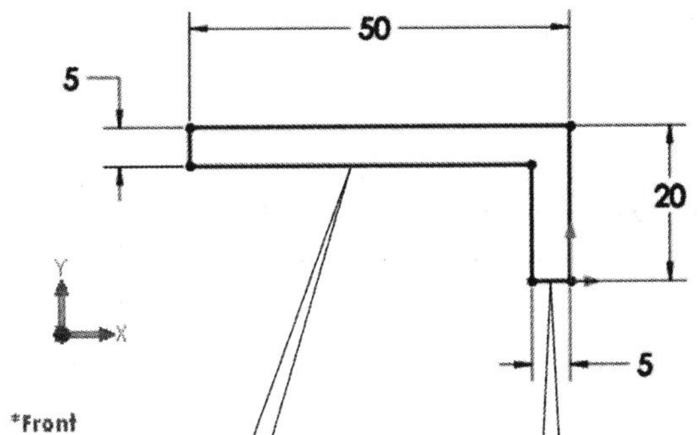

[4] On the **Front** plane, draw a sketch like this.

[6] This line is used as the **Axis of Revolution**.

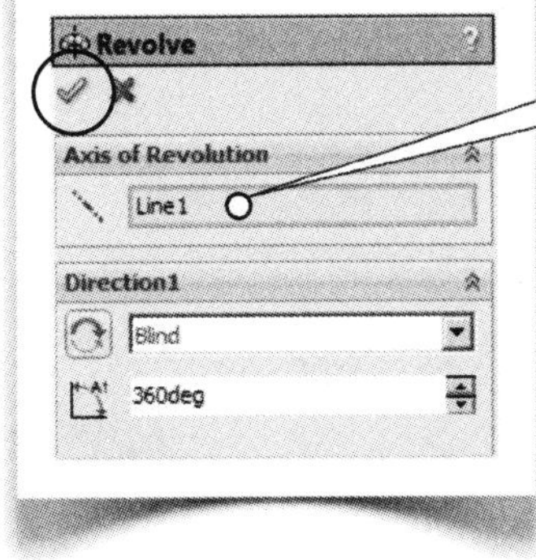

[5] **Revolve** the sketch 360 degrees using the line on X-axis [6] as the **Axis of Revolution**.

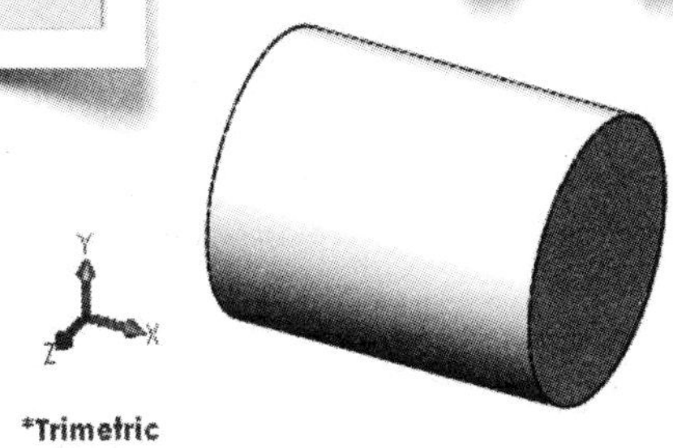

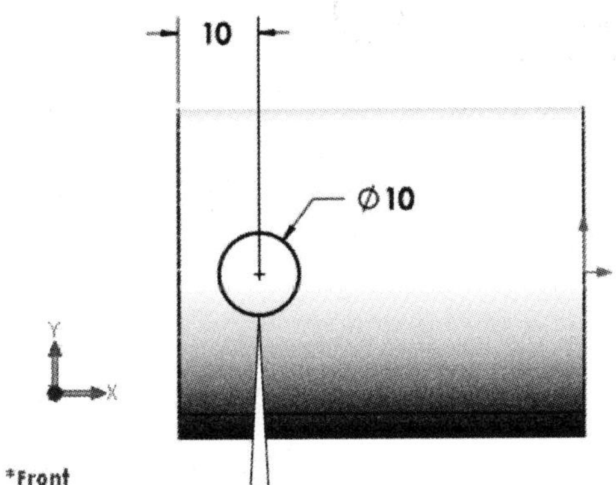

[7] On the **Front** plane, draw a circle like this.

[8] In the **Features Toolbar**, click **Extruded Cut**.

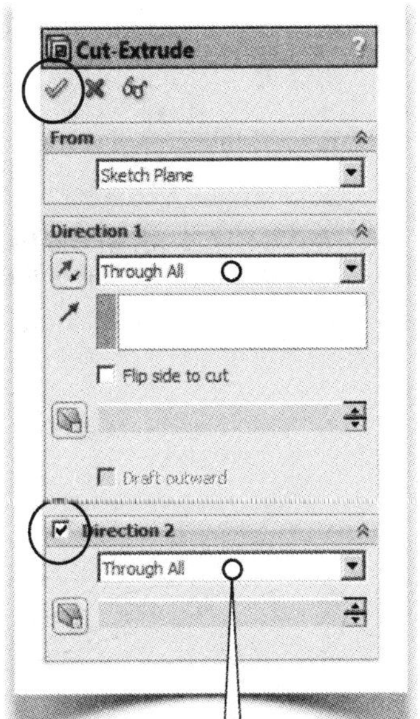

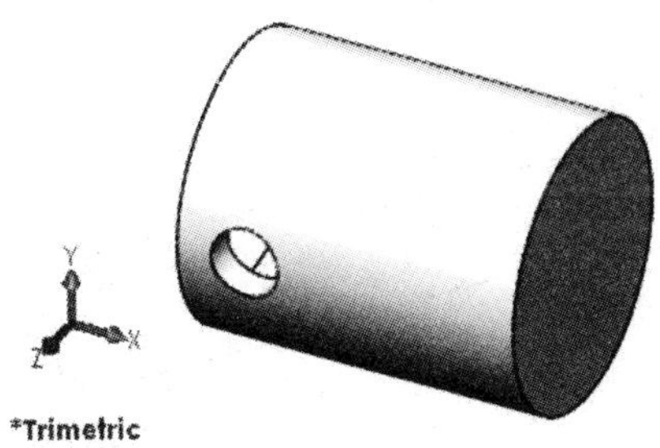

[9] Use **Through All** option for both sides. #

5.1-5 Create an Assembly: **Crank-Link-Piston**

[1] Click **New** and create an **Assembly**.

[4] Save the **Assembly** with the name **Crank-Link-Piston**.

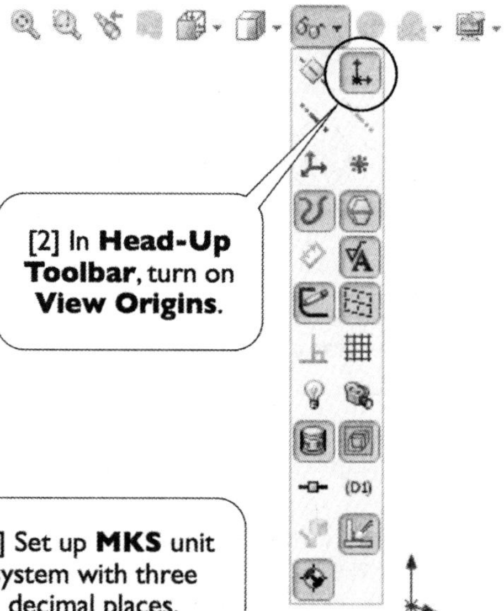

[2] In **Head-Up Toolbar**, turn on **View Origins**.

[3] In the **Begin Assembly Property Box**, select **Crank** and click the assembly's **Origin**.

[5] Set up **MKS** unit system with three decimal places.

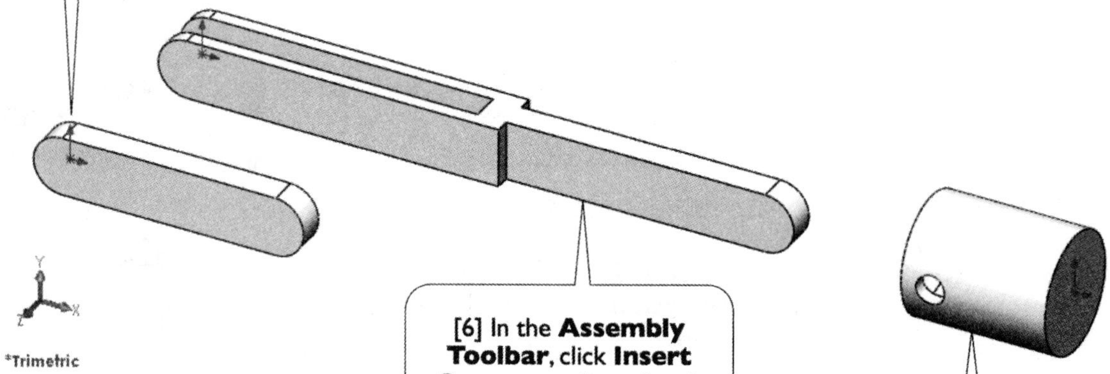

[6] In the **Assembly Toolbar**, click **Insert Components** and park **Link** here.

[7] Click **Insert Components** again and park **Piston** here.

[8] Right-click **Crank<1>** and select **Float**.

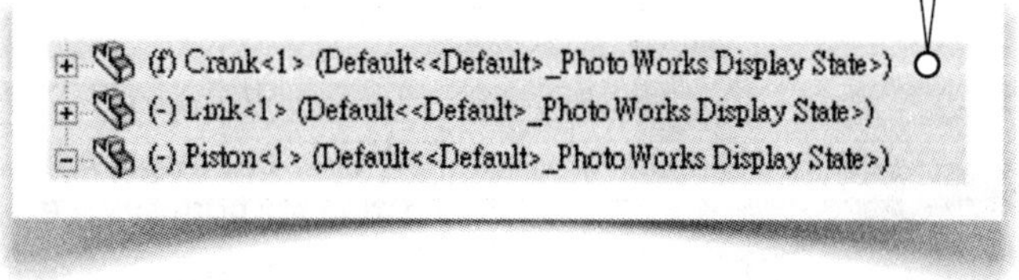

[9] In **Assembly Toolbar**, click **Mate**.

[10] We'll create these 8 **Mates** in [11-25].

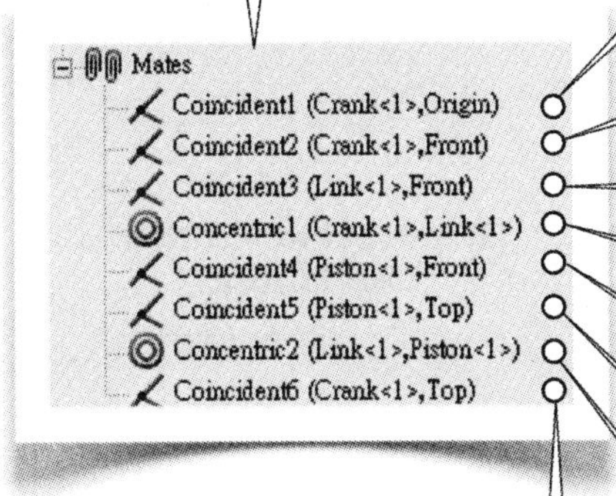

[11] The **Assembly's** and the **Crank's Origins** are **Coincident**. Before clicking **OK**, uncheck **Align axes** (see [12]).

[13] The **Assembly's** and the **Crank's Front** planes are **Coincident**.

[14] The **Assembly's** and the **Link's Front** planes are **Coincident**.

[15] **Concentric1** establishes a revolute joint between the **Crank** and the **Link**, see [16, 17].

[18] The **Assembly's** and the **Piston's Front** planes are **Coincident**.

[19] The **Assembly's** and the **Piston's Top** planes are **Coincident**. Now, the piston can move along *X*-axis only.

[20] **Concentric2** establishes a revolute joint between the **Link** and the **Piston**, see [21, 22].

[24] Finally, the **Assembly's** and the **Crank's Top** planes are **Coincident**. This is the initial configuration (see [25]). We'll suppress this **Mate** later.

[12] Uncheck **Align axes**.

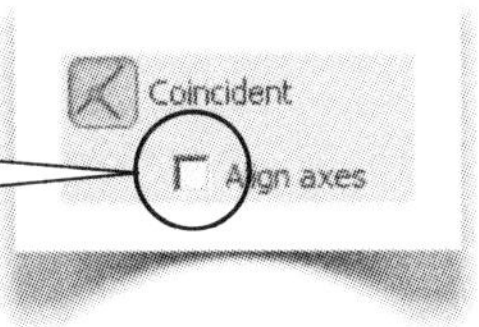

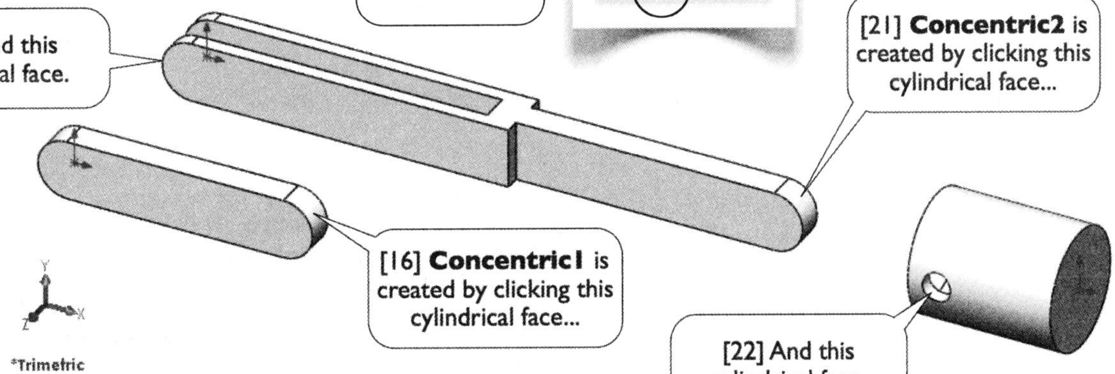

[17] And this cylindrical face.

[21] **Concentric2** is created by clicking this cylindrical face...

[16] **Concentric1** is created by clicking this cylindrical face...

[22] And this cylindrical face.

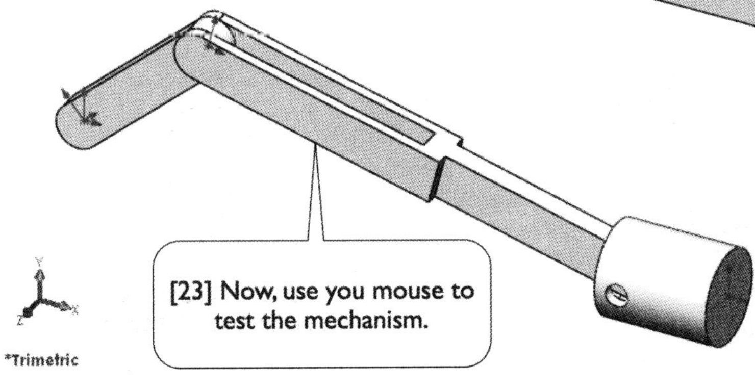

[23] Now, use you mouse to test the mechanism.

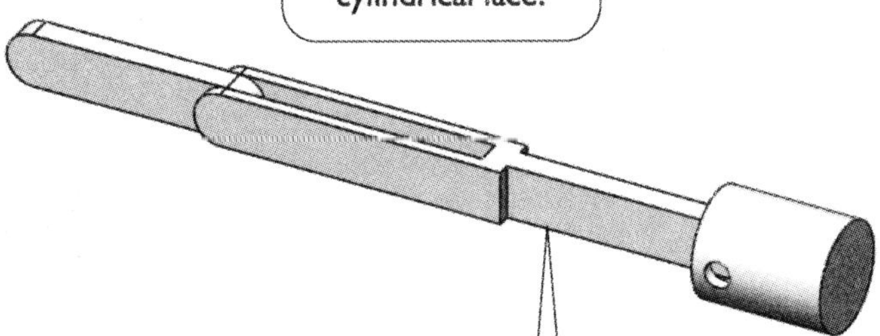

[25] This is the initial configuration. Turned off **View Origins**. #

5.1-6 Create a **Motion Study** and Set Up **Motor**

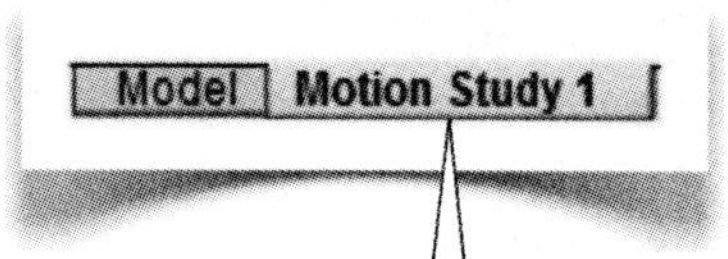

[1] Click **Motion Study 1** tab.

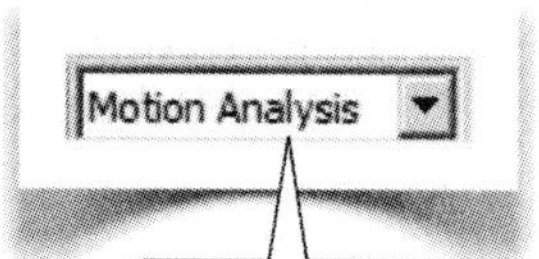

[2] Select **Motion Analysis**.

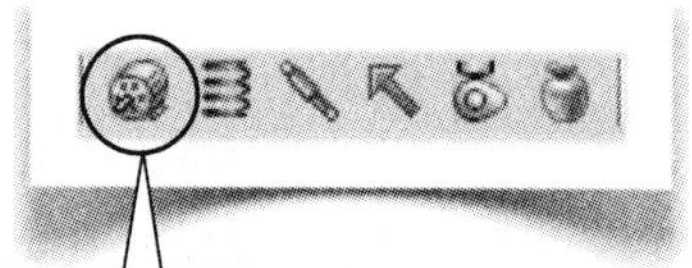

[3] In **Motion Toolbar**, click **Motor**.

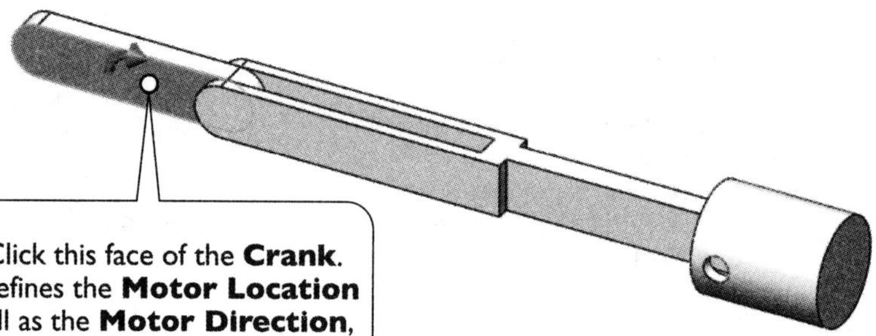

[4] Click this face of the **Crank**. This defines the **Motor Location** as well as the **Motor Direction**, see [5, 6].

[9] Click **OK**. #

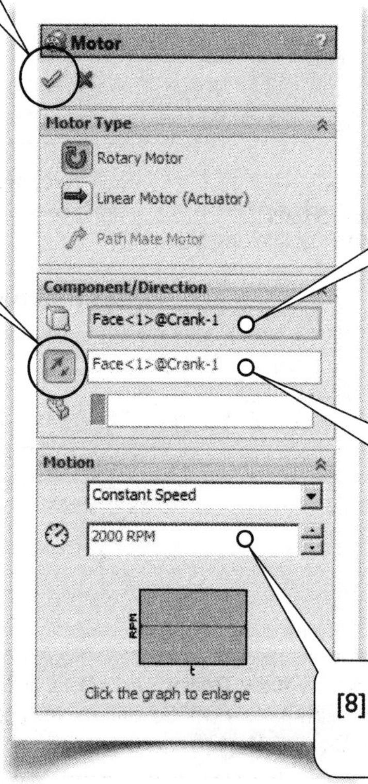

[7] Click **Reverse Direction**.

[5] The **Crank** becomes the **Motor Location**.

[6] The face defines the **Direction** of the **Rotary Motor**; i.e., Z-direction.

[8] Type 2000 (RPM) for **Speed**.

5.1-7 Calculate and Animate **Results**

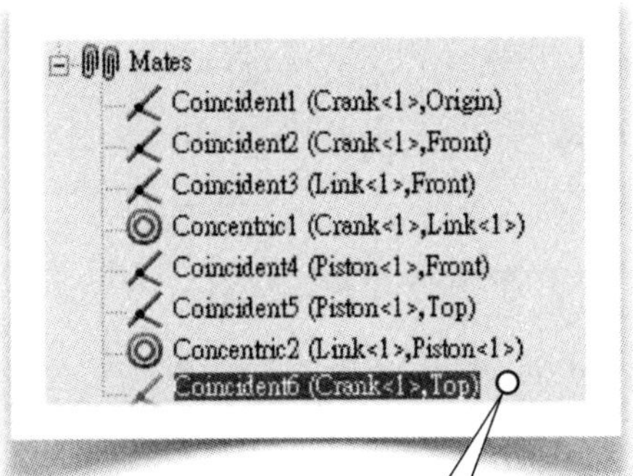

[1] In the **Assembly Tree**, under **Mates**, suppress **Coincident6** (see 5.1-5[24], page 105).

[2] In the **Motion Toolbar**, Click **Motion Study Properties**.

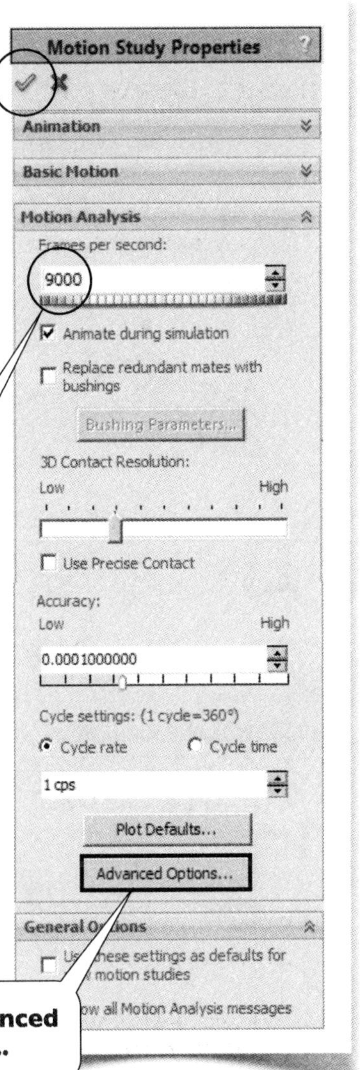

[3] Type 9000 for **Frames per second**. We want the **CSV** file report results every 1/9000 sec. Note that $\theta = 40^\circ$ (see 5.1-1, page 100) corresponds to $t = 8/300$ seconds ($(360^\circ - 40^\circ) \div (2000 \times 360^\circ \div 60) = 8/300$ sec).

[4] Click **Advanced Options...**

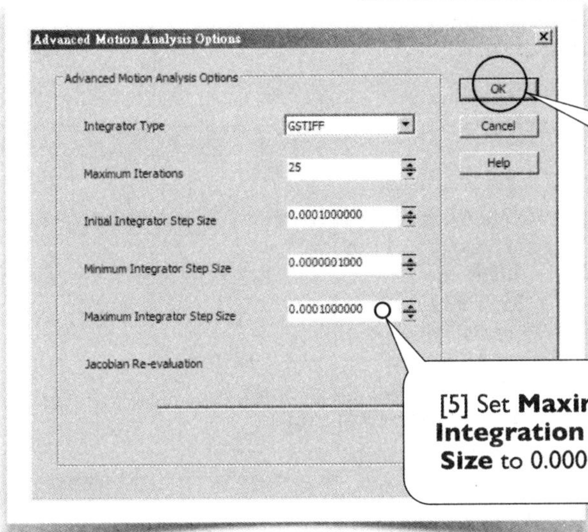

[5] Set **Maximum Integration Step Size** to 0.0001 sec.

[6] Click **OK**.

[7] Click **OK**.

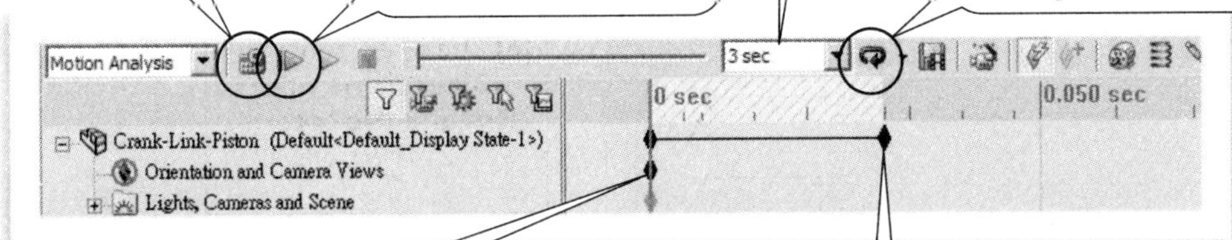

[8] Right-click this **Key Point** and select **Edit Key Point Time** and type 0.03 (sec). The simulation will be one cycle (2000 rpm = 0.03 sec/cycle). Click **Time Scale Zoom Buttons** to zoom-in the time scale (1.1-11[2], page 14).

[9] Set **Playback Speed** to **3 sec**. A cycle will play 3 sec.

[10] Select **Loop** for **Playback Mode**.

[11] Right-click this **Key Point** and select **View Orientation>Isometric**.

[12] Click **Calculate**.

[13] Click **Play from Start**. Click **Stop** after viewing the animation. #

5.1-8 Results: Angular Velocity and Acceleration of the **Link**

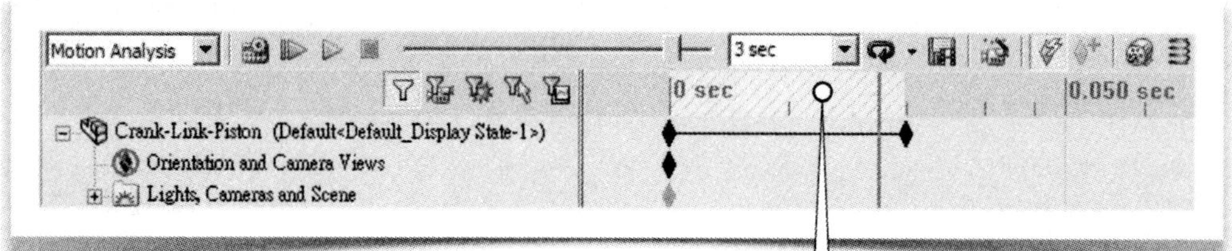

[1] Right-click the yellow area and select **Move Time Bar** and type 0.026667 (s).

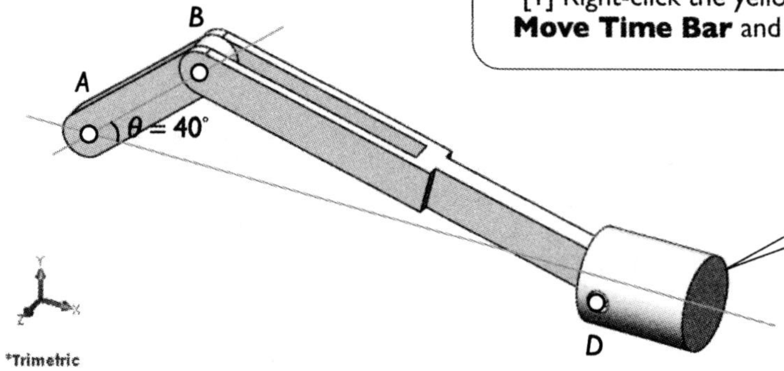

[2] The configuration at t = **0.026667 sec**.

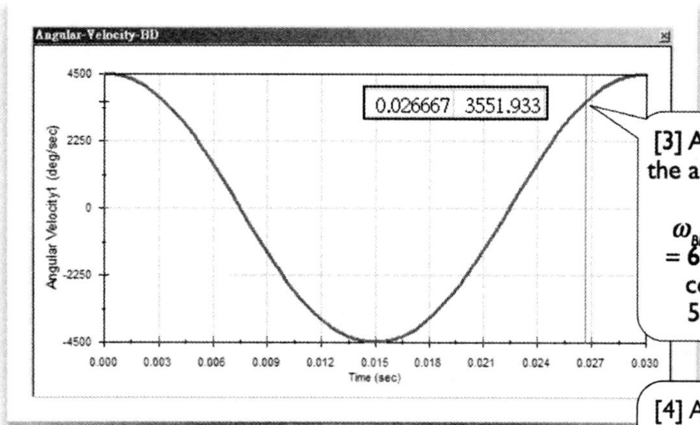

[3] At 0.026667 seconds, the angular velocity of the **Link** is ω_{BD} = **3551.933 deg/s** = **61.99 rad/s**, which is consistent with Eq. 5.1-1(1), page 100.

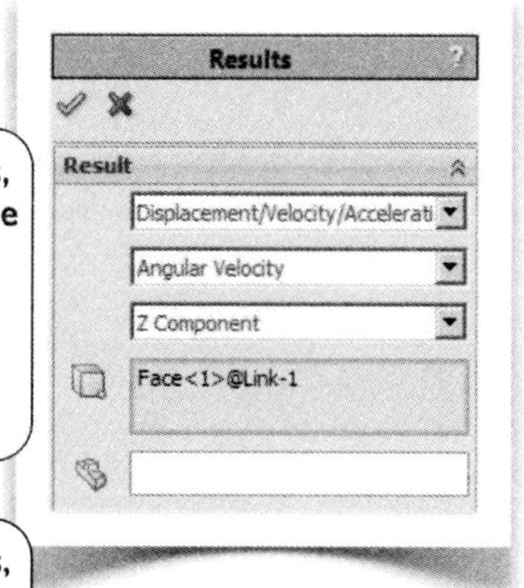

[4] At 0.026667 seconds, the angular acceleration of the **Link** is α_{BD} = **569529.4 deg/s^2** = **9940.16 rad/s^2**, which is consistent with Eq. 5.1-1(2), page 100. #

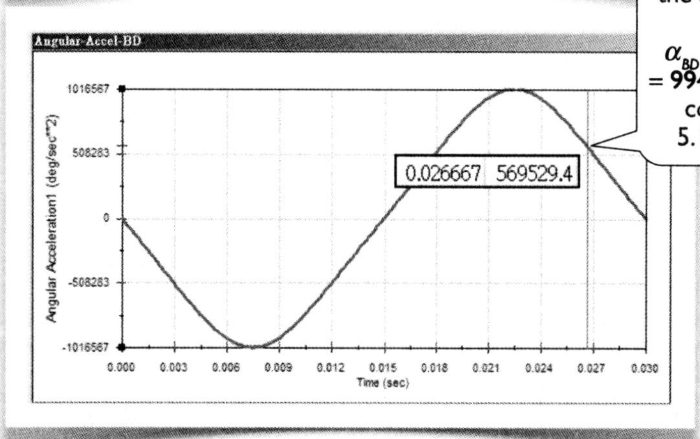

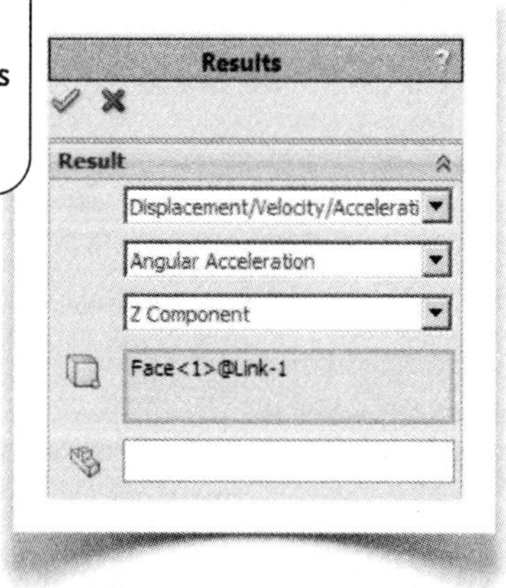

5.1-9 Results: Linear Velocity and Acceleration of the **Piston**

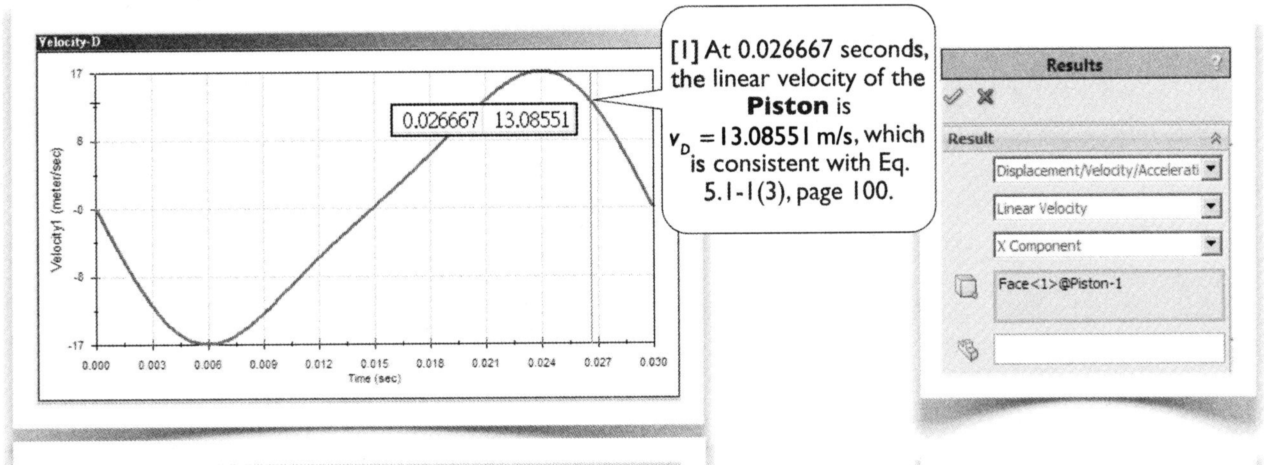

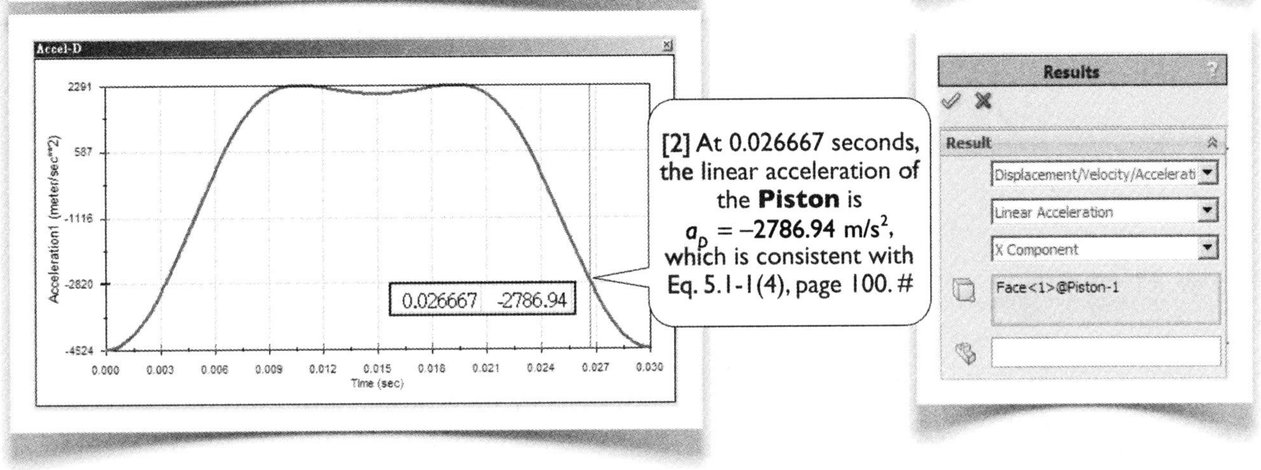

5.1-10 Results: Linear Velocity and Acceleration at *B*

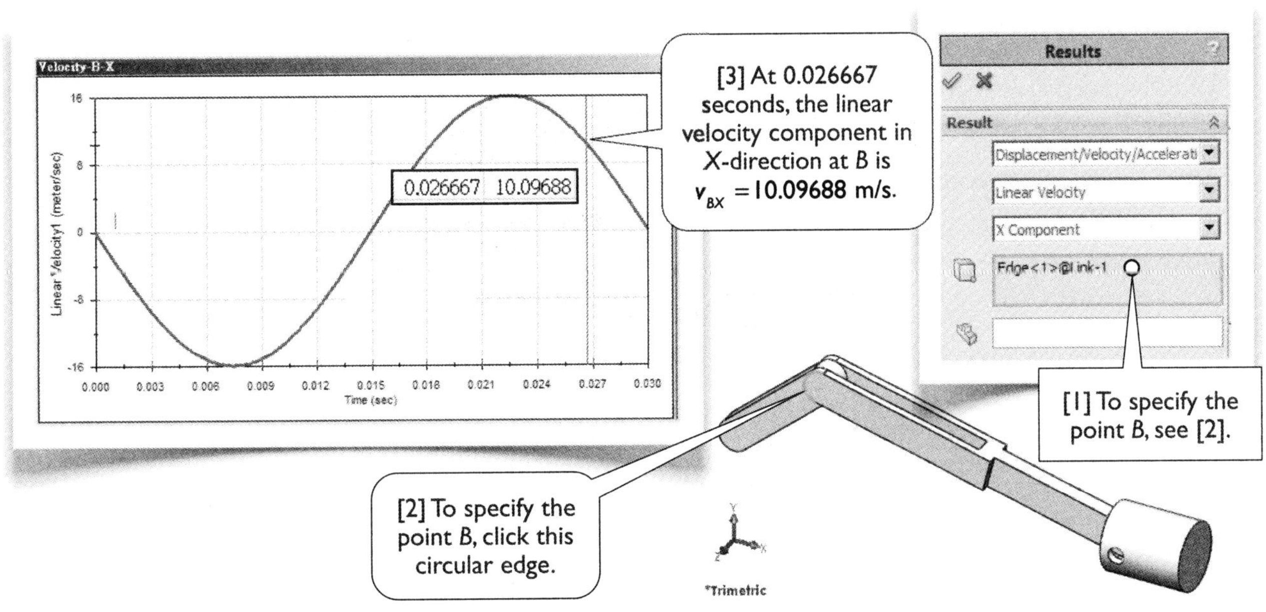

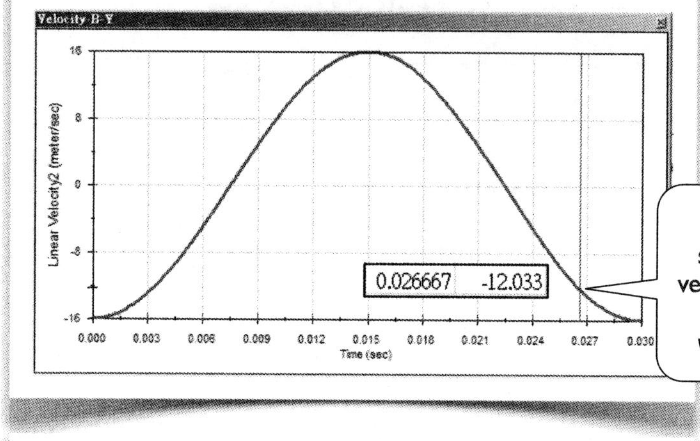

[4] At 0.026667 seconds, the linear velocity component in *Y*-direction at *B* is $v_{BY} = -12.033$ m/s.

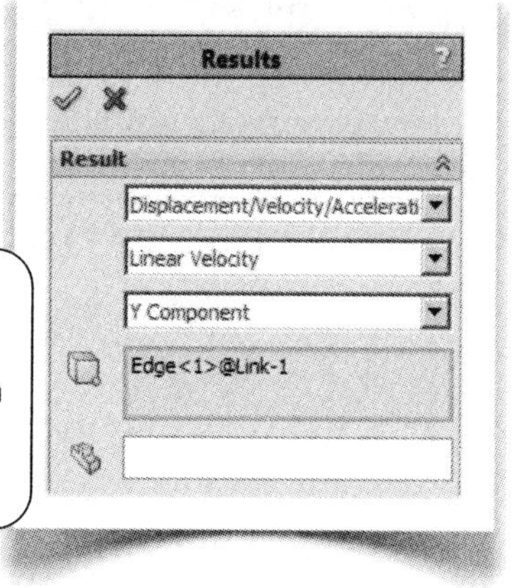

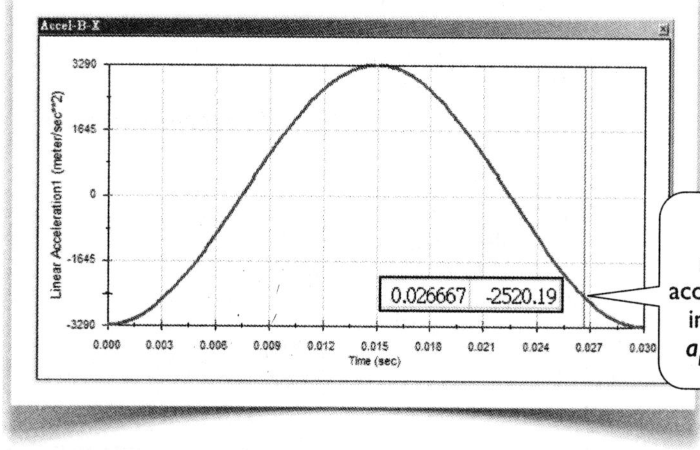

[5] At 0.026667 seconds, the linear acceleration component in *X*-direction at *B* is $a_{BX} = -2520.19$ m/s^2.

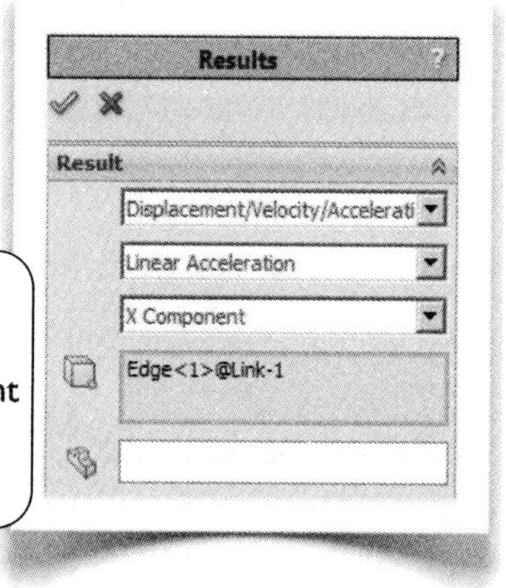

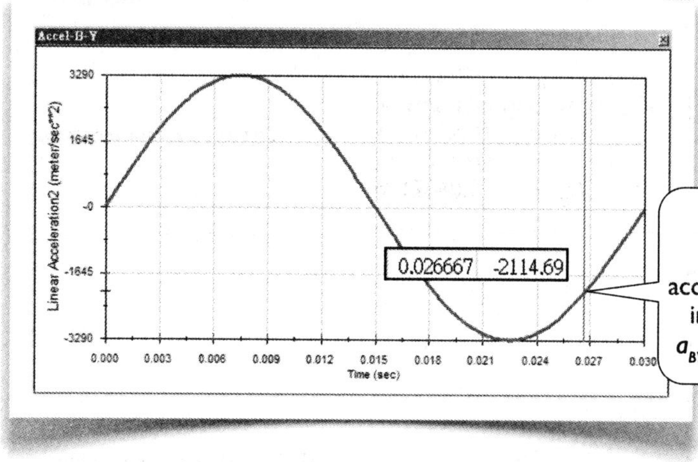

[6] At 0.026667 seconds, the linear acceleration component in *Y*-direction at *B* is $a_{BY} = -2114.69$ m/s^2. #

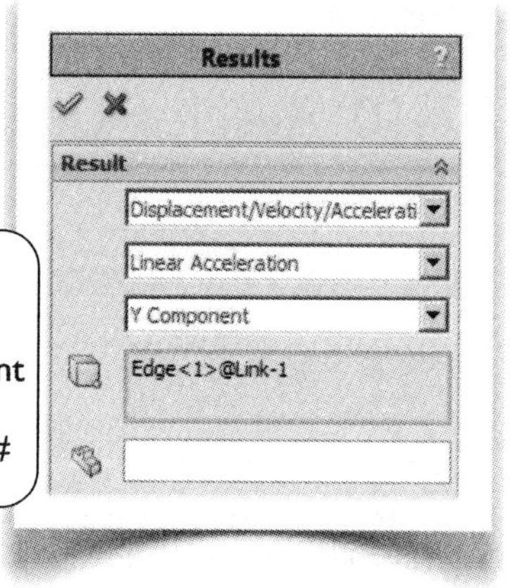

5.1-11 Results: Position Vector of D relative to B

[1] Click **Results and Plots**.

[2] To specify the position of D relative to B see [3, 4].

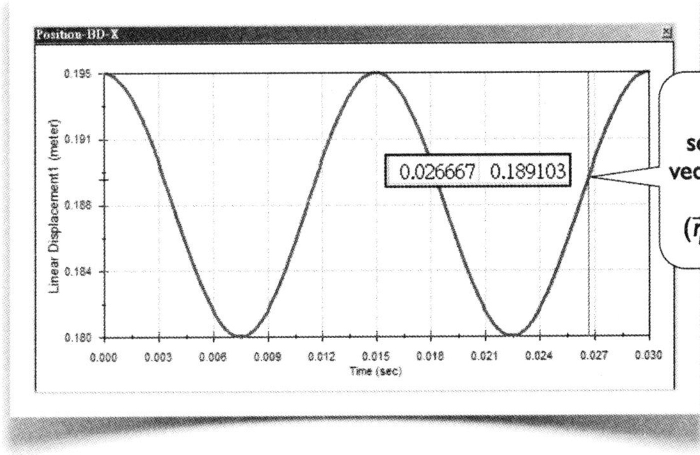

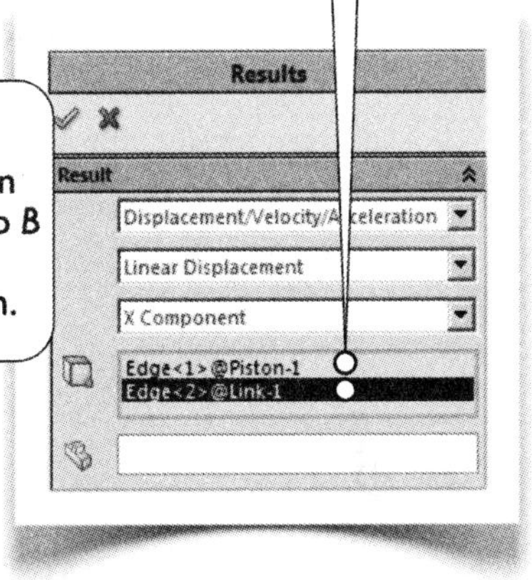

[5] At 0.026667 seconds, the position vector of D relative to B in X-direction is $(\vec{r}_{D/B})_X = 0.189103$ m.

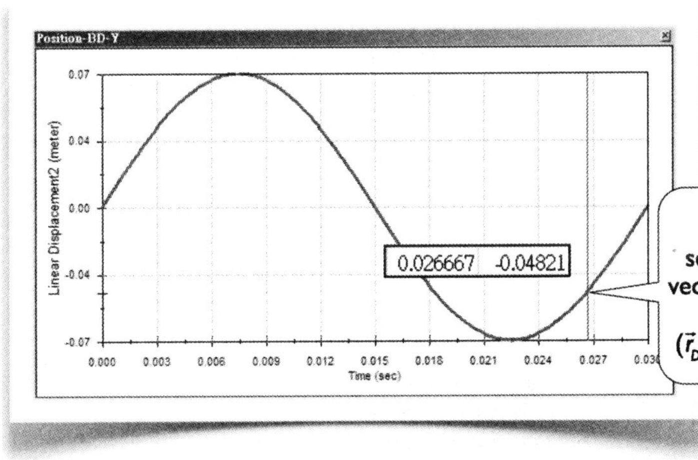

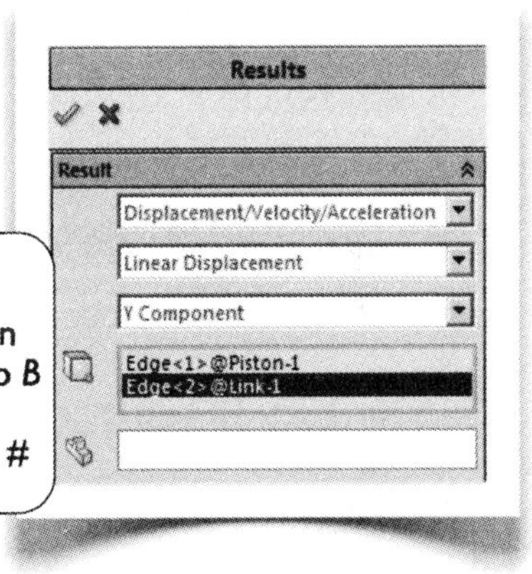

[6] At 0.026667 seconds, the position vector of D relative to B in Y-direction is $(\vec{r}_{D/B})_Y = -0.04821$ m. #

[4] And then click this circular edge to define B.

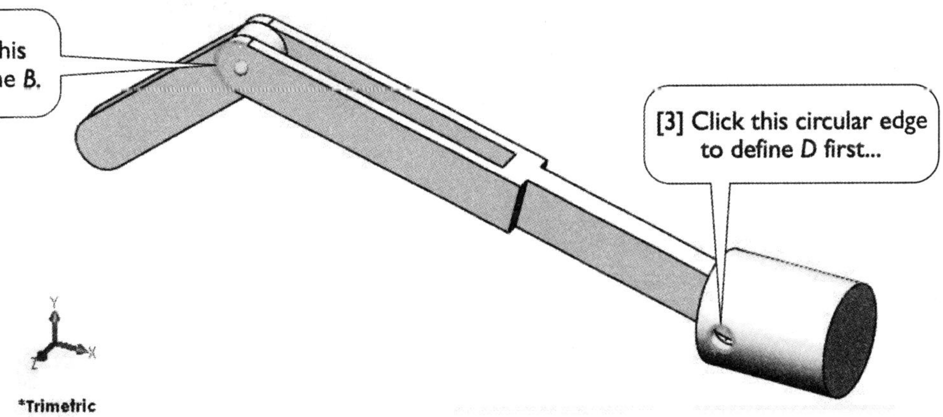

[3] Click this circular edge to define D first...

5.1-12 Verify Eqs. 5.1-1(5, 6)

[1] Let's summarize the results in 5.1-8 through 5.1-11: at 0.26667 seconds,

The angular velocity of the **Link**	$\vec{\omega}_{BD} = 61.99\ \vec{k}$ (rad/s)	(5.1-8[3], page 108)
The angular acceleration of the **Link**	$\vec{\alpha}_{BD} = 9940.16\ \vec{k}$ (rad/s^2)	(5.1-8[4], page 108)
The velocity of the **Piston**	$\vec{v}_D = 13.08551\ \vec{i}$ (m/s)	(5.1-9[1], page 109)
The acceleration of the **Piston**	$\vec{a}_D = -2786.94\ \vec{i}$ (m/s^2)	(5.1-9[2], page 109)
The linear velocity at *B*	$\vec{v}_B = 10.09688\ \vec{i} - 12.033\ \vec{j}$ (m/s)	(5.1-10[3, 4], pages 109-110)
The linear acceleration at *B*	$\vec{a}_B = -2520.19\ \vec{i} - 2114.69\ \vec{j}$ (m/s^2)	(5.1-10[5, 6], page 110)
The position of *D* relative to *B*	$\vec{r}_{D/B} = 0.189103\ \vec{i} - 0.04821\ \vec{j}$ (m)	(5.1-11[5, 6], page 111)

The right-hand-side of Eq. 5.1-1(5) (page 100) is

$$\begin{aligned}\vec{v}_B + \vec{\omega}_{BD} \times \vec{r}_{D/B} &= (10.09688\ \vec{i} - 12.033\ \vec{j}) + (61.99\ \vec{k}) \times (0.189103\ \vec{i} - 0.04821\ \vec{j}) \\ &= (10.09688\ \vec{i} - 12.033\ \vec{j}) + (2.9885\ \vec{i} + 11.7225\ \vec{j}) \\ &= 13.0854\ \vec{i} - 0.3105\ \vec{j}\end{aligned}$$

which is close to the value of $\vec{v}_D$ above. The right-hand-side of Eq. 5.1-1(6) (page 100) is

$$\begin{aligned}&\vec{a}_B + \vec{\alpha}_{BD} \times \vec{r}_{D/B} + \vec{\omega}_{BD} \times \left(\vec{\omega}_{BD} \times \vec{r}_{D/B}\right) \\ &= (-2520.19\ \vec{i} - 2114.69\ \vec{j}) + (9940.16\ \vec{k}) \times (0.189103\ \vec{i} - 0.04821\ \vec{j}) + (61.99\ \vec{k}) \times (2.9885\ \vec{i} + 11.7225\ \vec{j}) \\ &= (-2520.19\ \vec{i} - 2114.69\ \vec{j}) + (479.22\ \vec{i} + 1879.71\ \vec{j}) + (-726.68\ \vec{i} + 185.26\ \vec{j}) \\ &= -2767.65\ \vec{i} - 49.72\ \vec{j}\end{aligned}$$

which is close to the value of $\vec{a}_D$ above. #

5.1-13 Do It Yourself

[1] Eqs. 5.1-1(5, 6) (page 100) are two of the most fundamental kinematic equations for a rigid body. To make sure that you are comfortable with these equations, you should practice these equations at least one more time on your own, at different time than 0.26667 seconds.

[2] Wrap Up

Save all files and exit **SolidWorks**. #

Section 5.2

Geneva Mechanism

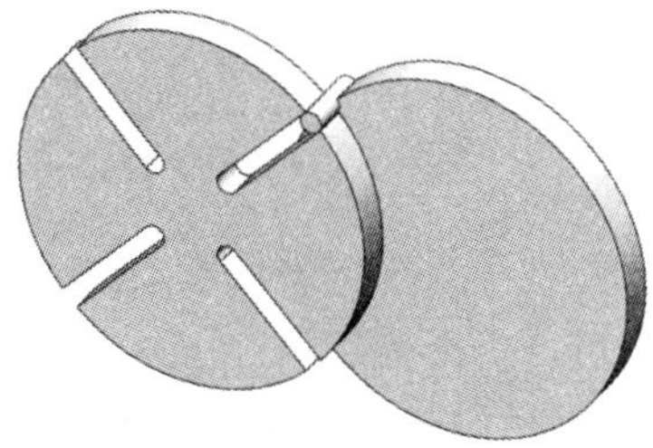

5.2-1 Introduction

[1] A geneva mechanism translates a continuous rotation of a **Driver** wheel [2] into an intermittent rotation of a **Slot** wheel [3, 4]. This problem is adapted from Sample Problem 15.9, *Vector Mechanics for Engineers: Dynamics, 9th ed. in SI Units*, by F. P. Beer, E. R. Johnston, Jr., and P. J. Cornwell. Some of the quantities calculated by the textbook are: when $\phi = 150^\circ$,

The angular velocity of the **Slot** wheel $\vec{\omega}_S = -4.08\,\vec{k}$ (rad/s) (1)

The angular acceleration of the **Slot** wheel $\vec{\alpha}_S = -233\,\vec{k}$ (rad/s^2) (2)

Note that the negative signs indicate that both the angular velocity and angular acceleration are in a clockwise sense.

In this section, we'll perform a simulation for the Geneva mechanism and validate the results with the values in Eqs. (1, 2).

[3] The objective of this simulation is to find the angular velocity and angular acceleration of the **Slot** wheel.

[4] Initially, the **Pin** is at a position $\phi = 135^\circ$.#

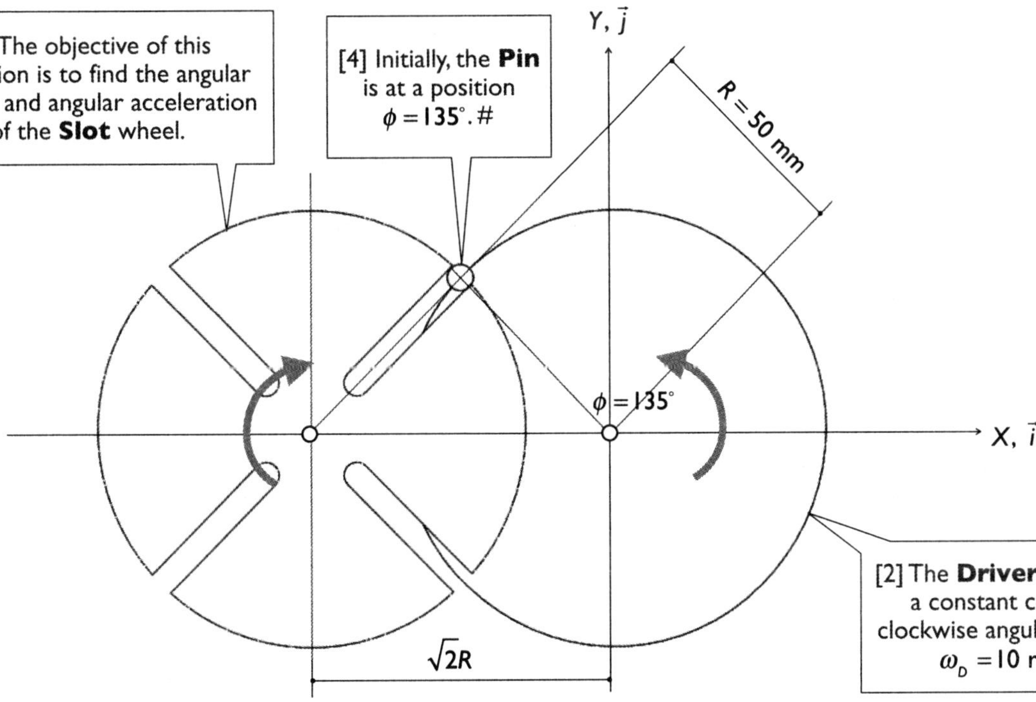

[2] The **Driver** wheel has a constant counter-clockwise angular velocity $\omega_D = 10$ rad/s.

5.2-2 Start Up and Create a Part: **Driver**

[2] Save the **Part** with the name **Driver**.

[1] Launch **SolidWorks** and click **New** to create a new **Part**.

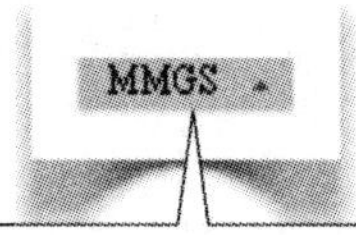

[3] Set up **MMGS** unit system with default decimal places.

[4] On **Front** plane, draw a circle like this.

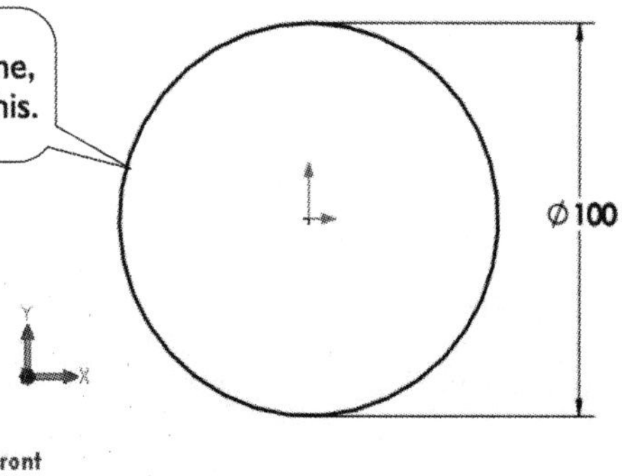

[5] Extrude the sketch 10 mm.

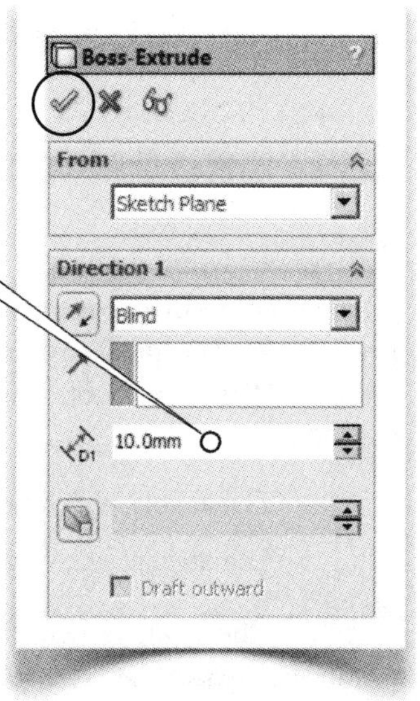

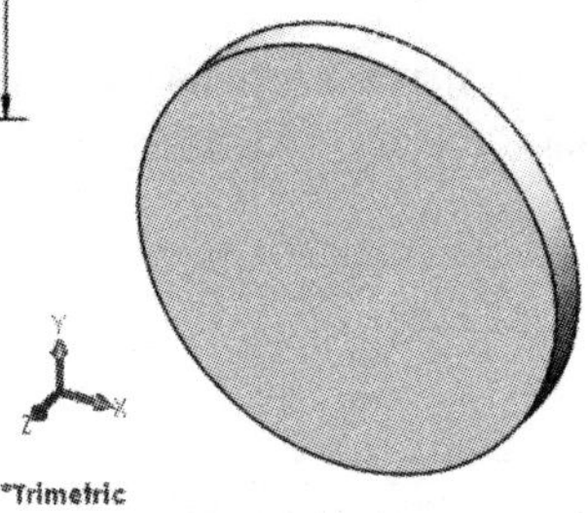

[6] On **Front** plane, draw a small circle and two **Centerlines** like this.

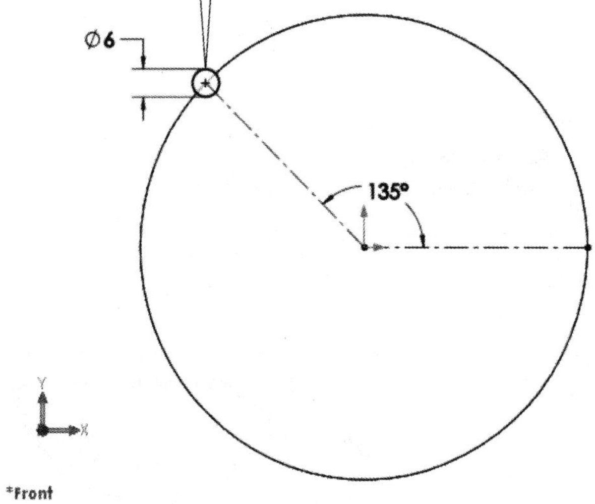

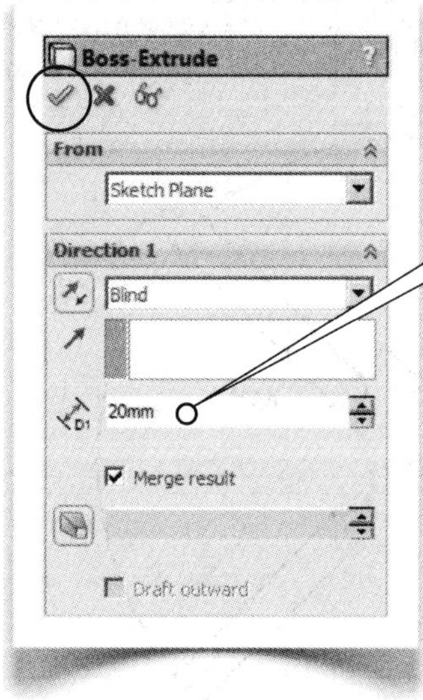

[7] Extrude the sketch 20 mm. #

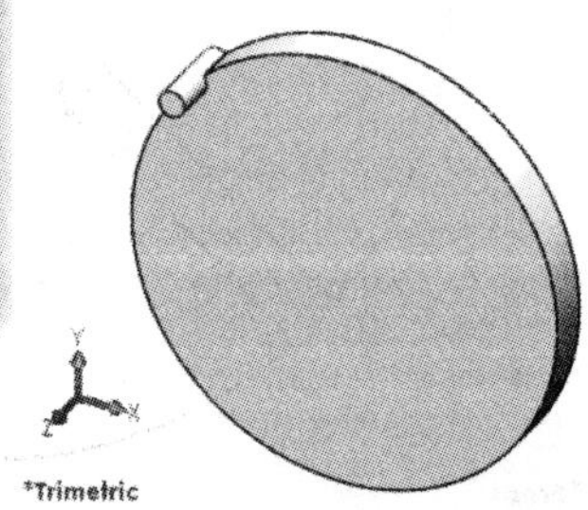

5.2-3 Create a Part: **Slot**

[3] Set up **MMGS** unit system with default decimal places.

[2] Save the **Part** with the name **Slot**.

[1] Click **New** to create a new **Part**.

[5] **Trim** away segments outside the circle (see [6]).

[4] Create a sketch on **Front** plane. Draw a **Circle**, two **Centerlines**, and a **Straight Slot**. The length of the **Straight Slot** is not important.

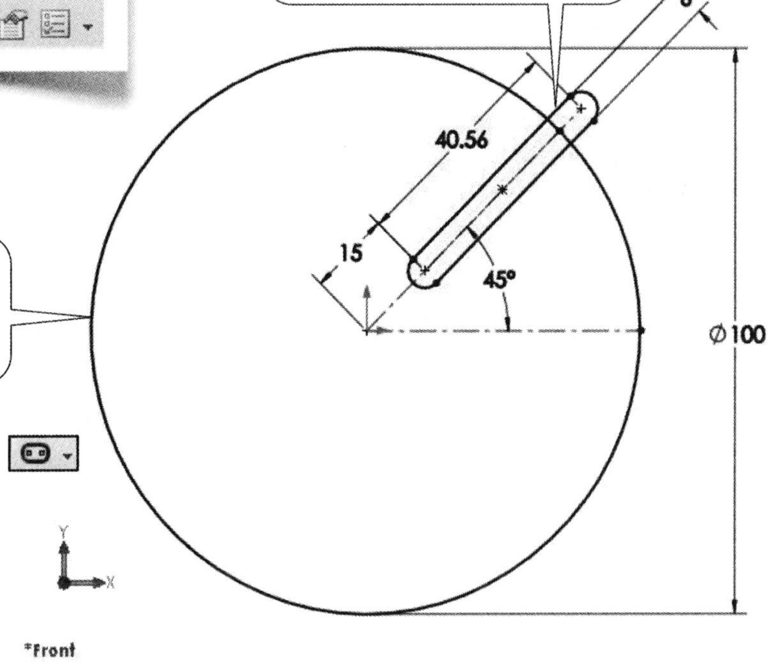

[6] After trimming, fix all entities. Remember, you can drag a blue-colored entity to figure out what relations you should add. In this case, you may add two **Parallel** and two **Tangent** relations to fix all entities except this point, which is not relevant.

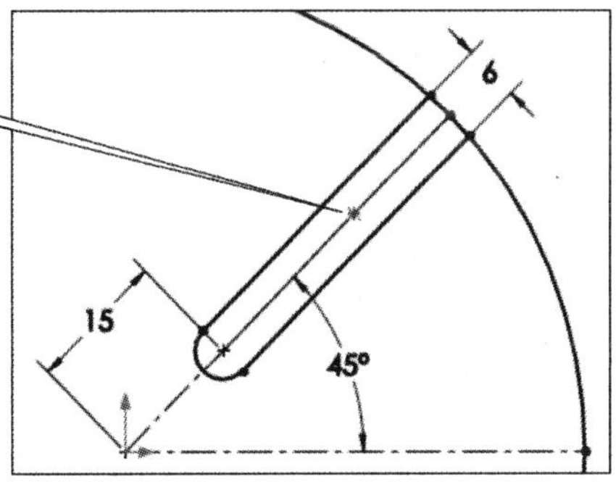

[7] Use **Circular Sketch Pattern** to duplicate the slot (including the **Centerline**). **Trim** away unwanted segments like this.

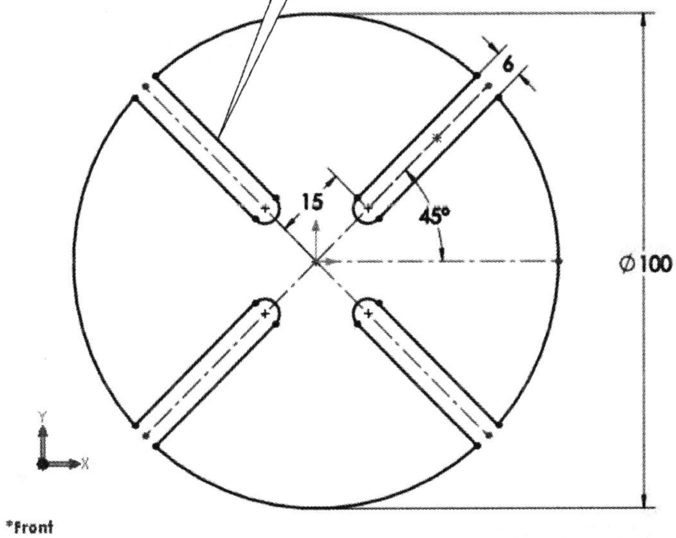

[8] Extrude the sketch 10 mm. #

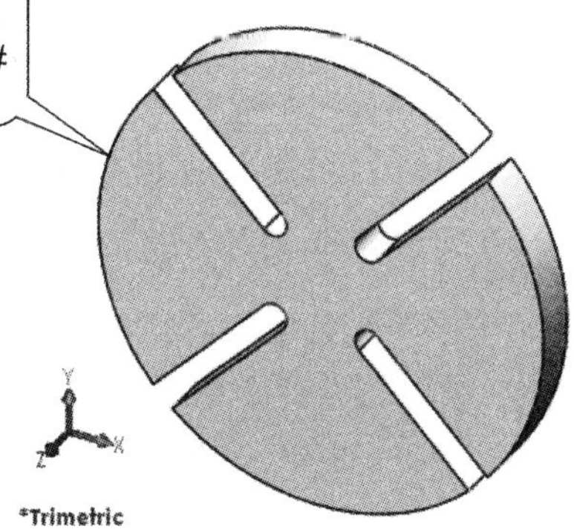

5.2-4 Create an Assembly: **Geneva**

[1] Click **New** and create an **Assembly**.

[4] Save the **Assembly** with the name **Geneva**.

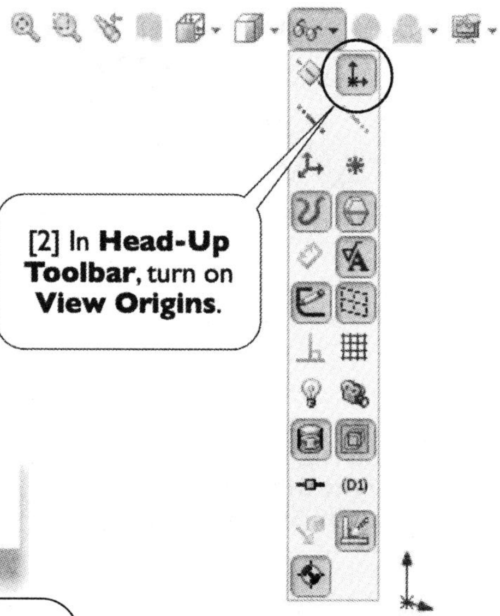

[2] In **Head-Up Toolbar**, turn on **View Origins**.

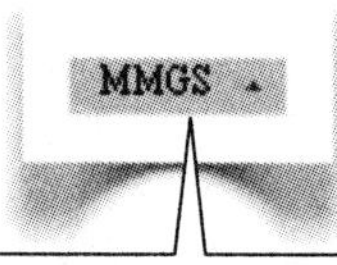

[5] Set up **MMGS** unit system with default decimal places.

[6] In the **Assembly Toolbar**, click **Insert Components** and park **Slot** anywhere.

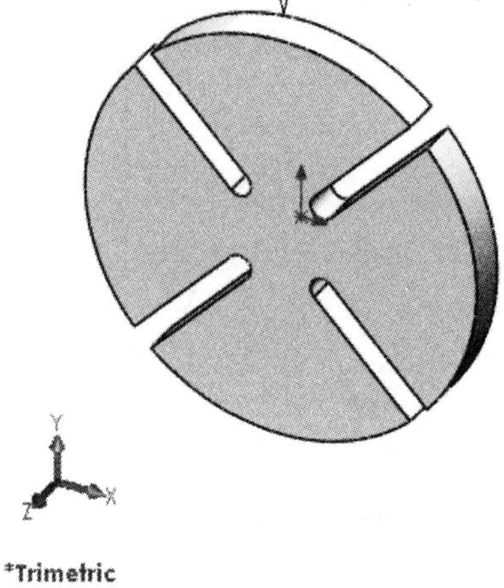

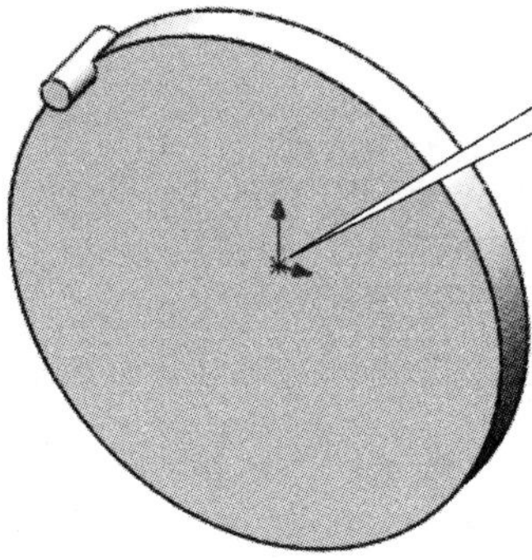

[3] In the **Begin Assembly Property Box**, select **Driver** and click the assembly's **Origin**.

[7] Right-click **Driver<1>** and select **Float**.

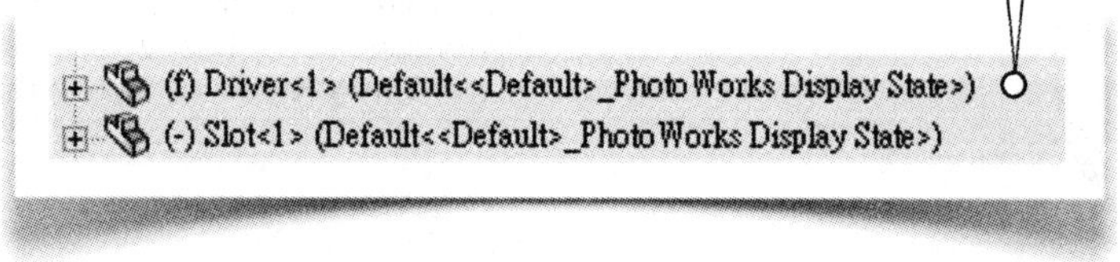

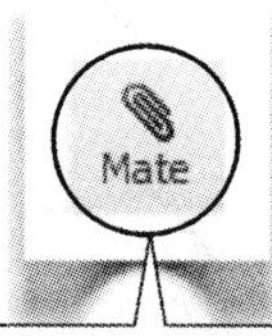

[8] In **Assembly Toolbar**, click **Mate**.

[9] We'll create these 7 **Mates** in [10-21].

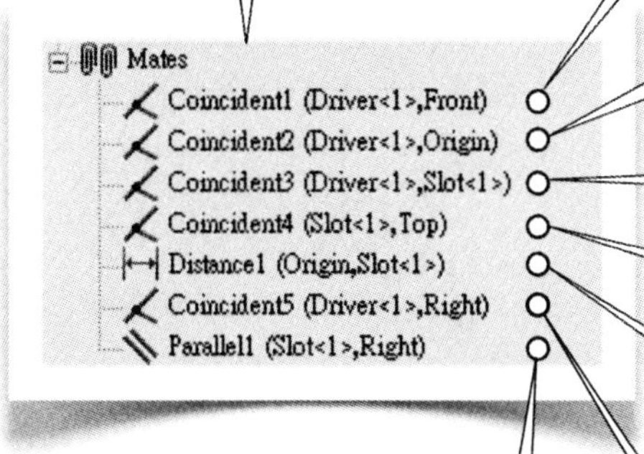

[10] The **Assembly's** and the **Driver's Front** planes are **Coincident**.

[11] The **Assembly's** and the **Driver's Origins** are **Coincident**. Before clicking **OK**, uncheck **Align axes** (see [12]).

[13] The **Driver's** frontal face and the **Slot's** backside face are **Coincident** (see [14, 15])

[16] The **Slot's Origin** and the **Assembly's Top** plane are **Coincident**.

[17] The **Assembly's** and the **Slot's Origins** has a **Distance** of 71.414 mm. This distance is calculated by: $\sqrt{2R^2 + (10\ \text{mm})^2} = 71.414\ \text{mm}$, where $R = 50$ mm.

[19] The **Assembly's** and the **Driver's Right** planes are **Coincident**. This is the initial configuration of the **Driver**. We'll suppress this **Mate** later.

[20] The **Assembly's** and the **Slot's Right** planes are **Parallel**. This is the initial configuration of the **Slot**. We'll suppress this **Mate** later.

[12] Uncheck **Align axes**.

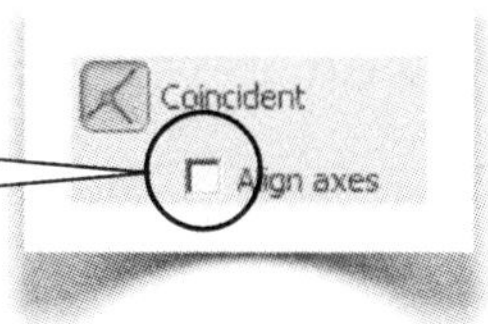

[15] The **Slot's** backside face.

[14] The **Driver's** frontal face.

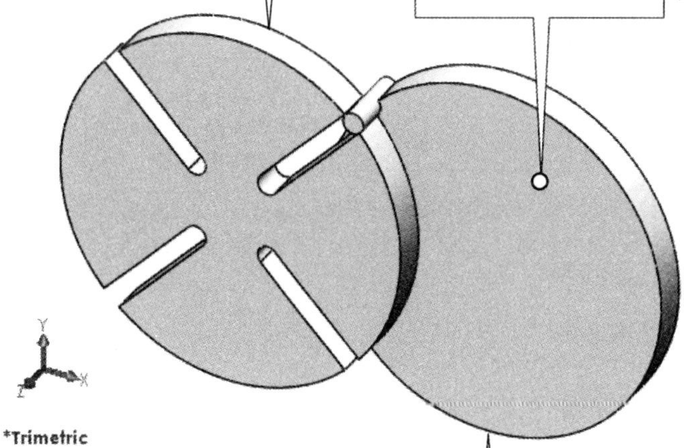

[21] This is the initial configuration. Turned off **View Origins**. #

[18] Now, use you mouse to rotate the **Driver** and the **Slot**.

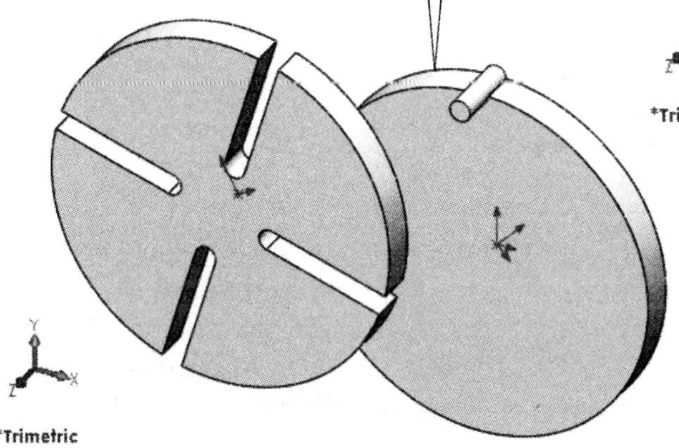

5.2-5 Create a **Motion Study**, Set Up **Contact** and **Motor**

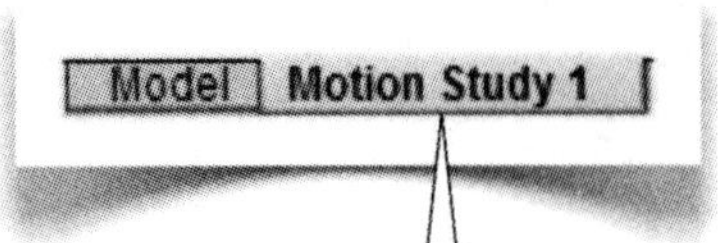

[1] Click **Motion Study 1** tab.

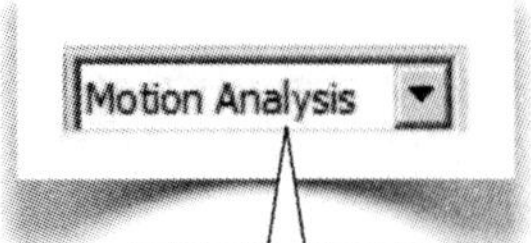

[2] Select **Motion Analysis**.

[3] In **Motion Toolbar**, click **Contact**.

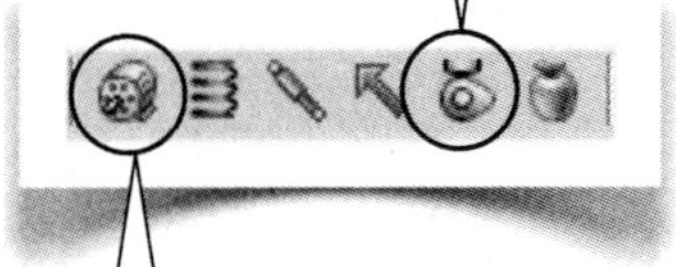

[8] Click **Motor**.

[7] Click **OK**.

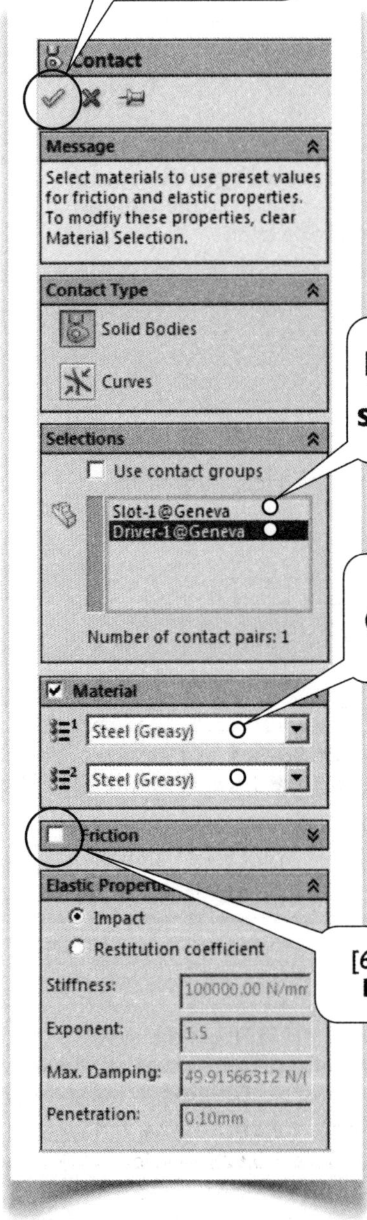

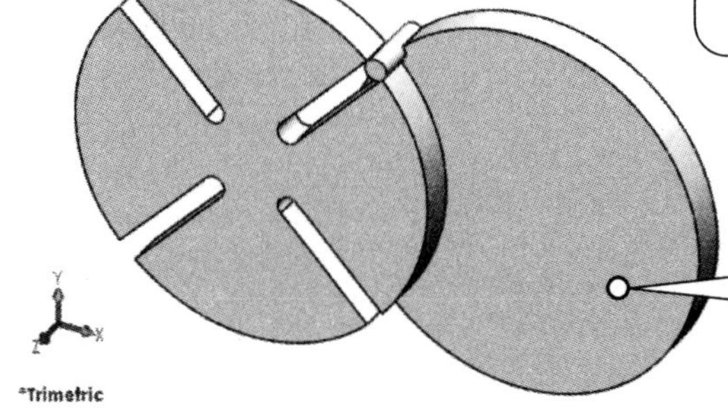

[9] Click this face of the **Driver**. This defines the **Motor Location** as well as the **Motor Direction**, see [10, 11].

[4] In the **Graphics Window**, click the **Slot** and the **Driver**.

[5] Select **Steel (Greasy)** for both materials.

[6] Uncheck **Friction**.

[13] Click **OK**. #

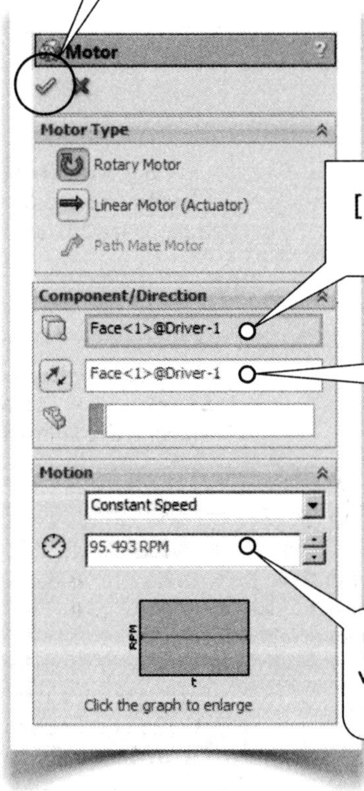

[10] The **Driver** is the **Motor Location**.

[11] The face normal is the **Direction** of the **Rotary Motor**; i.e., *Z*-direction.

[12] Type 95.493 (RPM), which equals to 10 rad/s, for **Speed**.

5.2-6 Calculate and Animate **Results**

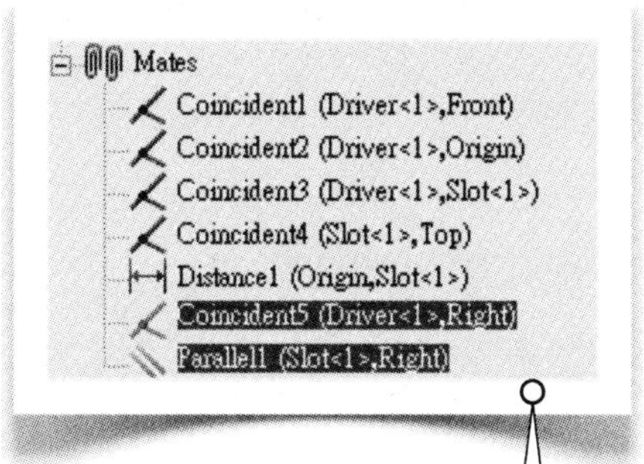

[1] In the **Assembly Tree**, under **Mates**, suppress **Coincident5** and **Parallel1** (see 5.2-4[19, 20], page 117).

[2] In the **Motion Toolbar**, Click **Motion Study Properties**.

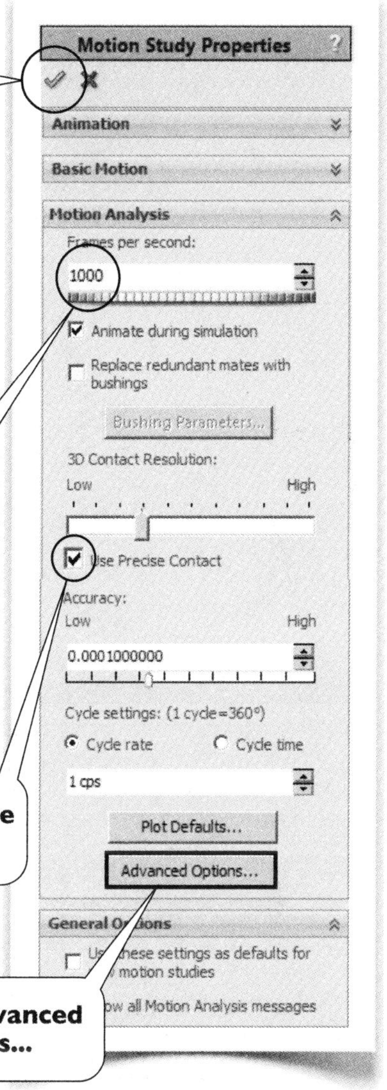

[3] Type 1000 for **Frames per second**.

[4] Click **Use Precise Contact**.

[5] Click **Advanced Options...**

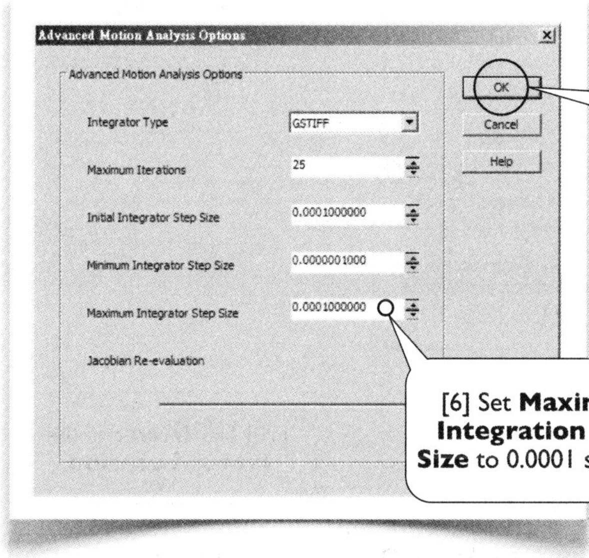

[6] Set **Maximum Integration Step Size** to 0.0001 seconds.

[7] Click **OK**.

[8] Click **OK**.

[9] Right-click this **Key Point** and select **Edit Key Point Time** and type 0.628 (s). The simulation will be one cycle (10 rad/s = 0.628 s/cycle). Click **Time Scale Zoom Buttons** to enlarge the time scale (1.1-11[2], page 14).

[10] Set **Playback Speed** to **3 sec**. A cycle will play 3 sec.

[11] Select **Loop** for **Playback Mode**.

[12] Right-click this **Key Point** and select **View Orientation>Front**.

[13] Click **Calculate**.

[14] Click **Play from Start**. Click **Stop** after viewing the animation. #

5.2-7 Results: Angular Velocity and Acceleration of the **Slot**

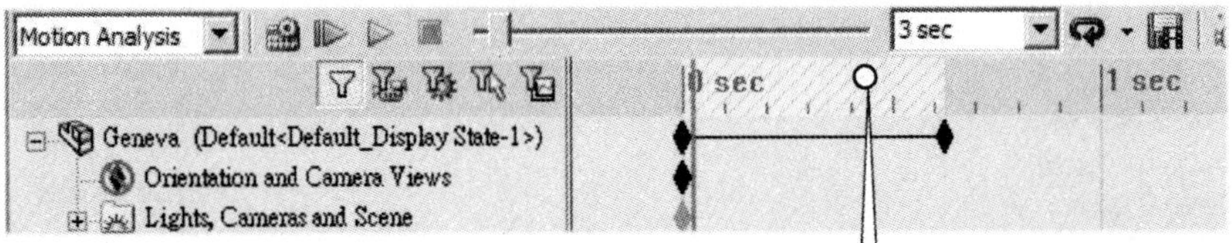

[1] Right-click the yellow area and select **Move Time Bar** and type 0.0262 (s).

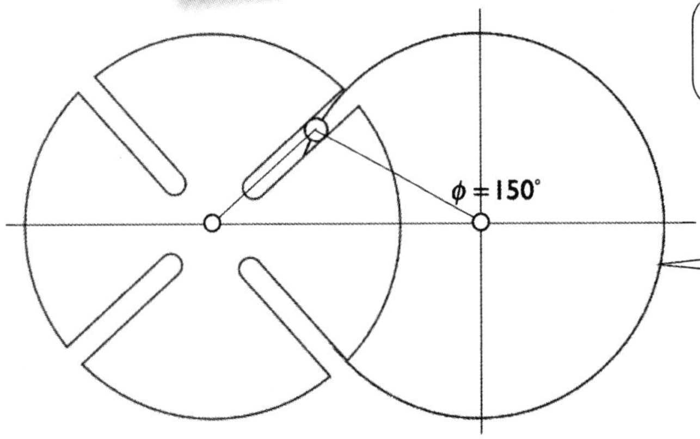

[2] The configuration at $t = 0.0262$ sec ($\phi = 150^\circ$).

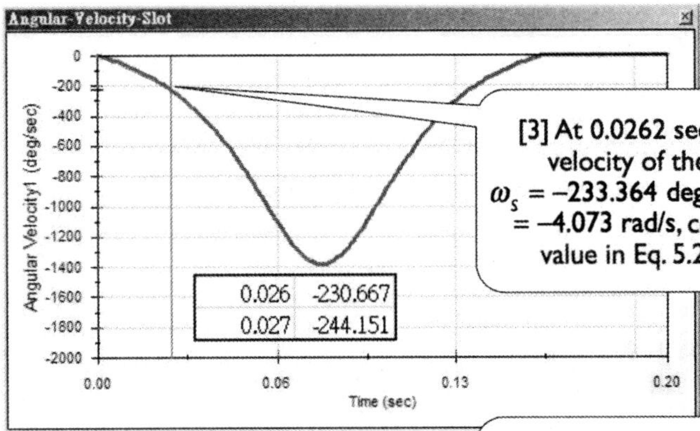

[3] At 0.0262 seconds, the angular velocity of the **Slot** wheel is $\omega_s = -233.364$ **deg/s** (by interpolation) $= -4.073$ **rad/s**, consistent with the value in Eq. 5.2-1(1), page 113.

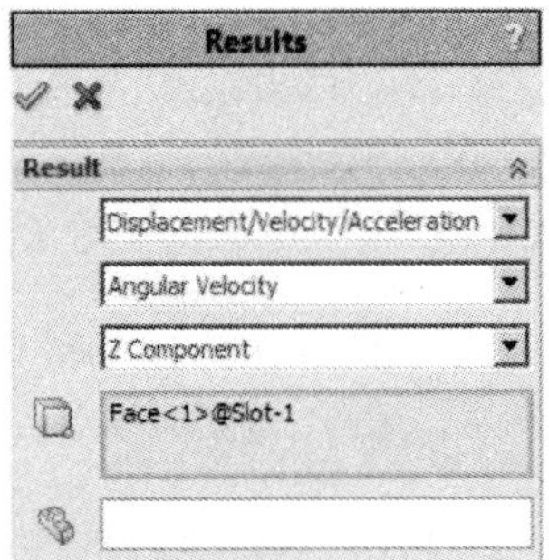

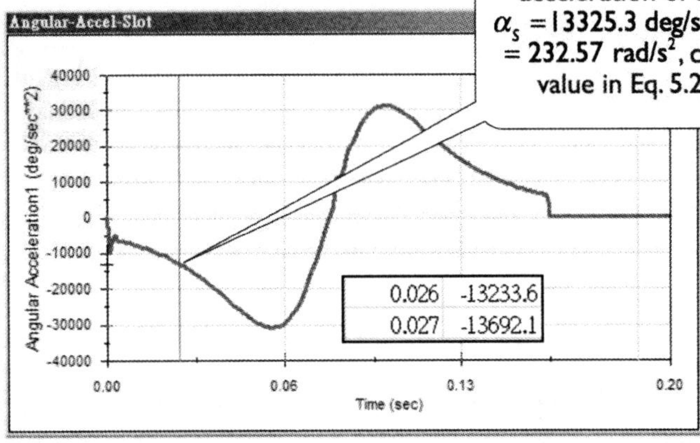

[4] At 0.0262 seconds, the angular acceleration of the **Slot** wheel is $\alpha_s = 13325.3$ **deg/s²** (by interpolation) $= 232.57$ **rad/s²**, consistent with the value in Eq. 5.2-1(2), page 113.

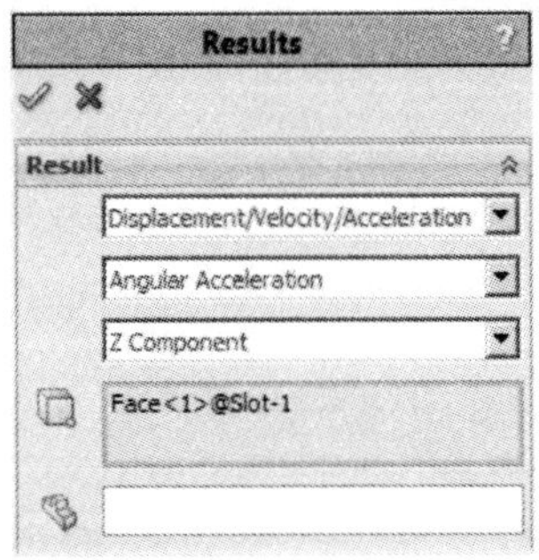

[5] Wrap Up

Save all files and exit **SolidWorks**. #

Chapter 6

Planar Rigid Body Dynamics: Force and Acceleration

Newton's 2nd Law

As mentioned (page 99), the Newton's 2nd Law for a rigid body in plane motion can be expressed as

$$\sum F_x = m\bar{a}_x, \ \sum F_y = m\bar{a}_y, \ \sum M_G = \bar{I}\alpha \tag{1}$$

This chapter will demonstrate how Eq. (1) is applied to rigid bodies in plane motion.

Alternative Form

The third equation in Eq. (1) can be replaced by the following equation

$$\sum M_O = I_O\alpha \tag{2}$$

where

$\sum M_O$ is the resultant moment acting on the body with respect to a FIXED point O in the space.
I_O is the moment of inertia of the body with respect to an axis passing through O and normal to the xy-plane;

Eq. (2) is useful when a rigid body rotates about a fixed axis passing through the point O.

Section 6.1

Newton's 2nd Law: Double Pendulum

6.1-1 Introduction

[1] Consider a **Double Pendulum** consisting of a **Link** and a **Plate** [2, 3]. The system is released from an initial configuration in which the **Link** forms 45° with a vertical plane and the **Plate** forms 30° with the **Link**.

In this section, we'll perform a simulation for this system and demonstrate how the dynamic behavior is governed by the Newton's 2nd Law:

$$\sum F_X = m\bar{a}_X,\ \sum F_Y = m\bar{a}_Y,\ \sum M_G = \bar{I}\alpha \qquad (1)$$

where XY-plane is the motion plane, m is the mass of the body, $\bar{a}_X$ and $\bar{a}_Y$ are the acceleration components at the mass center, α is the angular acceleration of the body, and $\bar{I}$ is the moment of inertia with respect an axis perpendicular to the motion plane and passing through the mass center G. The SI unit for $\bar{I}$ is kg-m^2.

The geometry details of the **Link** and the **Plate** (including the locations of mass center and the moment of inertia $\bar{I}$) are not shown in this page, but will be illustrated later.

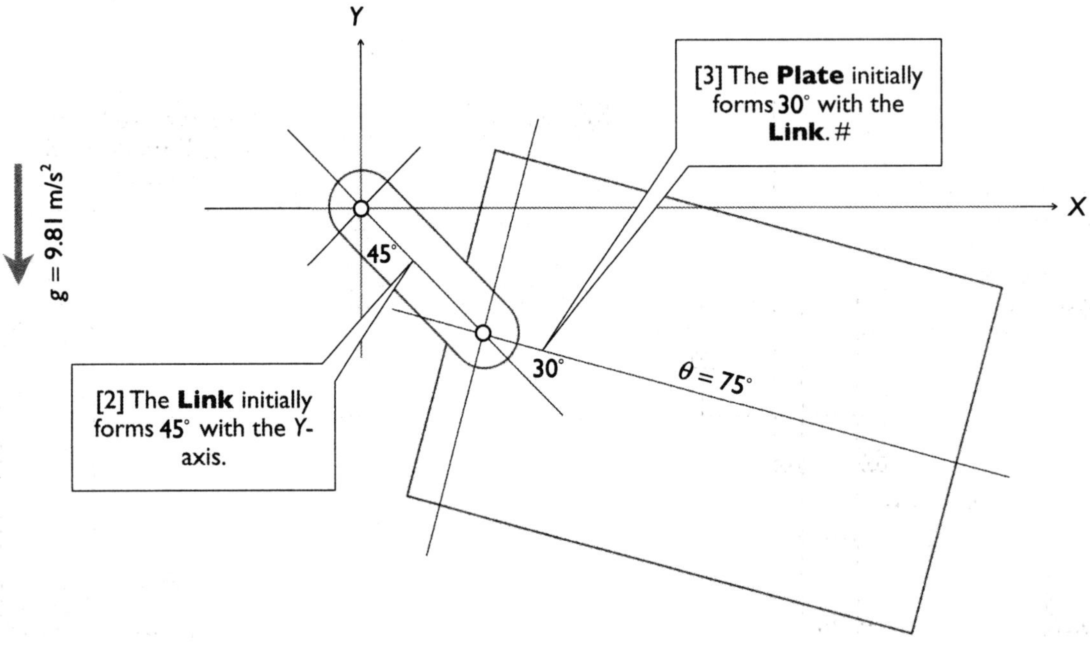

6.1-2 Start Up and Create a Part: **Link**

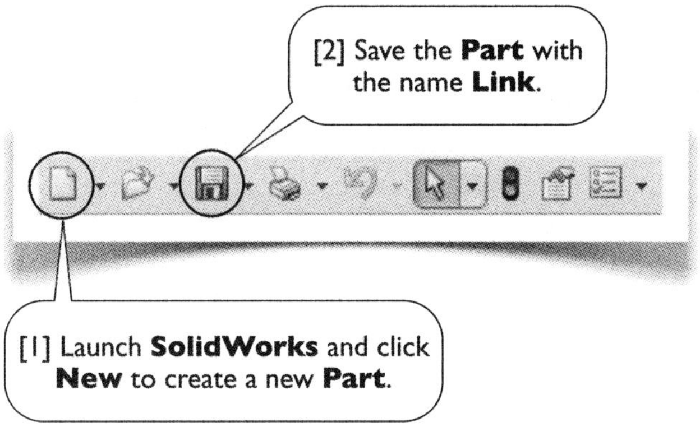

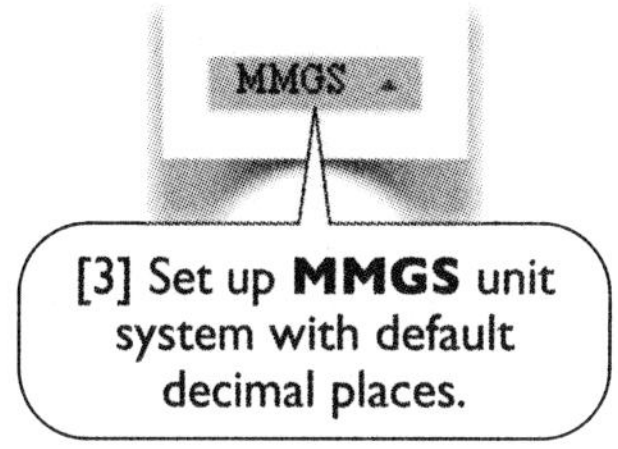

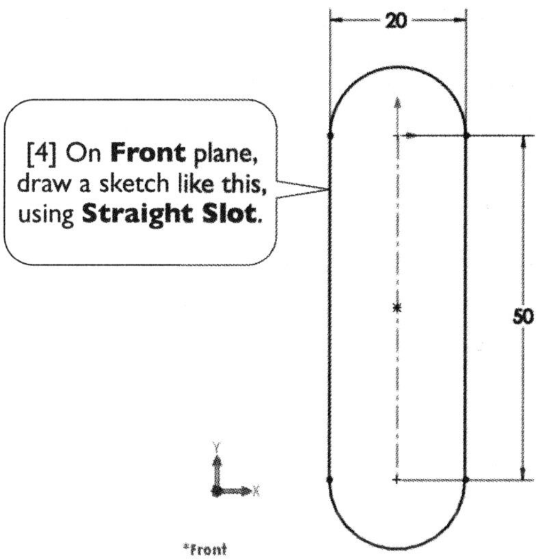

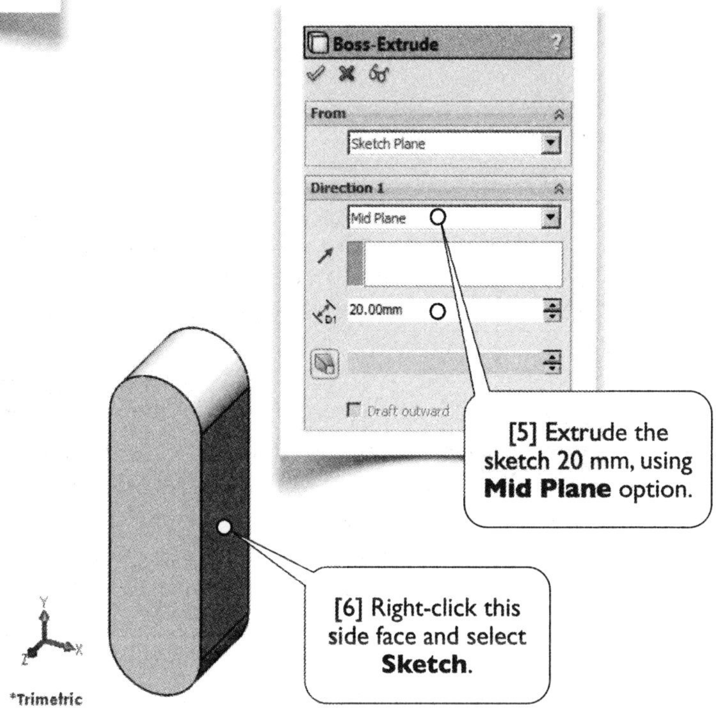

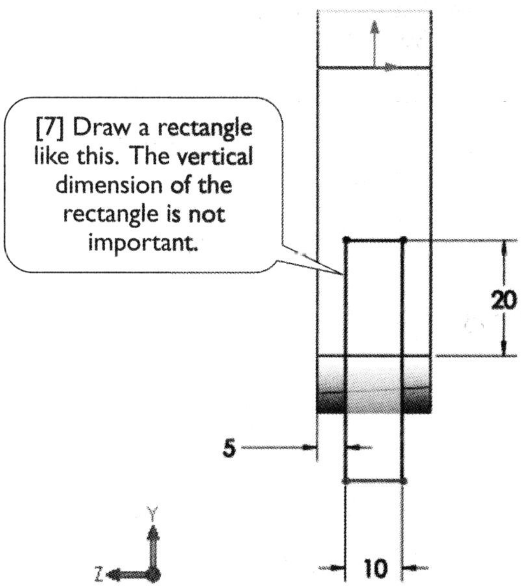

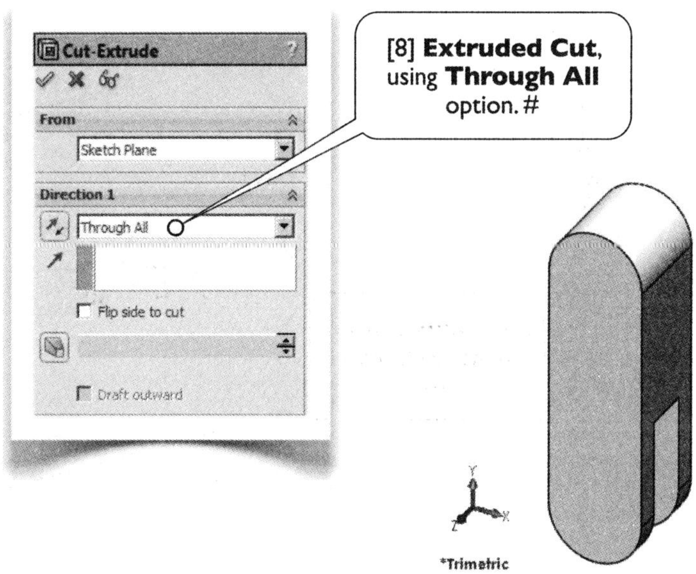

6.1-3 Create a Part: **Plate**

[1] Click **New** to create a new **Part**.

[2] Save the **Part** with the name **Plate**.

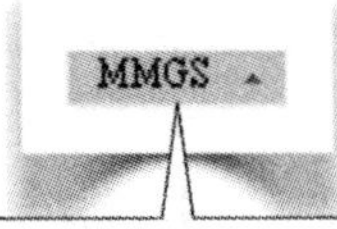

[3] Set up **MMGS** unit system with 5 decimal places for **Length** in **Mass/Section Properties.**

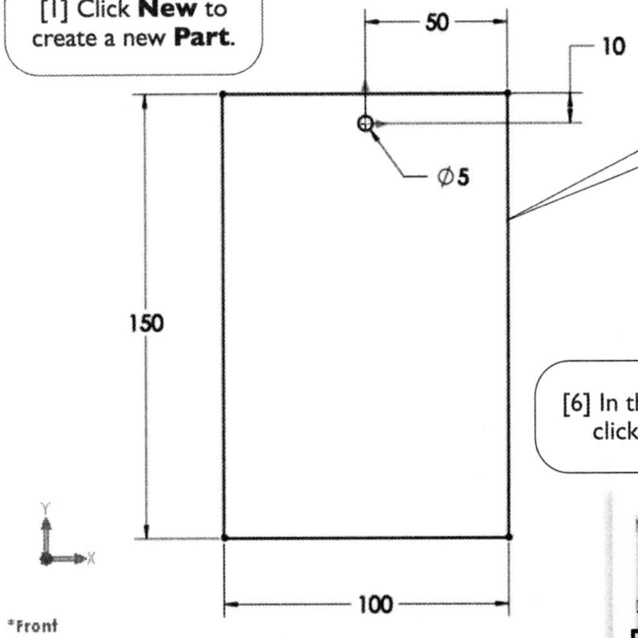

[4] On **Front** plane, draw a sketch like this.

[5] Extrude the sketch 10 mm, using **Mid Plane** option.

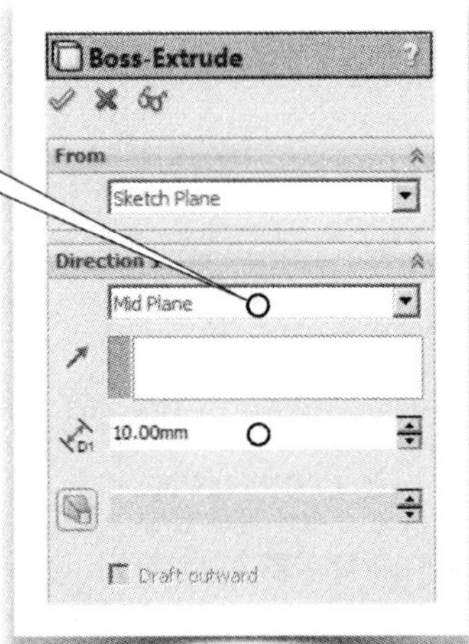

[6] In the **Evaluate Toolbar**, click **Mass Properties**.

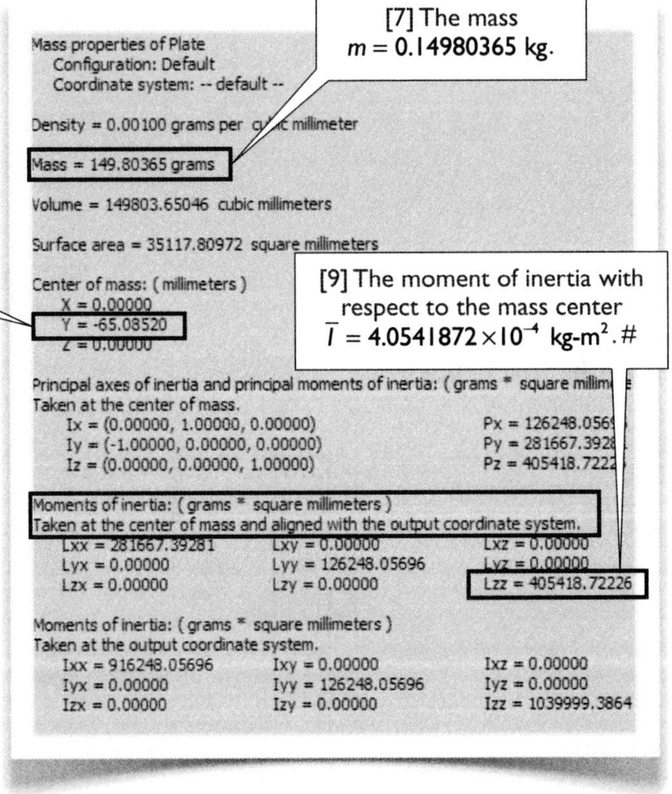

[7] The mass $m = 0.14980365$ kg.

[8] The mass center locates at $Y = -65.08520$ mm.

[9] The moment of inertia with respect to the mass center $\bar{I} = 4.05441872 \times 10^{-4}$ kg-m^2. #

6.1-4 Create an Assembly: **Pendulum**

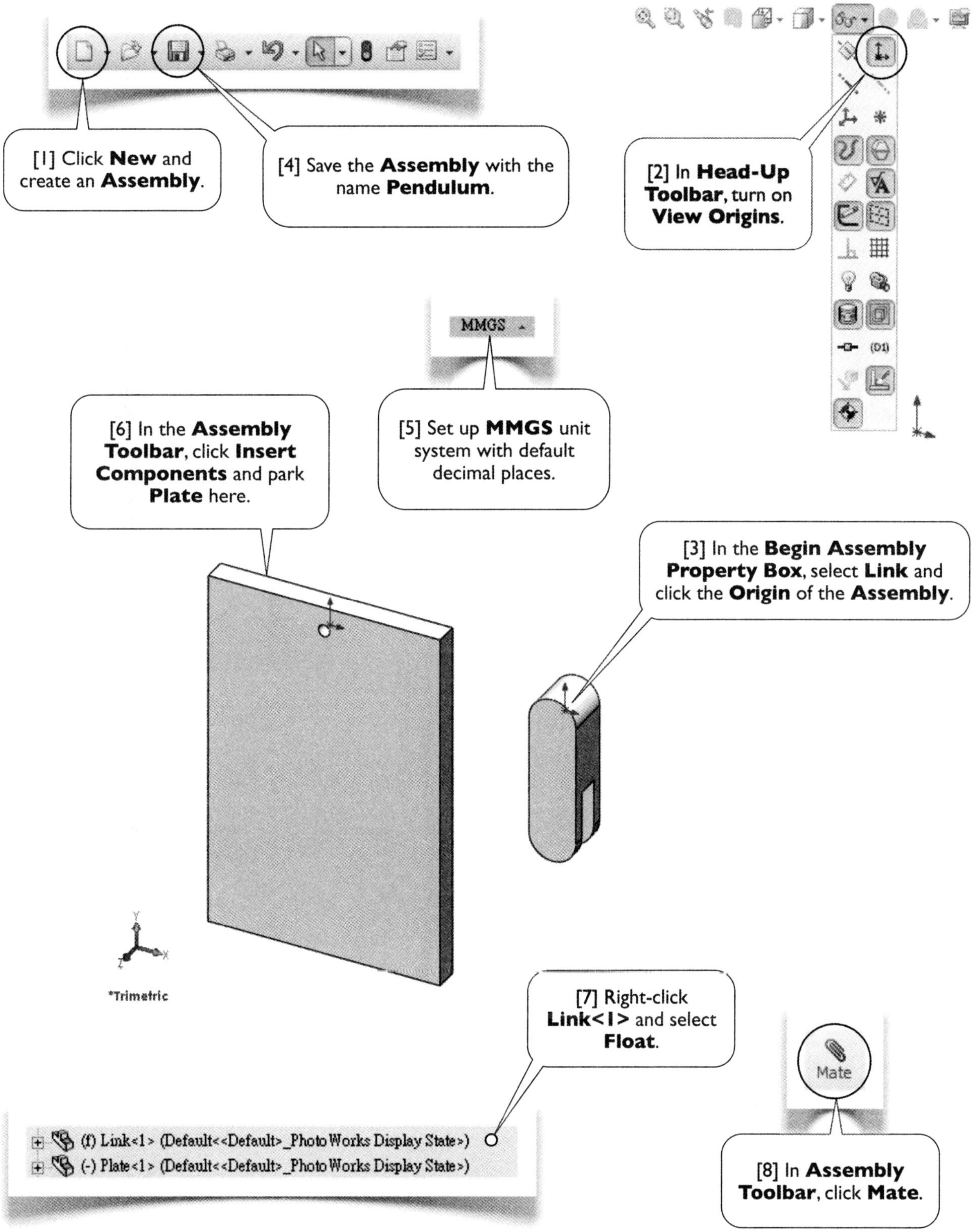

[9] We'll create these 6 **Mates** in [10-22].

[10] The **Plate** and the **Link** are connected with a revolute joint (see [11, 12]).

[13] The **Link's** inner frontal face [14] and the **Plate's** backside face [15] are **Coincident**.

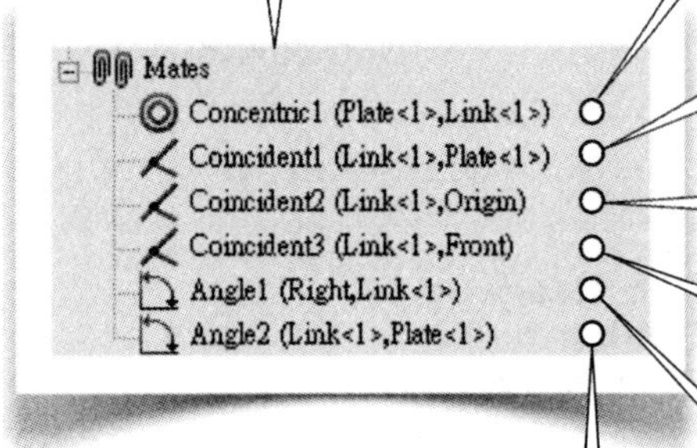

[16] The **Links's** and the **Assembly's Origins** are **Coincident**. Uncheck **Align axes** (see [17]) before clicking **OK**.

[18] The **Link's** and the **Assembly's Front** planes are **Coincident**.

[20] The **Assembly's** and the **Link's Right** planes form an **Angle** of 45 degrees. Click **Flip dimension** if necessary. This is the initial configuration of the **Link**. We'll suppress this **Mate** later.

[21] The **Link's** and the **Plate's Right** planes form form an **Angle** of 30 degrees. Click **Flip dimension** if necessary. This is the initial configuration of the **Plate**. We'll suppress this **Mate** later.

[15] The **Plate's** backside face.

[11] **Concentric1** is created by clicking this cylindrical face...

[14] The **Link's** inner frontal face.

[12] And this cylindrical face.

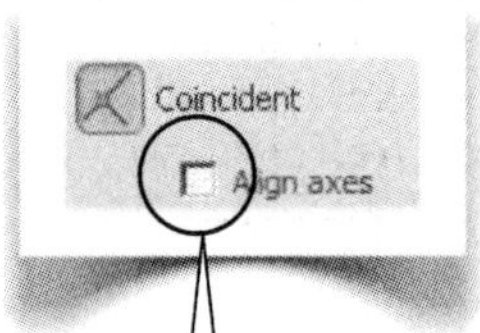

[17] Uncheck **Align axes**.

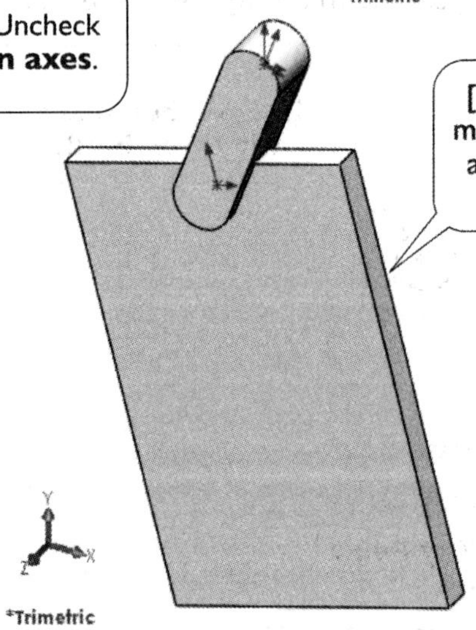

[19] Now, use you mouse to make sure all the **Mates** are correct.

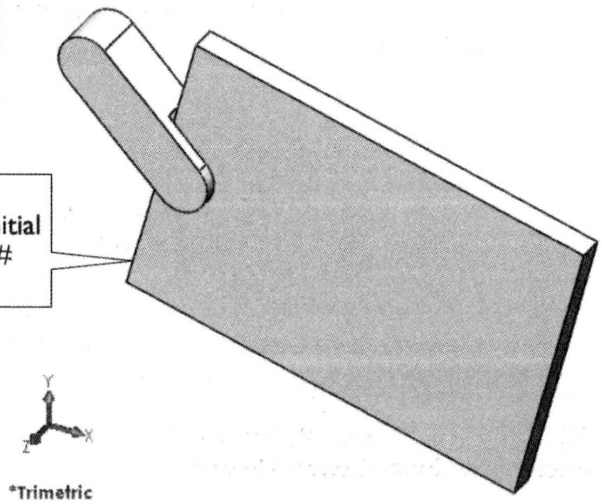

[22] This is the initial configuration. #

6.1-5 Create a **Motion Study** and Set Up **Gravity**

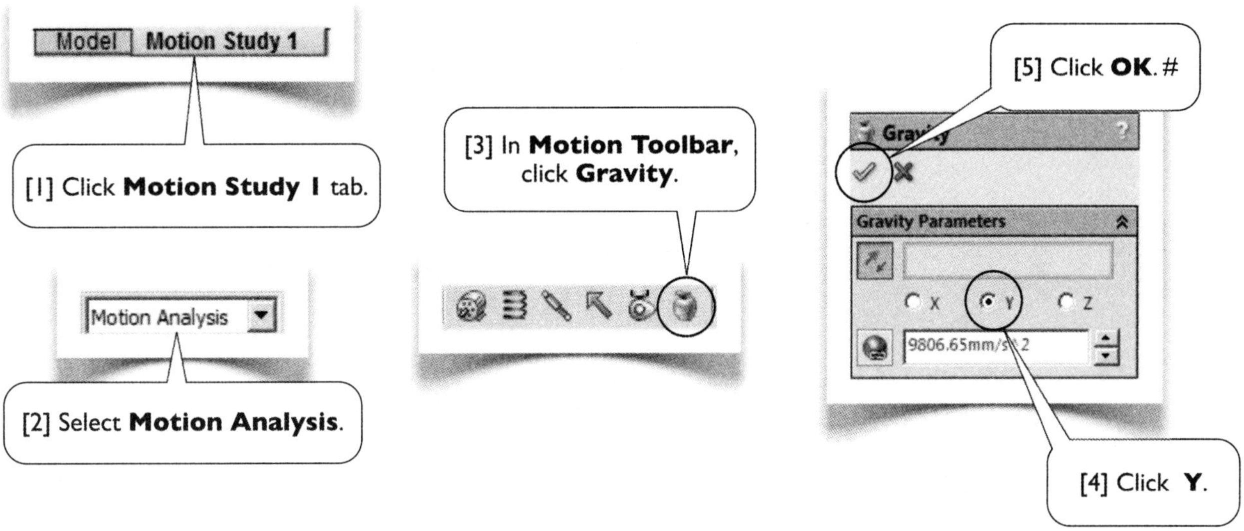

6.1-6 Calculate and Animate **Results**

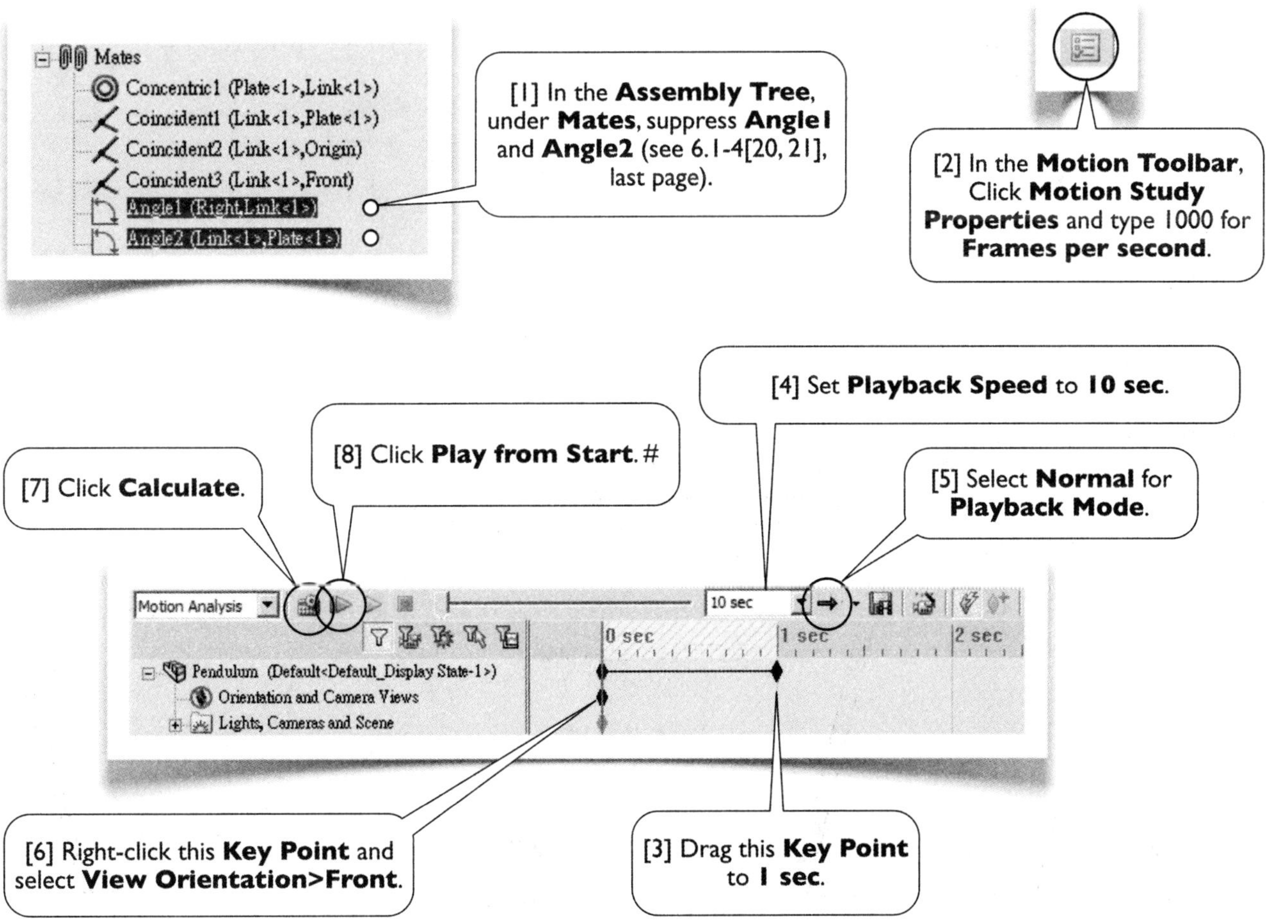

6.1-7 Results: Linear and Angular Accelerations of the **Plate**

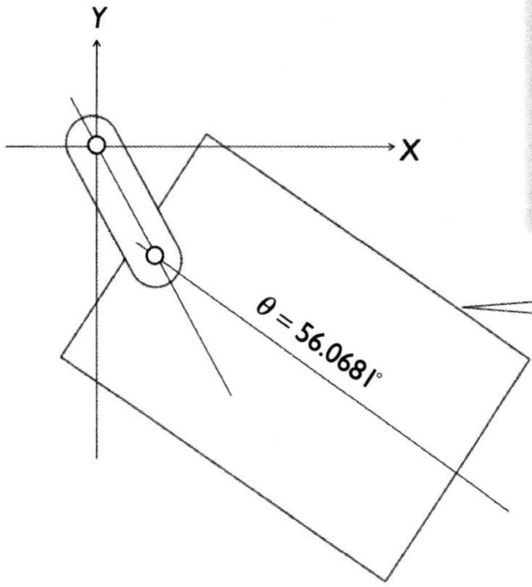

[1] Click at 0.1 sec. This time point is arbitrarily choosen.

[2] At t = 0.1 sec, the **Plate** forms an angle θ = 56.0681° with the Y-axis (see 6.1-8[1], next page)

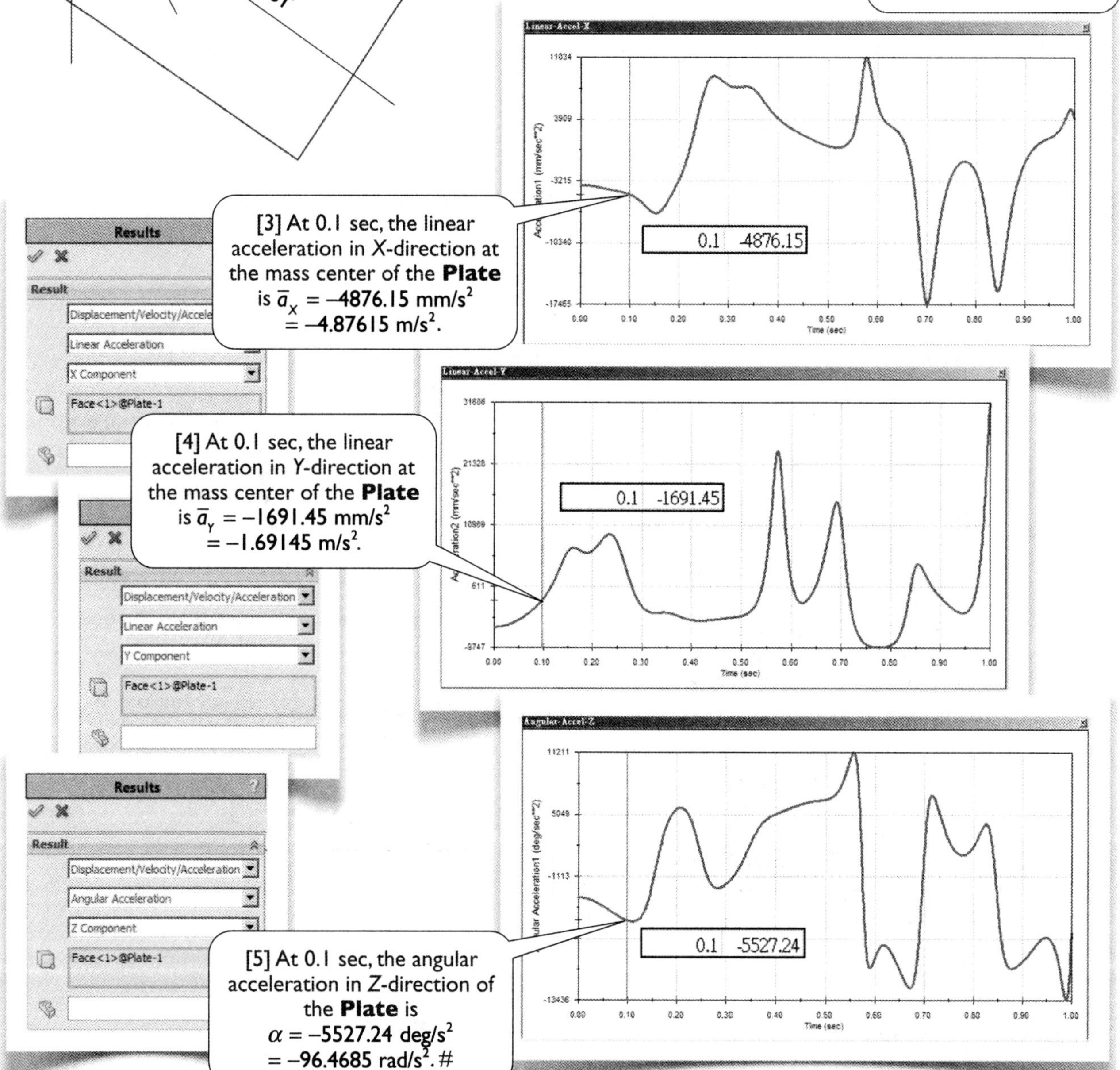

[3] At 0.1 sec, the linear acceleration in X-direction at the mass center of the **Plate** is $\bar{a}_X$ = −4876.15 mm/s^2 = −4.87615 m/s^2.

[4] At 0.1 sec, the linear acceleration in Y-direction at the mass center of the **Plate** is $\bar{a}_Y$ = −1691.45 mm/s^2 = −1.69145 m/s^2.

[5] At 0.1 sec, the angular acceleration in Z-direction of the **Plate** is α = −5527.24 deg/s^2 = −96.4685 rad/s^2. #

6.1-8 Results: Angular Displacement of the **Plate**

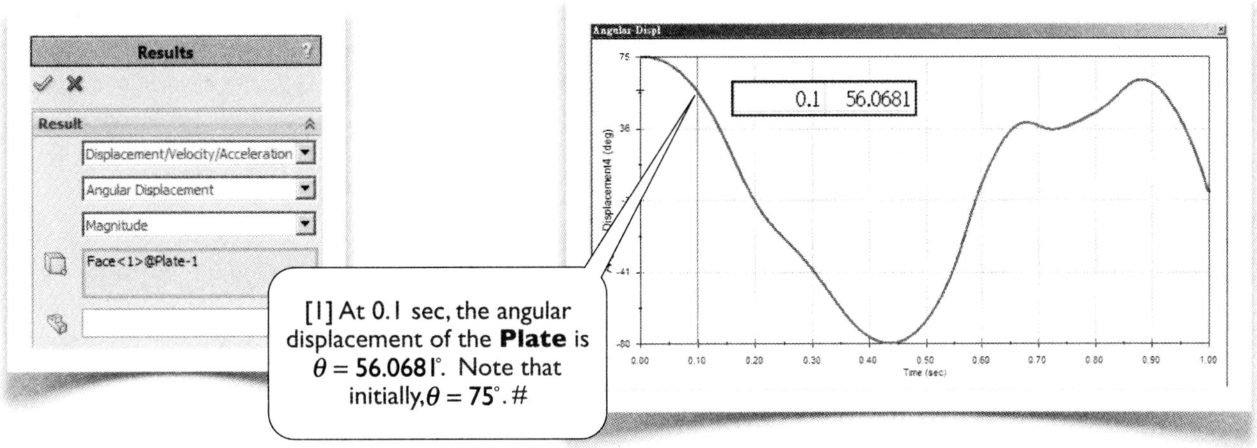

6.1-9 Results: Reaction Forces at **Concentric1**

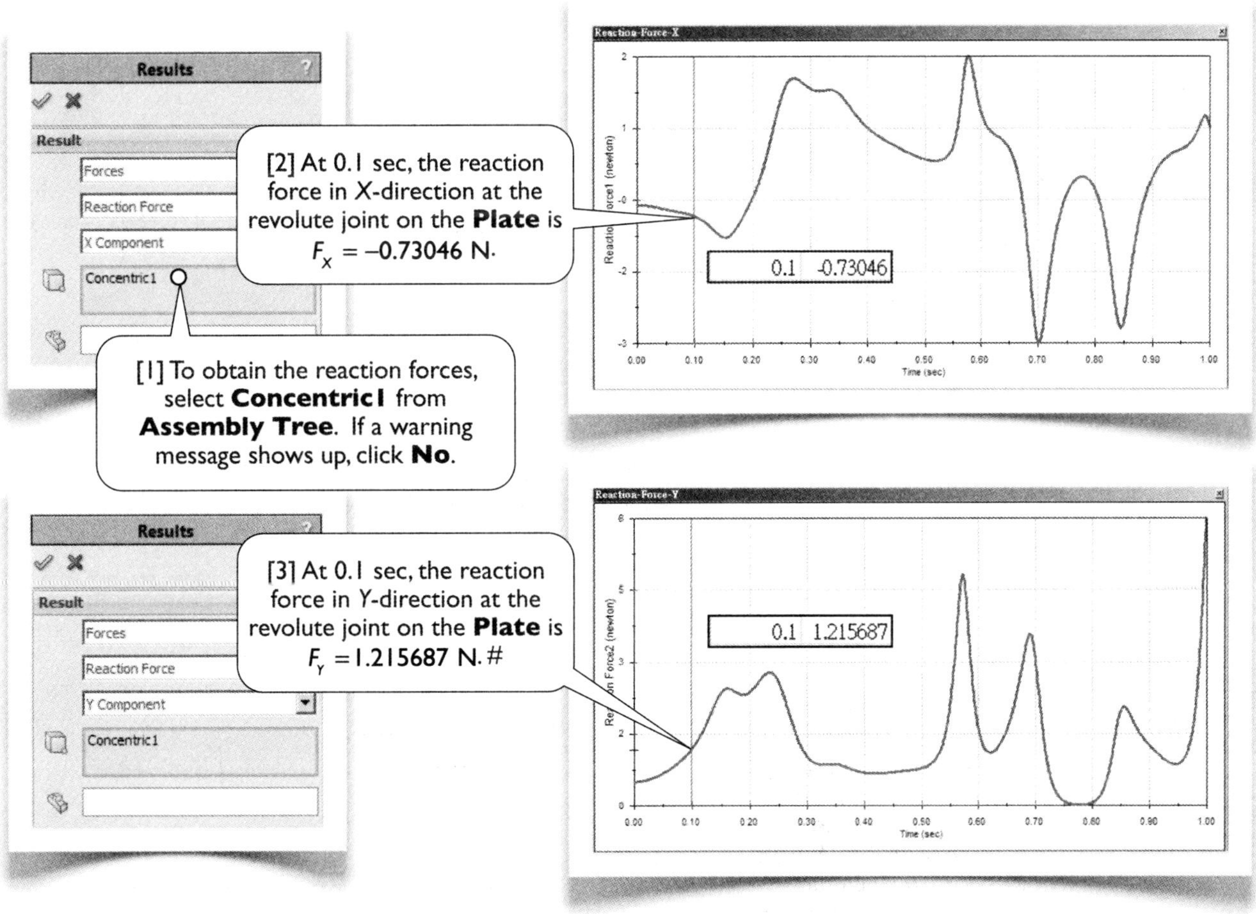

6.1-10 Newton's 2nd Law: **Plate**

[1] Newton's 2nd Law for a rigid body in plane motion (Eq. 6.1-1(1), page 122) states that *the external forces and moments acting on a rigid body is equivalent to the* **effective force and moments** *acting on the particle. The effective force of a rigid body is simply the product of its mass and the acceleration at the mass center; the effective moment of a rigid body is the product of its moment of inertia* $\bar{I}$ *and the angular acceleration* α.

The external forces acting on the **Plate** and the effective forces and moment on the **Plate** are shown in [2-8]. It's easy to confirm that these forces and moments indeed satisfy Newton's 2nd Law; i.e., in *X*-direction,

$$-0.73046 \approx (0.14980365)(-4.87615)$$

In *Y*-direction,

$$1.215687 - (0.14980365)(9.80665) \approx (0.14980365)(-1.69145)$$

Taking the moment about the mass center, we have

$$(0.73046)(0.0650852\cos 56.0681^\circ) - (1.215687)(0.0650852\sin 56.0681^\circ) \approx -(4.0541872\times 10^{-4})(96.4685)$$

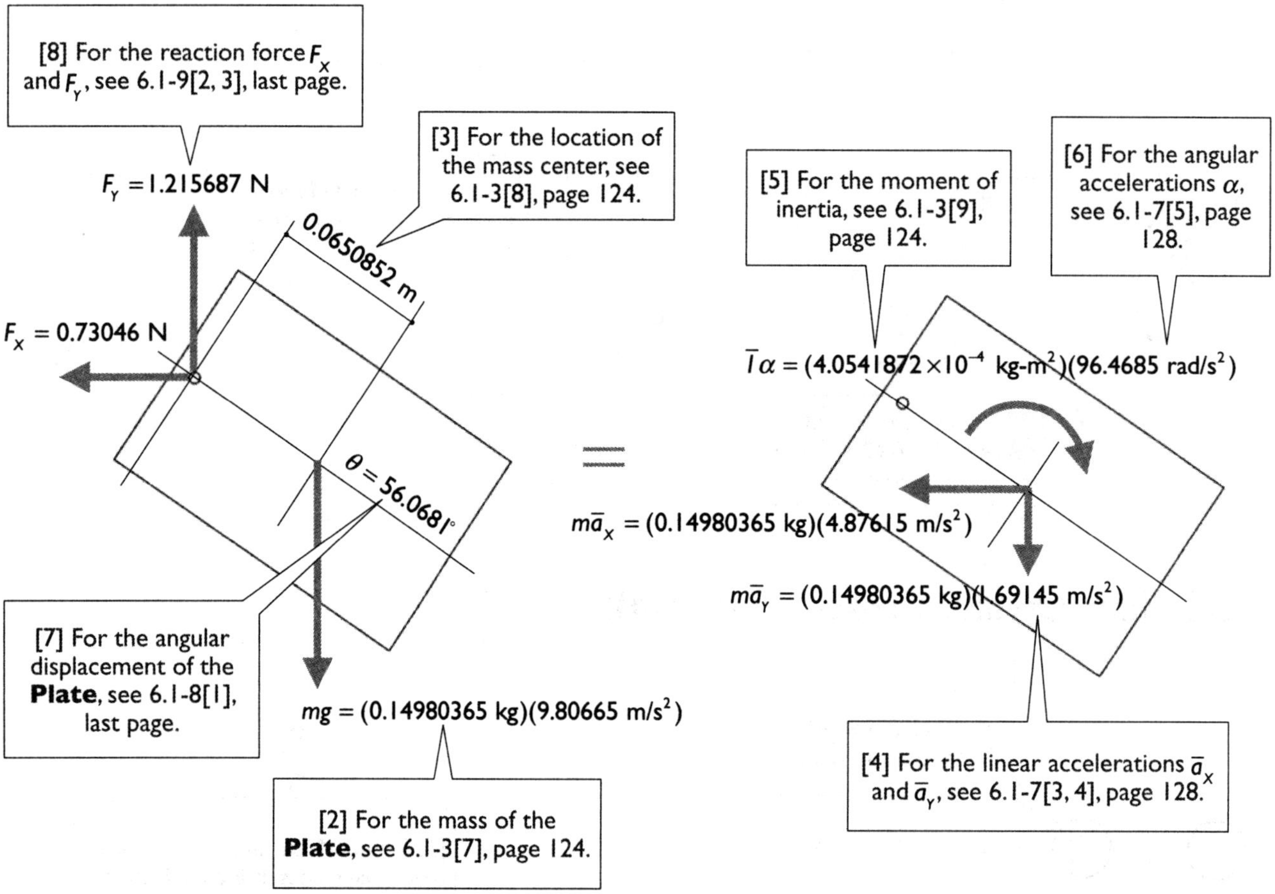

[9] Wrap Up

Save all files and exit **SolidWorks**. #

Section 6.2

Sliding and Rolling: Bowling Ball

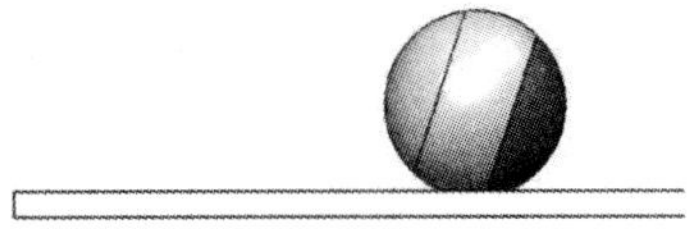

6.2-1 Introduction

[1] A **Ball** of radius $r = 11$ **cm** is projected along a floor with a linear velocity $\vec{v}_0$ = **5 m/s** and no angular velocity [2, 3]. The **Ball** is made of a PBT (polybutylene terephthalate) plastic which has a mass density of **1300 kg/m^3**.

In this section, we'll perform a simulation for this scenario and illustrate how the Newton's 2nd Law govern the behavior.

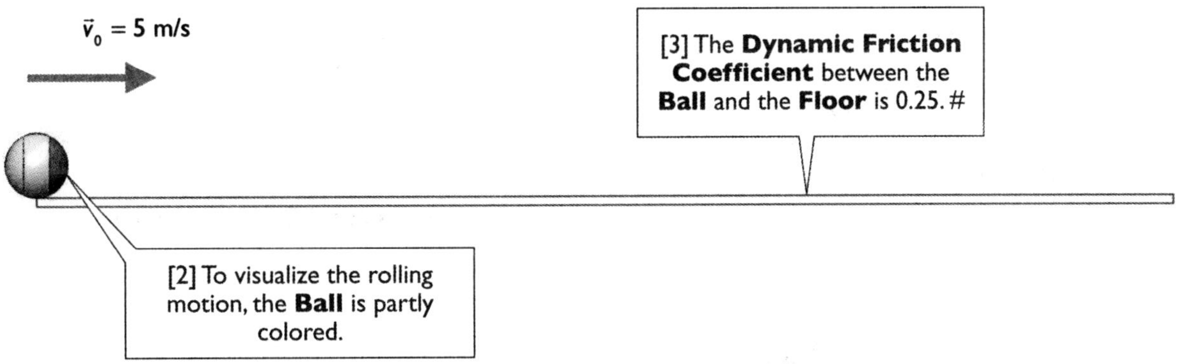

6.2-2 Start Up and Create a Part: **Ball**

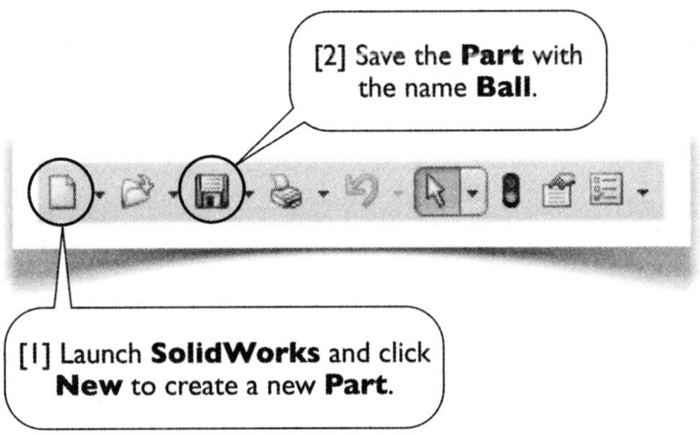

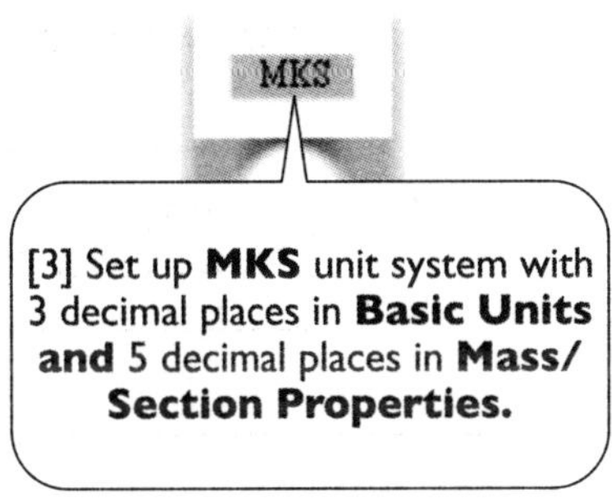

[4] On **Front** plane, draw a sketch like this.

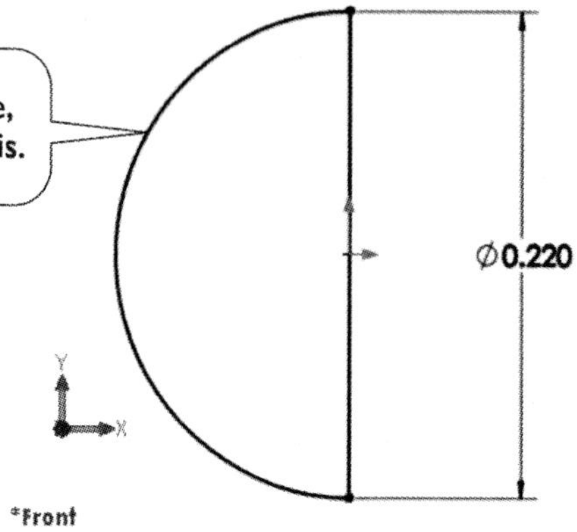

[5] Revolve the sketch 360°, using the straight line as the **Axis of Revolution**.

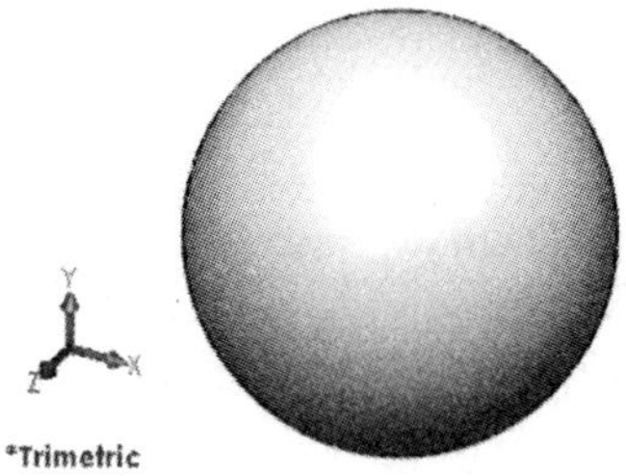

[6] On **Right** plane, draw a circle like this. Click **Exit Sketch**.

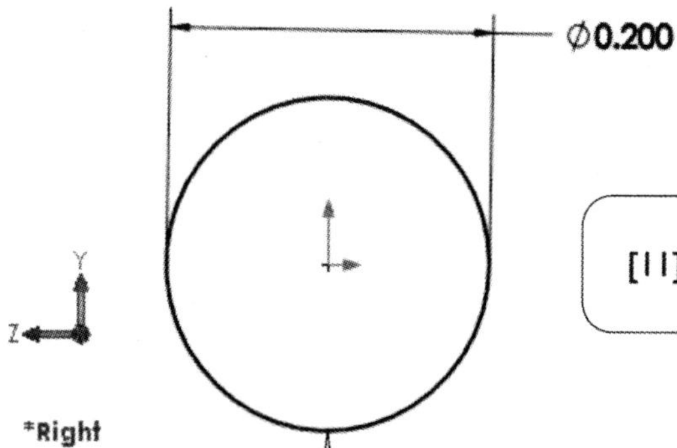

[7] In the **Features Toolbar**, select **Curves>Split Line**.

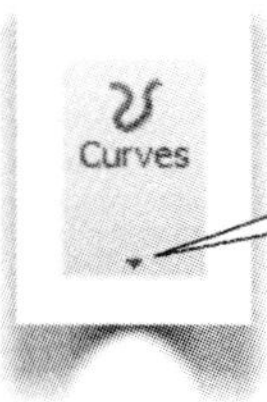

[8] Make sure **Projection** is selected.

[9] By default, the newly created sketch is used as the **Sketch to Project**.

[10] In the **Graphics Window**, click the spherical face for **Faces to Split**.

[11] Click **OK**.

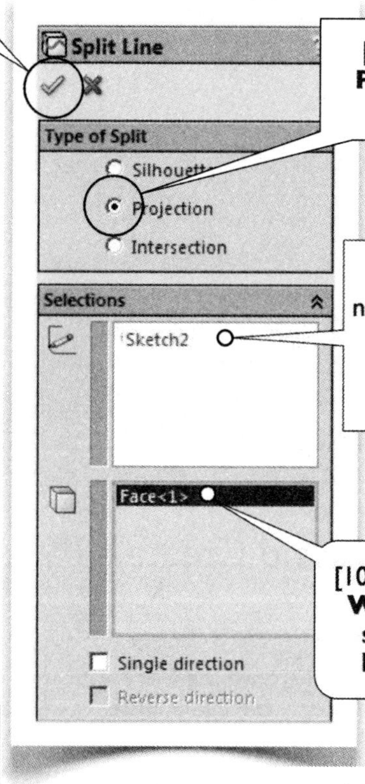

[12] Right-click this face and select **Appearance>Face<1>@Split Line1**. Select a color (e.g., red) and click **OK**.

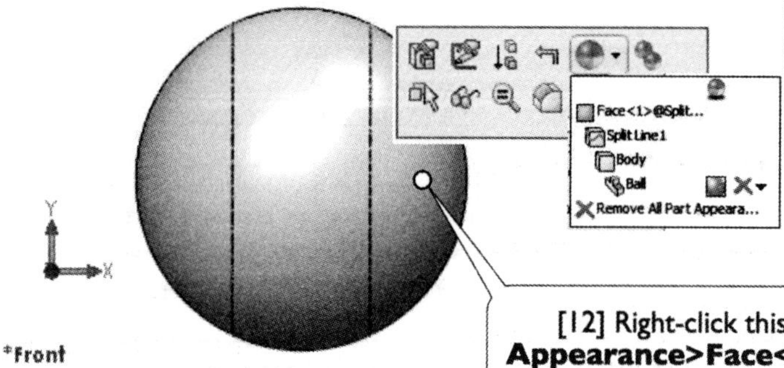

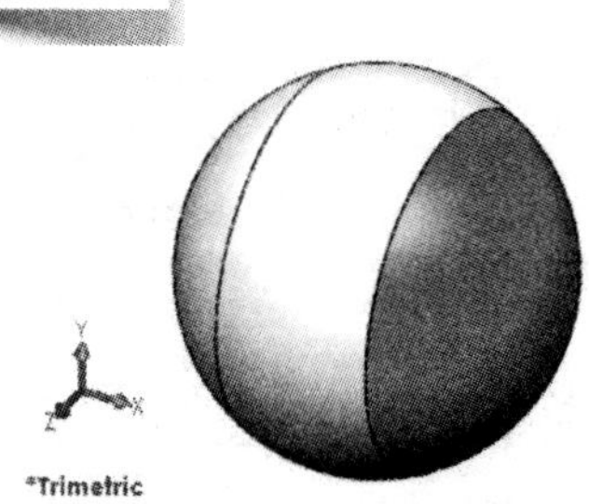

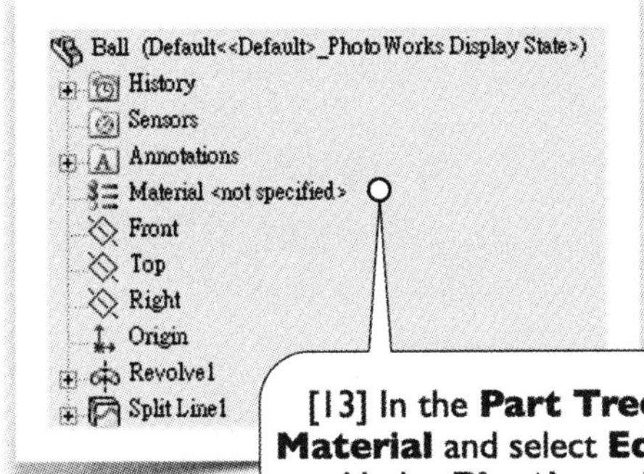

[13] In the **Part Tree**, right-click **Material** and select **Edit Material**. Under **Plastics**, select **PBT General Purpose** (see [14]).

[15] In the **Evaluate Toolbar**, select **Mass Properties...**

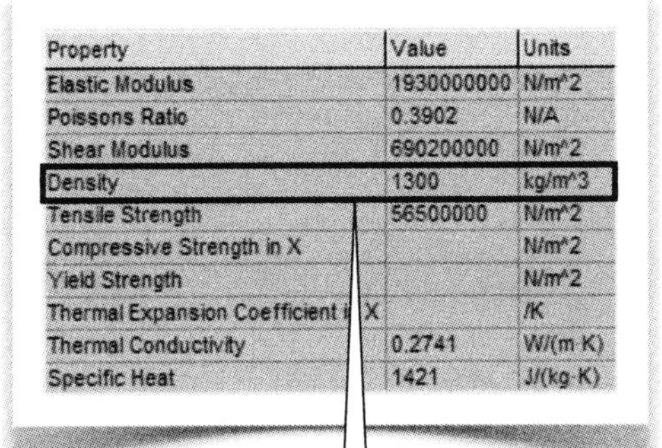

Property	Value	Units
Elastic Modulus	1930000000	N/m^2
Poissons Ratio	0.3902	N/A
Shear Modulus	690200000	N/m^2
Density	1300	kg/m^3
Tensile Strength	56500000	N/m^2
Compressive Strength in X		N/m^2
Yield Strength		N/m^2
Thermal Expansion Coefficient in X		/K
Thermal Conductivity	0.2741	W/(m·K)
Specific Heat	1421	J/(kg·K)

[14] Make sure the **Density** is 1300 kg/m^3. Click **Apply**. Click **Close**.

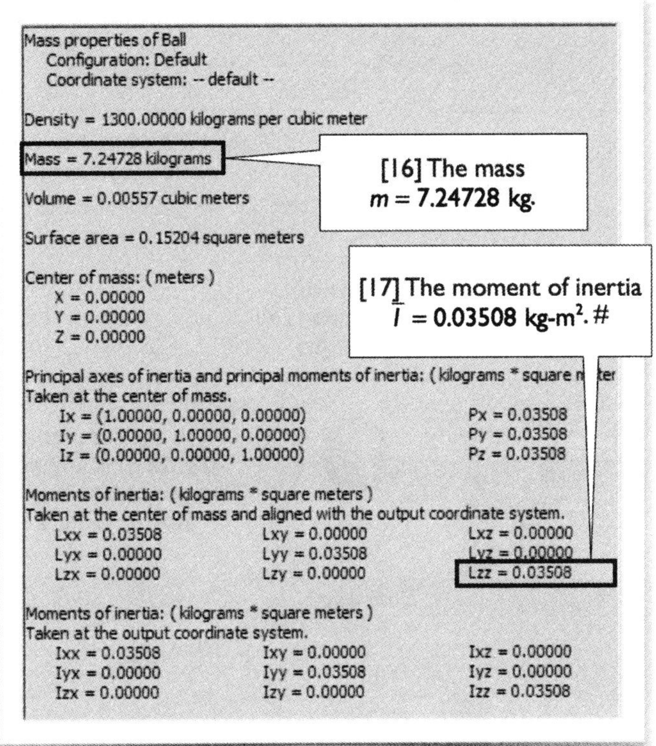

Mass properties of Ball
Configuration: Default
Coordinate system: -- default --

Density = 1300.00000 kilograms per cubic meter

Mass = 7.24728 kilograms

Volume = 0.00557 cubic meters

Surface area = 0.15204 square meters

Center of mass: (meters)
X = 0.00000
Y = 0.00000
Z = 0.00000

Principal axes of inertia and principal moments of inertia: (kilograms * square meters)
Taken at the center of mass.
Ix = (1.00000, 0.00000, 0.00000) Px = 0.03508
Iy = (0.00000, 1.00000, 0.00000) Py = 0.03508
Iz = (0.00000, 0.00000, 1.00000) Pz = 0.03508

Moments of inertia: (kilograms * square meters)
Taken at the center of mass and aligned with the output coordinate system.
Lxx = 0.03508 Lxy = 0.00000 Lxz = 0.00000
Lyx = 0.00000 Lyy = 0.03508 Lyz = 0.00000
Lzx = 0.00000 Lzy = 0.00000 Lzz = 0.03508

Moments of inertia: (kilograms * square meters)
Taken at the output coordinate system.
Ixx = 0.03508 Ixy = 0.00000 Ixz = 0.00000
Iyx = 0.00000 Iyy = 0.03508 Iyz = 0.00000
Izx = 0.00000 Izy = 0.00000 Izz = 0.03508

[16] The mass $m = 7.24728$ kg.

[17] The moment of inertia $\bar{I} = 0.03508$ kg-m^2. #

6.2-3 Create a Part: **Floor**

[1] Click **New** to create a new **Part**.

[2] Save the **Part** with the name **Floor**. Set up **MKS** unit system with 3 decimal places.

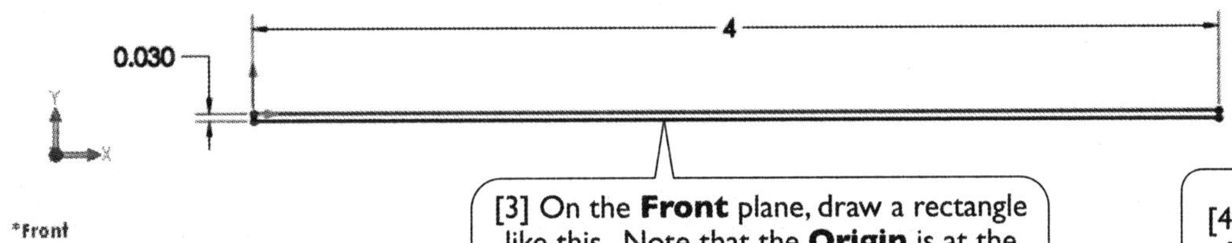

[3] On the **Front** plane, draw a rectangle like this. Note that the **Origin** is at the upper-left corner of the rectangle.

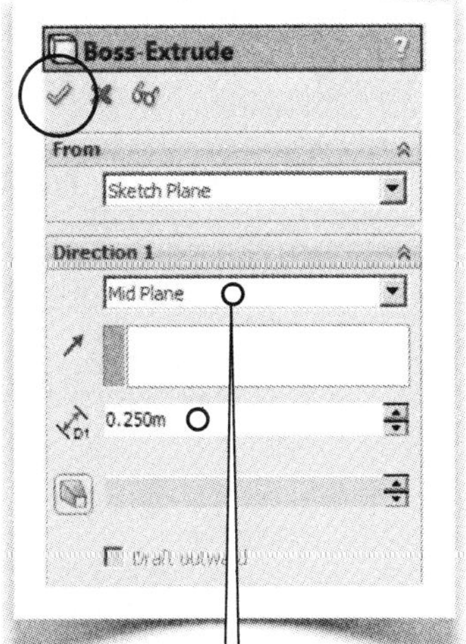

[4] Extrude 0.25 m, using **Mid Plane** option. #

6.2-4 Create an Assembly: **Bowling**

[1] Click **New** and create an **Assembly**.

[4] Save the **Assembly** with the name **Bowling**.

[2] In **Head-Up Toolbar**, turn on **View Origins**.

[3] In the **Begin Assembly Property Box**, select **Floor** and click the assembly's **Origin**.

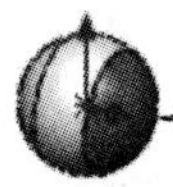

[6] In the **Assembly Toolbar**, click **Insert Components** and park **Ball** anywhere.

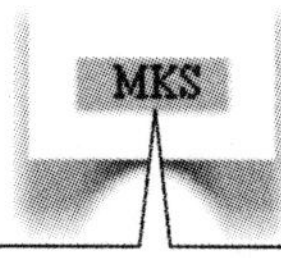

[5] Set up **MKS** unit system with default decimal places.

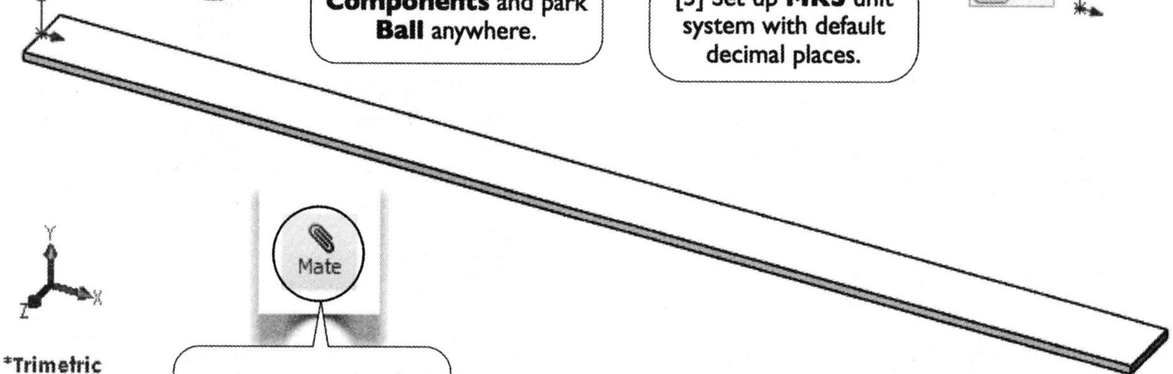

*Trimetric

[7] In **Assembly Toolbar**, click **Mate**.

[8] We'll create these 3 **Mates** in [9-11].

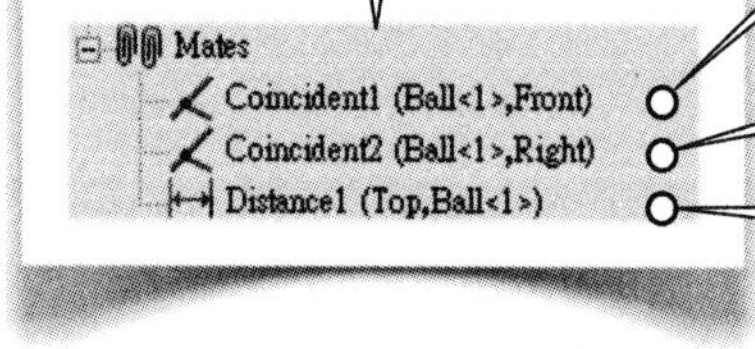

[9] The **Ball's** and the **Assembly's Front** planes are **Coincident**.

[10] The **Ball's** and the **Assembly's Right** planes are **Coincident**. This is an initial condition of the **Ball**. We'll suppress this **Mate** later.

[11] The **Ball's** and the **Assembly's Top** planes has a **Distance** of 0.11 m. This is an initial condition of the **Ball**. We'll suppress this **Mate** later. #

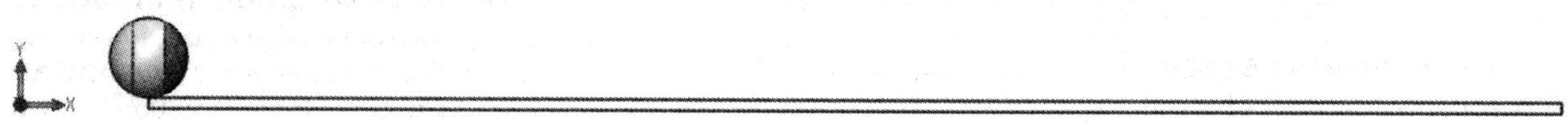

*Front

6.2-5 Create **Motion Study**; Set Up **Gravity**, **Contact**, and **Initial Velocity**

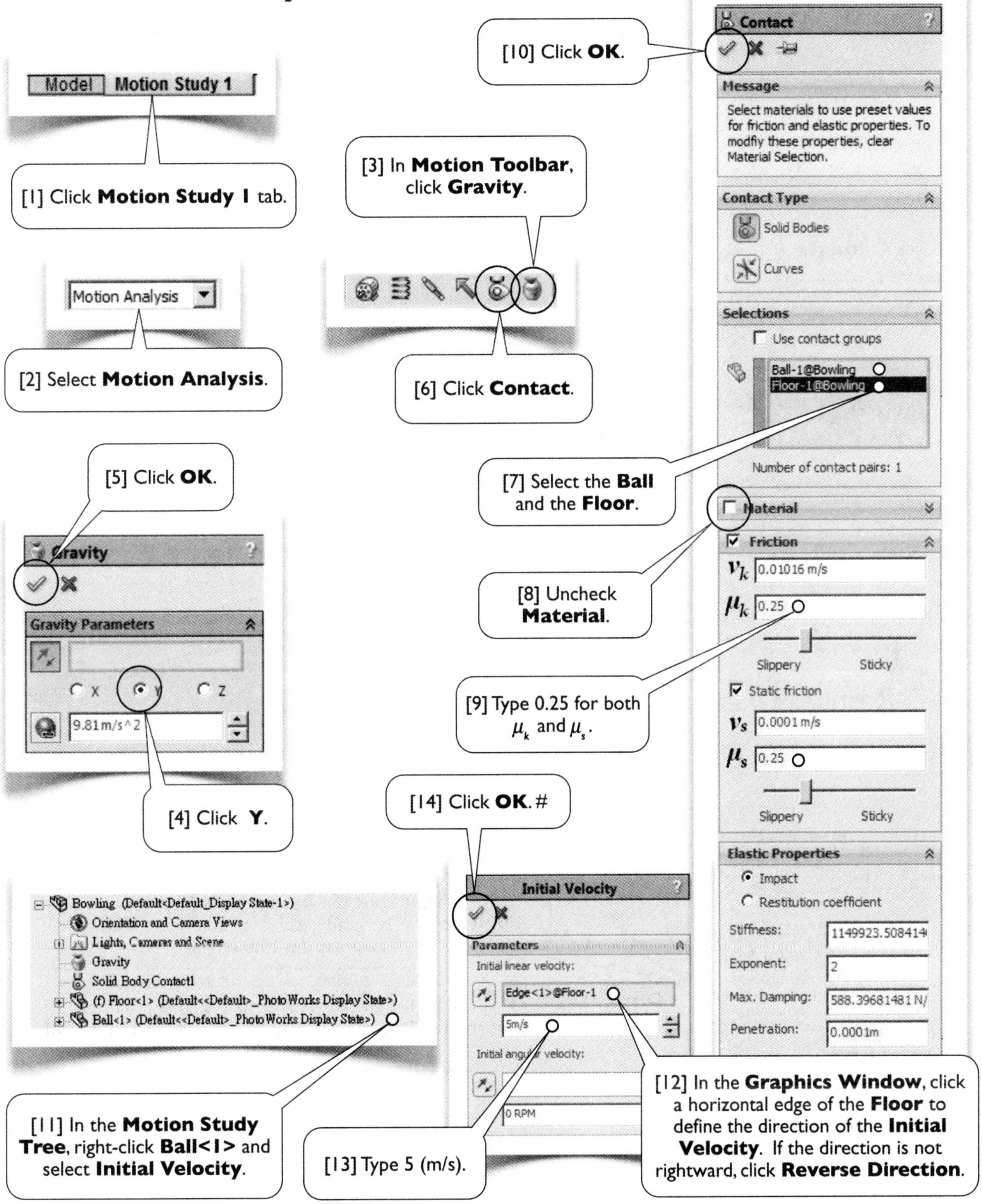

6.2-6 Calculate and Animate **Results**

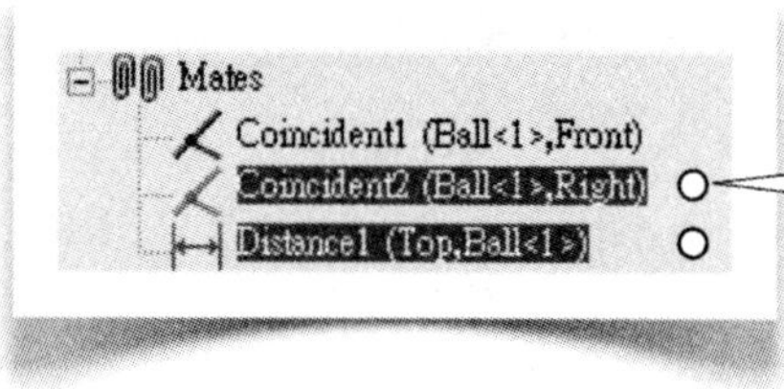

[1] In the **Assembly Tree**, under **Mates**, suppress **Coincident2** and **Distance1** (see 6.2-4[10, 11], page 134).

[2] In the **Motion Toolbar**, Click **Motion Study Properties**. Type 1000 for **Frames per second** and turn on **Use Precise Contact** (5.2-6[3, 4], page 119).

[3] Drag this **Key Point** to **0.8 sec**.

[4] Set **Playback Speed** to **10 sec**.

[5] Select **Normal** for **Playback Mode**.

[6] Right-click this **Key Point** and select **View Orientation>Front**.

[7] Click **Calculate**.

[8] Click **Play from Start**. #

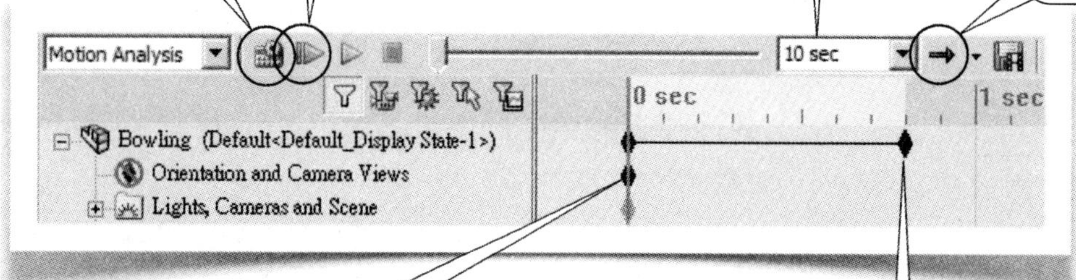

6.2-7 Results: Linear and Angular Velocity of the **Ball**

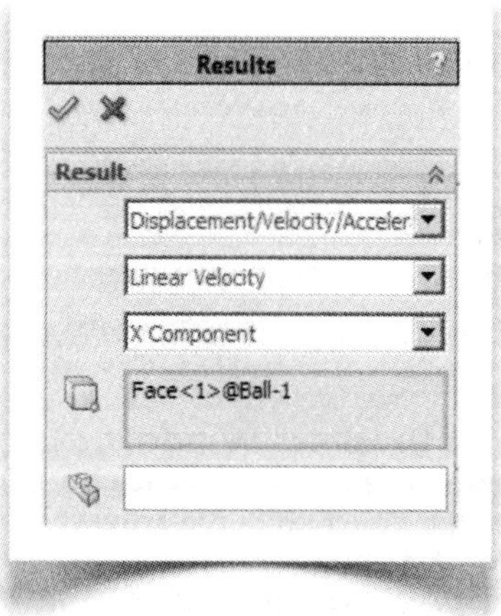

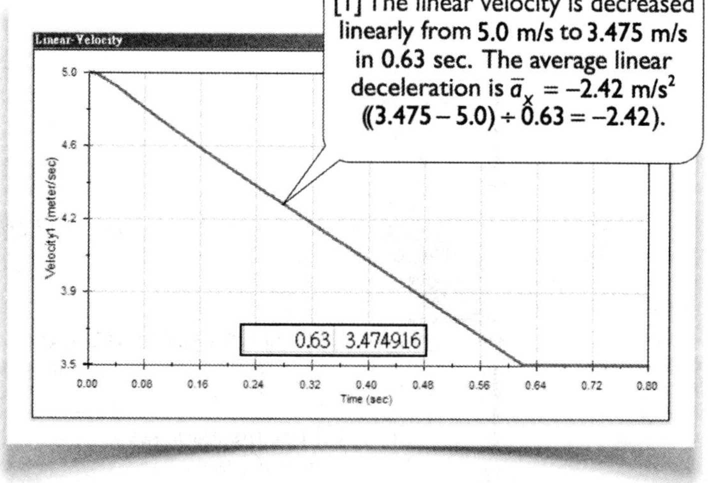

[1] The linear velocity is decreased linearly from 5.0 m/s to 3.475 m/s in 0.63 sec. The average linear deceleration is $\bar{a}_x = -2.42\ \text{m/s}^2$ $((3.475 - 5.0) \div 0.63 = -2.42)$.

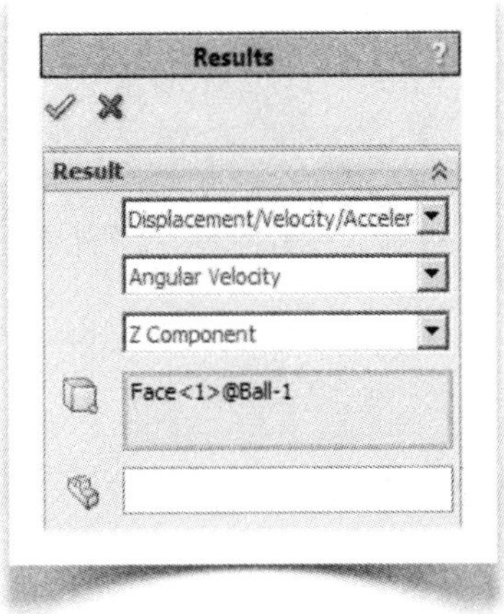

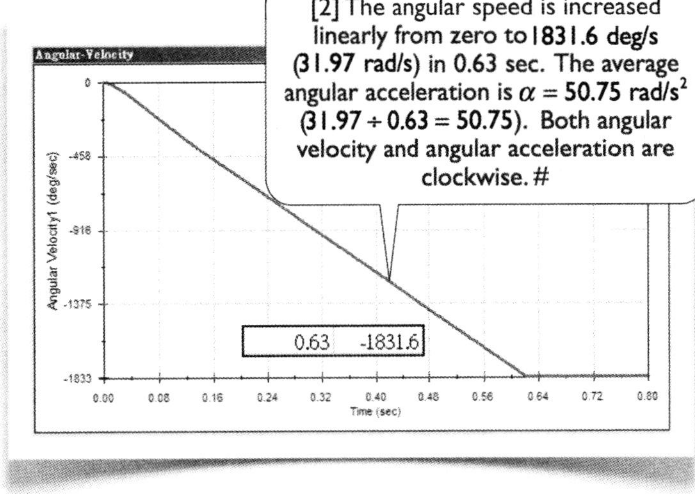

[2] The angular speed is increased linearly from zero to **1831.6 deg/s (31.97 rad/s)** in **0.63 sec**. The average angular acceleration is α = **50.75 rad/s²** (**31.97 ÷ 0.63 = 50.75**). Both angular velocity and angular acceleration are clockwise. #

6.2-8 Newton's 2nd Law: **Ball**

[1] Before 0.63 sec

Before 0.63 sec, the ball slides and rolls simultaneously. The sliding speed is decreasing while the rolling speed is increasing. At 0.63 seconds, the linear speed $\bar{v}_x$ and the angular speed ω reach a condition $\bar{v}_x = r\omega$ (3.475 m/s ≈ (0.11 m)(31.97 rad/s)) which is a pure rolling motion.

Now, let's calculate the theoretical values of linear deceleration $\bar{a}_x$ and the angular acceleration α, and compare the theoretical values with those in 6.2-7[1, 2] (last page and this page).

The external forces acting on the **Ball** and the effective force and moment on the **Ball** are shown in [2, 3]. In X-direction,

$$0.25(7.24728\text{ kg})(9.80665\text{ m/s}^2) = (7.24728\text{ kg})a_x$$

Solving, we have $\bar{a}_x = 2.45\text{ m/s}^2$ (= $\mu_k g$), which is close to the value in 6.2-7[1], last page. Taking the moment about the mass center, we have

$$0.25(7.24728\text{ kg})(9.80665\text{ m/s}^2)(0.11\text{ m}) = (0.03508\text{ kg-m}^2)\alpha$$

Solving, we have $\alpha = 55.7\text{ rad/s}^2$, which is close to the value in 6.2-7[2].

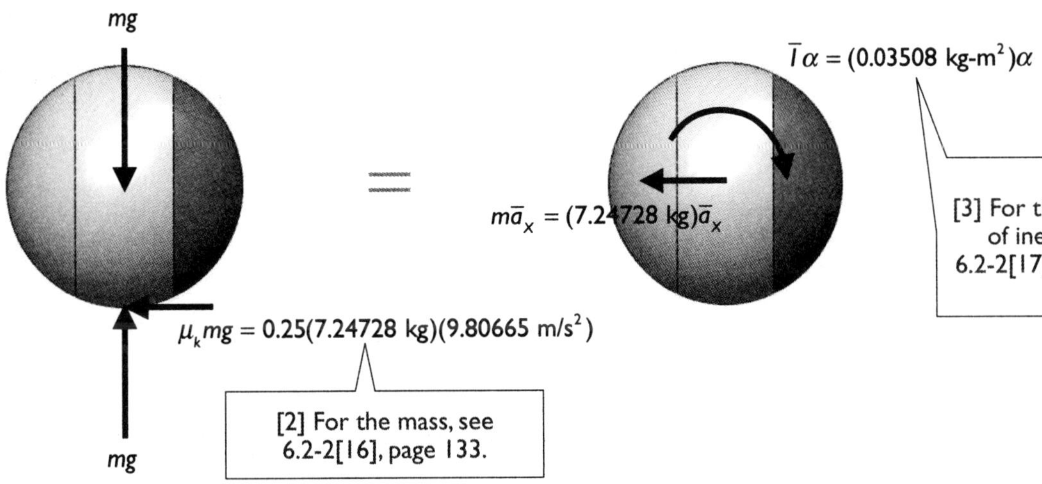

[2] For the mass, see 6.2-2[16], page 133.

[3] For the moment of inertia, see 6.2-2[17], page 133.

[4] After 0.63 sec

At 0.63 sec, the linear speed $\bar{v}_x$ and the angular speed ω reach a pure rolling condition $\bar{v}_x = r\omega$. In a pure rolling motion, because of no sliding, there must be no dynamic friction. And because of no external horizontal forces, there must be no static friction. In fact, the only external forces acting on the **Ball** are the gravitational force and the reaction force from the **Floor** [5]. Accordingly, the effective forces and moment must be zeros. That implies the linear acceleration and the angular acceleration are zeros; i.e., the linear velocity and the angular velocity are constant.

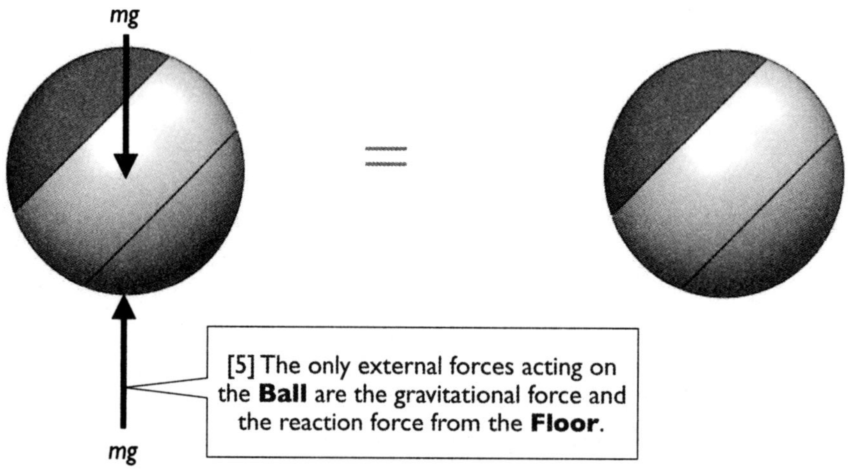

[5] The only external forces acting on the **Ball** are the gravitational force and the reaction force from the **Floor**.

[6] Remark: Will it roll forever after 0.63 sec?

It won't. In the simulation, we didn't consider rolling resistance (or rolling friction); therefore, it rolls forever after 0.63 sec. However, it'll eventually stop if the rolling resistance is taken into account.

[7] Wrap Up

Save all files and exit **SolidWorks**. #

Chapter 7

Planar Rigid Body Dynamics: Work and Energy

Kinetic Energy

A body can be thought of as a system of particles. Let m_i and $\vec{v}_i$ be the mass and the velocity of an arbitrary particle. A velocity $\vec{v}_i$ can be expressed as the sum of the velocity $\bar{\vec{v}}$ of the mass center G and the velocity $\vec{v}_i'$ of the particle relative to G; i.e., $\vec{v}_i = \bar{\vec{v}} + \vec{v}_i'$. The kinetic energy T of the body is the sum of the kinetic energy of each particle:

$$T = \frac{1}{2}\sum m_i(\vec{v}_i \cdot \vec{v}_i) = \frac{1}{2}\sum m_i(\bar{\vec{v}} + \vec{v}_i')\cdot(\bar{\vec{v}} + \vec{v}_i') \tag{1}$$

For a rigid body in plane motion, after some mild manipulations, Eq. (1) will become

$$T = \frac{1}{2}m\bar{v}^2 + \frac{1}{2}\bar{I}\omega^2 \tag{2}$$

where

m is the mass of the body;

$\bar{v}$ is the linear speed of the mass center G of the body;

$\bar{I}$ is the moment of inertia of the body with respect to an axis passing through G and normal to the motion plane;

ω is the angular speed of the body.

Principle of Work and Energy

The principle of work and energy for a particle, Eq. 3(5) (page 58), is still valid for a rigid body

$$T_1 + V_1 + U_{1\to 2} = T_2 + V_2 \tag{3}$$

However, all quantities in Eq. (3) must include rotational quantity. For example, kinetic energy must include rotational kinetic energy (Eq. (2)); work done must also consider the work done by moments.

This chapter will demonstrate how Eq. (3) is applied for rigid bodies in plane motion.

Section 7.1

Principle of Work and Energy: Crank-Link-Piston Mechanism

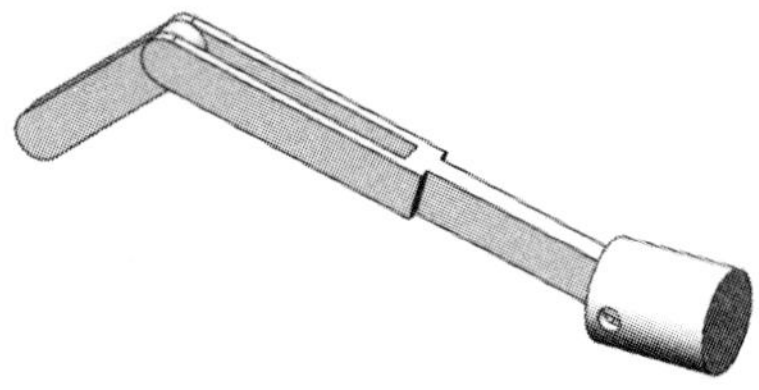

7.1-1 Introduction

In this section, we'll revisit the **Crank-Link-Piston** example, introduced in Section 5.1. We'll replace the **Motor**, which has a constant clockwise angular velocity of 2000 rpm, with a constant clockwise **Torque** $M = 5$ N·m. Using this example, we'll illustrate the **principle of Work and Energy** for a mechanical system consisting of rigid bodies in plane motion, which states

$$T_0 + V_0 + U_{0\to t} = T_t + V_t \quad (1)$$

where T_0 and V_0 are respectively the initial kinetic energy and potential energy of the system, and T_t and V_t are respectively the kinetic energy and potential energy of the system at time t, and $U_{0\to t}$ is the work done by non-conservative force (work done by conservative forces always can be expressed as potential energies). This statement appears to be identical to the statement in 3.1-1[1] (page 59), which is the **principle of Work and Energy** for a system of particles. However, when applying to rigid bodies, calculations of work or energy must include rotational quantities. For example, the kinetic energy of a rigid body in plane motion is calculated as

$$T = \frac{1}{2}m\bar{v}^2 + \frac{1}{2}\bar{I}\omega^2 \quad (2)$$

where m is the mass of the body, $\bar{v}$ is the linear speed at the mass center, $\bar{I}$ is the moment of inertia with respect to an axis passing through the mass center and normal to the motion plane, and ω is the angular speed of the rigid body.

In this case, we neglect the gravitational potential energy (i.e., $V_0 = V_t = 0$) and $T_0 = 0$. The work done by the constant **Torque** is $U_{0\to t} = M\theta_t$, where θ_t is the rotating angle at time t; therefore, Eq. (1) reduces to

$$T_t = M\theta_t \quad (3)$$

Eq. (3) holds for any time t. In this exercise, we'll verify it at t = **0.01 sec** only, which is arbitrarily chosen. We leave it for you to check other time points.

7.1-2 Open the File **Crank-Link-Piston.SLDASM**

[1] Launch **SolidWorks** and open the file **Crank-Link-Piston.SLDASM**, which is saved in Section 5.1.#

7.1-3 Create a New **Motion Study**

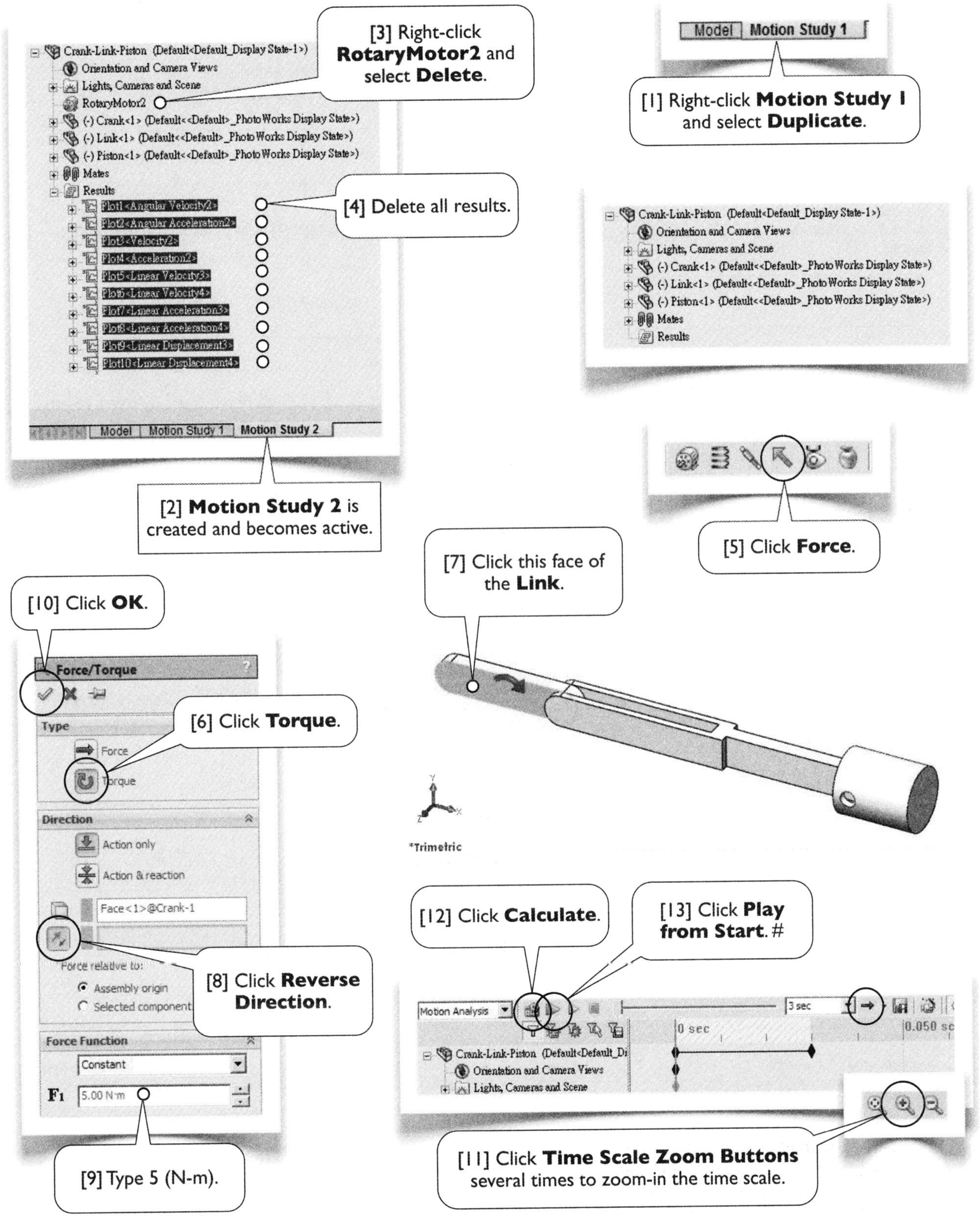

7.1-4 Mass and Moment of Inertia

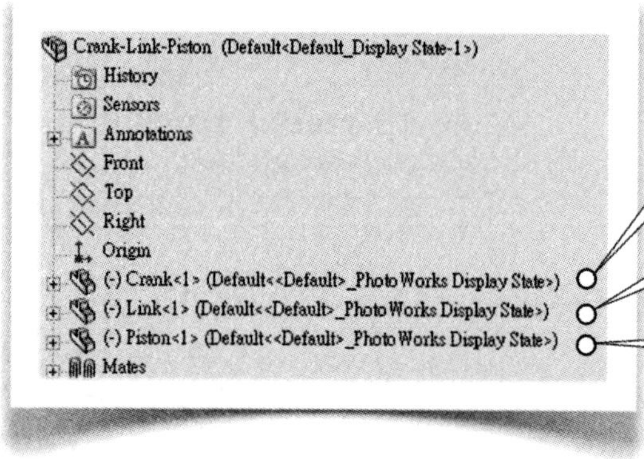

[1] In **Assembly Tree**, right-click **Crank<1>** and select **Open Part**.

[4] Right-click **Link<1>** and select **Open Part**.

[7] Right-click **Piston<1>** and select **Open Part**.

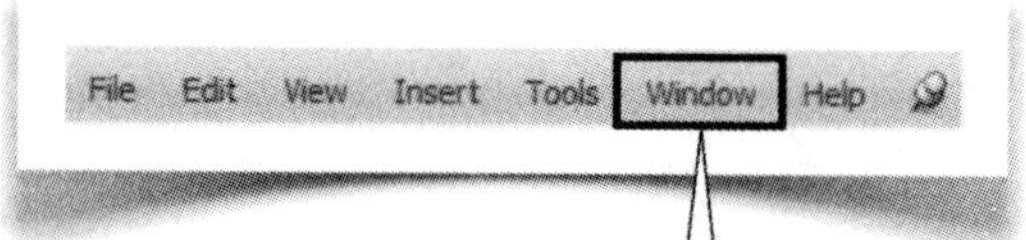

[2, 5, 8] In the **Evaluate Toolbar**, click **Mass Properties** and record the mass and the moment of inertia at the mass center. For **Piston**, the moment of inertia is not needed.

[3, 6, 9] From **Pull-Down Menus**, select **Window>Crank-Link-Piston** to return to the assembly.

	Crank	Link	Piston
Mass (gram)	18.14159	45.14159	30.2295
Moment of Inertia (gram-mm^2)	13106.19	169037.46	

[10] Click **Motion Study 2**. #

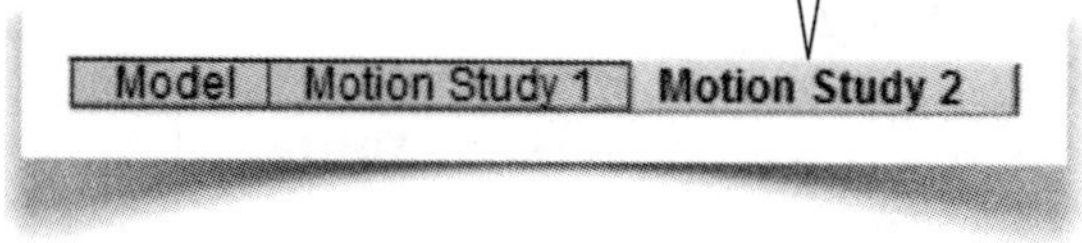

7.1-5 Results: Linear and Angular Speed of **Crank**

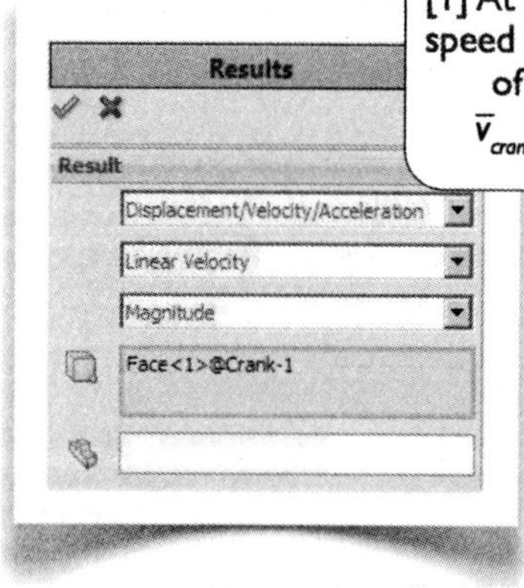

[1] At 0.01 sec, the linear speed at the mass center of the **Crank** is $\bar{v}_{crank} = 5.7262$ m/s.

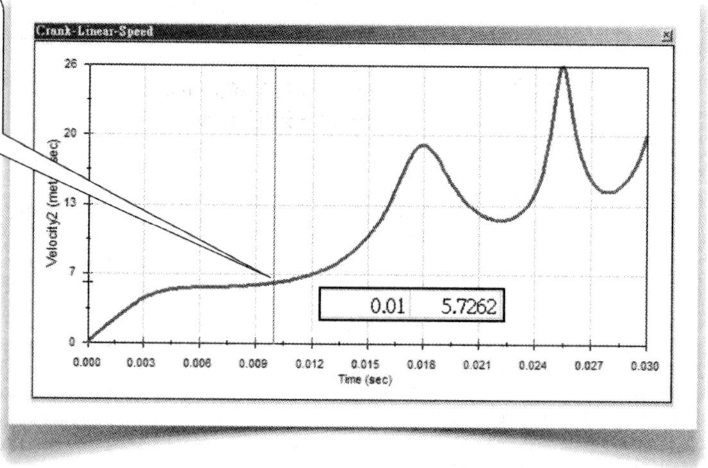

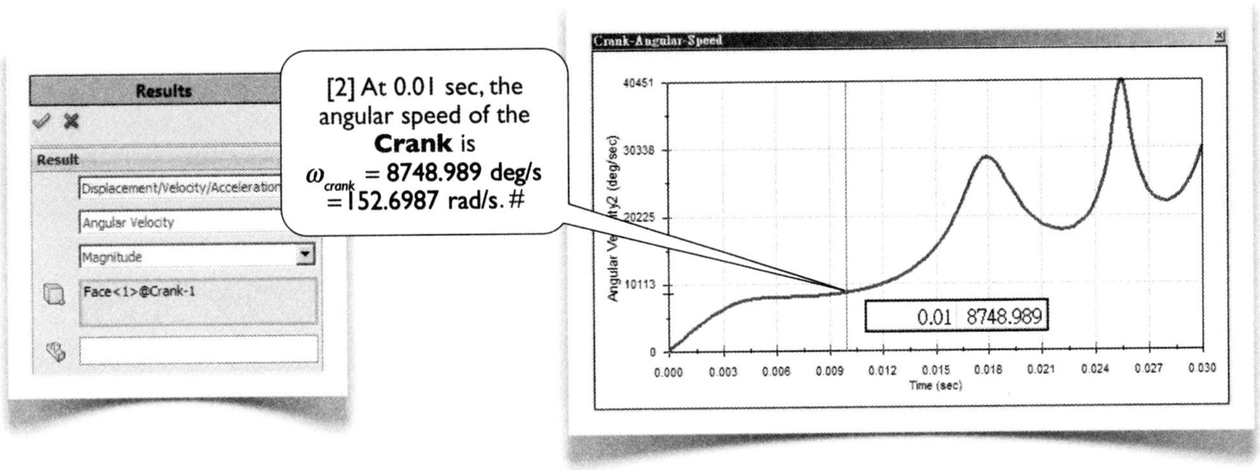

7.1-6 Results: Linear and Angular Speed of **Link**

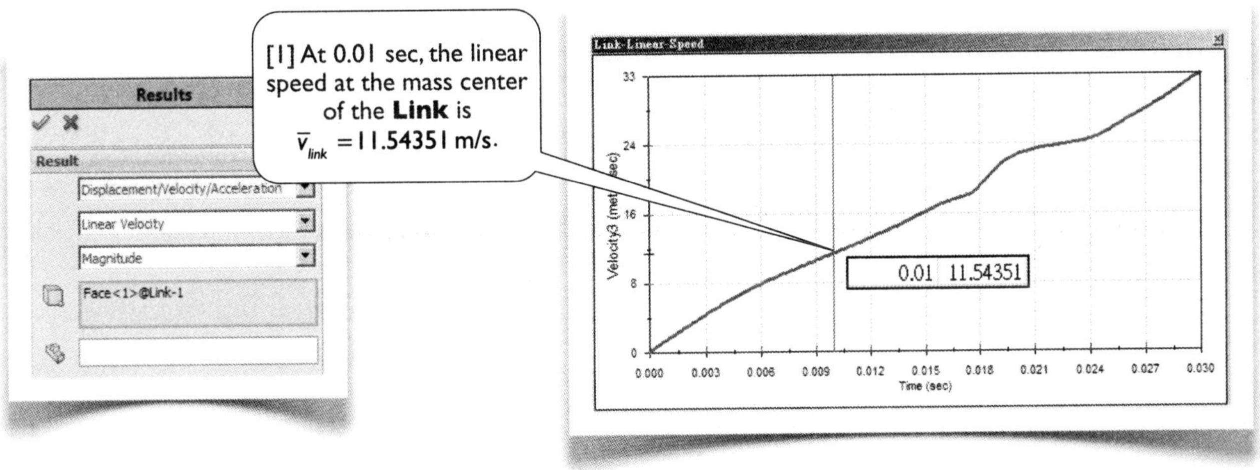

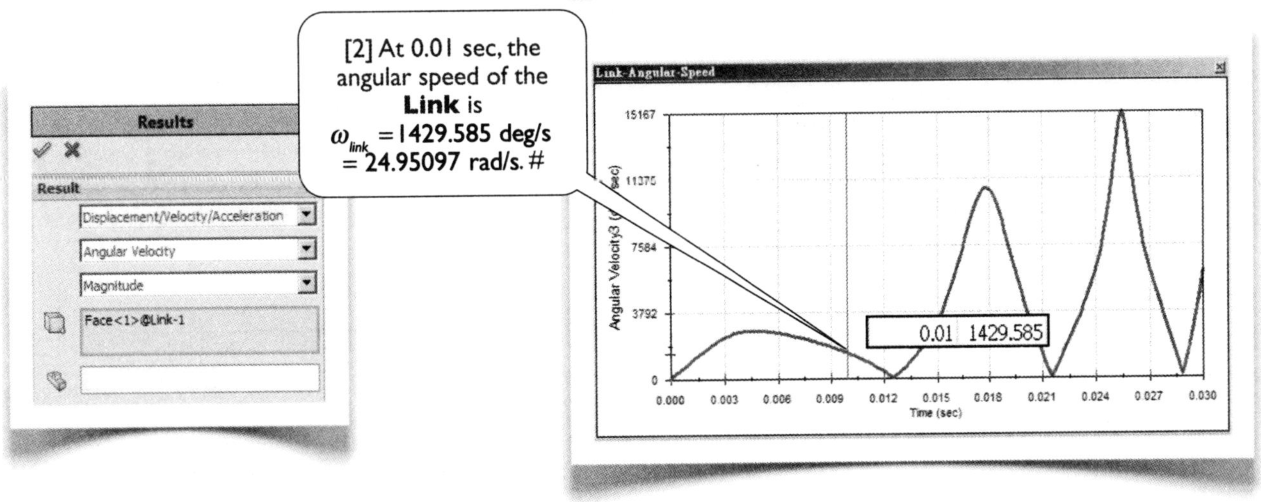

7.1-7 Results: Linear Speed of **Piston**

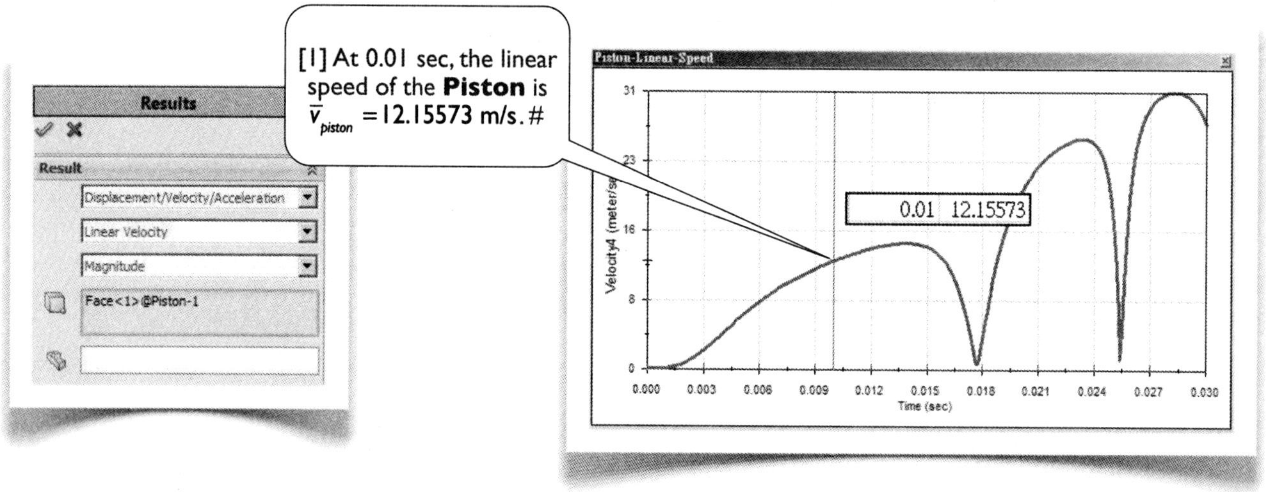

7.1-8 Results: Angular Displacement of **Crank**

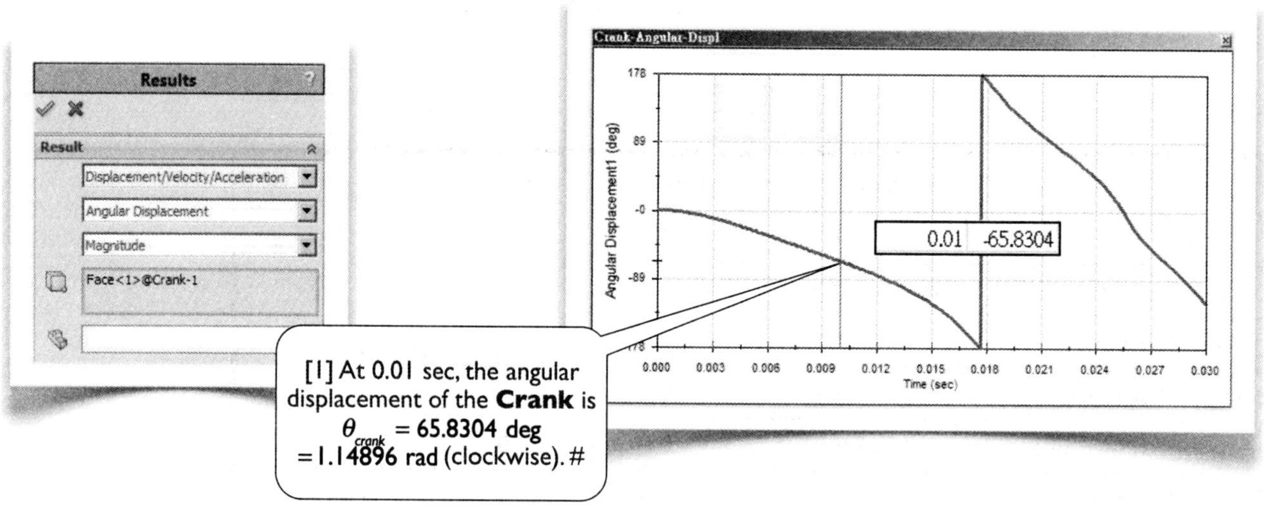

7.1-9 Principle of Work and Energy: **Crank-Link-Piston**

[1] The work done by the moment $M = 5\ \text{N}\cdot\text{m}$, from $t = 0$ to $t = 0.01$ s is

$$U_{0\to 0.01} = M\theta_{0.01} = (5\ \text{N}\cdot\text{m})(1.14896\ \text{rad}) = 5.745\ \text{J}$$

For the **Crank**, the kinetic energy is

$$\begin{aligned} T_{crank} &= \frac{m_{crank}\bar{v}^2_{crank}}{2} + \frac{\bar{I}_{crank}\alpha^2_{crank}}{2} \\ &= \frac{(0.01814159\ \text{kg})(5.7262\ \text{m/s})^2}{2} + \frac{(13106.19\times 10^{-9}\ \text{kg-m}^2)(152.6987\ \text{rad/s})^2}{2} \\ &= 0.450223\ \text{J} \end{aligned}$$

For the **Link**, the kinetic energy is

$$\begin{aligned} T_{link} &= \frac{m_{link}\bar{v}^2_{link}}{2} + \frac{\bar{I}_{link}\alpha^2_{link}}{2} \\ &= \frac{(0.04514159\ \text{kg})(11.54351\ \text{m/s})^2}{2} + \frac{(169037.46\times 10^{-9}\ \text{kg-m}^2)(24.95097\ \text{rad/s})^2}{2} \\ &= 3.060435\ \text{J} \end{aligned}$$

For the **Piston**, the kinetic energy is

$$T_{piston} = \frac{m_{piston}\bar{v}^2_{piston}}{2} = \frac{(0.0302295\ \text{kg})(12.15573\ \text{m/s})^2}{2} = 2.233382\ \text{J}$$

The total kinetic energy is

$$T_{0.01} = T_{crank} + T_{link} + T_{piston} = 0.450223\ \text{J} + 3.060435\ \text{J} + 2.233382\ \text{J} = 5.744\ \text{J}$$

We have

$$T_{0.01} \approx M\theta_{0.01}$$

	Crank	Link	Piston	Total
Mass (kg)	0.01814159	0.04514159	0.03022950	
Moment of Inertia (kg-m^2)	0.00001310619	0.00016903746		
Linear Speed (m/s)	5.726200	11.54351	12.15573	
Angular Speed (deg/s)	8748.989	1429.585	0	
Angular Speed (rad/s)	152.6987	24.9510	0	
Linear Kinetic Energy (J)	0.2974256	3.007617	2.233384	5.538426
Angular Kinetic Energy (J)	0.1527977	0.05261717	0	0.205415
Kinetic Energy (J)	0.4502233	3.060234	2.233384	5.743841

[2] This is a summary of the calculations in [1].

[3] Wrap Up

Save all files and exit **SolidWorks**. #

Section 7.2

Conservation of Energy: Double Pendulum

7.2-1 Introduction

[1] In this section, we'll revisit the **Double Pendulum** example, introduced in Section 6.1. The only external forces involved in this system are gravitational forces, which are conservative and their work done can be expressed in potential energy. Therefore, Eq. 7.1-1(1) (page 140) reduces to

$$T_0 + V_0 = T_t + V_t \qquad (1)$$

which is often referred to as the **principle of Conservation of Energy**: In a mechanical system in which no external non-conservative forces are involved, the **total mechanical energy** (the sum of kinetic energy and potential energy) remains constant over time; i.e.,

$$T_t + V_t = \text{const} \qquad (2)$$

In this exercise, we'll calculate the total mechanical energy at $t = 0$, 0.2, 0.4, 0.6, 0.8, 1.0 sec, and confirm that Eq. (2) holds over time for the **Double Pendulum** system. The baseline (i.e., $V = 0$) of gravitational potential energy is conveniently chosen at assembly's **Top** plane. #

7.2-2 Open **Pendulum.SLDASM** and Create a New Study

[1] Launch **SolidWorks** and open the file **Pendulum.SLDASM**, which is saved in Section 6.1.

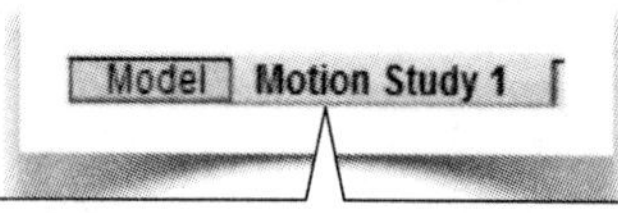

[2] Right-click **Motion Study 1** and select **Duplicate**.

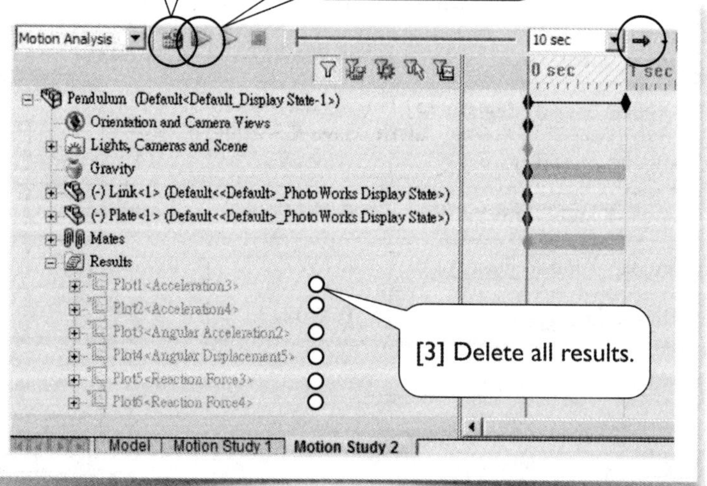

[3] Delete all results.

[4] Click **Calculate**.

[5] Click **Play from Start**. #

7.2-3 Results: **Link**

[1] In **Assembly Tree**, right-click **Link** and select **Open Part**. In the **Evaluate Toolbar**, click **Mass Properties** and record the mass m_{link} = 20.71239 g and the moment of inertia at the mass center $\bar{I}_{link}$ = 7305.70 g-mm^2.

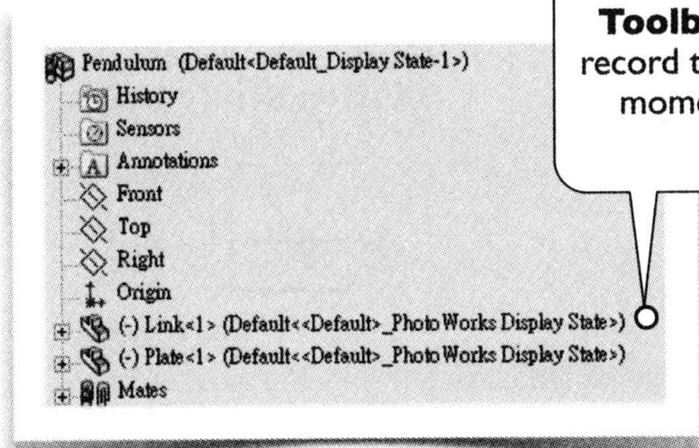

[2] From **Pull-Down Menus**, select **Window>Pendulum** to return to the assembly. Click **Motion Study 2** tab.

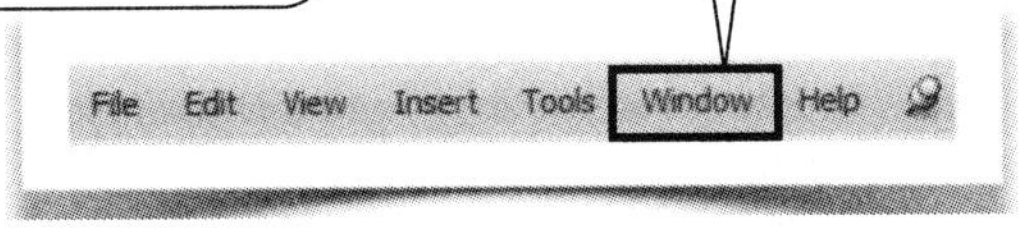

[3] The elevation of the mass center of **Link**. (The baseline is on the **Top** plane.) Save **CSV** file.

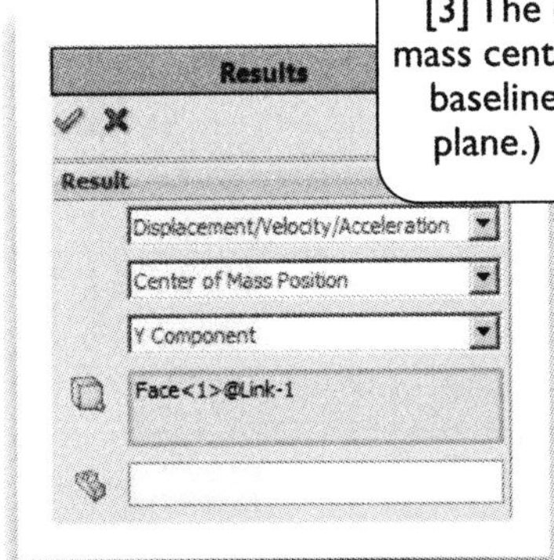

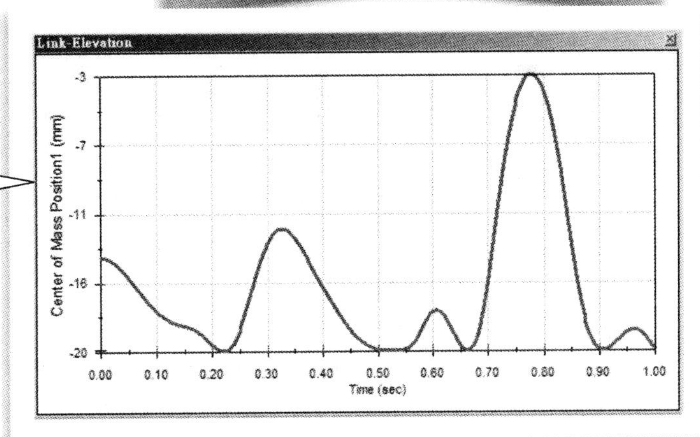

[4] The linear speed of the mass center of **Link**. Save **CSV** file.

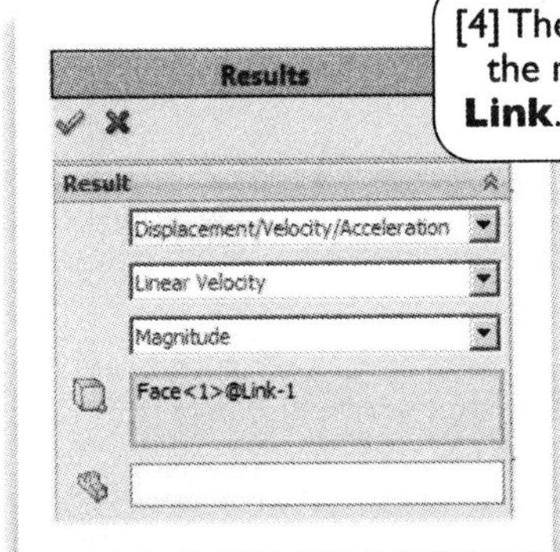

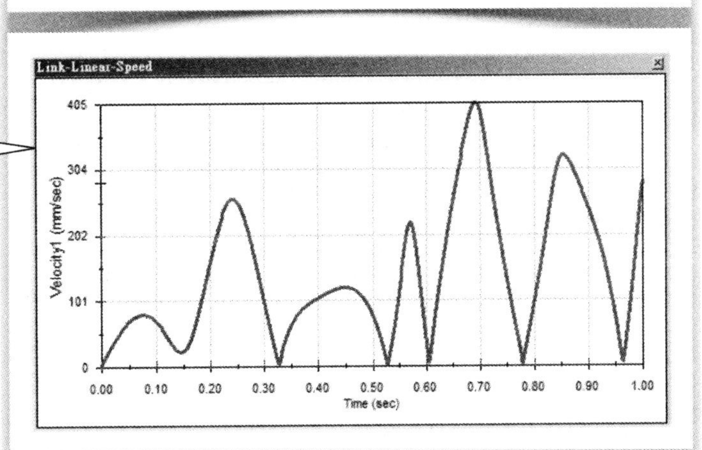

[5] The angular speed of **Link**. Save **CSV** file. #

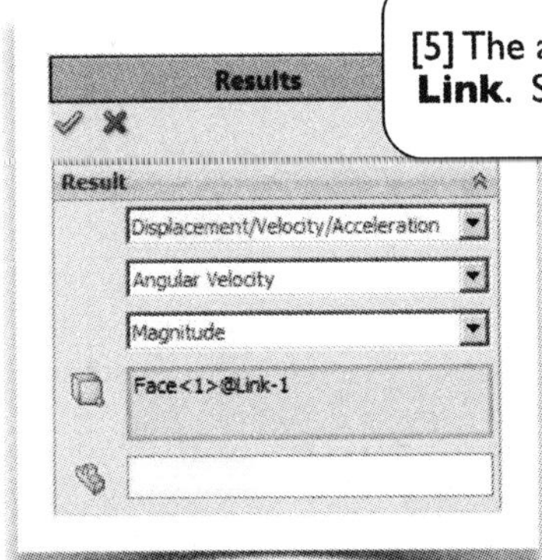

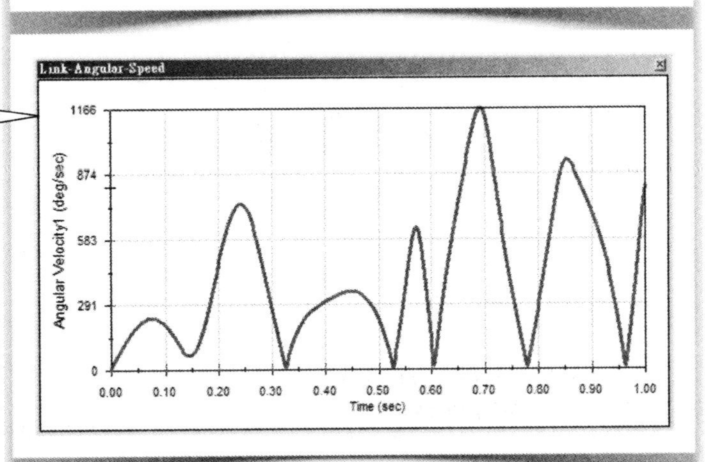

7.2-4 Results: **Plate**

[1] In **Assembly Tree**, right-click **Plate** and select **Open Part**. In the **Evaluate Toolbar**, click **Mass Properties** and record the mass m_{plate} = 149.80365 g and the moment of inertia I_{plate} = 405418.72 g-mm^2.

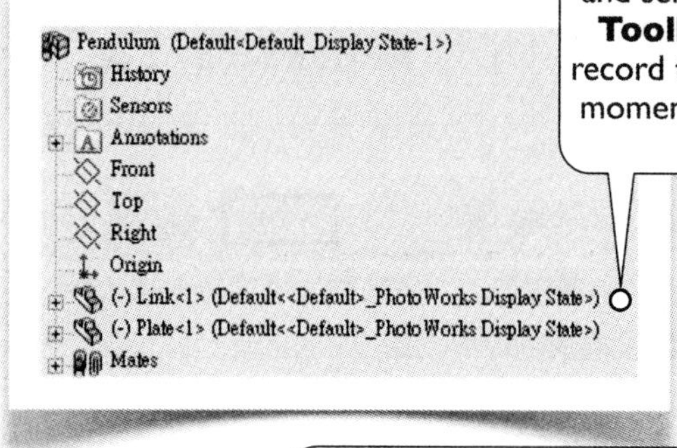

[2] From **Pull-Down Menus**, select **Window>Pendulum** to return to the assembly. Click **Motion Study 2** tab.

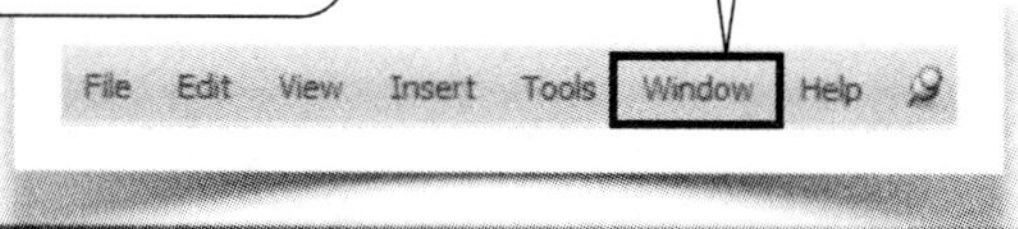

[3] The elevation of the mass center of **Plate**. (The baseline is on the **Top** plane.) Save **CSV** file.

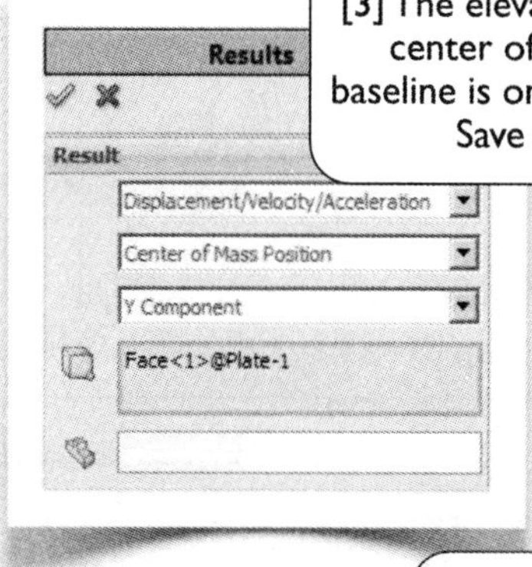

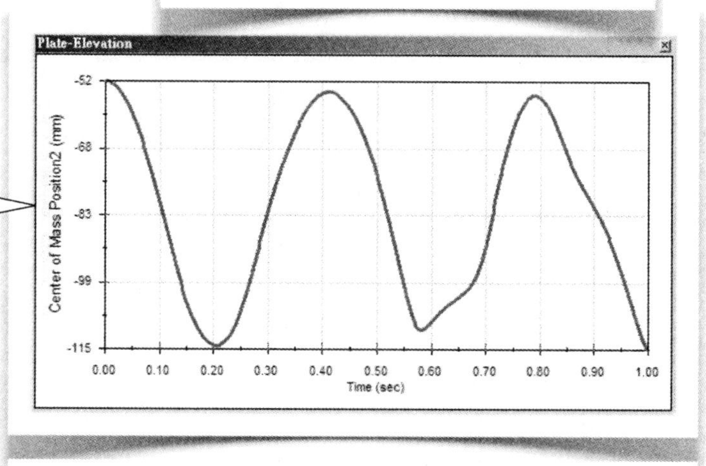

[4] The linear speed of the mass center of **Plate**. Save **CSV** file.

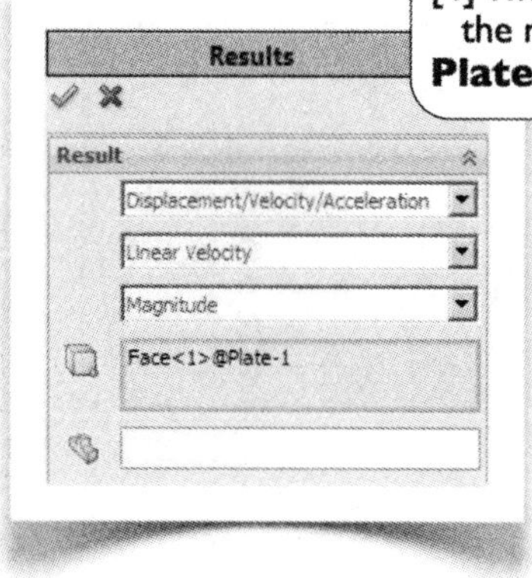

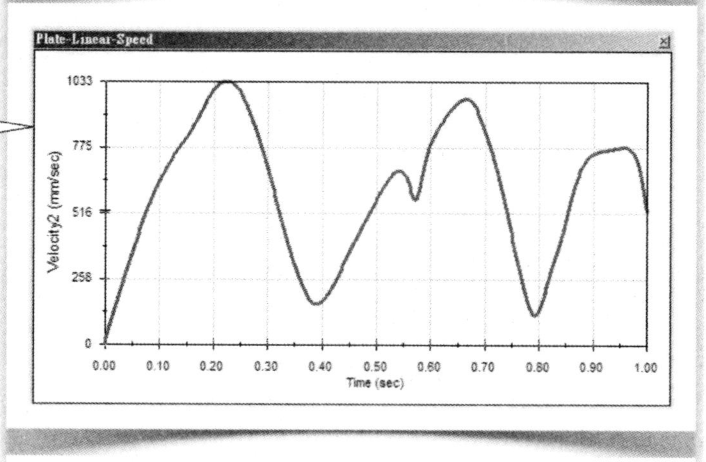

[5] The angular speed of **Plate**. Save **CSV** file. #

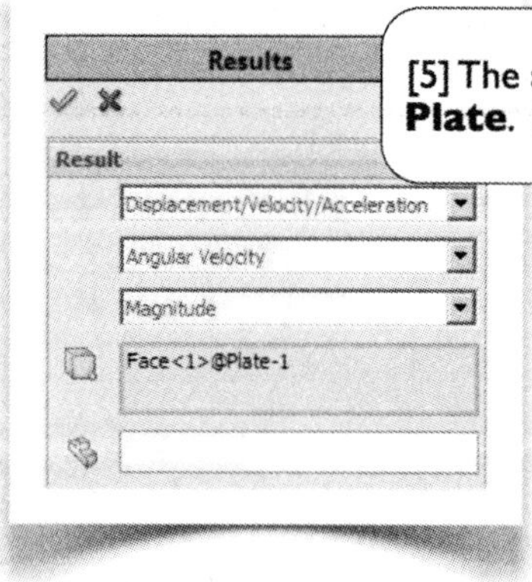

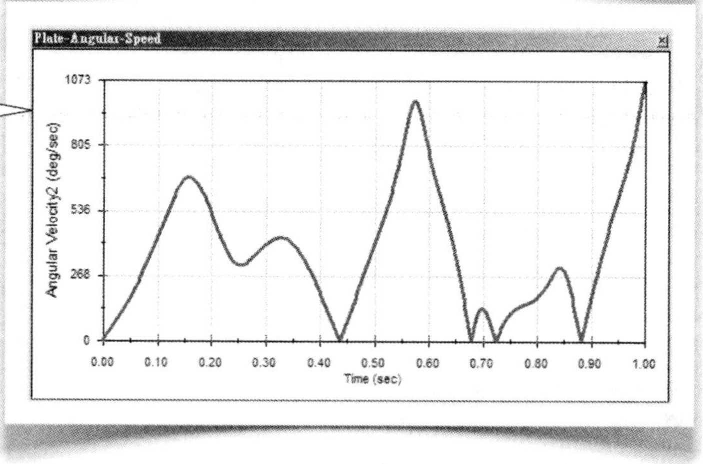

7.2-5 Calculations of Mechanical Energy

[1] The calculations of mechanical energy are tabulated here.

	time (sec)	0	0.2	0.4	0.6	0.8	1.0
Link	Elevation (mm)	-14.0611	-19.4635	-15.8337	-17.5036	-3.7317	-19.7780
	Linear Speed (mm/s)	0	159.9065	103.2962	49.0980	91.6721	282.9333
	Angular Speed (deg/s)	0	460.7306	297.6253	141.4658	264.1338	815.1668
	Angular Speed (rad/s)	0	8.0413	5.1945	2.4690	4.6100	14.2273
	Potential Energy (mJ)	-2.8560	-3.9534	-3.2161	-3.5553	-0.7580	-4.0172
	Linear Kinetic Energy (mJ)	0	0.2648	0.1105	0.0250	0.0870	0.8290
	Angular Kinetic Energy (mJ)	0	0.2362	0.0986	0.0223	0.0776	0.7394
	Total Energy (mJ)	-2.8560	-3.4524	-3.0070	-3.5080	-0.5933	-2.4488
Plate	Elevation (mm)	-52.2006	-113.9314	-55.1728	-108.8007	-55.9685	-114.7990
	Linear Speed (mm/s)	0	994.1924	165.8069	785.9524	132.4961	521.0872
	Angular Speed (deg/s)	0	528.3980	199.4554	779.4670	177.5273	1072.9739
	Angular Speed (rad/s)	0	9.2223	3.4812	13.6043	3.0984	18.7269
	Potential Energy (mJ)	-76.6857	-167.3718	-81.0520	-159.8344	-82.2208	-168.6463
	Linear Kinetic Energy (mJ)	0	74.0344	2.0592	46.2684	1.3149	20.3382
	Angular Kinetic Energy (mJ)	0	17.2405	2.4565	37.5166	1.9461	71.0897
	Total Energy (mJ)	-76.6857	-76.0969	-76.5362	-76.0493	-78.9599	-77.2183
Total Energy (mJ)		-79.5417	-79.5492	-79.5433	-79.5574	-79.5532	-79.6672

[2] The bottom line shows that the mechanical energy remains constant over time.

[3] Wrap Up

Save all files and exit **SolidWorks**. #

Chapter 8

Planar Rigid Body Dynamics: Impulse and Momentum

Linear Momentum and Angular Momentum

As mentioned (page 139), a rigid body can be thought of as a system of particles. Let m_i and $\vec{v}_i$ be the mass and the velocity of an arbitrary particle. A velocity $\vec{v}_i$ can be expressed as the sum of the velocity $\vec{\bar{v}}$ of the mass center G and the velocity $\vec{v}_i'$ of the particle relative to G; i.e., $\vec{v}_i = \vec{\bar{v}} + \vec{v}_i'$. The linear momentum $\vec{L}$ of the body is the sum of the linear momentum of each particles:

$$\vec{L} = \sum m_i \vec{v}_i = \sum m_i (\vec{\bar{v}} + \vec{v}_i') = \sum m_i \vec{\bar{v}} + \sum m_i \vec{v}_i' = m\vec{\bar{v}} + 0$$

where m is the mass of the body. We write

$$\vec{L} = m\vec{\bar{v}} \tag{1}$$

The angular momentum $\vec{H}_G$ of the body about the mass center G is the sum of the angular momentum of each particles about G. Let $\vec{r}_i'$ be the position vector of each particle relative to G, then for a rigid body in plane motion,

$$\vec{H}_G = \sum \vec{r}_i' \times m_i \vec{v}_i = \sum \vec{r}_i' \times m_i (\vec{\bar{v}} + \vec{v}_i') = \sum \vec{r}_i' \times m_i \vec{\bar{v}} + \sum \vec{r}_i' \times m_i \vec{v}_i' = (\sum m_i \vec{r}_i') \times \vec{\bar{v}} + \sum \vec{r}_i' \times m_i \omega \vec{r}_i' = 0 + \omega \sum m_i (r_i')^2$$

where ω is the angular speed of the body. The sum in the right-hand side equals to $\bar{I}$, the moment of inertia of the body with respect to an axis passing through G and normal to the motion plane. We write

$$\vec{H}_G = \bar{I}\omega \tag{2}$$

Principle of Impulse and Momentum

The principle of impulse and momentum for a particle, Eq. 4(2) (page 82), is still valid for a rigid body in plane motion,

$$m\vec{v}_1 + \sum \overrightarrow{Imp_{1\to 2}} = m\vec{v}_2 \tag{3}$$

In addition, there is an equation accounting for the relation between angular momentum and angular impulse in the direction normal to the motion plane:

$$H_1 + \sum AngImp_{1\to 2} = H_2 \tag{4}$$

This chapter will demonstrate the meaning of Eqs. (3, 4) for rigid bodies in plane motion.

Section 8.1

Principle of Impulse and Momentum: Crank-Link-Piston Mechanism

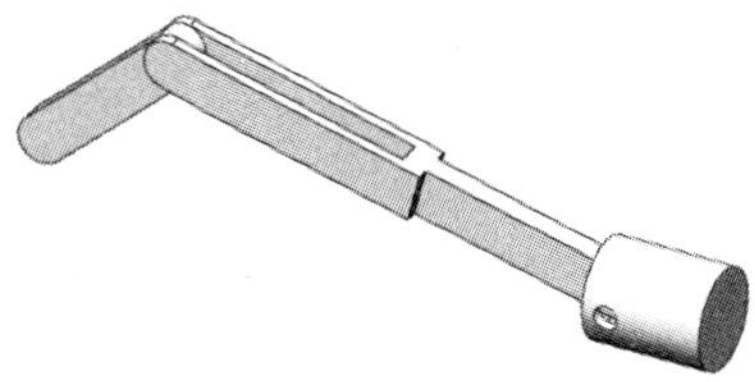

8.1-1 Introduction

[1] In this section, we'll revisit the **Crank-Link-Piston** example again. We'll use the same scenario in Section 7.1 to illustrate the **principle of impulse and momentum** for a system of rigid bodies in plane motion, which can be represented in a mathemastics form:

$$\sum m\vec{v}_0 + \sum \overrightarrow{Imp}_{0\to t} = \sum m\vec{v}_t \tag{1}$$

$$\sum H_0 + \sum AngImp_{0\to t} = \sum H_t \tag{2}$$

In practical calculation, we usually draw a diagrammatic form. For example, in this case, assuming $t = 0.01$ sec, Eq. (1, 2) are diagrammatically represented as below [2, 3]. Note that the initial linear momentum $\sum m\vec{v}_0 = 0$ and initial angular momentum $\sum H_0 = 0$; they are not shown in the diagram.

This section will demonstrate the calculation of each item in [2, 3] and confirm the equality relation, so that the students will fully understand the use of Eqs. (1, 2) and their diagrammatic form.

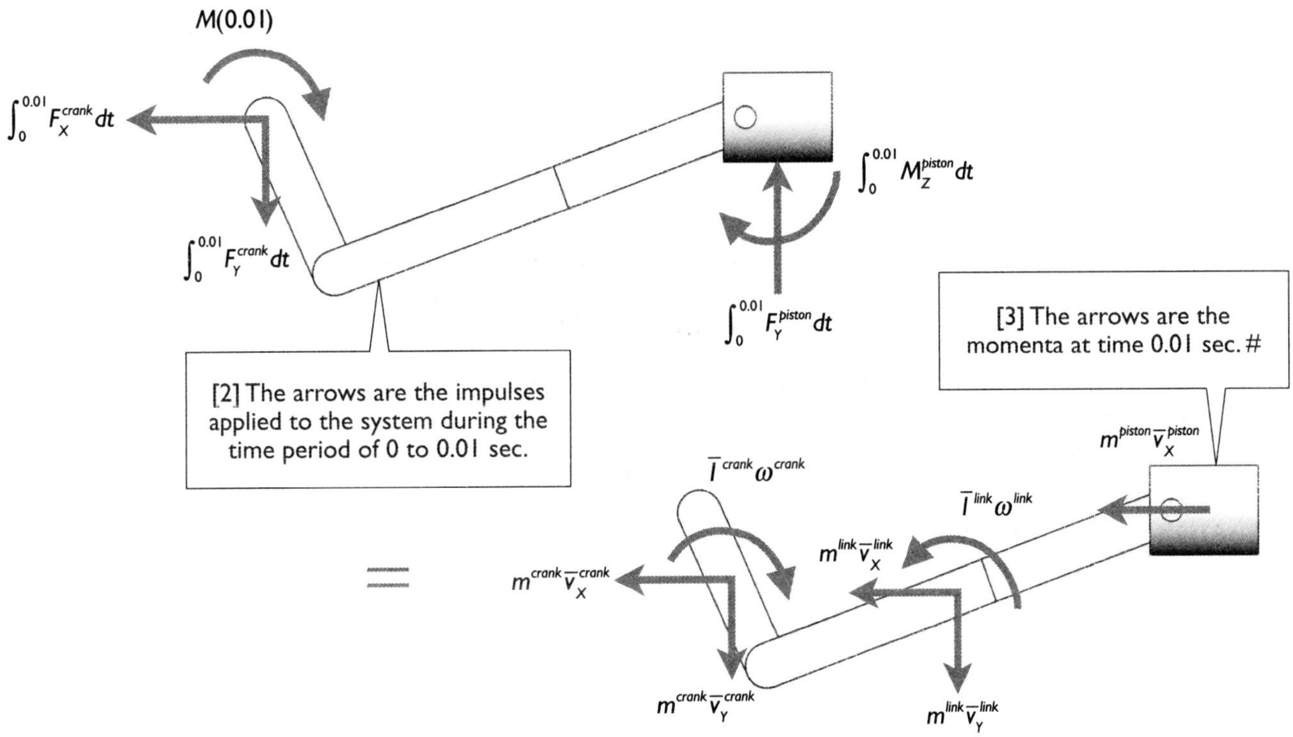

8.1-2 Open the File **Crank-Link-Piston.SLDASM**

[1] Launch **SolidWorks** and open the file **Crank-Link-Piston.SLDASM**, which was saved in Section 7.1.

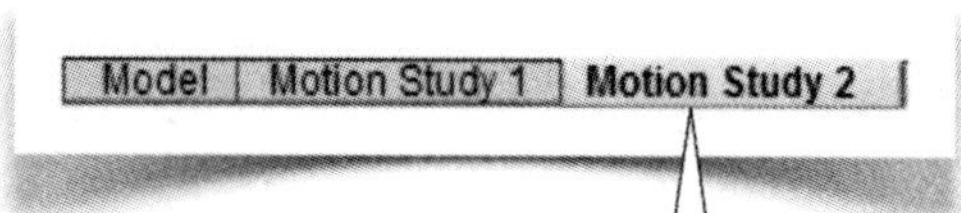

[2] Click **Motion Study 2**. #

8.1-3 Reaction Forces/Moments and Impulses

[1] To obtain the reaction force at the pivot of **Crank**, select **Coincident1** (see 5.1-5[11], page 105).

[2] This is a plot of F_X^{crank} (see 8.1-1[2], last page). The impulse $\int_0^{0.01} F_X^{crank} dt$ is the area below the curve and to the left of 0.01 sec. With the **CSV** file, it can be calculated to be 0.97665 N-s leftward. To do this, simply sum up the forces up to 0.01 sec and multiply by 1/9000 (remember that the results are reported every 1/9000 sec; see 5.1-7[3], page 107).

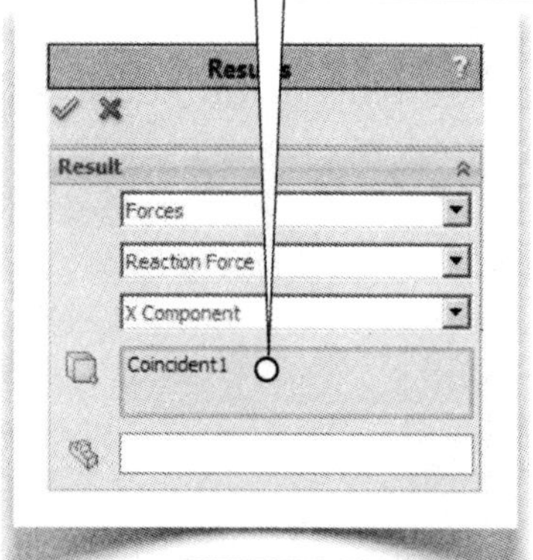

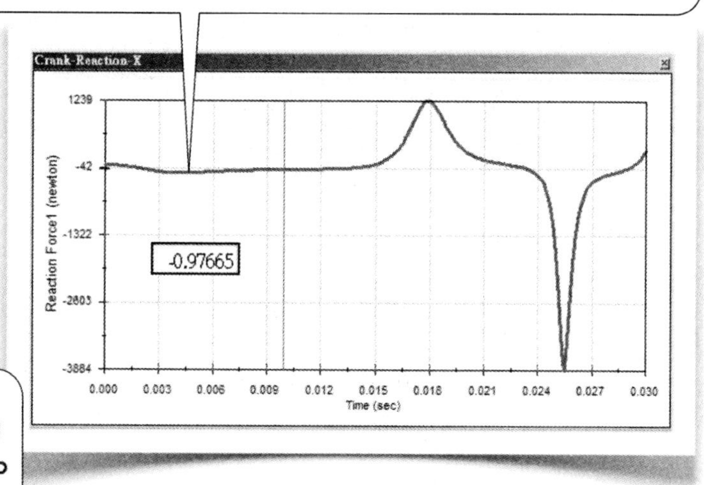

[3] This is a plot of F_Y^{crank}. The impulse $\int_0^{0.01} F_Y^{crank} dt$ is the area below the curve and to the left of 0.01 sec, which is calculated to be 0.22149 N-s downward (see [2]).

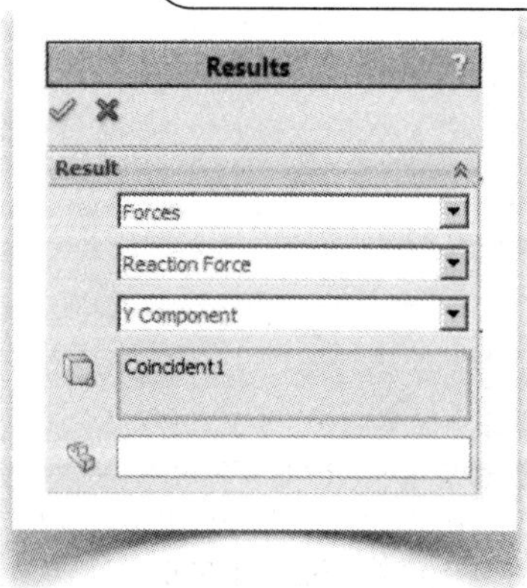

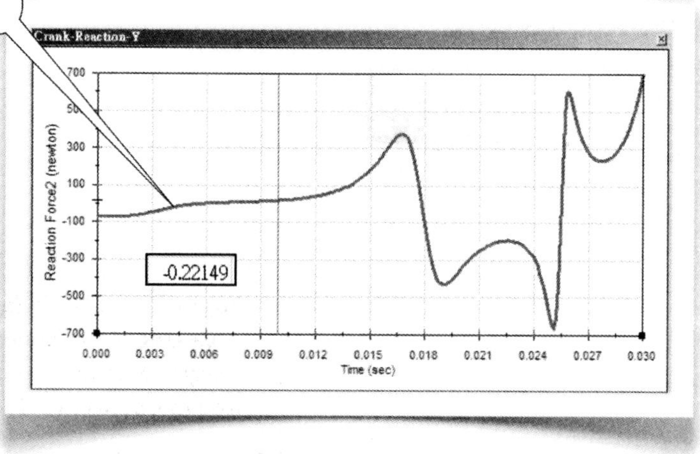

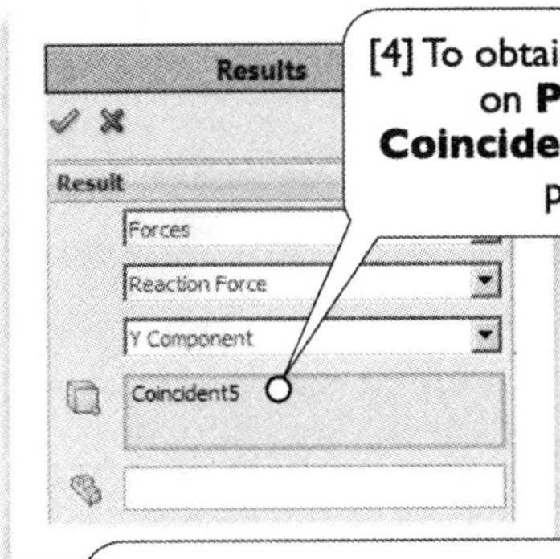

[4] To obtain the reaction force on **Piston**, select **Coincident5** (see 5.1-5[19], page 105).

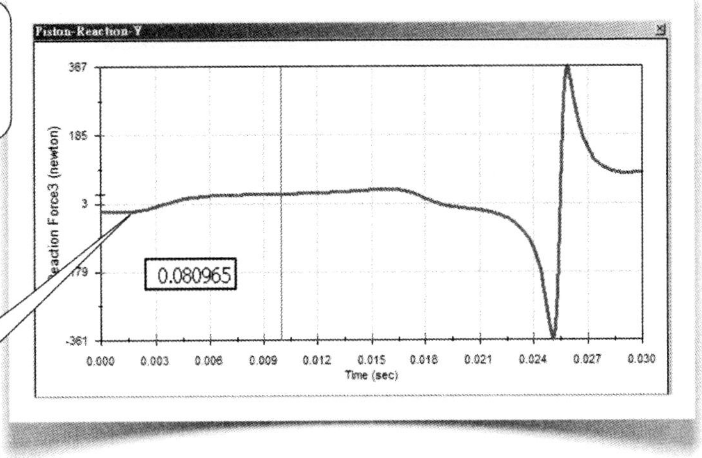

[5] This is a plot of F_Y^{piston}. The impulse $\int_0^{0.01} F_Y^{piston} dt$ is the area below the curve and to the left of 0.01 sec, which is calculated to be 0.080965 N-s upward (see [2], last page).

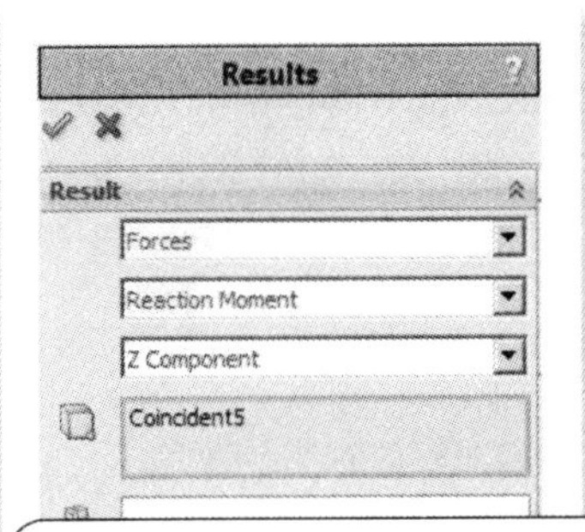

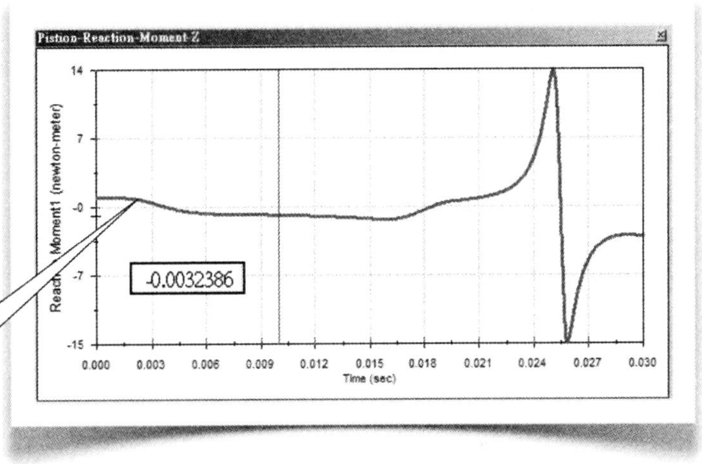

[6] This is a plot of M_Z^{piston}. The impulse $\int_0^{0.01} M_Z^{piston} dt$ is the area below the curve and to the left of 0.01 sec, which is calculated to be 0.0032386 N-m-s clockwise (see [2], last page).

[7] This is a summary of the Impulses during the time period 0 to 0.01 second.

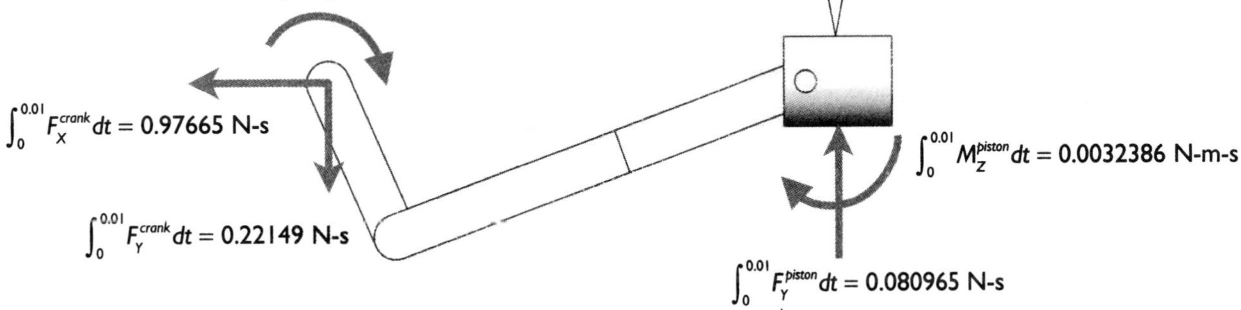

[8] Later in 8.1-6[9] (page 159), we'll take the moment about the pivot of **Crank**. Calculation of the moment of this impulse about the pivot is challenging because the horizontal distance to the pivot varies with time; i.e., we need to calculate $\int_0^{0.01} F_Y^{piston} X^{piston} dt$. We'll show this in 8.1-6[1, 2], page 158. #

8.1-4 Linear/Angular Velocities and Momenta

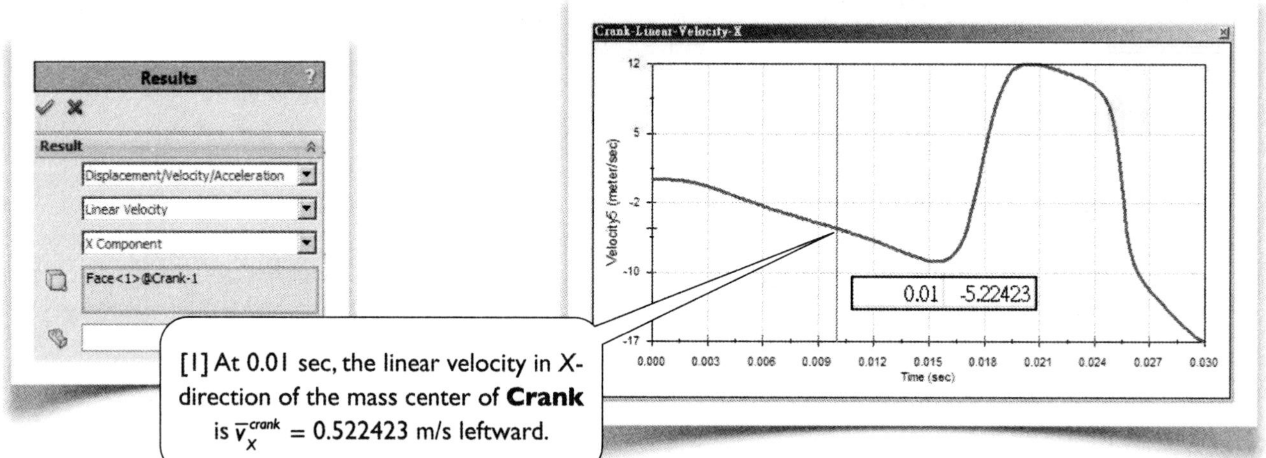

[1] At 0.01 sec, the linear velocity in X-direction of the mass center of **Crank** is $\bar{v}_X^{crank}$ = 0.522423 m/s leftward.

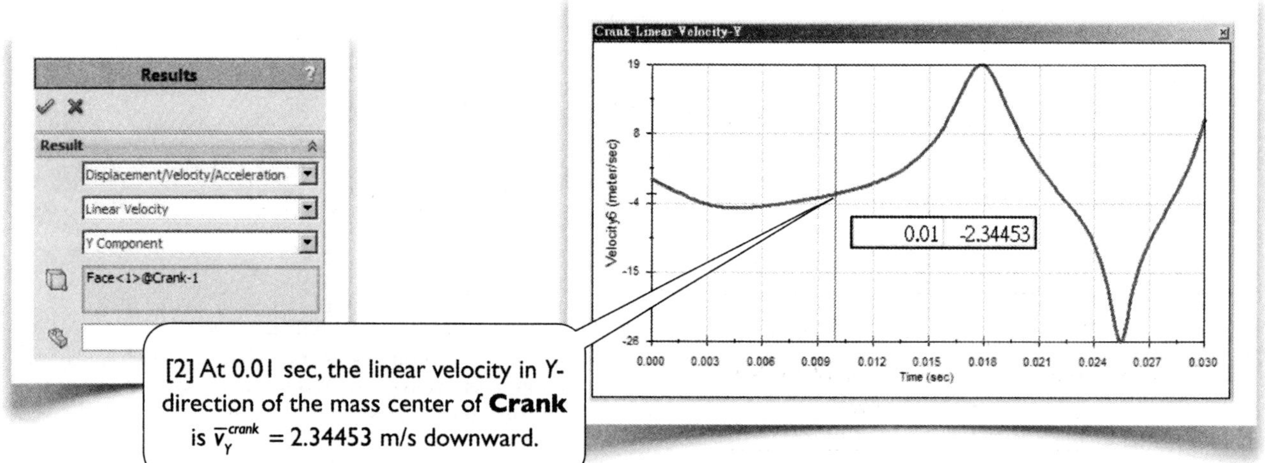

[2] At 0.01 sec, the linear velocity in Y-direction of the mass center of **Crank** is $\bar{v}_Y^{crank}$ = 2.34453 m/s downward.

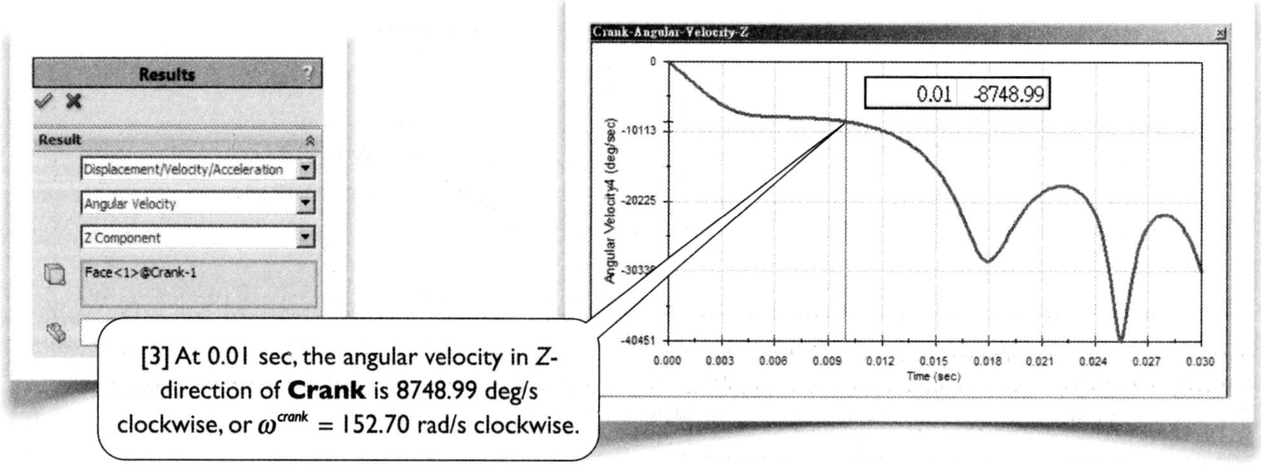

[3] At 0.01 sec, the angular velocity in Z-direction of **Crank** is 8748.99 deg/s clockwise, or ω^{crank} = 152.70 rad/s clockwise.

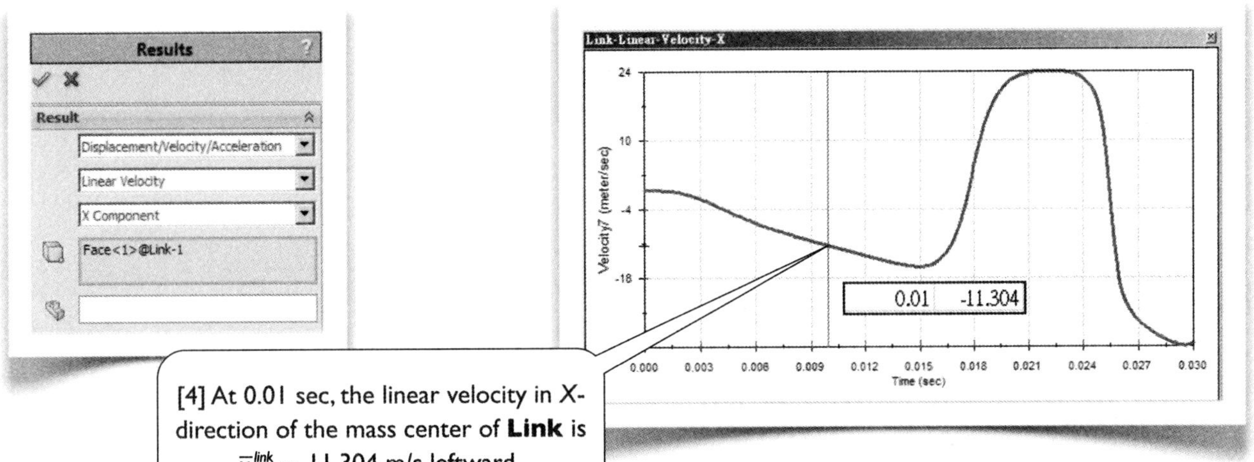

[4] At 0.01 sec, the linear velocity in *X*-direction of the mass center of **Link** is $\bar{v}_X^{link}$ = 11.304 m/s leftward.

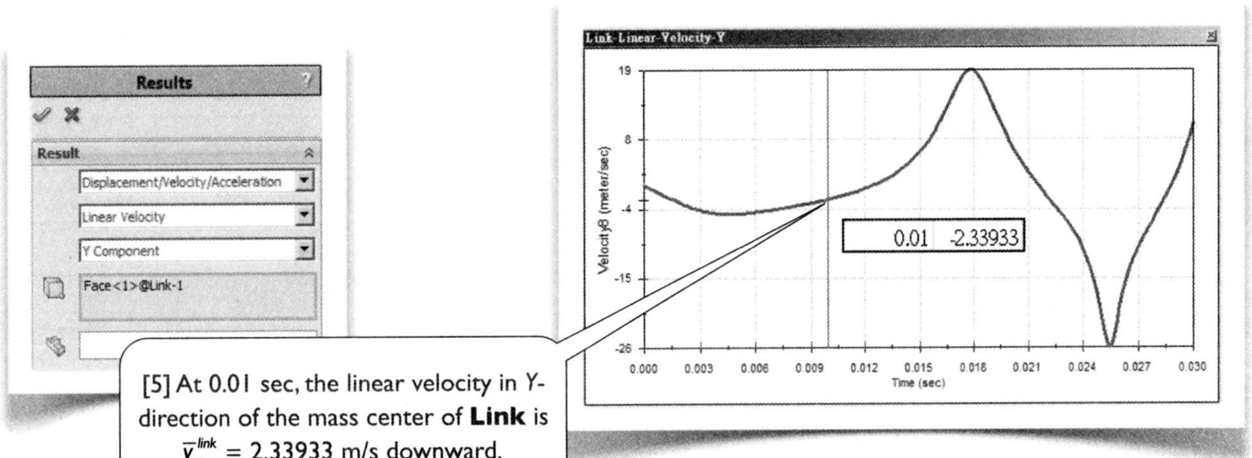

[5] At 0.01 sec, the linear velocity in *Y*-direction of the mass center of **Link** is $\bar{v}_Y^{link}$ = 2.33933 m/s downward.

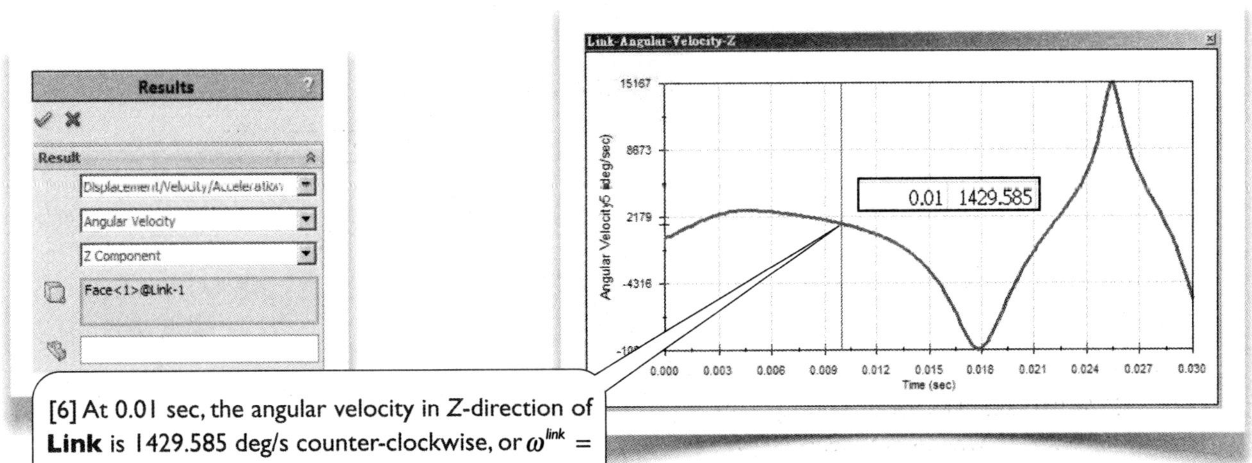

[6] At 0.01 sec, the angular velocity in *Z*-direction of **Link** is 1429.585 deg/s counter-clockwise, or ω^{link} = 24.951 rad/s counter-clockwise.

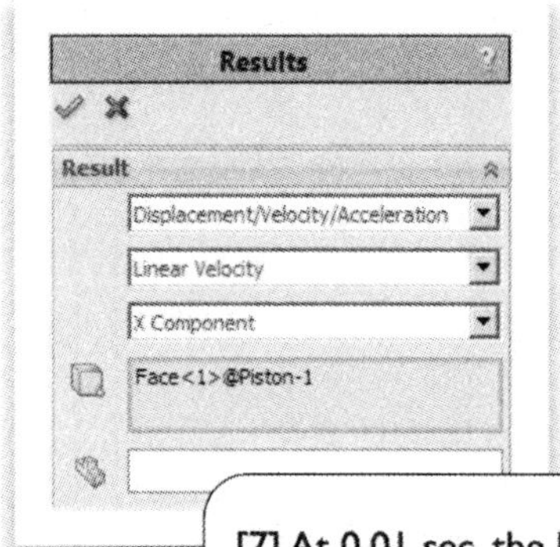

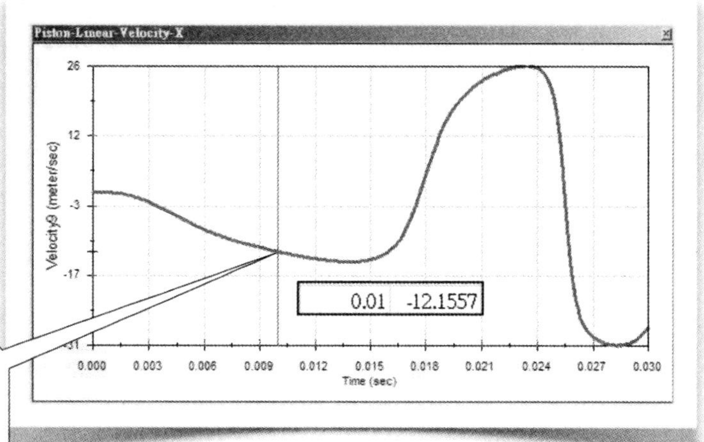

[7] At 0.01 sec, the linear velocity in X-direction of the mass center of **Piston** is $\bar{v}_X^{piston}$ = 12.1557 m/s leftward.

[8] Calculations of linear and angular momenta are tabulated here.

	Crank	Link	Piston
Mass (kg)	0.018142	0.045142	0.030230
Moment of Inertia (kg-m^2)	0.000013106	0.00016904	
Linear Velocity X (m/s)	-5.2242	-11.3040	-12.156
Linear Velocity Y (m/s)	-2.3445	-2.3393	
Angular Velocity Z (deg/s)	-8749.0	1429.6	
Angular Velocity Z (rad/s)	-152.70	24.951	
Linear Momentum X (N-s)	-0.094776	-0.51028	-0.36746
Linear Momentum Y (N-s)	-0.042533	-0.10560	
Angular Momentum Z (N-m-s)	-0.0020013	0.0042176	

[10] Later in 8.1-6[9] (page 159), we'll take the moment about the pivot of **Crank**. We thus need to know the positions of the mass centers of **Crank** and **Link**. We'll show this in 8.1-6[3-6], pages 158-159.#

[9] This is a summary of momenta at 0.01 sec.

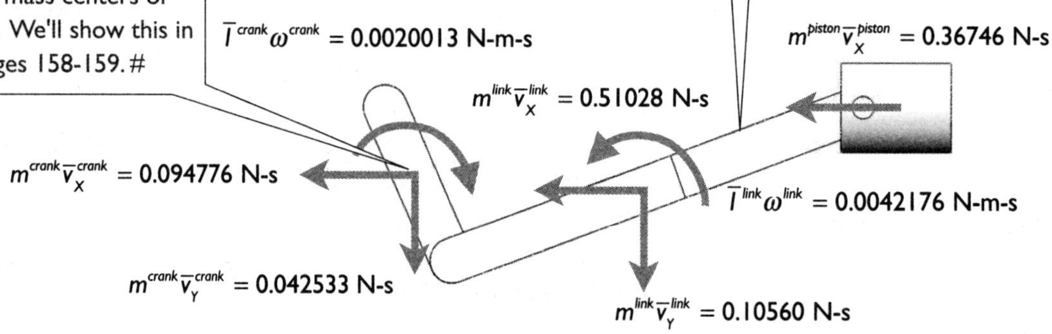

8.1-5 Principle of Impulse and Momentum: Linear Impulses and Linear Momenta

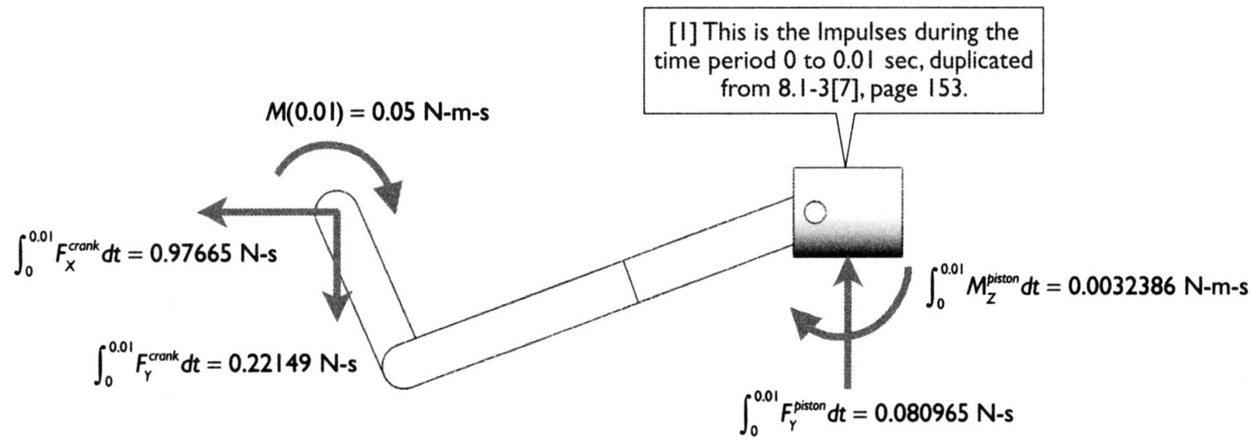

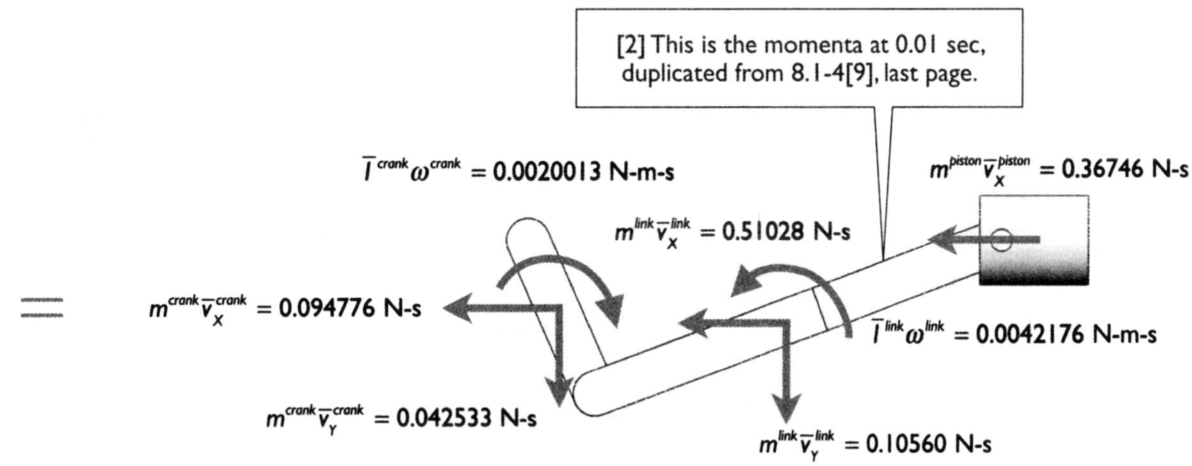

[3] With the diagrams [1, 2], it is easy to confirm that Eq. 8.1-1(1) (page 151) holds for the linear impulses and the linear momenta. In X-direction,

$$-0.97665 \approx -0.094776 - 0.51028 - 0.36746$$

And in Y-direction,

$$-0.22149 + 0.080965 \approx -0.042533 - 0.10560$$

#

8.1-6 Principle of Impulse and Momentum: Angular Impulses and Angular Momenta

[1] To verify the balance between angular impulses and angular momenta, we may conveniently take the moment about the pivot of **Crank**. As mentioned in 8.1-3[8] (page 153), we need to know the horizontal location of the mass center of **Piston** in order to calculate $\int_0^{0.01} F_Y^{piston} X^{piston} dt$ [2]. Also, we need to know the locations of the mass centers of **Crank** and **Link** [3-6].

[2] This is a plot of X^{piston}. The quantity $\int_0^{0.01} F_Y^{piston} X^{piston} dt$ can be calculated in the **CSV** files by summing up the multiplication of X^{piston} and the F_Y^{piston} (8.1-3[5], page 153), and then multiply by 1/9000. The result is

$$\int_0^{0.01} F_Y^{piston} X^{piston} dt = 0.019813 \text{ N}\cdot\text{m}\cdot\text{s}$$

counter-clockwise.

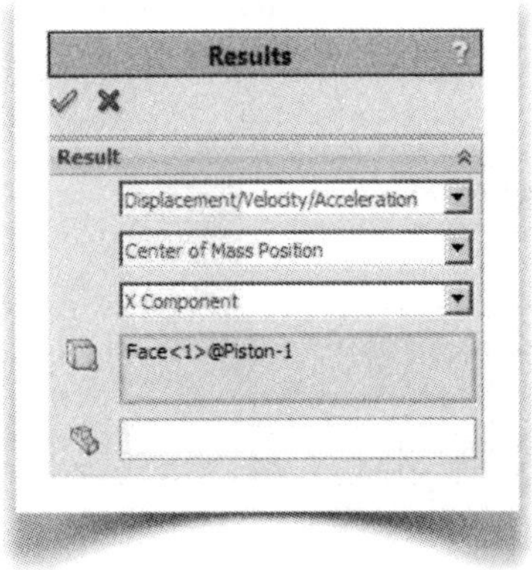

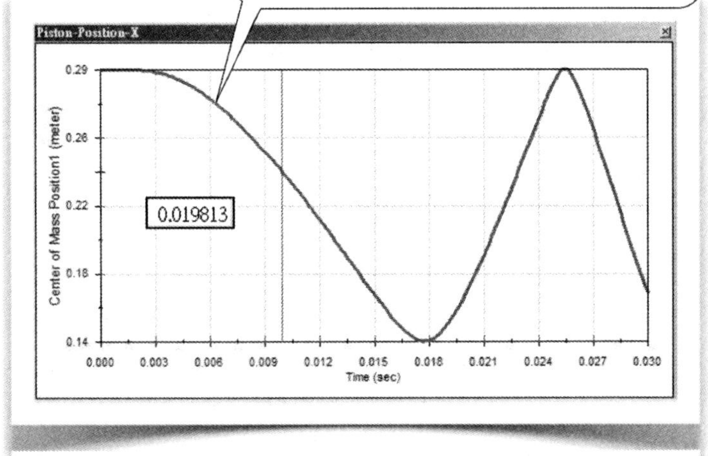

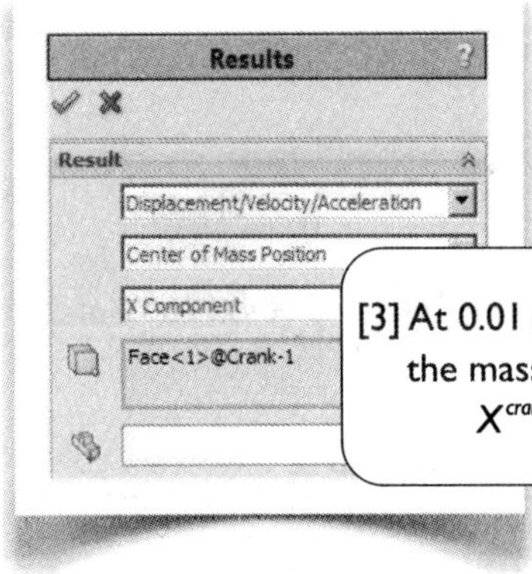

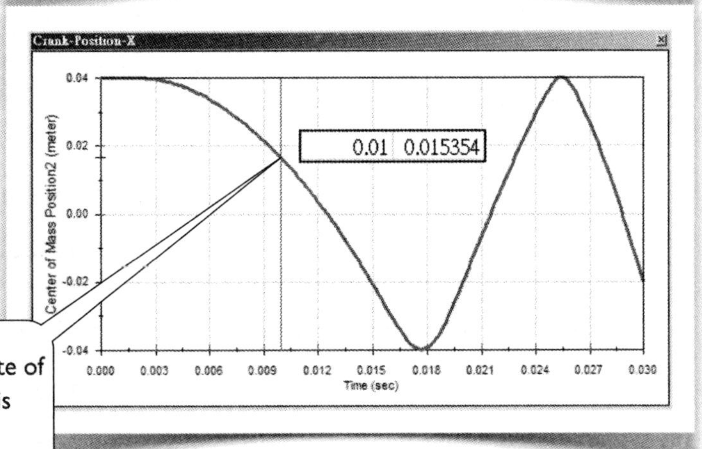

[3] At 0.01 sec, the X-coordinate of the mass center of **Crank** is $X^{crank} = 0.015354$ m.

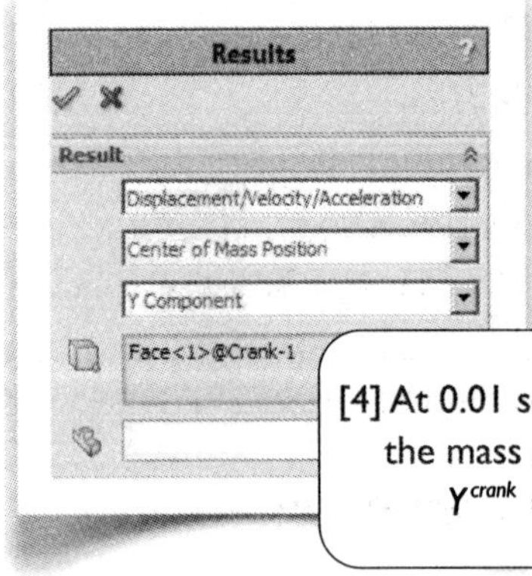

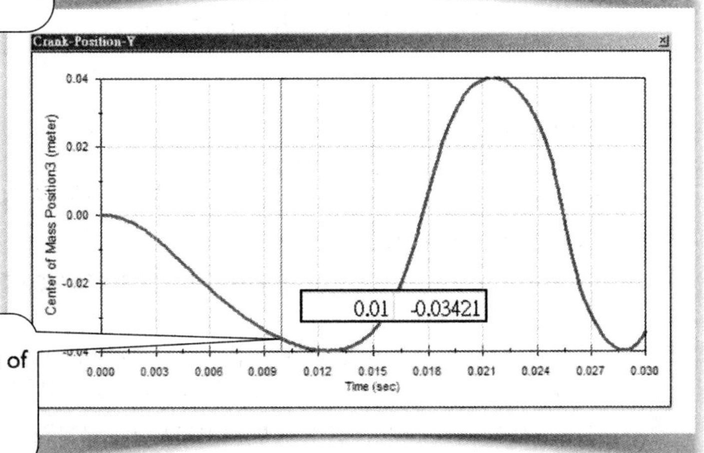

[4] At 0.01 sec, the Y-coordinate of the mass center of **Crank** is $Y^{crank} = -0.034213$ m.

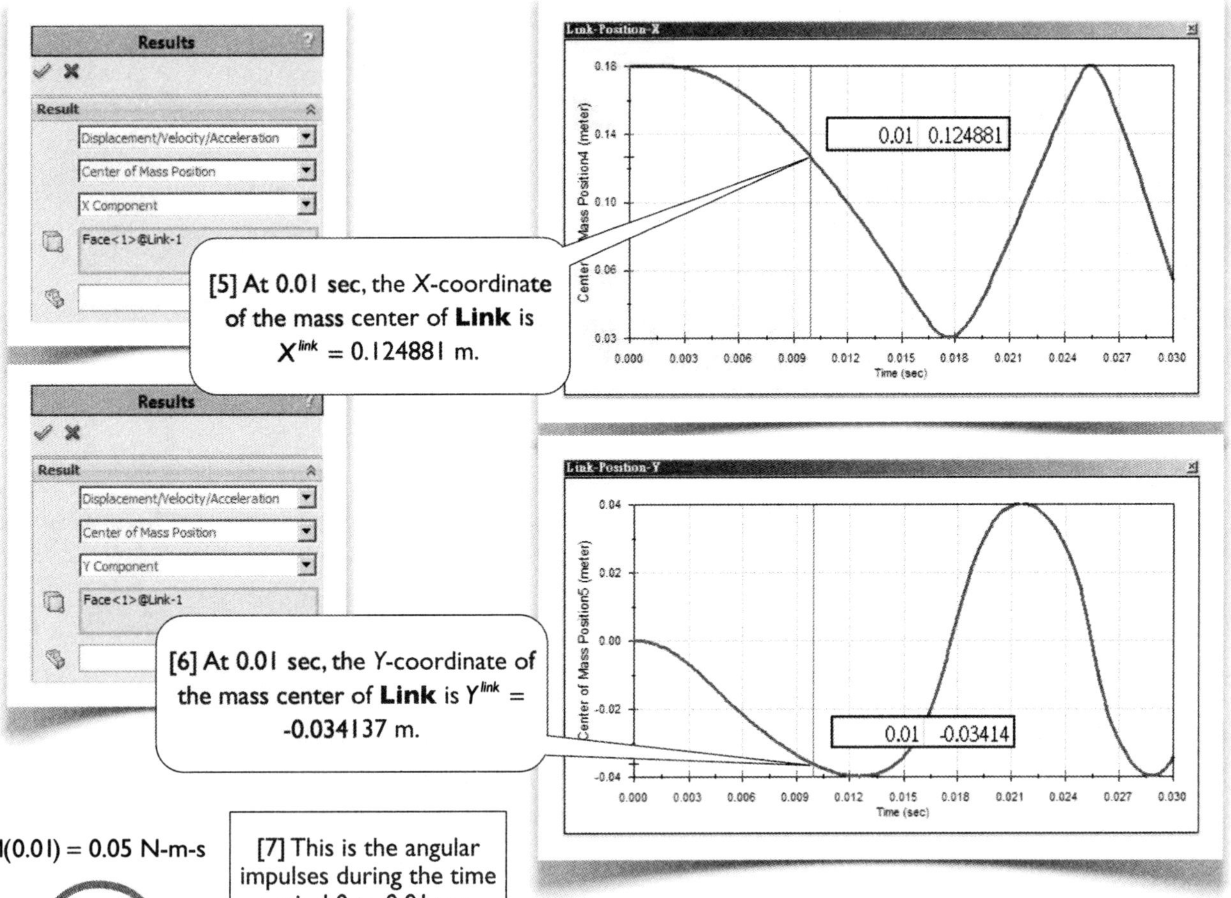

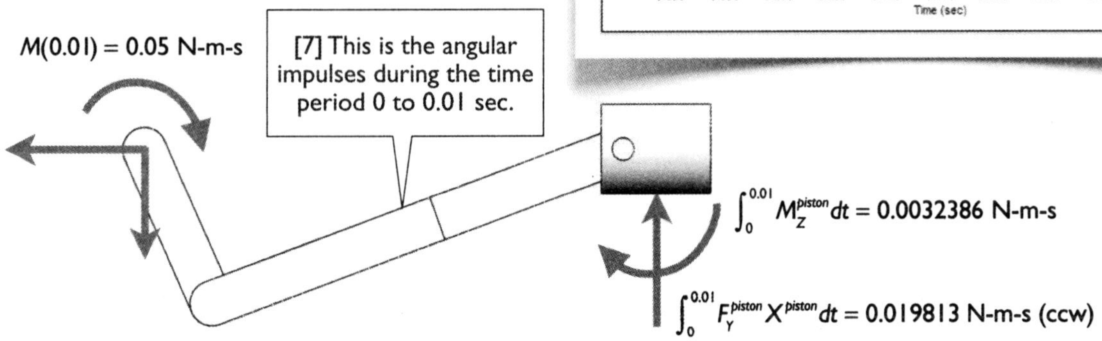

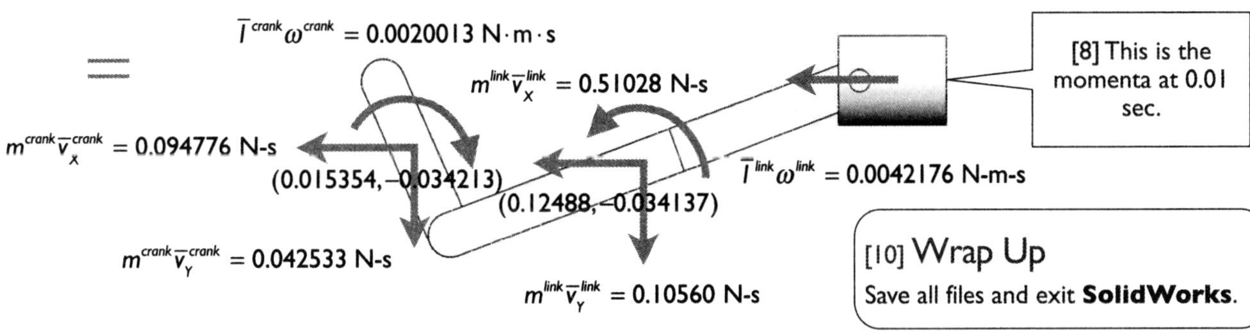

[10] Wrap Up

Save all files and exit **SolidWorks**.

[9] With the diagrams [7, 8], it is easy to confirm that Eq. 8.1-1(2) (page 151) holds for the angular impulses and the angular momenta,

$$-0.05 - 0.0032386 + 0.19813 \approx -0.0020013 + 0.0042176 - 0.094776(0.034213) - 0.042533(0.015354)$$
$$-0.51028(0.034137) - 0.10560(0.12488) \quad \#$$

Section 8.2

Conservation of Momentum: Impact of Ball and Bar

8.2-1 Introduction

[1] In this section, we'll simulate an impact between a **Ball** and a **Bar** [2, 3]. The **Restitution coefficient** between the **Ball** and the **Bar** is 0.2. During the impact, there are no external forces involved: therefore, Eqs. 8.1-1(1, 2) (page 151) reduces to

$$\sum m\vec{v}_0 = \sum m\vec{v}_t \quad (1)$$

$$\sum H_0 = \sum H_t \quad (2)$$

Eqs. (1, 2) is called the **principle of conservation of momenta** for rigid bodies in plane motion: If there are no external forces involved, a system's linear momentum and angular momentum remain constant.

We'll confirm the conservation of momenta during the impact. We'll also point out that, since this case is not an elastic impact, the energy is NOT conserved.

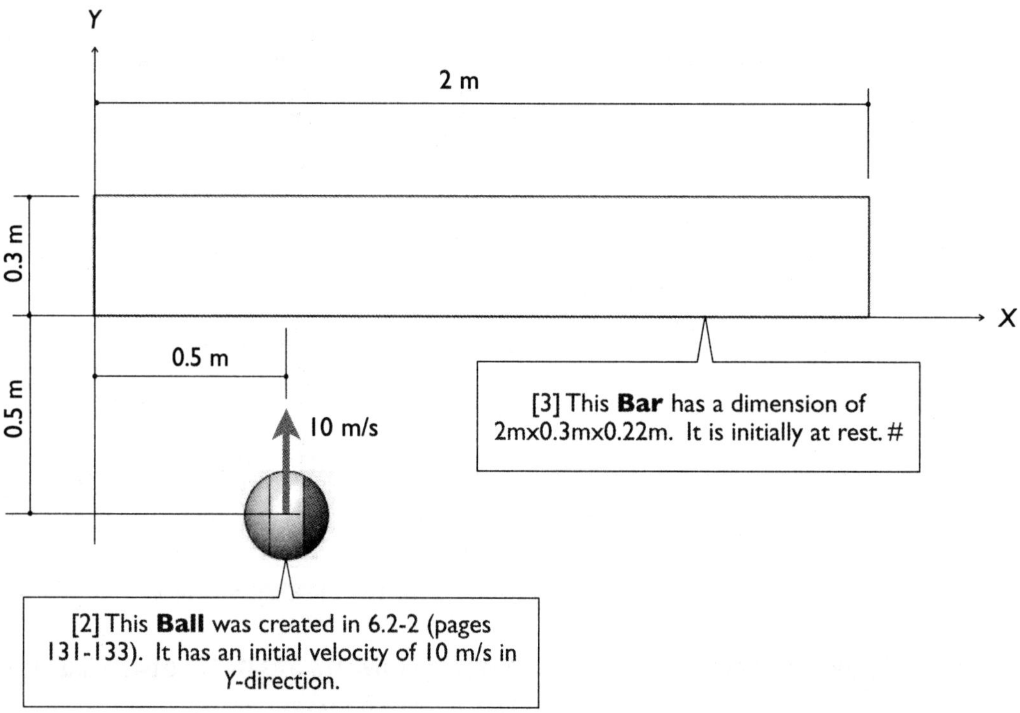

8.2-2 Open the File **Ball.SLDPRT**

[1] Launch **SolidWorks** and open the file **Ball.SLDPRT**, which is saved in Section 6.2. #

8.2-3 Create a Part: **Bar**

[1] Click **New** to create a new **Part**.

[2] Save the **Part** with the name **Bar**. Set up **MKS** unit system with default decimal places.

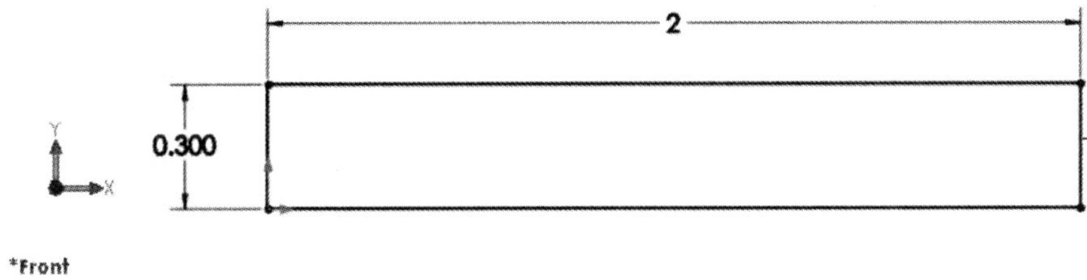

[3] On the **Front** plane, draw a rectangle like this.

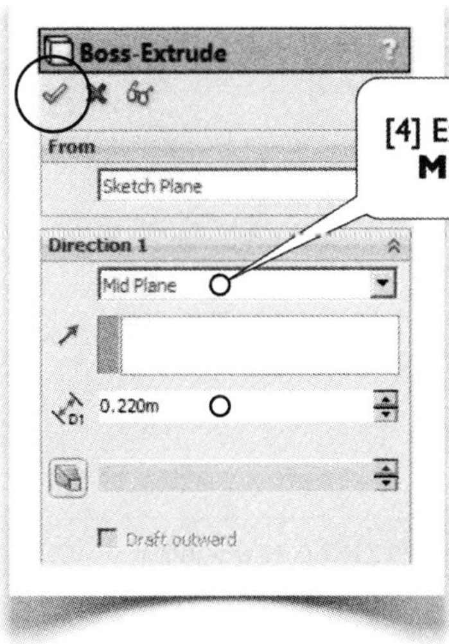

[4] Extrude 0.22 m, using **Mid Plane** option.

[5] In the **Evaluate Toolbar**, click **Mass Properties**.

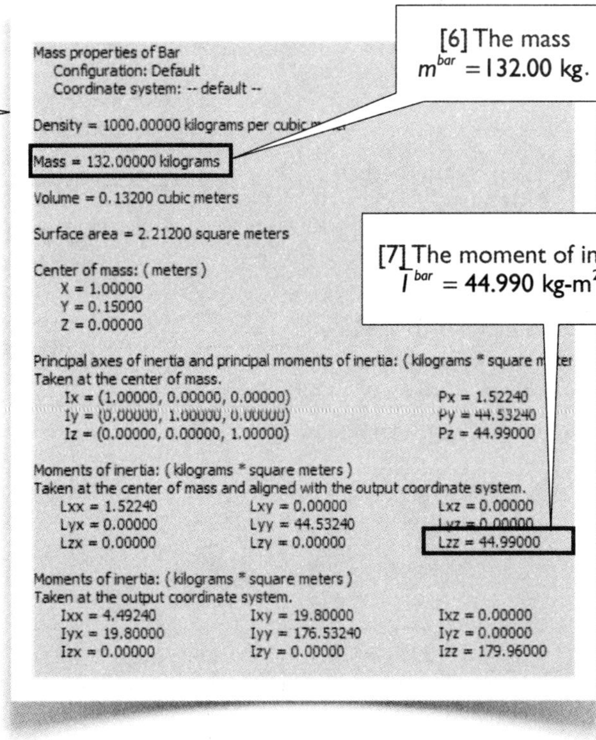
Mass properties of Bar
Configuration: Default
Coordinate system: -- default --

Density = 1000.00000 kilograms per cubic meter

Mass = 132.00000 kilograms

Volume = 0.13200 cubic meters

Surface area = 2.21200 square meters

Center of mass: (meters)
X = 1.00000
Y = 0.15000
Z = 0.00000

Principal axes of inertia and principal moments of inertia: (kilograms * square meters)
Taken at the center of mass.
Ix = (1.00000, 0.00000, 0.00000) Px = 1.52240
Iy = (0.00000, 1.00000, 0.00000) Py = 44.53240
Iz = (0.00000, 0.00000, 1.00000) Pz = 44.99000

Moments of inertia: (kilograms * square meters)
Taken at the center of mass and aligned with the output coordinate system.
Lxx = 1.52240 Lxy = 0.00000 Lxz = 0.00000
Lyx = 0.00000 Lyy = 44.53240 Lyz = 0.00000
Lzx = 0.00000 Lzy = 0.00000 Lzz = 44.99000

Moments of inertia: (kilograms * square meters)
Taken at the output coordinate system.
Ixx = 4.49240 Ixy = 19.80000 Ixz = 0.00000
Iyx = 19.80000 Iyy = 176.53240 Iyz = 0.00000
Izx = 0.00000 Izy = 0.00000 Izz = 179.96000

[6] The mass $m^{bar} = 132.00$ kg.

[7] The moment of inertia $\bar{I}^{bar} = 44.990$ kg-m^2. #

8.2-4 Create an Assembly: **Ball-And-Bar**

[1] Click **New** and create an **Assembly**.

[4] Save the **Assembly** with the name **Ball-And-Bar**.

[2] In **Head-Up Toolbar**, turn on **View Origins**.

[3] In the **Begin Assembly Property Box**, select **Bar** and click the assembly's **Origin**.

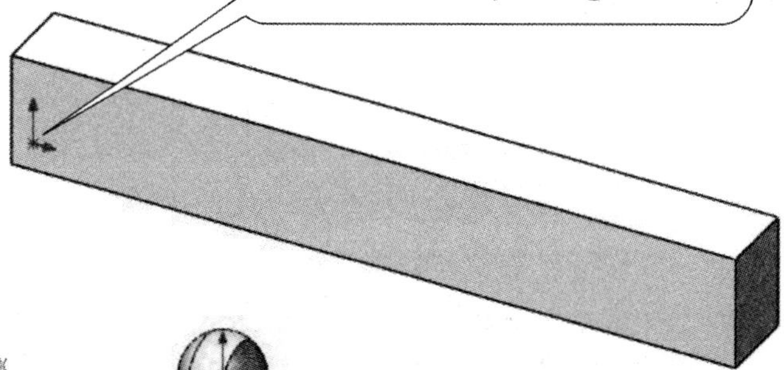

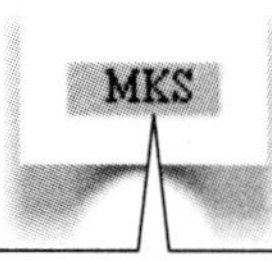

[5] Set up **MKS** unit system with default decimal places.

*Trimetric

[6] In the **Assembly Toolbar**, click **Insert Components** and park **Ball** anywhere.

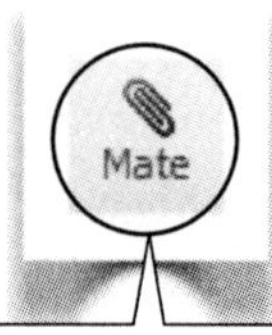

[7] In **Assembly Toolbar**, click **Mate**.

[8] We'll create these 3 **Mates** in [9-12].

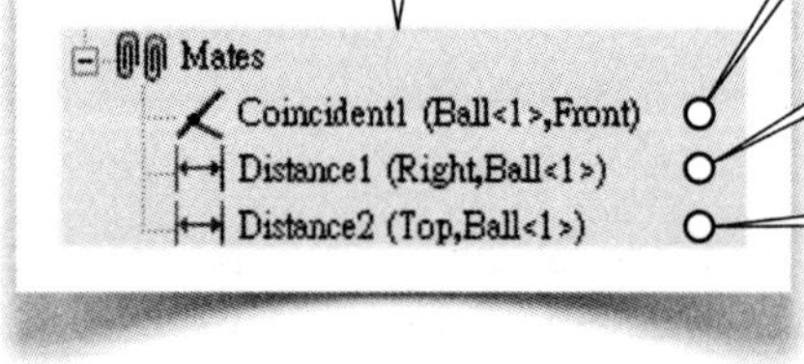

[9] The **Ball's** and the **Assembly's Front** planes are **Coincident**.

[10] The **Assembly's** and the **Ball's Right** planes have a **Distance** of 0.5 m. We'll suppress this **Mate** later.

[11] The **Assembly's** and the **Ball's Top** planes has a **Distance** of 0.5 m. We'll suppress this **Mate** later.

*Front

[12] This is the initial configuration of the system. #

8.2-5 Create **Motion Study**; Set Up **Contact** and **Initial Velocity**

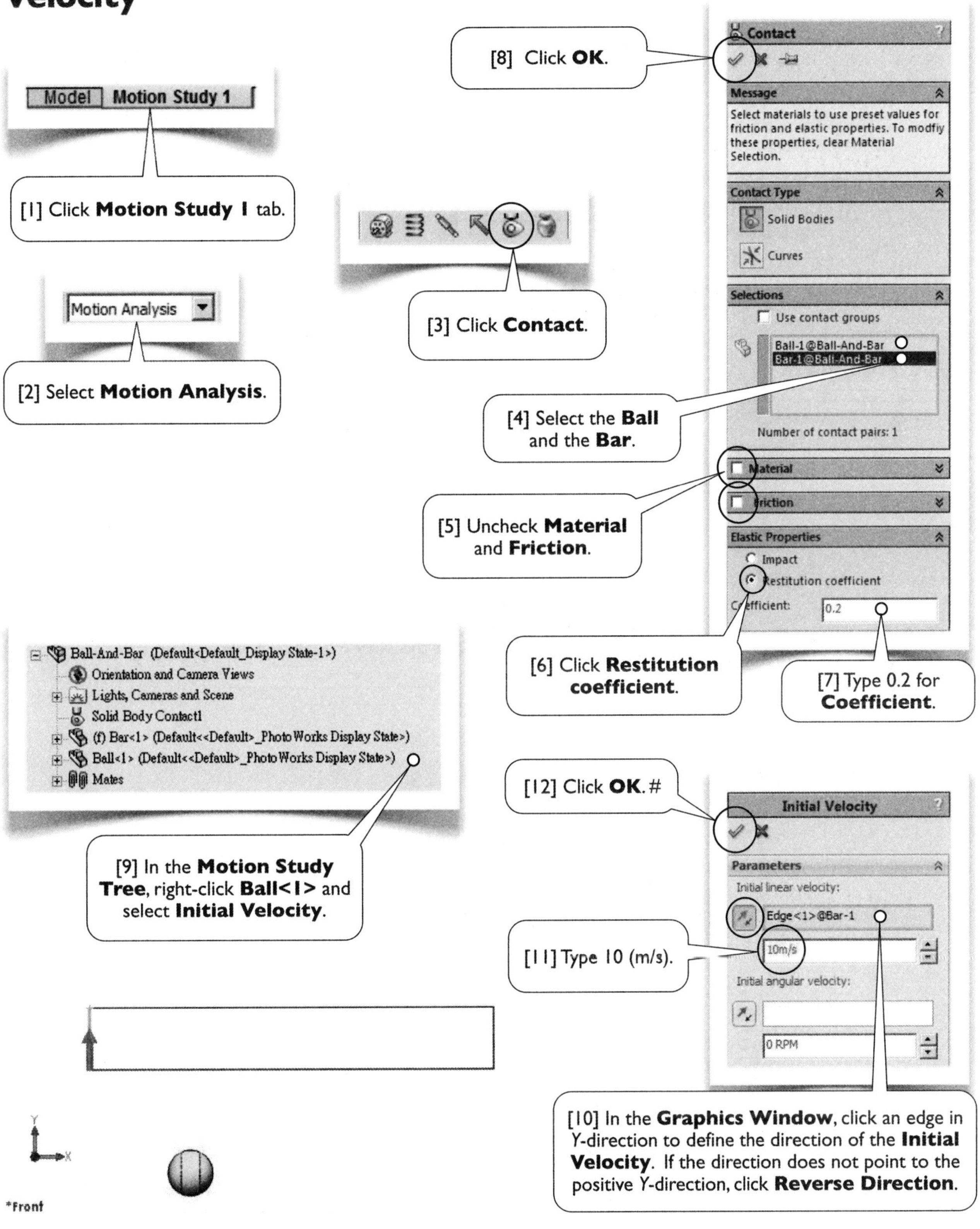

8.2-6 Calculate and Animate **Results**

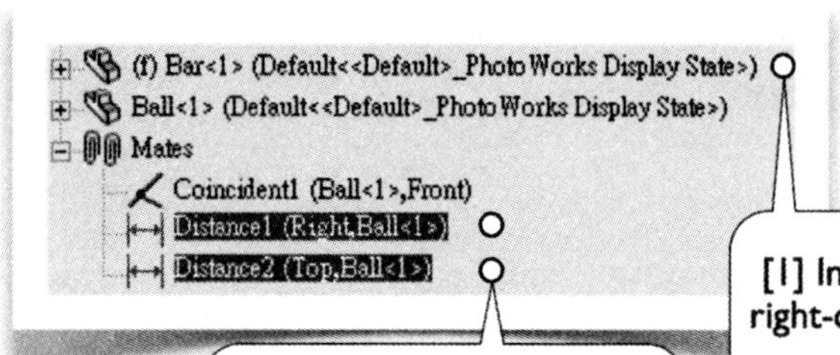

[1] In the **Assembly Tree**, right-click **Bar<1>** and select **Float**.

[2] Suppress **Distance1** and **Distance2**.

[3] In the **Motion Toolbar**, Click **Motion Study Properties**. Type 1000 for **Frames per second** and turn on **Use Precise Contact** (see 5.2-6[3, 4], page 119).

[5] Set **Playback Speed** to **5 sec**.

[9] Click **Play from Start**. #

[8] Click **Calculate**.

[6] Select **Normal** for **Playback Mode**.

[7] Right-click this **Key Point** and select **View Orientation>Front**.

[4] Drag this **Key Point** to **1 sec**.

8.2-7 Results: Linear and Angular Velocities

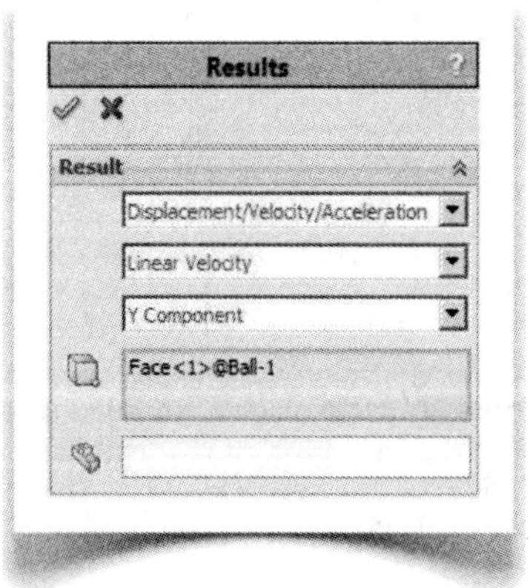

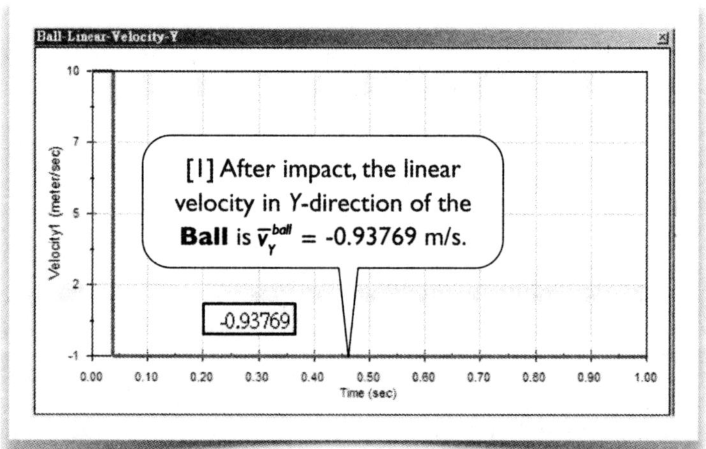

[1] After impact, the linear velocity in *Y*-direction of the **Ball** is $\overline{v}_Y^{ball}$ = -0.93769 m/s.

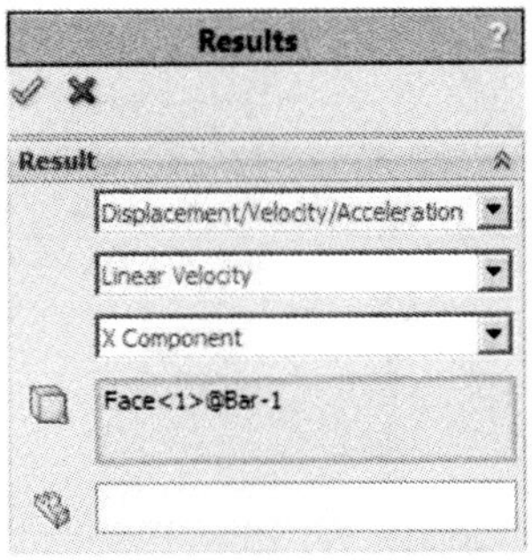
Results
Result
Displacement/Velocity/Acceleration
Linear Velocity
X Component
Face<1>@Bar-1

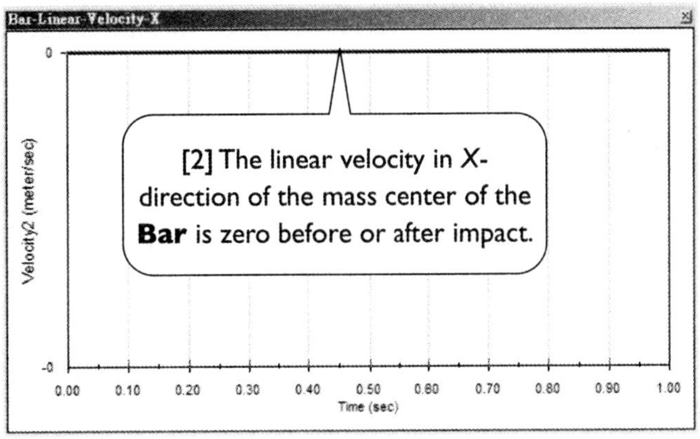
Bar-Linear-Velocity-X
Velocity2 (meter/sec)
Time (sec)
[2] The linear velocity in X-direction of the mass center of the **Bar** is zero before or after impact.

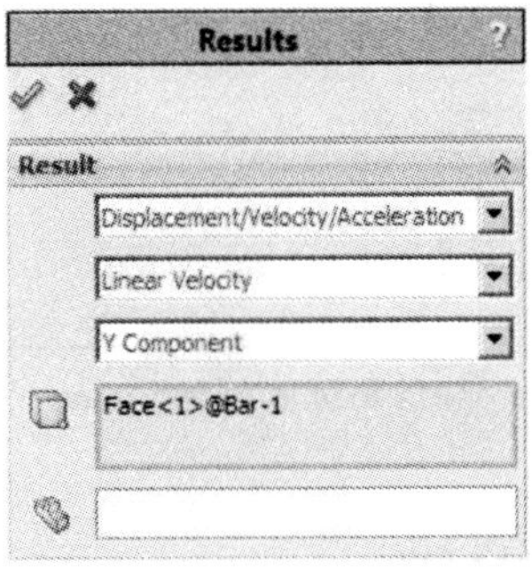
Results
Result
Displacement/Velocity/Acceleration
Linear Velocity
Y Component
Face<1>@Bar-1

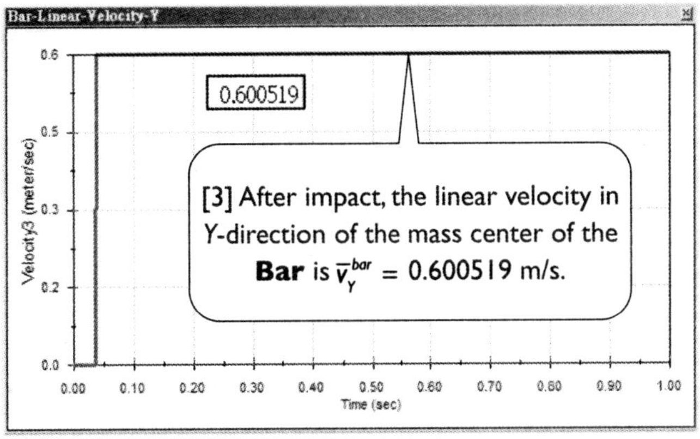
Bar-Linear-Velocity-Y
Velocity3 (meter/sec)
Time (sec)
0.600519
[3] After impact, the linear velocity in Y-direction of the mass center of the **Bar** is $\bar{v}_Y^{bar}$ = 0.600519 m/s.

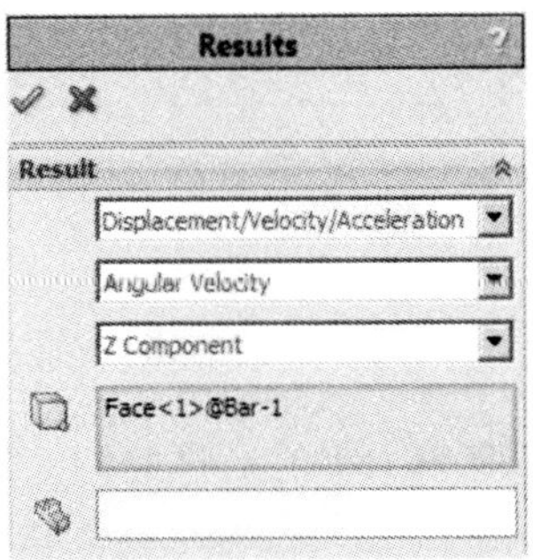
Results
Result
Displacement/Velocity/Acceleration
Angular Velocity
Z Component
Face<1>@Bar-1

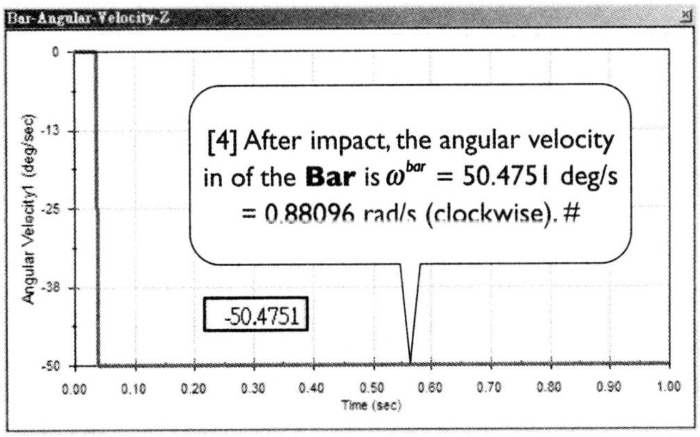
Bar-Angular-Velocity-Z
Angular Velocity1 (deg/sec)
Time (sec)
-50.4751
[4] After impact, the angular velocity in of the **Bar** is ω^{bar} = 50.4751 deg/s = 0.88096 rad/s (clockwise). #

8.2-8 Conservation of Momentum

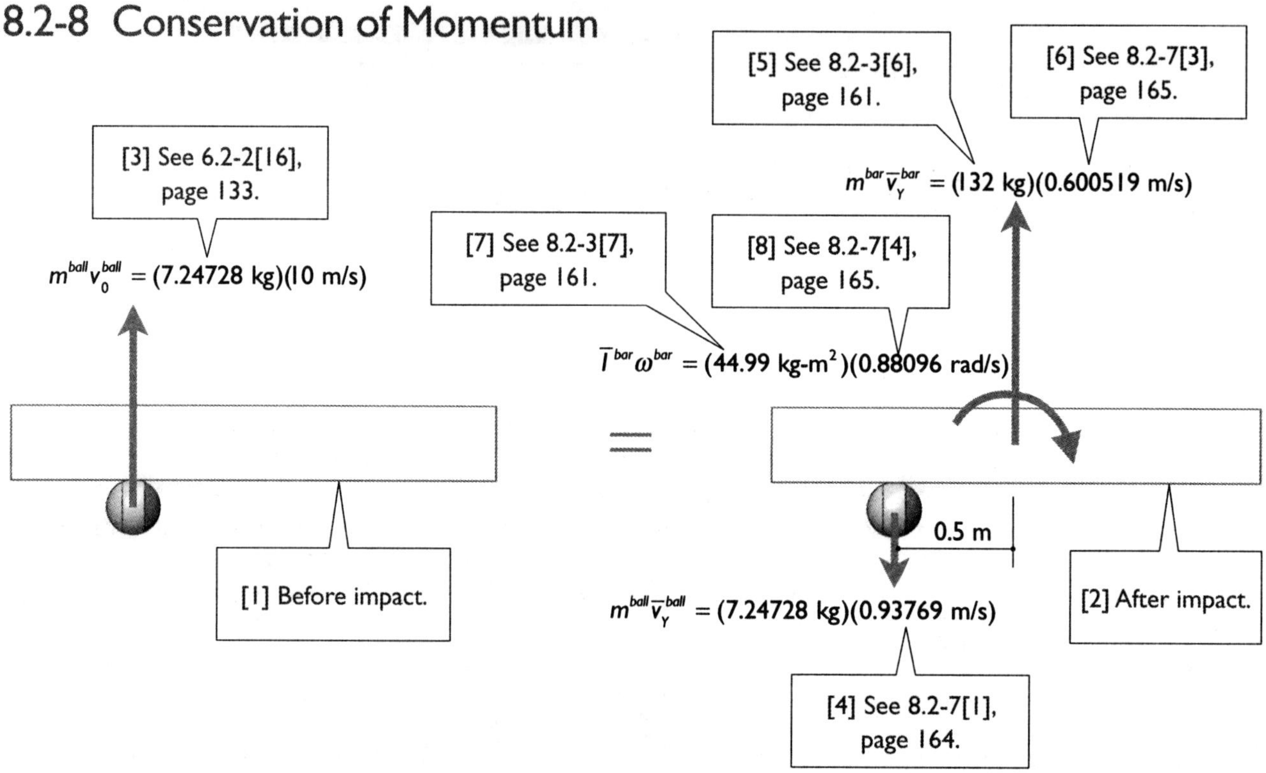

[9] With the diagrams [1-8], it is easy to confirm Eqs. 8.2-1(1, 2) (page 160). The linear momenta in X-direction are trivial. The linear momenta in Y-direction,

$$(7.24728 \text{ kg})(10 \text{ m/s}) \approx -(7.24728 \text{ kg})(0.93769 \text{ m/s}) + (132 \text{ kg})(0.600519 \text{ m/s})$$

For angular momenta (in Z-direction), we may conveniently sum up angular momenta about the mass center of the **Ball**,

$$0 \approx -(44.99 \text{ kg-m}^2)(0.88096 \text{ rad/s}) + (132 \text{ kg})(0.600519 \text{ m/s})(0.5 \text{ m})$$ #

8.2-9 Energy Loss

[1] Before impact, the kinetic energy is

$$T^{before} = \frac{1}{2}(7.24728 \text{ kg})(10 \text{ m/s})^2 = 362.36 \text{ J}$$

After impact, the kinetic energy is

$$T^{after} = \frac{1}{2}(7.24728 \text{ kg})(0.93769 \text{ m/s})^2 + \frac{1}{2}(132 \text{ kg})(0.600519 \text{ m/s})^2 + \frac{1}{2}(44.99 \text{ kg-m}^2)(0.88096 \text{ rad/s})^2 = 44.445 \text{ J}$$

The energy loss is

$$\frac{T^{before} - T^{after}}{T^{before}} = \frac{362.36 - 44.445}{362.36} = 87.7\%$$

[2] Wrap Up

Save all files and exit **SolidWorks**. #

Chapter 9

3D Rigid Body Kinematics

The next two chapters will devote to the study of rigid bodies in general 3D motions. In general, the principles learned earlier for particles (chapters 1-4) and rigid body in plane motion (chapters 5-8) can be used for rigid bodies in general 3D motion. In fact, the **SolidWorks Motion** solves all types of problemds (particles, 2D rigid bodies, or 3D rigid bodies) using the same procedure. However, many phenomena in 3D dynamics are interesting and do not presented in 2D dynamics. An example is the precession of a gyroscope (Section 10.3). Study of 3D dynamics needs much more elaboration but is rewarding, since, as an engineer, you are able to create some innovative mechanical systems using these 3D dynamic phenomena.

Section 9.1

Disk-Link-Collar Mechanism

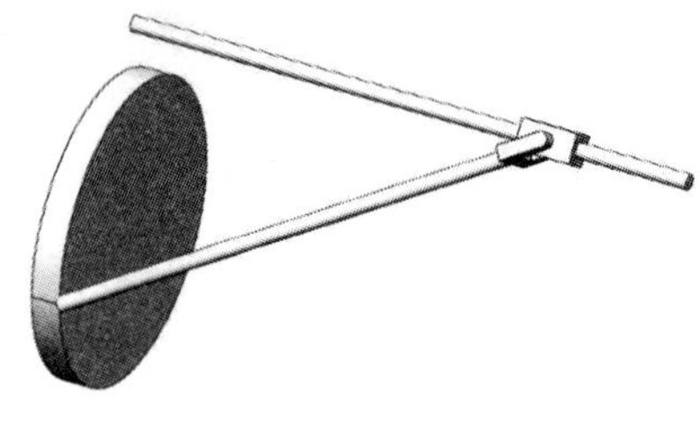

9.1-1 Introduction

[1] Consider a **Disk-Link-Collar** mechanism [2-6]. This problem is adapted from Sample Problem 15.12, *Vector Mechanics for Engineers: Dynamics, 9th ed in SI Units.*, by F. P. Beer, E. R. Johnston, Jr., and P. J. Cornwell. Some of the quantities calculated by the textbook are: For the position shown below,

The linear velocity of the **Collar** $\vec{v}_B = -300\,\vec{i}$ (mm/s) (1)

The angular velocity of the **Link** $\vec{\omega}^{link} = 3.69\,\vec{i} + 1.846\,\vec{j} + 2.77\,\vec{k}$ (rad/s) (2)

In this section, we'll perform a simulation for this system and validate the results using the values in Eqs. (1-2). As mentioned in 5.1-1 (page 100) that Eqs. 5.1-1(5, 6) are also valid for rigid bodies in general 3D motions (not restricting to plane motions). As an exercise, we'll leave you to verify that, for the position shown below,

$$\vec{v}_B = \vec{v}_A + \vec{\omega}^{link} \times \vec{r}_{B/A} \quad (3)$$

$$\vec{a}_B = \vec{a}_A + \vec{\alpha}^{link} \times \vec{r}_{B/A} + \vec{\omega}^{link} \times \left(\vec{\omega}^{link} \times \vec{r}_{B/A}\right) \quad (4)$$

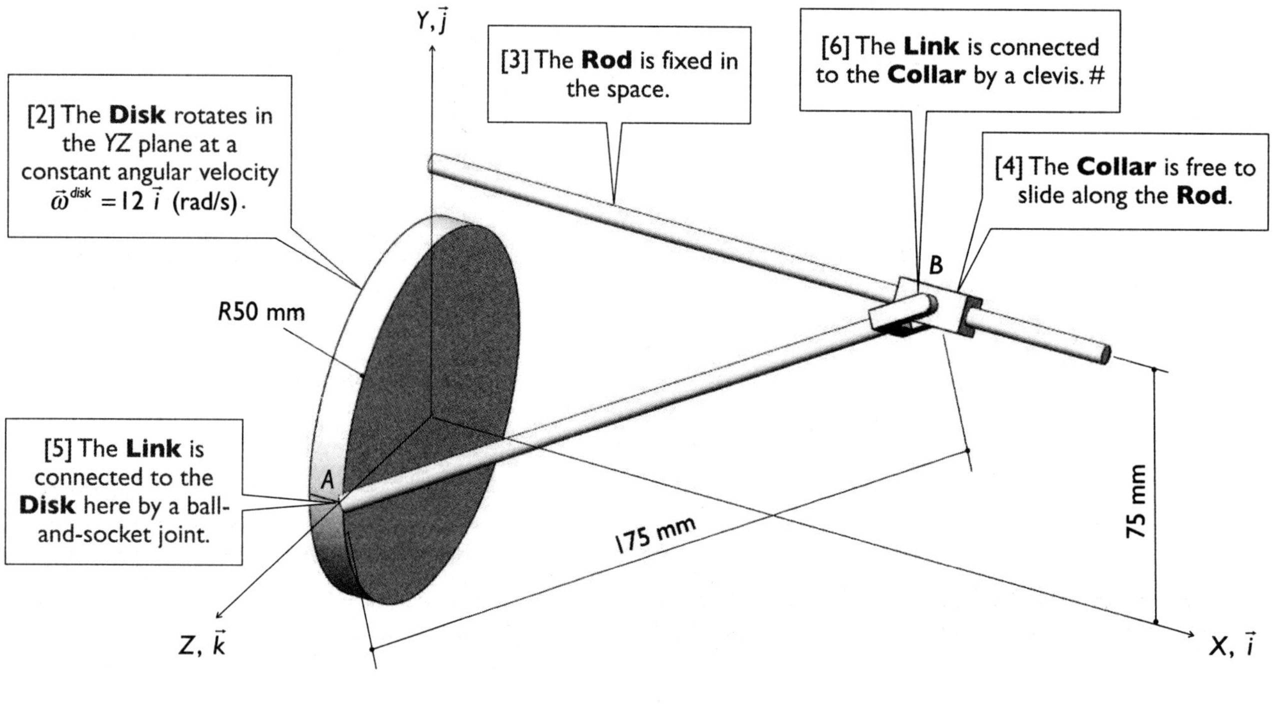

9.1-2 Start Up and Create a Part: **Disk**

[1] Launch **SolidWorks** and click **New** to create a new **Part**.

[2] Save the **Part** with the name **Disk**.

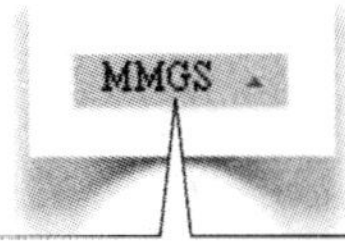

[3] Set up **MMGS** unit system with default decimal places.

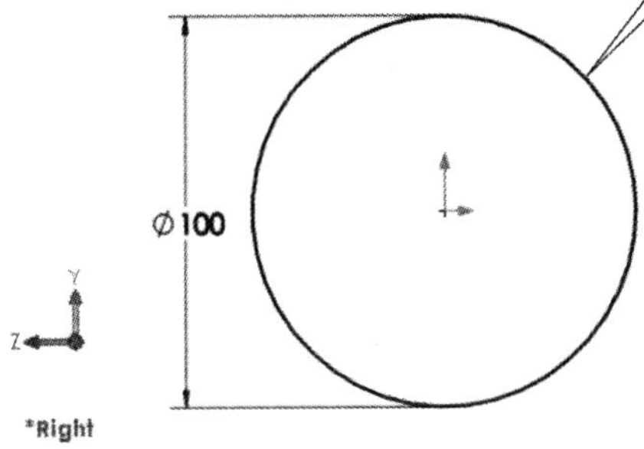

[4] On the **Right** plane, draw a circle like this.

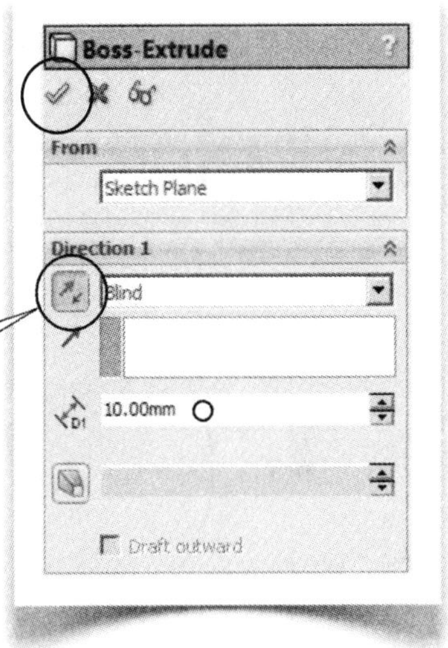

[5] Extrude the sketch 10 mm, click **Reverse Direction**.

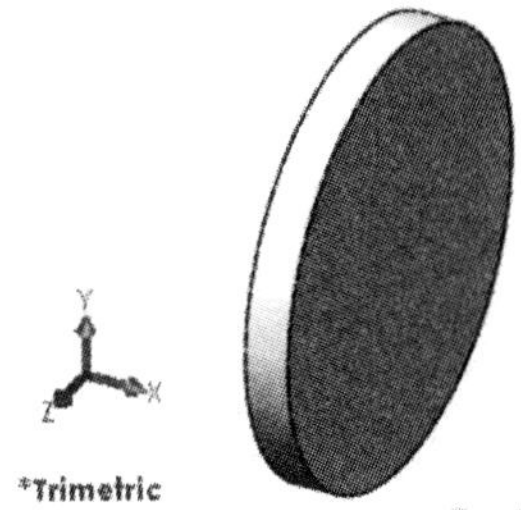

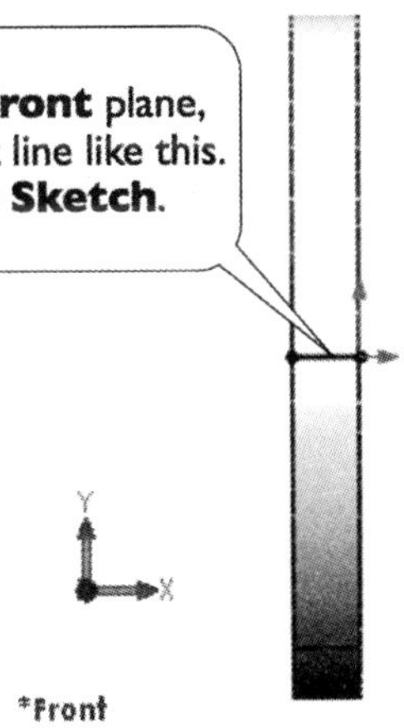

[6] On the **Front** plane, sketch a short line like this. Click **Exit Sketch**.

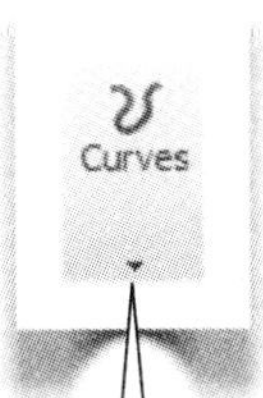

[7] In the **Features Toolbar**, select **Curves>Split Line**.

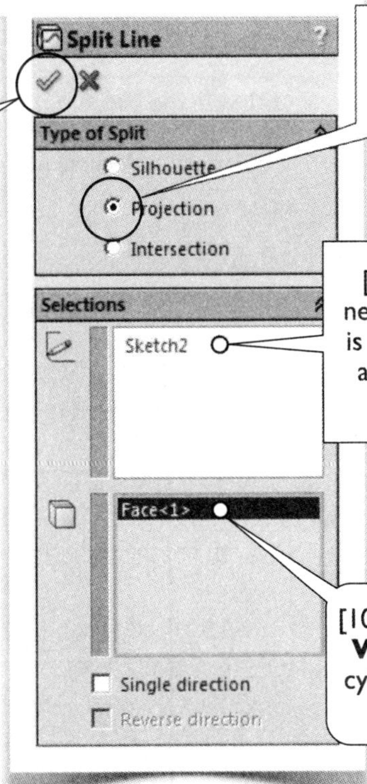

[8] Make sure **Projection** is selected.

[9] By default, the newly created sketch is automatically used as the **Sketch to Project**.

[10] In the **Graphics Window**, click the cylindrical face of the **Disk**.

[11] Click **OK**.

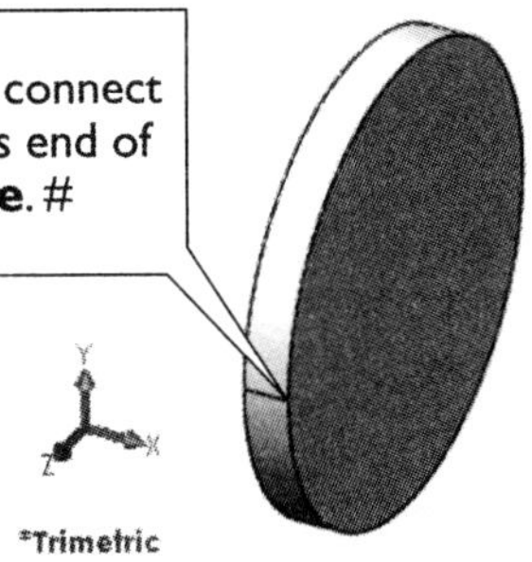

[12] The **Link** will connect to the **Disk** at this end of the **Split Line**. #

9.1-3 Create a Part: **Rod**

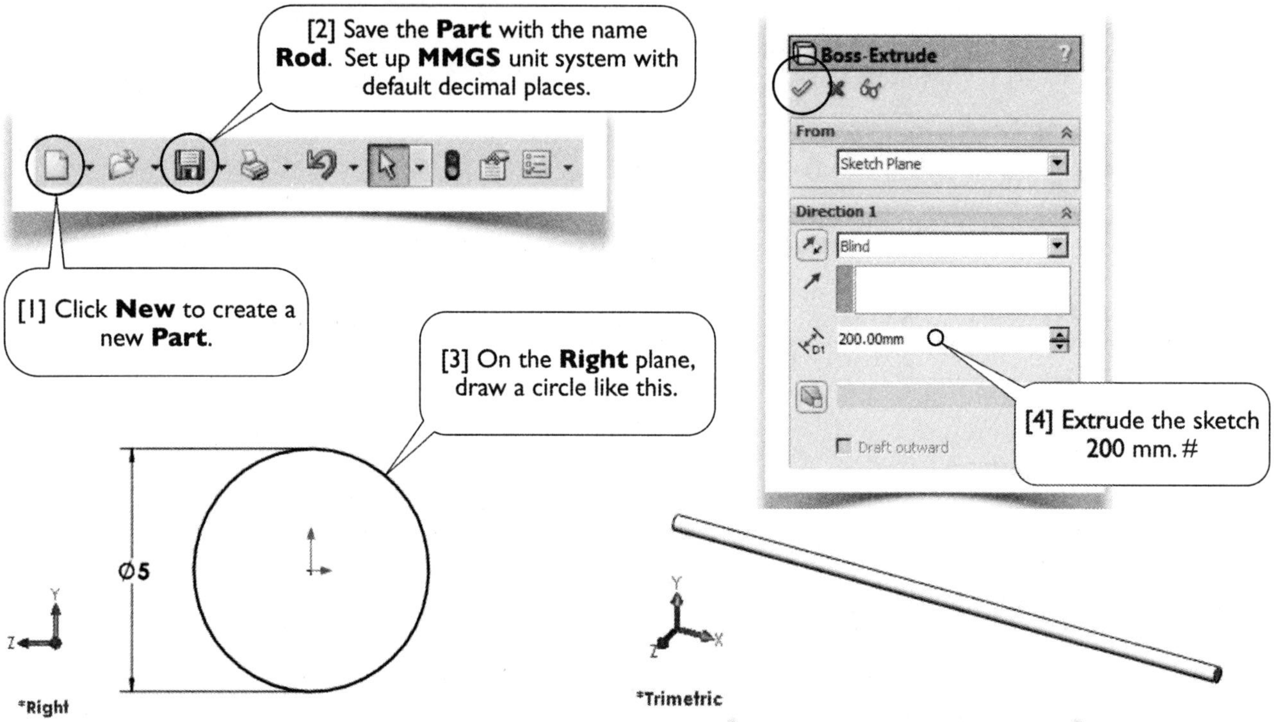

9.1-4 Create a Part: **Collar**

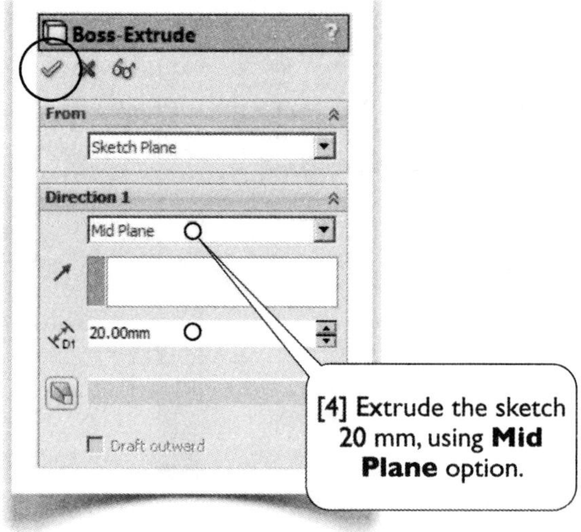

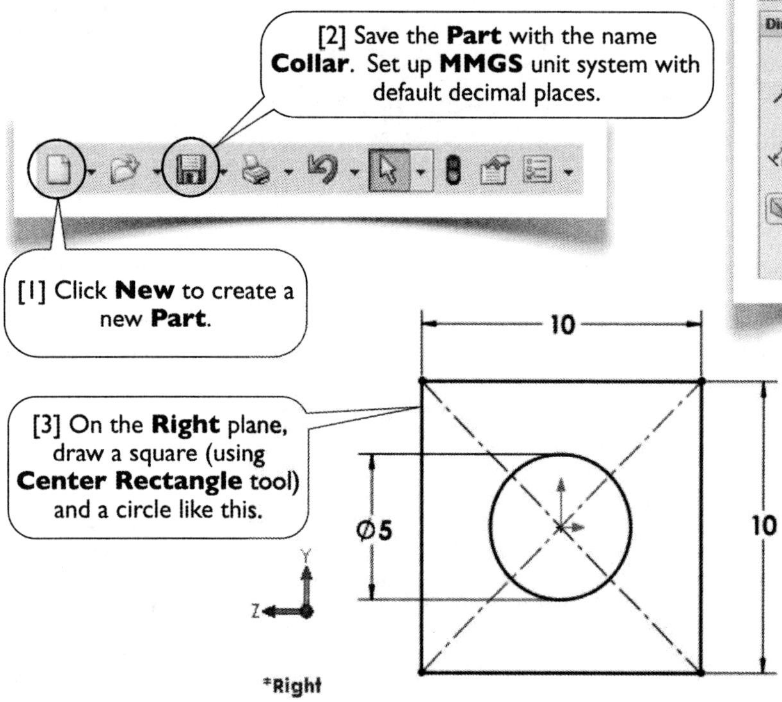

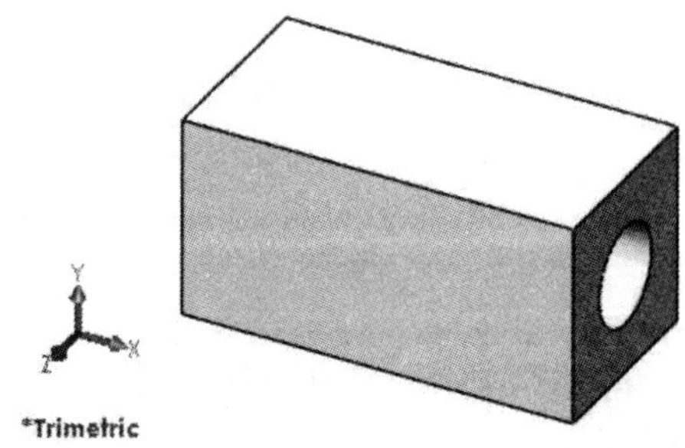

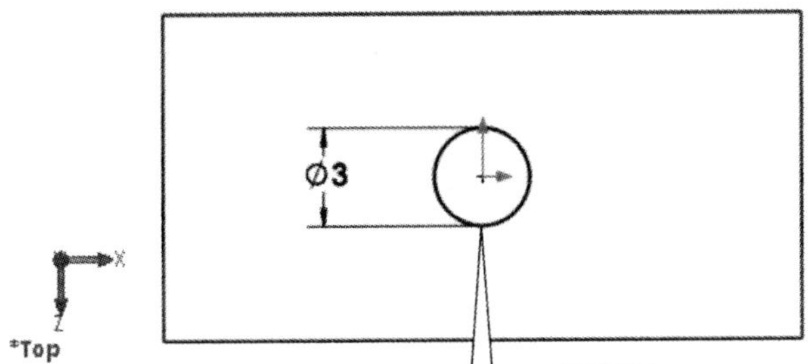

[5] On the **Top** plane, draw a circle like this.

[6] **Extruded Cut**, using **Through All** option for both directions. #

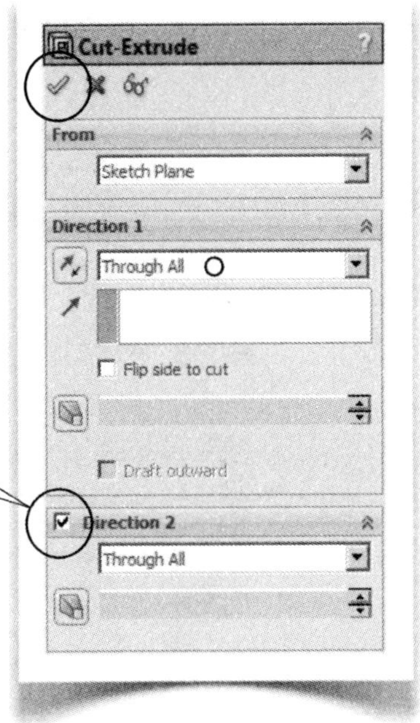

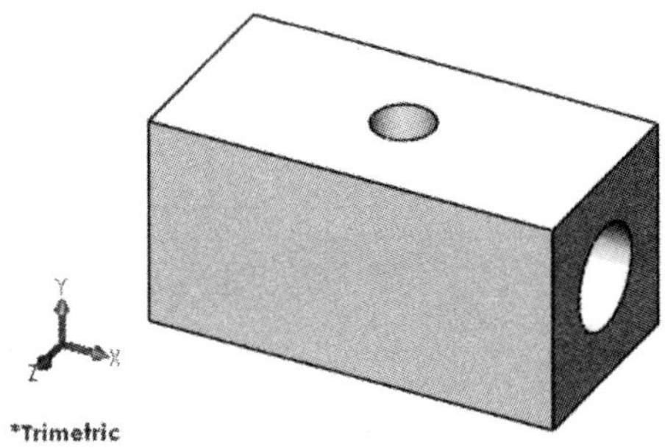

9.1-5 Create a Part: **Link**

[2] Save the **Part** with the name **Link**. Set up **MMGS** unit system with default decimal places.

[1] Click **New** to create a new **Part**.

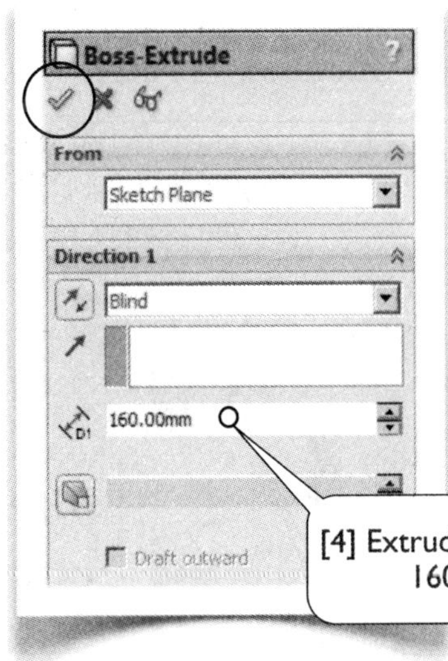

[3] On the **Right** plane, draw a circle like this.

[4] Extrude the sketch 160 mm.

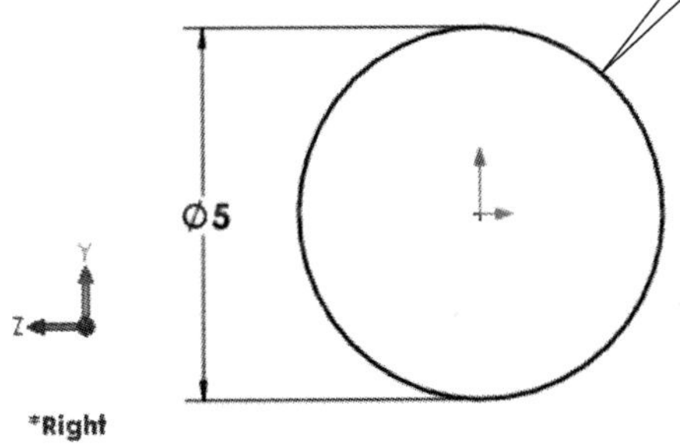

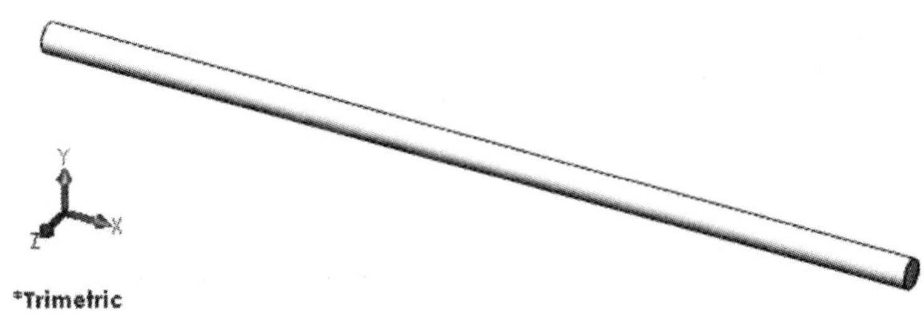

[5] On the **Front** plane, draw a sketch like this. The **Centerline** is used as the line of symmetry.

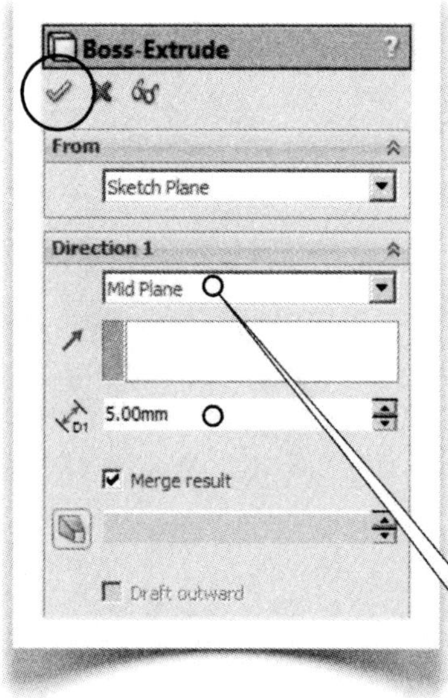

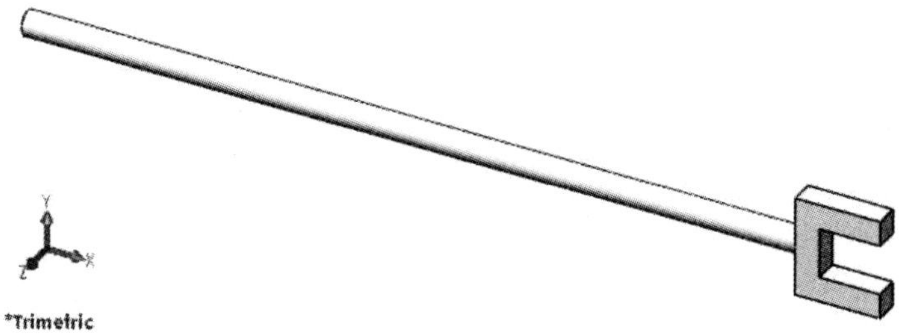

[6] Extrude the sketch 5 mm, using **Mid Plane** option.

[7] In the **Features Toolbar**, click **Fillet**.

[8] Click **Full round fillet**.

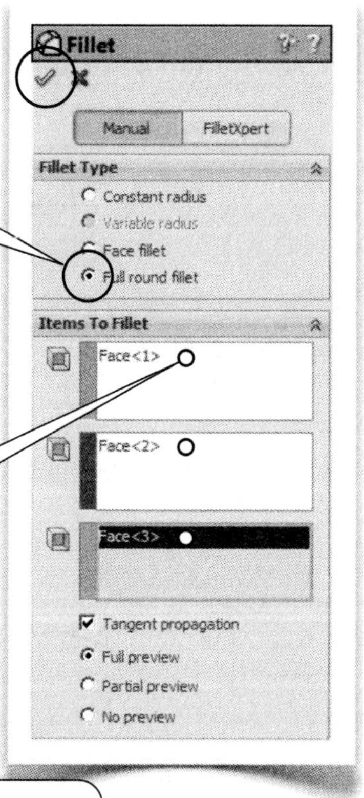

[12] **Face<3>** is on the backside. You need to rotate the view.

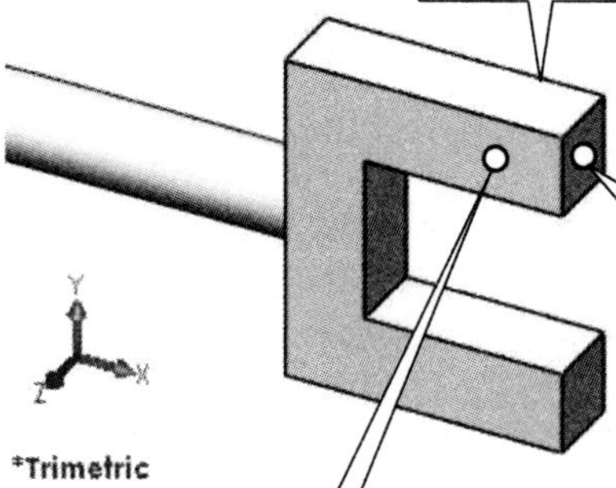

[11] **Face<2>**.

[9] Select three faces (see [10-12]) to create a **Full round fillet**.

[10] **Face<1>**.

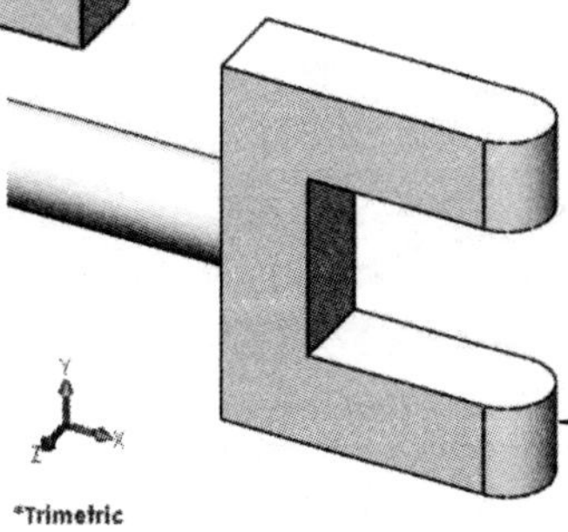

[13] Repeat steps [7-9] to create a second **Full round fillet**. #

9.1-6 Create an Assembly: **Disk-Link-Collar**

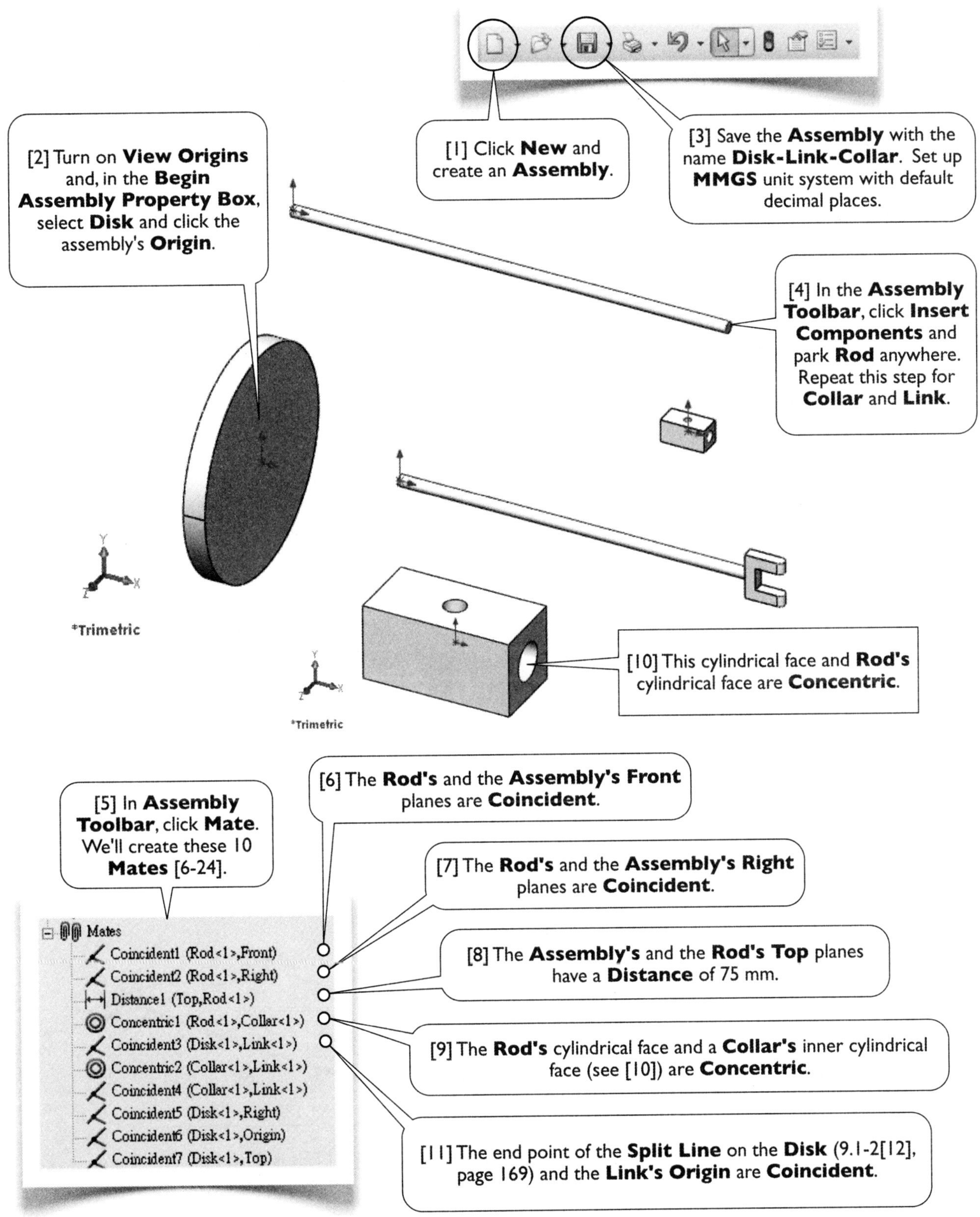

[12] A cylindrical face of the **Collar** (see [13]) and a cylindrical face of the **Link** (see [14]) are **Concentric**.

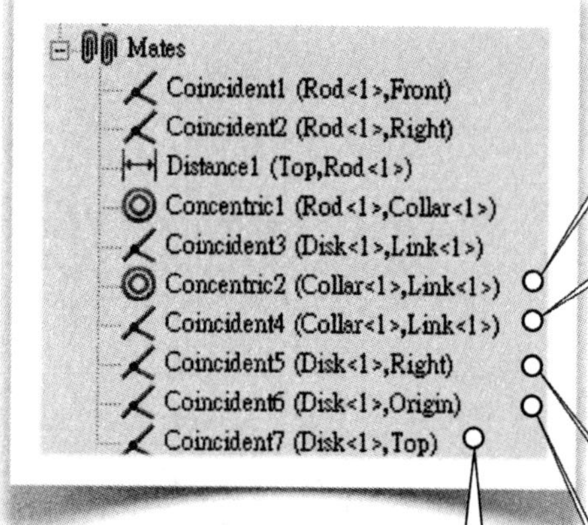

[15] The upper face of the **Collar** (see [16]) and a face of the **Link** (see [17]) are **Coincident**.

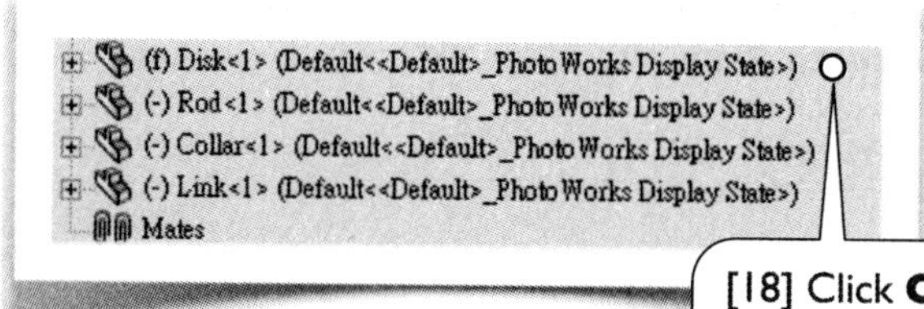

[18] Click **OK** to dismiss **Mate** and right-click **Disk** and select **Float**.

[23] Finally, the **Disk's** and the **Assembly's Top** planes are **Coincident**. We'll suppress this **Mate** later.

[19] The **Disk's** and the **Assembly's Right** planes are **Coincident**.

[20] The **Disk's** and the **Assembly Origins** are **Coincident**. Before clicking **OK**, uncheck **Align axes** (see [21]).

[13] This cylindrical face...

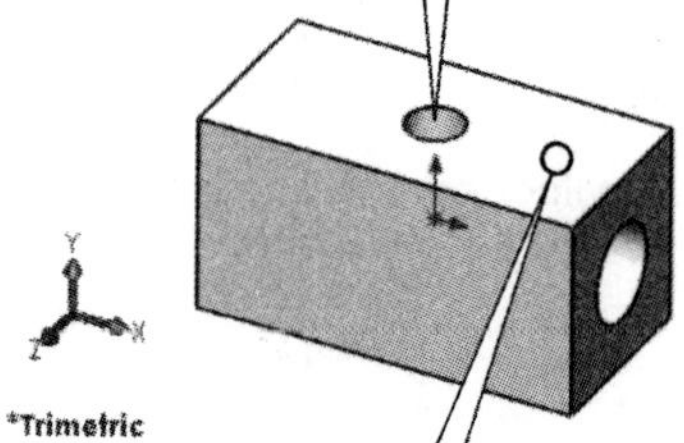

[14] And this cylindrical face are **Concentric**.

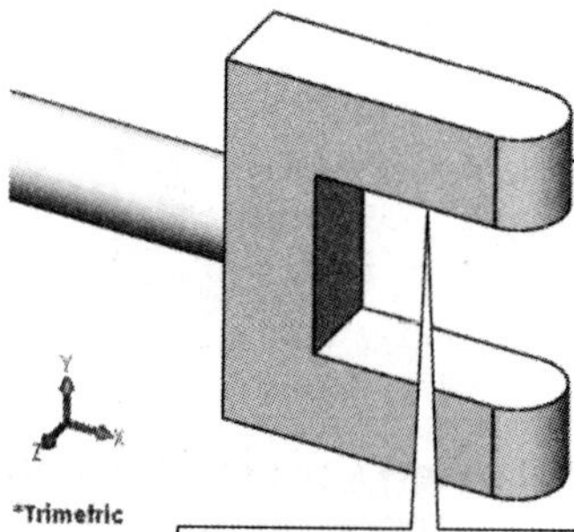

[16] This face...

[17] And this bottom side face are **Coincident**. You need to rotate the view.

[21] Uncheck **Align axes**.

[22] Now, use you mouse to test the mechanism.

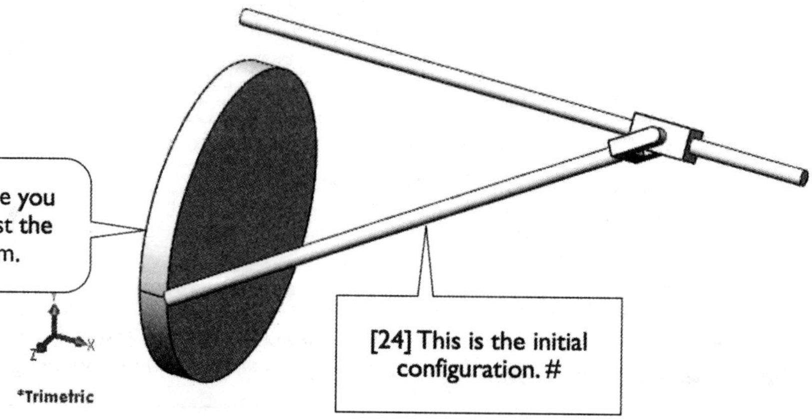

[24] This is the initial configuration. #

9.1-7 Create **Motion Study**, Set Up **Motor**, and Run the Simulation

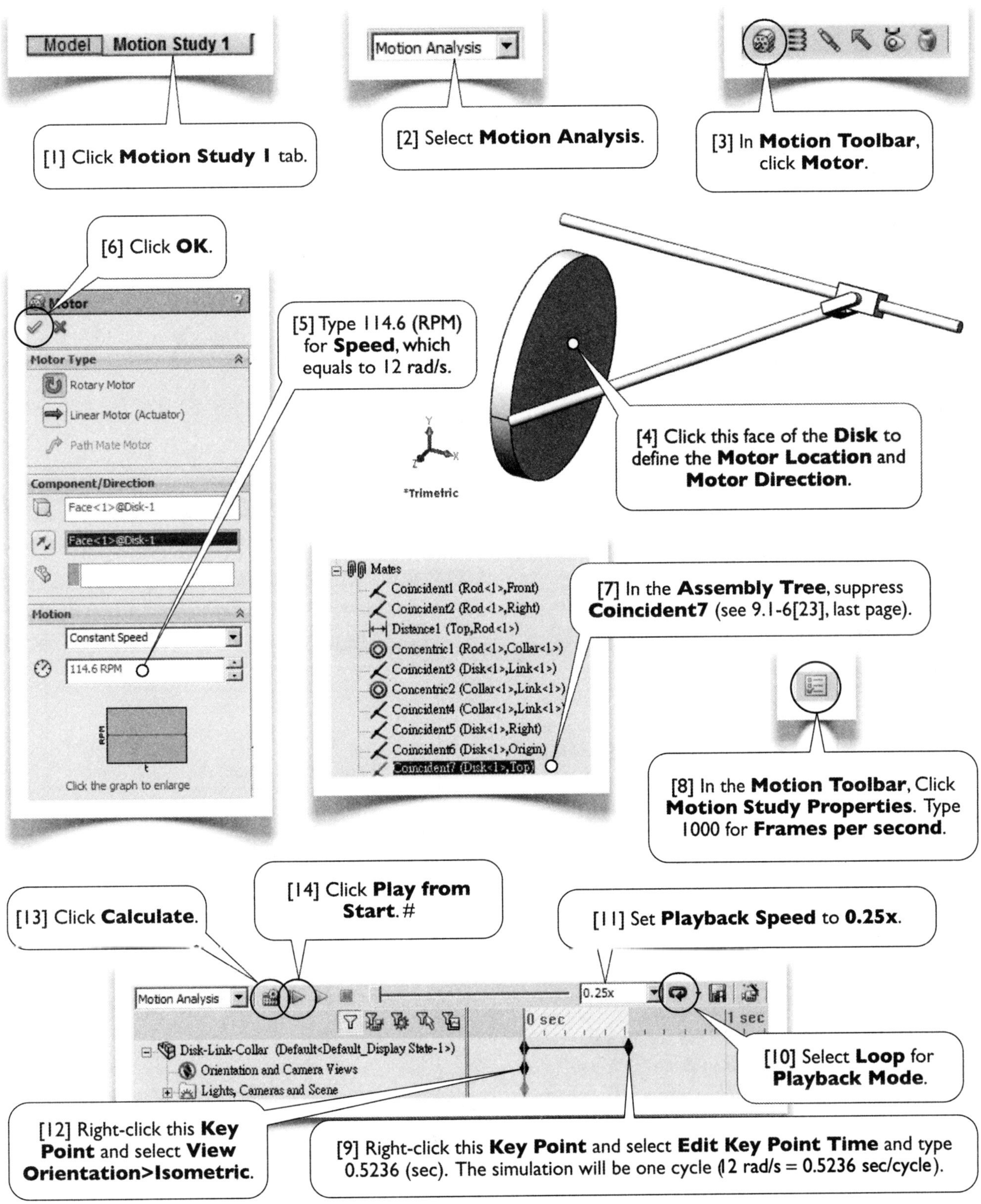

9.1-8 Results

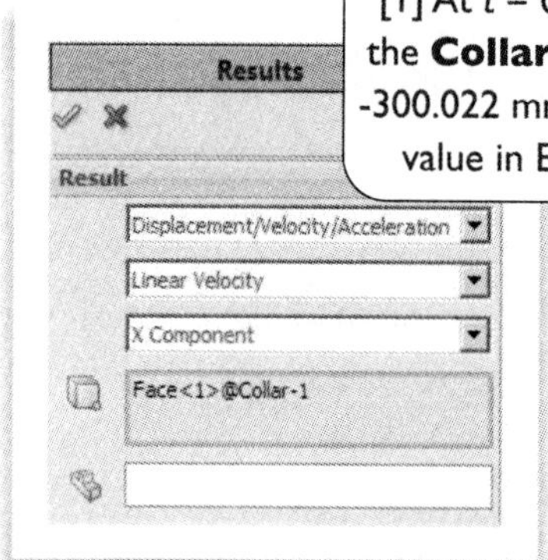

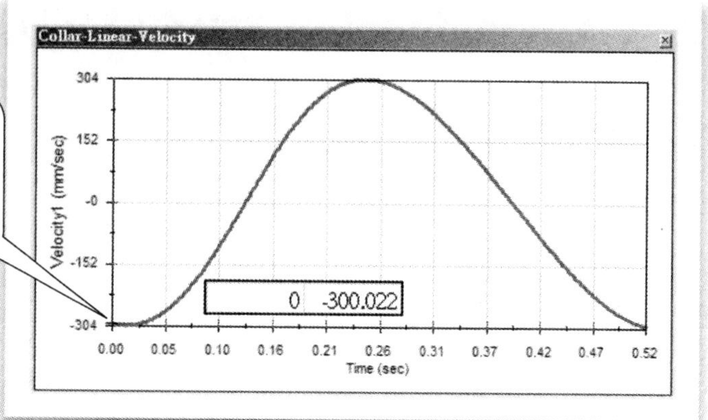

[1] At $t = 0$, the linear velocity of the **Collar** in X-direction is v_{BX} = -300.022 mm/s, consistent with the value in Eq. 9.1-1(1), page 168.

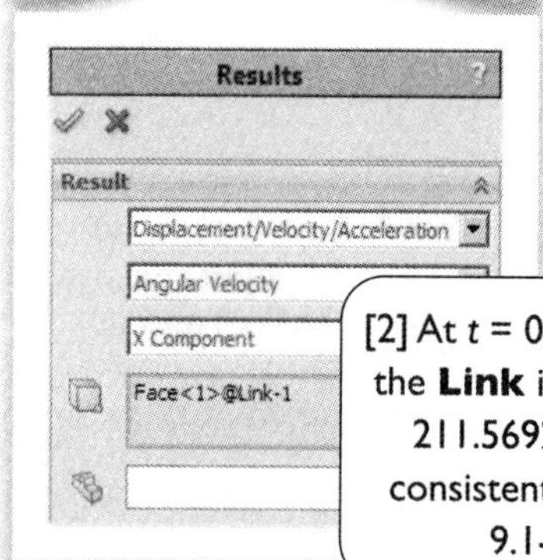

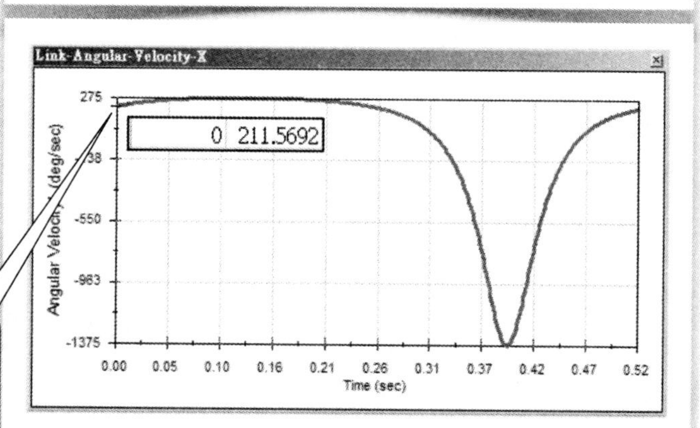

[2] At $t = 0$, the angular velocity of the **Link** in X-direction is ω_X^{link} = 211.5692 deg/s = 3.69 rad/s, consistent with the value in Eq. 9.1-1(2), page 168.

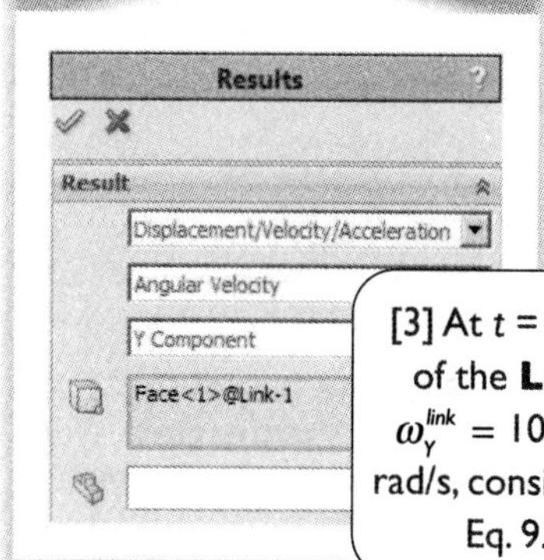

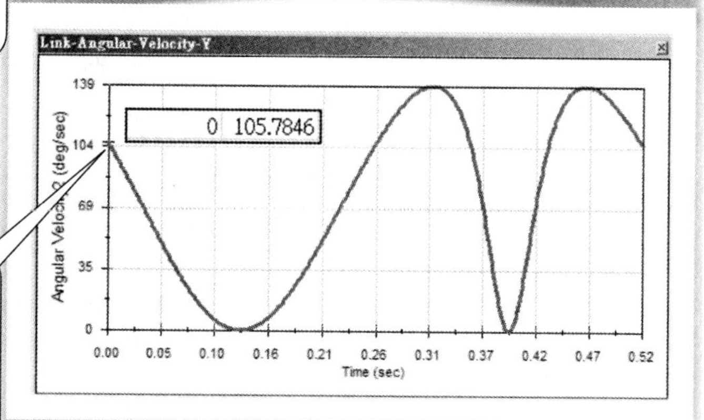

[3] At $t = 0$, the angular velocity of the **Link** in Y-direction is ω_Y^{link} = 105.7846 deg/s = 1.846 rad/s, consistent with the value in Eq. 9.1-1(2), page 168.

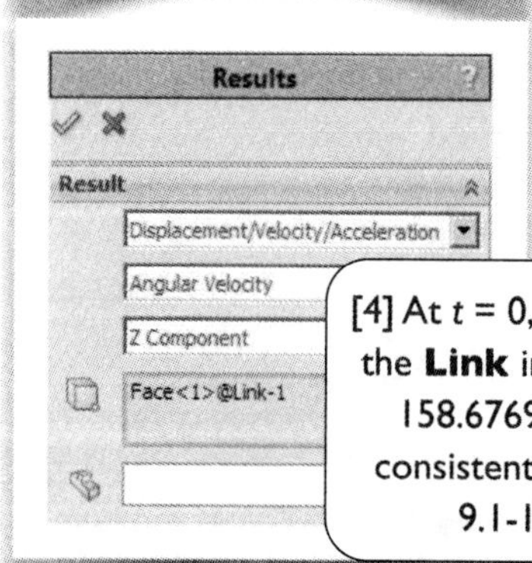

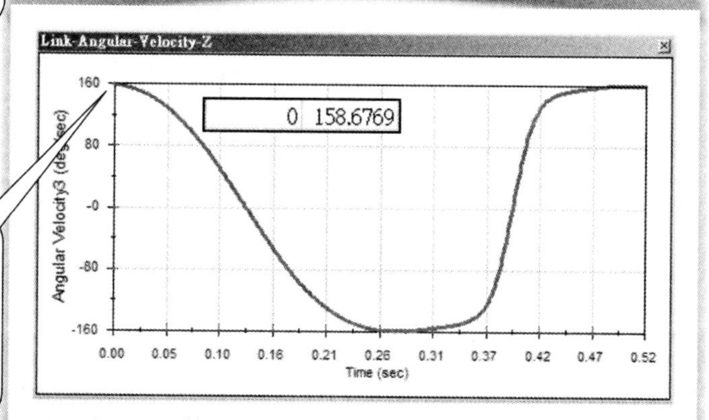

[4] At $t = 0$, the angular velocity of the **Link** in Z-direction is ω_Z^{link} = 158.6769 deg/s = 2.77 rad/s, consistent with the value in Eq. 9.1-1(2), page 168. #

9.1-9 Do It Yourself: Eqs. 9.1-1(3, 4)

[1] Validate Eqs. 9.1-1(3, 4), page 168, at $t = 0$.

$$\vec{v}_B = \vec{v}_A + \vec{\omega}^{link} \times \vec{r}_{B/A}$$ Copy of Eq. 9.1-1(3)

$$\vec{a}_B = \vec{a}_A + \vec{\alpha}^{link} \times \vec{r}_{B/A} + \vec{\omega}^{link} \times \left(\vec{\omega}^{link} \times \vec{r}_{B/A}\right)$$ Copy of Eq. 9.1-1(4)

Note that, at $t = 0$, the position vector $\vec{r}_{B/A}$ is

$$\vec{r}_{B/A} = 150\,\vec{i} + 75\,\vec{j} - 50\,\vec{k} \text{ (mm)}$$

[2] Wrap Up

Save all files and exit **SolidWorks**. #

Section 9.2

Robot

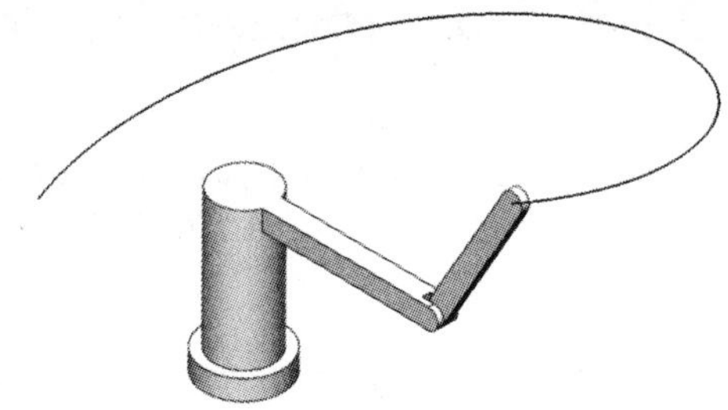

9.2-1 Introduction

[1] Consider a **Robot** consisting of a **Base**, an **Arm**, and a **Boom** [2-5]. This problem is adapted from Problem 15.234, *Vector Mechanics for Engineers: Dynamics, 9th ed in SI Units.*, by F. P. Beer, E. R. Johnston, Jr., and P. J. Cornwell. Some of the quantities calculated by the textbook are: For the position shown below,

The angular acceleration of the **Boom** $\vec{\alpha}^{boom} = -0.27\,\vec{i}$ (rad/s^2) (1)

The linear velocity of D $\vec{v}_D = 155.9\,\vec{i} - 90\,\vec{j} - 420\,\vec{k}$ (mm/s) (2)

The linear acceleration of D $\vec{a}_D = -290\,\vec{i} - 70\,\vec{j} - 190\,\vec{k}$ (mm/s^2) (3)

In this section, we'll perform a simulation for this system and validate the results using the values in Eqs. (1-3). As an exercise, we'll leave you to confirm that, for the position shown below,

$$\vec{v}_D = \vec{v}_C + \vec{\omega}^{boom} \times \vec{r}_{D/C} \quad (4)$$

$$\vec{a}_D = \vec{a}_C + \vec{\alpha}^{boom} \times \vec{r}_{D/C} + \vec{\omega}^{boom} \times \left(\vec{\omega}^{boom} \times \vec{r}_{D/C}\right) \quad (5)$$

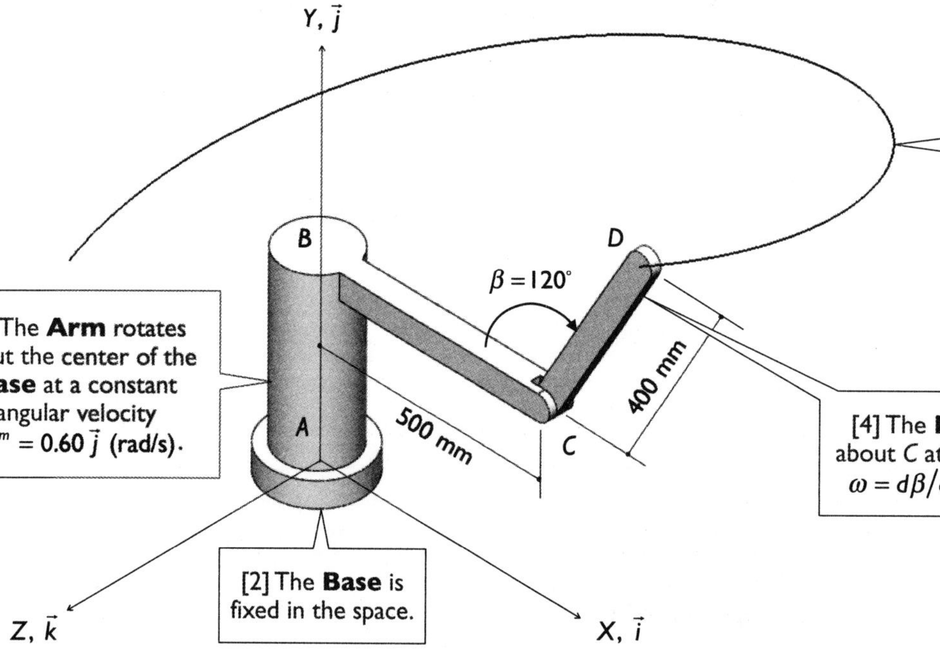

[2] The **Base** is fixed in the space.

[3] The **Arm** rotates about the center of the **Base** at a constant angular velocity $\vec{\omega}^{arm} = 0.60\,\vec{j}$ (rad/s).

[4] The **Boom** rotates about C at a constant rate $\omega = d\beta/dt = 0.45$ rad/s.

[5] This is the **Trace Path** of D. #

9.2-2 Start Up and Create a Part: **Base**

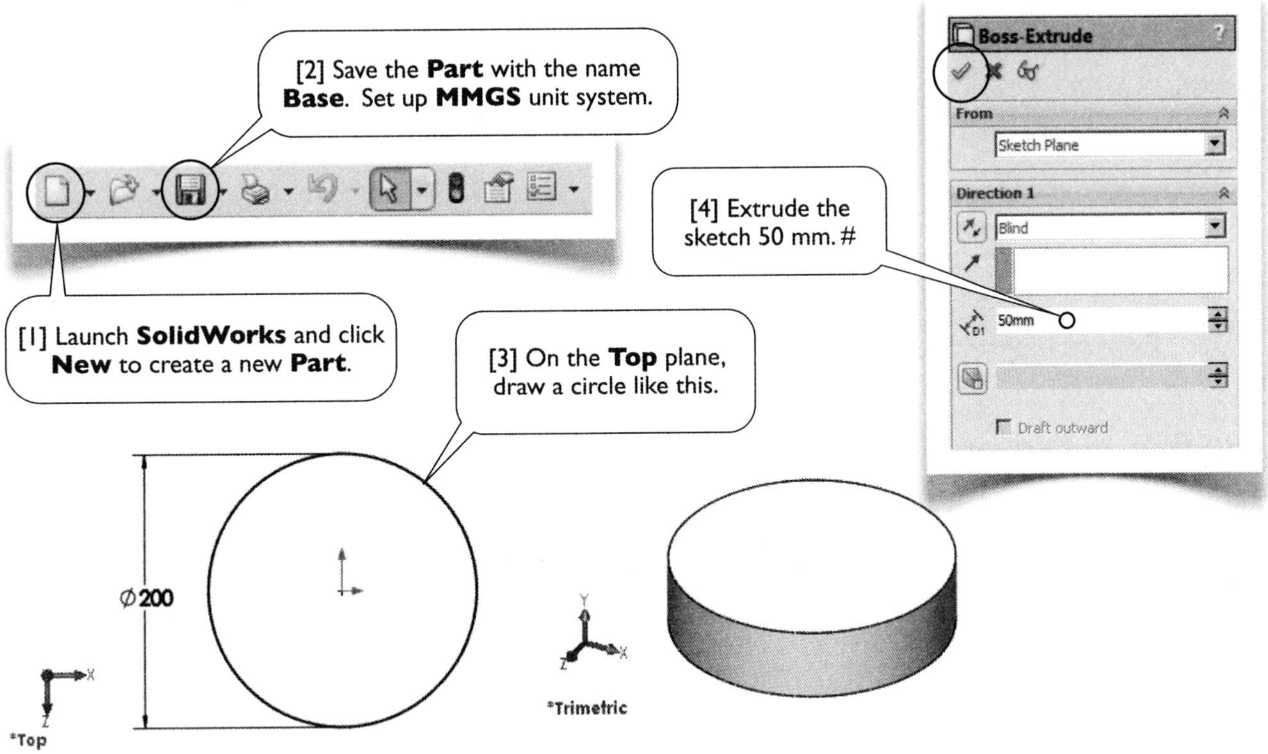

9.2-3 Create a Part: **Arm**

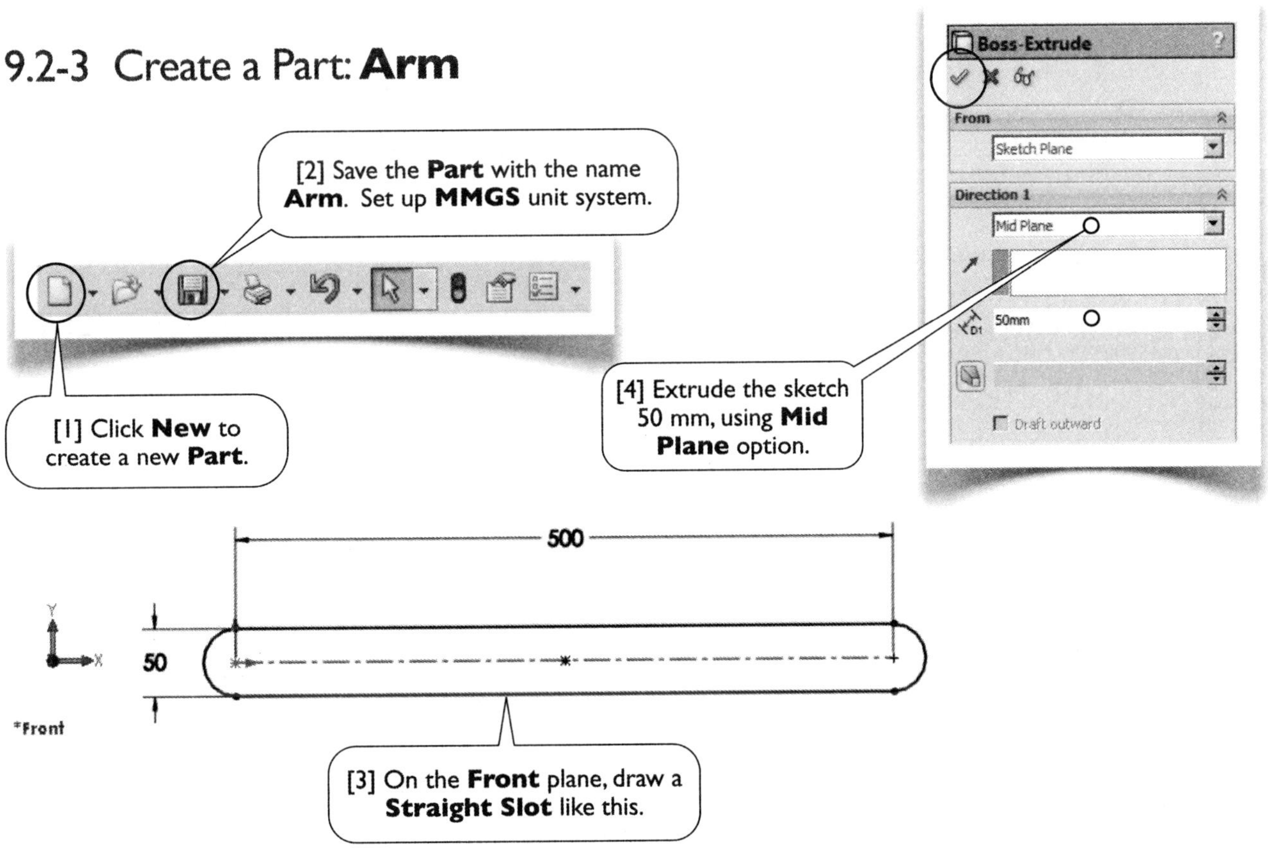

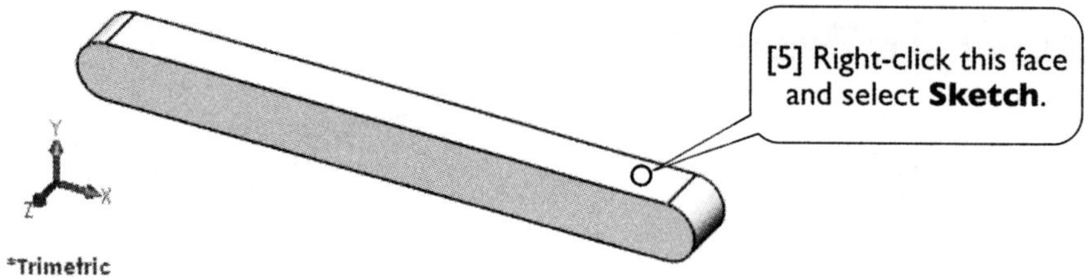
[5] Right-click this face and select **Sketch**.
*Trimetric

30
15
20
[6] Draw a rectangle like this.

Cut-Extrude
From
Sketch Plane
Direction 1
Through All
Flip side to cut
Draft outward
[7] **Extruded Cut**, using **Through All** option.

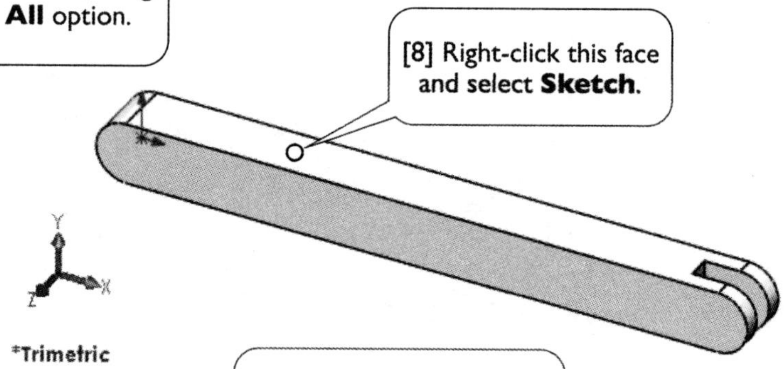
[8] Right-click this face and select **Sketch**.
*Trimetric

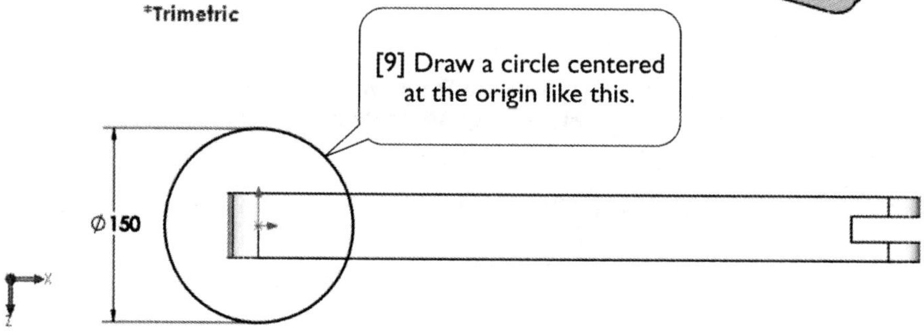
[9] Draw a circle centered at the origin like this.
∅150

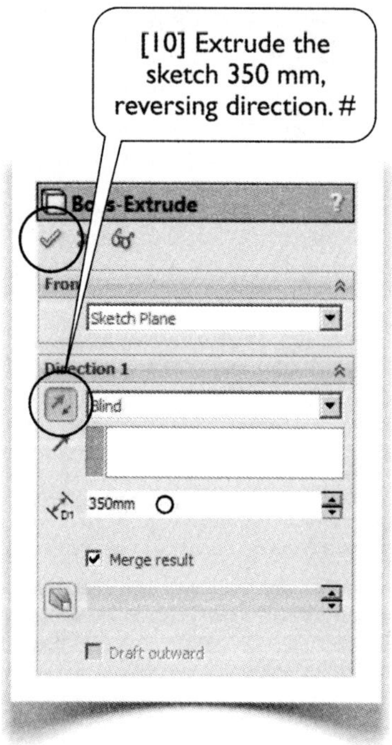
[10] Extrude the sketch 350 mm, reversing direction. #
Sketch Plane
Blind
350mm
Merge result
Draft outward

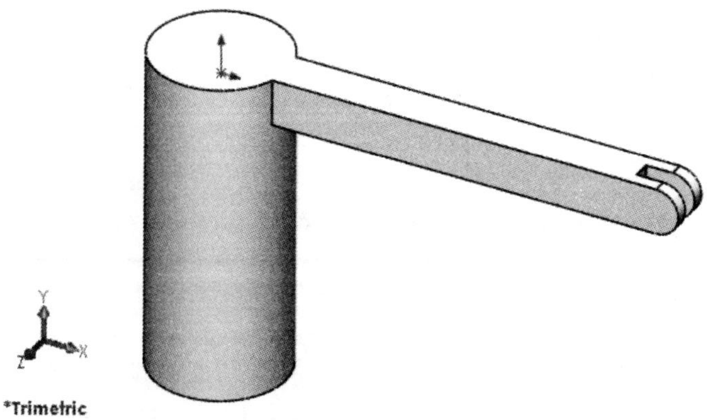
*Trimetric

9.2-4 Create a Part: **Boom**

[1] Click **New** to create a new **Part**.

[2] Save the **Part** with the name **Boom**. Set up **MMGS** unit system.

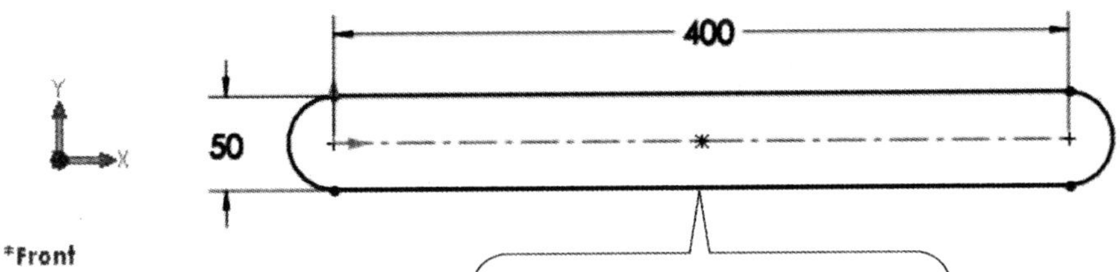

[3] On the **Front** plane, draw a **Straight Slot** like this.

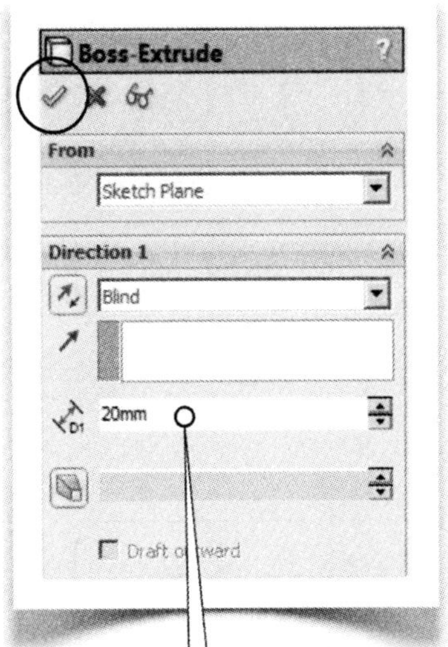

[4] Extrude the sketch 20 mm.

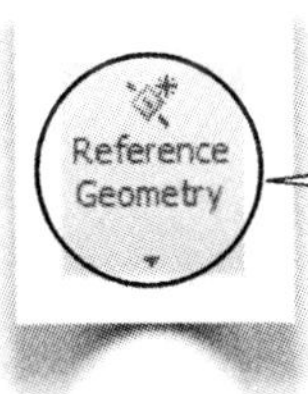

[5] In the **Features Toolbar**, select **Reference Geometry>Point**.

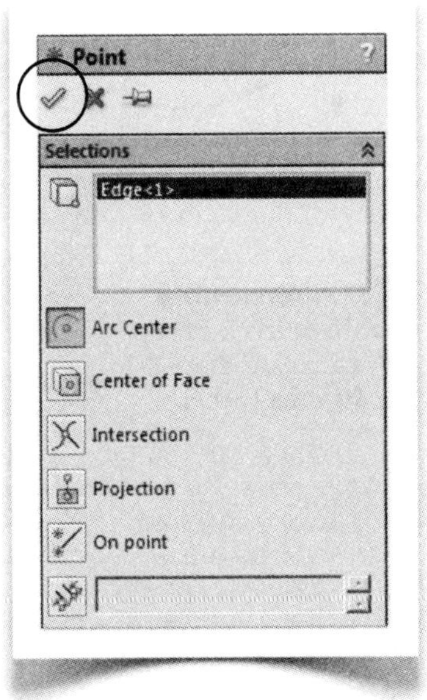

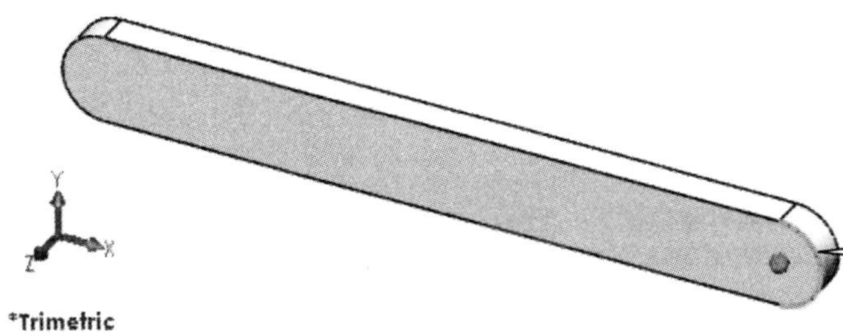

[6] Click this arc to define point *D*, of which the velocity and acceleration will be investigated. #

9.2-5 Create an Assembly: **Robot**

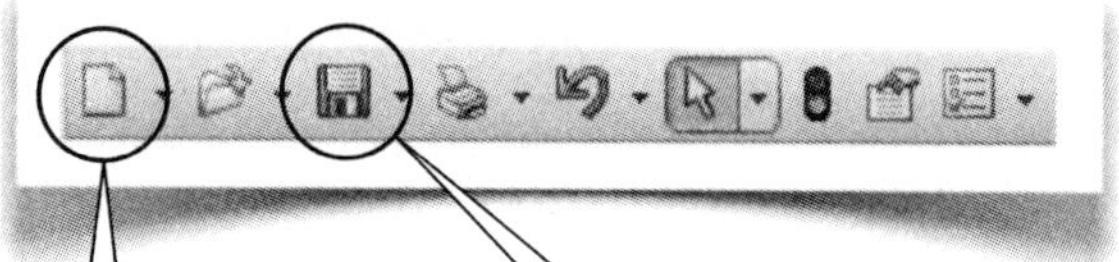

[1] Click **New** and create an **Assembly**.

[2] Turn on **View Origins** and, in the **Begin Assembly Property Box**, select **Base** and click the assembly's **Origin**.

[3] Save the **Assembly** with the name **Robot**. Set up **MMGS** unit system.

[4] In the **Assembly Toolbar**, click **Insert Components** and park **Arm** anywhere. Repeat this step for **Boom**.

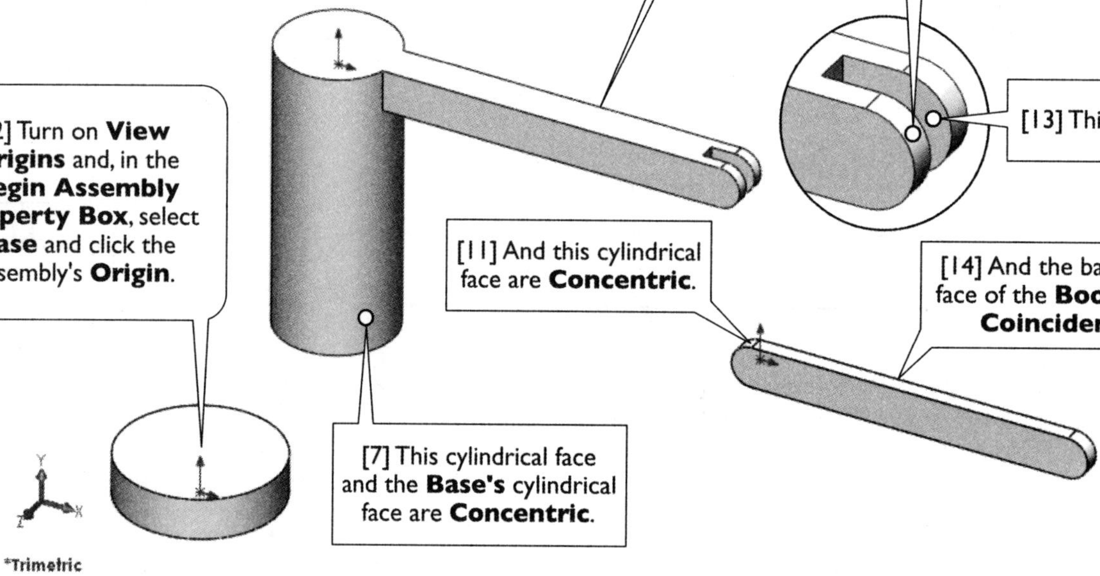

[5] In **Assembly Toolbar**, click **Mate**. We'll create these 6 **Mates** [6-17].

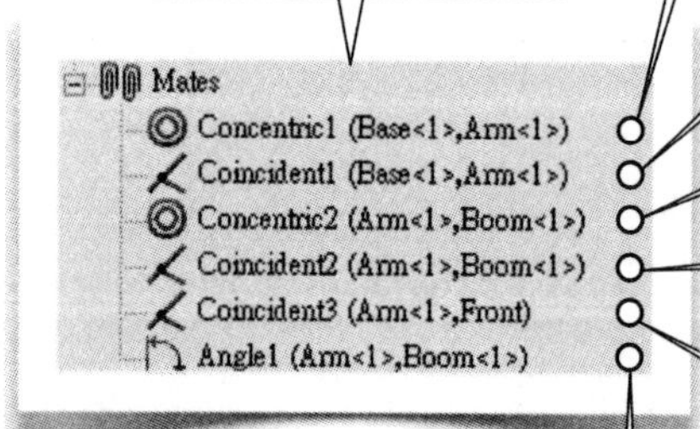

[6] The **Base's** cylindrical face and an **Arm's** cylindrical face (see [7]) are **Concentric**.

[7] This cylindrical face and the **Base's** cylindrical face are **Concentric**.

[8] The **Base's** upper face and the **Arm's** bottom side face are **Coincident**.

[9] An **Arm's** cylindrical face (see [10]) and a **Boom's** cylindrical face (see [11]) are **Concentric**.

[10] This cylindrical face...

[11] And this cylindrical face are **Concentric**.

[12] An **Arm's** face (see [13]) and a **Boom's** face (see [14]) are **Coincident**.

[13] This face...

[14] And the backside face of the **Boom** are **Coincident**.

[15] Now, use you mouse to test the mechanism.

[16] The **Arm's** and the **Assembly's Front** planes are **Coincident**. We'll suppress this **Mate** later.

[17] The **Arm's** and the **Boom's Top** planes form an angle of 60 degrees. We'll suppress this **Mate** later. #

9.2-6 Create **Motion Study**, Set Up **Motor**, and Run the Simulation

[1] Click **Motion Study 1** tab.

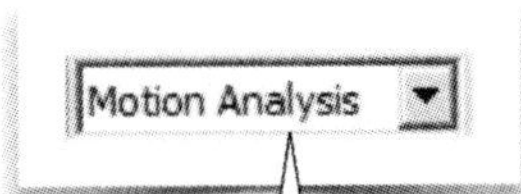

[2] Select **Motion Analysis**.

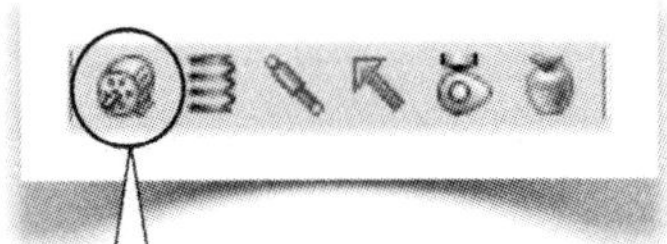

[3, 5] In **Motion Toolbar**, click **Motor**.

[4] Click this face of the **Arm** to define the **Motor Location** and **Motor Direction**. Type 5.7296 (RPM) for **Speed**, which equals to 0.60 rad/s. Click **OK**.

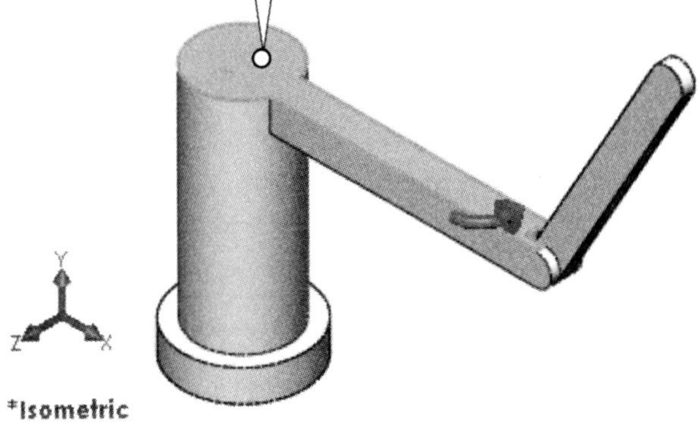

[6] Click this face of the **Boom** to define the **Motor Location** and **Motor Direction**. Click **Reverse Direction**. Type 4.2972 (RPM) for **Speed**, which equals to 0.45 rad/s. Click **OK**.

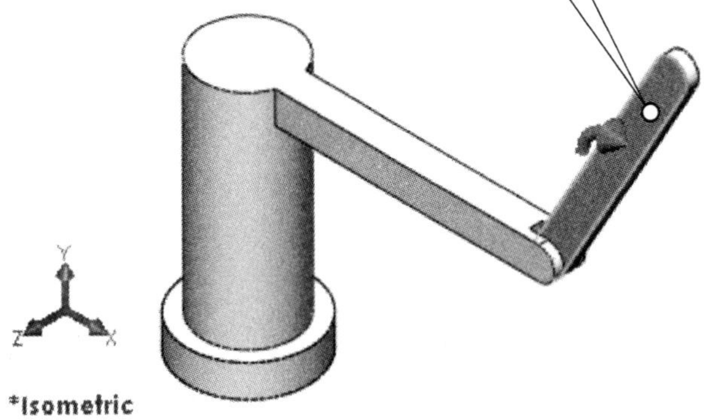

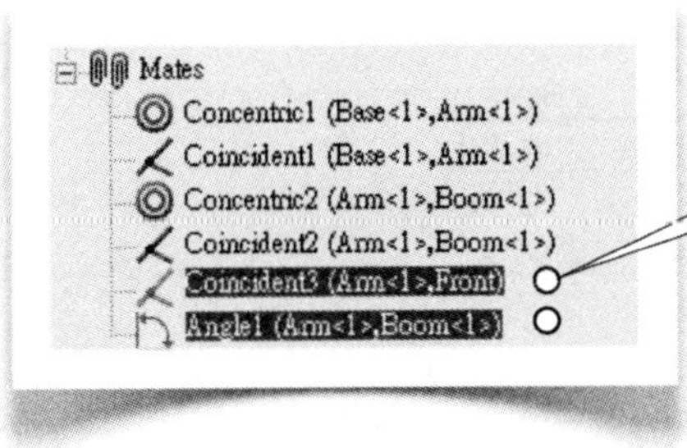

[7] Suppress **Coincident3** and **Angle1** (see 9.2-5[15, 16], last page).

[8] In the **Motion Toolbar**, Click **Motion Study Properties**. Type 100 for **Frames per second**.

[11] Click **Calculate**.

[12] Click **Play from Start**. #

[9] Select **Normal** for **Playback Mode**.

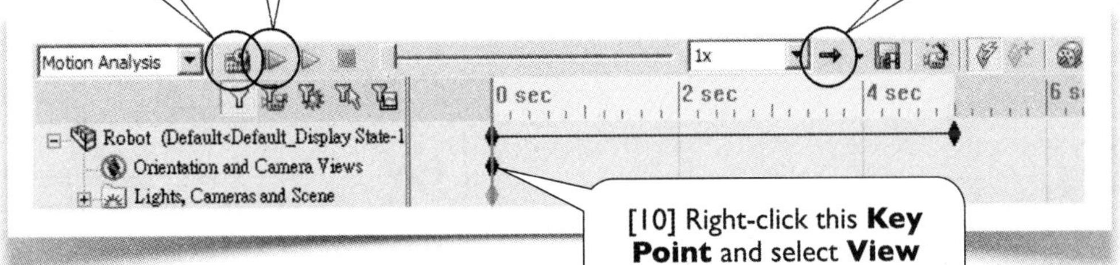

[10] Right-click this **Key Point** and select **View Orientation>Isometric**.

9.2-7 Results: Trace Path

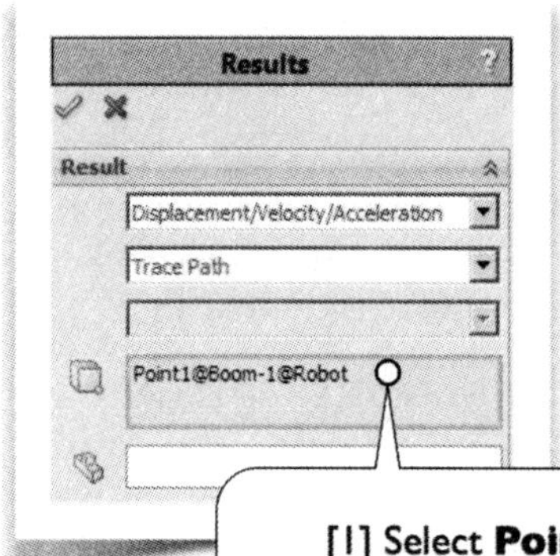

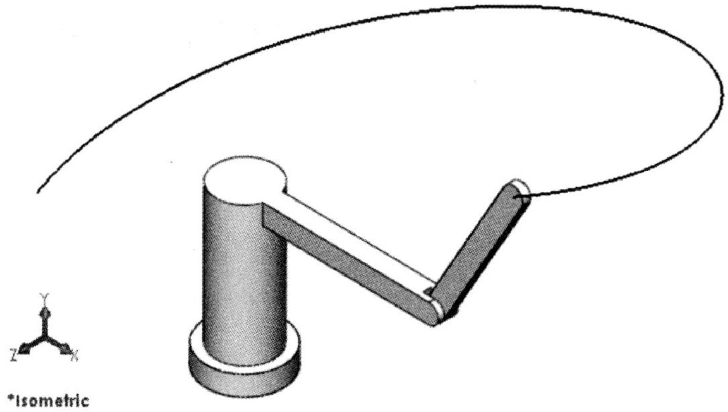

[1] Select **Point1** either from **Assembly Tree** (under **Boom<1>**) or **Graphics Window** (you need to turn on **View Points**). #

9.2-8 Results: Angular Acceleration of the **Boom**

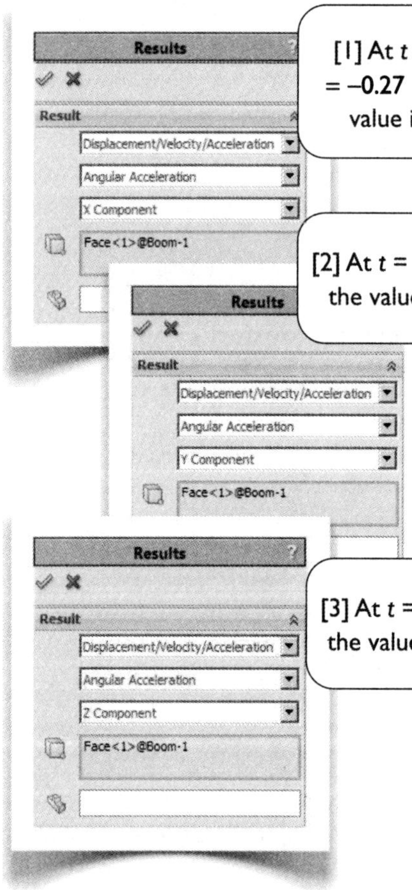

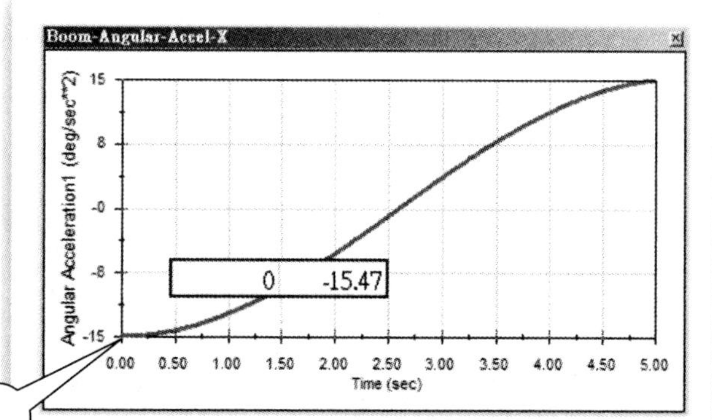

[1] At $t = 0$, $\alpha_X^{boom} = -15.47$ deg/s^2 $= -0.27$ rad/s^2, consistent with the value in Eq. 9.2-1(1), page 178.

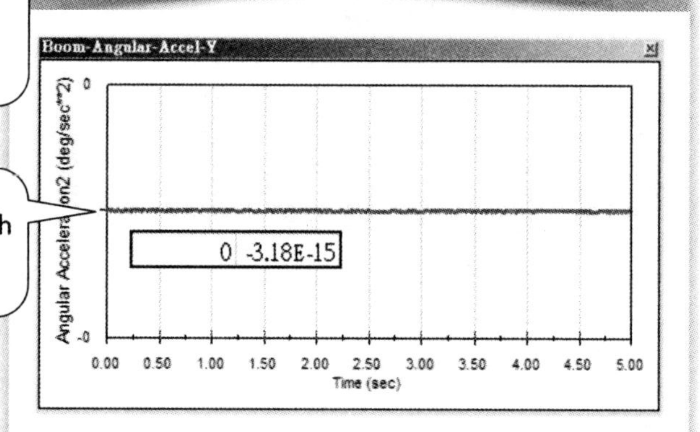

[2] At $t = 0$, $\alpha_Y^{boom} = 0$, consistent with the value in Eq. 9.2-1(1), page 178.

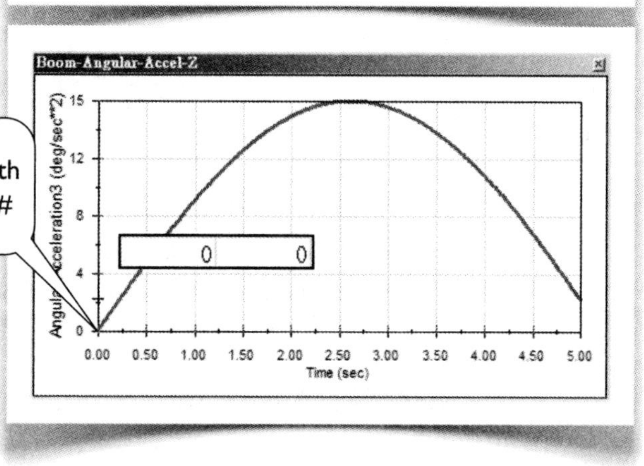

[3] At $t = 0$, $\alpha_Z^{boom} = 0$, consistent with the value in Eq. 9.2-1(1), page 178. #

9.2-9 Results: Linear Velocity and Acceleration at Point D

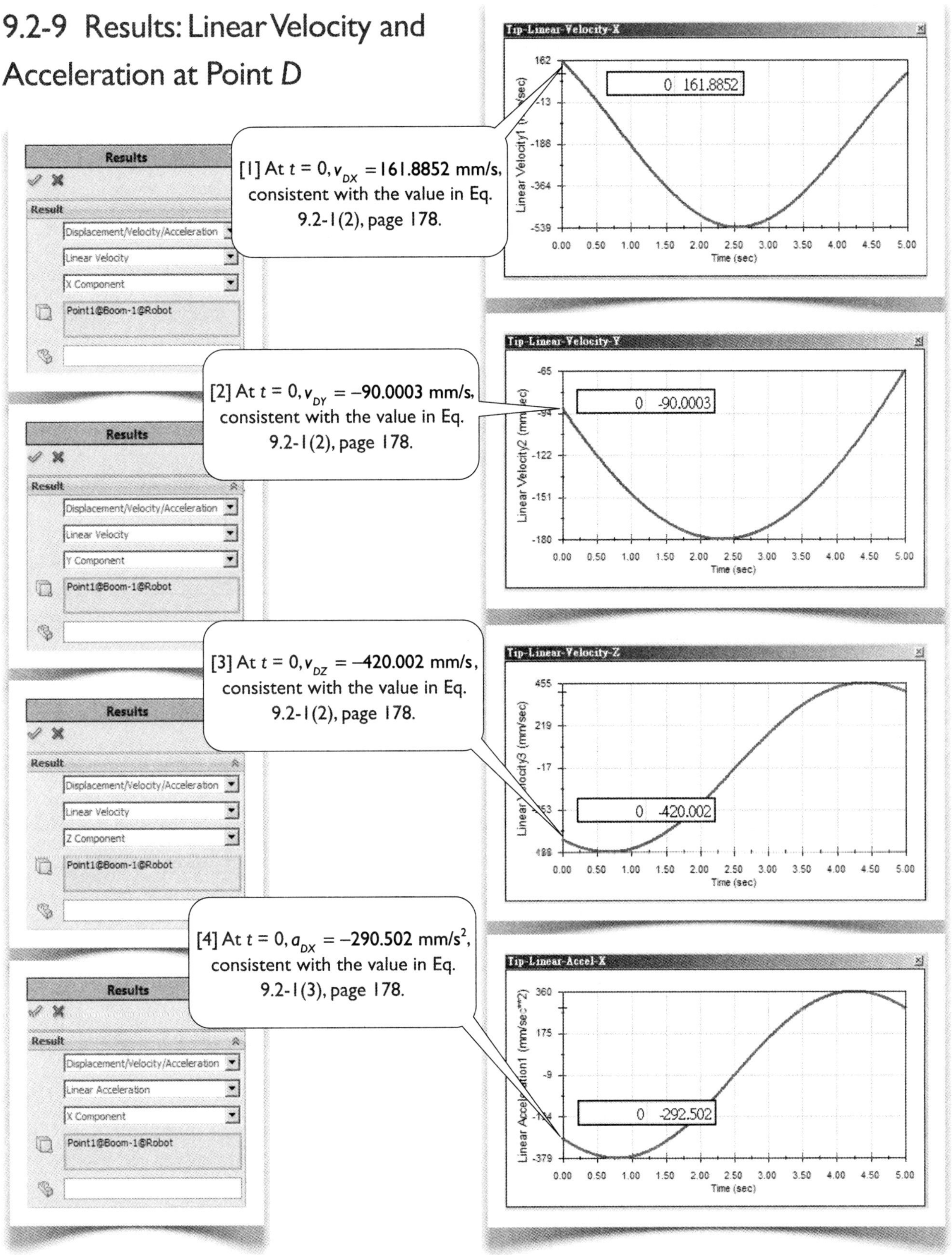

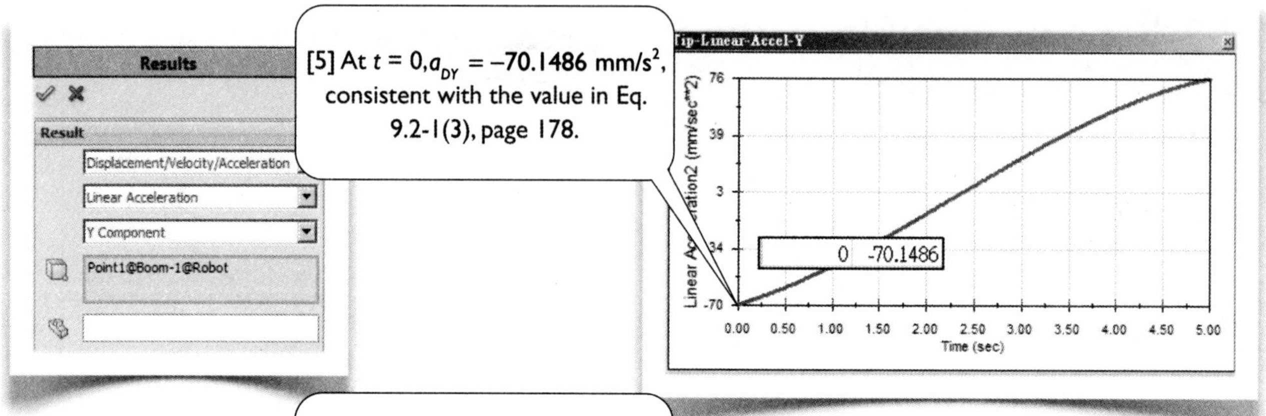

[5] At $t = 0, a_{DY} = -70.1486$ mm/s^2, consistent with the value in Eq. 9.2-1(3), page 178.

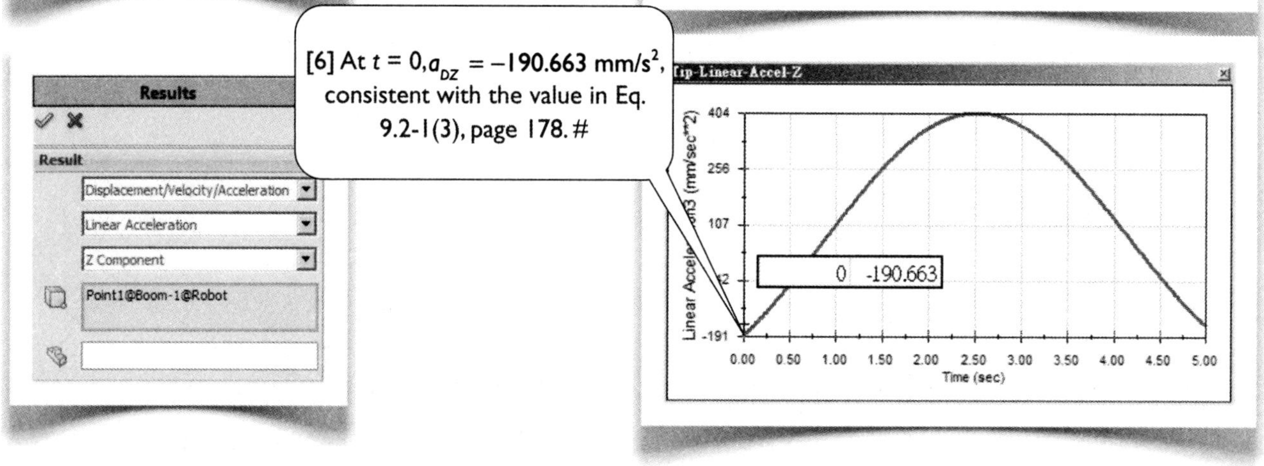

[6] At $t = 0, a_{DZ} = -190.663$ mm/s^2, consistent with the value in Eq. 9.2-1(3), page 178. #

9.2-10 Do It Yourself: Eqs. 9.2-1(4, 5)

[1] Validate Eqs. 9.2-1(4, 5), page 178, at $t = 0$.

$$\vec{v}_D = \vec{v}_C + \vec{\omega}^{boom} \times \vec{r}_{D/C} \quad \text{Copy of Eq. 9.2-1(4)}$$

$$\vec{a}_D = \vec{a}_C + \vec{\alpha}^{boom} \times \vec{r}_{D/C} + \vec{\omega}^{boom} \times \left(\vec{\omega}^{boom} \times \vec{r}_{D/C}\right) \quad \text{Copy of Eq. 9.2-1(5)}$$

[2] Wrap Up

Save all files and exit **SolidWorks**. #

Chapter 10

3D Rigid Body Dynamics

Newton's 2nd Law for a rigid body in general 3D motion can be expressed in the following form:

$$\sum \vec{F} = m\bar{\vec{a}} \tag{1}$$

$$\sum \vec{M}_O = \dot{\vec{H}}_O \tag{2}$$

where

$\sum \vec{F}$	is the resulting force acting on the body;
m	is the mass of the body;
$\bar{\vec{a}}$	is the linear acceleration of the mass center of the body;
$\sum \vec{M}_O$	is the resulting moment acting on the body about a fixed point O in the space.
$\dot{\vec{H}}_O$	is the rate of change of angular momentum of the body about the fixed point O.

It is worth to emphasize that the point O must be a FIXED point in the space. However, it turns out that Eq. (2) still holds if O is replaced by the mass center G of the body (which is a moving point); i.e.,

$$\sum \vec{M}_G = \dot{\vec{H}}_G \tag{3}$$

Eq. (3) can be used in general cases (Section 10.1), while Eq. (2) can be more useful when a body rotates about a fixed point or rotates about a fixed axis passing through O. An example of using Eq. (2) will be given in Section 10.2.

Section 10.1

Newton's 2nd Law: Disk-Link-Collar Mechanism

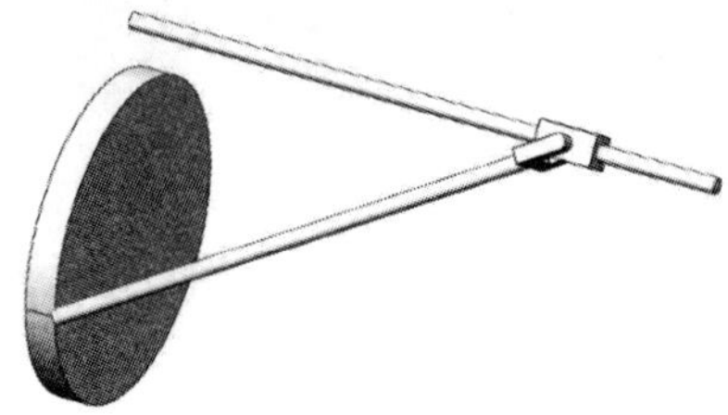

10.1-1 Introduction

[1] As mentioned in the last page, Newton's 2nd Law for a rigid body in general 3D motion can be expressed in the following form:

$$\sum \vec{F} = m\vec{\bar{a}} \tag{1}$$

$$\sum \vec{M}_G = \dot{\vec{H}}_G \tag{2}$$

where G is the mass center of the body. Note that $\dot{\vec{H}}_G$ is the rate of change of the angular momentum of the body about the moving point G, observed in a FIXED frame. It is more convenient to observe it in a moving frame xyz attached to the body. It can be proved that

$$\dot{\vec{H}}_G = (\dot{\vec{H}}_G)_{xyz} + \vec{\omega} \times \vec{H}_G \tag{3}$$

where

- $(\dot{\vec{H}}_G)_{xyz}$ is the rate of change of angular momentum of the body about its mass center, observed in the frame xyz, which is attached to and moving with the body.
- $\vec{\omega}$ is the angular velocity of the body.
- $\vec{H}_G$ is the angular momentum of the body about its mass center, which can be calculated by

$$\vec{H}_G = \begin{pmatrix} \bar{I}_x & -\bar{I}_{xy} & -\bar{I}_{xz} \\ -\bar{I}_{yx} & \bar{I}_y & -\bar{I}_{yz} \\ -\bar{I}_{zx} & -\bar{I}_{zy} & \bar{I}_z \end{pmatrix} \begin{pmatrix} \omega_x \\ \omega_y \\ \omega_z \end{pmatrix} \tag{4}$$

where all quantities are referring to the xyz coordinate system, and the moments/products of inertia are calculated at the mass center of the body. Also note that the products of moments are symmetric; i.e., $\bar{I}_{xy} = \bar{I}_{yx}, \bar{I}_{yz} = \bar{I}_{zy}, \bar{I}_{zx} = \bar{I}_{xz}$. Eq. (2) then can be written as

$$\sum \vec{M}_G = (\dot{\vec{H}}_G)_{xyz} + \vec{\omega} \times \vec{H}_G \tag{5}$$

[2] If the x, y, z axes are chosen to coincide with the principal axes of inertia of the body (i.e., $\bar{I}_{xy} = \bar{I}_{yz} = \bar{I}_{zx} = 0$), then Eq. (4) reduces to

$$\vec{H}_G = \bar{I}_x \omega_x \vec{i} + \bar{I}_y \omega_y \vec{j} + \bar{I}_z \omega_z \vec{k} \tag{6}$$

where $\vec{i}$, $\vec{j}$, $\vec{k}$ are unit vectors in x-, y-, z-direction respectively. Let α_x, α_y, α_z be the angular acceleration components in xyz coordinate system. The two terms in the right-hand-side of Eq. (5) then become

$$(\dot{\vec{H}}_G)_{xyz} = \bar{I}_x \alpha_x \vec{i} + \bar{I}_y \alpha_y \vec{j} + \bar{I}_z \alpha_z \vec{k} \tag{7}$$

$$\vec{\omega} \times \vec{H}_G = \begin{vmatrix} \vec{i} & \vec{j} & \vec{k} \\ \omega_x & \omega_y & \omega_z \\ \bar{I}_x \omega_x & \bar{I}_y \omega_y & \bar{I}_z \omega_z \end{vmatrix} = -(\bar{I}_y - \bar{I}_z)\omega_y \omega_z \vec{i} - (\bar{I}_z - \bar{I}_x)\omega_z \omega_x \vec{j} - (\bar{I}_x - \bar{I}_y)\omega_x \omega_y \vec{k} \tag{8}$$

Substitution of Eqs. (7, 8) into Eq. (5) yields

$$\begin{aligned} \sum M_{Gx} &= \bar{I}_x \alpha_x - (\bar{I}_y - \bar{I}_z)\omega_y \omega_z \\ \sum M_{Gy} &= \bar{I}_y \alpha_y - (\bar{I}_z - \bar{I}_x)\omega_z \omega_x \\ \sum M_{Gz} &= \bar{I}_z \alpha_z - (\bar{I}_x - \bar{I}_y)\omega_x \omega_y \end{aligned} \tag{9}$$

Eq. (9) is called the **Euler's equations of motion**, named after the Swiss mathematician Leonhard Euler.

In this section, we'll revisit the **Disk-Link-Collar** example, introduced in 9.1, and demonstrate how Eqs. (1, 5-9) apply to the **Link** [3] at $t = 0$.

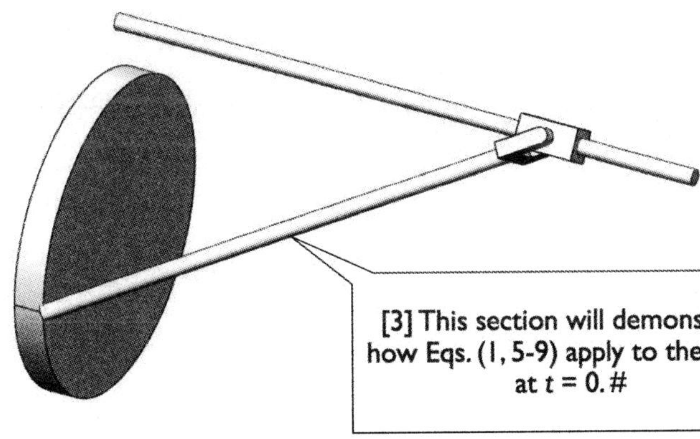

[3] This section will demonstrate how Eqs. (1, 5-9) apply to the **Link** at $t = 0$.#

10.1-2 Open the File **Disk-Link-Collar.SLDASM**

[1] Launch **SolidWorks** and open the file **Disk-Link-Collar.SLDASM**, which was saved in Section 9.1.#

10.1-3 The Mass and Moments of Inertia of the **Link**

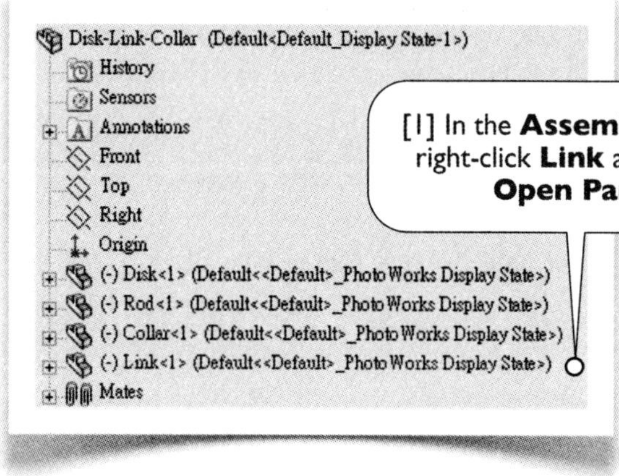

[1] In the **Assembly Tree**, right-click **Link** and select **Open Part**.

[2] In the **Evaluate Toolbar**, click **Mass Properties**.

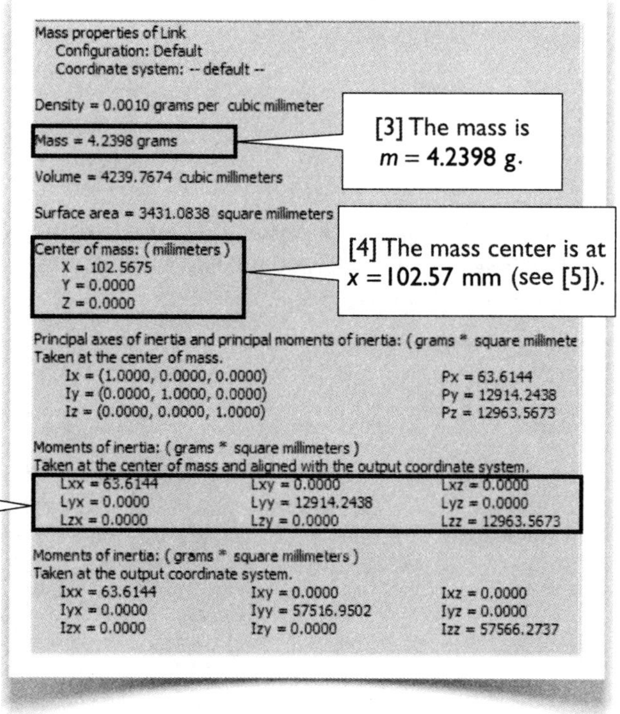

Mass properties of Link
Configuration: Default
Coordinate system: -- default --

Density = 0.0010 grams per cubic millimeter

Mass = 4.2398 grams

Volume = 4239.7674 cubic millimeters

Surface area = 3431.0838 square millimeters

Center of mass: (millimeters)
X = 102.5675
Y = 0.0000
Z = 0.0000

Principal axes of inertia and principal moments of inertia: (grams * square millimete
Taken at the center of mass.
Ix = (1.0000, 0.0000, 0.0000) Px = 63.6144
Iy = (0.0000, 1.0000, 0.0000) Py = 12914.2438
Iz = (0.0000, 0.0000, 1.0000) Pz = 12963.5673

Moments of inertia: (grams * square millimeters)
Taken at the center of mass and aligned with the output coordinate system.

Lxx = 63.6144	Lxy = 0.0000	Lxz = 0.0000
Lyx = 0.0000	Lyy = 12914.2438	Lyz = 0.0000
Lzx = 0.0000	Lzy = 0.0000	Lzz = 12963.5673

Moments of inertia: (grams * square millimeters)
Taken at the output coordinate system.

Ixx = 63.6144	Ixy = 0.0000	Ixz = 0.0000
Iyx = 0.0000	Iyy = 57516.9502	Iyz = 0.0000
Izx = 0.0000	Izy = 0.0000	Izz = 57566.2737

[3] The mass is $m = 4.2398$ g.

[4] The mass center is at $x = 102.57$ mm (see [5]).

[6] The moments of inertia taken at the mass center and aligned with the **Part's** coordinate system are $\bar{I}_x = 63.614$ g-mm^2, $\bar{I}_y = 12914$ g-mm^2, $\bar{I}_z = 12964$ g-mm^2. All products of inertia are zeros, meaning the principal axes are aligned with **Link's** coordinate system.

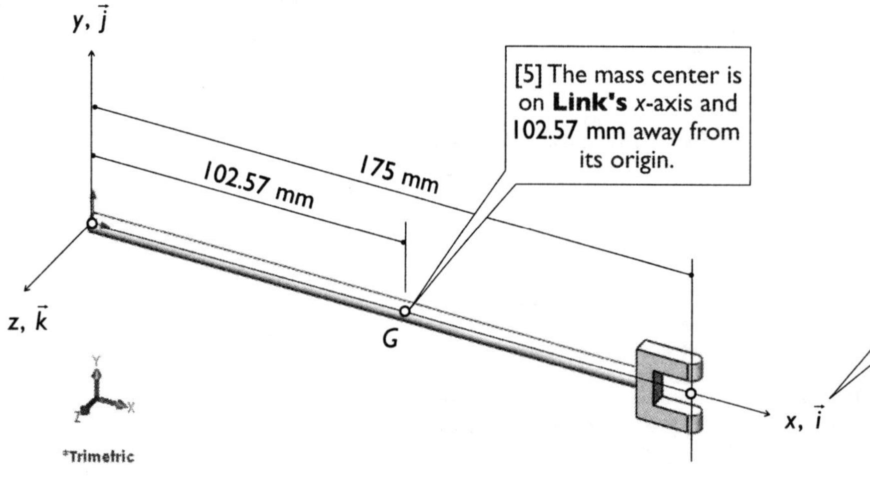

[5] The mass center is on **Link's** x-axis and 102.57 mm away from its origin.

[7] In this chapter, we'll use lower case letters (x, y, z) for **Part's coordinates** to distinguish them from **Assembly's coordinates**, in which upper case letters (X, Y, Z) are used. The unit vectors ($\vec{i}, \vec{j}, \vec{k}$) are in x, y, z directions respectively. #

10.1-4 Return to the Assembly

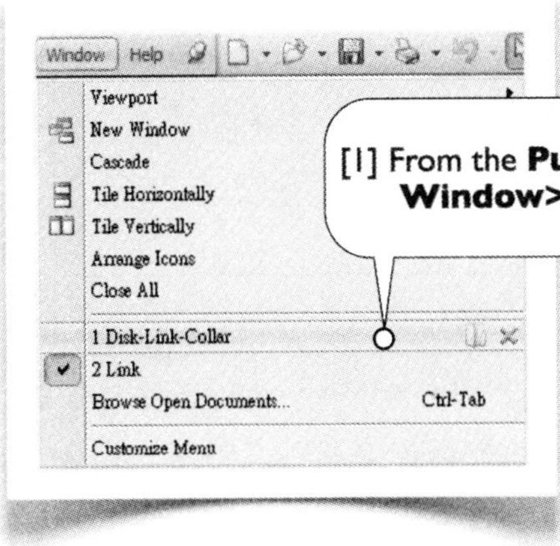

[1] From the **Pull-Down Menus**, select **Window>Disk-Link-Collar**.

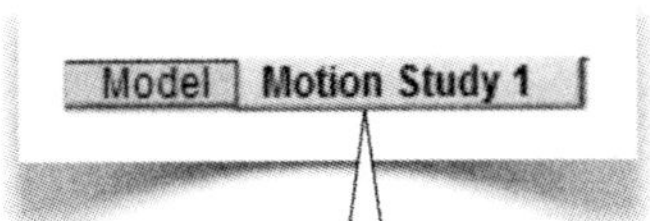

[2] Click **Motion Study 1**.#

10.1-5 External Forces on the **Link**

[3] At $t = 0$, the reaction force in x-direction on the **Disk** by the **Link** is $F_x^{disk/link} = 365\ \mu N$.

[1] To obtain forces between the **Disk** and the **Link**, select **Coincident3** (see 9.1-6[11], page 173).

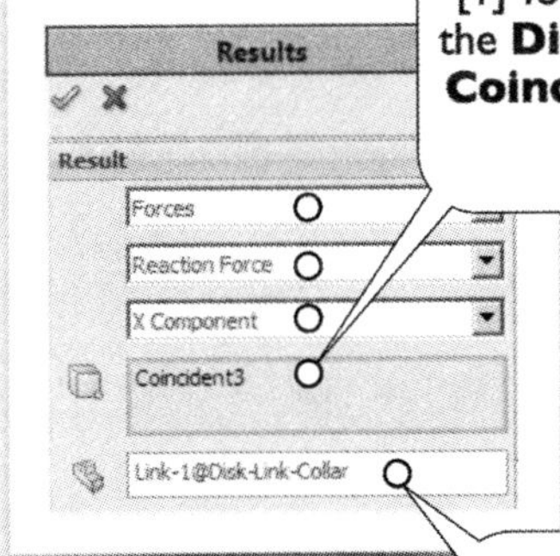

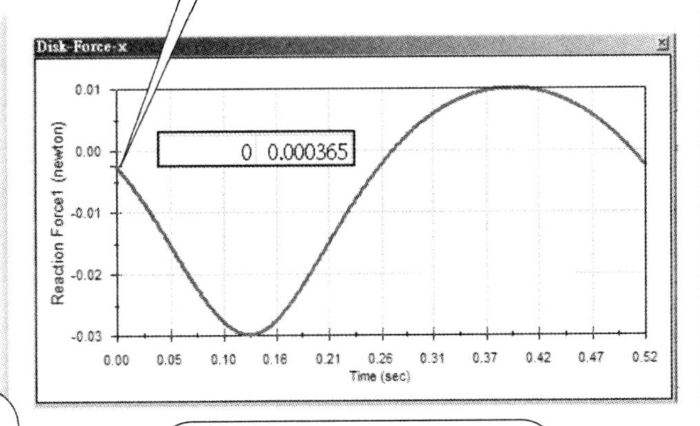

[2] In the **Graphics Window**, click the **Link**. The **Link's** coordinate system will be used as the **reference coordinate system**. For the rest of this section, we always use this reference coordinate system and use lower case letter (x, y, z) for the three directions.

[4] At $t = 0$, the reaction force in y-direction on the **Disk** by the **Link** is $F_y^{disk/link} = 6903\ \mu N$.

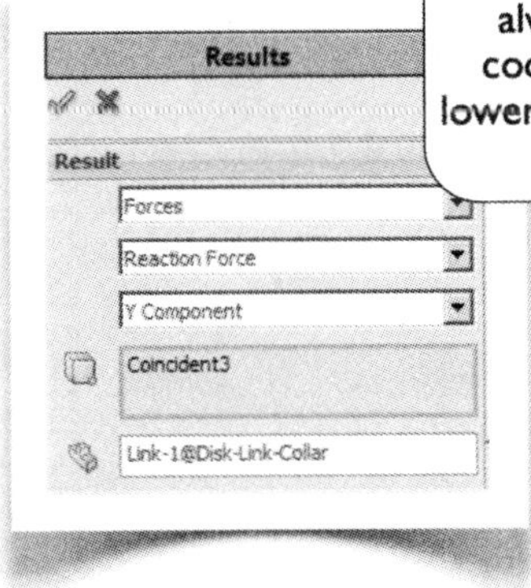

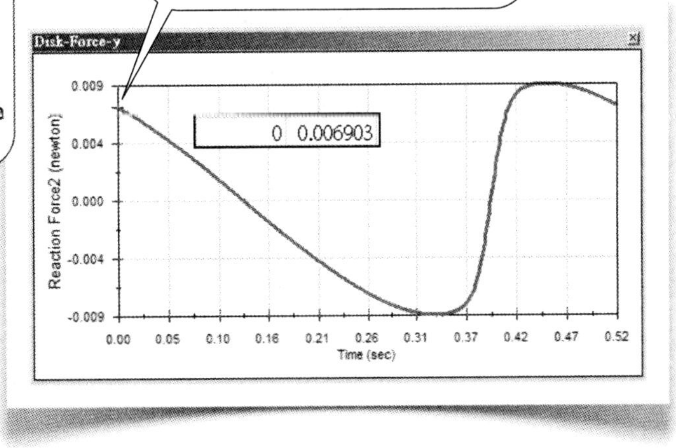

[5] At t = 0, the reaction force in z-direction on the **Disk** by the **Link** is $F_z^{disk/link}$ = 4118 μN.

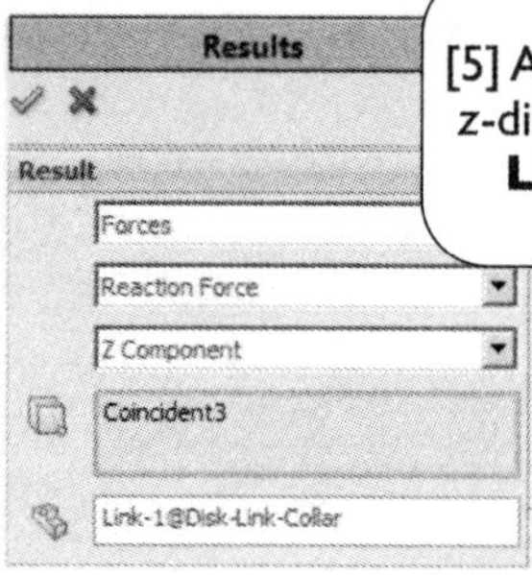

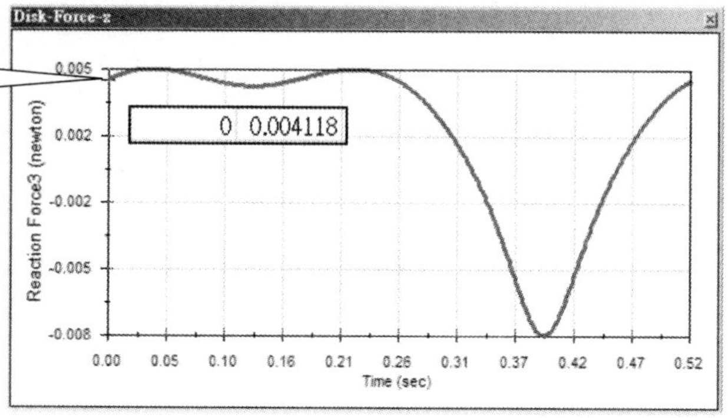

[6] Select **Concentric2** (see 9.1-6[12], page 174); the results will be the reaction forces on the **Collar** by the **Link**.

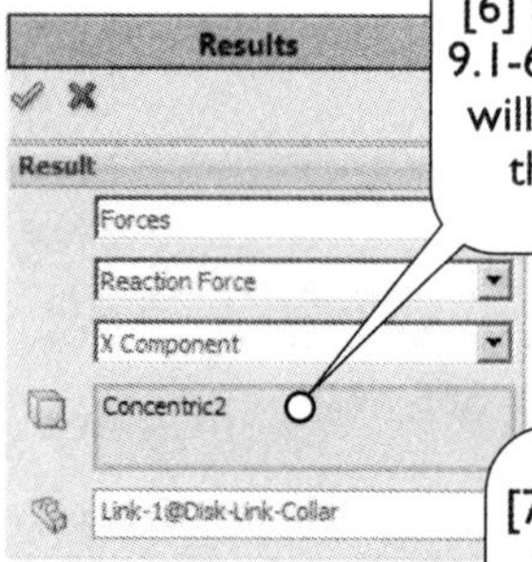

[7] At t = 0, the reaction force in x-direction on the **Collar** by the **Link** is $F_x^{collar/link}$ = –2700 μN.

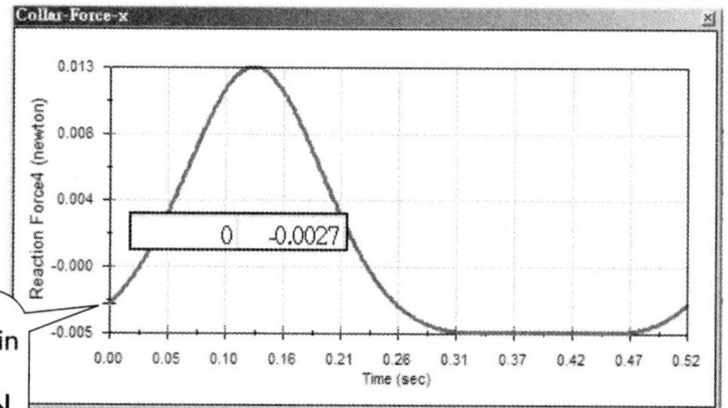

[8] At t = 0, the reaction force in z-direction on the **Collar** by the **Link** is $F_z^{collar/link}$ = 2659 μN.

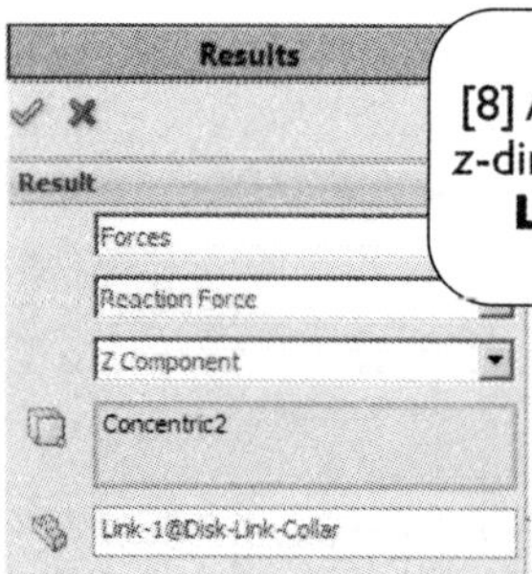

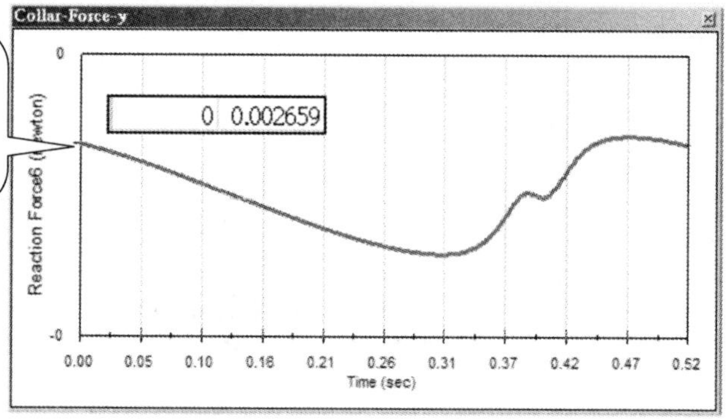

[9] Select **Coincident4** (see 9.1-6[15], page 174); the results will be the reaction forces on the **Collar** by the **Link**.

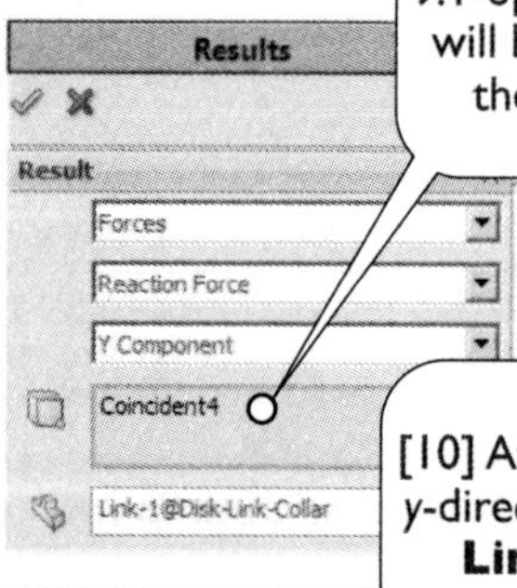

[10] At t = 0, the reaction force in y-direction on the **Collar** by the **Link** is $F_y^{collar/link}$ = 3612 μN.

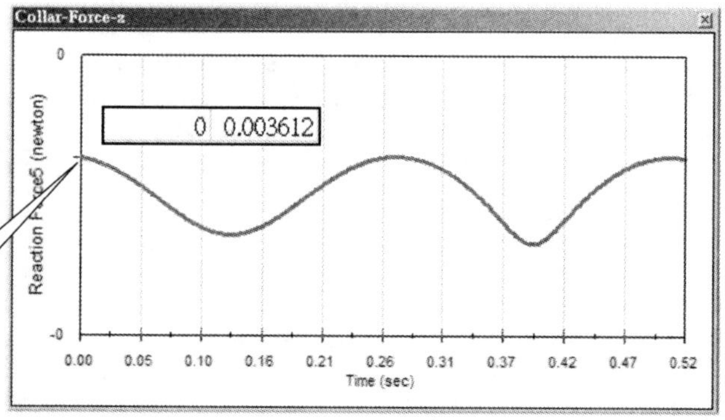

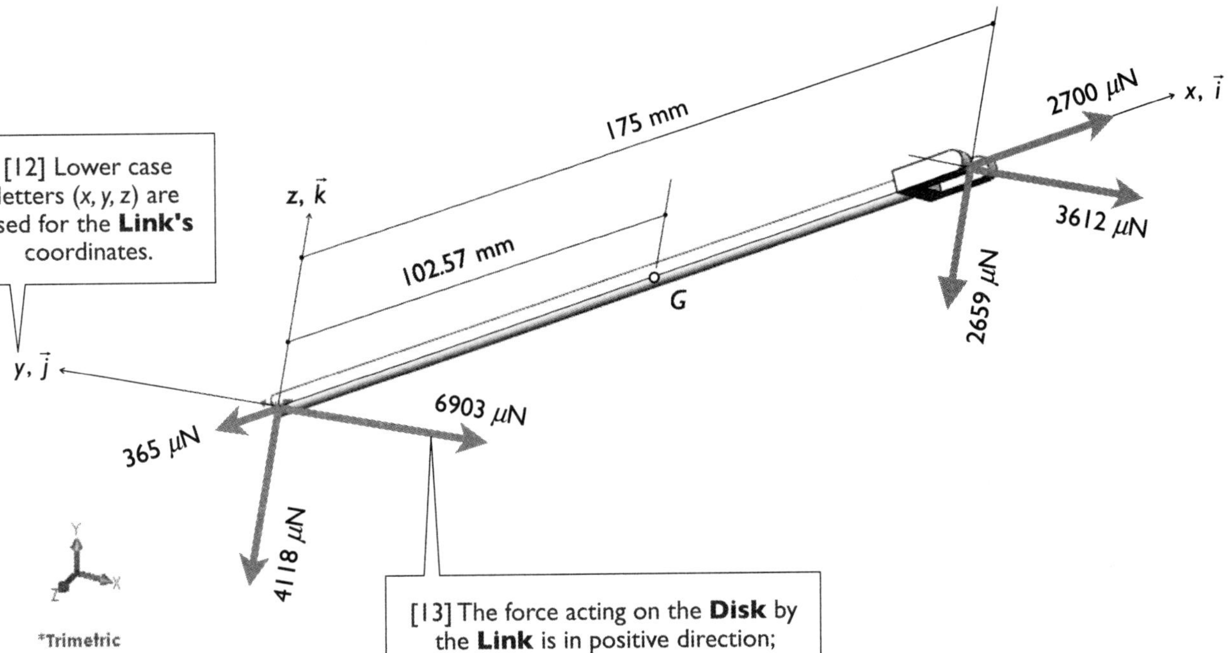

[12] Lower case letters (*x, y, z*) are used for the **Link's** coordinates.

[13] The force acting on the **Disk** by the **Link** is in positive direction; therefore, the force acting on the **Link** by the **Disk** is in negative direction.

[11] The **Assembly's** coordinate system.

[14] The resultant force and moment (about *G*) are calculated as follows:

$$\vec{F}^{link/disk} = -365\ \vec{i} - 6903\ \vec{j} - 4118\ \vec{k}\ (\mu\text{N})$$

$$\vec{F}^{link/collar} = 2700\ \vec{i} - 3612\ \vec{j} - 2659\ \vec{k}\ (\mu\text{N})$$

$$\sum \vec{F} = \vec{F}^{link/disk} + \vec{F}^{link/collar} = 2335\ \vec{i} - 10515\ \vec{j} - 6777\ \vec{k}\ (\mu\text{N}) \quad (1)$$

$$\vec{r}^{disk/G} = -102.57\ \vec{i}\ (\text{mm})$$

$$\vec{r}^{collar/G} = (175 - 102.57)\ \vec{i} = 72.42\ \vec{i}\ (\text{mm})$$

$$\sum \vec{M}_G = \vec{r}^{disk/G} \times \vec{F}^{link/disk} + \vec{r}^{collar/G} \times \vec{F}^{link/collar} = -229820\ \vec{j} + 446460\ \vec{k}\ (\mu\text{N-mm}) \quad (2)$$

#

10.1-6 Effective Force on the **Link**

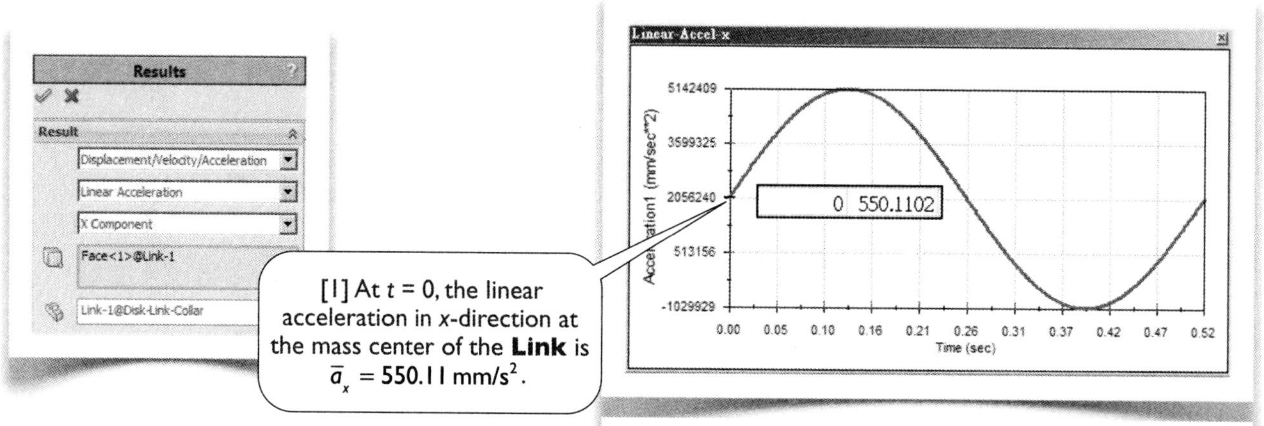

[1] At t = 0, the linear acceleration in x-direction at the mass center of the **Link** is $\bar{a}_x = 550.11$ mm/s^2.

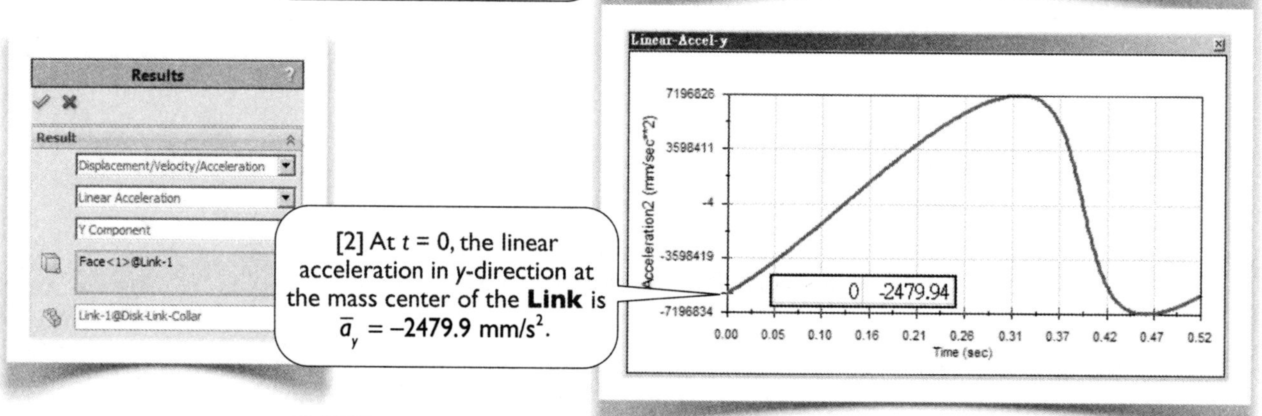

[2] At t = 0, the linear acceleration in y-direction at the mass center of the **Link** is $\bar{a}_y = -2479.9$ mm/s^2.

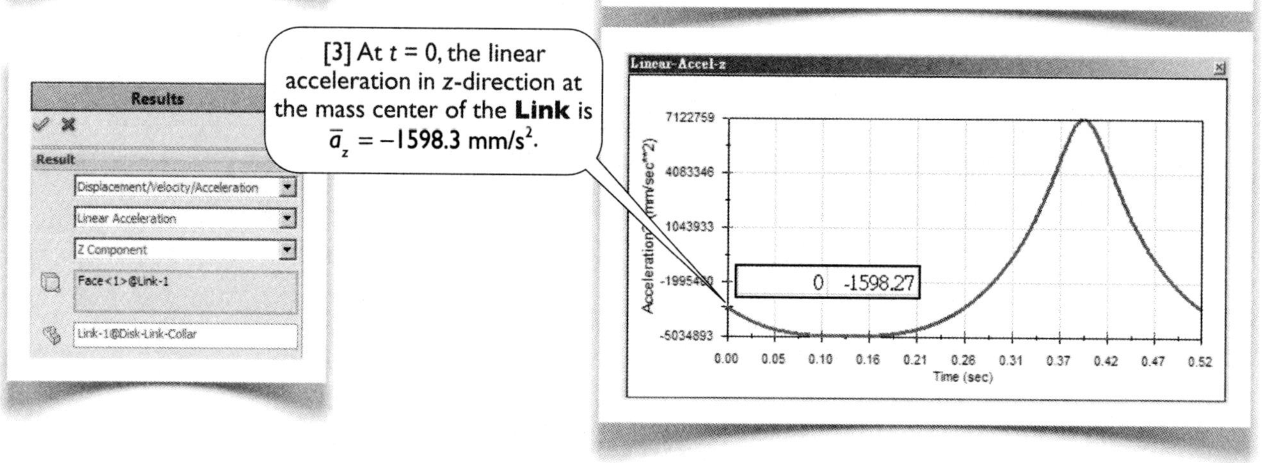

[3] At t = 0, the linear acceleration in z-direction at the mass center of the **Link** is $\bar{a}_z = -1598.3$ mm/s^2.

[4] The effective force on the **Link** are calculated as follows.

$$\vec{\bar{a}} = 550.11\,\vec{i} - 2479.9\,\vec{j} - 1598.3\,\vec{k}\ (\text{mm/s}^2)$$

$$m = 4.2398 \text{ g} \quad (\text{see 10.1-3[3], page 190})$$

$$m\vec{\bar{a}} = 2332\,\vec{i} - 10514\,\vec{j} - 6776\,\vec{k}\ (\mu\text{N}) \qquad (1)$$

Comparing Eq. (1) with Eq. 10.1-5(1) (page 193), we conclude that Eq. 10.1-1(1) (page 188) is indeed satisfied. #

10.1-7 Angular Momentum of the **Link**

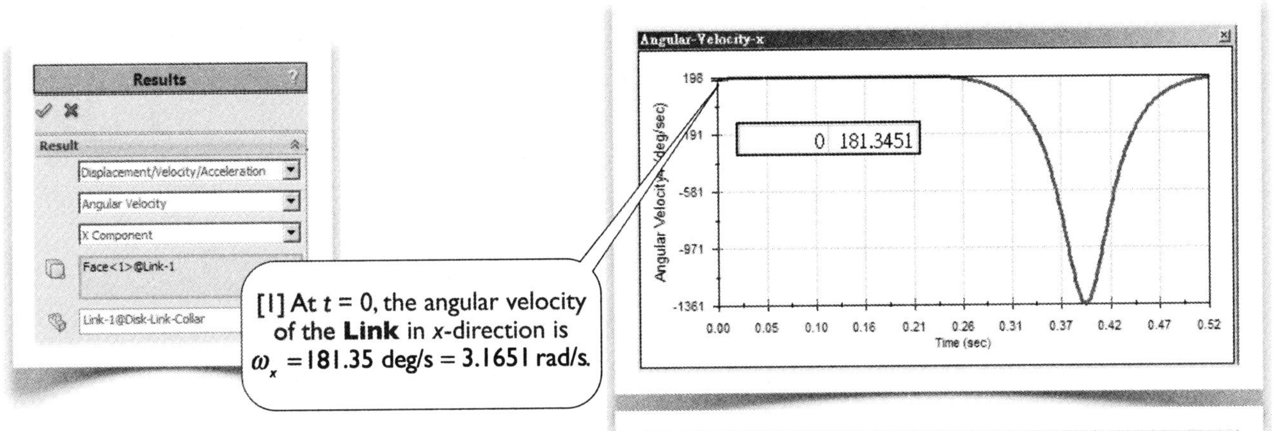

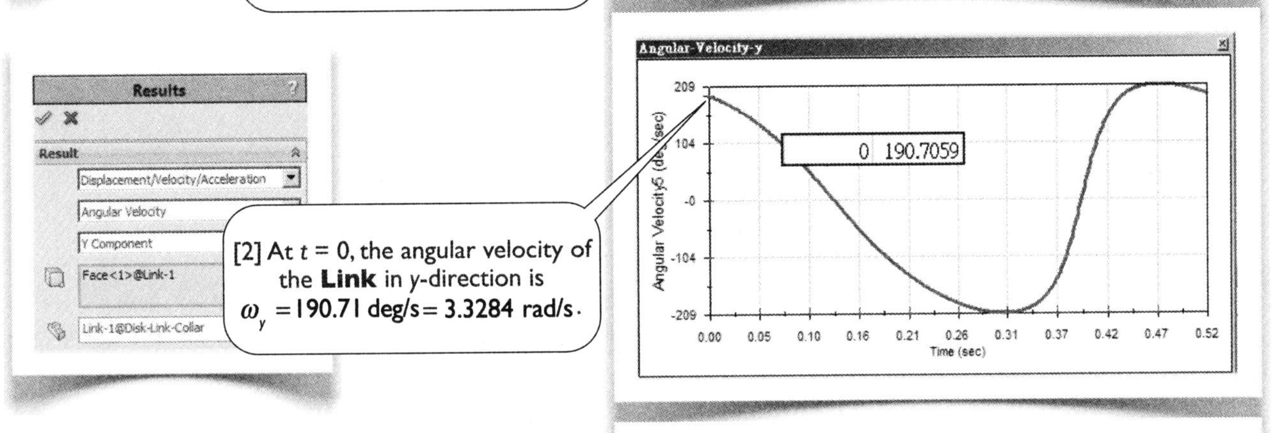

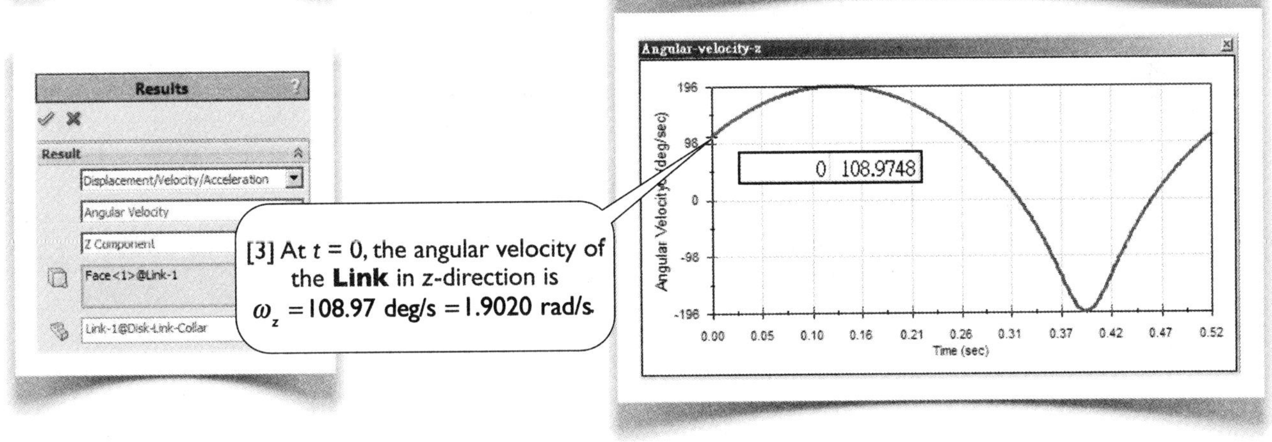

[4] The angular momentum about the mass center G can be calculated according to Eq. 10.1-1(6), page 189:

$$\vec{\omega} = 3.1651\,\vec{i} + 3.3284\,\vec{j} + 1.9020\,\vec{k} \text{ (rad/s)}$$

$$\bar{I}_x = 63.614 \text{ g-mm}^2,\ \bar{I}_y = 12914 \text{ g-mm}^2,\ \bar{I}_z = 12964 \text{ g-mm}^2. \text{ (see 10.1-3[6], page 190)}$$

$$\vec{H}_G = \bar{I}_x\omega_x\vec{i} + \bar{I}_y\omega_y\vec{j} + \bar{I}_z\omega_z\vec{k} = 201.34\,\vec{i} + 42983\,\vec{j} + 24658\,\vec{k} \ (\mu\text{N-mm-s}) \qquad (1)$$

The angular momentum $\vec{H}_G$ actually can be reported by **SolidWorks Motion** (see [5-8], next page).

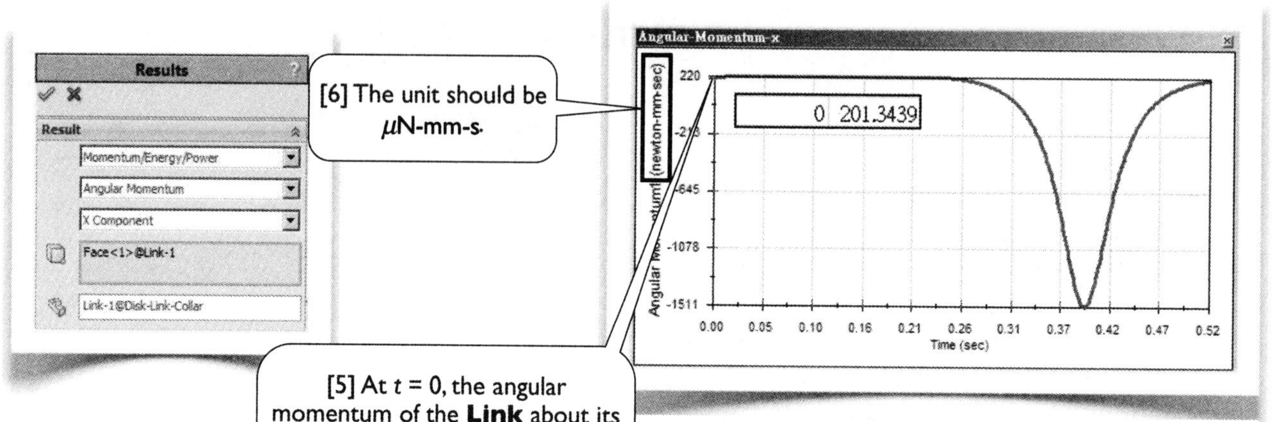

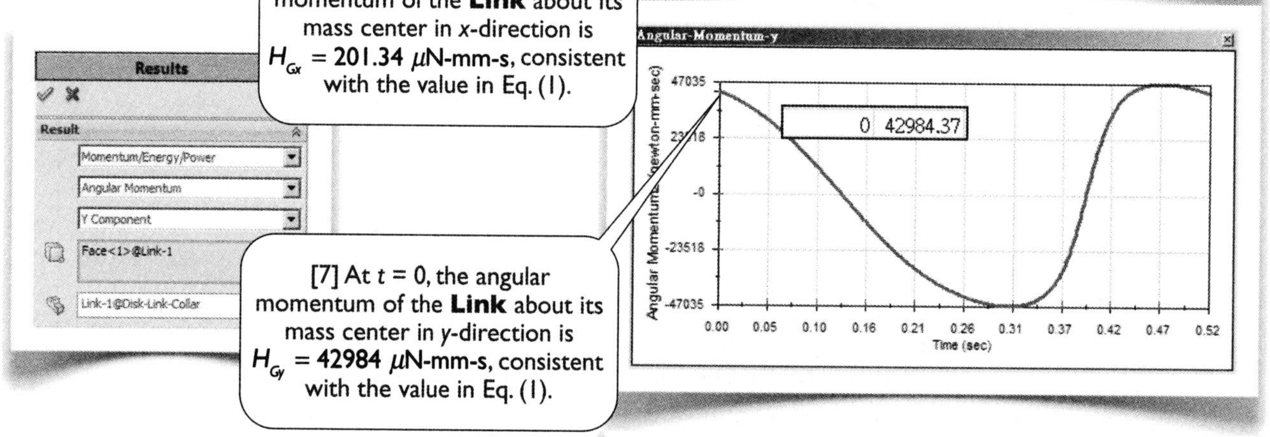

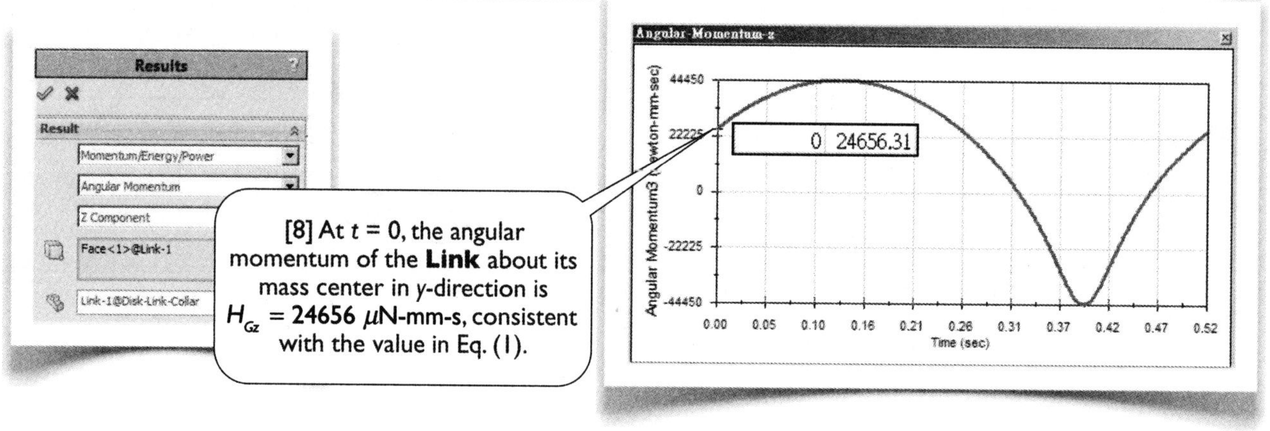

[9] The quantity $\vec{\omega} \times \vec{H}_G$ (Eq. 10.1-1(8), page 189) is calculated as follows:

$$\vec{\omega} = 3.1651\,\vec{i} + 3.3284\,\vec{j} + 1.9020\,\vec{k} \text{ (rad/s)}$$

$$\vec{H}_G = 201.34\,\vec{i} + 42984\,\vec{j} + 24656\,\vec{k} \text{ (μN-mm-s) (see [5-8])}$$

$$\vec{\omega} \times \vec{H}_G = 309.46\,\vec{i} - 77656\,\vec{j} + 135379\,\vec{k} \text{ (μN-mm)} \quad (2)$$

#

10.1-8 Rate of Change of Angular Momentum $(\dot{\vec{H}}_G)_{xyz}$

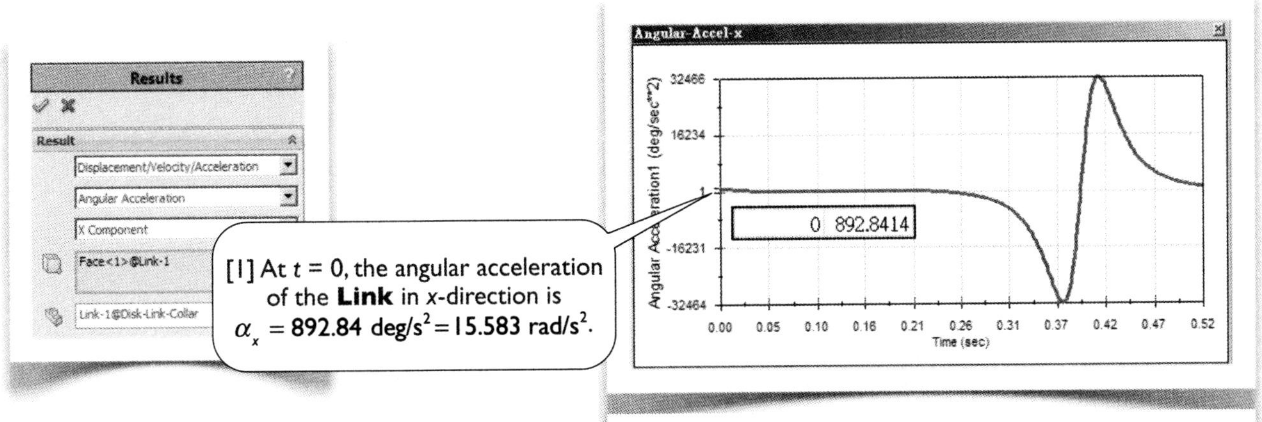

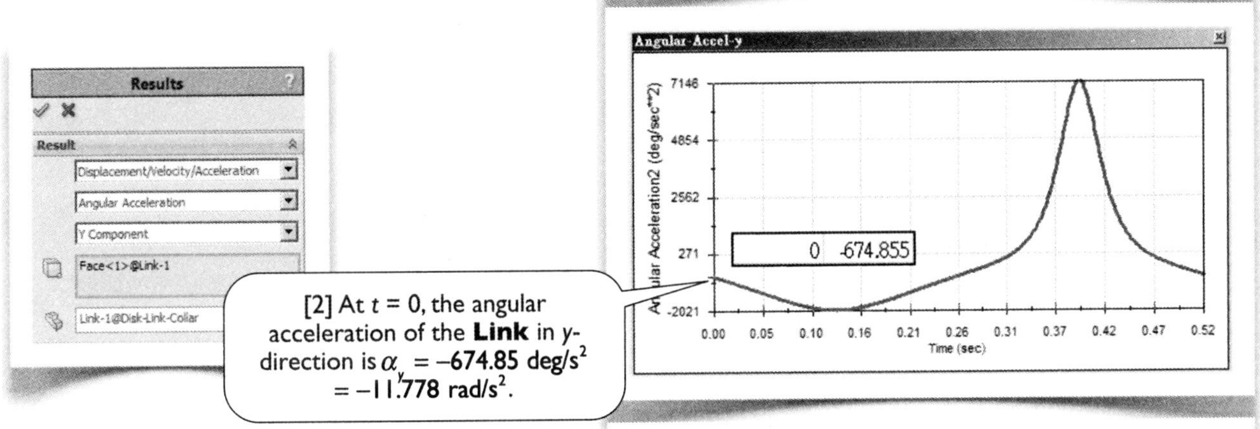

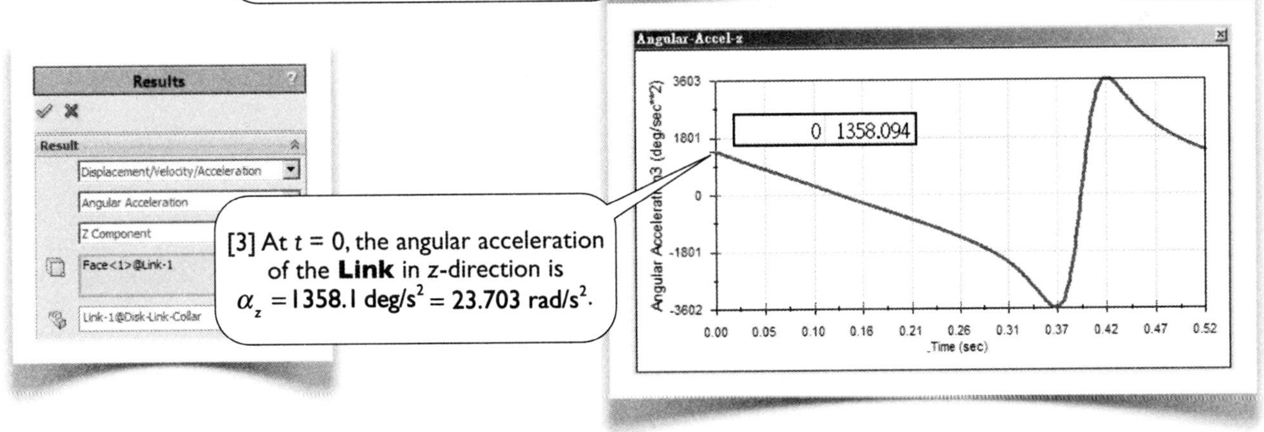

[4] The rate of change of angular momentum observed in xyz frame, $(\dot{\vec{H}}_G)_{xyz}$, according to Eq. 10.1-1(7) (page 189),

$$\vec{\alpha} = 15.583\,\vec{i} - 11.778\,\vec{j} + 23.703\,\vec{k}\ (\text{rad/s}^2)$$

$$\bar{I}_x = 63.614\ \text{g-mm}^2,\ \bar{I}_y = 12914\ \text{g-mm}^2,\ \bar{I}_z = 12964\ \text{g-mm}^2.\ \text{(see 10.1-3[6], page 190)}$$

$$(\dot{\vec{H}}_G)_{xyz} = \bar{I}_x\alpha_x\vec{i} + \bar{I}_y\alpha_y\vec{j} + \bar{I}_z\alpha_z\vec{k} = 991.30\,\vec{i} - 152101\,\vec{j} + 307286\,\vec{k}\ (\mu\text{N-mm}) \qquad (1)$$

#

10.1-9 Effective Moment on the **Link**

[1] The right-hand side of Eq. 10.1-1(5), page 188, is

$$\begin{aligned}(\dot{\vec{H}}_G)_{xyz} + \vec{\omega}\times\vec{H}_G &= (991.30\,\vec{i} - 152101\,\vec{j} + 307286\,\vec{k}) + (309.46\,\vec{i} - 77656\,\vec{j} + 135379\,\vec{k}) \\ &= 1300.8\,\vec{i} - 229757\,\vec{j} + 442665\,\vec{k}\ (\mu\text{N-mm})\end{aligned} \tag{1}$$

Comparing Eq. (1) with Eq. 10.1-5(2) (page 193), we conclude that Eq. 10.1-1(5), page 188, is indeed satisfied.

[2] Wrap Up

Save all files and exit **SolidWorks**. #

Section 10.2

Unbalanced Shaft

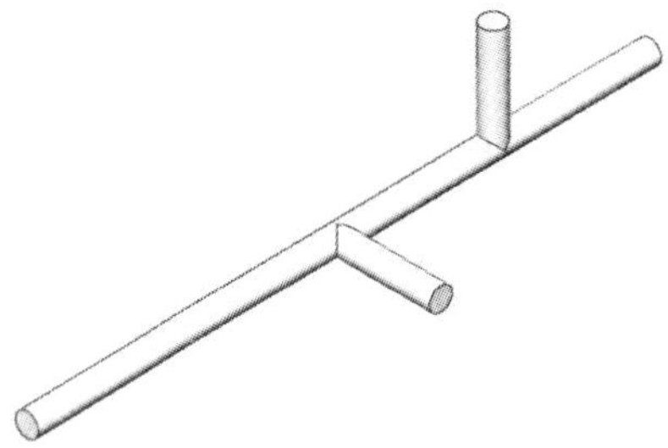

10.2-1 Introduction

[1] As mentioned in page 187, Newton's 2nd Law for a rigid body in general 3D motion can be expressed in the following form:

$$\sum \vec{F} = m\vec{\bar{a}} \tag{1}$$

$$\sum \vec{M}_O = \dot{\vec{H}}_O \tag{2}$$

where O is a fixed point in the space. It is usually more convenient to observe it in a moving frame xyz which is attached to the body. It can be proved that

$$\dot{\vec{H}}_O = (\dot{\vec{H}}_O)_{xyz} + \vec{\omega} \times \vec{H}_O \tag{3}$$

where

$(\dot{\vec{H}}_O)_{xyz}$ is the rate of change of angular momentum of the body about the fixed point O, observed in the frame xyz, which is attached to the body.

$\vec{\omega}$ is the angular velocity of the body.

$\vec{H}_O$ is the angular momentum of the body about the fixed point O, which can be calculated by

$$\vec{H}_O = \begin{pmatrix} I_x & -I_{xy} & -I_{xz} \\ -I_{yx} & I_y & -I_{yz} \\ -I_{zx} & -I_{zy} & I_z \end{pmatrix} \begin{pmatrix} \omega_x \\ \omega_y \\ \omega_z \end{pmatrix} \tag{4}$$

where the moments/products of inertia are calculated at the point O. Also note that the products of moments are symmetric; i.e., $I_{xy} = I_{yx}, I_{yz} = I_{zy}, I_{zx} = I_{xz}$. Eq. (2) then can be written as

$$\sum \vec{M}_O = (\dot{\vec{H}}_O)_{xyz} + \vec{\omega} \times \vec{H}_O \tag{5}$$

Eqs. (1, 5) are useful when applying to a rigid body rotating about a fixed point O or about a fixed axis passing through the point O. In particular, consider a **Shaft** rotating about a fixed Z-axes [2-6] (next page) with an angular velocity $\vec{\omega} = \omega\vec{k}$ and an angular acceleration $\vec{\alpha} = \alpha\vec{k}$. In this case, Eq. (4) reduces to

$$\vec{H}_O = -I_{xz}\omega\vec{i} - I_{yz}\omega\vec{j} + I_z\omega\vec{k} \tag{6}$$

where $\vec{i}$, $\vec{j}$, $\vec{k}$ are unit vectors in x-, y-, z-direction respectively. Eq. (5) then reduces to

$$\begin{aligned} \sum \vec{M}_O &= (\dot{\vec{H}}_O)_{xyz} + \vec{\omega} \times \vec{H}_O \\ &= (-I_{xz}\alpha\vec{i} - I_{yz}\alpha\vec{j} + I_z\alpha\vec{k}) + (\omega\vec{k}) \times (-I_{xz}\omega\vec{i} - I_{yz}\omega\vec{j} + I_z\omega\vec{k}) \\ &= (-I_{xz}\alpha + I_{yz}\omega^2)\vec{i} + (-I_{yz}\alpha - I_{xz}\omega^2)\vec{j} + (I_z\alpha)\vec{k} \end{aligned} \tag{7}$$

In this section, we'll show how these equations apply to the **Shaft** when it reaches an angular velocity of 1200 rpm.

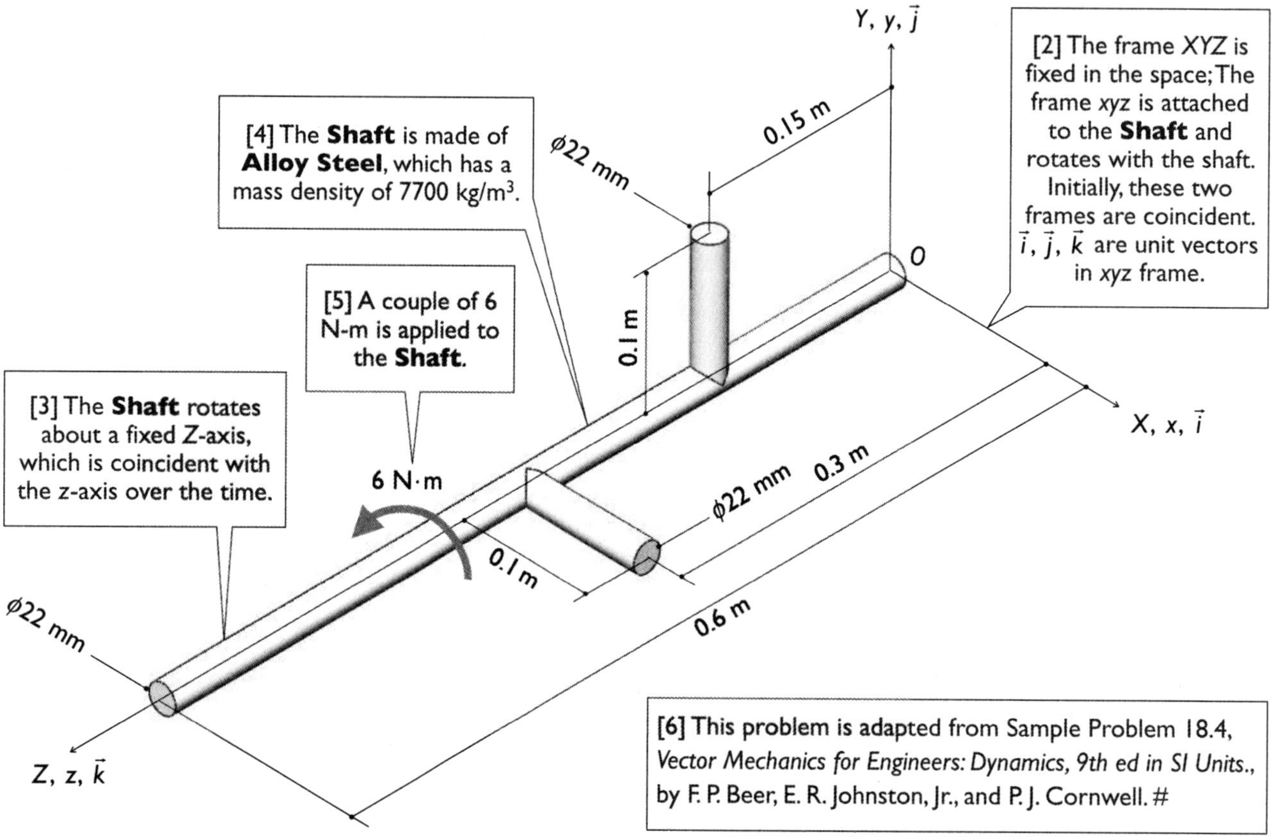

10.2-2 Start Up and Create a Part: **Shaft**

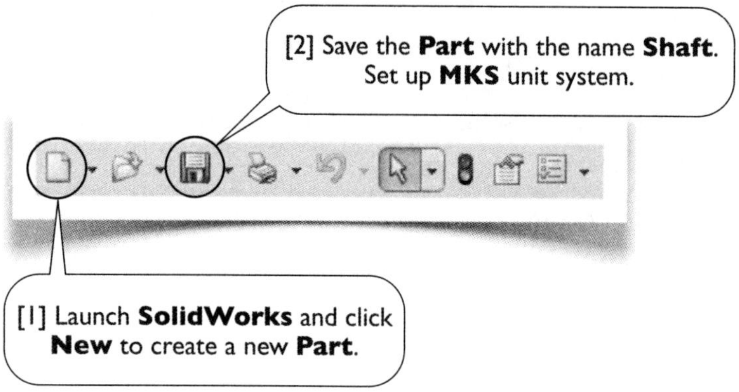

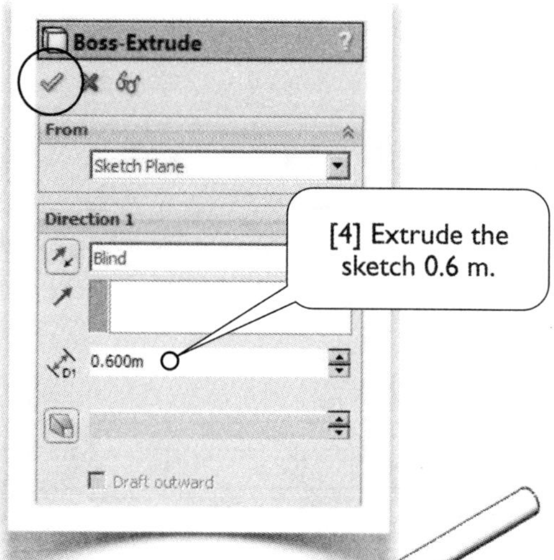

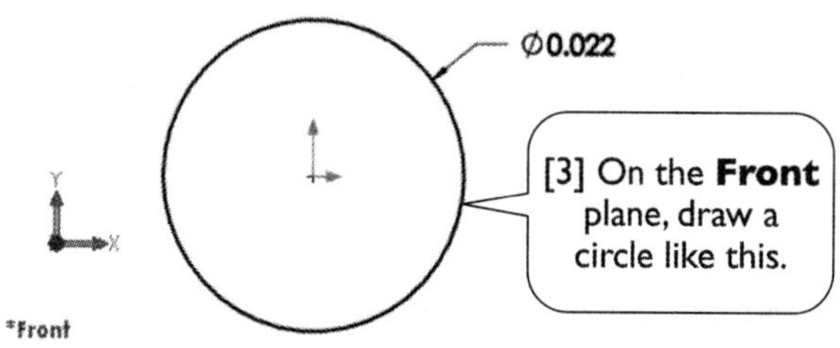

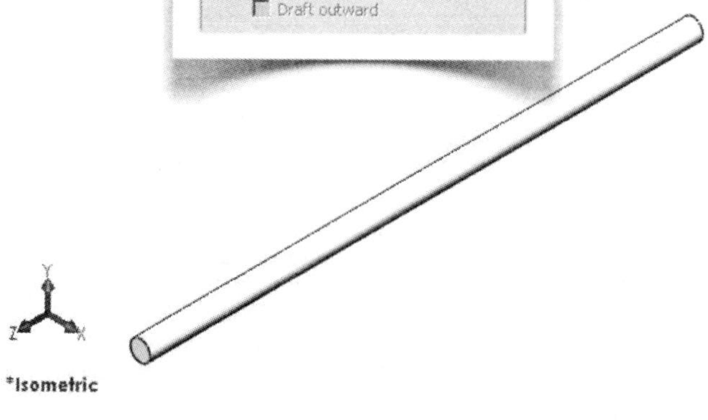

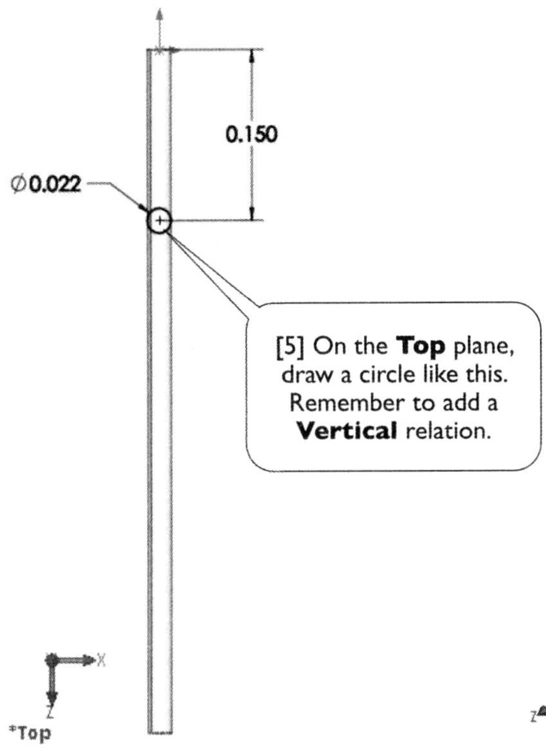
0.150
∅0.022
[5] On the **Top** plane, draw a circle like this. Remember to add a **Vertical** relation.
*Top

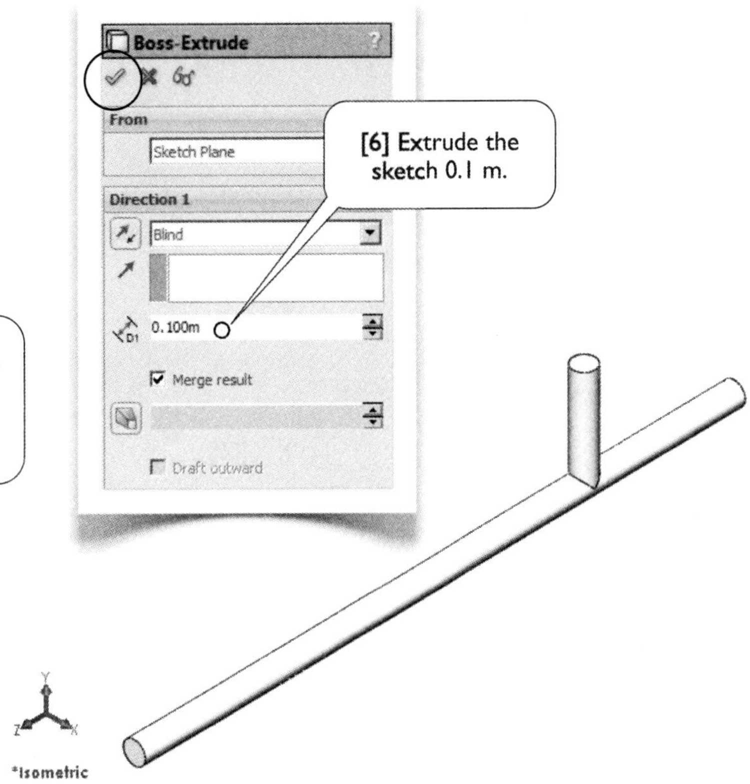
Boss-Extrude
From
Sketch Plane
Direction 1
Blind
0.100m
Merge result
Draft outward
[6] Extrude the sketch 0.1 m.
*Isometric

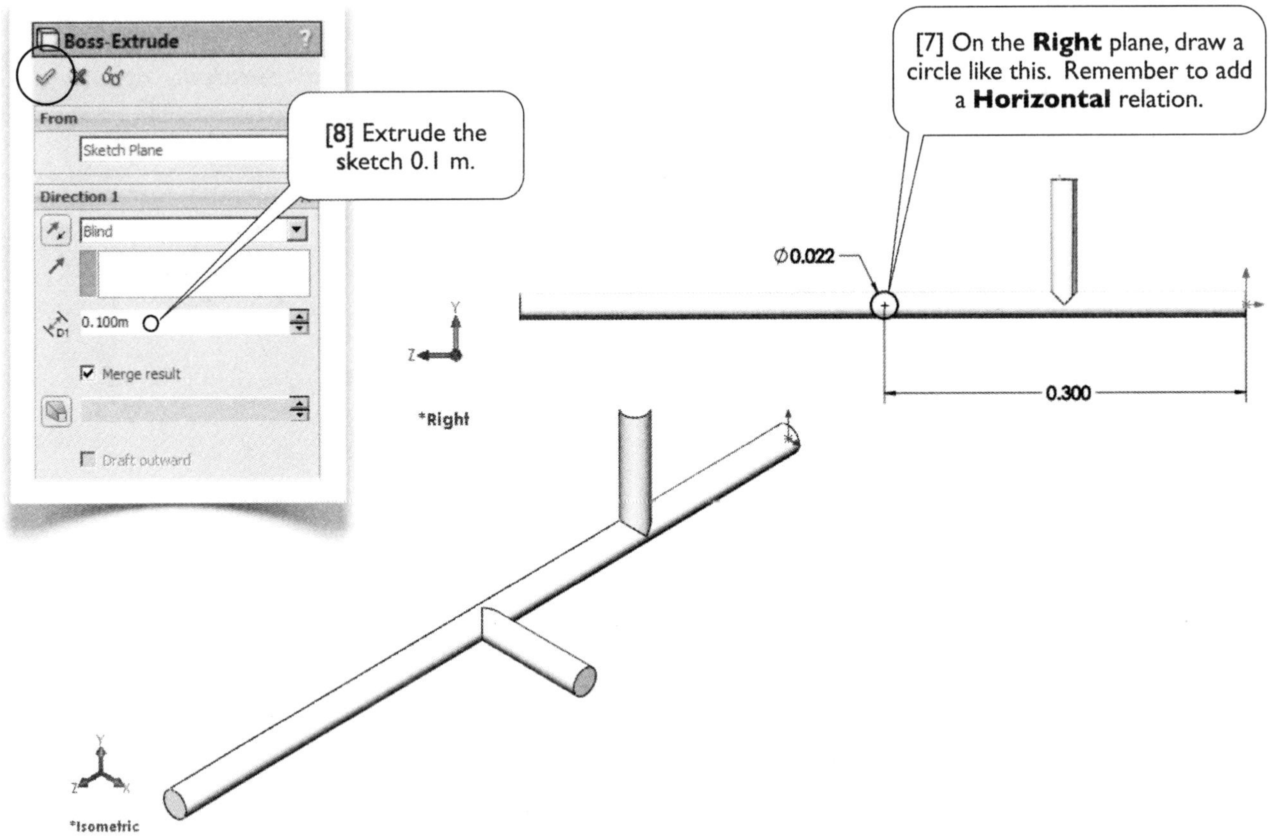
Boss-Extrude
From
Sketch Plane
Direction 1
Blind
0.100m
Merge result
Draft outward
[8] Extrude the sketch 0.1 m.
[7] On the **Right** plane, draw a circle like this. Remember to add a **Horizontal** relation.
∅0.022
0.300
*Right
*Isometric

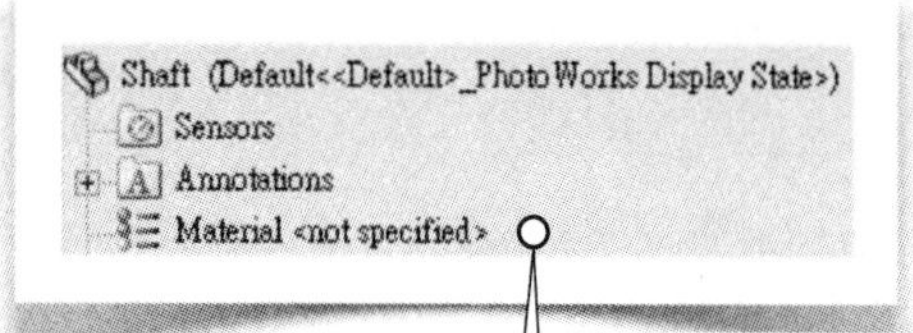

[9] In the **Part Tree**, right-click **Material** and select **Edit Material**.

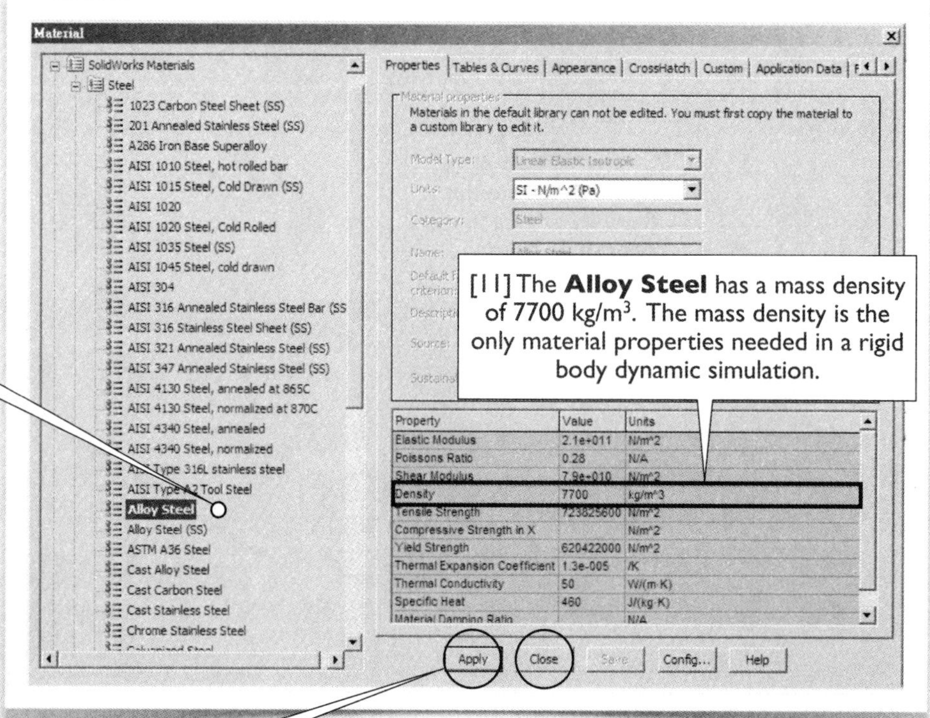

[10] Select **Alloy Steel**, which is under the **Steel** category.

[11] The **Alloy Steel** has a mass density of 7700 kg/m^3. The mass density is the only material properties needed in a rigid body dynamic simulation.

[12] Click **Apply**, and then click **Close**.

[13] In the **Evaluate Toolbar**, click **Mass Properties**.

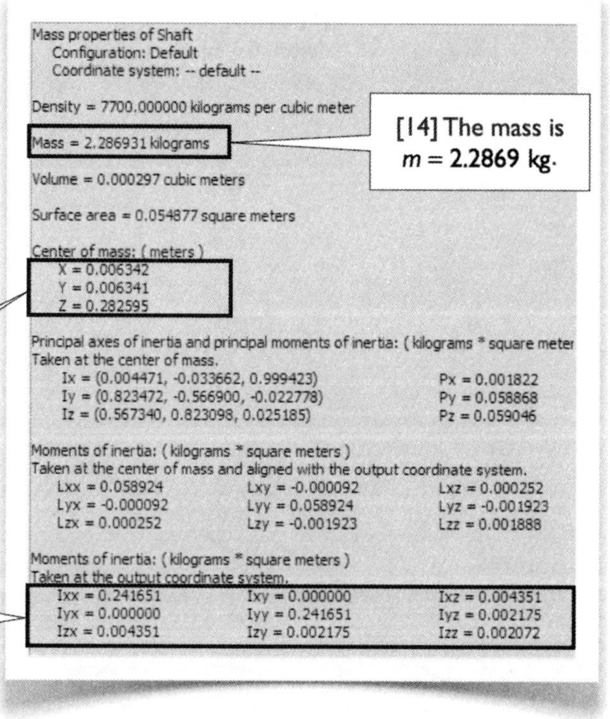

[14] The mass is $m = 2.2869$ kg.

[15] The mass center is not on the z-axis. It is this eccentricity that generates reaction forces at bearings.

[16] These are the moments of inertia and products of inertia taken at the **Shaft's Origin** and aligned with its coordinate system. #

10.2-3 Create an Assembly: **Rotating-Shaft**

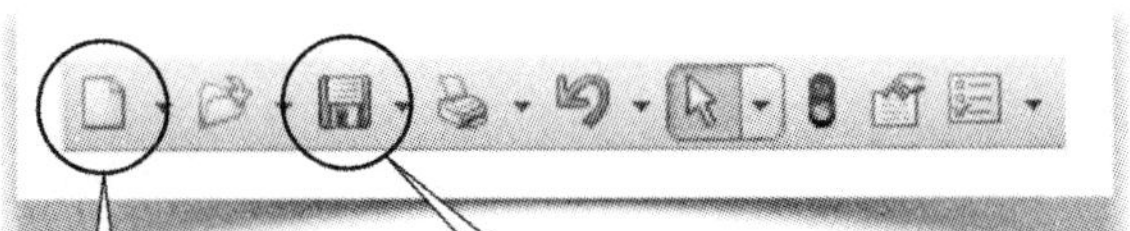

[1] Click **New** and create an **Assembly**.

[2] Turn on **View Origins** and, in the **Begin Assembly Property Box**, select **Shaft** and click the **Origin** of the **Assembly**.

[3] Save the **Assembly** with the name **Rotating-Shaft**. Set up **MKS** unit system.

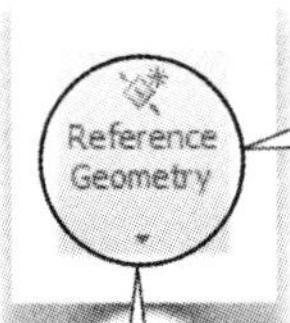

[4] In **Assembly Toolbar**, select **Reference Geometry>Plane.**

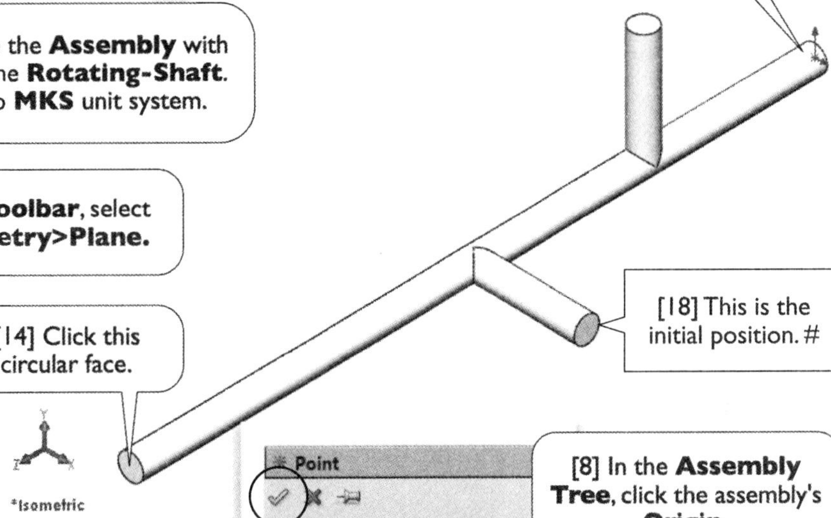

[14] Click this circular face.

[18] This is the initial position. #

[7] Select **Reference Geometry>Point.**

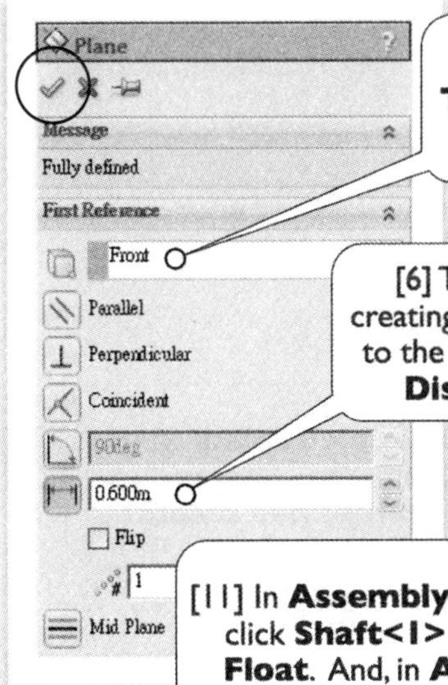

[5] In the **Assembly Tree**, click the assembly's **Front** plane.

[6] Type 0.6 m. We're creating a new plane parallel to the **Front** plane with a **Distance** of 0.6 m.

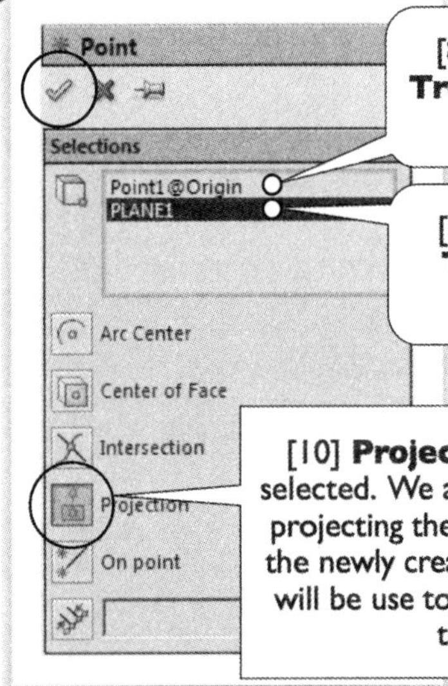

[8] In the **Assembly Tree**, click the assembly's **Origin**.

[9] In the **Assembly Tree**, click the newly created plane.

[10] **Projection** is automatically selected. We are creating a **Point** by projecting the assembly's **Origin** to the newly created plane. This **Point** will be use to **Mate** with an end of the **Shaft**.

[11] In **Assembly Tree**, right-click **Shaft<1>** and select **Float**. And, in **Assembly Toolbar**, click **Mate**. We'll create these 3 **Mates** [12-17].

[12] The **Shaft's** and the assembly's **Origin** are **Coincident**. Before clicking **OK**, uncheck **Align axes** (see 9.1-6[21], page 174)

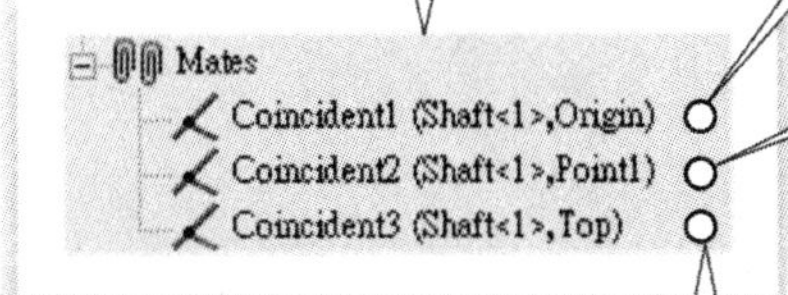

[13] A **Shaft's** circular end face (see [14]) and **Point1** (created in [7-10]) are **Coincident**.

[15] Now, use you mouse to rotate the **Shaft**.

[16] The **Shaft's** and the assembly's **Top** planes are coincident. Click **Aligned** if the initial position is not correct (see [17]). We'll suppress this **Mate** later.

[17] Click **Aligned** if the initial position [18] is not correct.

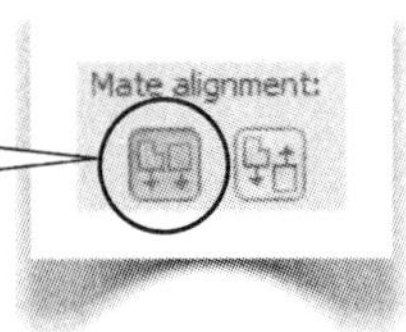

10.2-4 Create **Motion Study**, Set Up **Torque**, and Run the Simulation

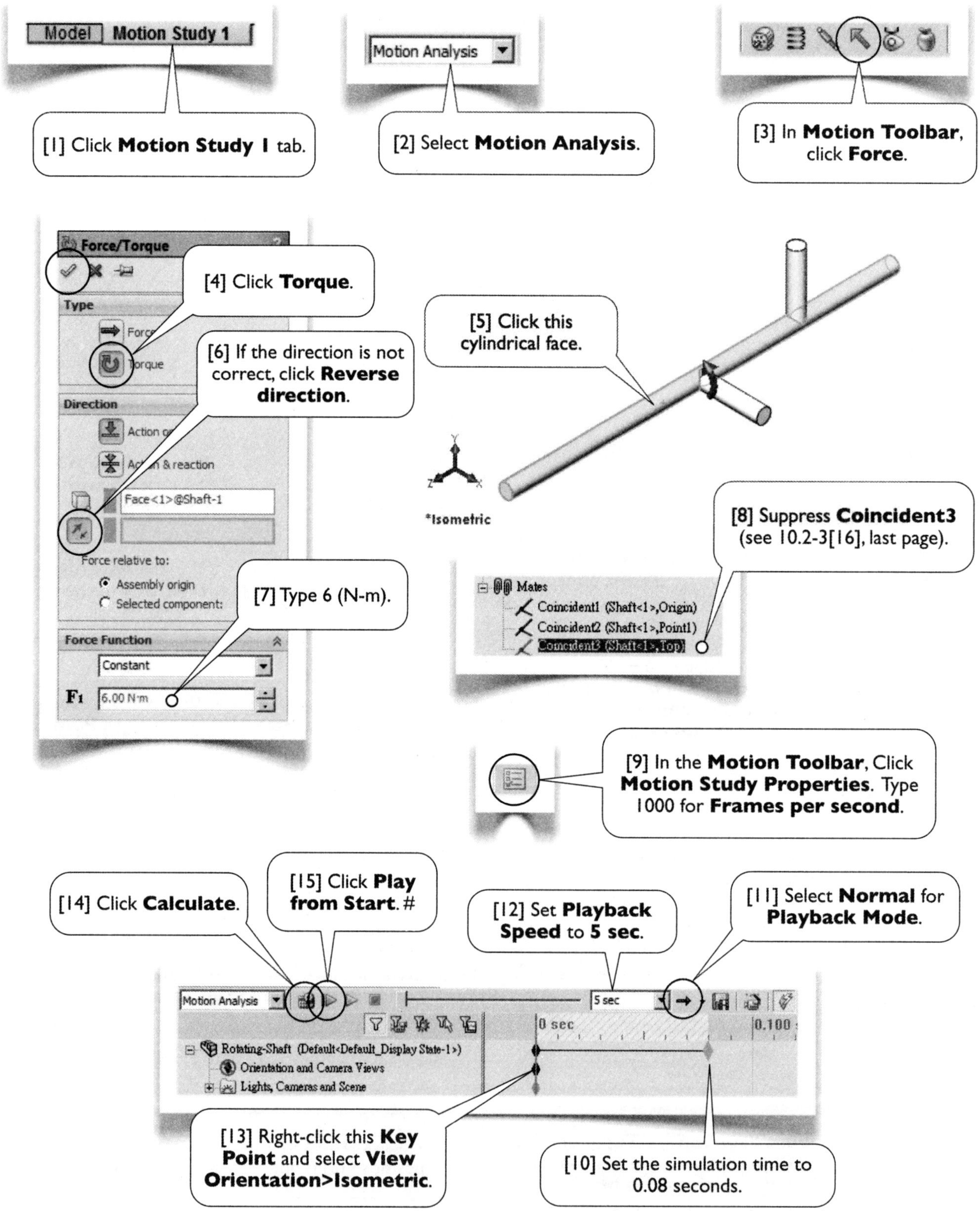

10.2-5 Angular Velocity

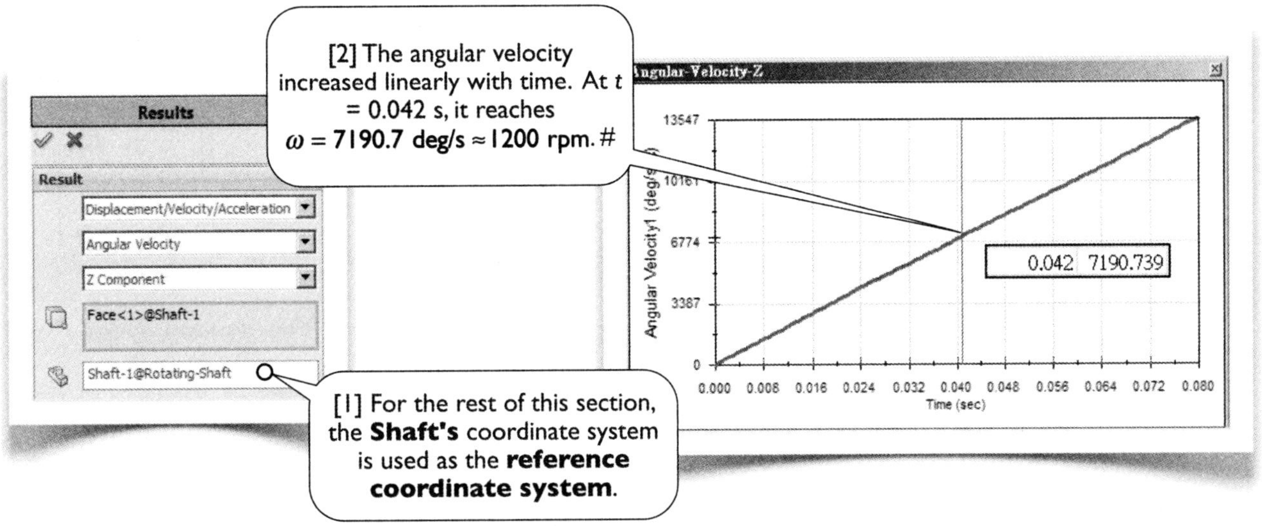

10.2-6 Reaction Forces

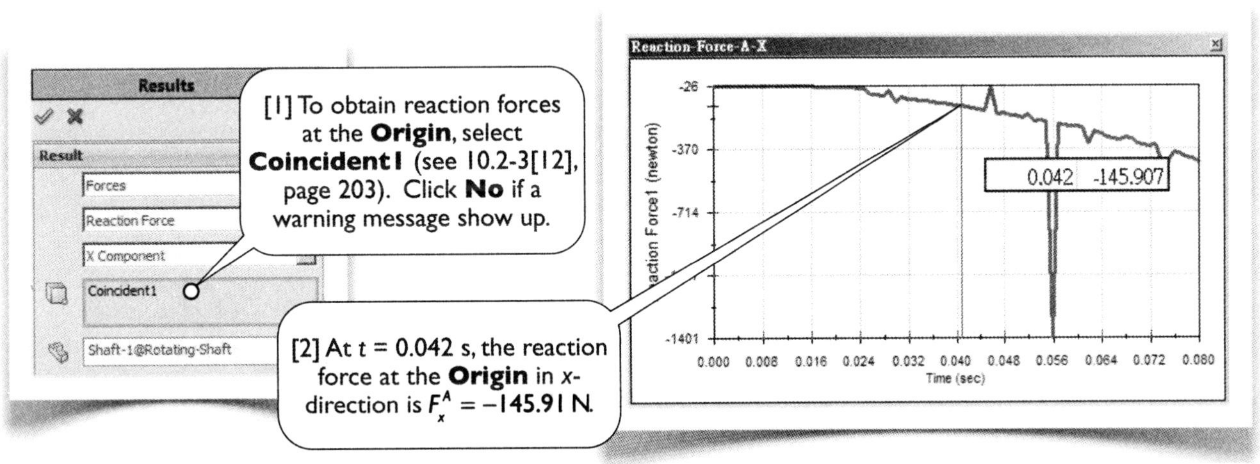

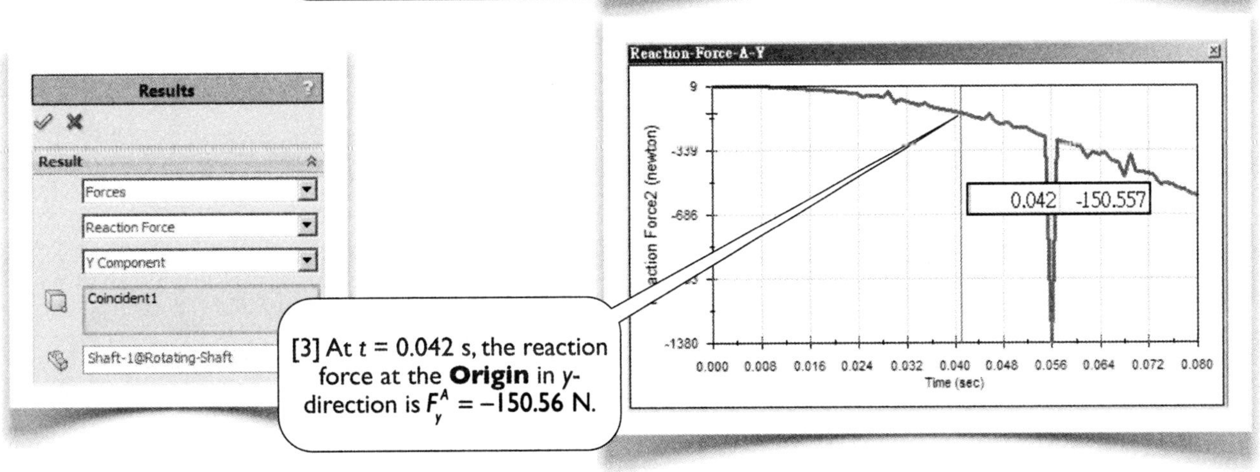

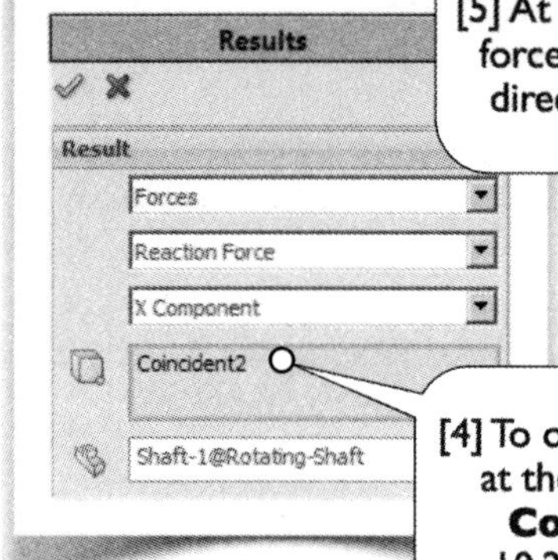

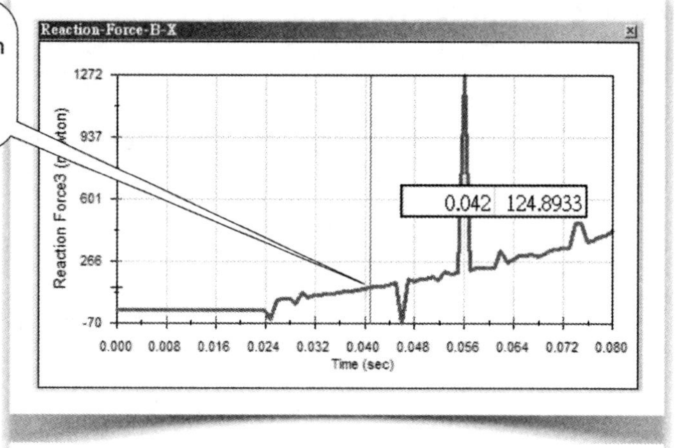

[5] At t = 0.042 s, the reaction force at the other end in x-direction is $F_x^B = 124.89$ N.

[4] To obtain reaction forces at the other end, select **Coincident2** (see 10.2-3[13], page 203).

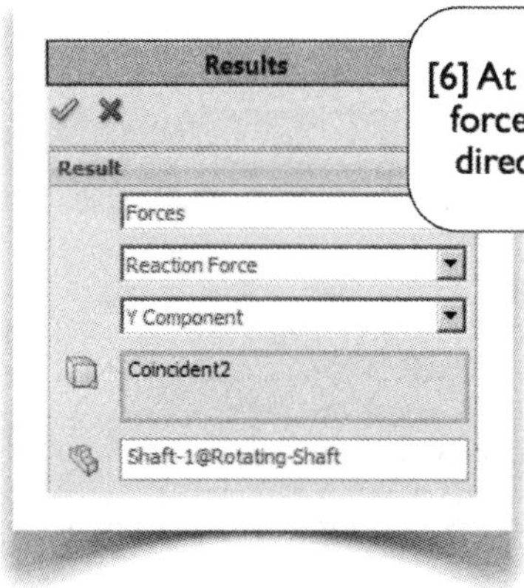

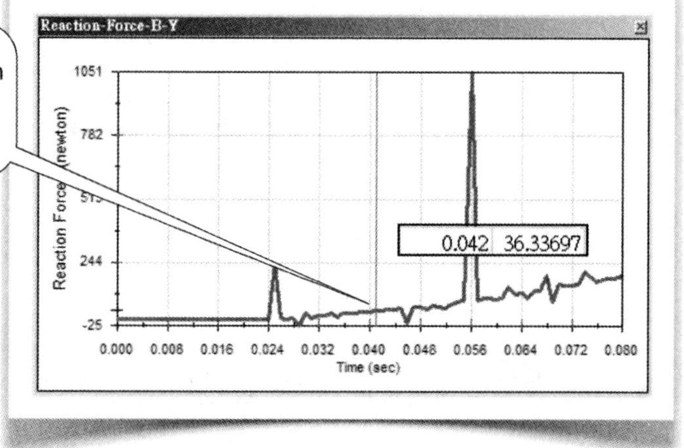

[6] At t = 0.042 s, the reaction force at the other end in y-direction is $F_y^B = 36.337$ N.

[9] The resultant force are calculated as follows:

$$\vec{F}^A = -145.91\,\vec{i} - 150.56\,\vec{j}\ \text{(N)}$$

$$\vec{F}^B = -124.89\,\vec{i} - 36.337\,\vec{j}\ \text{(N)}$$

$$\sum \vec{F} = \vec{F}^A + \vec{F}^B = -270.80\,\vec{i} - 186.90\,\vec{j}\ \text{(N)} \qquad (1)$$

[7] This is the fixed frame XYZ.

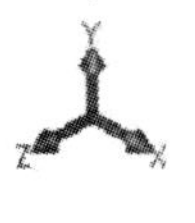

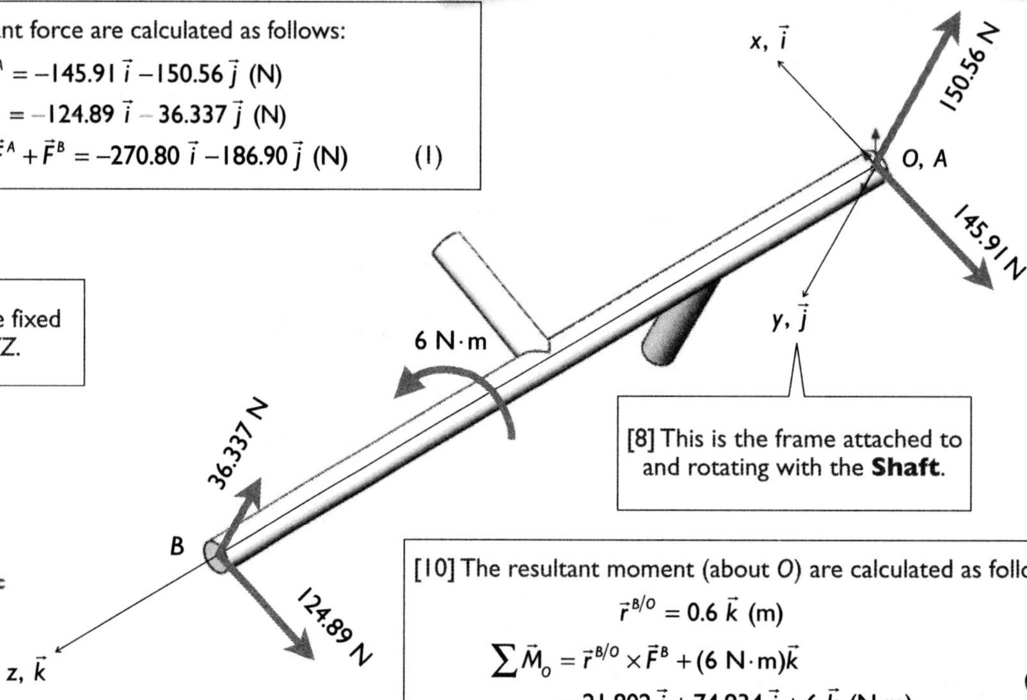

[8] This is the frame attached to and rotating with the **Shaft**.

[10] The resultant moment (about O) are calculated as follows:

$$\vec{r}^{B/O} = 0.6\,\vec{k}\ \text{(m)}$$

$$\sum \vec{M}_O = \vec{r}^{B/O} \times \vec{F}^B + (6\ \text{N}\cdot\text{m})\vec{k} = 21.802\,\vec{j} + 74.934\,\vec{j} + 6\,\vec{k}\ \text{(N-m)} \qquad (2)$$

#

10.2-7 Effect Forces

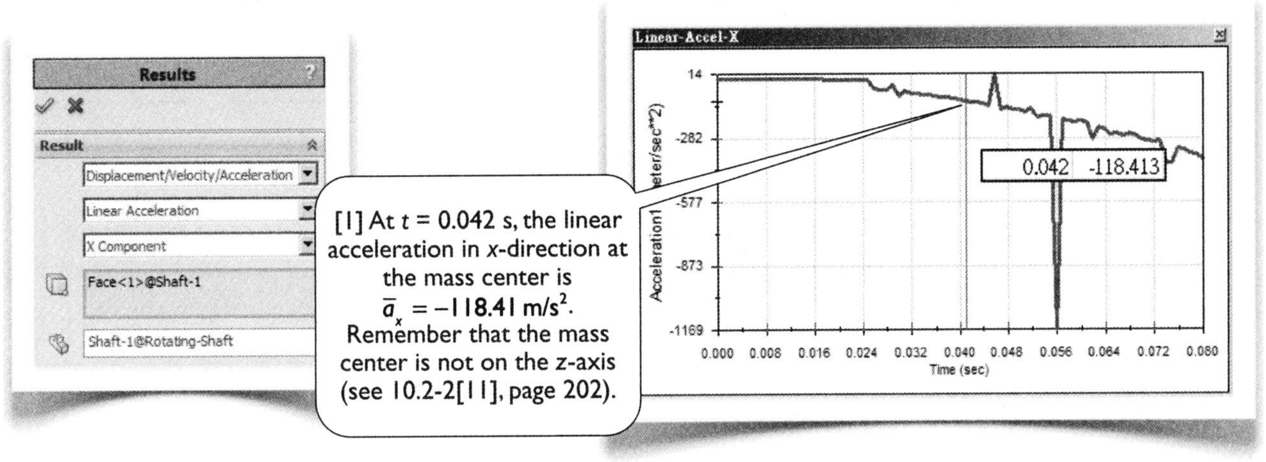

[1] At t = 0.042 s, the linear acceleration in x-direction at the mass center is $\bar{a}_x = -118.41$ m/s^2. Remember that the mass center is not on the z-axis (see 10.2-2[11], page 202).

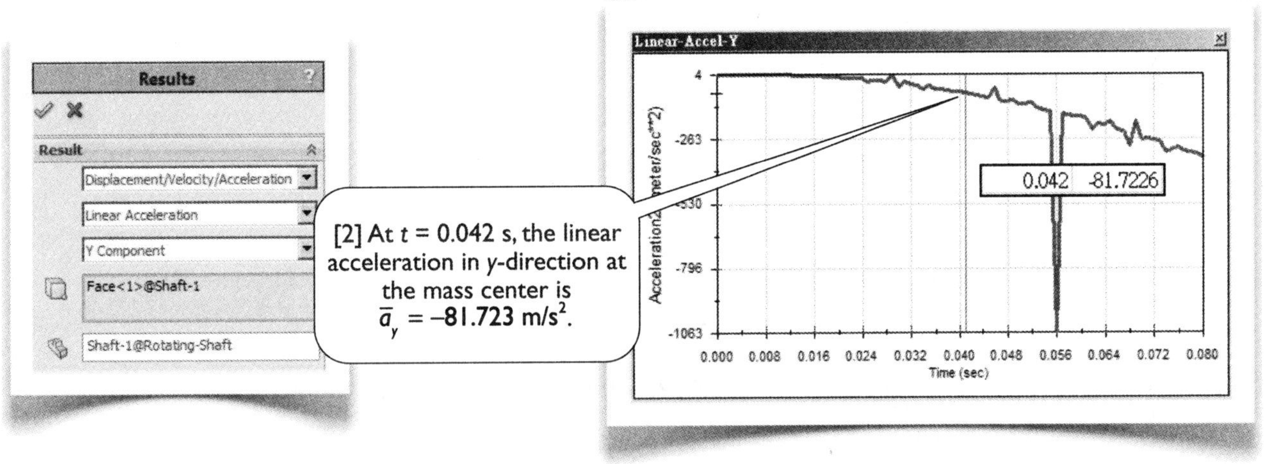

[2] At t = 0.042 s, the linear acceleration in y-direction at the mass center is $\bar{a}_y = -81.723$ m/s^2.

[3] The effective force on the **Shaft** are calculated as follows.

$$\vec{\bar{a}} = -118.41\,\vec{i} - 81.723\,\vec{j} \ \ (\text{m/s}^2)$$

$$m = 2.2869 \text{ kg} \quad (\text{see } 10.2\text{-}2[10], \text{page } 202)$$

$$m\vec{\bar{a}} = -270.79\,\vec{i} - 186.89\,\vec{j} \ \ (\text{N}) \qquad (1)$$

Comparing Eq. (1) with Eq. 10.2-6(1) (last page), we conclude that Eq. 10.2-1(1) (page 199) is indeed satisfied. #

10.2-8 Effect Moments

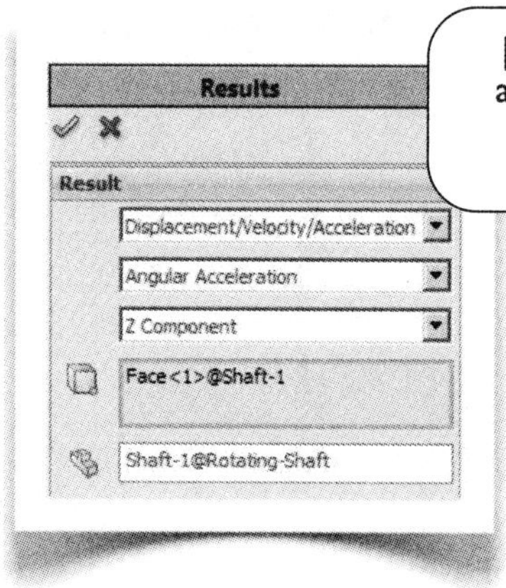

[1] At t = 0.042 s, the angular acceleration is $\alpha = 165918$ deg/s^2 = 2895.8 rad/s^2

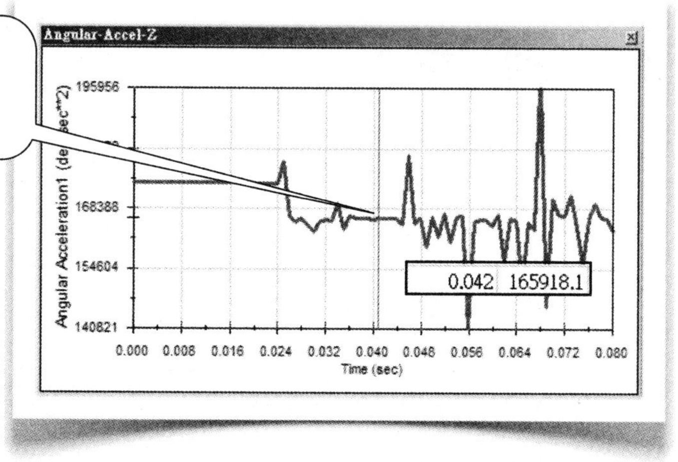

[2] The right-hand-side of Eq. 10.2-1(7) (page 199) is calculated as follows:

$$\omega = 7190.7 \text{ deg/s} = 125.5 \text{ rad/s (see 10.2-5[2], page 205)}$$

$$\alpha = 2895.8 \text{ rad/s}^2 \text{ (see[1])}$$

$$I_z = 0.002072 \text{ kg}\cdot\text{m}^2,\ I_{xz} = 0.004351 \text{ kg}\cdot\text{m}^2,\ I_{yz} = 0.002175 \text{ kg}\cdot\text{m}^2. \text{ (see 10.2-2[16], page 202)}$$

$$-I_{xz}\alpha + I_{yz}\omega^2 = -0.004351(2895.8) + 0.002175(125.5)^2 = 21.66 \text{ (N}\cdot\text{m)}$$

$$-I_{yz}\alpha - I_{xz}\omega^2 = -0.002175(2895.8) - 0.004351(125.5)^2 = 74.83 \text{ (N}\cdot\text{m)}$$

$$I_z\alpha = 0.002072(2895.8) = 6.000 \text{ (N}\cdot\text{m)}$$

$$(\dot{\vec{H}}_O)_{xyz} + \vec{\omega} \times \vec{H}_O = 21.66\,\vec{i} + 74.83\,\vec{j} + 6.000\,\vec{k} \text{ (N-m)} \quad (1)$$

Comparing Eq. (1) with Eq. 10.2-6(2) (page 206), we conclude that Eq. 10.2-1(5), page 199, is indeed satisfied.

[3] Wrap Up

Save all files and exit **SolidWorks**. #

Section 10.3

Spinning Top

10.3-1 Introduction

[1] Precession is the slow motion of the axis of a spinning body due to a torque (caused by, for example, gravitational force) to change the direction of the axis. In this section, we'll simulate a **Top** spinning about an axis passing through a fixed point [2-5]. The **Trace Path** of the upper tip [6] will be drawn to observe the precession.

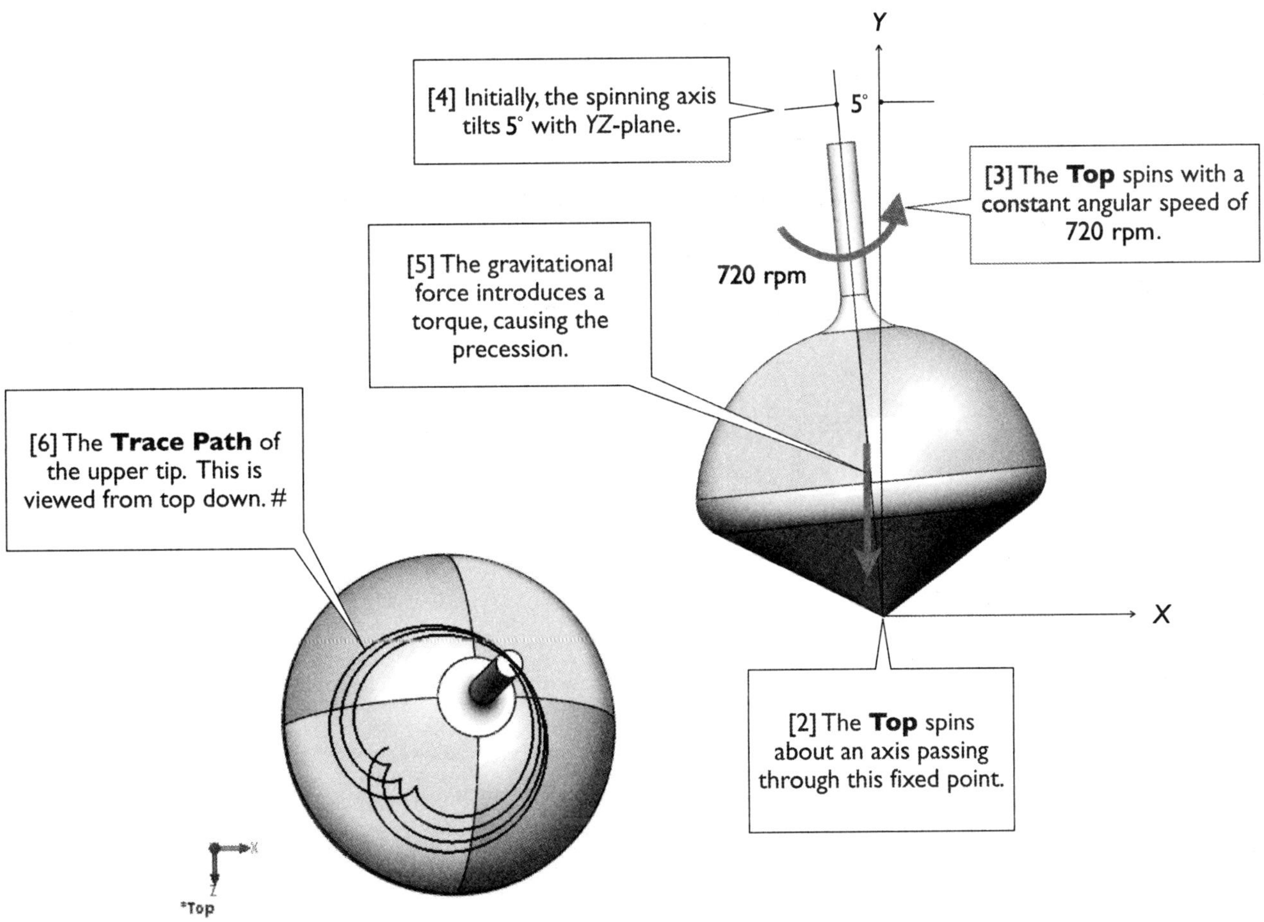

10.3-2 Start Up and Create a Part: **Top**

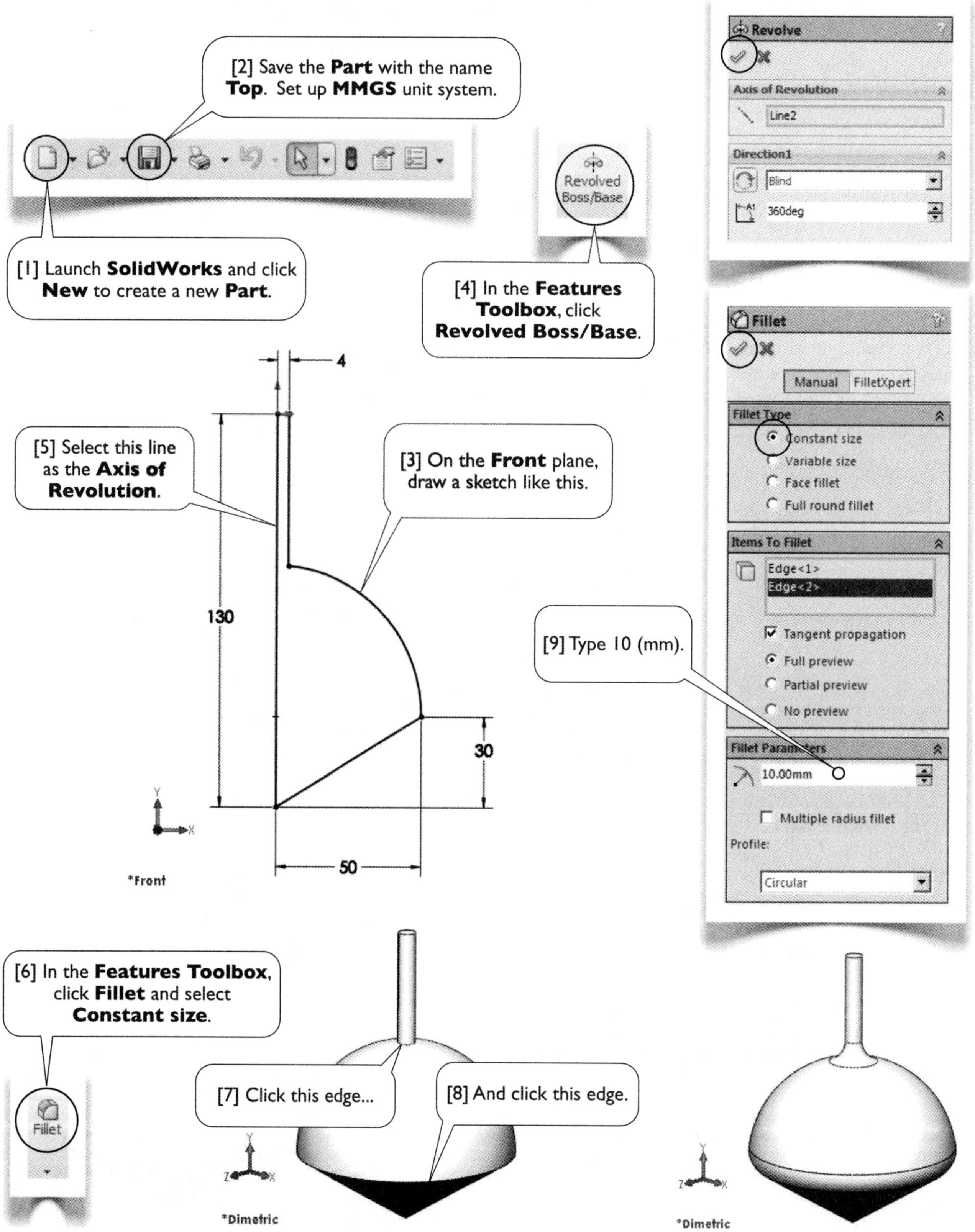

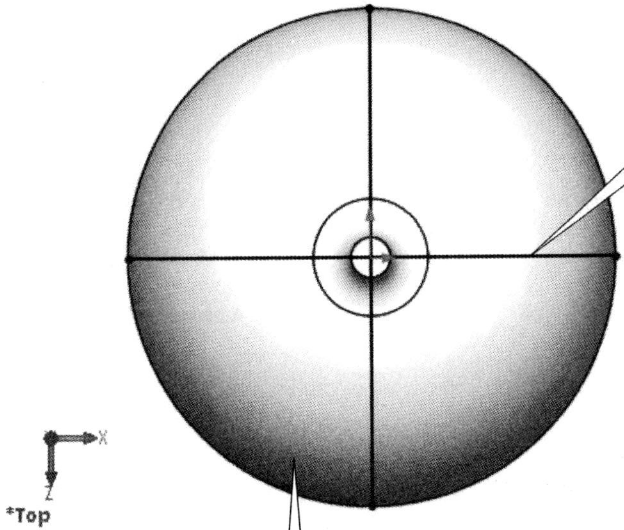

[10] On the **Top** plane, draw two lines orthogonal at the origin like this. Click **Exit Sketch**.

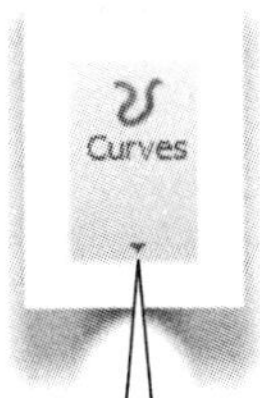

[11] In the **Features Toolbox**, select **Curves>Split Line**.

[14] **Face<1>**.

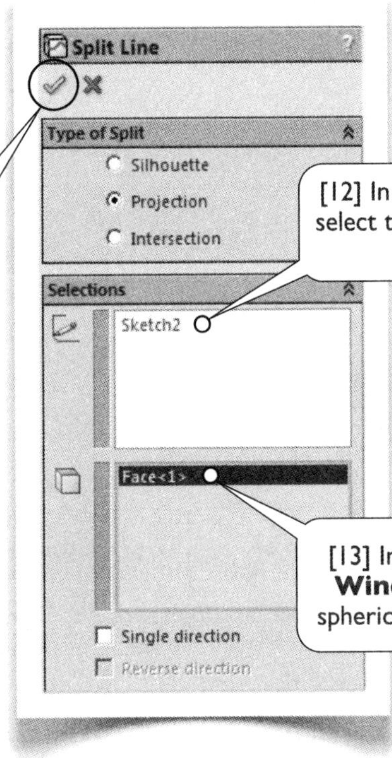

[15] Click **OK**.

[12] In the **Part Tree**, select the newly created sketch.

[13] In the **Graphics Window**, select the spherical face (see [14]).

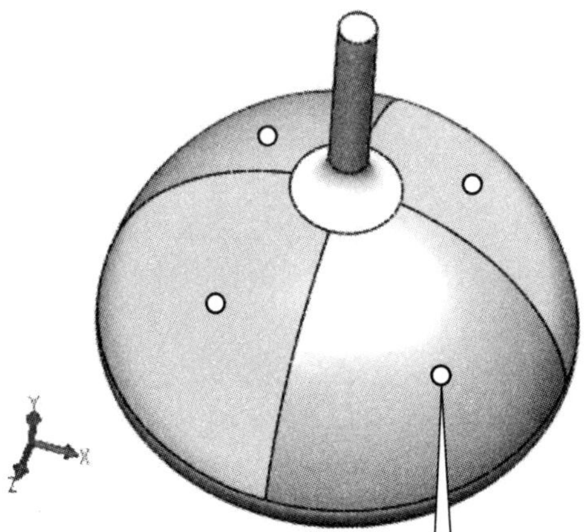

[16] Right-click this face and select **Appearance>Face<1>**. Select a color and click **OK**. Repeat this step for other 3 faces. The reason to color these faces is for the visual effects when the **Top** spins. #

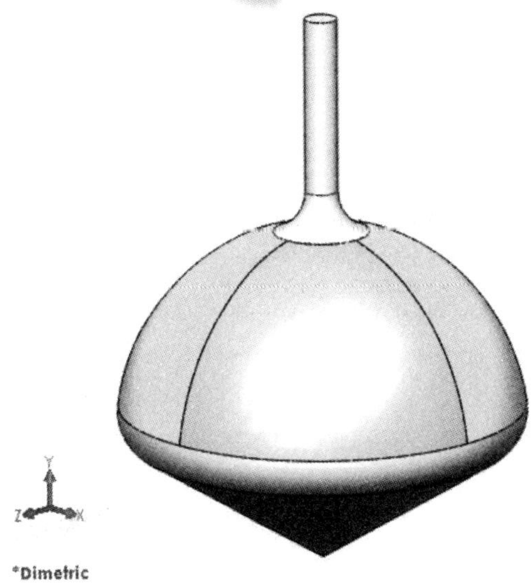

10.3-3 Create an Assembly: **Spinning-Top**

[1] Click **New** and create an **Assembly**.

[3] Save the **Assembly** with the name **Spinning-Top**. Set up **MKS** unit system.

[2] In the **Begin Assembly Property Box**, select **Top** and place it anywhere in the **Graphics Window**.

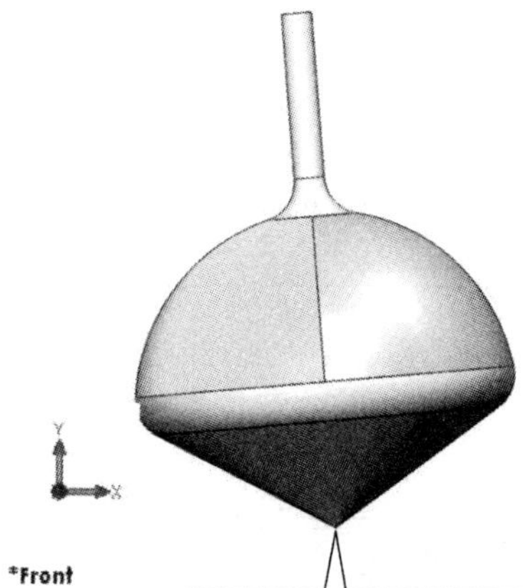

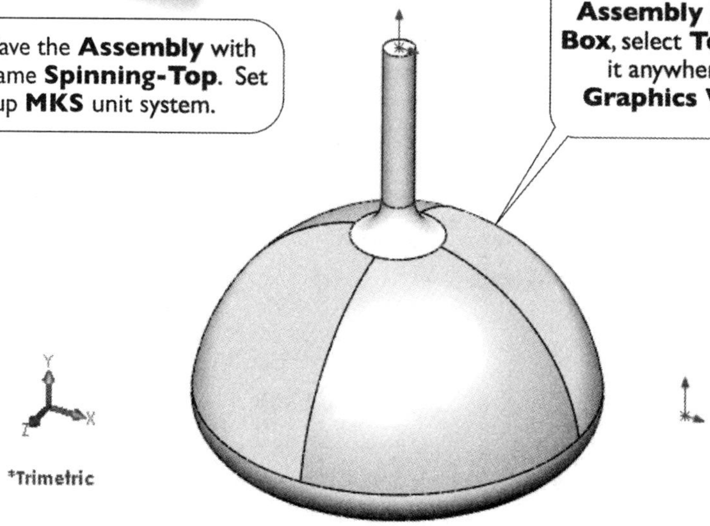

[6] This tip is to be **Coincident** with the assembly's **Origin**.

[9] In the **Front** view, the **Top** should tilt left (see [6]). If not, click **Flip dimension**. #

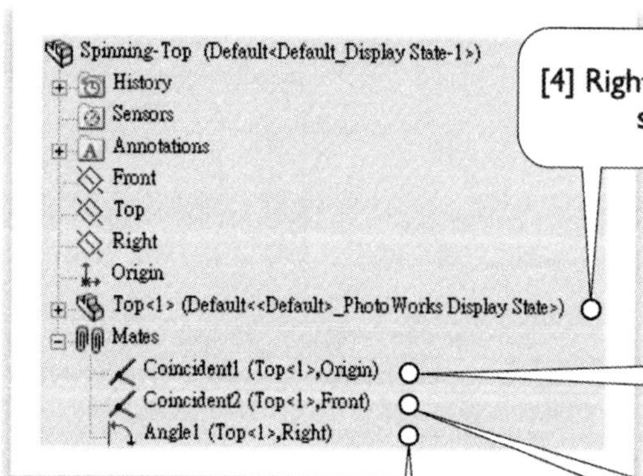

[4] Right-click **Top<1>** and select **Float**.

[5] The **Top's** bottom tip (see [6]) and the assembly's **Origin** are **Coincident**.

[8] The **Top's** and the assembly's **Right** planes form an angle of 5 degrees. We'll suppress this **Mate** later.

[7] The **Top's** and the assembly's **Front** planes are **Coincident**. We'll suppress this **Mate** later.

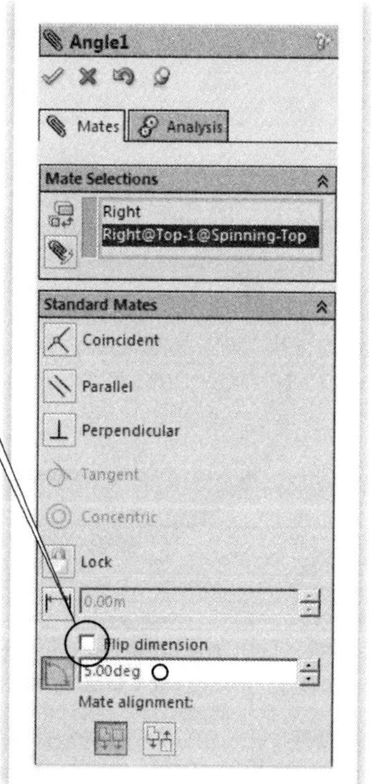

10.3-4 Create **Motion Study**, Set Up **Motor**, and Run the Simulation

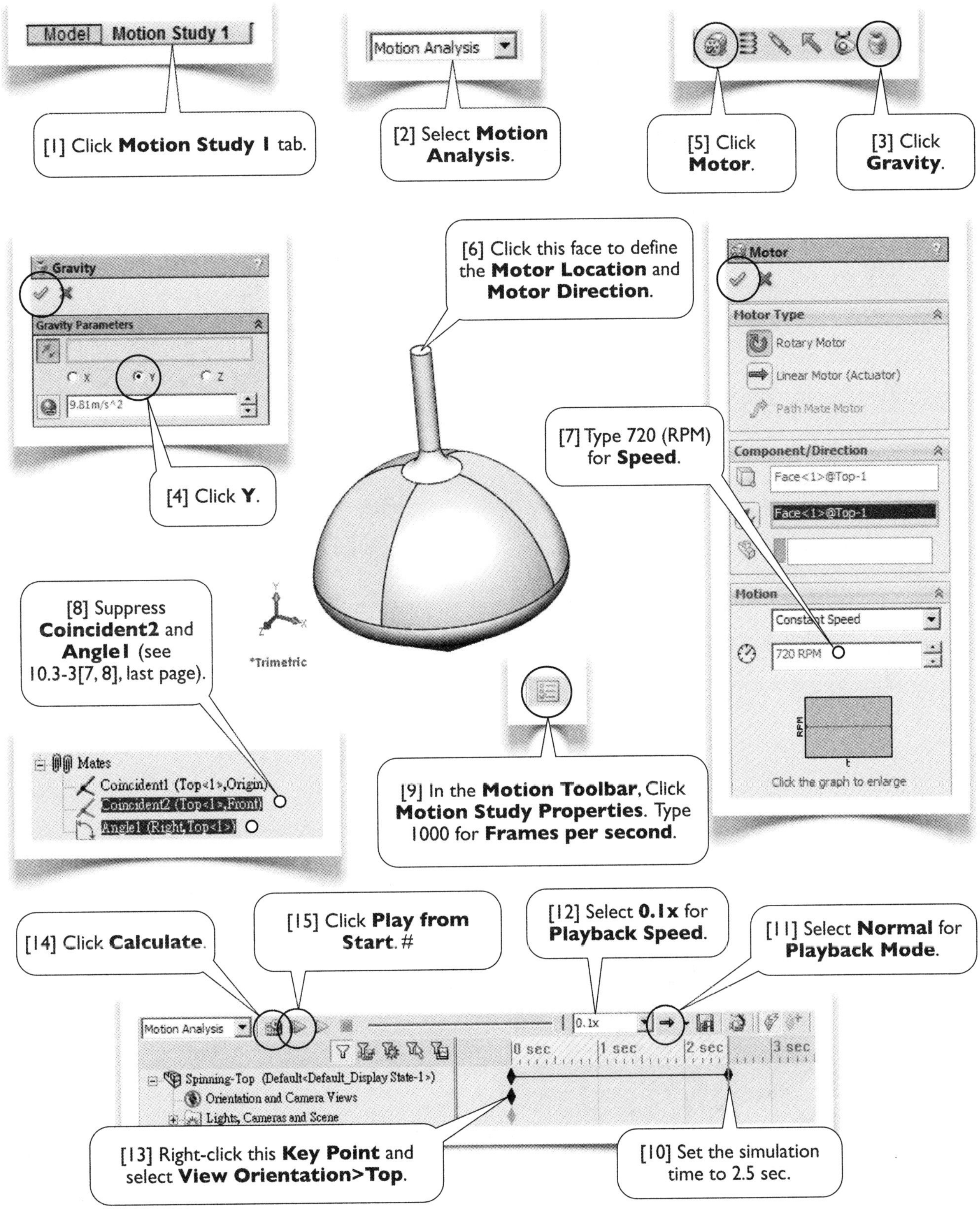

10.3-5 Results: Trace Path

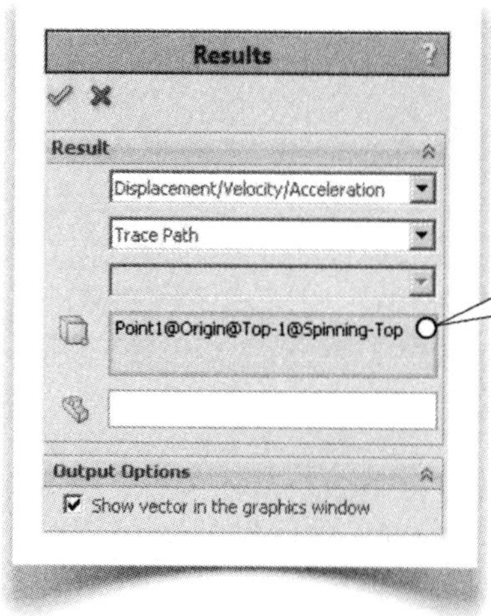

[1] Select the **Top's Origin** either from the **Asembly Tree** or **Graphics Window** (you need to turn on **View Origins**). You also can select the circular edge of the top surface.

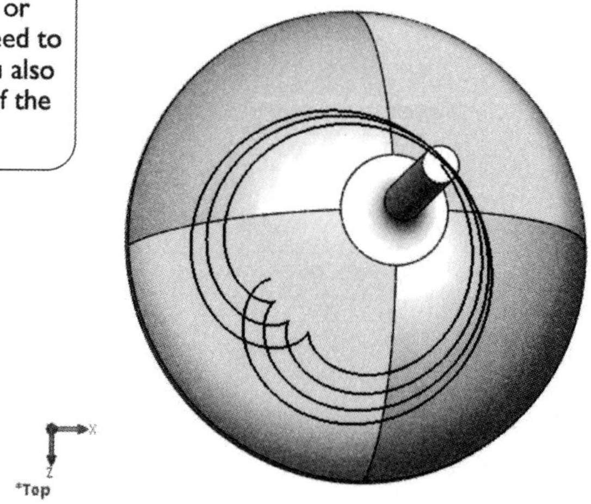

[2] Turn on **RealView Graphics** and **Shadows In Shaded Mode**. #

Chapter 11

Vibrations

In this chapter, we'll study vibrations of a mechanical system, including free vibrations, damped vibrations, and harmonically forced vibrations. The cases studied in this chapter involve only single degree of freedom. However, if you can perform problems of single degree of freedom, it is not difficult to extend the experience for much more complicated problems.

Section 11.1

A Mass-Spring-Damper System

11.1-1 Introduction

[1] Consider a **Mass-Spring-Damper** system [2-5]. The **Spring** is stretched 0.2 m and then released [6] and a harmonic force $F = F_m \sin(\omega_f t)$ is applied on the **Mass** [7].

Undamped Free Vibration

When $F = 0$ and $c = 0$, it is called a **undamped free vibration**. Application of Newton's 2nd law on the **Mass** yields

$$m\ddot{y} + ky = 0 \qquad (1)$$

The solution is

$$y = R \sin \omega_n t \qquad (2)$$

where the **natural frequency** is

$$\omega_n = \sqrt{\frac{k}{m}} = \sqrt{\frac{100 \text{ N/m}}{1 \text{ kg}}} = 10 \text{ rad/s} \qquad (3)$$

The **natural period** is

$$T_n = \frac{2\pi}{\omega_n} = 0.628 \text{ s} \qquad (4)$$

Damped Free Vibration

When $F = 0$ and $c \neq 0$, it is called a **damped free vibration**. Newton's 2nd law yields

$$m\ddot{y} + c\dot{y} + ky = 0 \qquad (5)$$

Note that we assume the damping force is linearly proportional to the velocity $\dot{y}$ with a proportional constant c.

There exists a critical damping $c_c = 2m\omega_n$ such that when $c > c_c$, the **Mass** doesn't oscillate and it is called an **over-damped vibration**. When $c < c_c$, the **Mass** oscillates and it is called an **under-damped vibration**. When $c = c_c$, the **Mass** also doesn't oscillate and it is called a **critically-damped vibration**. In our case

$$c_c = 2m\omega_n = 2(1 \text{ kg})(10 \text{ rad/s}) = 20 \text{ N/(m/s)} \qquad (6)$$

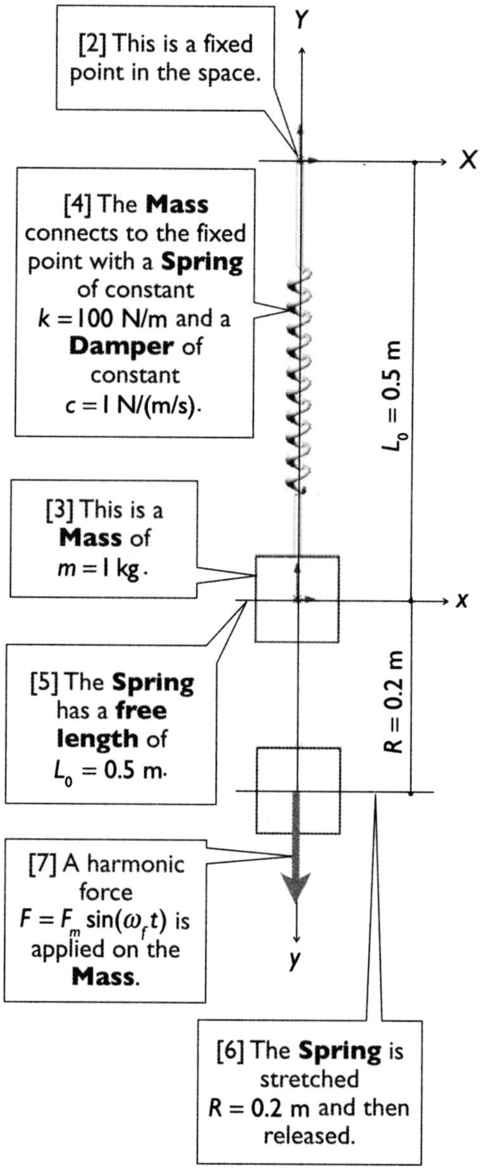

[8] Damping constant c is often used to represent an overall energy loss rate due to internal or external frictions. A typical structural or mechanical system surrounding by air has a damping constant no more than 10% of critical damping; i.e., $c < 0.1c_c$. In our case, $c = 0.05c_c$ (see [4] and Eq. (6)). The solution for an under-damped case is

$$y = e^{\frac{-ct}{2m}} R \sin \omega_d t \tag{7}$$

where ω_d is called the **damped frequency**,

$$\omega_d = \omega_n \sqrt{1 - \left(\frac{c}{c_c}\right)^2} \tag{8}$$

In our case, $\omega_d = 0.999\omega_n$: the damped frequency ω_d and the natural frequency ω_n are practically identical.

Note that the vibrations will eventually vanish ($y = 0$) after a long period of time. The ratio of amplitudes between two successive periods can be calculated by

$$r = \frac{y_{t+T_n}}{y_t} \approx e^{\frac{-cT_n}{2m}} = e^{\frac{-(1)(0.628)}{2(1)}} = 0.73 \tag{9}$$

Note that, by measuring the ratio, Eq. (9) can also be used to estimate the damping constant c.

Harmonically Forced Vibration

Now consider that, in addition to the stretch of $R = 0.2$ m, a harmonic force $F = F_m \sin(\omega_f t)$ is applied on the **Mass**. Newton's 2nd law yields

$$m\ddot{y} + c\dot{y} + ky = F_m \sin(\omega_f t) \tag{10}$$

To be more specific, assume $F_m = 2$ N and $\omega_f = 1 \text{ Hz} = 2\pi$ rad/s. With such a small force, the displacement is initially dominated by Eq. (7), which will eventually vanish after a long period of time, and then the vibration reaches a steady state:

$$y = y_m \sin(\omega_f t - \varphi) \tag{11}$$

where

$$y_m = \frac{F_m/k}{\sqrt{\left[1 - (\omega_f/\omega_n)^2\right]^2 + \left[2(c/c_c)(\omega_f/\omega_n)\right]^2}} \tag{12}$$

$$\varphi = \tan^{-1} \frac{2(c/c_c)(\omega_f/\omega_n)}{1 - (\omega_f/\omega_n)^2} \tag{13}$$

In our case, $c/c_c = 0.05$ and $\omega_f/\omega_n = 0.628$, therefore

$$y_m = \frac{2/100}{\sqrt{\left[1 - (0.628)^2\right]^2 + \left[2(0.05)(0.628)\right]^2}} = 0.0328 \text{ m} \tag{14}$$

$$\varphi = \tan^{-1} \frac{2(0.05)(0.628)}{1 - (0.628)^2} = 5.92^\circ \tag{15}$$

Since the period of the harmonic force is $T_f = 1$ s, the phase angle of 5.92° equals to a time difference of $T_f \times (5.92^\circ/360^\circ) = 0.016$ s. This section is designed to help students understand these equations. #

11.1-2 Start Up and Create a Part: **Mass**

[2] Save the **Part** with the name **Mass**. Set up **MKS** unit system.

[1] Launch **SolidWorks** and click **New** to create a new **Part**.

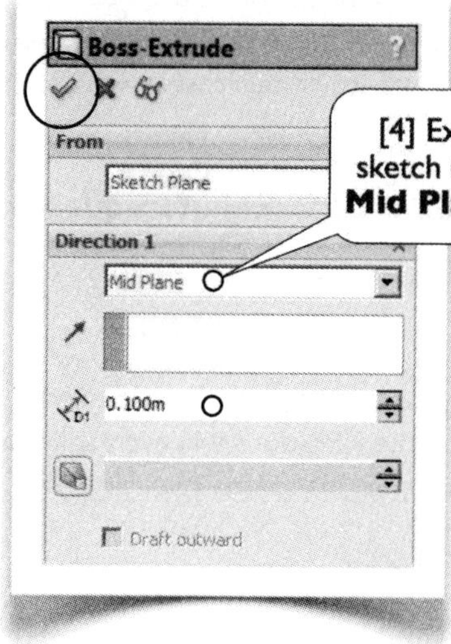

[4] Extrude the sketch 0.1 m, using **Mid Plane** option.

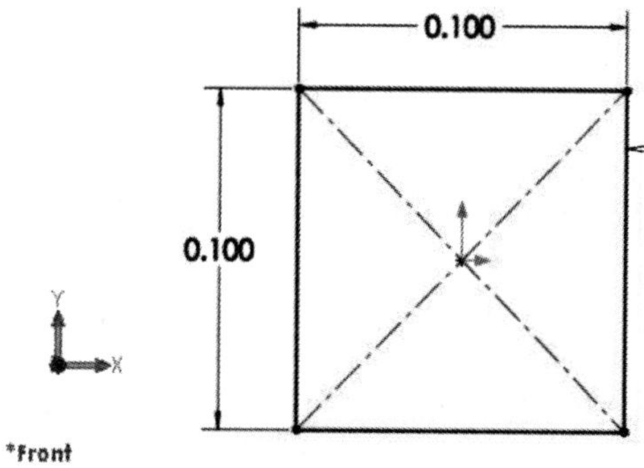

[3] On the **Front** plane, draw a rectangle (using **Center Rectangle** tool) like this.

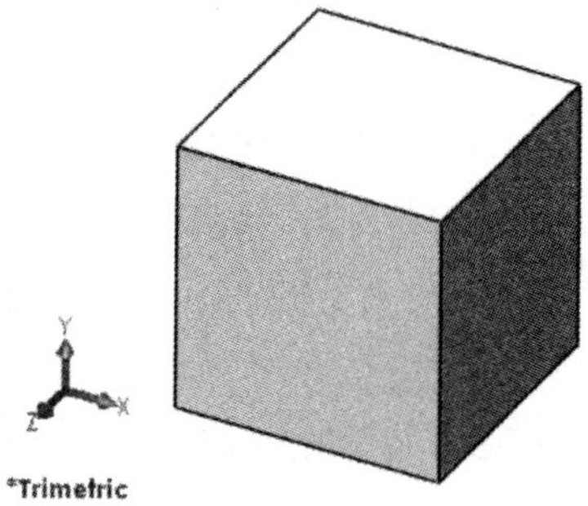

[5] In the **Evaluate Toolbar**, click **Mass Properties**.

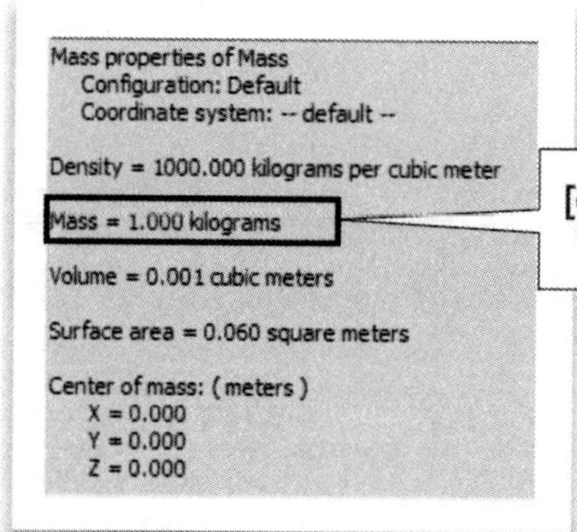

Mass properties of Mass
Configuration: Default
Coordinate system: -- default --

Density = 1000.000 kilograms per cubic meter

Mass = 1.000 kilograms

Volume = 0.001 cubic meters

Surface area = 0.060 square meters

Center of mass: (meters)
X = 0.000
Y = 0.000
Z = 0.000

[6] Make sure the mass $m = 1$ kg. #

11.1-3 Create an Assembly: **Mass-Spring-Damper**

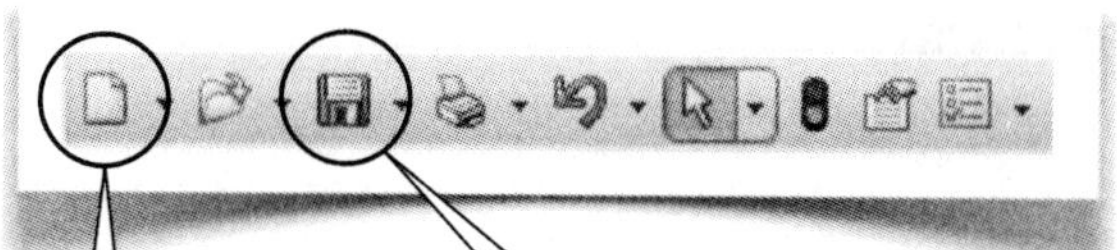

[1] Click **New** and create an **Assembly**.

[2] In the **Begin Assembly Property Box**, select **Mass** and place it anywhere in the **Graphics Window**.

[3] Save the **Assembly** with the name **Mass-Spring-Damper**. Set up **MKS** unit system.

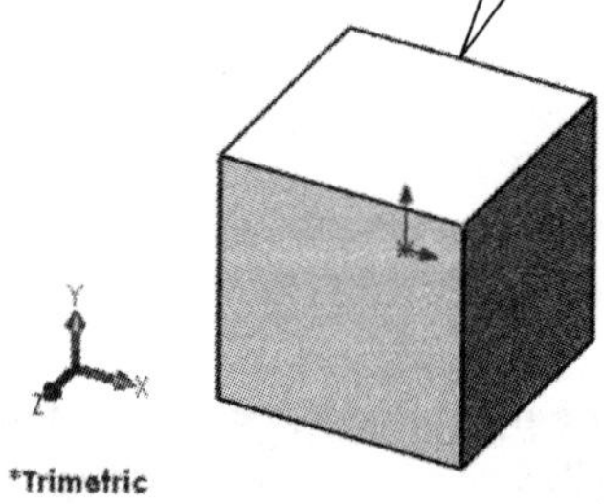

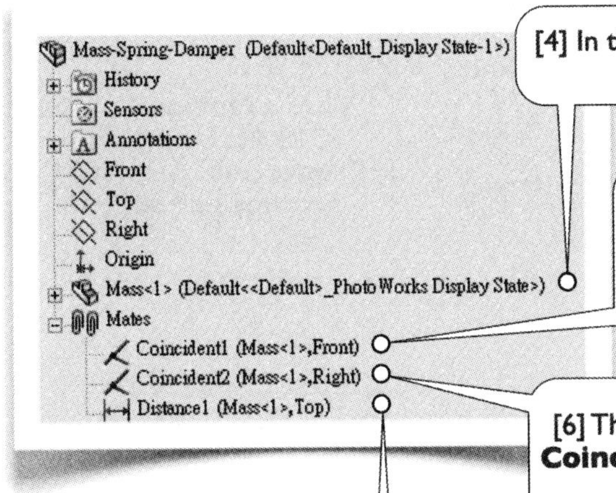

[4] In the **Assembly Tree**, right-click **Mass** and select **Float**.

[5] The **Mass's Front** plane is **Coincident** with the assembly's **Front** plane.

[6] The **Mass's Right** plane is **Coincident** with the assembly's **Right** plane.

[7] The **Mass's Top** plane has a **Distance** of 0.5 m below the assembly's **Top** plane (see [8]). This **Mate** will be suppressed later.

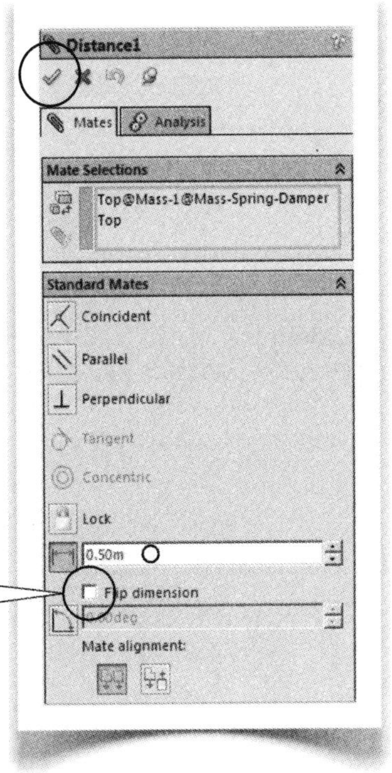

[8] The **Mass** should be BELOW the assembly's **Top** plane. If not, click **Flip dimension** to fix it. #

11.1-4 Create a Motion Study: **Free Vibration**

[1] Click **Motion Study 1** tab and rename it to **Free Vibration**.

[2] Select **Motion Analysis**.

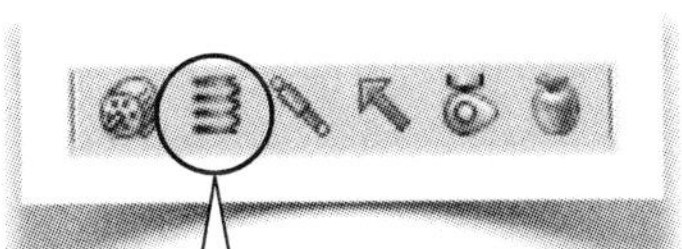

[3] In **Motion Toolbar**, click **Spring** to create a **Linear Spring**.

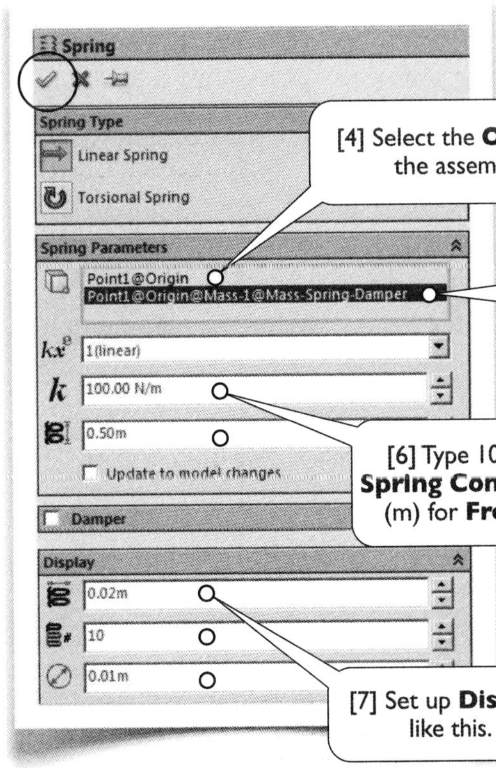

[4] Select the **Origin** of the assembly.

[5] Select the **Origin** of the **Mass**.

[6] Type 100 (N/m) for **Spring Constant** and 0.5 (m) for **Free Length**.

[7] Set up **Display** like this.

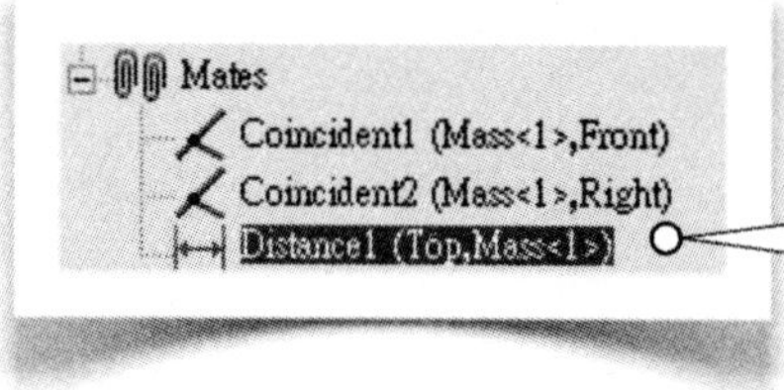

[8] In the **Assembly Tree**, ight-click **Distance1** and select **Edit Feature**. Change the **Distance** to 0.7 m. Suppress **Distance1**.

[9] In the **Motion Toolbar**, Click **Motion Study Properties**. Type 1000 for **Frames per second**.

[17] Click **Calculate**.

[18] Click **Play from Start**. As you play, click **LinearSpring1** to make it visible. #

[12] Set **Playback Speed** to **0.25x**.

[11] Select **Normal** for **Playback Mode**.

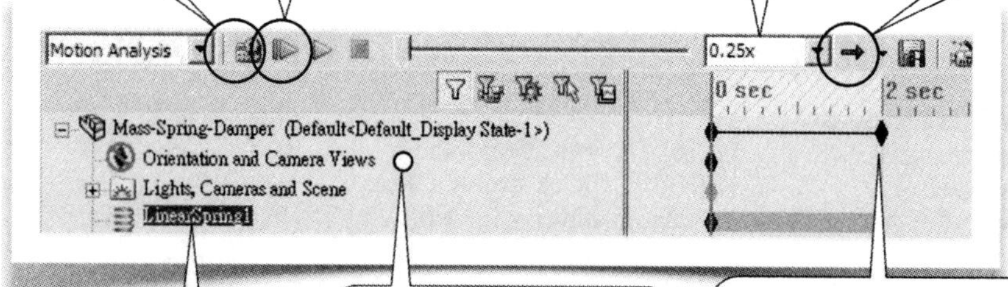

[14] Click to highlight **LinearSpring1**, so that the **Spring** can be seen in the **Graphics Window**.

[13, 16] Right-click **Orientation and Camera View** and select **Disable View Key Creation**.

[10] Set the simulation time to 2 seconds.

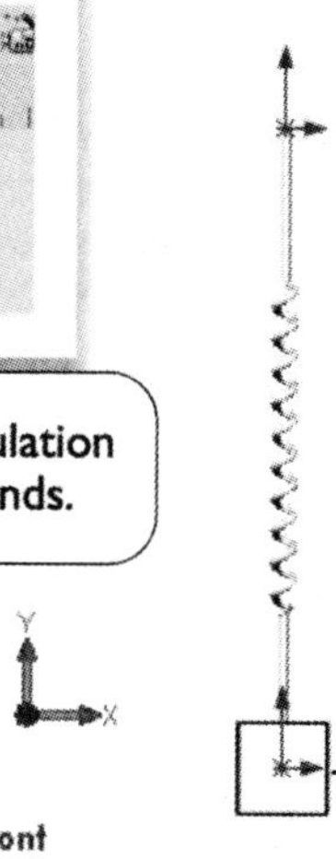

[15] Adjust to a **Front** view like this.

11.1-5 Results: Free Vibration

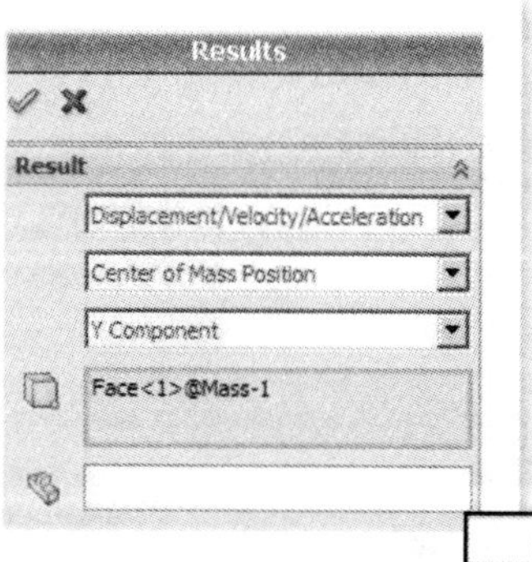

0.627	-0.69998
0.628	-0.7
0.629	-0.7
0.63	-0.69997

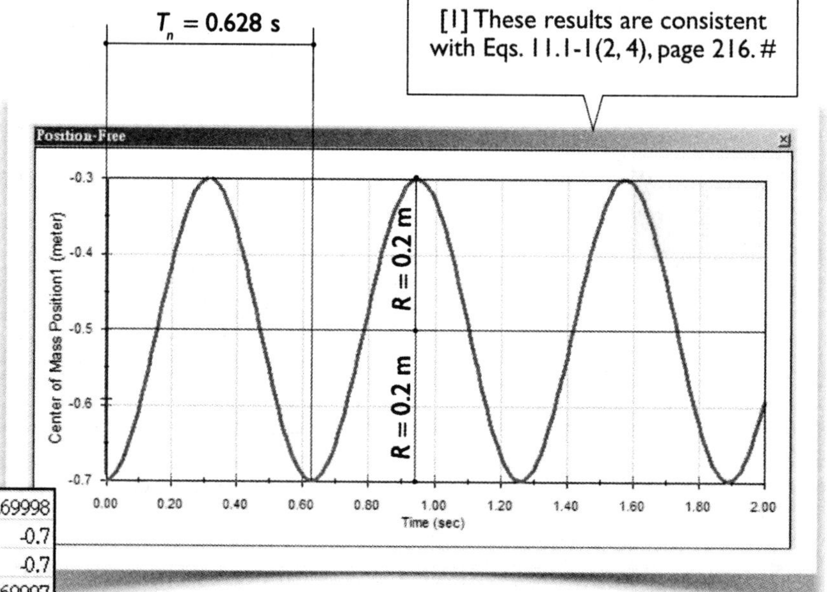

[1] These results are consistent with Eqs. 11.1-1(2, 4), page 216. #

11.1-6 Create a Motion Study: **Damped Free Vibration**

[1] Right-click **Free Vibration** and select **Duplicate**.

[2] Rename the new study as **Damped Free Vibration**.

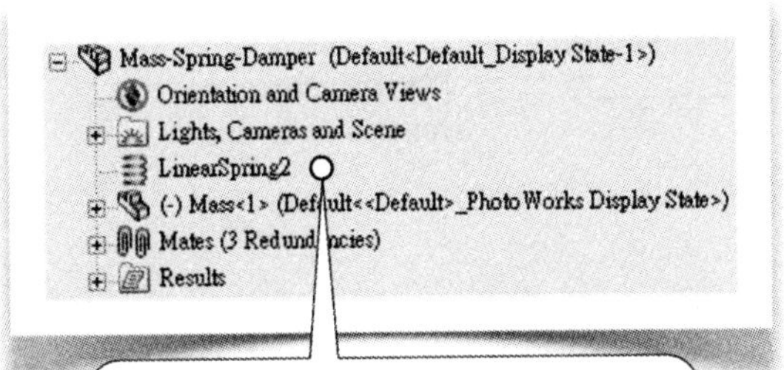

[3] Right-click **LinearSpring2** and select **Edit Feature**.

[4] Click **Damper**.

[5] Type 20 (N/(m/s)) for **Damping Constant**. This is the critical damping constant (see Eq. 11.1-1(6), page 216).

[6] Set the simulation time to 10 seconds.

[7] Click **Calculate**.

[8] Click **Play from Start**. #

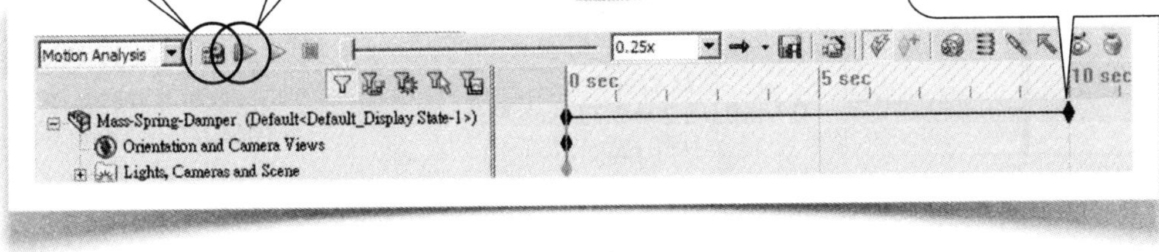

11.1-7 Results: Critically-Damped Vibration

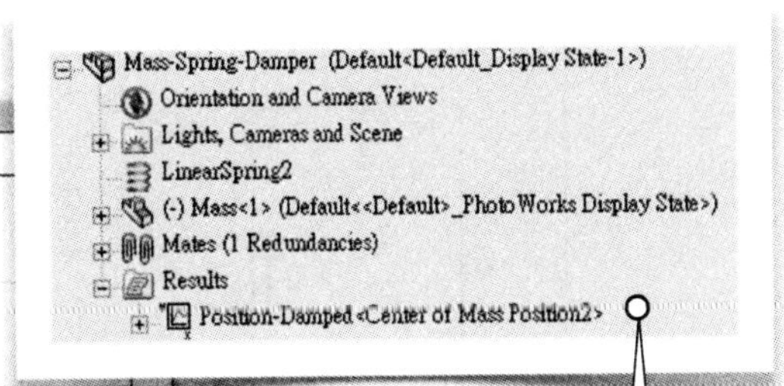

[1] Change the name like this and right-click-select **Show Plot**.

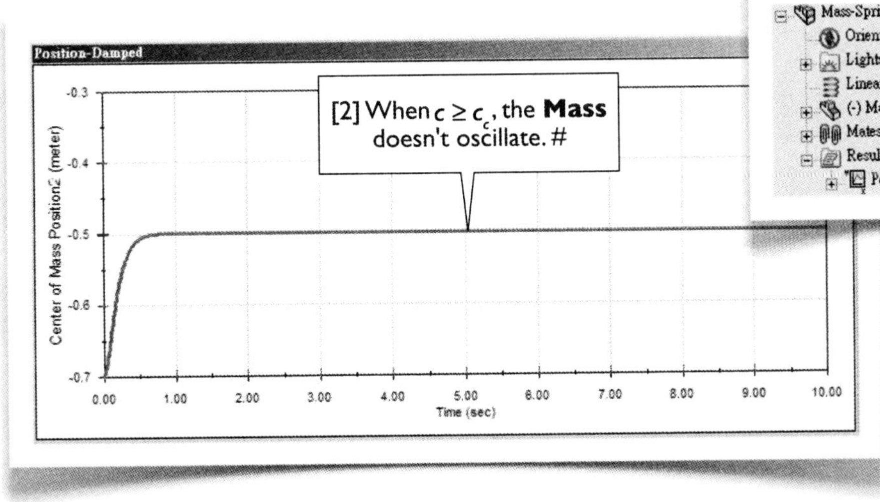

[2] When $c \geq c_c$, the **Mass** doesn't oscillate. #

11.1-8 Results: Under-Damped Vibration

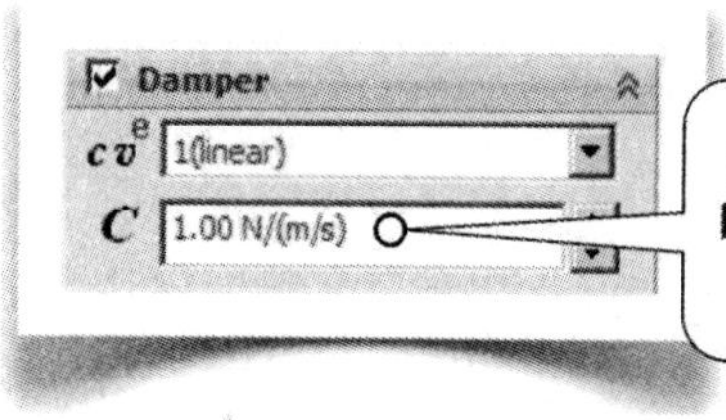

[1] Edit **LinearSpring2** and change **Damping Constant** to 1 (N/(m/s)) and click **Calculate**.

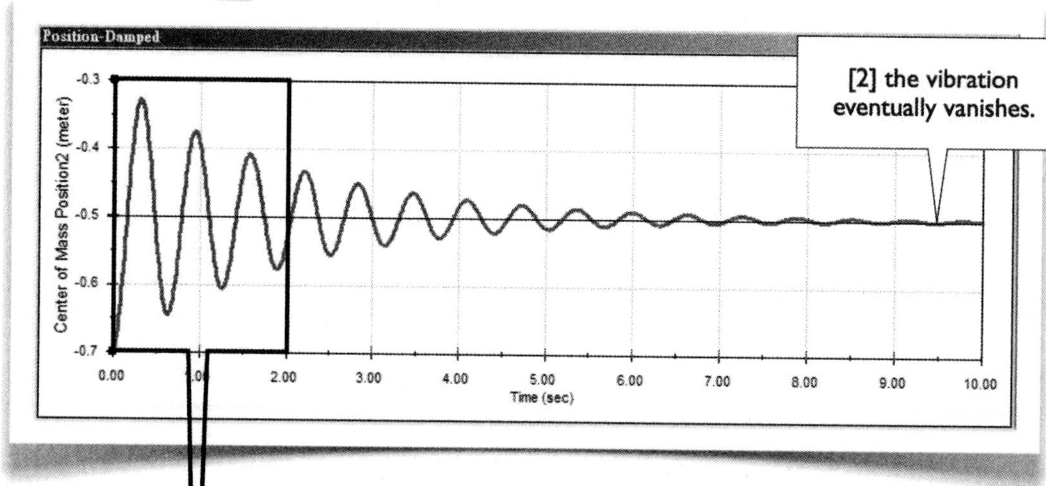

[2] the vibration eventually vanishes.

[4] The ratio of amplitudes between the second and the first crests is **0.14603/0.2 = 0.73 (see Eq. 11.1-1(9), page 217).**

[5] The ratio of amplitudes between the third and the second crests is **0.10662/0.14603 = 0.73**.

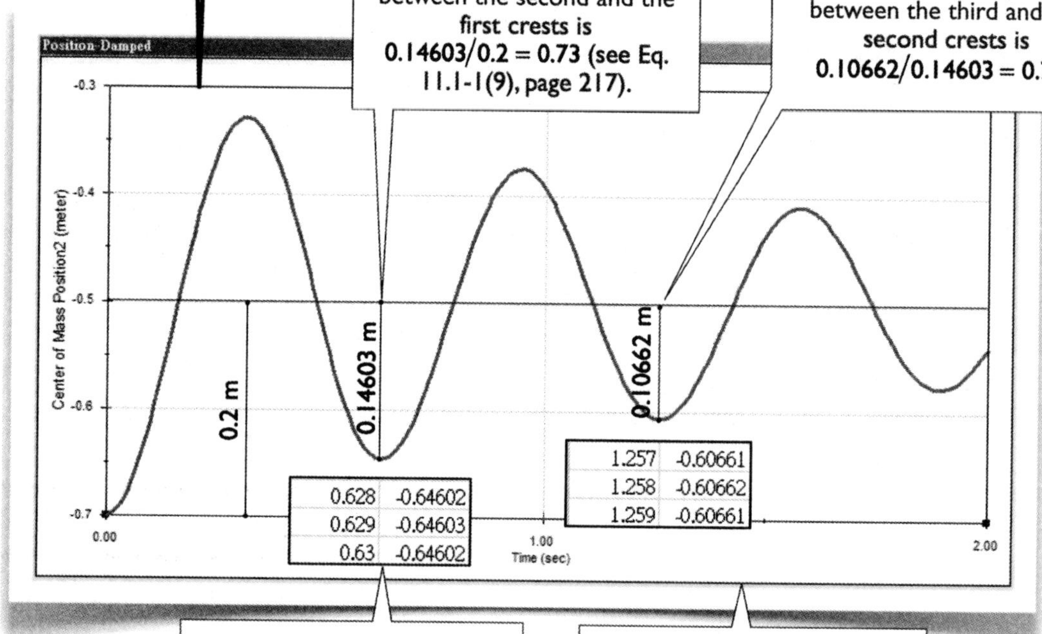

[3] The period of damped vibration is almost identical to that of the free vibration.

[6] In summary, these results are consistent with Eqs. 11.1-1(8, 9), page 217.#

11.1-9 Create a Motion Study: **Forced Vibration**

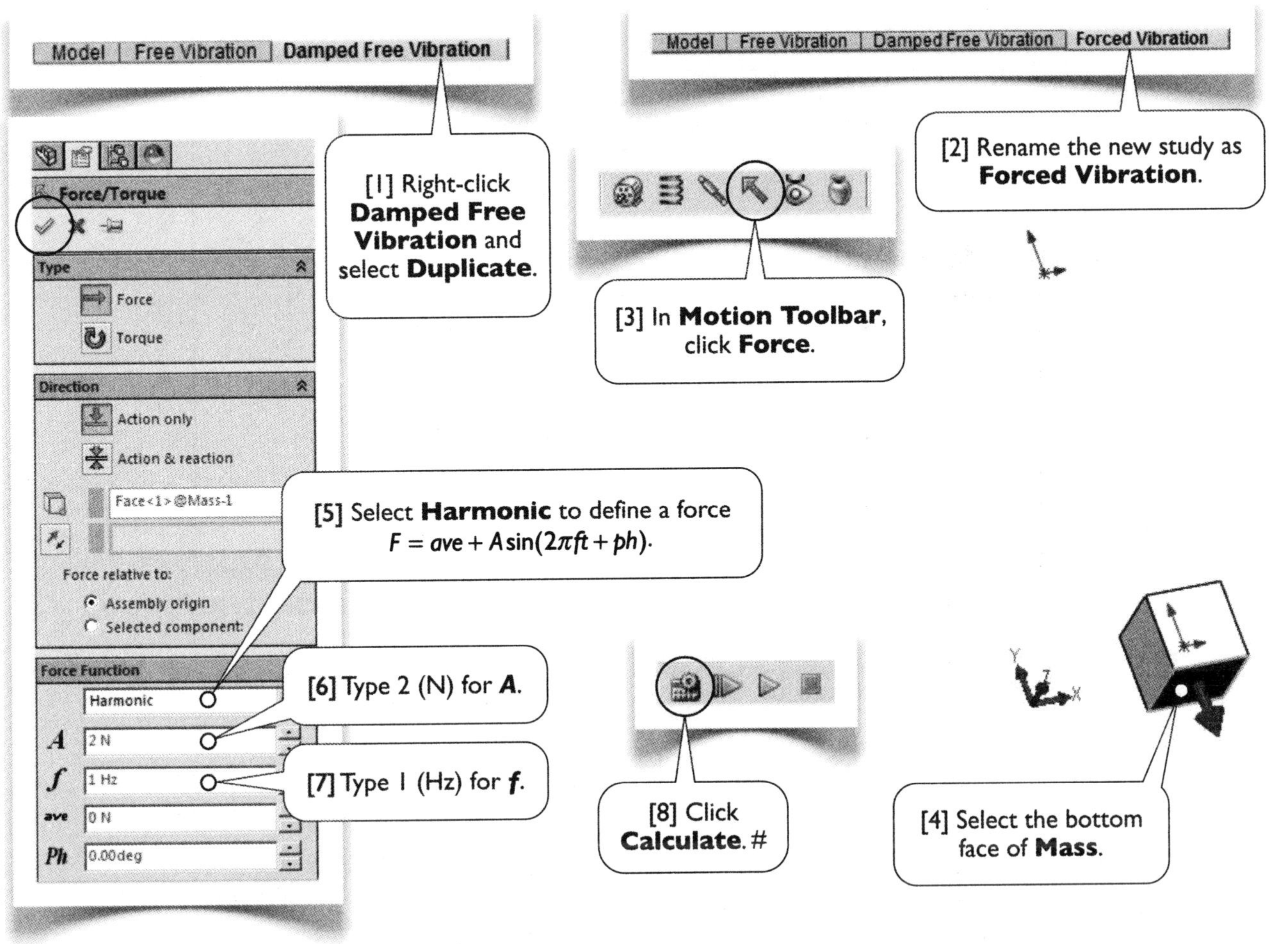

11.1-10 Results: Forced Vibration

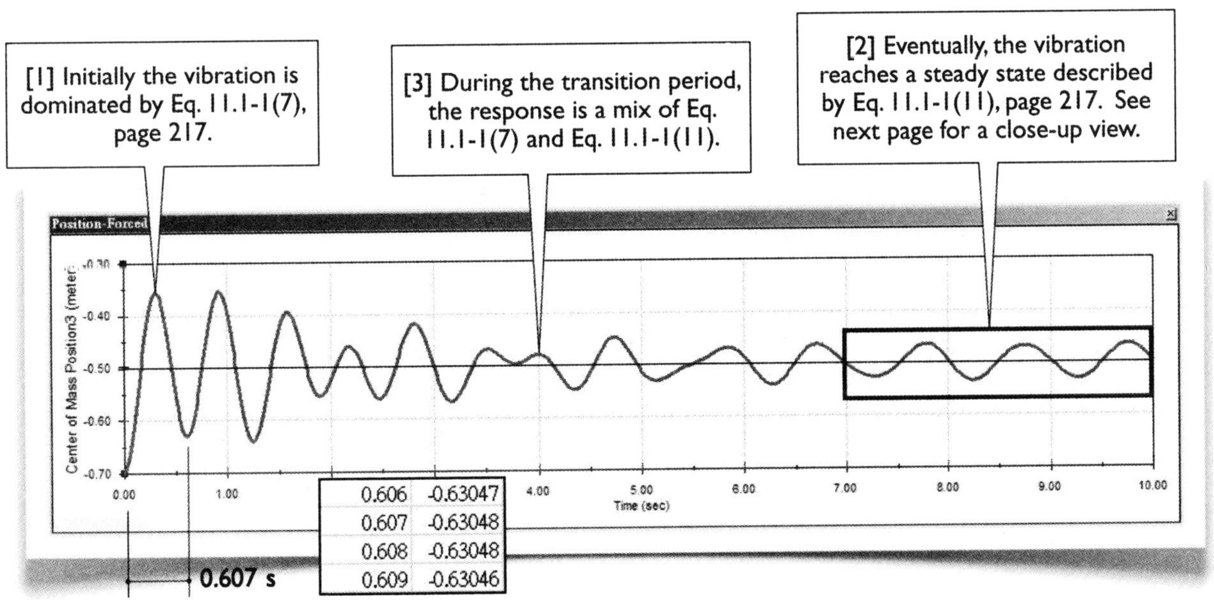

[4] This is a close-up view of [2] in the last plot.

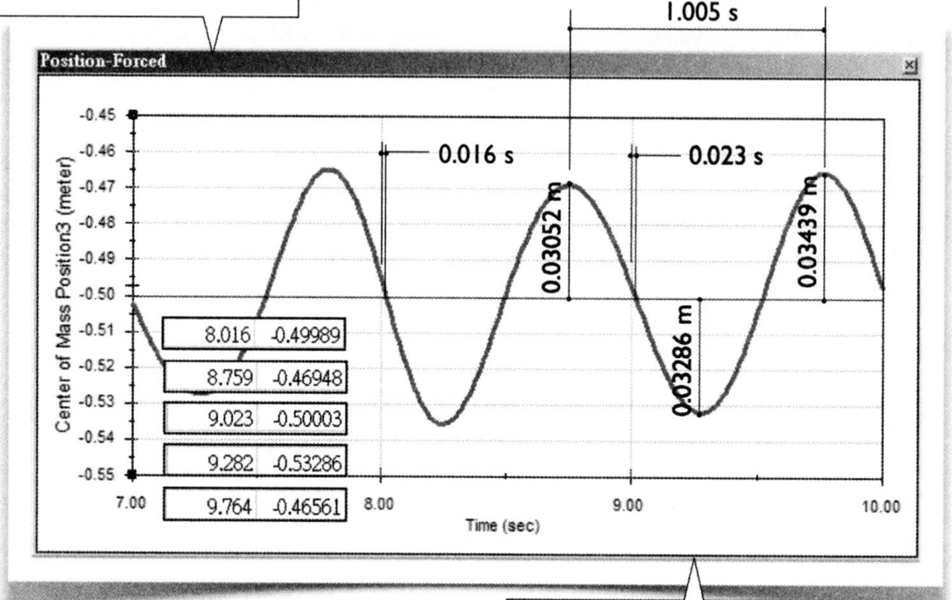

[5] These results are consistent with Eqs. 11.1-1(14, 15), page 217.

[6] Wrap Up

Save all files and exit **SolidWorks**. #

Section 11.2

Eccentric Rotor

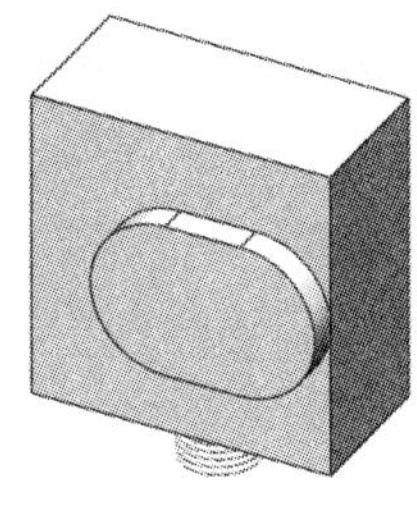

11.2-1 Introduction

[1] Consider a **Housing** seated on a base with a **Spring** [2-4]. A **Rotor** is attached to the **Housing**, rotating eccentrically [5]. The eccentric rotation generates a harmonic force $\vec{F}$ on the spring

$$\vec{F} = F_m \sin(\omega_f t)\,\vec{j} \tag{1}$$

where

$$F_m = mr\omega_f^2 = (0.25708\text{ kg})(0.025\text{ m})(125.66\text{ rad/s})^2 = 101.49\text{ N} \tag{2}$$

The natural frequency is

$$\omega_n = \sqrt{\frac{k}{M+m}} = \sqrt{\frac{10000\text{ N/m}}{4\text{ kg} + 0.25708\text{ kg}}} = 48.467\text{ rad/s} \tag{3}$$

The critical damping constant is

$$c_c = 2(M+m)\omega_n = 2(4\text{ kg} + 0.25708\text{ kg})(48.467\text{ rad/s}) = 412.66\text{ N/(m/s)} \tag{4}$$

In this case, we use a **Damper** of $c = 400$ N/(m/s), which is approximately equal to the critical damping constant in Eq. (4), so that the transient free vibration will be damped out very quickly.

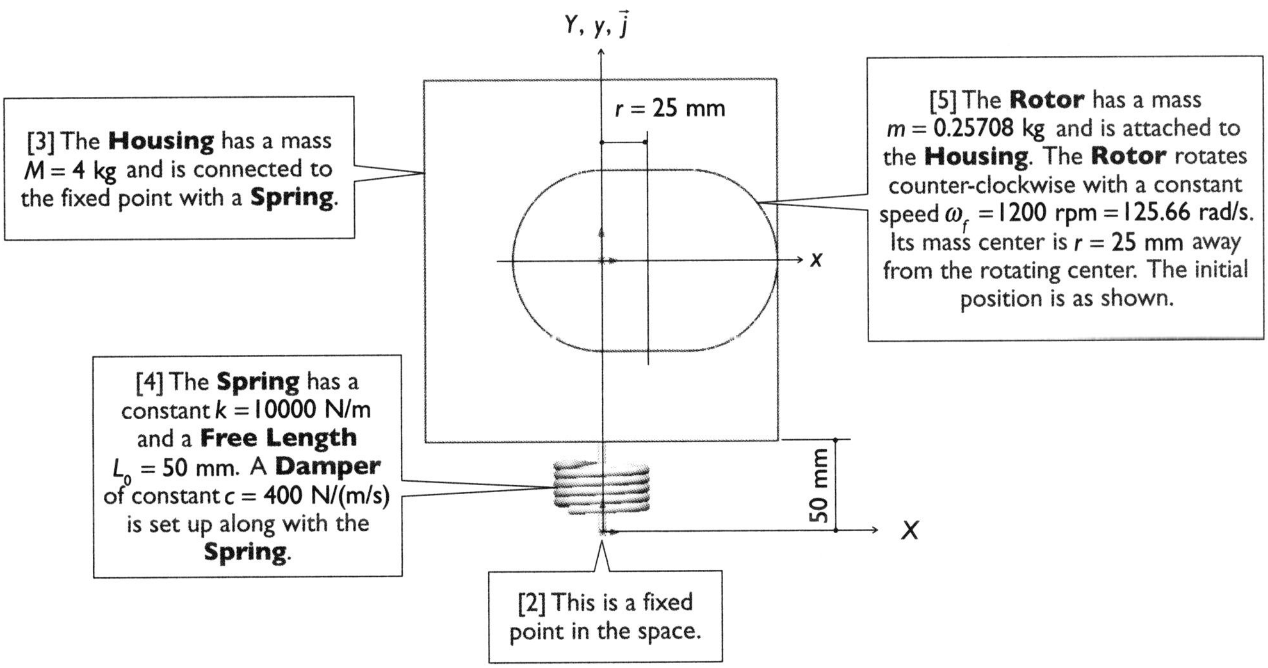

[6] According to Eqs. 11.1-1(11-13) (page 217), the displacement of the **Housing** is

$$y = y_m \sin(\omega_f t - \varphi) \tag{5}$$

where

$$y_m = \frac{F_m/k}{\sqrt{\left[1-(\omega_f/\omega_n)^2\right]^2 + \left[2(c/c_c)(\omega_f/\omega_n)\right]^2}} = 0.001333 \text{ m} \tag{6}$$

$$\varphi = \tan^{-1}\frac{2(c/c_c)(\omega_f/\omega_n)}{1-(\omega_f/\omega_n)^2} = -41.296^\circ \tag{7}$$

Since the period of the harmonic force is $T_f = 0.05$ s, the phase angle of -41.296° equals to a time difference of $T_f \times (41.296^\circ/360^\circ) = -0.005736$ s. This section performs a simulation for this system and validate the results with the values in Eqs. (6, 7). #

11.2-2 Start Up and Create a Part: **Housing**

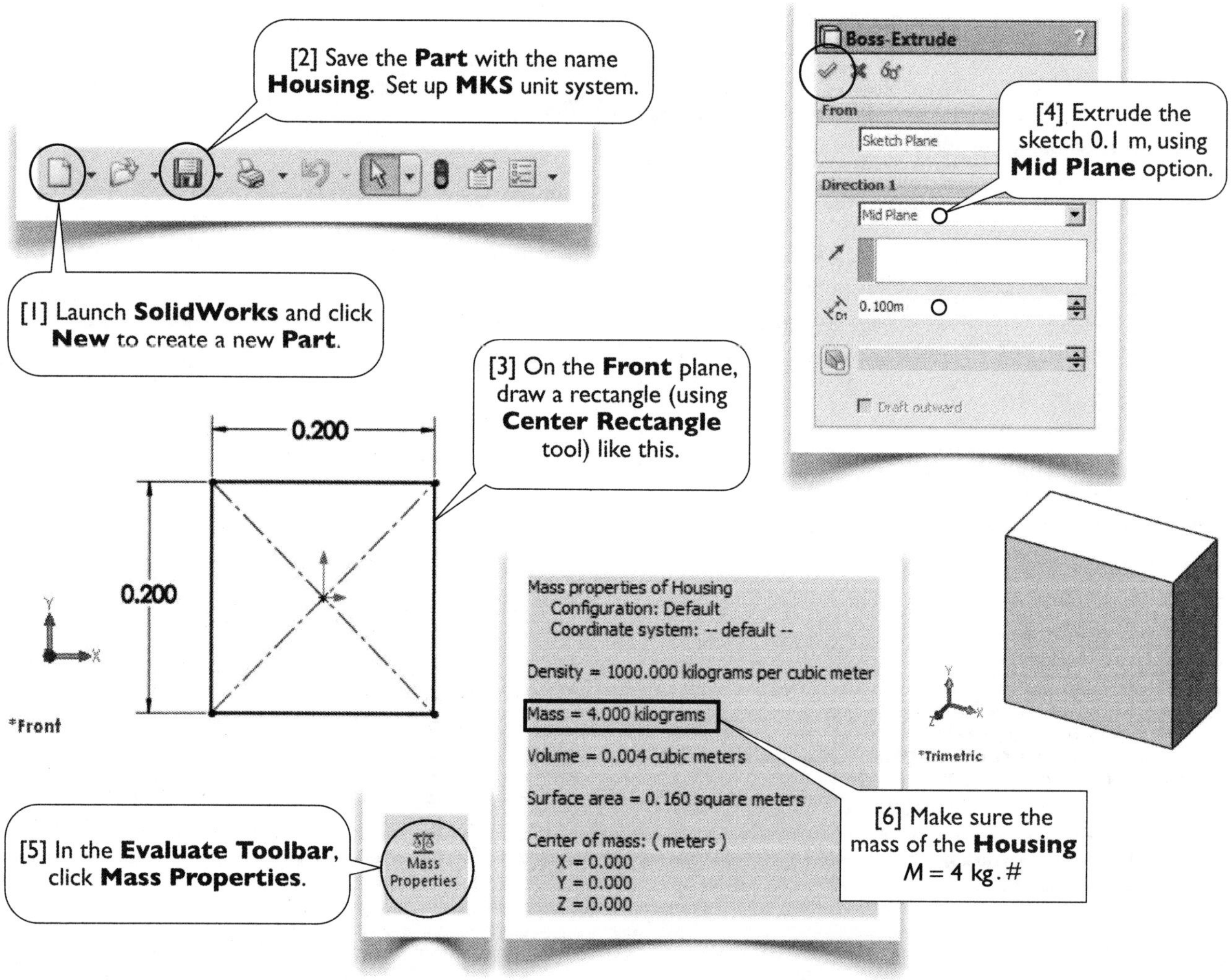

11.2-3 Create a Part: **Rotor**

[2] Save the **Part** with the name **Rotor**. Set up **MKS** unit system.

[1] Click **New** to create a new **Part**.

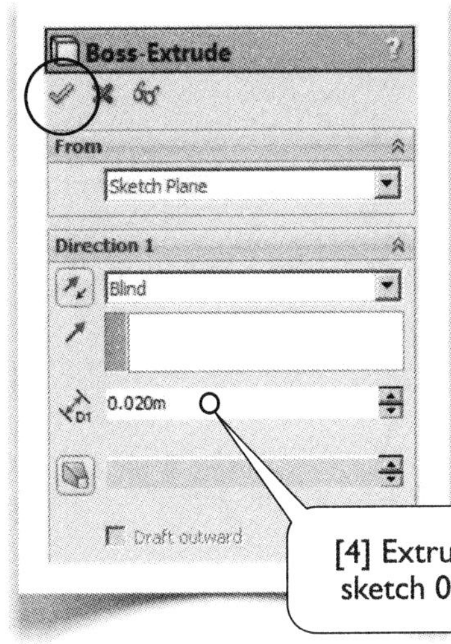

[4] Extrude the sketch 0.02 m.

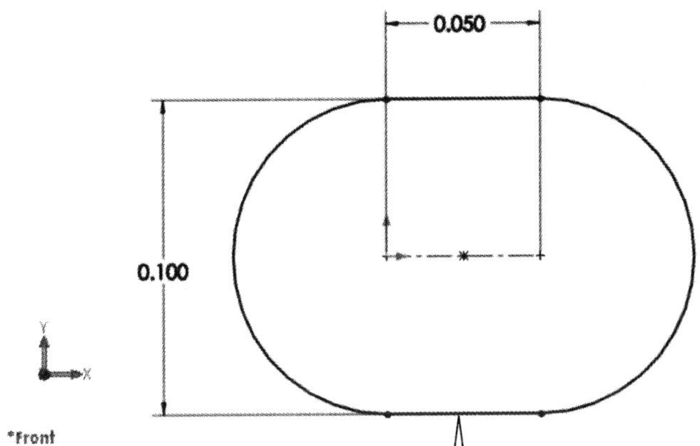

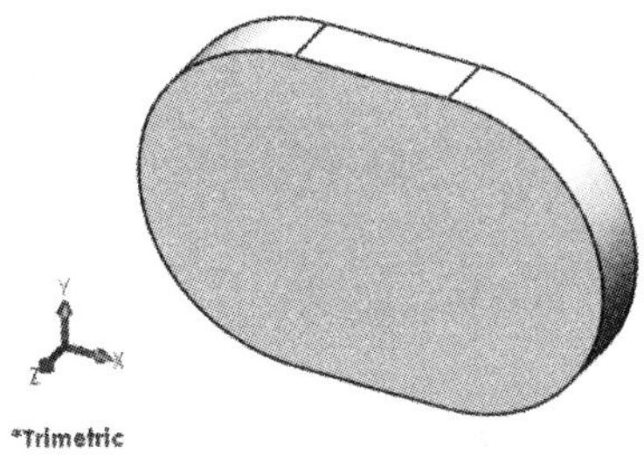

[3] On the **Front** plane, draw a **Straight Slot** like this.

[5] In the **Evaluate Toolbar**, click **Mass Properties**.

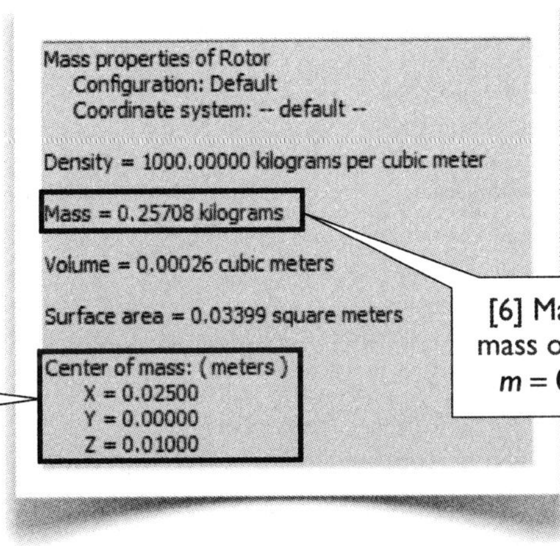

[7] Make sure the location of the mass center is like this. #

[6] Make sure the mass of the **Rotor** $m = 0.25708$ kg.

11.2-4 Create an Assembly: **Eccentric-Rotor**

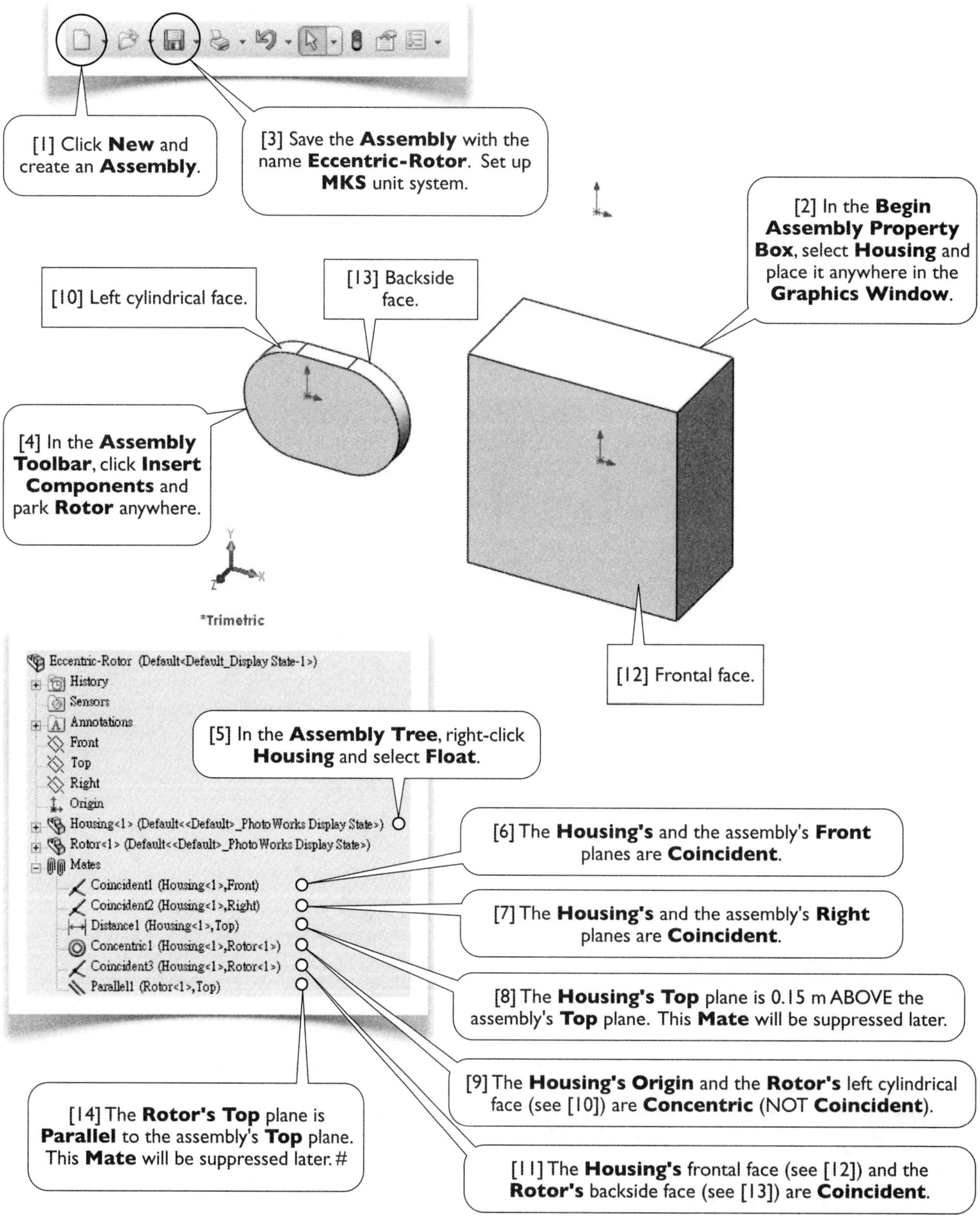

11.2-5 Create a Motion Study; Set Up **Spring** and **Motor**

[1] Click **Motion Study 1** tab.

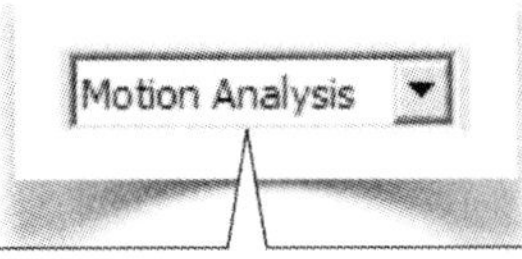

[2] Select **Motion Analysis**.

[3] In **Motion Toolbar**, click **Spring** to create a **Linear Spring**.

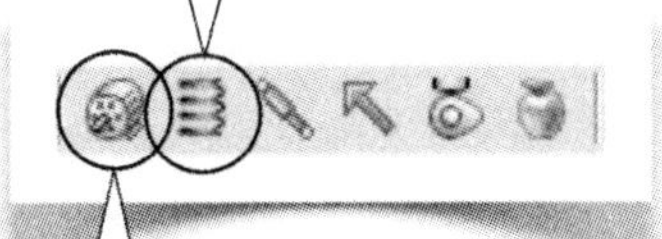

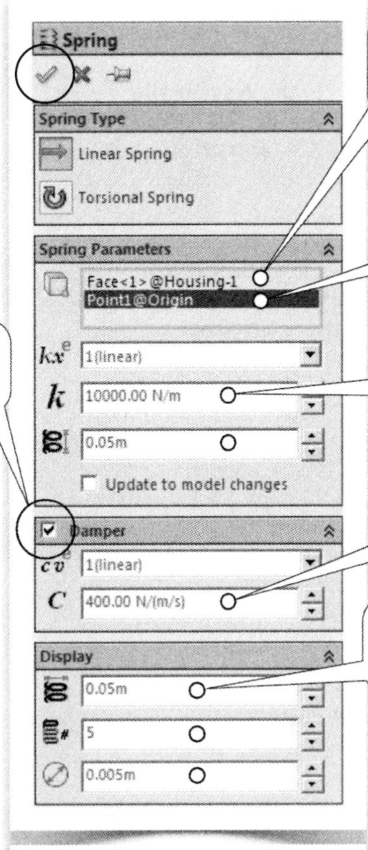

[4] Select the bottom face of the **Housing** (see [5]).

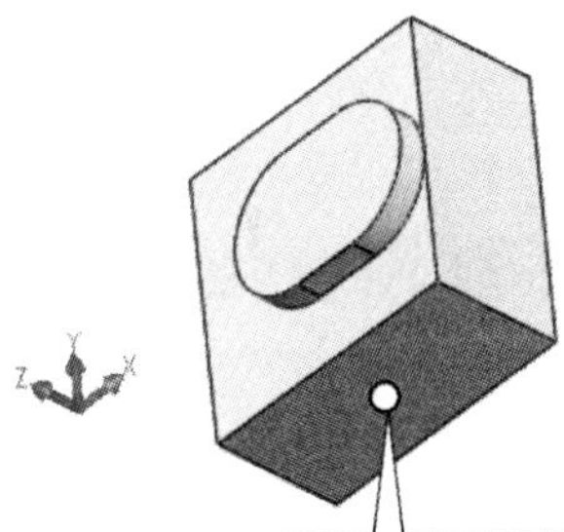

[5] Bottom face.

[6] Select the **Origin** of the assembly.

[7] Type 10000 (N/m) for **Spring Constant** and 0.05 (m) for **Free Length**.

[8] Click **Damper**.

[9] Type 400 (N/(m/s)) for **Damping Constant**.

[10] Set up **Display** like this.

[11] Click **Motor** to create a **Rotary Motor**.

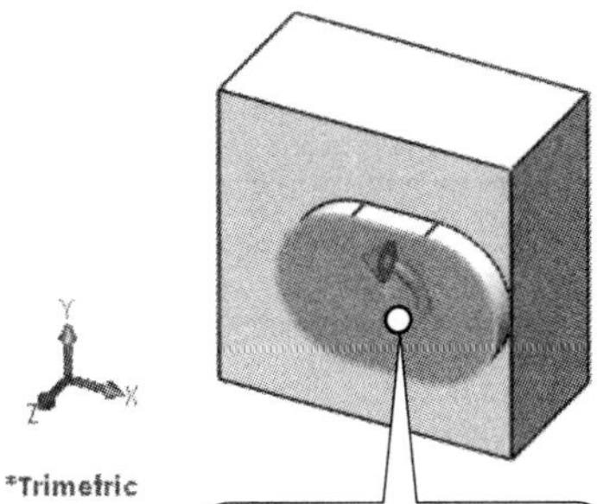

[12] Click this face of the **Rotor**.

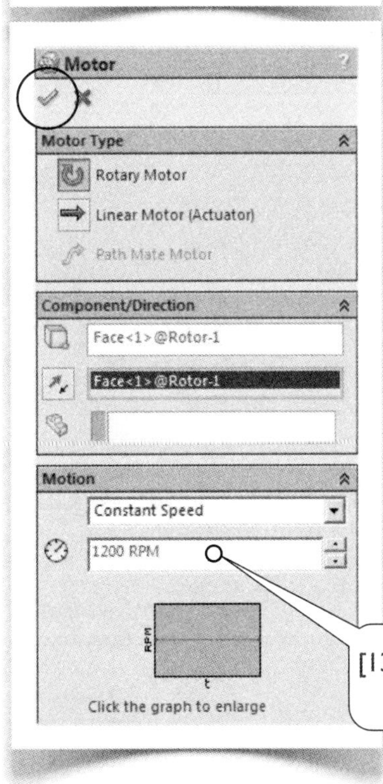

[13] Type 1200 (RPM) for **Speed**. #

11.2-6 Run the Simulation

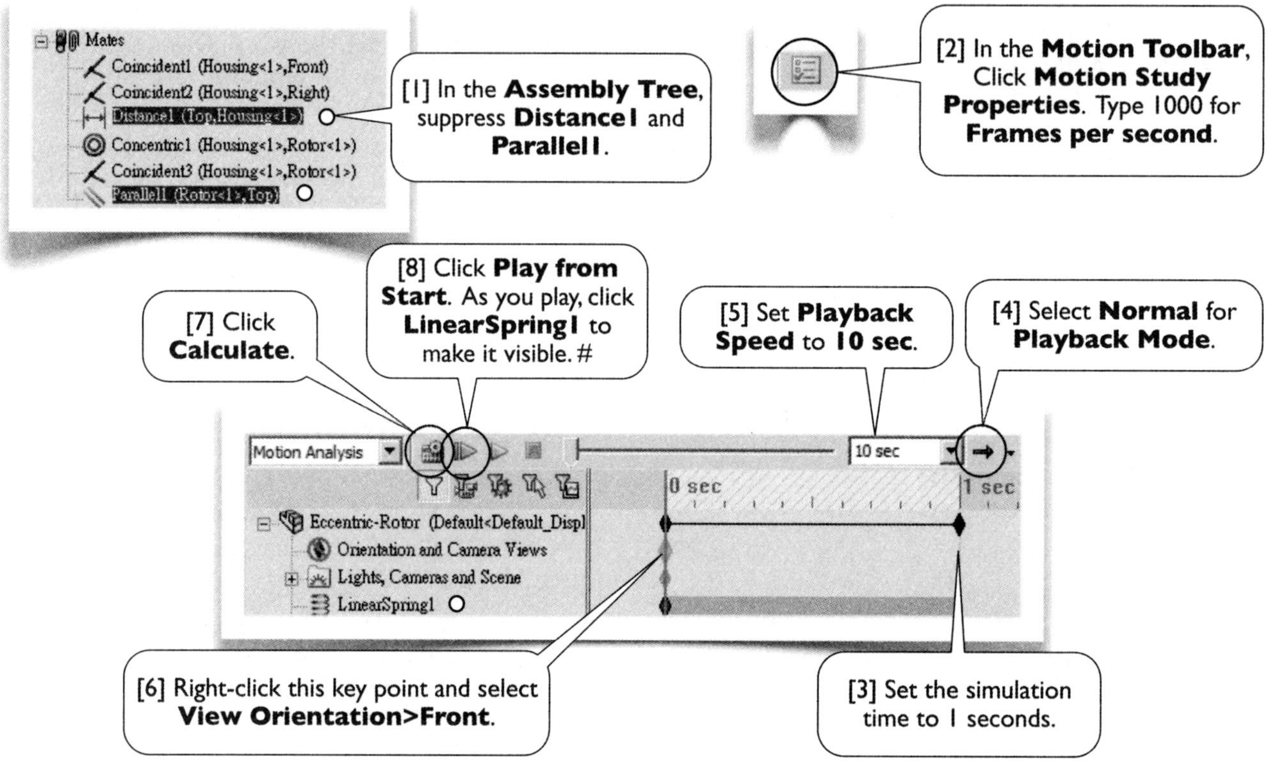

11.2-7 Results

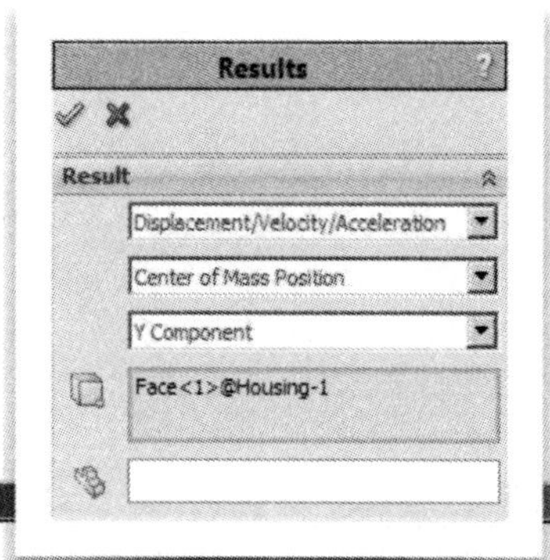

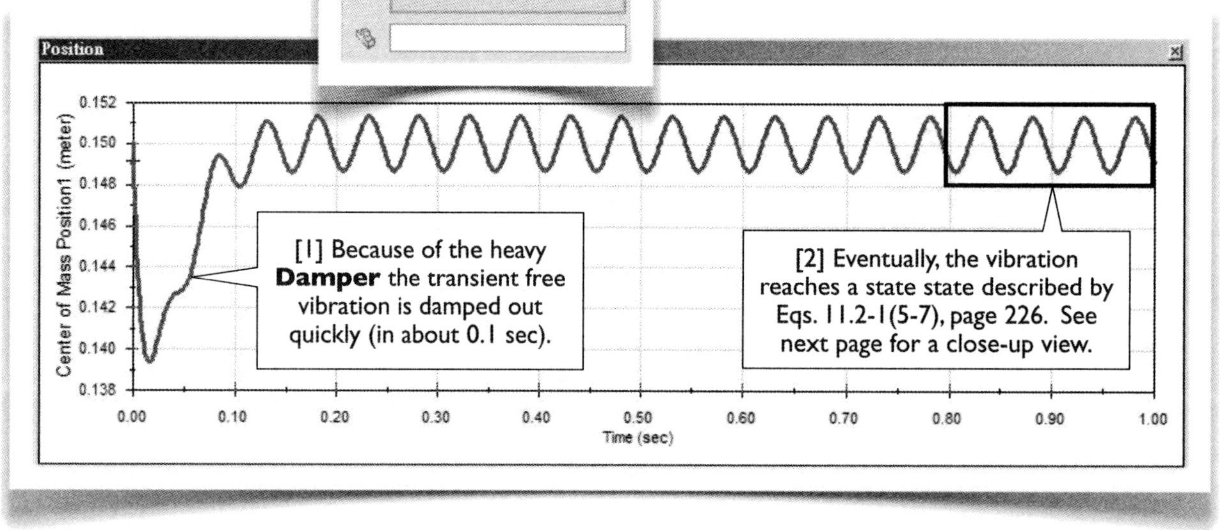

[3] This is a close-up view of the last plot.

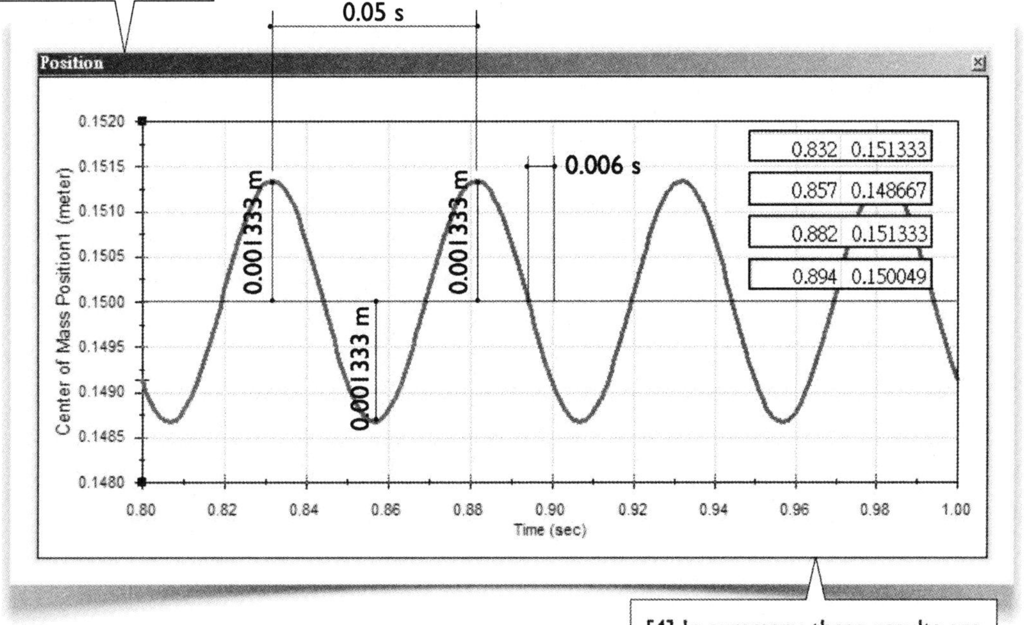

[4] In summary, these results are consistent with Eqs. 11.2-1(5-7), page 226.

[5] Wrap Up

Save all files and exit **SolidWorks**. #

Index